CÉ

TIME-COMPRESSED SPEECH:

An Anthology and Bibliography
in Three Volumes

by
SAM DUKER

Volume I

The Scarecrow Press, Inc.
Metuchen, N.J.   1974

348892

Other Scarecrow books by Sam Duker:

Listening: Readings [Vol. 1]. 1966.

Listening: Bibliography. 2d ed. 1968.

Individualized Reading: An Annotated Bibliography. 1968.

Individualized Reading: Readings. 1969.

Listening: Readings, Vol. 2. 1971.

Teaching Listening in the Elementary School: Readings. 1971.

Individualized Instruction in Mathematics. 1972.

Library of Congress Cataloging in Publication Data

Duker, Sam, 1905-
    Time-compressed speech: an anthology and bibliog-
raphy.

    1. Speech processing systems. 2. Speech processing
systems--Bibliography. 3. Speech perception. 4. Speech
perception--Bibliography. I. Title.
TK7882. S65D84   001. 54'2   73-8756
ISBN 0-8108-0643-6
ISBN 0-8108-0644-4 (Vol. III)

Copyright 1974 by Sam Duker

ii

IN MEMORIAM

H. S. v. H. D.

W. F. v. H. D.

BRIEF TABLE OF CONTENTS

Volume 1

PART III.   PRACTICAL APPLICATIONS

PART IV.   PATENTS

Volume 3

PART V.   ANNOTATED BIBLIOGRAPHY

FULL TABLE OF CONTENTS

vii

PART V.   ANNOTATED BIBLIOGRAPHY

PREFACE

We live in an era which is dependent upon communication in a way that is unparalleled in the history of mankind. Not only is communication more rapid than ever before, but the proliferation of communicative material is indescribable in any sort of meaningful terms. To a large extent, modern technology is a major causal factor in this situation. It hardly seems necessary to describe the role of the printing press and all its refinements in this process. The telegraph and all the subsequent developments of its principles have, of course, added immeasurably to the rate at which messages are transmitted. Witness, for example, the millions who heard the words of Astronaut Armstrong as he first stepped on the moon. The time lapse, in fact, was so small that, for all practical purposes, the transmission and reception were simultaneous.

While the role of modern technology should not be minimized, we are also living in a world that has many times the population ever known before. This fact, of course, deeply affects the communication problem as the last three decades of our century begin. It is obvious that the potential number of transmitters and especially of receivers of messages is a major factor in the present dependence on efficient, effective, and dependable means of communication.

Aside from primitive pictographic types of information-sharing, early man's only means of communication was non-written, being in large part oral. In historical times handwritten records followed (a redundancy, as we date historical time from the discovery of a means of keeping written records.) As writing was succeeded by printing, human use of written communications and dependency on reading increased sharply.

Now, in the 1970's, we find ourselves swamped in the morass of printed material produced in ever increasing quantities. The quality of much of this overwhelming flood of books, booklets, journals, pamphlets, and the like does not justify its preservation. Despite the introduction and increasing use of micro-storage technology, libraries are bulging while individuals are deluged with more reading material than they can possibly absorb. One means of maximizing the ability to cope, albeit not a sufficient one, has been the development of techniques to increase the speed of reading. In recent years an increasing awareness of the need to acquire the ability to read rapidly has become widespread. Nevertheless, resistance to the idea of rapid reading has persisted in some quarters. Such resistance is strong in many of our schools, where the notion persists that careful reading must be slow reading.

Of course the ability to read is not evenly distributed. Here in the United States an incredibly large number of people are, functionally speaking, non-readers. It would be gratifying to find that the inability to read was confined to those who have not shared the benefits of modern American education. Yet, unfortunately, this is not true. Throughout the United States (not only in the inner-city of large urban centers, as some would have us believe) there are those who notwithstanding eight, ten, or even 12 years of schooling, are still functional non-readers. To one who has been professionally engaged in the training of teachers for a number of decades, it is tempting to dwell on this topic. Suffice it to note that in the rest of the world non-readers far outnumber those who are able to read. The need for efficient and effective oral communication is self-evident.

Anyone curious as to how reading skills are acquired inevitably becomes interested in oral communication skills because, after all, these skills are much more widely needed than reading skills. The amount of oral communication, even in a country such as ours--a so-called "literate" one--far exceeds the amount of written communication. On a worldwide basis, the preponderance of oral communication is even greater.

Technological ingenuity which spawned the printing press and the linotype has contributed to an even greater degree, if that is possible, to facilitation of oral communication. The radio, television, microphone, and tape recorder are only a few of the many 20th-century developments that have increased the use of oral communication far beyond the wildest dreams of their inventors. Just as reading and writing, using these terms in their broadest sense, comprise the basic skills required for written communication, so speech and listening form the bases of oral communication. Of these, reading and listening are receptive skills with a great many factors in common.

One common element is the fact that in a technological civilization the amount of communicative material far exceeds the individual's capacity to cope with it. We have already considered the matter of rapid reading by a very brief mention. Years ago, Ralph Nichols pointed out that the listener's thought processes are able to operate much more rapidly than the speech produced by human vocal chords. The truth of this statement is evident to anyone who notes that the human mind has ample opportunity to wander while listening, even when the speaker is talking rapidly. In fact on many lists of desirable listening skills that should be developed such mind-wandering rates special attention. Rather than allowing the mind to wander and thus to distract one from the listening task, good use can be made of this phenomenon by forming mental images, by promulgating mental questions, by reviewing what has already been said, and by deducing what will be said next. In other words, the listener can avoid turning his thoughts toward matters other than the subject of the listening activity. Obviously, therefore, rapid listening would not only be a time-saving device but would also, very likely, lead to more efficient listening. The listener cannot control the rate, as the reader can, but he must learn to employ the rate at which the transmission is made.

The degree to which speech can be speeded up by the human speaker without very seriously affecting intelligibility is quite limited. Obviously, then, any meaningful change in the speed of listening will have to depend upon the use of recorded speech. The most obvious way to speed up a tape, for example, is to play it back at a rate that is greater than the rate at which it was recorded. This would be a very satisfactory process, placing the rate under the control of the listener, were it not for one obstacle. Due to the inevitable shift in frequency as the rate increases, we soon get what has been called the "Donald Duck effect."

As a result of research that began in the late 1940's various means of changing the rate of recorded material without a corresponding shift in frequency began to be discovered. This process has continued to the present day. The product of this rate-changing process is commonly called compressed speech. This is not a satisfactory term because of its common use in connection with bandwidth compression, a process not closely related to rate changing in the sense with which we are concerned. The terms accelerated speech, rapid speech, rate-altered speech and others have all been used to some extent but not on a widespread basis. The term that we have adopted in the title of this work, time-compressed speech, is only a slight improvement but it has, I believe, acquired the greatest general acceptance.

This work is a collection of writings about time-compressed speech. Part I for the first time reproduces and presents in one convenient place the most frequently cited documents on this subject. Few of these are readily available and therefore it seemed to me useful to provide access to them in this manner. In addition to these basic documents, Part I includes a number of shorter articles dealing with what I feel are fundamental kinds of information concerning time-compressed speech which are of importance to every serious student of this topic. Part II is concerned with the presentation of selections from representative research having to do with the investigation of various aspects of compressed speech. Some of the research concerns the manner of accomplishing a change of rate; other research is directed to an examination of the effect of various types of material or content; and still other research investigates the effect on the communication process of the audience which receives the rate-altered messages.

Part III is made up of descriptions of practical applications. Much of the material in these chapters was written especially for this work. Part IV provides copies of most of the patents related to the subject of time-compressed speech. Part V, a separate volume, is an annotated bibliography of much of the material that

has been written on the subject.   Because I have had some experience in the area of bibliographing, I know better than to claim
either comprehensiveness or complete accuracy for this part of this
collection of material.   I can, however, state: this bibliography is
the most comprehensive one available to date and no item has been
included which has not been personally examined and read by me.
Scattered throughout this work are references to this bibliography,
in brackets like this: [B193].   The number refers to entry number
in the bibliography volume (number 3).   It has been my purpose to
prepare these volumes in such a way that readers with a variety of
divergent purposes may find them useful as a starting point for
further investigations in accordance with their individual needs.

ACKNOWLEDGMENTS

This anthology and bibliography on the theories, applications, and potentials of altering the rate of listening to speech has been possible only through the cooperation of the writers of the material especially written for this work, or reprinted, excerpted, or cited in the following pages. While I do not belong to the school of thought which says that the compilation of a work of this kind involves little effort, I am keenly aware that my efforts constitute only a small fraction of the sum total of the effort put forth by all those writers in the preparation and writing of what is reproduced here.

It is, therefore, an especially pleasant task for me to acknowledge with great gratitude the cooperation of those whose works are included in one way or another in these volumes. I must make special mention of the fact that permissions, help, and cooperation were not only given when requested but were given promptly, willingly, and with an incomparable spirit of interest in and kind support for my project.

My interest in compressed speech, an inexact term to be sure, arose naturally from my long standing interest in listening. As I have done before, I must therefore once again acknowledge the long-time support and encouragement of the man who, above all others, has made "listening" a respectable household word in the educational world and in training programs of all kinds and varieties: MR. LISTENING himself, Ralph G. Nichols, head of the Department of Rhetoric on the St. Paul campus of the University of Minnesota. It was he who first called attention to the discrepancy between the speed of speech and the speed of thought as a factor adding to the difficulty of effective listening.

I owe many debts to those who helped me learn about accelerated listening but two people stand out: David B. Orr, formerly of the American Institutes of Research and now president of Scientific Educational Systems of Silver Spring, Maryland, who is entitled to my special additional thanks for his willingness to write an introduction to this work and, of course, Emerson Foulke of the Perceptual Alternatives Laboratory at the University of Louisville in Kentucky. If there is a MR. COMPRESSED SPEECH, Emerson Foulke is certainly he. Not only has he carried out extensive research on various facets of compressed speech but also has been the one prime disseminator of information on this subject through his writing as well as through the conferences on this subject which he has promoted and implemented.

Others who served with me as members of the advisory board of the Center for Rate Controlled Recordings have also been most supportive as well as informative in my process of studying and reading about compressed speech. These include Robert S. Bray, chief of the Division for the Blind and Physically Handicapped of the Library of Congress; the late John K. Dupress of the Sensory Aids Center at Massachusetts Institute of Technology; Dr. Anthony Holbrook of the Speech and Hearing Science Laboratory at Florida State University; Dr. Lawson Hughes, professor of education at Indiana University; Dr. Murray Miron, professor of psychology at Syracuse University; Dr. Carson Y. Nolan of the American Printing House for the Blind; Dr. Richard Woodcock, formerly professor of education at Peabody and now associated as editor and director of research with the American Guidance Service of Minneapolis; and Dr. Willard Zemlin of the Speech Research Laboratory and Hearing Clinic at the University of Illinois.

Librarians, office colleagues, secretarial staffs, and typists, both at Brooklyn College and elsewhere, have been most helpful in more ways than can be enumerated or described here. To each individual a heartfelt "thank you."

It is a very satisfying duty to make the following formal acknowledgments to those whose writings are included in this anthology. A number of individuals have kindly responded to my invitation to write material especially for this anthology: Robert S. Bray has written on "Uses of Compressed Speech." He has already been identified.

Professor Edward W. Brombach has written "Use of Time Expansion in Studying Portamento" which is related to his doctoral thesis completed at the University of Rochester in 1969. He is presently professor of music at New York State University College at Potsdam.

Dr. Ronald P. Carver who is a Senior Research Scientist associated with the American Institutes for Research in their Washington office in Silver Spring, Maryland, has contributed a short article entitled "Using Time-Compressed Speech to Present a Convention Paper."

Dr. Emerson Foulke of the University of Louisville, who has already been identified, has contributed a thoughtful and what I consider to be an outstanding review of compressed speech insofar as it relates to the blind.

Dr. Sanford E. Gerber and Miss Frances F. Pezzullo, who completed her master's thesis Speech Time Compression: A Study of the Intelligibility of Rapid Speech under his direction in 1970, have contributed an article on the important topic, "Limits of Speech Time Compression," which in part summarizes the findings in the Pezzullo thesis. Dr. Gerber is professor of speech at the University of California at Santa Barbara and is presently working on the final stages of a book on the subject of compressed speech.

Professor Gerald Gleason of the Department of Educational Psychology at the University of Wisconsin at Milwaukee together with two of his colleagues, Roland Callaway and Robert Lakata, has contributed an interesting paper on "Effects of Audio-Rate Compression on Student Comprehension and Attitudes."

Professor Gerald M. Goldhaber, presently teaching in the Speech Department at the University of New Mexico, contributed an article especially written for this Anthology about his experiments concerning the use of time-compressed speech in the Navajo and Spanish languages and about how this compares to its use in English. Professor Goldhaber has been interested in time-compressed speech for some time now and has contributed to the knowledge about this subject in other writing as well as in the article included in this work.

Mr. Robert Good of New York's Compressed Time, Inc., contributed a paper describing a newly developed speech compressor, for which a patent application is pending, and which he hopes will be in production in the near future.

Mr. Wayne Graham of Discerned Sound, Inc., of Hollywood, California, contributed information concerning his "Whirling Dervish" speech compressor on which the description of that speech compressor by Emerson Foulke is based.

Mr. Richard Koch of Lynbrook, N. Y. contributed an article in which he described the "AmBiChron," a speech compressor which he has invented and on which a patent has been applied for.

Dr. Norman J. Lass, professor of speech pathology and audiology at the University of West Virginia's Medical School, and Miss Cheryl J. Cain, who is completing her master's thesis under his direction, contributed a paper, entitled "Listening Rate Preference in Adults," based on that master's thesis.

In addition to the foregoing, Professor Lass has also contributed a paper, "Consistency of Speech Rate Evaluations of Experienced and Inexperienced Listeners," jointly with Miss Vicki L. Goff who recently completed her master's thesis under his direction.

Dr. James A. Libby, professor of veterinary medicine at the University of Minnesota, contributed an article entitled, "Use of Time-Compressed Speech in Auto-Tutorial Instruction of Veterinary Food Hygiene."

Dr. Robert D. McDonald, who is affiliated with Syracuse Psychiatric Hospital, Frani R. Cummings of Marcy State Hospital, and Shirley A. Greiff of the Upstate Medical Center of the State University of New York have contributed a paper on "Schizophrenia and Compressed Speech."

Professor Murray Miron of the Psychology Department at Syracuse University, whom I have already mentioned, and Professor Eric W. Brown of New York University contributed the paper entitled, "Durational Variables in Speech Compression."

Dr. J. M. Pickett, professor of speech communication research at Gallaudet College in Washington, D. C., kindly revised and updated a paper on "Sound Patterns of Speech" which had originally appeared in the March 1968 issue of Annals of the Deaf.

Dr. Barbara G. Parkhurst of the Queens College Speech Department, who recently completed her doctorate at the City University of New York, contributed a paper on "Effect of Time-Altered Speech Stimuli on Auditory Comprehension of Adult Aphasics."

Professor Thomas K. Perry, who is with the Department of Communication Arts of the University of West Florida in Pensacola, wrote an article especially for this work entitled "Effects of a Compressed Slide-Audio Tape Presentation in a Learning Carrel," based largely on his 1970 Michigan State University doctoral thesis.

Dr. Emma E. Plattor, professor of education at the University of Calgary, and her colleague Waldemar R. Unruh contributed a description of an experiment conducted by them and entitled, "Effects of Differential Speech-Rate Training on Comprehension of School Children."

Mr. Shadid U. Qureshi of the Department of Electrical Engineering at the University of Toronto kindly contributed an article, "Speech Compression by Computer," which is based in part on his master's thesis recently completed at Toronto.

Professor Sarah Short of the Department of Health at Syracuse University describes an experiment in the use of compressed speech for instructional purposes in a specially written paper, "Use of Compressed-Rate Speech Tapes in a Self-Instruction Laboratory.'

Professor Walter F. Stromer was kind enough to contribute an article, "A Forerunner of Time Compression." He is with the Speech Department of Cornell College in Iowa.

Mr. Ching Yee Suen and Professor Michael P. Beddoes of the Department of Electrical Engineering at the University of British Columbia contributed an article, "Some Applications of a Small Digital Computer in Speech Processing."

An article on "Responses to Time-Expanded Speech in Presbycusic and Normal-Hearing Males" was contributed by Mr. Barry B. Wass, on whose University of South Florida master's thesis the article was based, and Professor Randall K. Beedle of the Audiology Department of that university.

Mr. Bob Wakeman of Los Angeles kindly contributed an

article entitled "Time Compression of Religious Sermons on Radio."

Dr. Meredith A. Watts, Jr., director of research of the Learning Center at Air University in Birmingham, Alabama, contributed an article entitled "Use of Compressed Speech to Teach Instructional Methodology."

Professor Lawrence R. Wheeless, who is director of undergraduate studies in speech at Illinois State University at Normal, contributed a provocative article, "Persuasive Effects of Time-Compressed Speech."

To all those just listed I express my deep appreciation for their generous contributions to this anthology which is greatly enriched because of the inclusion of their material.

The remainder of this anthology is composed of reprinted and excerpted materials. I acknowledge with gratitude and thanks the contributions made by the authors of this material.

Two excerpts from the 1963 Ohio State University doctoral dissertation entitled, A Study of Intra- and Inter-Phrasal Pauses and Their Relationship to the Rate of Speech, are used with the kind permission of the author, Professor Joseph G. Agnello of the Department of Speech at the University of Cincinnati.

An article, "Retention as a Function of Rate of Information Transmission and Degree of Comprehension," which appeared in the January 1967 issue of the Florida Journal of Research, is reprinted with the permission of the journal and of the two authors, John E. Allen of Salt Lake City, Utah and Professor R. M. Travers of the Department of Education at Western Michigan University.

Professor Morton W. Altshuler of the Speech Department of Temple University in Philadelphia granted permission to use excerpts from his doctor's thesis, Responses to Expanded Speech by Hard-of-Hearing Aged Subjects, completed at Boston University in 1964.

Dr. Daniel S. Beasley, professor of audiology and voice sciences at Michigan State University, completed his doctoral dissertation, Auditory Analysis of Time-Varied Sentential Approximations, at the University of Illinois in 1970. Excerpts are used with his permission.

The article, "Flexible Analog Time Compression of Short Utterances" which first appeared in March 1968 in IEEE Transactions on Audio and Electroacoustics AU16:12-20, is reprinted with the permission of the Institute of Electrical and Electronic Engineers as well as of the authors, Drs. David H. Beetle, Jr., and William D. Chapman, both of whom are associated with the Systems Development Division of International Business Machines at Research Triangle Park, North Carolina.

Excerpts from a 1964 Wayne State University doctoral thesis, The Effect of an Alteration in the Time-Frequency Characteristics of Selected Speech Samples on Pathological Ears, are used with the permission of the author, Dr. Philip A. Bellefleur, who is presently headmaster of the Pennsylvania School for the Deaf.

The reprint of the article, "The Harmonic Compressor: A System for Doubling Information Rates of Speech," which appeared in 1969 as an Audio Engineering Society Preprint No. 658(c-1), is made possible through the kind permission of the Society as well as of John W. Breuel and Leo M. Levens, both affiliated with the research activities of the American Foundation for the Blind.

Dr. Richard A. Bruland, author of Listening and Listening-Reading at Two Rates of Presentation by Fifth Grade Pupils, a 1970 Syracuse University doctoral dissertation, kindly allowed the use of excerpts from his work. He is presently on the staff of the University of Wisconsin at Green Bay.

Substantial excerpts from an article by Professors C. Calearo of the University of Ferrara and A. Lazzaroni of the Department of Otolaryngology of the University of Milan, which first appeared in the May 1957 Laryngoscope, are used with the permission of the two authors and of the publishers of the journal.

Mr. John L. Davy, curriculum coordinator of the Industrial Technology Department of Hanover High School in New Hampshire, kindly gave permission to use a brief excerpt from his master's thesis, The Efficacy of Compressed-Speech as a Means of Increasing Comprehension of Children Having Reading Problems.

Two excerpts from a 1968 Stanford University doctoral thesis, Fusion in Dichotic Listening, are used with the permission of the author, Professor Ruth S. Day of the Yale University Psychology Department.

Permission to reprint was given by the authors C. F. Diehl, presently director of the Speech and Hearing Center of the University of Kentucky; R. C. White, now professor of homiletics at the Lexington Theological Seminary of Kentucky; and K. W. Burk, professor of audiology at Purdue University; as well as by the American Speech Association, publishers of Speech Monographs, in which the article, "Rate and Communication," originally appeared in August 1959.

Excerpts from the 1970 U. S. C. doctoral dissertation, Learning in Multi-Media Programmed Instruction as a Function of Aptitude and Instruction Rate Controlled by Compressed Speech, are used with the permission of the author, Professor Wymond W. Eckhardt, now affiliated with the Instructional Media Center at Fresno State College in California.

Professor Mitat A. Enç of the Department of Education of

xxvi

Ankara University in Turkey gave permission for use of excerpts from his 1958 University of Illinois doctoral dissertation, The Effect of Two Different WPM Listening Rates on Learning and Retention of Blind Children.

The late Dr. Grant Fairbanks, formerly a professor at the University of Illinois and at Stanford University, was author or co-author of six articles which are reprinted almost in their entirety in this anthology. While no permission was obtainable from him or on his behalf, as I was unable to locate any literary heir, I must acknowledge my profound sense of appreciation for his work, which made incomparable contributions to thinking about time-compressed speech, and for the quality of his lucid descriptions of that work.

The article "Effects of Time Compression and Expansion of Speech" which appears in Experimental Phonetics: Selected Articles, edited and compiled by Murray Miron and published by the University of Illinois Press in 1966, is used with the permission of the publisher.

The article, "Method for Time or Frequency Compression-Expansion of Speech," which appeared in 1954 in Transactions of the Institute of Radio Engineers, Professional Group on Audio, was written by Dr. Fairbanks and two co-authors. It is reprinted with the kind permission of the Institute of Radio Engineers and of the co-authors, Professor W. L. Everitt of the Department of Electric Engineering at the University of Illinois and R. P. Jaeger, who is affiliated with Litton Industries in Chatsworth, California.

Since it is the policy of the Journal of Speech and Hearing Disorders to allow reprinting of articles that have appeared in that journal when permission is obtained from the authors, the article by Dr. Grant Fairbanks entitled "Systematic Research in Experimental Phonetics: 1. A Theory of the Speech Mechanism as a Servo-System," which appeared in that journal in 1954, is reprinted in this anthology without any specific permission.

Three articles by Fairbanks which also appeared in the Journal of Speech and Hearing Disorders in 1957 were co-authored by Drs. Newman Guttman, now a member of the technical staff of Bell Telephone Laboratories, and Murray Miron, now of Syracuse University. These articles were entitled: "Effects of Time Compression Upon the Comprehension of Connected Speech"; "Auditory Comprehension of Repeated High-Speed Messages"; and "Auditory Comprehension in Relation to Listening Rate and Selective Verbal Redundancy." These three items are reprinted with the kind permission of the two co-authors.

"Theory of Communication" by Dr. D. Gabor is reprinted with the kind permission of the author and of the Journal of the Institution of Electrical Engineers in which it originally appeared in 1946.

Dr. William D. Garvey of Johns Hopkins University gave his permission to use substantial excerpts from both his master's and his doctoral theses, completed at the University of Virginia. His master's thesis, completed in 1949, was entitled Duration Factors in Speech Intelligibility and his doctoral, completed in 1953, was An Experimental Investigation of the Intelligibility of Speeded Speech.

Permission to use excerpts from Difficulty of Material and Retention of Compressed Speech, his 1970 Indiana University doctoral dissertation, was granted by Professor Robert G. George now of the Department of Education of that University.

Professor Frieda Goldman-Eisler's article, "The Determinants of the Rate of Speech Output and their Mutual Relations," which appeared in the Journal of Psychosomatic Research in 1956, is reprinted with the kind permission of the author and of the Pergamon Press, publishers of the Journal.

Substantial excerpts from his 1940 Teachers College, Columbia University doctoral thesis, Reading and Listening Comprehension at Various Controlled Rates, are used in this anthology with the kind permission of the author, Harry Goldstein.

Permission was given to use excerpts from his doctoral thesis, An Experimental Study of the Effects of Rate of Speaking upon Listenability, completed at U.S.C. in 1956 by Leo Goodman-Malamuth II, who is now academic vice president of California State College at Long Beach.

Excerpts from "Automatic Evaluation of Time-Varying Communication Systems," which appeared in 1968 in IEEE Transactions on Audio and Electroacoustics AU16:100-105, are used with the permission of the Institute of Electrical and Electronic Engineers and the three authors, Dr. Michael H. Hecker of the Stanford Research Institute in Menlo Park, California; Dr. Gottfried von Bismarck of the Institut für Electroakustic in Munich, Germany; and Dr. Carl E. Williams, head of Acoustics and Audiology at the Naval Aerospace Medical Research Laboratory at Pensacola, Florida.

Professor William G. Henry, Jr., now with the Education Department of Southwest Texas State University, gave permission for the use of excerpts from his 1967 Indiana University doctoral dissertation, Recognition of Time Compressed Speech as a Function of Word Length and Frequency of Use.

Excerpts from his 1964 Wayne State University doctoral thesis, Speech Intelligibility in Presbycusis under Conditions of Simultaneous Time and Frequency Distortion, are used with permission of Dr. Milton J. Hill, presently an audiologist with the Oakland, Michigan schools.

Permission to use excerpts from An Experimental Study of the Effects of Repetitive Compressed Speech on Listening

Comprehension was given by Dr. Fred W. Hopkins, Jr., author of that doctoral thesis which was completed in 1970 at the University of Maryland.

Permission to use excerpts from a 1954 University of Illinois thesis completed under the direction of Grant Fairbanks and entitled A Psychological Study of Speech Rate was given by the author, Professor Charles L. Hutton, Jr., now with the Department of Education of Emory University in Georgia.

Professor Robert E. Jester, now with the Department of Education of the University of Florida, granted permission to use excerpts from his 1966 University of Utah dissertation entitled, Comprehension of Connected Meaningful Discourse as a Function of Individual Differences and Rate and Modality of Presentation.

Professor Robert T. Jones, now director of the Learning Resources Center at Worcester State College in Massachusetts, wrote The Effect of Multi-Channel Audio Stimuli on Learning Efficiency as his doctoral dissertation at Syracuse University in 1969. Excerpts from it are used with his permission.

"Intelligibility of Time-Compressed Speech," which originally appeared in the Journal of the Acoustical Society of America in 1961, is reprinted in this collection with the consent of the Journal and of the two co-authors, Roy G. Klumpp, who is now affiliated with the Naval Undersea Research and Development Center in San Diego, and J. C. Webster, who is an engineering psychologist with the Naval Electronics Laboratory Center in the same city.

Professor Francis Kodman, Jr., now of the Department of Psychology at Murray State University in Kentucky, gave me permission to use substantial excerpts from his 1954 University of Illinois doctoral dissertation which was sponsored by Grant Fairbanks and entitled An Investigation of Word Intelligibility as a Function of Time Compression.

The extensive excerpts from yet another doctoral thesis sponsored by Grant Fairbanks are used with the permission of the author, George H. Kurtzrock, now director of audiology at the University of Florida. It was completed at the University of Illinois in 1956 and was entitled The Effects of Time and Frequency Distortion upon Word Intelligibility.

Dr. Robert P. Langford, now with the Maine Institute for the Blind, kindly gave permission for the use of excerpts from his 1968 New York University doctoral dissertation, The Effect of Compressed Speech on Listening Comprehension.

Excerpts from An Experimental Study of Some Effects of Time Compression upon the Comprehension and Retention of Visually Augmented Televised Speech, which was written as his doctoral dissertation at U.S.C. in 1967 by James L. Loper, now general

xxix

manager of the non-commercial television station, KCET, in Hollywood, are used with the author's permission.

Excerpts from the 1966 University of Kansas doctoral dissertation by Thomas C. Levitt, which was entitled Narrative Rate Preference in Normal and Retarded Males as Assessed by Conjugate Reinforcement, are used with the kind permission of the author who is presently a professor at the University of Washington in Seattle.

Excerpts from the 1971 University of Illinois doctoral dissertation, An Exploration of Comprehension Differences in Time Compressed Japanese, Chinese, Hindi, and English Speech, are used with the kind permission of the author, Marion D. Meyerson, now associated with the Department of Communication Disorders at Fresno State College in California.

The well-known article by Professor George A. Miller, "The Magical Number Seven, Plus or Minus Two: Some Limits on Our Capacity for Processing Information," which originally appeared in the Psychological Review, 1956, is reprinted with the consent of the author and of the American Psychological Corporation, publisher of the Review.

"The Intelligibility of Interrupted Speech" which appeared in the Journal of the Acoustical Society of America in 1950 is reprinted with the kind permission of the Journal and of the two co-authors, Professor George A. Miller of Rockefeller University and J. C. R. Licklider of Massachusetts Institute of Technology.

Professor Fred D. Minifie, who completed his doctorate at the University of Iowa in 1963 and is now with the Department of Speech at the University of Washington, gave permission for the use of excerpts from his dissertation entitled, An Analysis of the Durational Aspects of Connected Speech Samples By Means of an Electronic Speech Duration Analyzer.

Professor H. G. Moll, who is now with the Department of Education at Western Illinois University, gave permission to use excerpts from his 1968 Indiana University doctoral dissertation, The Effect of Selective Elimination of Speech Sounds on the Comprehension of Compressed Speech.

Reprinting of the article, "Note on Thought Rate as a Function of Reading and Listening Rates" is made possible by the kind permission of the author, Dr. David B. Orr, and of Perceptual and Motor Skills, in which it originally appeared in 1964. Also, Dr. Orr, as the senior author of "Trainability of Listening Comprehension of Speeded Discourse," which appeared in the Journal of Educational Psychology in 1965, has given permission for the reprinting of this article, as has the American Psychological Association, publishers of the Journal.

Professor Clement C. Parker of Tarrant County Junior

College in Texas has kindly given me permission to include in this anthology excerpts from his 1970 North Texas University doctoral dissertation entitled, Effect of Rate of Compression and Mode of Presentation on the Comprehension of a Recorded Communication to Junior College Students of Varying Aptitudes.

The Significance of Various Portions of the Wave Length in the Minimum Duration Necessary for the Recognition of Vowel Sounds was the title of a 1939 Louisiana State University dissertation by the late Gordon E. Peterson. Excerpts from it are included through the gracious permission of Mrs. Peterson.

Dr. Ronald H. Reid kindly gave his consent to the inclusion in this collection of excerpts from his 1968 Indiana University doctoral dissertation which had the title: Comprehension of Compressed Speech as a Function of Difficulty of Material.

Dr. Saralou L. Reid, the other half of this husband and wife doctoral team, was equally generous in allowing me to use excerpts taken from her thesis, The Effect on Reading Achievement of Reading Paced by Compressed Speech, accepted in 1971 by Indiana University.

Sister Mary L. Reiland gave her permission to use excerpts from her 1970 Rutgers University doctorate, The Effect of Compressed Speech on Reading and Listening Abilities of Sixth-Grade Children.

Excerpts from the Effects of Training on the Intelligibility and Comprehension of Frequency Shifted Time-Compressed Speech by the Blind are included in this collection with permission of the author, Professor Paul E. Resta, who is presently a member of the staff of the University of New Mexico's College of Education. He completed his doctorate at Arizona State University in 1968.

Professor Peter S. Robinson who is on the teaching staff of Northern Michigan University kindly allowed me to use excerpts from his 1971 University of Utah doctoral dissertation, Some Effects of Listening to Speeded Speech on the Listening and Reading Behavior of Sixth Grade Boys.

Professor Charles M. Rossiter, Jr., who obtained his doctorate from Ohio University and who is now on the faculty of the Department of Communications of the University of Wisconsin at Milwaukee, allowed the inclusion of excerpts from his thesis, The Effects of Rate of Presentation on Listening Test Scores for Recall of Facts, Recall of Ideas, and Generation of Inferences.

Professor Terry D. Schon gave me permission to use excerpts from his 1968 Syracuse University doctoral thesis, The Effects of Speech Compression and Expansion on Normal Hearing, Hard of Hearing, and Aged Males. Dr. Schon is presently on the staff of Lehman College, New York City.

An article, "A Device for Time Expansion Used in Sound Recording," which appeared in Transactions of the Institute of Radio Engineers, Professional Group on Audio AU2:12-15 in 1954, is reprinted with the kind permission of the Institute of Radio Engineers. I have been unsuccessful in my efforts to locate the author, H. Schiesser.

Drs. M. R. Schroeder, B. F. Logan, and A. J. Prestigiacomo, all affiliated with Bell Telephone Laboratories, kindly gave me their permission to reprint a paper on "New Methods for Speech Analysis-Synthesis and Bandwidth Compression" which they presented at a Speech Communication Seminar in Stockholm sponsored by the Royal Institute of Technology in 1962.

Permission to include in this anthology major excerpts from his dissertation Speech Compression was given by the author, Hideo Seo who completed his doctorate at the University of South Carolina in 1967 and is now professor of engineering at the Middletown campus of Pennsylvania State University.

Professor Howard Spicker of the Department of Special Education of Indiana University kindly permitted me the use of excerpts from his 1963 George Peabody College for Teachers doctoral dissertation, Listening Comprehension and Retention of Intellectually Normal and Retarded Children as Functions of Speaking Rate and Passage Difficulty.

Dr. Thomas G. Sticht, senior scientist with the Human Resources Research Organization (HumRRO) at Monterey, California, has generously allowed me to use excerpts from "Some Interactions of Speech Rate, Signal Distortion, and Certain Linguistic Factors in Listening Comprehension," which was published as HumRRO Professional Paper 39-68 in 1968.   The article, "Studies on the Efficiency of Learning by Listening to Time Compressed Speech, which appeared as HumRRO's Professional Paper 4-70 in February 1970, is also used with the kind permission of Dr. Sticht, its author.

Mr. Kenneth H. Thames of the Speech Department of the University of Wisconsin at Milwaukee kindly gave permission for the use of excerpts from his master's thesis, The Effect of Training with Compressed Speech on Reading Rate and Listening Comprehension.

Excerpts from a 1965 Wayne State University doctoral thesis, Simultaneous Time and Frequency Distortion as a Diagnostic Test of Speech Intelligibility are included with the permission of the author, Dr. John I. Tschantz.

Mr. Howard M. Wasserman, who teaches in the Department of Educational Psychology at the University of Arizona, permitted me to use excerpts from his 1970 Southern Methodist University master's thesis, Effect of Increased Stimulus Rate Presentation Rate Upon Visual and Audio Perception.

Excerpts from "Differences in Learning Through Compressed Speech as a Function of Presentation Strategy and Rate Among Culturally Disadvantaged Fourth Grade Children," by Richard W. Woodcock and Charlotte R. Clark are included with the kind permission of the senior author. This material originally appeared in an "IMRID" Report at George Peabody College for Teachers.

A brief excerpt from Speech Perception: A Study of Time Altered Selected Voiceless Fricatives, Dr. Barbara R. Zimmerman's doctoral thesis, is used with her permission.

GENERAL INTRODUCTION

David B. Orr
(Scientific Educational Systems, Inc.
Silver Spring, Md.)

Having accepted Professor Duker's kind invitation to prepare a General Introduction to these volumes, I have been forced to think back over developments in the field of time-compressed speech during the past few years. My own involvement in the field dates back over 10 years from the time at which I write these words. At that time only the groundwork had been laid. The milestone publications of Goldstein, Diehl, Garvey, Miller and Licklider, and Fairbanks and his students (reviewed later in this volume) had appeared, and Foulke had just published his first report of his investigations with blind students at the University of Louisville (Bixler, Foulke, et al., Comprehension of Rapid Speech by the Blind, Cooperative Research Project # 1005, U. S. Office of Education, Washington, 1961). The technology of the field was limited to Fairbanks' device at the University of Illinois, a crude and unsuccessful commercial adaptation of it, and a few units of the similar, early device invented by the German inventor, Anton Springer.

Almost no one had ever heard of time-compressed speech.

I felt (and still do) that the creative potentialities of this technology were enormous, and began a program of research at the American Institutes for Research in Washington, D. C., which was designed to explore some of the possibilities, and to take us beyond the specialized interests of some of the previous work. The field was almost uncharted, and the research which I initiated was only capable of broad-scale generalizations and hypothesis-generation, which we and others have subsequently pursued up through the present. However, I believe we established two over-riding facts which assure the ultimate importance of time-compressed speech; first, that the naive listener is capable of comprehending a significant degree of time-compression of connected discourse without comprehension loss; and second, that even greater degrees of compression, although resulting in comprehension decrements, can be offset at least in part by practice and training in listening to compressed materials.

And still almost no one had heard of time-compressed speech.

However, in the fall of 1965 I organized a symposium for the Annual Convention of the American Psychological Association in

Chicago entitled, "Recent Research on the Comprehension of Time-Compressed (Speeded) Speech." The participants included Dr. Robert M. W. Travers, University of Utah; Dr. Herbert L. Friedman, American Institutes for Research; Roy O. Freedle, American Institutes for Research; H. Leslie Cramer, Harvard Graduate School of Education; Dr. Emerson Foulke, University of Louisville; Professor Sam Duker, Brooklyn College; and myself as chairman. For some reason as yet unknown to me this symposium caught the attention of the public press, and suddenly articles occurred in all of the major newspapers coast-to-coast, culminating with a December appearance on the CBS Television Evening News with Walter Cronkite showing our staff at work on time-compressed speech research. Some 4000 cards and letters were received from the viewing audience as a result of this coverage. But much to my regret, I was unable to discern much impact on the growth of research in the field as a result of this exposure. It still seemed as though almost no one had ever heard of time-compressed speech.

In the fall of 1966 a more significant event for the future of the field took place. With the help of Dr. Robert Bray of the Library of Congress, Professor Foulke organized the first Louisville Conference on Time-Compressed Speech at the University of Louisville. While this Conference did not receive the publicity of the previous year's meetings, it reached a higher proportion of those more directly interested in the possibilities of time-compressed speech. It resulted in several major accomplishments: a Proceedings which effectively reviewed the state-of-the-art in time-compressed speech and its applications; the establishment of a Center for Rate Controlled Recordings under the direction of Professor Foulke at the University of Louisville with a board of trustees including Professor Duker, Professor Foulke, myself, Dr. Bray, and several others dedicated to the advancement of the field; and a Newsletter which I initiated at the American Institutes for Research and which is currently published by the Center at Louisville. The circulation of the Newsletter is itself evidence that interest in time-compressed speech has grown steadily over the years; it began with a circulation of less than 200 and is now well over 1000.

Further evidence of the growth of interest and significance of the field of time-compressed speech in the last few years can be assessed by an examination of the volume of research literature being produced in the field. In 1968 Professor Duker, who was then the general editor of the Journal of Communication asked me to guest-edit an entire issue of the Journal devoted to time-compressed speech (September 1968). Though it was not difficult to obtain sufficient research papers of high quality to fill this issue, I can say that there was not a great overabundance of them, and a look at the issue bibliography discloses 76 titles. This may be compared to the contents of the present work and its bibliography of 456 items.

And yet, even today, it seems that almost no one has ever heard of time-compressed speech, at least in terms of the impact of the field on practical affairs. Later in this introduction I will tell you why I think that this situation is about to change. But before venturing such a prediction, I should like to digress to a brief discussion of several related topics.

Perhaps something should be said about what time-compressed speech is, and what it is not. Basically, time-compression as used here is the process of transmitting human speech at a rate faster than its original production rate. It must be understood that a variety of technical methods can be used to accomplish this end. However, no one of these methods can be applied to the compression of speech simultaneously with its production, since obviously there is no external process which can speed up the source (speaking) rate. It is of course true that one can simply request the speaker to speak (or read) faster. However, there are distinct limitations on the rate at which the human speaker can produce connected discourse with acceptable enunciation; and though these limitations are subject to individual differences from person to person, in general they tend to restrict sustained oral productions to rates under 200 words per minute. For very many people, such rates are well below their demonstrated (through reading) capacities for processing and comprehending verbal material.

Thus, if one wishes to speed up discourse significantly in the time dimension, one must first record it and then subject it to subsequent processing (time-compression). As mentioned above, there are a number of ways of accomplishing this end, some of which are more satisfactory than others for a variety of reasons. A fuller discussion of this matter is presented by Foulke (in Horton, David L. and Jenkins, James J. eds.) Perception of Language, Columbus, Ohio: Charles E. Merrill, 1971, p. 80-84) and by Orr (Ibid., p. 108-111). Suffice it to say that the bulk of the existing research on the intelligibility, comprehension, and application of time-compressed speech in recent years has been carried out using devices which employ an electromechanical sampling technique.

No attempt will be made here to go into the technical details of the electromechanical technique, but it may be briefly described as follows. The tape recording of the material to be compressed is played through the compression device at a rate of speed which is a pre-selected amount faster than the original recording rate of the tape. The device reads alternate portions of the tape in a manner which preserves the pitch and sound characteristics of the original tape, but totally discards alternate portions in order to compensate for the excess speed. The portions read (sampling intervals) are blended into a continuous output signal, and the portions discarded (discard intervals) are totally lost. The output signal may be recorded for later playback on any standard tape player, or amplified and played as it is being produced.

Certain characteristics of time-compressed speech produced in this fashion should be noted. The discard intervals are short, generally shorter than any single speech sound, so that no entire speech sound is lost from the speech record. The discard intervals (and sampling intervals) occur in a fixed relationship across time, but are entirely independent of the contents of the speech record. The output produced in this way is pitch-normal and tends to preserve the stress and intonation patterns, pausing, and phrasing of the original speech record. The audio quality of such compressed speech is quite good up to about twice normal rates, but increasingly high degrees of compression result in some distortions. The equipment necessary to produce it is quite expensive.

In summary, time-compressed speech requires pre-recorded material as input, expensive equipment, and, as usually used, produces pitch-normal output very similar in sound patterns to the original.

We may now ask why such a process should be regarded as important in the first place. I answered this question in the special issue of the Journal of Communication in 1968, and I feel that the same considerations are still true (p. 290-291): "Basically, the significance of compressed speech lies primarily in two directions, one related to applied areas, and one related to basic research areas. Both of these avenues are of importance. ... the use of compressed speech as a tool to study the basic nature of human information processing provides a degree of control over a dimension of human communication hitherto determined exclusively by natural conditions. ... The applied dimension lies most clearly in the realm of education. Today's pressures on education, created by the burgeoning knowledge and culture to be transmitted to the next generation demand an efficient educational process. ... It is clear that auditory educational methods are assuming a larger and larger role in our educational process since some children learn better auditorially; since the use of audio-visuals is growing; and since the new educational technologies such as computer-assisted instruction, dial-access tape lectures, telelectures, etc., involve auditory presentations."

A glance at the research section (Part II) of the present work shows that the research community has indeed been busy in the last several years. However, I find less there than I would like to see dealing with the more basic processes of human information processing. In most cases the research which is covered here pertains to the interaction of time-compression with other speech variables and with traditional educational questions. I fear that we have yet to fully appreciate the potential value of time-compressed speech as a tool to study more basic functions of human cognitive processing such as auditory mediation, cognitive processing time, and short term memory. For example, what happens to cognitive processing when it is consistently overloaded with material which is perfectly comprehensible (such as normal speech) but simply coming in too fast? What are the nature of the distortions? Is the

cognitive processing rate itself amenable to increase through practice on cognitive processing? To what extent can time-compressed
presentations be used to assess an individual's tolerance for cognitive overloads of other kinds? What about more studies on the
diotic and dichotic listening dimensions? I have myself had the
experience of listening to short bursts of material at speeds in excess of my processing capability (at about 925 words/minute) and
found myself reading back unprocessed material into consciousness
from short term memory, during the pauses in the presentation.
Surely further studies along these lines could contribute much to
our understanding of the human communication process, for whatever
applied ends.

    With respect to the applied area, the research reported
herein exhibits a clear growth, both in quantity and in quality and
sophistication. Of course the application of time-compressed
speech implies a clear commitment to the importance of listening
in human affairs. Professor Duker has already made this point in
his discussion above, but I would like to underline it. It is indeed
true that much of the world's intercommunication takes place on an
oral-aural basis. Of course I would not suggest that time-compressed
speech should be interjected into all such situations, but much of
the time we spend listening to tapes (and speakers) could just as
easily be time-compressed, both within education and in other areas.
The rapid growth of taped newsletters, magazines, and professional
digests, not to mention correspondence courses and the usual educational materials provides ample opportunity for the application of
time-compression technology.

    Indeed, in many instances the need is for caution. Those of
us who believe in listening and in time-compression as important
processes may often push too hard and too fast for the uninitiated.
Time-compression has its limitations, both in terms of rate and in
terms of material. There are many things which probably should
not be compressed, both for esthetic and intrinsic reasons. Poetry
and mathematics texts, for example. And that which is to be compressed for popular consumption probably should be compressed
only moderately to take advantage of the efficiencies of the process
without creating comprehension difficulties. For example, most
lecture-type presentations could probably be compressed to 65 to
75 percent of their original lengths without creating strain and loss
of comprehension, thus saving a very significant 15 to 20 minutes
out of every hour of listening time. However, further compression,
particularly if instituted too rapidly, could cause problems. If
there is ever any question, it is better to choose the slower rate,
allowing the receivers to demand a faster one when ready. In one
of our studies (Orr, et al., "Self-Pacing Behavior in the Use of
Time-Compressed Speech," J. of Educ. Psychol., 1969, 60, 28-31)
we discovered that subjects who had complete control of the rate of
presentation of some historical passages averaged a rate of about
150 percent of normal presentation rates. This study suggests that
the process is compatible with the needs of subjects, so that if people are not antagonized by being forced along too rapidly, they will

find time-compressed presentations useful and desirable.

Thus it may be seen that in these applications of time-compressed speech technology it is efficiency in the communication of information for which we must work, rather than for sheer speed itself. Indeed, it may be argued that the entire force of the "educational revolution" of current times is primarily directed at raising the efficiency of time spent at the educational enterprise with respect to the attainment of the output knowledges, skills, goals, etc. Properly applied, time-compression fits well with this emphasis. It should continue to fit well as we move into the era of improved audio technology, long-line transmission, interlibrary networks, and home information consoles.

One further thought occurs to me as I examine the material presented in these volumes. That is the dearth of research and application of "expanded" (slowed) speech. While the prospects for the slowed end of the rate-controlled speech continuum may not be as exciting as those for speeding, more attention to expansion appears to be warranted. I shall not attempt to catalogue the possibilities, but there are obvious applications to the study of various speech variables, and, perhaps, to the teaching of second languages. For example, in a paper presented to the XIth Interamerican Congress of Psychology ("Improving the Comprehension of a Second Language Through Training with Rate-Controlled Speech," Memorias Del XI Congreso Interamericano de Psicologia, Mexico City, December 1967, Section 88) I suggested the following hypothesis for text: "Given second language students who have mastered the fundamentals of the target language, their auditory comprehension of connected discourse will be greatly improved if they are given practice in listening to connected discourse at a rate of speed at which they can fully comprehend the message, and thus take full advantage of the contextual cues in the message." Using expanded speech, of course. While we did make some effort to explore the validity of this contention at the American Institutes for Research, I believe the issue remains open. This and related problems would make ideal areas in which to pursue the unique advantages of rate-controlled speech at the slower end of the scale.

And still it seems that almost no one has ever heard of time-compressed (or expanded) speech. But I return to my earlier contention that this is about to change.

Certainly one of the foremost restraints upon the growth of the field of rate-controlled recordings in general, and time-compressed speech in particular, has been the fact that speech compression equipment has been both scarce and expensive. At the present time, there is only one very small manufacturer who can supply equipment of the electromechanical sampling type, and that at a cost of several thousands of dollars or more. The German machine is no longer being produced, and was even more expensive; and other devices are one-of-a-kind, laboratory developments. Thus research, and more particularly applications, has been restricted to institutions which could afford and obtain the required equipment. The situation has been eased somewhat by the fact that the Center for Rate-Controlled Recordings at the University of Louisville has offered a service in preparing limited amounts of compressed tape for research purposes, at cost. But the fact of the matter is that few if any individuals have had the opportunity to work with compressed speech outside of the meager number of institutions possessing the equipment.

However, in the very near future, perhaps even by the time this book is distributed, concrete steps will be under development to bring to the public market a speech compressor with state-of-the-art quality at a price that individuals can afford, perhaps $300 to $500. This machine already exists, though it has not yet gone into production. And in the not too distant future, developments now well advanced in several laboratories promise an even less expensive model. The importance of these developments can scarcely be overemphasized. One division director of a government agency has written to me (personal communication) that he regards the development of an inexpensive home speech compressor as "the breakthrough we have been waiting for."

Thus, it is my promised prediction that, once these inexpensive home compressors are available (which should be within a year or two), it will seem that everybody has heard of time-compressed speech, and that every school and most people will eventually have one.

I have taken some space in this introduction reviewing some of the historical background of developments in time-compressed speech, addressing some of the strengths and weaknesses in the field, and presenting evidence for the importance of developments in this field. I have done so in an effort to underline the importance of these volumes. In my opinion, Professor Duker has done his usual excellent job on a task of Herculean size. In the field of time-compressed and rate-controlled speech, which is now growing rapidly and may soon boom, this work will undoubtedly assume landmark proportions.

Part I

BASICS

The larger portion of this part, the first 12 chapters, consists of the reproduction of major works that have been frequently
cited by those developing new concepts in regard to speech compression. A few, but only a few, of these items are readily accessible.
On the other hand, a substantial number of items are difficult to obtain in a readily usable form.

The compilation of an anthology or book of readings often
subjects one to the basic criticism that no new contribution is being
made. It is not possible to dispute the fact that the text in such a
compilation is not the original work of the compiler. No such claim
is made. On the other hand, there are, what seem to me, some
compelling advantages for the reader as well as for the research
worker that result from the existence of such collections. Mention
has already been made of the question of accessibility. It might be
argued that if the compiler of an anthology could obtain a document
for the purpose of reproducing it, then the reader or student could
do the same. True! The considerable effort involved in first locating and then obtaining the material would have to be duplicated by
each person interested in a particular item. That expenditure of
time and energy seems unjustified.

Most items that are included here are excerpted in order to
avoid repetition and the recital of the kind of meticulous detail that
would be of little interest to most users of a work such as this one.
I have not used the customary dots to indicate deletions because it
is my feeling that they tend to distract rather than help. I assume
that the serious researcher will use these excerpts, extensive though
some of them may be, for the primary purpose of determining
whether or not it would be profitable from his own particular standpoint and purposes to obtain and study the original document. The
more or less casual reader would not be concerned with the exact
places where some material has been deleted.

It seems obvious from the literature in the field of compressed speech that the late Professor Grant Fairbanks was the outstanding pioneer in that area. It is certainly true that research
since then has taken us much farther along the road, but little of
this work can be traced to a source other than the work done by or
sponsored by Grant Fairbanks at the University of Illinois. A very
substantial portion of the first 12 chapters is therefore given over to
his work. The last four chapters in Part I are concerned with a

variety of fundamental issues which will be of importance to the research worker who is engaged in investigation and development of various aspects of compressed speech.

For the uninitiated, a careful perusal of Part I will make the remainder of this book more understandable and significant. For those already knowledgeable in the area, it is hoped that Part I will serve as a useful and convenient reference source.

Chapter 1

EARLY BEGINNINGS

The two selections included in this chapter do not concern themselves with what we now think of as time compressed speech. They are, however, concerned with alteration of speech rate. The first excerpted selection, by Dr. Harry Goldstein, is probably the most frequently cited early work on altering the rate of presentation of oral material. The excerpts are taken from Goldstein's 1940 doctoral dissertation written under the direction of Professor Irving A. Lorge at Teachers College, Columbia University. An interesting sidelight is the use of subjects who were paid by public funds as part of one of the work-relief programs of New Deal days.

Goldstein was primarily concerned with a comparison of the efficacy of written and oral materials. He postulated that one of the ways of reaching the best possible judgment concerning the relative effect on comprehension of visual and aural presentations would be to vary the rate. Even the early efforts of such pioneers as Garvey [B167, 168] and Fairbanks [B99-109] were still far in the future so that speech compression by the sampling method was not available to Goldstein. He therefore adjusted the rate of visual material by varying the rate of projection on a screen; the rate of aural material by means of a combination of rapid speaking and playback at a rate more rapid than the recording rate.

Goldstein's work perforce was original and was carefully planned and executed. In a real sense it has served as a model for the research in a number of later studies. Certainly it has been one of the most frequently cited items in the field of rate alteration. This excerpt deserves careful examination even today by every serious student of the subject. This is so despite the mass of material that has subsequently become available on the relative merits of written and oral stimuli in producing comprehension. (For an early review of such studies see, for example, Willard F. Day and Barbara R. Beach, "A Survey of the Research Literature Comparing the Visual and Auditory Presentation of Information," A. F. Technical Report no. 5921, November 1950. Since that review, many further studies have been produced.)

The second excerpt in this chapter, by Diehl, White, and Burk, is included--even though it was published as late as 1959-- because of the important issues it raises for the first time. Both Garvey's and Fairbank's works, which are excerpted in later chapters, were investigations of the increase of rate produced by

45

random deletions from the spoken text.   The present study is concerned with determination of the effect on comprehension of altering
the length of pauses rather than the length of words.   The basic
questions raised in this study are of primary importance.   Over and
over again we will encounter in this book discussions about and
studies of the effect of altering pause time and of making random
deletions as opposed to making deletions at specific points in the
text.   In this study the rates were so near to each other that the
failure to obtain significant differences may be accounted for in this
way.

READING AND LISTENING COMPREHENSION

Harry Goldstein

In our society, reading and listening constitute the basic tools
of learning as well as the prime media of social intercourse.   In the
fulfillment of these roles, the importance of reading has never been
questioned.

Summary of Related Findings

The literature in the field, when restricted to published
studies involving comprehension of meaningful material, reveals contradictory findings.   These studies favor the auditory mode, while
an equal number favors the visual mode.   One research finds a reversal of superiority between the fifth and ninth grades, with the
visual mode superior in the high grades; another finds the auditory
mode superior for college students and the visual mode superior for
non-college adults; a third finds that for rapid readers in college the
visual mode is superior and for slow readers the auditory mode is
superior.   The three studies testing for association-recall (rather
than comprehension) are all in agreement in finding the auditory mode
to be reliably superior.   In the unpublished minor investigations performed under the writer's supervision, the auditory mode is superior
in two cases; in the third case, modality superiority is conditioned
by the reading ability of the subjects.

The factors responsible for the discrepancies in the findings
are difficult to disentangle since they are interwoven in the various
experiments.   Included among these are the nature and difficulty of
the material, the social and educational background of the experimental subjects, the quality of the auditory and visual situations, the
rates of speech and reading, and the method of equating the modalities.   In this investigation the last two factors are subjected to
rigorous control.

Points of Departure of the Present Experiment

Two basic limitations are common to all of the experiments cited. (1) Equation of conditions, where attempted at all, involved control in terms of keeping time or number of presentations constant. Neither method presents analogous audio-visual situations, since, where time is kept constant, the number of presentations varies; and where the number of presentations is kept constant, time varies. (2) A single rate was utilized, the rate being purely arbitrary, and frequently not even stated. The selected rate may, conceivably, have favored one or the other mode.

The present experiment provides: (1) superior equation of conditions by means of synchronous control of the rate factor and (2) inclusion of various speeds of presentation.

The justification of the present investigation lies not only in the construction of techniques devised especially to procure proper rate control, but in the change of perspective afforded audio-visual comparisons of the utilization of various speeds; to wit, if faster rates of presentation are relatively more favorable to one mode, that fact constitutes a point of superiority for that mode--at least from the point of view of educational economy. Educationally, as well as physically, rate times time equals distance. For theoretical reasons, rates of speech not ordinarily attainable (as high as 322 words per minute) were included in the present experiment. The future may see acceleration of speeds of communication (and learning) in every form.

The Problem

The basic problem of the experiment was to compare reading and listening comprehension at various rates of presentation. Schematically, the problem may be presented as follows, with x_1, x_2, ... x_7 and y_1, y_2, ... y_7 representing reading and listening comprehension, respectively, at seven specified rates, and x and y representing the average comprehension achievement.

Mode	Rates							Average
	1	2	3	4	5	6	7	
Reading comprehension	x_1	x_2	x_3	x_4	x_5	x_6	x_7	$\bar{x}$
Listening comprehension	y_1	y_2	y_3	y_4	y_5	y_6	y_7	$\bar{y}$

As indicated, the experiment actually consisted of several sections. A horizontal analysis shows how comprehension in each modality varies with rate. A vertical analysis provides a comparison of reading and listening comprehension at each of the several rates. In addition, certain other aspects of the problem were treated. These included:

1. The effect of difficulty of material upon relative modality differences.
2. The distribution of abilities in each mode.
3. The extent of individual differences in relative ability in the two modes.
4. The detection of possible optimum rates of presentation.
5. The relationship between reading and listening comprehension.
6. The relationship between intelligence and comprehension in each mode.
7. The relationship between reading-speed and comprehension in each mode.
8. The effect of intelligence and of reading-speed upon the direction and extent of audio-visual differentials in comprehension.
9. The effect of intelligence upon easy-hard passage differentials within each mode.
10. The effect of intelligence upon modality differentials on easy versus difficult materials.
11. The equivalence of passages in both modalities.
12. The reliability and validity of the experimental data.

The Modalities Defined

The exigencies of the experimental situation, which required strict rate control, precluded the use of the usual print-reading and audience-speaker situations. To a degree, therefore, naturalness was sacrificed for control. In this experiment, the visual mode of presentation consisted of motion film projection of meaningful type-written material upon a screen. The auditory mode of presentation consisted of phonographic reproduction of the identical material, electrically transcribed.

Fully natural conditions do not obtain even in the usual comparative audio-visual studies, where the customary procedure is to present material once orally to the subjects and then have the subjects read comparable material once only. The auditory presentation in this respect is less atypical than the visual, since a speaker does not ordinarily repeat various sections of his presentation; the visual presentation, in excluding the opportunity for rereading, to that extent differs from the typical reading situation, where rereading is a matter of personal wish.

In the present study, the experimental situations were even less natural. The auditory situation, involving the use of mechanical media, differed from the usual audience-speaker situation, where visual cues may aid in the interpretation of speech. However, the speech heard in the present experiment was of exceptional quality, and the phonograph records were superior to the usual radio situation where static and distortion may tend to hinder speech intelligibility. As for the reading situation, not only were the subjects permitted just one reading of each passage, but their reading rate was "paced";

that is, they were required to read at an externally controlled rate rather than at their own convenient rate. The usual print-reading situation was replaced by a film-reading situation which changed color of print, size of letters, length of line, and focal distance. In addition, the stationary visual field was replaced by a moving field since the lines of the passages moved continuously up the screen.

Nevertheless, despite these superficial differences, it is a fair assumption that the visual mode did provide a true reading situation: (1) studies have demonstrated the importance of context over structural factors in influencing reading rate and comprehension; (2) the correlations between film-reading and standardized reading test scores obtained in the present investigation were as high as the correlations among standardized reading measures.

Materials

Of the available standardized reading material, the McCall-Crabbs Standard Test Lessons in Reading were most easily adaptable for the purposes of the present experiment. There is a distribution of grade norms for each passage, scaled in terms of tenths of a grade, based upon the number of questions answered correctly. Only general type narrative and descriptive passages were selected. Fourteen passages presumably easy and 14 passages presumably difficult were selected. The chosen passages averaged 119 words in length for the easy level and 213 words for the difficult level. The questions on each passage were scrutinized. Occasionally questions were added, sometimes to measure comprehension of the main thought, and sometimes to compensate for questions dealing with word meaning rather than paragraph comprehension. The 28 passages contained a total of 314 questions which were answered on special score sheets.

Subjects

A group of 280 subjects, male and female, ranging in age from 18 to 65 years, and showing wide scatter on a variety of standardized measures, was utilized in this experiment. Table 1 presents relevant information concerning the nature and background of the group. Assuming 14 years as the average mental age of the adult population (Pintner) and eighth-grade ability as the average achievement level, it appears that the group is somewhat above average in intelligence and school achievement. The size of the standard deviation indicates the variability of the group.

Experimental Apparatus and Design

The proper control of rate necessitated the formulation of techniques in both the visual and auditory areas. Films and records were selected as offering the most practical means of control. The selection of rates was conditioned chiefly by two factors: (1) the

Table 1

BACKGROUND DATA CONCERNING THE EXPERIMENT GROUP

	Mean	S. D.	Norm Equivalent
Age......................	34. 27	12. 13	
Intelligence			
Otis Self-Administering Tests of Mental Higher Examination: Form A	34. 45	10. 85	15-9 (M. A.)
I. E. R. Intelligence Scale CAVD, Levels M-Q, Form II	391. 49	14. 08	not available
Reading			
Thorndike-McCall Reading Scale, Forms I, IV, VI, VII, VIII			
I..................	27. 80	3. 61	9. 02 (Grade score)
VI.................	28. 09	3. 84	9. 22 (Grade score)
VII................	29. 61	4. 50	9. 28 (Grade score)
IV-VIII............	27. 47	4. 60	8. 64 (Grade score)
Gates Reading Survey for Grades 3 to 10, Form I			
Speed..............	43. 72	13. 10	10. 09 (Grade score)
Comprehension	72. 09	8. 97	10. 42 (Grade score)
Vocabulary..........	74. 87	8. 25	11. 79 (Grade score)
Gates Reading Survey for Grades 3 to 10, Form II			
Speed..............	40. 55	10. 90	8. 86 (Grade score)
Comprehension	74. 22	9. 19	10. 84 (Grade score)
Vocabulary	73. 18	11. 30	11. 62 (Grade score)
Traxler Silent Reading Test, Form I (designed for use in grades 3 to 10)			
Speed	34. 66	9. 44	8. 5 (Grade score)
Sentence Compr	12. 17	5. 21	12. 19 (Grade score)
Vocabulary.........	35. 75	9. 28	beyond 10th grade
Paragraph Compr...	27. 11	7. 12	10th grade
Thorndike Test of Word Knowledge, Form C............	76. 00	16. 22	beyond 9th grade
Am. Council on Educ. Co-op. General Culture Test, Revised Series, Form O			
Social Science........	31. 95	24. 23	50th %-ile coll. fresh.
Foreign Literature....	26. 90	21. 03	54th %-ile coll. fresh.
Fine Arts............	39. 33	23. 71	62nd %-ile coll. fresh.
Science	30. 42	16. 97	15th %-ile coll. fresh.
Mathematics.........	9. 14	8. 38	20th %-ile coll. fresh.

practical speed limits, at either end, of intelligible, fluent speech; and (2) the number of distinct differentiations in speaking rate that appeared feasible. Preliminary trials indicated that clear and intelligible speech could be obtained within a range of from 100 to 285 words per minute; and further, that speaking rate could be differentiated conveniently into six speed groups at successive increments of 37 words per minute. It was found, too, that an additional increment of 37 words per minute could be obtained, without undue distortion, by means of controlled phonographic acceleration. Consequently, the reading and listening rates of speed used in this study, were: 100, 137, 174, 211, 248, 285, and 322 words per minute.

In fairness to the auditory mode, it was necessary that optimum speech conditions prevail. Mr. Alwyn Bach, the winner of the 1931 gold medal award of the American Academy of Arts and Letters for good diction on the air, was engaged to make the experimental records. The renditions were delivered in an objective tone, avoiding undue emphases or pauses. They were electrically recorded on wax at 33.33 revolutions per minute, yielding eight double-sided 12-inch records. Guided by a stop watch, the speaker practiced each rate, beginning with the slowest one. When the timing was found to be accurate, the recordings were begun. All the passages were delivered at the first rate of 100 words per minute. The speaker then practiced the next rate, had recordings made, and continued this procedure until all the passages had been recorded at six rates.

Construction of Rate of Comprehension Test Films

After considering various possible ways of presenting a rate-controlled natural reading situation, a moving passage technique involving screen projection was decided upon. In brief, this technique involved the photographing of "justified" typewritten script (that is, a script on which all lines are equal in length) which wound around a speed-controlled paper-drive equipment. The passages were typewritten in pica type on ordinary adding-machine paper, three and one-half inches in width, the length of line being two and one-quarter inches. The lines averaged four to five words in length. Each passage was filmed at each rate, with the camera running at a constant speed.

Design of the Experiment

The duration of the experiment was approximately thirty working days, and the average testing time was three hours. Each weekday a different group of ten people met in the experimental room. When the subjects entered the room, they found closed looseleaf booklets and two answer sheets, upon which they were asked to give such information as name, age, and date. The general tenor of the instructions given to all groups was as follows:

"The purpose of this experiment is to determine the effect of the rate of presenting material to you upon your understanding of the material. This is to be obtained for both reading and listening. For reading, the passages will be presented on the screen, the lines of each passage moving up until they have disappeared at the top of the screen. Some of the passages will move up very slowly; some will move up very rapidly. You will not know in advance the order in which speeds will be presented, so you must be prepared for any speed. For the slow speeds, you will find that you can read down faster than the lines move up. Please try to stay up at the top of the screen, else you will penalize yourself by not taking the full time, since you cannot begin answering questions until the lights go on. Also, by finishing faster, you have more time in which to lose the thought. As for the fast passages, you don't need any instructions since you will have difficulty enough staying up at the top of the screen. For listening, the passages will be presented to you by means of phonograph records, also at different rates of speed and in random order. Each passage will be preceded and followed by the sound of a bell, to signal the beginning and end of the passage.

"When the passage has been presented, I will call out the number of that passage and you are to turn to that page in the book on the desk and start answering the questions. The pages are in straight numerical order. The questions will all deal with the passage you have just read or heard. All questions are of a multiple-choice type, that is, each question is followed by four possible answers, only one of which is correct. Put the letter of the correct answer in the box next to the number of that question. Each box must have the letter A, B, C, or D in it, until you have answered all the questions of that passage. If you have any trouble in finding the correct answer, please use your best judgment, and select the one that appears most nearly correct. Answer the first passage in the first column, going down the page; the second passage in the second column, and so until you have worked your way across the page.

"Please use capital letters only, since it is sometimes hard to tell the difference between a small "a" and a small "d." When you have finished, please close the book as the signal for the next passage to begin.

"I am sure that many of you would like to know how you score. When the experiment is over, and the tests have all been marked, I'll be glad to let you know how you did in comparison to the rest of the members of the whole group of some 280 people.   Also, if you are interested, I can let you know how you made out in reading compared to listening.   Incidentally, it is hoped that the findings of this experiment may be used in connection with the Adult Education Reading Project. Your sincere cooperation will be appreciated.

"Please do not discuss the nature of the passages with any other members of the project, since they may answer the questions in light of what they heard about the passages, rather than from what they were able to understand by themselves. Is it all clear?   Are there any questions?"

Questions were few, and covered quickly.   Two assistants observed the subjects, and made sure that the directions were followed. The variables operating in the experiment were:
1.   Subjects: 28 groups of ten subjects, each subject of the group representing a different decile ranking in intelligence.
2.   Difficulty levels: two levels of difficulty, corresponding on the average to grade 3.5 and 7.5.
3.   Passages within levels: 14 passages of each level of difficulty.
4.   Rates of presentation: seven rates, ranging in increment of 37 words per minute from 100 to 322 words per minute.
5.   Serial orders of presentation: 28 random orders of presentation of the passages and rates for each group.
6.   Modes of presentation: visual and auditory.

The randomization of all variables was attempted through the use of 16 seven-way Graeco-Latin Squares, which were presented in random orders.   Since the squares themselves constitute a system of complete randomization, the experimental design provided for rotation both within and among squares.   The experimental design adopted neutralizes possible inequalities within each variable, balancing possible practice, carry-over, or fatigue effects which may operate to the advantage or disadvantage of one or the other modality, specific rates, or patricular passages.   It minimizes possible differences in difficulty of the passages at each level; possible differences in the ability of the experimental groups; and possible experimental variation in rates of presentation.   In addition, it lends itself to appropriate statistical treatment and interpretation.

The Data and Their Treatment

The requisite data for answering the problems of this investigation are presented in the succeeding tables.   Preliminary inspection of the scores for passages revealed that, despite the care in selecting

Table 2

HARD READING COMPREHENSION SCORES IN A GRAECO-LATIN SQUARE

Groups	Rates 1	2	3	4	5	6	7	Sum	
1	d-3 209.7	e-1 215.0	f-4 218.1	a-5 200.7	b-2 212.4	c-7 215.8	g-6 190.3	1462.0	Correction (C): $\frac{(10206.3)^2}{49} = 2125889$ *
2	a-7 207.1	c-6 210.3	b-3 219.8	e-2 192.1	f-1 202.4	g-4 199.7	d-5 196.2	1427.6	Total: $2131456 - C = 5567$
3	b-5 220.7	g-1 228.1	d-7 217.5	c-4 206.9	a-6 208.0	e-3 192.1	f-2 194.7	1468.0	Groups: $\frac{14888694.33}{7} - C = 1067$
4	e-4 220.6	d-2 208.5	c-5 208.0	f-6 211.5	g-7 212.4	b-1 185.6	a-3 200.8	1447.4	Passages: $\frac{14881972.11}{7} - C = 107$
5	g-5 228.2	f-7 230.9	e-6 230.1	d-1 211.9	c-3 212.5	a-2 211.6	b-4 204.2	1529.4	Rates: $\frac{14899650.99}{7} - C = 2633$
6	f-3 216.8	a-4 199.1	g-2 204.0	b-7 209.2	e-5 212.5	d-6 204.0	c-1 201.5	1447.1	Orders: $\frac{14882434.75}{7} - C = 173$
7	c-2 208.0	b-6 211.5	a-1 215.2	g-3 203.9	d-4 204.0	f-5 198.1	e-7 184.1	1424.8	Remainder = 1587
Sum	1511.1	1503.4	1512.7	1436.2	1464.2	1406.9	1371.8	10206.3	

			Summary by Passages					Sum
Passages	a	b	c	d	e	f	g	
Sum	1442.5	1463.4	1463.0	1451.8	1446.5	1472.5	1466.6	10206.3

			Summary by Orders					Sum
Orders	1	2	3	4	5	6	7	
Sum	1459.7	1431.3	1455.6	1452.6	1464.4	1465.7	1477.0	10206.3

Note: The letter and number at the top of each cell represent passage and order respectively.
* Figures are given to the nearest whole number.

Table 2 (cont.)

ANALYSIS OF VARIANCE

Source of Variation	Degrees of Freedom	Sum of Squares	Mean Square	F	$F_{.05}$	$F_{.01}$
Total.................	48	5567				
Groups (1-7).........	6	1067	178	2.69*	2.51	3.67
Rates................	6	2633	439	6.65**	2.51	3.67
Passages (a-g)........	6	107	18	−3.67	3.84	7.31
Orders...............	6	173	29	−2.28	3.84	7.31
Error................	24	1587	66			

*Significant; $F > F_{.05}$
**Highly significant; $F > F_{.01}$
—Minus F values indicate that the variance is less than
   error variance. (The use of negative signs in this
   fashion is not customary in the literature.)

them, they were apparently not equivalent at each level. In order
to equate the passages, they were scaled by means of the regression
equation technique against a reading criterion consisting of a composite of four forms of the Thorndike-McCall Reading Scale. (The
scaled scores were derived from coded scores representing the composite Thorndike-McCall criterion measure.) In order to avoid
forcing a possibly spurious identity between the reading and listening
scores on the passages, only the reading scores were scaled, and
the scale equivalents were then applied to the raw reading and listening scores. The advantages of using scaled rather than raw scores
are (1) the scores can be interpreted more meaningfully in terms of
the grade level equivalents; (2) the passages are equated; (3) the
equation of passages permits a more valid correlation between reading and listening.

The basic statistical treatment consisted of an analysis of
variance of data in the Graeco-Latin Squares.

The Problems Treated

Problem 1a. Are reading and listening comprehension affected
significantly by: Rate of presentation? Serial order of presentation?
The nature of the passages? The composition of the groups?

Table 2 illustrates the Graeco-Latin Square experimental design and the accompanying analysis of variance procedure for the
solution of the problem. The scores in each cell represent the sum
of the coded scores earned by a particular group for a particular
passage presented at a particular rate in a particular order. The
columns represent rate scores; the rows, group scores. The letter
and number at the top of each cell represent passage and order, respectively. The computation of the sum of squares for each variable

is presented in the upper right-hand side and the analysis of variance appears in the lower section of the table.

It is evident that the composition of the groups is a significant source of variation, the F value exceeding the $F_{.05}$ value. This indicates not only that the experimental groups were not strictly equated, but that the inequality among the groups is accompanied by differences in degree of comprehension. The nature of the groups influences the findings. Rate is highly significant, as indicated by the fact that the F value is considerably higher than the $F_{.01}$ value. Rate of presentation is therefore very important in influencing comprehension attainment. The passages and orders of presentation are an inconsequential source of variation, indicating the success of the scaling procedure used in equating the passages and the efficacy of randomization in the Graeco-Latin Squares.

The essential data of the 16 Graeco-Latin Squares, comprising the F values of each of the variables, are presented in Table 3.

Table 3

THE RATIO OF VARIANCE AMONG DESIGNATED SOURCES
TO ERROR VARIANCE

Squares with Level and Mode	ANALYSIS OF VARIANCE (F VALUES)			
	Groups	Rates	Passages	Orders
Easy reading				
1....................	15.33**	10.95**	−2.67	1.12
2....................	6.30**	9.78**	−1.83	1.00
3....................	3.30*	4.34**	−5.75†	−2.56
4....................	3.65*	3.34*	−2.82	2.29
Hard reading				
5....................	2.69*	6.65**	−3.67	−2.28
6....................	3.65*	10.47**	−2.86	3.40*
7....................	4.85**	12.26**	−1.70	2.47
8....................	8.29**	7.58**	−4.83†	2.33
Easy listening				
9....................	−1.11	15.38**	5.61**	1.51
10....................	5.20**	18.75**	5.95**	2.85*
11....................	2.39	6.54**	1.02	−1.10
12....................	4.84**	5.72**	1.56	−1.02
Hard listening				
13....................	8.22**	16.05**	9.33**	1.30
14....................	12.56**	18.26**	−1.35	1.47
15....................	4.01**	11.73**	2.51*	2.91*
16....................	5.78**	8.37**	3.31*.	−2.22

*Significant; $F > F_{.05}$
**Highly significant; $F > F_{.01}$
†Significant negatively; variance less than would be expected by chance.
††Highly significant negatively; variance much less than would be expected by chance.

Square 5 is the one given in Table 2.   The factor of rate is obviously significant.   Not only is it found to be highly significant in 15 of
the 16 Graeco-Latin Squares, and significant in one, but the degree
of significance $(F > F_{.01})$ in most of the cases is so great that the null
hypothesis may be rejected with a confidence greater than .99.

Variation among groups is highly significant in ten squares,
significant in four, and not significant in two.   Evidently, the composition of the groups is a significant factor in determining the results.
Passages are found to be highly significant positively in three cases,
significant positively in two and not significant in 11.   This is undoubtedly due to the scaling of the passages and indicates that the
scaling procedure was highly successful.   It does not mean that passages constitute an insignificant source of variation outside of the
present experiment.   Serial order of presentation was so well randomized that in no square is it found to be highly significant; it is
significant in three squares, and not significant in 13 squares.   Apparently, serial order of presentation is not a significant source of
variation.

Problem 1b.   What is the effect of the experimental variables
as a function of modality, and difficulty of material?

As stated above, it was demonstrated that groups and rates of
presentation are significant factors in influencing comprehension.
Passages and order of presentation were shown to be insignificant
factors.   In order to note possible differential effects of these variables as a function of modality, and difficulty of material, the analysis of variance was undertaken separately for the easy and hard
reading and listening passages.   The essential data are presented in
Table 4.

Table 4

ANALYSIS OF VARIANCE OF THE EASY AND HARD READING AND LISTENING
COMPREHENSION SCORES

Source of Variation	ANALYSIS OF VARIANCE (F VALUES)			
	Easy Reading	Hard Reading	Easy Listening	Hard Listening
Groups	5.46*	5.33*	2.76*	6.65*
Rates	5.74*	8.52*	9.15*	12.54*
Passages	−2.81†	−3.24†	2.43*	3.99*
Orders	1.47	1.99*	1.19	1.60

* Highly significant.
† Highly significant negatively.

Rates are a highly significant source of variation for both
modalities at both difficulty levels.   They are apparently more significant in influencing listening than reading comprehension, and they

exert more pressure at the difficult than at the easy level. Groups are also a highly significant source of variation for both easy and hard reading and listening comprehension. They appear to be about equally significant for easy and hard reading comprehension but considerably more significant for hard than for easy listening comprehension. In other words, different groups will show greater differences in listening comprehension for hard than for easy material.

Passages show a particularly interesting effect. For reading comprehension, the passage variance is considerably less than the error variance. However, for listening comprehension the passage variance is highly significant. Apparently, the scaling of the passages for the reading scores equated them so well that their variation is significantly less than would be expected even from a group of homogeneous passages. But the fact that the passages are thoroughly equated for reading does not insure equivalence for listening comprehension. The identical passages which are an insignificant source of variation of reading comprehension are a highly significant source of variation of listening comprehension. Serial order of presentation (which is not a pure function, being a conglomerate of order of presentation of passages and order of presentation of rates) has been effectively randomized, and is an insignificant source of variation except for hard reading comprehension, where it exceeds the $F_{.01}$ value of 1.98 by .01. Since the same system of randomization was used in all cases, the discrepancy is difficult to explain.

Problem 2a. Are there any reading-listening differentials in comprehension, in general?

In order to determine the relative efficacy of reading and listening presentation, the mean scores for each mode, based upon the total reading and listening scores earned by each individual at both levels of difficulty and at all rates of presentation, were compared and the difference tested for reliability. The results are given in Table 5.

Table 5

RELIABILITY OF DIFFERENCE BETWEEN READING AND LISTENING COMPREHENSION

Mode	N	Mean	S. D.	$S.E._M$	D	$S.E._D$*	D/SE_D
Listening....	280	295.4	22.3	1.33	3.7	.97	3.8
Reading.....	280	291.7	25.8	1.54			

$$*S.E._D = \sqrt{S.E._{M(R)}^2 + S.E._{M(L)}^2 - 2r_{RL} S.E._{M(R)} S.E._{M(L)}}, \text{ where } r_{RL} = .78$$

Since the critical ratio (represented by the ratio of the obtained difference to the standard error of the difference) is greater than three, it is significant, the chances of a true difference being 99.9 out of 100.   Apparently, then, under the conditions of the present experiment, listening comprehension is reliably superior to reading comprehension although quantitatively the difference is very slight. The educational significance of the obtained difference of 3.7 points is more readily interpretable in terms of grade scores.   The average code comprehension scores for the visual and auditory modes are 20.84 and 21.08 respectively.   (See Table 6.)

Table 6

AVERAGE READING AND LISTENING COMPREHENSION SCORES AT THE SEVEN RATES
OF PRESENTATION

Mode	Rates							Average
	1	2	3	4	5	6	7	
Listening	21.91	21.69	21.65	21.50	20.70	20.56	19.56	21.08
Reading..........	21.62	21.28	21.32	21.07	20.69	20.30	19.60	20.84
Listening superior.	.29	.41	.33	.43	.01	.26		.24
Reading superior..							.04	

Problem 2b.   Are there any reading-listening differentials in comprehension as a function of the difficulty of material?

In order to determine whether size of auditory superiority is conditioned by the level of difficulty of the passages, a distribution of reading-listening differences for each subject was drawn up, separately for the easy and hard passages, and the mean differences were compared to the standard errors of the respective distributions of differences.   The data are presented in Table 7.

Table 7

RELIABILITY OF THE DIFFERENCE BETWEEN
READING AND LISTENING COMPREHENSION
FOR EASY AND HARD PASSAGES

Passages	N	Mean Diff.	S. D.	$S.E._M$	$M/S.E._M$	Mode Favored
Easy.................	280	2.79	9.82	.59	4.73	Auditory
Hard...............	280	.89	10.66	.64	1.39	Auditory

It is clear that the relative difference between reading and listening comprehension is a function of the level of difficulty of material. For the easy passages, the difference in favor of listening is decidedly significant; for the difficult passages the difference is not reliable.

Problem 2c. Are there any reading-listening differentials in comprehension as a function of rate of presentation?

The rate factor was shown to be highly significant in affecting both reading and listening comprehension. In order to determine whether there are any reading-listening differentials in comprehension as a function of the rate of presentation, the average reading and listening comprehension scores were computed for each rate, combining the hard and easy passages. The data are presented in Table 6.

Reading and listening comprehension show a decline with rate. For four of the seven rates listening comprehension is superior to reading comprehension. For rate five there is practically no difference and for rate seven the difference is very slightly superior for reading comprehension, the small difference probably being attributable to chance. A smoothing of the reading-listening differential curves would apparently indicate that, for the first four rates, listening comprehension is superior to reading comprehension, and for the last three rates the differences are negligible.

Problem 2d. Are there any reading-listening differentials in comprehension, as a function of difficulty of material, at the various rates?

In order to determine whether there are any reading-listening

Table 8

AVERAGE EASY AND HARD READING AND LISTENING SCORES AT THE SEVEN RATES
OF PRESENTATION

Mode	Rates							Average
	1	2	3	4	5	6	7	
Listening—easy...	21.99	21.81	21.84	21.62	21.00	20.68	19.61	21.22
Reading—easy....	21.48	21.24	21.32	21.08	20.78	20.40	19.76	20.87
Listening superior.	.51	.57	.52	.54	.22	.28		.35
Reading superior..							.15	
Listening—hard...	21.84	21.57	21.45	21.38	20.41	20.43	19.52	20.94
Reading—hard....	21.75	21.31	21.33	21.07	20.59	20.19	19.43	20.81
Listening superior.	.09	.26	.12	.31		.24	.09	.13
Reading superior..					.18			

differentials in comprehension as a function of the difficulty of material at the various rates, the average reading and listening comprehension scores were computed for the easy and difficult series. The data appear in Table 8.

For both easy and difficult materials, listening comprehension is superior to reading comprehension, the difference being more marked for the easy materials. For the easy passages, the differential appears to decline after the fourth rate, and at the seventh rate it is slightly favorable to reading comprehension. For the difficult materials, the differences in favor of listening are slight all the way through with no consistency of trend noticeable. The differential appears to be least at the first and seventh--the slowest and the fastest rates. At rate five there is a reversal in favor of reading, but since this is slight, and righted again at the next rate, it is probably unreliable.

Problem 2e. Are there any reading-listening differentials in comprehension, as a function of intelligence, at the various rates?

The total group of 280 subjects was divided into deciles on the basis of the Otis Intelligence Score, and the average easy and hard reading and listening scores were computed separately for each decile group, number one representing the highest decile. Tables 9 and 10 present the final data.

The easy comprehension scores indicate that, for all but the fourth deciles, listening comprehension averages higher than reading comprehension; it is probable that a chance fluctuation accounts for the reversal at the fourth decile. Although the figures are irregular, there is an apparent trend toward greater reading-listening differentials in favor of listening comprehension at the lower deciles of intelligence, and a decrease in reading-listening differential at the faster rates. The most consistent reversal in favor of reading comprehension occurs at the seventh rate, but is apparently not related to decile since the reversals hold for the first, second, fourth, eighth, and ninth deciles.

For the hard passages listening comprehension is not as consistently superior to reading comprehension as it is for the easy passages. Listening comperhension averages higher than reading comprehension in seven of the ten deciles, but the average differences favoring either mode are slight in most cases. No trend of differential with rate is apparent. There is a continuous decrease in reading and listening comprehension score with successively lower decile groups.

Table 11 presents the number of intelligence deciles favoring each mode of presentation at each rate. It is apparent that the number of deciles favoring listening over reading is greater at the slower rates.   [cont. on p. 64]

Table 9

Intelligence Decile	Mode	1	2	3	4	5	6	7	Average
1	Listening...	22.88	22.67	22.98	22.66	22.48	22.29	20.29	22.32
	Reading....	22.66	22.69	22.10	22.21	22.21	21.93	21.62	22.20
	Listening superior..	.22		.88	.45	.27	.36		.12
	Reading superior..		.02					1.33	
2	Listening...	22.63	22.45	22.29	22.52	21.87	21.63	20.03	21.92
	Reading....	22.02	21.87	21.79	22.26	21.64	21.78	21.29	21.81
	Listening superior..	.61	.58	.50	.26	.23			.11
	Reading superior..						.15	1.26	
3	Listening...	22.54	22.15	22.67	22.25	21.81	21.87	21.18	22.07
	Reading....	22.31	21.75	22.36	21.71	22.33	21.20	20.81	21.78
	Listening superior..	.23	.40	.31	.54		.67	.37	.29
	Reading superior..					.52			
4	Listening...	22.84	22.13	22.21	21.83	21.62	21.45	19.69	21.68
	Reading....	22.22	22.48	22.33	21.85	21.62	21.45	21.34	21.90
	Listening superior..	.62				.00	.00		
	Reading superior..		.35	.12	.02			1.65	.22
5	Listening...	22.43	22.41	22.62	22.22	21.78	21.12	20.73	21.90
	Reading....	21.86	21.73	21.68	21.80	21.43	20.55	19.75	21.26
	Listening superior..	.57	.68	.94	.42	.35	.57	.98	.64
	Reading superior..								
6	Listening...	22.41	21.69	21.53	22.08	21.00	20.51	20.15	21.34
	Reading....	21.88	21.05	21.56	21.52	20.96	20.11	19.44	20.93
	Listening superior..	.53	.64		.56	.04	.40	.71	.41
	Reading superior..			.03					
7	Listening..	22.01	22.07	22.03	21.58	20.51	20.72	19.49	21.20
	Reading....	21.34	21.69	21.69	20.86	20.52	21.55	19.30	20.99
	Listening superior.	.67	.38	.34	.72			.19	.21
	Reading superior..					.01	.83		
8	Listening..	21.65	21.86	21.60	20.93	19.97	20.03	18.51	20.65
	Reading....	20.86	20.75	20.44	20.11	20.12	19.88	18.84	20.14
	Listening superior..	.79	1.11	1.16	.82		.15		.51
	Reading superior..					.15		.33	
9	Listening...	21.17	20.69	21.28	20.72	20.05	19.47	18.14	20.22
	Reading....	20.33	20.25	20.43	19.38	19.17	18.73	18.48	19.54
	Listening superior..	.84	.44	.85	1.34	.88	.74		.68
	Reading superior..							.34	
10	Listening...	19.35	19.99	19.15	19.42	18.92	17.67	17.85	18.91
	Reading....	19.28	18.18	18.80	19.05	17.84	16.86	16.79	18.11
	Listening superior..	.07	1.81	.35	.37	1.08	.81	1.06	.80
	Reading superior..								

Table 10

Intelligence Decile	Mode	1	2	3	4	5	6	7	Average
1	Listening	23.56	23.61	23.46	22.71	22.46	22.61	22.06	22.92
	Reading	22.96	23.16	23.71	23.20	22.70	22.55	22.03	22.90
	Listening superior	.60	.45				.06	.03	.02
	Reading superior			.25	.49	.24			
2	Listening	23.43	23.04	22.54	22.51	21.88	21.90	20.24	22.22
	Reading	23.03	23.08	22.71	23.00	21.53	21.46	20.67	22.21
	Listening superior	.40				.35	.44		.01
	Reading superior		.04	.17	.49			.43	
3	Listening	23.08	22.74	22.95	22.23	21.90	22.04	21.10	22.29
	Reading	22.73	22.76	22.00	22.10	21.78	21.26	20.98	21.94
	Listening superior	.35		.95	.13	.12	.78	.12	.35
	Reading superior		.02						
4	Listening	22.89	22.14	22.65	22.27	21.90	20.67	20.11	21.80
	Reading	22.28	21.51	22.28	21.82	21.38	20.58	20.21	21.44
	Listening superior	.61	.63	.37	.45	.52	.09		.36
	Reading superior							.10	
5	Listening	21.56	21.13	21.83	21.50	20.79	21.45	19.59	21.12
	Reading	22.91	21.60	22.16	22.03	21.17	21.34	19.63	21.55
	Listening superior						.11		
	Reading superior	1.35	.47	.33	.53	.38		.04	.43
6	Listening	21.74	21.34	21.36	21.53	20.50	20.45	19.59	20.93
	Reading	22.06	21.44	20.90	21.14	20.60	20.29	19.44	20.84
	Listening superior			.46	.39		.16	.15	.09
	Reading superior	.32	.10			.10			
7	Listening	21.93	21.40	20.53	20.76	20.23	19.10	19.32	20.47
	Reading	21.76	21.08	21.70	20.71	20.90	19.14	18.59	20.55
	Listening superior	.17	.32		.05			.73	
	Reading superior		1.17			.67	.04		.08
8	Listening	21.15	20.25	20.79	20.69	18.51	19.01	18.84	19.89
	Reading	20.50	20.72	20.40	20.23	19.75	19.46	18.89	19.99
	Listening superior	.65		.39	.46				
	Reading superior		.47			1.24	.45	.05	.10
9	Listening	19.90	20.12	19.99	20.20	18.25	18.76	17.53	19.25
	Reading	20.25	19.53	19.13	20.01	19.03	18.78	17.38	19.16
	Listening superior		.59	.86	.19			.15	.09
	Reading superior	.35				.78	.02		
10	Listening	19.15	18.98	18.46	19.45	17.71	18.36	16.78	18.41
	Reading	19.08	18.25	18.30	17.92	17.11	17.03	16.50	17.74
	Listening superior	.07	.73	.16	1.53	.60	1.33	.28	.67
	Reading superior								

Table 11

NUMBER OF INTELLIGENCE DECILES FAVORING EACH MODE OF PRESENTATION AT
EACH RATE

Level and Mode	Rate							Total
	1	2	3	4	5	6	7	
Easy listening superior.........	10	8	8	9	6*	7*	5	53
Easy reading superior.........	0	2	2	1	3*	2*	5	15
Hard listening superior.........	7	5	6	7	4	7	6	42
Hard reading superior.........	3	5	4	3	6	3	4	28
Total listening superior......,..	17	13	14	16	10	14	11	95
Total reading superior.........	3	7	6	4	9	5	9	43

* The number of deciles does not equal ten because of tie scores.

Problem 2f.   Are there any reading-listening differentials in comprehension, as a function of reading speed, at the various rates?

In order to determine whether there are any reading-listening differentials in comprehension as a function of reading speed at the various rates, the 260 subjects for whom Gates speed of reading measures were available were divided into quintile groups, and the average easy and hard reading and listening scores were computed separately for each group.   These data are presented in Tables 12 and 13.

For the easy reading material, all the quintiles show listening superior to reading, the difference increasing steadily with each successively lower quintile.   For the hard reading material, the first and third quintiles show slight differences in favor of reading comprehension; the fifth quintile markedly favors listening comprehension. The data further reveal that in the first quintile group reading is superior to listening comprehension from the fifth through the seventh rates for the easy material, and from the fourth through the seventh rates for the hard material.   Apparently, for the faster readers, the faster rates tend to favor reading comprehension.

Problem 2g.   Are there any differentials between hard and easy passages, within each mode, as a function of intelligence?

Table 12

AVERAGE EASY READING AND LISTENING COMPREHENSION SCORES AT THE SEVEN
RATES OF PRESENTATION FOR GROUPS DIFFERING IN READING SPEED

Reading Speed Quintile	Mode	RATES							Average
		1	2	3	4	5	6	7	
1	Listening...	22.75	22.67	22.74	23.02	22.09	21.98	20.91	22.31
	Reading....	22.29	22.27	22.05	22.09	22.18	22.16	21.49	22.08
	Listening superior..	.46	.40	.69	.93				.23
	Reading superior..					.09	.18	.58	
2	Listening...	22.60	22.75	22.40	22.31	21.89	21.97	20.13	22.01
	Reading ...	22.05	22.29	22.06	21.92	21.86	21.42	20.75	21.76
	Listening superior..	.55	.46	.34	.39	.03	.55		.25
	Reading superior..							.62	
3	Listening...	22.11	21.68	21.83	21.91	20.67	20.72	20.28	21.31
	Reading ...	21.34	21.64	21.65	21.14	20.99	20.50	20.06	21.05
	Listening superior..	.77	.04	.18	.77		.22	.22	.26
	Reading superior..					.32			
4	Listening...	21.74	21.08	21.63	21.43	21.03	20.24	18.83	20.85
	Reading ...	21.56	20.90	21.31	20.48	19.99	19.71	18.67	20.37
	Listening superior..	.18	.18	.32	.95	1.04	.53	.16	.48
	Reading superior.								
5	Listening...	20.83	20.70	20.69	19.34	19.61	18.57	17.67	19.63
	Reading...	19.91	19.30	19.85	19.42	18.91	18.28	17.76	19.06
	Listening superior	.92	1.40	.84		.70	.29		.57
	Reading superior..				.08			.09	

In order to determine whether there are any differentials between hard and easy passages, within each mode, for groups differing in intelligence, the "average" columns of Tables 9 and 10, which
are presented for convenience in Table 14, were compared. It
should be remembered that the easy and hard passages were scaled
against the identical criterion, so that the grade scores would not
differ despite the differences in intrinsic difficulty of the passages.

The data for the listening mode indicate that the top four intelligence deciles score higher on the hard than on the easy passages
while the bottom six intelligence deciles score higher on the easy
than on the hard material. Similarly, for the reading mode, the
first three and the fifth intelligence deciles score higher on the hard
than on the easy material while the fourth and the last five intelligence deciles score higher on the easy than on the hard material.
The explanation of these findings may be that the motivation of the
more intelligent subjects was stronger for the more difficult passages,

Table 13

AVERAGE HARD READING AND LISTENING COMPREHENSION SCORES AT THE SEVEN
RATES OF PRESENTATION FOR GROUPS DIFFERING IN READING SPEED

Reading Speed Quintile	Mode	Rates							Average
		1	2	3	4	5	6	7	
1	Listening...	23.21	23.15	22.93	22.50	22.15	21.94	20.47	22.34
	Reading....	22.75	22.93	22.71	23.30	22.30	22.08	21.48	22.51
	Listening superior..	.46	.22	.22					
	Reading superior..				.80	.15	.14	1.01	.17
2	Listening...	23.15	22.56	22.17	22.20	21.47	21.41	21.19	22.02
	Reading...	22.78	22.26	22.64	21.89	21.86	21.26	20.11	21.83
	Listening superior..	.37	.30		.31		.15	1.08	.19
	Reading superior..			.47		.39			
3	Listening...	21.82	21.50	21.88	21.07	20.19	19.93	19.48	20.84
	Reading....	21.81	21.45	21.73	20.87	20.83	20.47	19.40	20.94
	Listening superior..	.01	.05	.15	.20			.08	
	Reading superior..					.64	.54		.10
4	Listening...	20.78	20.81	21.05	20.69	19.60	20.25	18.37	20.22
	Reading....	21.50	20.73	20.63	20.06	19.67	19.66	18.75	20.14
	Listening superior..		.08	.42	.63		.59		.08
	Reading superior..	.72				.07		.38	
5	Listening...	20.16	19.67	19.20	20.28	18.39	18.45	17.90	19.15
	Reading...	19.95	19.46	19.07	19.24	18.60	17.22	17.18	18.67
	Listening superior..	.21	.21	.13	1.04		1.23	.72	.48
	Reading superior..					.21			

and therefore they scored comparatively higher on them than on the less difficult passages. The less intelligent subjects, on the other hand, instead of being encouraged to further effort, may rather have been overwhelmed by more difficult passages.

Problem 2h. Are there any differences in the relative reading-listening differentials, for the easy and hard passages, as a function of intelligence?

The relative audio-visual differentials for the easy and for the hard passages, for groups differing in intelligence, are presented in Table 15. It is evident that the reading-listening differentials are greater for the less intelligent groups, the total differential being 3.28 as against 1.25 for the more intelligent groups. For the less intelligent groups, the reading-listening differentials are greater on the easy passages than on the difficult passages, the total differentials for the easy and difficult passages being 2.61 and 0.67, respectively. For

Table 14

AVERAGE EASY AND HARD COMPREHENSION SCORES IN EACH MODE FOR GROUPS
DIFFERING IN INTELLIGENCE

Intelligence Decile	LISTENING		READING	
	Easy	Hard	Easy	Hard
1	22.32	22.92	22.20	22.90
2	21.92	22.22	21.81	22.21
3	22.07	22.29	21.78	21.94
4	21.68	21.80	21.90	21.44
5	21.90	21.12	21.26	21.55
6	21.34	20.93	20.93	20.84
7	21.20	20.47	20.99	20.55
8	20.65	19.89	20.14	19.99
9	20.22	19.25	19.54	19.16
10	18.91	18.41	18.11	17.74

Table 15

AVERAGE MODALITY DIFFERENTIALS IN COMPREHENSION ON EASY AND HARD
MATERIAL FOR GROUPS DIFFERING IN INTELLIGENCE

Read.-List. Differentials	DECILES					Total	DECILES					Total
	1	2	3	4	5		6	7	8	9	10	
Easy	.12	.11	.29	−.22	.64	0.94	.41	.21	.51	.68	.80	2.61
Hard	.02	.01	.35	.36	−.43	0.31	.09	−.08	−.10	.09	.67	0.67
Total	.14	.12	.64	.14	.21	1.25	.50	.13	.41	.77	1.47	3.28

Note: Negative numbers refer to differentials favoring reading.

the more intelligent groups, the reading-listening differentials on the
easy and hard passages do not differ to any appreciable degree, the
total differentials being 0.94 and 0.31, respectively.

Problem 2i. Are there any reading-listening differentials, in
comprehension as a function of film-reading speed?

The reading-listening differential was found to favor listening
for even the most intelligent groups and the most rapid readers, intelligence and speed of reading being determined by means of stand-
tests. In order to determine whether the same holds true for film-

reading score in this experiment, and the reading-listening differentials for each quartile were computed. The data are given in Table 16.

Table 16

READING-LISTENING DIFFERENTIALS FOR QUARTILE GROUPS
DIFFERING IN FILM-READING COMPREHENSION

Mode Superiority	No.	Q_1 Diff.	No.	Q_2 Diff.	No.	Q_3 Diff.	No.	Q_4 Diff.
Listening.......	26	169.6	35	266.9	48	501.1	46	1211.6
Reading........	44	305.3	35	375.5	22	247.7	24	269.6
Difference favoring listening..					26	253.4	22	942.0
Difference favoring reading...	18	135.7		108.6				

For the highest reading quartile, the number of subjects with reading comprehension superior to listening comprehension is greater than the number of subjects with listening superior to reading, and the total difference is in favor of reading.   For the lower quartiles, however, the situation is decidedly reversed; the majority of subjects are superior in listening comprehension and the total difference in favor of listening is very large.   This is to be expected, since the process of selecting those cases who were highest in one modality loads the errors of measurement on one side.   Nevertheless, the difference between the standardized reading test results and the film test results would indicate that the two reading situations were not identical.   Identity obtains only for perfectly correlated measures.

Problem 3.   Are there any optimum rates of presentation for reading and listening: In general? As a function of difficulty of material? As a function of intelligence? As a function of reading-speed?

The data necessary for determining optimum rates have been presented, in connection with other problems, in Tables 7, 8, 9, 10, 12, 13.   Within the limits of the experiment, no optimum rates are apparent either for the group as a whole or for groups segregated on the basis of intelligence or reading speed.   Comprehension declines from the first through the seventh rates for all groups, with both modes of presentation, at both difficulty levels.

Problem 4.   What is the extent of decline with rate for easy and hard reading and listening comprehension: In general? As a function of intelligence? As a function of reading speed?

The code scores for the first and seventh rates classified according to intelligence grouping by deciles, and according to speed of reading grouping by quintiles, were converted by interpolation into equivalent grade scores. The grade scores, with their differences, appear in Tables 17 and 18.

The data in Tables 17 and 18 indicate the following: (1) The higher intelligence groups score higher at the fastest rate than do the less intelligent at the lowest rate. With the easy reading material, for example, the second and fourth intelligence deciles at rate seven equal the seventh decile at rate one. The third decile at rate seven is approximately equal to the eighth decile at rate one. The fifth decile at rate seven exceeds the tenth decile at rate one. Similar but less pronounced findings occur with the easy listening material. The first decile at rate seven exceeds the tenth decile at rate one. With hard reading material, the first decile at rate seven exceeds the seventh and lower deciles at rate one; and the second and third deciles at rate seven exceed the eighth, ninth, and tenth deciles at rate one. Similar findings obtain with hard listening material, but, as with the hard reading material, they are less accentuated. Likewise, the same general finding holds for the higher and lower quintile groups, segregated according to reading speed. (2) The first rate of presentation gives in all cases a slightly wider range of scores between the highest and lowest decile groups than does the seventh rate. (3) Surprisingly, there are greater comprehension losses with rate for the higher than for the lower intelligence decile and reading quintile groups, although the trend is irregular. This may be accounted for by the fact that differences in raw score at the higher levels correspond to greater differences in grade score equivalents than do those same differences at the lower levels, according to the Thorndike-McCall norms.

Within the limits of rates used in the present experiment (100 to 332 words per minute), the average decline of comprehension with rate appears to be a little over two annual high school grades. For the highest intelligence deciles, it is about three grades; and for the lowest decile groups, it is about one and a half grades. It should be remembered that these interpretations are based upon the norms for the tests although the experimental subjects were adults.

Problem 5. What are the various zero-order and first-order correlations between reading and listening comprehension, as measured in this experiment and: Intelligence, as measured by standardized tests? Reading comprehension, as measured by standardized tests? Reading speed, as measured by standardized tests?

The measures of reading and listening comprehension used to compute the correlations were obtained by summing up, separately for each mode, all the subject's scores for both levels of difficulty and all rates of presentation. The combining of scores for all rates of presentation was considered advisable for two reasons: (1) it reduced the number of correlation coefficients to be computed; (2) it furnished a more reliable measure, being based upon seven times as many scores. The contamination of the correlation coefficient by the rate factor may tend to obscure somewhat the true correlation. On

Table 17

DIFFERENCES IN EASY READING AND LISTENING COMPREHENSION GRADE SCORES
BETWEEN SLOWEST AND FASTEST RATES OF PRESENTATION FOR GROUPS DIFFERING
IN INTELLIGENCE AND READING SPEED

Factor	Easy Reading			Easy Listening		
	Rate 1	Rate 7	Diff.	Rate 1	Rate 7	Diff.
Intelligence decile						
1..............	12.22	10.63	1.59	12.49	9.11	3.38
2..............	11.28	10.15	1.13	12.08	8.87	3.21
3..............	11.68	9.50	2.18	11.95	9.98	1.97
4..............	11.55	10.15	1.40	12.35	8.73	3.62
5..............	11.12	8.78	2.34	11.82	9.42	2.40
6..............	11.12	8.59	2.53	11.82	9.03	2.79
7..............	10.15	8.54	1.61	11.28	8.64	2.64
8..............	9.58	8.26	1.32	10.79	8.06	2.73
9..............	9.11	8.06	1.05	9.98	7.77	2.21
10..............	8.54	7.28	1.26	8.59	7.67	.92
Average..............	10.74	9.09	1.64	11.32	8.73	2.59
Reading speed quintile						
1..............	11.68	10.47	1.21	12.35	9.58	2.77
2..............	11.41	9.50	1.91	12.08	8.95	3.13
3..............	10.15	8.95	1.20	11.41	9.11	2.30
4..............	10.63	8.19	2.44	10.79	8.26	2.53
5..............	8.82	7.63	1.19	9.50	7.60	1.90
Average..............	10.54	8.94	1.59	11.23	8.70	2.53

the other hand, the correlation may be unduly high in view of the
fact that the questions were presented visually for both modes.   A
poor reader may appear to be a poor listener because of difficulty
in interpreting the written questions.   Table 19 presents the obtained
correlations.

The raw correlation of .78 between reading and listening comprehension is quite high, particularly in view of the fact that the
comprehension scores are contaminated by rate.   The size of the
correlation coefficient is indicative of the fact that reading is largely
a central rather than a peripheral activity.   This is substantiated in
part by the reduction when intelligence is held constant.   However,
the net correlation is still quite high, indicating that reading and
listening comprehension are related in some way other than through
general intelligence.

Reading and listening comprehension, as measured in this ex-

Table 18

DIFFERENCES IN HARD READING AND LISTENING COMPREHENSION GRADE SCORES
BETWEEN SLOWEST AND FASTEST RATES OF PRESENTATION FOR GROUPS DIFFERING
IN INTELLIGENCE AND READING SPEED

Factor	Mode					
	Hard Reading			Hard Listening		
	Rate 1	Rate 7	Diff.	Rate 1	Rate 7	Diff.
Intelligence decile						
1	12.62	11.28	1.34	12.99	11.41	1.58
2	12.62	9.42	3.20	12.87	9.03	3.84
3	12.22	9.66	2.56	12.66	9.82	2.84
4	11.68	9.03	2.65	12.49	8.95	3.54
5	12.49	8.68	3.81	10.63	8.68	1.95
6	11.41	8.59	2.82	10.79	8.68	2.11
7	10.96	8.12	2.84	11.12	8.54	2.58
8	9.27	8.33	.94	9.98	8.26	1.72
9	9.11	7.48	1.63	8.82	7.52	1.30
10	8.45	7.20	1.25	8.49	7.28	1.21
Average	11.08	8.78	2.30	11.08	8.81	2.27
Reading speed quintile						
1	12.35	10.47	1.88	12.74	9.27	3.47
2	12.35	8.95	3.40	12.74	9.98	2.76
3	10.96	8.59	2.37	10.96	8.64	2.32
4	10.47	8.26	2.21	9.50	7.99	1.51
5	8.87	7.41	1.46	9.03	7.67	1.36
Average	11.00	8.74	2.26	10.99	8.71	2.28

periment, have a high correlation with intelligence as measured by
both the Otis and the CAVD tests; and with reading comprehension
and reading rate as measured by the Thorndike-McCall and the Gates
tests, respectively. The correlations with these tests are practically identical for reading and for listening comprehension. The film
and record scores appear to correlate somewhat higher with reading
comprehension than with reading rate. The Gates tests, it should be
noted, do not minimize comprehension, but actually measure rate of
comprehension.

Problem 6. Are the data obtained in the present investigation
reliable?

The analysis of variance presented in Table 3 (see page 56)
supplies one indication of the reliability of the data. In order to
furnish additional information as to the consistency of the experimental findings, data from the first fourteen groups are compared with

Table 19

ZERO-ORDER AND FIRST-ORDER CORRELATIONS BETWEEN EXPERIMENTAL READING
AND LISTENING COMPREHENSION SCORES AND STANDARDIZED READING AND
INTELLIGENCE MEASURES

Factors	
Reading and listening	.78
Reading and Otis	.75
Listening and Otis	.72
Reading and CAVD	.68
Listening and CAVD	.70
Reading and Thorndike-McCall	.76
Listening and Thorndike-McCall	.76
Reading and Gates	.67*
Listening and Gates	.68*
Reading and listening (Otis constant)	.50
Reading and listening (CAVD constant)	.60
Reading and listening (Th.-McC. constant)	.54
Reading and listening (Gates constant)	.58

* Correlation based upon 260 cases; all other correlations based upon 280 cases.

Table 20

CONSISTENCY OF RESULTS AS EVIDENCED BY COMPARISON OF FIRST AND LAST HALVES
OF THE EXPERIMENT

Mode	Section of Experiment	RATES						
		1	2	3	4	5	6	7
Easy listening	1st half	1386	1350	1341	1331	1268	1227	1126
	2nd half	1342	1338	1345	1327	1253	1229	1116
Easy reading	1st half	1301	1275	1274	1252	1237	1198	1109
	2nd half	1313	1299	1314	1286	1239	1182	1165
Hard listening	1st half	1118	1070	1055	1058	943	962	851
	2nd half	1113	1090	1081	1063	976	958	858
Hard reading	1st half	1087	1067	1059	977	971	920	839
	2nd half	1111	1065	1059	1059	983	925	852

data from the last fourteen groups. The figures, which represent total raw scores (unscaled), are given separately for both modes of presentation and for both levels of difficulty in Table 20. The similarity of the results is a gratifying indication of minimum experimental error. If the figures were presented as averages rather than as totals, the discrepancies would appear microscopic.

Findings

Bearing in mind the fact that the reading and listening situations, particularly the former, are not quite typical, a concise listing of the findings is presented below, classified according to the variables operating in the experiment. Because of the interaction among the variables, overlapping is inevitable.

Modes

1. Listening comprehension is, in general, superior to reading comprehension.
2. The superiority of listening comprehension is decidedly more marked for the easy than for the difficult materials.
3. The relative superiority of listening comprehension is in inverse proportion to the intelligence and reading-speed of the groups.
4. The relative superiority of listening over reading comprehension declines with increased rate of presentation.
5. Reading comprehension is more variable than listening comprehension.
6. Modality superiority is, to a certain extent, a function of "individual idiosyncrasy" of the subjects.

Rates

7. Reading and listening comprehension show a consistent decline with increased rate.
8. The decline of reading and listening comprehension with increased rate is slight for the first few rates but becomes accelerated at the faster speeds.
9. The average decline of comprehension between the slowest and most rapid rates of presentation appears to be slightly over two annual high school grades.
10. Within the limits of the rates used in the experiment, optimum rates of presentation are not manifested for the group as a whole, or for groups segregated according to intelligence or reading-speed.

Groups

11. The composition of the groups is a highly significant factor in influencing comprehension achievement.

12. Groups are more variable in reading than in listening comprehension.

13. Groups are apparently more variable at the slower than at the faster rates of presentation, but this may be conditioned by the difference in the grade level achievement at these rates.

14. The more intelligent and more rapid-reading groups score higher in both reading and listening comprehension than do the less intelligent groups.

15. Within each mode, the more intelligent groups score relatively higher on the difficult than on the easy passages; the reverse holds true for the less intelligent groups.

16. The more intelligent and more rapid-reading groups score higher for both modalities at the fastest rate than the less intelligent and slower-reading groups do at the slowest rate.

17. The fast readers find reading more effective than listening at the fast rates, although the reverse is true for the fast readers at the slow rates.

18. The grade level decline in comprehension with rate is apparently greater for the more intelligent than for the less intelligent groups, but this may be a result of the inequality of score units at the higher and lower levels of achievement.

19. The reading-listening differential favors listening in general and increases inversely in proportion to the intelligence and reading speed of the groups.

20. The upper quartile groups in film-reading comprehension find film-reading comprehension superior to listening comprehension; for the lower quartiles this situation is emphatically reversed.

21. Modality preference is apparently conditioned in some degree by "individual idiosyncrasy" of the subjects, the range of individual differences being far greater than the difference between mean modality scores.

Passages

22. Passages, when properly equated by scaling, are not a significant source of variation in comprehension.

23. Equivalence of passages for reading comprehension does not insure their equivalence for listening comprehension.

24. The superiority of listening over reading comprehension is more marked for the easy than for the difficult passages.

25. The easy passages give greater reading-listening differentials than the difficult passages, particularly for the less intelligent groups.

Orders

26. Serial order of presentation, when properly randomized, is not a significant source of variation in comprehension.

Correlations

27. Reading and listening comprehension are highly correlated, indicating the importance of central over peripheral activity.

28. If standardized measures are valid criteria, the test scores for the films and records are satisfactory indices of reading and listening comprehension.

29. If standardized measures are valid criteria, the test scores for the films and records are satisfactory indices of intelligence.

RATE AND COMMUNICATION

Charles F. Diehl, Richard C. White, Kenneth W. Burk

Rate can be altered by a speaker in several ways: by prolonging or shortening the pause time between words, phrases, or sentences, by introducing new pauses, and by prolonging or shortening syllables and words within phrases. Relationship of rate of speech to effective communication has been studied in various ways. The present study inquires into the relationship of rate of speech and listener comprehension by altering only pause time, a technique not previously used in rate studies.

Procedure

To alter pause time, it was necessary first to establish a communication pattern as a control point for all alterations. Therefore, a 14-minute informative-type lecture on "birds" was practiced and tape recorded by one of the experimenters. This recording was then judged by three speech specialists with the objective of guiding the speaker to the very best speech of which he was capable. After four such listening sessions, suggestions for improvement having been incorporated into each new recording, the judges agreed that the lecture was being delivered effectively by the speaker and that additional recordings would probably show little or no improvement. This tape was called the "master tape." The rate of speech on the master tape was 145 wpm.

To determine where a pause was to be altered, the experimenters listened to the master tape, each identifying what he considered to be pause points. All of these points were then inspected by actual linear measurement of the corresponding points on the tape. It was discovered that none of the tape lengths between pauses was less than 2.5 inches. At a tape rate of 7.5 inches per second, the rate at which the master tape was recorded, 2.5 inches represents 1/3 second. Therefore, 2.5 inches of tape (or 1/3 second) was accepted as the minimum separation for pauses, and only pauses of at

least this length were altered.   Throughout the experiment, linear
measurement of the tape was used in altering all pauses.   It was arbitrarily decided to alter pause time of the master tape in four ways:
by removing 75 per cent of pause, and removing 50 per cent, thus
yielding a faster wpm rate; and by adding 75 per cent, and adding
50 per cent, thus yielding a slower wpm rate.

In preparing the experimental tapes, five exact electronic reproductions of the master tape were made.   From tape A, 75 per
cent of pause was removed; from tape B, 50 per cent of pause time
was removed; to tape C, 75 per cent of pause time was added; to
tape D, 50 per cent of pause time was added.   Tape E was unaltered.
The removal or addition of pause time was accomplished in all cases
by the removal or addition of the appropriate percentages of actual
tape at each pause point.   In all, 181 pause alterations were made
in each tape.   After all pauses had been altered, tape A had a wpm
rate of 172; tape B, 160; tape C, 135; and tape D, 126.   Tape E remained at the original 145 wpm rate.

Four experimental groups (A, B, C, D) and one control group
(E) to which the final recordings were administered were selected
from students enrolled in various courses in two liberal arts colleges
and one university in Kentucky.   On each of the three campuses the
procedure was identical: Group A listened to tape A, Group B to
tape B, Group C to tape C, Group D to tape D, and Group E to tape
E.   These data were then pooled for all subjects, yielding an approximate N of 75 for each group with a total of N of 371.

To evaluate the effect of altered pause time on the comprehension of the lecture by the listeners and their reactions to the "quality" of the delivery, they completed a two-part test immediately after
hearing the recorded lecture.   Part I was a completion-type test of
49 questions based on lecture content.

Table 1

Mean Information Test Scores for Five Experimental Groups Where Pause Time Was
Altered: (A) Less 75% Pause Time, (B) Less
50% Pause Time, (C) 75% Pause Time
Added, (D) 50% Pause Time Added,
and (E) Unaltered Pause Time.

Groups	A	B	C	D	E
N	81	81	71	64	74
Mean	26.82	26.06	27.49	26.04	28.57

Results

The mean comprehension scores (Table 1) of the five groups ranged from 26.04 to 28.57. The results of an analysis of variance of the mean comprehension scores (Table 2) revealed no significant differences between groups.

Table 2

Summary of Analysis of Variance for Testing
Differences Among Comprehension Scores of
Five Experimental Groups Who Listened
to Recordings of a Lecture Presented
at Different Rates.

Source	df	ms	F
Between groups	4	83.03	1.07*
Within groups	366	77.96	
Total	370		

*Not significant.

Conclusions and Discussions

On the basis of the results and within the limitations of the study, it appears that altering rate from 126 wpm to 172 wpm by altering pause time as described in this experiment does not interfere with listener comprehension and does not effect listeners' ratings of the quality of a speaker's delivery.

Although the procedure for altering rate in this study differed from those used in previous research, the results add support to the conclusions previously reached, that rate may range from 125 wpm to 225 wpm without appreciable loss in comprehension. The relationship between pause time and phonation time in connected speech can, apparently, be altered with no appreciable loss in comprehension. This suggests that the listening mechanism is highly adaptable.

The altering rate through altering pause time by the removal or addition of actual tape is suggested as a useful technique for studying various aspects of rate. Its use insures validity by eliminating the voice variables introduced through the use of different speakers, or of one practiced speaker presenting material at various rates. Its use is suggested to study a more radical alteration of pause time beyond the 75 per cent alterations reported here. The effect of altered pause time on the comprehension of more difficult lecture material is also suggested.

Chapter 2

CUT AND SPLICE

The excerpt which constitutes this chapter is taken from a
master's thesis by William D. Garvey which was completed at the
University of Virginia in 1949. Like the Goldstein study in the previous chapter, this work has been cited in almost all later studies
relating to change of speech rate. Prior to the Garvey study it had
been determined by a number of experimenters that speech could be
interrupted by deleting segments from recorded discourse without affecting either intelligibility or comprehension. This was found to be
so even when a large proportion of spoken material was omitted.
Garvey's contribution was the proposition that if the remaining portions of the discourse were abutted, increased intelligibility would
result. In addition to this, another advantage of abutting would be a
saving of time. In the previous work the time for reproduction was
the same for interrupted material as for the original uninterrupted
material. Since Garvey's work was sponsored by the Air Force
which was anxious to find ways to speed up communication to moving
aircraft, the factor of time was naturally of prime importance.

Confusion is often caused by the use of the terms, "intelligibility" and "comprehension." The distinction between these two
terms must be thoroughly understood by the careful reader of this
work. This distinction has been excellently explained by Kenneth A.
Harwood ["A Concept of Listenability," Western Speech 14(2):10-12,
March 1950]. Garvey's study is concerned solely with the matter of
intelligibility and comprehension is not involved in his experiment.
Because intelligibility was the focus of this investigation the material
used was a word list rather than connected discourse. Except for
the first deletion made at the beginning of each word the remaining
deletions were made on a random basis. This excerpt is a carefully
written description of a meticulously performed experiment which required great persistence, care, and preciseness. It is well worth
reading and studying.

DURATION FACTORS IN SPEECH INTELLIGIBILITY

William D. Garvey

The present emphasis upon the development of high speed air-craft creates the necessity for shortening the time consumed in the process of aviation communication.   Because of the relative slow-ness of presenting and receiving messages through the auditory sense channel, aeronautical engineers have proposed employing a system of visual message presentation.   However, in order to determine the relative practicability of auditory and visual message presentation, possibilities of speeding up recorded speech should be more fully ex-plored.   Under contract with the Air Force, the University of Vir-ginia is investigating the practical limits to which recorded speech can be speeded up without undue sacrifice of intelligibility.   Previous methods of speeding up speech have led to attendant distortion of the speech pattern.   The present thesis describes a new procedure and reports the preliminary results in the use of this procedure.   This technique is designed so that recorded speech can be speeded up to any desired rate without attendant distortion.

History of Problem

H. Goldstein [B193] reports a study in which the experimenters read aloud paragraphs from several reading comprehension tests at various rates of speed 100, 137, 174, 248, 285, and 322 words per minute.   The results indicated that clear and intelligible speech could be obtained from 100 to 322 words per minute.   It appears that the reader could read clearly up to the rate of only about 285 words per minute.   An additional increment of 37 words per minute was added to the 285 by recording the paragraphs read at 285 words per minute and then speeding up the playback turntable.   This additional speed up was accomplished without undue distortion.   Comprehension scores for these various rates showed only very slight loss from the increases in speed.

E. D. Steinberg, in "Effects of Distortion on Speech and Mu-sic" [Electrical Engineer's Handbook, ed. H. Pender & K. McIlwain, New York: Wiley, 1936; p. 932-38], reports the speeding up of re-corded speech on recording discs and sound film.   In this study the technique employed to speed up the recorded speech was to increase the speed of the sound film or disc above that used during recording. Steinberg reports that with continuous speech large losses in intelli-gibility were obtained for increases of 14, 28, and 48 per cent in speed.   Some of these large losses in intelligibility undoubtedly were due to factors other than the mere speeding up of the recorded speech.   In the technique described by Steinberg the speed-up is ac-companied by a frequency shift.   When the speed of a turntable is increased over the speed used during recording, the frequency shifts upward, the amount depending on the speedup (i. e. final frequency equalling original frequency multiplied by turntable speed-up).

George A. Miller, in "Intelligibility of Speech: Effects of
Distortion" [Combat Instrumentation II, ed. G. E. Waring, Wash.,
D. C.: Gov. Print. Off., 1946; p. 88-109], reports an investigation
done at the Harvard Psycho-Acoustic Laboratory in which continuous
speech was chopped by means of cutting the speech on and off with
an electronic switch. It was found, with a chop rate of nine segments per second, that as much as 50 per cent of the original speech
could be removed with a loss of only 15 per cent intelligibility. This
finding suggested that if some means could be devised for chopping
segments from the speech record, removing the unrecorded portions,
then splicing together the remaining segments, the effect of speeding
up the speech could be obtained without the usual frequency distortion.

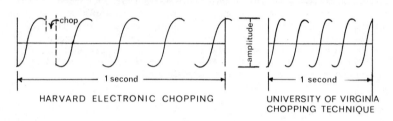

HARVARD ELECTRONIC CHOPPING   UNIVERSITY OF VIRGINIA
                                     CHOPPING TECHNIQUE

Figure 1.   Illustration of the effect of chopping segments from a
pure tone.

It may be seen from Figure 1 that by removing 50 per cent
of a tone in successive chops and then bringing the remaining portions of it back together the effect of a 100 per cent speed-up has
been accomplished, (i. e., one second of tone now is played back in
one half of a second). The same thing can be done for speech.

Before condemning auditory communication and adapting some
visual method, it is important that further possibilities of speeding
up auditory communication should be explored. Rather than assume
that our present auditory communication methods are operating at
their most efficient level with the human operators, an investigation
should be made to determine if voice communication can be speeded
up by increasing the speed of speech. If it can be shown that speech
can be speeded up twice, or even one and a half times, the present
communication speed, then a great deal of the need for replacing
auditory communication with visual means of communication will be
eliminated.

PROCEDURE

Method of Chopping

Preliminary experimentation indicated that a new technique involving the removing of small sections of recording tape with consequent splicing so as to achieve a continuous record, was a technique which would give speed-ups of any desired rate without attendant distortion. At a conference with Dr. John W. Black, Dr. Black explained that he was working on a technique in which he was removing small portions of words to determine the effect of certain vowels and consonants on the intelligibility of these words. By using recording tapes he found that no effect, other than that caused by removal of parts of speech, was made on the speech by the splicing technique. Dr. Black further suggested that some means might be devised whereby a cutting-splicing technique could be used for the speeding up of recorded speech. The spondaic words from the Harvard Psycho-Acoustic Laboratory Auditory Test No. 14 were re-recorded on plastic base tape. The position of the words on the tape was determined next by slowly passing the tape over the magnetic playback head of the recorder. The beginning and ending of each word thus could be clearly determined and marked. Once the position of the words on the tape had been determined the sections to be removed were marked on the tape with a soft pencil. If an amount of speed-up of 100 per cent was desired, this could be accomplished by removing one centimeter and leaving one centimeter in or removing two centimeters and leaving two centimeters in; or any other one-to-one ratio could be used. In order to be systematic in chopping the words, the chopping always commenced at the beginning of the word; e. g. , if the ratio was one centimeter removed to every one centimeter, the first centimeter of the word was removed, the second left in and spliced to the point of the tape where the word originally began; the third centimeter was removed, the fourth left in and connected to the end of the second centimeter removed, and so forth. If the ratio was one centimeter removed to every three centimeters then the same procedure was followed.

Apparatus

Using a regular 78 r. p. m. turntable the first 50 spondaic words of the Harvard Psycho-Acoustic Laboratory Test No. 14 were transcribed onto 11 plastic base recording tapes.

In order that the speed of the tape passing the recording head on the Brush Recorder might be increased, a larger capstan was made to replace the standard pulling mechanism. By means of this new capstan it was found that 38. 9 centimeters of tape per second passed the recording head as compared with 19. 0 centimeters per second with the standard capstan. This meant that the average recorded spondaic word would cover about 33 centimeters of the tape as compared with approximately 16 centimeters of tape covered by use of the original capstan. This alteration enabled the experimenter to have a greater length of tape with which to work in the chopping and splicing technique. Preliminary experimentation indicated that by chopping at the rate of one centimeter removed for every one centimeter, less than 60 per cent intelligibility of the words was obtained with the original slower capstan. With the new faster capstan chopping at the same rate, intelligibility scores above 98 per cent were obtained. This would seem to indicate that if larger capstans could be provided with the subsequent speeding up of the tape passing the recording head even higher intelligibility scores might be obtained.

After the tapes had been chopped at their various rates and spliced back together, they were transcribed onto a second tape. It was found that the speed of the tape passing the recording head on the tape recorder was the same as that on the Brush when the original small capstan was used. Thus by replacing the original capstan on the Brush recorder the tapes recorded on the Webster Ekotape could be played back to the subjects on the Brush Sound Mirror at standard speed.

The auditory pretest tape and the experimental tapes were presented to the subjects by means of the following apparatus.

1. The tapes were played to the subjects on a Brush Sound Mirror.
2. From the Sound Mirror the signal entered the attenuator where tne proper attenuation was added to present a signal to the subjects at an intensity level of 42 decibels above threshold. The signal on leaving the attenuator entered an impedance matcher and thence went to the earphones of the subject and the experimenter. The proper intensity level was maintained at all times by controlling the primary voltage and decreasing or increasing the volume of the signal when necessary as indicated by the voltage monitor system.
3. The subjects received the tests monaurally over earphones.
4. The words spoken by the subjects were picked up by a microphone and recorded by a Soundscriber.

Variables Investigated

The primary purpose of this experiment was to investigate the effect of speeding up of speech on its intelligibility. By varying the size of the chop removed and the size of the unremoved segment, further variables could be investigated. It thus was considered important to set up the experiment so as to be able to investigate such variables as:

1. The relationship between intelligibility and the size of the removed chop.
2. The relationship between intelligibility and the size of the removed chop, with the per cent of speed-up held at a con-

stant level.
3. The relationship between intelligibility and the size of the unremoved chop.
4. The relationship between intelligibility and the per cent of the word removed.

Experimental Design

All of these factors could be investigated by the preparation of 11 experimental tapes. Each tape is chopped at a different rate. (See Table 1.) All tapes were recorded at the same intensity level,

Table 1

DESCRIPTION OF EXPERIMENTAL TAPES

Tape No.	Chop Rate*	% Speed-up	% Of Word Removed	% Of Word Remaining
1	1cm/2cm	50	33.33	66.67
2	1cm/1cm	100	50.00	50.00
3	1.5cm/2cm	75	42.86	57.14
4	1.5cm/1.5cm	100	50.00	50.00
5	1.5cm/1cm	150	60.00	40.00
6	2cm/1cm	200	66.67	33.33
7	2cm/2cm	100	50.00	50.00
8	2cm/3cm	67	40.00	60.00
9	2.5cm/1cm	250	71.43	28.51
10	2.5cm/2.5cm	100	50.00	50.00
11	3cm/1cm	300	75.00	25.00

*The numerator equals the size of the chop removed and the denominator equals the size of the segment left in.

and all tapes had recorded on them the first 50 spondaic words from the Harvard Psycho-Acoustic Laboratory Auditory Test No. 14. Systematic chopping, as described in the previous section of this paper, was applied to all tapes. In investigating the relationship between speed-up and intelligibility all 11 tapes were used. Thus a range of rates of speed-up was obtained from 50 to 300 per cent. To determine the effect on intelligibility of the size of chop removed, the unremoved portion of the tape was held at a constant one centimeter and tapes number two (1cm/1cm), five (1.5cm/1cm), six (2cm/1cm), nine (2.5cm/1cm), and 11 (3cm/1cm) were used.

In ascertaining the relationship between intelligibility and the size of the chop removed, with the rate of speed-up held at a constant rate of 100 per cent, tapes number two (1cm/1cm), four (1.5 cm/1.5cm), seven (2cm/2cm), and ten (2.5cm/2.5cm) were used.

[cont. on p. 86]

Table 2

INDIVIDUAL ACUITY AND INTELLIGIBILITY SCORES
(Presented for Each Experimental Tape)

Tape # 1

Subject	Acuity Scores	Experimental Tape Scores
1	19	98
2	15	96
3	23	98
4	21	100
5	16	100
6	16	100
TOTAL	110.00	592.00
MEAN	18.33	98.67
S. D.	2.93	1.49

Tape # 2

Subject	Acuity Scores	Experimental Tape Scores
1	23	98
2	18	94
3	20	94
4	16	92
5	20	96
6	15	98
TOTAL	112.00	572.00
MEAN	18.67	95.33
S. D.	2.68	2.23

Tape # 3

Subject	Acuity Scores	Experimental Tape Scores
1	20	98
2	24	100
3	19	94
4	15	96
5	18	88
6	19	98
TOTAL	115.00	574.00
MEAN	19.67	95.67
S. D.	2.72	3.90

Tape # 4

Subject	Acuity Scores	Experimental Tape Scores
1	23	98
2	20	92
3	16	98
4	22	94
5	15	94
6	16	98
TOTAL	112.00	574.00
MEAN	18.67	95.67
S. D.	3.14	2.34

Tape # 5

Subject	Acuity Scores	Experimental Tape Scores
1	20	94
2	19	98
3	18	94
4	19	96
5	20	90
6	20	88
TOTAL	116.00	560.00
MEAN	19.33	93.33
S. D.	.75	3.39

Tape # 6

Subject	Acuity Scores	Experimental Tape Scores
1	23	62
2	20	78
3	16	88
4	23	68
5	17	88
6	17	86
TOTAL	116.00	470.00
MEAN	19.33	78.33
S. D.	2.87	13.05

Table 2 (cont.)

	Tape # 7			Tape # 8	
Subject	Acuity Scores	Experimental Tape Scores	Subject	Acuity Scores	Experimental Tape Scores
1	21	92	1	16	96
2	16	92	2	18	92
3	16	98	3	20	96
4	21	96	4	18	90
5	20	94	5	16	92
6	19	98	6	21	94
TOTAL	113.00	570.00	TOTAL	109.00	560.00
MEAN	18.83	95.00	MEAN	18.17	93.33
S. D.	2.2	2.52	S. D.	1.94	2.26

	Tape # 9			Tape # 10	
Subject	Acuity Scores	Experimental Tape Scores	Subject	Acuity Scores	Experimental Tape Scores
1	19	48	1	16	82
2	20	58	2	19	88
3	20	66	3	19	92
4	20	62	4	16	80
5	16	50	5	19	86
6	19	64	6	16	86
TOTAL	114.00	348.00	TOTAL	105.00	514.00
MEAN	19.00	58.00	MEAN	17.53	85.67
S. D.	1.14	6.38	S. D.	1.5	3.91

	Tape # 11	
Subjects	Acuity Scores	Experimental Tape Scores
1	19	44
2	16	40
3	20	40
4	24	38
5	16	38
6	20	40
TOTAL	115.00	240.00
MEAN	19.17	40.00
S. D.	2.88	2.00

Tapes number six (2cm/1cm), seven (2cm/2cm), and eight (2cm/3 cm) were used to study the effect on intelligibility of the unremoved portion, with the removed portion held at a constant figure of two centimeters. Since the speed-up was directly related to the amount of the word removed, the effect of the percentage of the word removed was investigated by use of all the experimental tapes; this gave a range of the amount of the word removed from 33.33 to 75.00 per cent.

Statistical Design

Sixty-six male college students were used as subjects for the experiment. The experiment was designed for analysis of variance of the intelligibility scores. In doing this each experimental tape was considered one condition, and six subjects were used in each condition. Each group of six subjects for a specific condition was then considered a "cell." Since there were 11 experimental tapes, it resulted in 11 experimental conditions or 11 cells. All subjects were tested before the experiment for auditory acuity. Thus it was assured that all subjects had normal hearing.

Presentation of Experimental Tapes

A level of 42 decibels above threshold was selected, and all experimental tapes were presented to the subjects at this level. The subjects were assigned to the various experimental tapes at random. This was accomplished by first drawing numbers from a table of random numbers, and assigning them as they were drawn to the various condition "cells." Then as each subject reported in for the experiment he was assigned to a cell corresponding to his sequence number.

In order to prevent possible learning effects, no subject listened to more than one of the experimental tapes. All instructions were recorded on each of the 11 experimental tapes. The subject repeated each word, as heard, into the microphone in front of him. His responses were recorded by a disc recorder and later scored for accuracy. The score for these tests was given in terms of the per cent of correct responses made to the total presentation of 50 words. A tabulation was made of all words that were missed. If there was any consistency in incorrect responses, note of this was made too.

RESULTS

The results obtained were quite clear-cut, the subjects showing remarkable agreement within any single cell, yet there were wide differences among some of the experimental tapes. The results may be seen in Table 2.

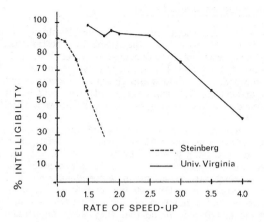

Figure 2. The relationship between intelligibility and the rate of speed-up. The broken line is a plot of the results obtained by Steinberg. The solid line is a plot of the results obtained with the chopping technique described in this thesis.

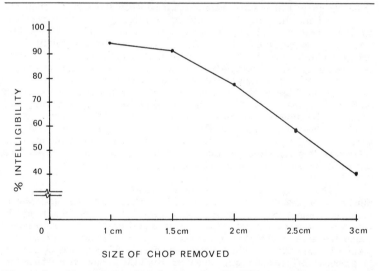

Figure 3. The relationship between intelligibility and the size of the chop removed, with the size of the unremoved segment held at the constant one centimeter.

Effect of Speed-Up on Intelligibility

Figure 2 shows the relationship of intelligibility to the rate of speed-up. It may be seen from the graph that better than 95 per cent intelligibility was obtained for speed-ups of 1. 5, 1.75, and 2. 0. For speed-ups of 1.67 and 2. 5 intelligibility scores above 90 per cent were obtained. It would seem that for discrete words the critical point is around the 2. 5 speed-up point, for it is not until this point is reached that the intelligibility scores show a significant drop.

At a speed-up rate of 3. 0 times the original speed, intelligibility scores of slightly above 78 per cent were still obtained. When the words had been speeded up to a rate of 3. 5, 50 per cent intelligibility was still obtained. When 75 per cent of the original word had been removed, resulting in a speed-up rate of 4. 0, a mean intelligibility score of less than 40 per cent was obtained. The intelligibility scores as a function of speed-up were tested for statistical significance and it was found that they were significant beyond the 1 per cent level.

Relationship Between Intelligibility and Size of Chop Removed

Figure 3 shows the relationship between the size of chop removed and intelligibility. By holding the size of the unremoved segment constant and varying the size of the removed chop, this relationship could be investigated. As would be expected logically from the graph in Figure 2, the size of chop is a critical factor determining intelligibility, since speed-up is a function of the size of chop removed. Figure 3 shows that when the unremoved segment is held at a constant size of one centimeter, intelligibility decreases abruptly with an increase in size of the removed chop. It, however, was not until the size of the removed chop (3cm) was three times as large as the unremoved section (1cm) that the mean intelligibility score dropped below the 50 per cent level. This would indicate that relatively large portions of the speech pattern may be removed from the word before appreciable losses in intelligibility occur.

The intelligibility scores as a function of the size of chop removed, with the size of the unremoved portion held constant, were tested for statistical significance and were found to be significant beyond the 1 per cent level. The highly significant relationship between the size of the chop removed and the intelligibility would explain why tape No. 8 with a speed-up of only 67 per cent of the original speed received a lower mean intelligibility score than those tapes giving 75, 100, and 150 per cent speed-ups. In order to obtain a speed-up of 67 per cent, a chop rate of two centimeters removed to three centimeters unremoved was made. In the speed-up rates of 75, 100, and 150 per cent the largest size of the removed chop was only one and a half centimeters. This would seem to indicate that the size of the chop removed is as critical a factor in determining intelligibility as the rate of speed-up. Actually, as will be shown later, intelligibility is a function of both, or either.

Relationship Between Intelligibility and Size of Unremoved Segment (with Removed Chop Held at a Constant Two Centimeters)

By retaining the size of the removed chop at a constant two centimeters it was possible to investigate the effect of the size of the unremoved segment on intelligibility. The results shown in Figure 4 are not as clear-cut as the other data; but it is logical from the previous graphs to expect that the more of the word left intact, the greater the intelligibility will be. The fact that intelligibility is higher when the size of the unremoved section is only two centimeters than when the size of the unremoved segment is three centimeters may be explained by the fact that more critical parts of the words were removed in the latter tape.

The intelligibility scores as a function of the size of the unremoved portion, with the removed chop held at a constant size of two centimeters, were tested for statistical significance and found to be significant at the 5 per cent level.

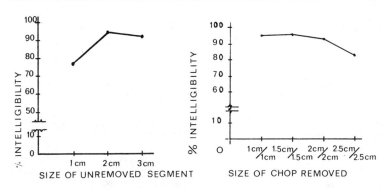

Figure 4. The relationship between intelligibility and the size of the unremoved section with the size of the removed chop held at a constant size of two centimeters.

Figure 5. The relationship between intelligibility and the size of the chop removed, with the rate of speed-up held at a constant level of 100 per cent.

Relationship Between Intelligibility and Size of Chop Removed (with Percentage of Speed-Up Held at a Constant 100 per cent)

By selecting chop rates so that the ratio of the removed chop to the unremoved segment was always a one-to-one ratio, it was possible to investigate this relationship. (See Figure 5.) As would be expected from previous findings, intelligibility is an inverse function of the size of the chop removed. The size of the chop is not the only variable that contributes to the degree of intelligibility. Intel-

ligibility in the graph in Figure 5 is a function only of the size of
the removed chop, for the rate of speed-up is held constant. It is
apparent that with the increase of rate of speed-up, intelligibility decreases not only because of the fact that more of the word is removed per chop, to obtain this increase in speed-up, but also because of the speed-up factor itself. (In other words, it also depends
on how often this chop is taken out.) The intelligibility scores as a
function of the size of the removed chop, with the rate of speed-up
held constant, were tested for statistical significance and found to be
significant at the 2 per cent level.

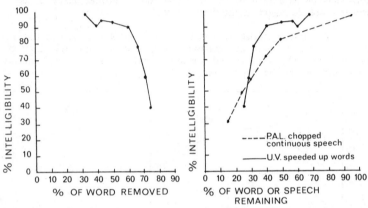

Figure 6. The relationship between intelligibility and per cent
of word removed.

Figure 7. The relationship between intelligibility and per cent
of speech or word remaining
after chopping. The broken line
is a plot of the results obtained
at the Harvard P.A.L. using an
electronic chopping technique on
continuous speech. The solid
line is a plot of the results obtained with the use of the technique described in this paper,
using discrete words.

Relationship Between Intelligibility and Percentage of the Word Removed

The graph in Figure 6 shows this relationship and the results
are quite striking. For it is not until more than 60 per cent of the
original word is removed that an appreciable effect is made on the
intelligibility of the word. It will be noticed from the graph that
even with the removal of over 71 per cent of the original words, 58
per cent intelligibility is still maintained. It is not until 75 per cent

of the word is removed that we receive mean intelligibility scores below the 50 per cent level. Since speed-up is directly related to amount of word removed, the graph in Figure 6 is a plot of the same function as in the graph in Figure 2.

DISCUSSION

Comparison of Harvard P. A. L. Chopping Technique with Continuous Speech and with Technique of Present Investigation

It will be remembered that the Harvard technique consisted of electronically chopping continuous speech so that blank spaces remained between the unchopped segments. The graph in Figure 7 shows a comparison between the results obtained at the Harvard Psycho-Acoustic Laboratory with chopped continuous speech and the results obtained with the technique involving the removing of small sections of recording tape with consequent splicing so as to give a continuous and interrupted record. Since the rate of speed-up in the latter technique is dependent on the amount of the word removed a more or less direct comparison may be made between it and the Psycho-Acoustic Laboratory technique. The broken line on the graph indicates the results obtained at the Psycho-Acoustic Laboratory when chopping continuous speech. The solid line indicates the results obtained at the University of Virginia when chopping discrete words. It may be seen that when less than 28 per cent of the speech or words remains, the Psycho-Acoustic Laboratory technique resulted in higher intelligibility scores. When more than 28 per cent of the speech or words remained, the University of Virginia technique shows the higher intelligibility scores. This comparison would imply that one or a combination of the following factors cause a difference in the resulting intelligibility obtained in the use of the two techniques: (1) intelligibility for continuous chopped speech is slightly lower than that for discrete words; (2) by removing the silent spaces in the speech and bringing the remaining portions of the speech together to form a continuous and uninterrupted speech pattern, the intelligibility of the speech has been increased.

Frequency Distortion

Technically, and as far as the experimenter and subjects were able to ascertain, the technique for speeding up speech presented in this paper eliminates the frequency shift which has accompanied the speeding up of recorded speech in previous studies. Steinberg reports that previous studies have shown that speeding up recorded speech on discs and sound film by increasing the rate of turntable or the rate of passage of the film (above the rate at which the speech was recorded), results in less than 50 per cent intelligibility for speed-ups of 50 per cent or more. By contrast the present results would tend to show that the loss in intelligibility is not due so much to the actual speeding up of the speech, but rather to the frequency shift that occurs when such techniques are used. If the frequency shift can be controlled, then it appears that the speed of the speech can be increased more than 100 per cent without undue losses in intelligibility.

Percentage of Word Removed

Figure 3 shows the relationship between intelligibility and the amount of the word removed. With the assumption that all the words on the Harvard Psycho-Acoustic Laboratory Auditory Test No. 14 were spoken at a normal speech rate, the results show that for words spoken at this rate over 60 per cent of the word may be removed with resulting mean intelligibility scores better than 90 per cent. The 50 per cent level of intelligibility is not approached until over 70 per cent of the word is removed. Such surprising results may indicate that words spoken at such a rate as the experimental words originally were spoken provide more cues than are necessary for understanding the words. Another interpretation that may be placed on these findings is that in the perceptual process there is a sort of "filling in" of the removed components of the words taking place. Whatever the explanation, the intelligibility scores are higher than would be expected from compressed speech.

Application or Significance of Findings

If the results obtained from the speeding up of discrete words are any indication of the amount that continuous speech can be speeded up, then the speed of auditory communication can be increased as much as 150 per cent without appreciable loss in intelligibility of the message. At the same time if auditory communication can be speeded up by this amount not only will the process of communication be speeded up but also more than twice as much additional transmission time will be made available for further transmission of auditory messages.

The speeding up of recorded messages may be applied to any type of routine communication such as landing instructions, weather reports, etc. where the messages can be recorded and stored up until proper time for transmission.

SUMMARY

A new technique has been devised for the speeding up of recorded speech without apparent distortion. This technique involves the systematic removal of small sections of recording tape with subsequent splicing so as to achieve a continuous record. It has been shown that through the use of the present technique, discrete words may be speeded up as much as 250 per cent of their original rate with less than 50 per cent loss of intelligibility. Although the present findings are limited to the use of discrete words, they were suggestive that recorded continuous speech may be greatly speeded up without great losses in intelligibility.

Chapter 3

CUT AND SPLICE REFINED

The excerpt in this chapter is taken from Garvey's doctoral dissertation completed in 1953 at the University of Virginia. The experiments reported here are based on the study reported in his master's thesis which was excerpted in the preceding chapter. A number of factors that went beyond the previously reported findings were introduced for investigation. Essentially however, this study, like the previous one, is concerned with the effects of deleting portions of tape-recorded oral material when the remaining portions of the text are then abutted.

It is interesting to note that the factors here introduced have continued to be the subjects of investigation in later research concerned with the control of message rate. This study introduces six new variables which are listed and briefly discussed here:

1. Garvey studied the effect of frequency shift on interrupted and abutted messages. Obviously this is an important factor for investigation, as the principal purpose of schemes for the compression of speech has been to alter the rate of speech without shifting the frequency of the original message.

2. The possible difference between intelligibility of words from a phonetically balanced list and the comprehension of short messages was investigated using sentences and words that had been interrupted and abutted in the manner previously described by Garvey.

3. Garvey reports on his study of the effects on intelligibility of different degrees of speed up of rate of presentation.

4. The effect of noise on intelligibility was an additional topic for investigation in the study described in the excerpt in this chapter.

5. Garvey reasoned that prior familiarity with a message might be a factor affecting intelligibility. He reports his findings on an investigation of this factor.

6. He further reports on his study of the effects of slow playback on intelligibility.

In addition to reporting on his experiments involving the six factors just listed, Garvey included an exhaustive phonetic analysis of errors made in intelligibility tests. Portions of this analysis are included in the excerpt which makes up this chapter.

AN EXPERIMENTAL INVESTIGATION OF THE
INTELLIGIBILITY OF SPEEDED SPEECH

William D. Garvey

With the outbreak of the Second World War the scientific study of speech was given new emphasis as it became increasingly clear that our communication systems were inadequate for the vast communication problems involved in a global mechanized war. As the engineers extended the limit of existing technical knowledge the psychologists were called upon to investigate further the human factor in auditory communication systems. In particular the war showed the need for research on the practical intelligibility limits of speech distorted in various ways in the transmission-presentation process.

The post war emphasis on the development of high-speed aircraft and attendant air traffic jamming at airports have created the problem of devising a more rapid system of communication between ground and air. The relative slowness of transmitting and receiving messages through the auditory sense channel is apparent in all phases of aviation communication, but it is especially striking in air traffic control, ground support, and interceptor operations (where radio channels are badly over-saturated). The idea occurred to aeronautical engineers that auditory communications might be supplemented or replaced by a system of presenting messages visually. In 1948 the Psychological Laboratory at the University of Virginia undertook a contract with the United States Air Force to investigate the possibilities of a visual message presentation system. Shortly after the start of this contract, research psychologists from the Virginia Laboratory devoted considerable time to visiting Air Force operating bases in order to get first-hand acquaintance with communications equipment and procedures currently in use. During these visits it was learned that the operating personnel generally were opposed to the idea of presenting messages visually in the aircraft because of the alleged danger of overcrowding the visual sense channel.

Following this line of argument it was frequently suggested by communications personnel at the operating bases that what was primarily needed was research designed to improve, and especially to speed up, auditory communication. It appeared rather obvious that an essential aspect of such research should be the determination of the practical limits of speeding up speech without undue sacrifice of intelligibility. Accordingly, one of the earlier projects under the contract was assigned to an investigation of the possibilities of speed-up of recorded speech. The research reported herein represents a continuation of research previously reported on the effect of speed-up on the intelligibility of recorded speech. A number of variables operating to affect the intelligibility of speeded speech have been investigated in the present study, including frequency shift, type of speech material, intensity, signal-noise ratio, familiarity of material to subjects, and slowdown (with frequency shift) of speeded speech material. In addition, an analysis has been made to determine the causes for lowered intelligibility of speeded words.

HISTORY

In recent years much research has been done on the effect of various kinds of distortion upon the intelligibility of speech. From this research it has become apparent that the speech wave pattern can be variously distorted without serious losses to the resulting intelligibility. The fact that speech can be distorted to a large degree and remain intelligible may be explained by the presence of an excess of cues in the "normal" speech patterns. The listeners respond most correctly when all these auditory cues are present, but a large number of these cues can be removed without greatly affecting intelligibility. These experimental results on the effects of distortion are relevant to our present problem of speeding speech, for speeding speech involves distorting the speech. Therefore, some of the most important findings on distortion in general will be reviewed briefly along with the results of previous attempts to speed speech.

Effects of Distortion on Speech Intelligibility

Amplitude Distortion: A severe distortion of the speech pattern can be obtained by means of an amplitude-selective device. Such a device passes only certain portions of the wave form through the communication system, and that portion which is passed depends upon its amplitude. J. C. R. Licklider ["Effects of Amplitude Distortion upon the Intelligibility of Speech," J. of Acoustical Soc. of Amer. 18:419-34, 1946] found that center clipping had a much more detrimental effect upon the listener's ability to understand the speech than did peak clipping. The differential effect of peak and center clipping is explained by the fact that the vowels are much more intense than the consonants, thus, in center clipping the critical (less intense) consonants are removed and the more intense vowels are permitted to remain as part of the speech pattern. In peak clipping the consonants are relatively untouched and the vowels are only reduced in power, thus the speech remains more intelligible.

Frequency Distortion: The frequency of the spectrum of the speech wave pattern may be limited by means of frequency-selective devices. N. R. French and J. C. Steinberg ["Factors Governing the Intelligibility of Speech Sounds," J. of Acoustical Soc. of Amer. 19:90-119, 1947] have shown that if only the frequencies of speech above 1900 cps. are passed, 67 per cent of the speech is understood. Also if only the frequencies below 1900 cps. are passed, 67 per cent of the speech is intelligible. This finding indicates that intelligibility of speech depends on both low and high frequencies. It also indicates that a considerable portion of the frequency spectrum can be eliminated, and still leave fair intelligibility.

Phase Distortion: Steinberg ["Effects of Phase Distortion on Telephone Quality," Bell System Tech. J. 9:550-56, 1930] separated the speech spectrum into high frequencies and low frequencies and

delayed one set of frequencies by a small fraction of a second before
he put the two sets back together again.   The high and low components then added together to give an entirely different wave form.
It was found that a delay in one half of the spectrum of as much as
0. 1 second did not affect the intelligibility of the speech significantly.

Frequency and Rate Distortion: Further evidence that considerable alteration of the speech pattern can be made without serious loss in intelligibility is indicated in the findings of another study
by Steinberg ["Effects of Distortion on Speech and Music, " in: Electrical Engineer's Handbook, ed. by H. Pender and K. McIlwain; New
York: Wiley, 1936; p. 932-38].   He has shown that when all the
component frequencies of speech are multiplied by a common factor,
such as is obtained when the rate of rotation of a phonographic recording is increased or decreased, the intelligibility of the speech
does not drop below 80 per cent until the component frequencies have
been multiplied by a factor of less than 0. 8 or more than 1. 4.

Interrupted Speech Patterns: Miller and Licklider [B283] have
recently reported a series of studies in which the speech pattern was
interrupted systematically during the course of its presentation to the
subjects.   Such an interruption was accomplished by means of an
electronic switch which turned the speech on and off at a desired
rate.   They reported that when the interruptions were made at a rate
of ten times per second, intelligibility of monosyllabic words did not
drop below 90 per cent until over 50 per cent of the original speech
pattern was removed.   It was not until 80 per cent of the speech pattern was removed that the resulting intelligibility dropped below 50
per cent.

Also Steinberg ["Effects of Distortion on Speech and Music"]
reported an experiment in which fractions of nonsense syllables were
removed before their presentation to the listener.   If the first half
of the consonant of the nonsense syllable was removed the subjects
were still able to understand the syllable correctly better than 50 per
cent of the time.   If meaningful material was used, and the whole
consonant was removed, the subjects were able to fill in the missing
element and understand the speech with approximately 90 per cent efficiency.

Presentation Rate: Although much thorough research has been
performed to determine the effects of various types of distortion upon
speech, research on the effect of presentation rate of speech upon intelligibility is meager.   Steinberg [B193] indirectly touched on the
problem of rate of presentation in his study of the effect of frequency
shifts.   He obtained his frequency shifts in the speech pattern at the
same time he increased or decreased the rate of presentation of the
speech elements.   Such increases or decreases in rate were obtained
by speeding up or slowing down recorded speech and discs of sound
film.   Large losses in intelligibility were not obtained until the speed
up was 1. 4 times that of the original speech speed.

Goldstein [B193] reported a study in which the experimenters read aloud paragraphs from several reading comprehension tests at various rates: 100, 137, 174, 248, 285, and 322 words per minute. Intelligibility scores (retention of the material as measured by recognition) remained remarkably high for the lower speed-up rates, and did not fall to zero even at the rapid rate of 322 words per minute. The experimenter could read clearly up to the rate of only about 285 words per minute, an additional increment of 37 words per minute was added to the 285 by recording the paragraphs read at 285 words per minute and then speeding up the playback turntable. This additional speed-up was reportedly accomplished without undue frequency shift.

The methods of speeding up the speech in these two studies have certain limitations. Steinberg's method is limited by the distortion effects resulting from the frequency shift. Goldstein's method is limited by the rate at which the talker is able to speak, and also by the changes in enunciating and timing involved in attempting to speak very rapidly.

It became one of the major problems of this project to determine a more efficient method of speeding up speech. A possible method was suggested from the general findings of the effects of various distortions on speech. Particularly from Miller and Licklider's [B283] work on interrupted speech, it appeared that the undistorted speech pattern affords an excess of cues, which may be utilized by the listener but are not essential to intelligibility. In their electronic chopping technique, the gaps in the speech record were not closed, hence no saving in time of presentation was achieved. It appeared possible, however, that if some means could be devised for removing the silent spaces, thus leaving an abbreviated speech record, the result would be an increase in the speech rate with no great losses in intelligibility for small chops. This method of speeding speech would not have the disadvantage of shifting the frequency.

The magnetic tape recorder afforded a means for solving this problem. Dr. J. W. Black, in research for the Navy on auditory communications, had successfully cut segments from a recording tape, with subsequent splicing together of the unremoved segments, to effect an abbreviated intact speech record. Dr. Black's objective had been an analysis of consonant and vowel contribution to the intelligibility of single words. It was determined to apply this method of tape chopping and splicing to attempt to speed up recorded speech. The method used was to record speech on the magnetic tape, then systematically cut out portions of the tape, and join together the remaining portions with Scotch tape. The results of a series of experiments on such speeded speech were reported in detail in an M.A. thesis [B167].

The results of these preliminary experiments have indicated the general effects of increasing the speed of speech by the new chopping technique. A further series of experiments was then designed to investigate variables which affect the intelligibility of the speeded speech. These experiments will be described in the following pages.

INVESTIGATION OF CERTAIN VARIABLES OPERATING
TO AFFECT THE INTELLIGIBILITY OF SPEEDED SPEECH

Several separate experiments were conducted to investigate
variables operating to affect the intelligibility of speeded speech; this
section of the report will take up these experiments individually.
These experiments were designed to determine the effect on speeded
speech of the following variables: (1) frequency shift, (2) type of
speech material, (3) intensity, (4) signal-noise ratio, (5) familiarity
of material to subjects and (6) slowdown (with frequency shift) of
speeded speech.

General Procedure

Subjects: The subjects for the following series of experiments
were male college students. In order to insure that the intelligibility
scores were not influenced by faulty hearing all subjects were tested
before the experiment proper for auditory acuity with the Harvard
P. A. L. Auditory Test No. 14. The subjects were assigned randomly to an experimental condition, and no subject was used more than
once in the series of experiments.

Apparatus: Recording of Speech Material: The speech material was recorded upon a master plastic base tape with a Brush Sound
Mirror (Model BK 403) magnetic tape recorder. The speech was
monitored as it was being recorded by measuring the average peak
voltage, in order that the material might be recorded at uniform intensity. Also, in order to have homogeneous articulation throughout,
the recorded material was played back and each word was examined
for good articulation. A re-recording was made if this seemed desirable. The original recording of the speech material was kept as
a master record tape. From the master tape the desired experimental records were made under identical recording conditions. The
various speech materials, i.e., single words, sentences, etc., were
all recorded and re-recorded under the conditions described.

Presentation of the Materials: Once the material had been recorded and speeded up by the chopping technique, it was again recorded onto an intact tape with an Eicor Sound Recorder (Model Number 15). The intact experimental tape was then presented to the subjects by means of the following apparatus (see Figure 1): (1) The
recorded speech material was played back to the subjects on an Eicor Sound Recorder. (2) From the Eicor Recorder the signal entered
the attenuator where the desired attenuation was added. The signal
on leaving the attenuator entered an impedance matching device before
going to the earphones of the subject and the experimenter. The
proper intensity was maintained at all times by monitoring the voltage of the speech signal from the tape. (3) The subjects received
the speech materials monaurally over Permoflux PRD No. 10 earphones. In order to insure uniformity all instructions were recorded.
At the end of the instructions the record was stopped and the subjects were given a chance to ask questions. After this period a warning was given and the experimental speech material was presented to

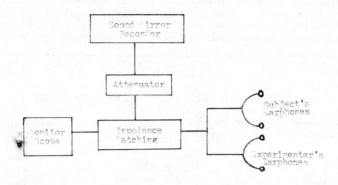

Figure 1. Block diagram showing arrangement of apparatus for presenting signal.

the subjects. After each presentation of a word or a sentence, a standard time was given the subjects to record the material that had been heard. Two methods of recording the subjects' responses were used: in the experiments with single words the subjects spoke the words aloud and these words were then recorded on discs; in the experiments with continuous speech the subjects were given time to write out the sentences.

Special details of procedure in addition to the general procedures in this section will be described for the following experiments where necessary.

Description of Separate Experiments

Frequency Shift: The results of the experiments on intelligibility of "chop-splice" speeded speech differed so greatly from the findings of Steinberg that it appeared advisable to investigate the effect of speed-up with accompanying frequency shift (Steinberg's technique), using the same speech that had been used in the earlier "chop-splice" speed-up experiments.

Statistical Design: Thirty male college students served as subjects. The experiment was designed for analysis of variance of the intelligibility scores. Five experimental conditions were used (speech material speeded up to rates 1.5, 1.67, 1.75, 2.00 and 2.5 times the original speed). Six subjects were assigned randomly to each of the experimental conditions (Table 1).

Apparatus and Procedure: Five experimental record tapes were prepared (see Table 1), using the Harvard P. A. L. Auditory Test No. 14 as the test material. This test is composed of 50 spondaic words and is the same material which was used in the orig-

inal experiments with the "chop-splice" speed-up technique.   Instead
of "chopping" the words to obtain the various speed-ups, the entire
list of words was presented to the subjects at the desired rate by
mechanically increasing the speed of the record tape past the magnetic recording pickup.   For this method of speed-up it was neces-

Table 1

DESCRIPTION OF EXPERIMENTAL RECORD TAPES

Experimental Condition	Speed-up of Presentation (No. of times original speed)	Resulting Frequency Shift
1	1.50	1.50
2	1.67	1.67
3	1.75	1.75
4	2.00	2.00
5	2.50	2.50

sary to prepare tapes with additional blank intervals spliced in between the words in order that the interval between the stimulus words
might be held constant.   The test material was presented to the subjects at an intensity level of 44 decibels above the threshold.

Results: The results are shown in Table 2 and are represented by the broken curve in the graph in Figure 1.   The difference between the intelligibility scores was tested for statistical significance
and it was found that they differed significantly beyond the 1 per cent
level of confidence.   Table 3 shows the details of a X^2 analysis.   A
comparison of the results for the two methods of speeding speech
can be made from the graph in Figure 1.   The upper solid line is
a plot of the results obtained in the earlier experiment; the lower
broken line is a plot of the results obtained from the experiment in
which a frequency shift accompanied the speed-up.

It is clear from Figure 2 that the frequency shift plays an
important role in determining the intelligibility of speeded up recorded speech.   At a speed-up of 1.75, using the same words and identical experimental procedure, the mean of the intelligibility scores,
with the concomitant frequency shift, was 90 per cent; for the same
speed-up with the chopping technique the mean intelligibility score
was 95 per cent.   For the speed-up of 2.00, intelligibility with the
frequency shift was 65 per cent, but was 95 per cent with the chop-
splice technique.   When the speed-up was increased to 2.50 a mean
intelligibility score of less than 10 per cent was obtained with the
frequency shift and a mean intelligibility score above 93 per cent
was obtained with the chopping technique.

Table 4 presents the statistical results of t-tests made on the
differences between the mean intelligibility scores for the two speed-
up methods at the various speed-up levels.   The differences between
(cont. on p. 103)

Table 2

INTELLIGIBILITY SCORES FOR SUBJECTS PRESENTED SPONDAIC WORDS SPEEDED WITH FREQUENCY SHIFT
(Details of Conditions are given in Table 1)

	Condition No. 1		Condition No. 2		Condition No. 3		Condition No. 4		Condition No. 5
Subject	Intelli-gibility	Subject	Intelli-gibility	Subject	Intelli-gibility	Subject	Intelli-gibility	Subject	Intelli-gibility
1	94%	1	82%	1	80%	1	68%	1	0
2	100	2	86	2	90	2	70	2	0
3	94	3	88	3	88	3	52	3	2
4	98	4	94	4	90	4	60	4	0
5	98	5	94	5	92	5	64	5	16
6	98	6	96	6	90	6	76	6	30
Total	582.0	Total	540.0	Total	530.0	Total	390.0	Total	48.0
Mean	97.0%	Mean	90.0%	Mean	88.33%	Mean	65.0%	Mean	8.0%
S.D.	2.24	S.D.	5.0	S.D.	3.9	S.D.	7.63	S.D.	11.4

Table 3

RESULTS OF STATISTICAL ANALYSIS OF THE
INTELLIGIBILITY SCORES OBTAINED AS A RESULT OF
SPEED-UP WITH FREQUENCY SHIFT

Computed X_r^2	X^2 (At 1% level)	Degree of Freedom	Level of Significance
19.23	13.28	4	.01

Table 4

STATISTICAL ANALYSIS OF THE DIFFERENCES IN SPEED-UP
EFFECTS WITH AND WITHOUT ATTENDANT FREQUENCY SHIFT

Speed-up (No. of times original speed)	Computed "t"	Level of Significance
1.50	1.39	--
1.67	1.36	--
1.75	3.00	.05
2.00	8.67	.01
2.50	17.63	.01

Table 5

DESCRIPTION OF THE EXPERIMENTAL RECORD TAPES
WHICH WERE USED IN EXPERIMENT
ON SPEEDED CONTINUOUS SPEECH

Condition	Chop-splice Ratio*	Resulting Speed-up
1 (control)	------	----
2	1.5cm/1.5cm	2.00
3	2.0cm/1.5cm	2.33
4	2.5cm/1.5cm	2.67

*The numerator equals the size of the chop removed and the denominator equals the size of the segment left in.

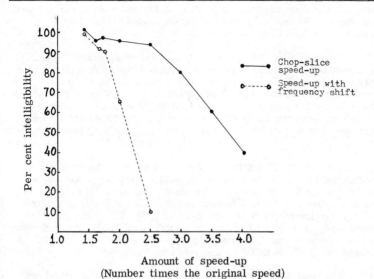

Figure 2. The relationship between intelligibility and the amount of speed-up. The broken line is a plot of the results obtained from speed-up with frequency shift. The solid line is a plot of the results obtained from speed-up without frequency shift.

the scores obtained for the speed-ups of 1.5 and 1.67 for the two methods were not found to be statistically significant at the 5 per cent level. For the speed-up of 1.75 the difference was found to be statistically significant at the 5 per cent level; for speed-ups of 2.00 and 2.50 the differences were found to be significant beyond the 1 per cent level of confidence.

Type of Speech Material: The speech material used in the previous research with the "chop-splice" technique was composed of 50 spondaic words. These words are double accented disyllabic words which are relatively easily understood when used in articulation testing situations. Since the majority of the Air Force messages are short sentences and since type of test material has been shown to be a variable in other investigations of speech intelligibility, an experiment was designed to determine the effect of speed-up on the intelligibility of continuous speech.

Statistical Design: Twenty-four male college students were used as subjects. One control and three experimental conditions were set up in an experiment designed for analysis of variance of the intelligibility scores. The control condition consisted of speech material which had not been speeded up by the chop-splice technique.

The three experimental conditions were conditions in which the speech material had been speeded up to 2.0, 2.33, and 2.67 times the original speed. Six subjects were assigned randomly to each of the four experimental conditions shown in Table 5.

Apparatus and Procedure: The same "chop-splice" technique for speeding up recorded speech which had been applied to discrete words in the earlier experiments was applied to the Harvard P. A. L. Sentence Intelligibility type of sentences. This group of 20 sentences was developed recently by the Harvard Psycho-Acoustic Laboratory for testing sentence intelligibility. Each of the 20 sentences contains five key words, four monosyllables and one disyllable, giving a total of 100 key words to be scored for intelligibility.

The details of the tape preparation were as follows: from the master speech record four additional record tapes were made; one of these four was used as a control, the other three were chopped and spliced at three different ratios, 1.5 centimeters removed and 1.5 centimeters left in (speed-up of 2.0), 2.0 centimeters removed and 1.5 centimeters left in (speed-up of 2.33), and 2.5 centimeters removed and 1.5 centimeters left in (speed-up of 2.67). A description of these tapes is presented in Table 5.

The sentences were presented to the subjects at an intensity level 44 decibels above threshold. At the end of each presentation of a test sentence an interval of ten seconds was given the subject to write what he had heard. At the end of the ten seconds a warning was given and the next sentence presented.

Results: The results are shown in Table 6. These results are represented graphically by the lower solid line in Figure 3. The intelligibility scores for the four conditions were tested to see if they differed significantly; they were found to differ significantly beyond the 1 per cent level of confidence. The results of the statistical analysis can be seen in Table 7.

Discussion of Results: Figure 2 shows the relationship between intelligibility and the amount of speed-up for continuous speech and for discrete words. At a speed of 2.0 times the original, a mean intelligibility score of 75.5 per cent was obtained for the continuous speech as compared to a mean of 95 per cent for the discrete words. When 57 per cent of the continuous speech was removed, resulting in a speed of 2.33 times the original speed, a mean intelligibility score of 60.5 per cent was obtained. With the discrete words, when 60 per cent of the word was removed (speed-up of 2.5) a mean intelligibility score of 95 per cent was obtained. At a speed of 2.67 times the original speed the mean intelligibility for the sentences dropped to 36.67 per cent. But, it was not until 75 per cent of the speech pattern of discrete words was removed, with a concomitant speed-up of 4.0, that the intelligibility scores reached a mean value of 40 per cent.

The results show then that speed-up has less effect upon the

Table 6

RESULTS OBTAINED
FROM SPEEDED UP CONTINUOUS SPEECH (44 db)

Control Condition No. 1		Experimental Condition No. 2	
Subject	Intelligibility	Subject	Intelligibility
1	100%	1	65%
2	97	2	75
3	97	3	78
4	98	4	77
5	96	5	80
6	99	6	78
Total	587.0	Total	453.0
Mean	97.83%	Mean	75.5%
S.D.	1.27	S.D.	4.92

Experimental Condition No. 3		Experimental Condition No. 4	
Subject	Intelligibility	Subject	Intelligibility
1	76%	1	35%
2	61	2	30
3	61	3	33
4	49	4	36
5	61	5	43
6	55	6	43
Total	363.0	Total	220.0
Mean	60.5%	Mean	36.67%
S.D.	8.2	S.D.	4.85

Table 7

RESULTS OF STATISTICAL ANALYSIS OF
INTELLIGIBILITY SCORES OBTAINED BY
SPEEDING UP CONTINUOUS SPEECH (44 DB)

Computed χ^2_r	χ^2 (At 1% Level)	Level of Confidence
17.00	11.34	.01

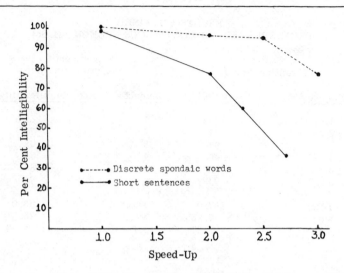

Figure 3. The relationship between intelligibility and the amount of speed-up. The dotted line is a plot of the results obtained with discrete spondaic words; the solid line, the results obtained with short sentences.

intelligibility of the discrete (spondaic) words than it does upon the continuous speech. (It must be kept in mind, however, that only key words in the present sentences were scored.) Such a finding suggests the hypothesis that continuous speech is more confusing to the listener because of the shortened time gaps between the words and the lack of time for the subject to "get set" for each new key word. (This apparently offsets the potential advantage offered by context.) Nevertheless, the problem of the type of words used in the sentences must be considered. In the present experiments the words used in the sentences were almost all monosyllabic. The question arises: are such monosyllabic words, when chopped and spliced singly, less intelligible than spondaic words similarly chopped?

    In an exploratory experiment to see an answer to this question, 20 monosyllabic words were taken from the Harvard PBL, 1a. These words were chopped at a rate of 1.5 centimeters removed to 1.5 centimeters left in, which resulted in an abbreviated speech record with a speed twice the original. The mean intelligibility score for four subjects, who were presented the words under the same experimental conditions as for the sentences and spondaic words, was found to be 85.25 per cent. This mean score is significantly less than the mean intelligibility score (95.67 per cent) of the spondaic words chopped at the same ratio and is significantly greater than the mean intelligibility score (75. 5 per cent) for the continuous speech with an identical chop ratio. The results of this brief experiment indicate that the lower intelligibility of the sentences is probably not due to the words used.

To the extent that the single monosyllabic words and the words used in the sentences are representative of speech sounds in general (and comparable in resistance to chopping damage) we can conclude that intelligibility for key words of sentences is less than for words presented singly when "chopping speed-up" is used.

Effect of Noise (Intensity): In order to determine the effect upon speeded speech of an intensity above this level, an experiment was conducted in which the speech materials were presented to the subjects at an intensity of 100 decibels above threshold. In statistical design, apparatus, speech material, and procedure were identical to those of the preceding experiment in which the effect of speedup on continuous speech was investigated. The present experiment, with the previous one, was designed so that an analysis of variance could be made on their combined intelligibility scores. A better understanding of this combined design can be obtained from Table 8.

Table 8

ANALYSIS OF VARIANCE DESIGN FOR THE EFFECT OF INTENSITY AND DEGREE OF SPEED-UP ON CONTINUOUS SPEECH

Intensity Level	Control (No Speed-Up)	Degree of Speed-Up 2. 0	2. 3	2. 8
44 db	Condition #1	Condition #2	Condition #3	Condition #4
100 db	Condition #5	Condition #6	Condition #7	Condition #8

Results: The results for the first four conditions (44 decibels) in Table 8 have been presented previously in Table 6. A tabulation of the results obtained for conditions 5, 6, 7, and 8 are given in Table 9.

The differences between the intelligibility scores for the four conditions (5, 6, 7, and 8) were tested for statistical significance with the Friedman ranking technique (5) and found to be significant beyond the 1 per cent level of confidence. The results of the statistical analysis may be seen in Table 10.

In order to make an adequate statistical analysis of the effect of intensity on the different degrees of speed-up of the speech materials, an analysis of variance was made of the data presented in Tables 6 and 9 as indicated in Table 8. A test for the homogeneity of variance was made on the data and the variance was found to be homogeneous. The results of the analysis of the variance are given in Table 11.

Table 9

TABULATION OF THE RESULTS OBTAINED FROM
SPEEDING UP CONTINUOUS SPEECH AT 100 DECIBELS

	Control Condition No. 5		Experimental Condition No. 6
Subject	Intelligibility	Subject	Intelligibility
1	97%	1	83%
2	98	2	75
3	97	3	83
4	93	4	78
5	94	5	74
6	99	6	90
Total	583.0	Total	483.0
Mean	97.17%	Mean	80.5%
S.D.	1.57	S.D.	5.48

	Experimental Condition No. 7		Experimental Condition No. 8
Subject	Intelligibility	Subject	Intelligibility
1	69%	1	24%
2	51	2	25
3	56	3	21
4	56	4	26
5	48	5	31
6	42	6	33
Total	322.0	Total	160.0
Mean	53.67%	Mean	26.67%
S.D.	3.78	S.D.	3.33

Table 10

RESULTS OF STATISTICAL ANALYSIS OF INTELLIGIBILITY
SCORES OBTAINED BY SPEEDING UP CONTINUOUS SPEECH
(100 DB)

Computed χ^2_r	χ^2 (At 1% Level)	Level of Confidence
18.00	11.34	.01

Table 11

ANALYSIS OF VARIANCE OF THE INTELLIGIBILITY SCORES OF
CONTINUOUS SPEECH SPEEDED AT 44 AND 100 db INTENSITY

	Source of Variation	Sum of Squares	df	Estimation of Variance
1.	Intensity	117.19	1	117.19
2.	Interaction	339.45	3	133.15
3.	Within groups	1,420.20	40	35.51

$$F_1 \text{ (Intensity)} = \frac{117.17}{133.15} = 0.88; P > .05$$

$$F_2 \text{ (Interaction)} = \frac{133.15}{33.51} = 3.75; .05 > P > .01$$

Discussion of Results: The analysis of variance of the intelligibility scores showed no overall significant differential effect of intensities at 44 and 100 decibels. However, the interaction between intensity and the various speed-ups was found to be significant at the
5 per cent level of confidence. An interpretation of this significance
may be made from a study of the graph in Figure 4. The broken
line in Figure 4 is a plot of the mean intelligibility scores obtained
at the various speed-up levels with an intensity of 44 decibels. The
solid line is a plot of the results when an intensity of 100 decibels

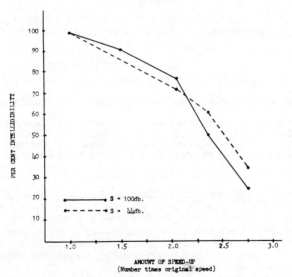

Figure 4. The relationship between intelligibility and amount of
speed-up at intensities of 44 decibels and 100 decibels above threshold of sensation. The broken line is a plot of the results obtained
with 44 decibels, the solid line for results obtained with 100 decibels.

was used. The significant interaction may be interpreted from the graph to mean that the effect of the intensity upon intelligibility of speeded speech depends on the amount of speed-up.

The effect of the increased intensity (100db) is to increase the intelligibility of the least speeded speech; it apparently has little or no effect on the moderately speeded speech (2.0 times the original speed), but when the speech is highly speeded, the increased intensity has a harmful effect upon the intelligibility. Signal-to-Noise Ratio: This experiment was designed to explore the effect of three signal-to-noise ratios upon the intelligibility of speeded continuous speech. Relatively high levels of noise were selected in order to make the experimental conditions comparable with those of actual Air Force operations.

Statistical Design: The experiment was set up in a complex analysis of variance design. A control tape (no speed-up) and four speed-up tapes, 1.5, 2.0, 2.3, and 2.7 times the speech rate of the control, were used in the experiment, and three signal-noise ratios, + 15 (105 db/90 db), + 10 (105 db/95 db), and +5 (105 db/100 db), and a control intensity of 100 db without noise, were used. The 20 different conditions resulting from the design can be seen in Table 12. Of the 120 subjects used, six were assigned randomly to each particular condition in the design.

Table 12

ANALYSIS OF VARIANCE DESIGN FOR THE EFFECT OF SIGNAL-NOISE RATIO AND DEGREE OF SPEED-UP ON CONTINUOUS SPEECH

Amount of Speed-Up (Number times orig-inal speed)		Control 100 db	Signal-Noise Ratio		
			+ 15	+ 10	+ 5
Control	1.0	Condition #1	Condition #6	Condition #11	Condition #16
	1.5	Condition #2	Condition #7	Condition #12	Condition #17
	2.0	Condition #3	Condition #8	Condition #13	Condition #18
	2.3	Condition #4	Condition #9	Condition #14	Condition #19
	2.7	Condition #5	Condition #10	Condition #15	Condition #20

Apparatus and Procedure: The apparatus for presenting the speech material was the same as in previous experiments. For example, when an analysis was made of the noise at 100 db, by measuring the number of decibels masking on particular frequencies, masking at the frequencies ranged from 11 decibels (at 70 c. p. s. to 85 db (at 8000 c. p. s.). The average masking frequencies within the speech range was 41.9 decibels.

The noise passed from noise generator to an attenuator, then entered a mixing transformer where it was mixed with the speech material coming from the Eicor recorder. Upon leaving the mixing

(cont. on p. 113)

Table 13

TABULATION OF THE RESULTS OBTAINED FROM
SPEEDING OF CONTINUOUS SPEECH UNDER CONDITIONS OF NOISE

Condition No. 1	Intelli-	Condition No. 2	Intelli-	Contition No. 3	Intelli-
Subject	gibility	Subject	gibility	Subject	gibility
1	97%	1	97%	1	83%
2	98	2	90	2	75
3	97	3	95	3	83
4	98	4	91	4	78
5	94	5	93	5	74
6	99	6	86	6	90
Total	583.0	Total	552.0	Total	483.0
Mean	97.17%	Mean	92.0%	Mean	80.5%
S.D.	1.57	S.D.	3.56	S.D.	5.48

Condition No. 4	Intelli-	Condition No. 5	Intelli-	Condition No. 6	Intelli-
Subject	gibility	Subject	gibility	Subject	gibility
1	69%	1	24%	1	96%
2	51	2	25	2	89
3	56	3	21	3	96
4	56	4	26	4	95
5	48	5	31	5	98
6	42	6	33	6	95
Total	322.0	Total	160.0	Total	569.0
Mean	53.67%	Mean	26.67%	Mean	94.83%
S.D.	3.78	S.D.	3.33	S.D.	2.80

Condition No. 7	Intelli-	Condition No. 8	Intelli-	Condition No. 9	Intelli-
Subject	gibility	Subject	gibility	Subject	gibility
1	67%	1	54%	1	31%
2	74	2	52	2	41
3	69	3	68	3	36
4	72	4	48	4	48
5	84	5	48	5	33
6	82	6	62	6	29
Total	448.0	Total	332.0	Total	218.0
Mean	74.67%	Mean	55.33%	Mean	36.33%
S.D.	6.31	S.D.	7.35	S.D.	5.54

Table 13 (cont.)

Condition No. 10		Condition No. 11		Condition No. 12	
Subject	Intelli-gibility	Subject	Intelli-gibility	Subject	Intelli-gibility
1	16%	1	97%	1	73%
2	20	2	97	2	82
3	16	3	97	3	59
4	18	4	92	4	61
5	17	5	96	5	61
6	21	6	93	6	53
Total	108.0	Total	572.0	Total	389.0
Mean	18.0%	Mean	95.33%	Mean	64.83%
S.D.	1.92	S.D.	2.05	S.D.	9.97

Condition No. 13		Condition No. 14		Condition No. 15	
Subject	Intelli-gibility	Subject	Intelli-gibility	Subject	Intelli-gibility
1	59%	1	22%	1	16%
2	49	2	30	2	17
3	43	3	32	3	10
4	47	4	36	4	15
5	42	5	27	5	13
6	45	6	24	6	12
Total	285.0	Total	171.0	Total	83.0
Mean	47.0%	Mean	28.50%	Mean	13.83%
S.D.	5.5	S.D.	4.75	S.D.	2.41

Condition No. 16		Condition No. 17		Condition No. 18	
Subject	Intelli-gibility	Subject	Intelli-gibility	Subject	Intelli-gibility
1	97%	1	69%	1	45%
2	93	2	46	2	33
3	95	3	60	3	27
4	98	4	46	4	23
5	98	5	46	5	29
6	96	6	78	6	33
Total	577.0	Total	345.0	Total	190.0
Mean	96.17%	Mean	57.50%	Mean	31.67%
S.D.	1.78	S.D.	12.61	S.D.	6.69

Table 13 (cont.)

| Condition No. 19 | | Condition No. 20 | |
Subject	Intelli-gibility	Subject	Intelli-gibility
1	17%	1	8%
2	15	2	8
3	20	3	10
4	21	4	7
5	21	5	15
6	19	6	9
Total	113.0	Total	57.0
Mean	18.83%	Mean	9.5%
S.D.	2.20	S.D.	2.64

transformer the noise, mixed with the signal, entered the earphones of the subject. The experimental procedure in this study was identical to that of the previous experiments on continuous speech.

Results: The results for each of the 20 experimental conditions indicated in Table 12 are presented in Table 13. A test for homogeneity of variance was made on the data and it was found that the variance was not homogeneous. From an observation of the standard deviations of the data presented in the conditions in Table 13 it appeared that the variance might be homogeneous if the data were broken down into two separate analysis of variance designs. (Table 14 shows the breakdown into the two designs, and presents a tabulation of the totals (T), means (M), and standard deviations (S.D.) of the conditions in each design.)

When the conditions were broken down into the two separate groups, A and B in Table 14, and tested for homogeneity of variance, it was found that the variance in each group was homogeneous. An analysis of variance was made on the data in Table 14-A, and the result of the analysis is presented in Table 15.

The analysis of variance of the intelligibility scores showed no overall significant effect of the three signal-noise ratios. The lack of significance is attributable to the ineffectiveness of the noise on the control (no speed-up) speech materials. This ineffectiveness may be explained by the type of the noise used in this experiment. It has been shown previously that with the more intense noise levels the best bands of noise for masking speech are below 1000 c.p.s. In the noise used in this experiment the average intensity of bands of frequencies below 1000 c.p.s. was approximately 30 decibels. However, the interaction between the intensity and the speed-up was found to be significant at the 1 per cent level of confidence. Also, the effect of speed-up was found to be significant at the 1 per cent level of confidence.

Table 14

BREAKDOWN OF ORIGINAL ANALYSIS OF VARIANCE DESIGN (TABLE 12) TO OBTAIN HOMOGENEITY OF VARIANCE

Part A

	Control 100 db	+ 15	Signal-Noise Ratio + 10	+ 5
	#1	#6	#11	#16
Control 1.0	T - 583.0 M - 97.17 SD - 1.57	T - 569.0 M - 94.83 SD - 2.80	T - 572.0 M - 95.33 SD - 2.05	T - 577.0 M - 96.17 SD - 1.78
	#5	#10	#15	#20
Speed-Up 2.7	T - 160.0 M - 26.67 SD - 3.33	T - 108.0 M - 18.0 SD - 1.92	T - 83.0 M - 13.83 SD - 2.41	T - 57.0 M - 9.5 SD - 2.64

Part B

	Control 100 db	+ 15	Signal-Noise Ratio + 10	+ 5
	#2	#7	#12	#17
Speed-Up 1.5	T - 552.0 M - 92.0 SD - 3.56	T - 448.0 M - 74.67 SD - 6.31	T - 389.0 M - 64.83 SD - 9.97	T - 345.0 M - 57.50 SD - 12.61
	#3	#8	#13	#18
Speed-Up 2.0	T - 483.0 M - 80.5 SD - 5.48	T - 332.0 M - 55.33 SD - 7.35	T - 285.0 M - 47.5 SD - 5.5	T - 190.0 M - 31.67 SD - 6.69
	#4	#9	#14	#19
Speed-Up 2.3	T - 322.0 M - 53.67 SD - 3.78	T - 218.0 M - 36.33 SD - 5.54	T - 171.0 M - 28.50 SD - 4.75	T - 113.0 M - 18.83 SD - 2.20

Table 15

ANALYSIS OF VARIANCE OF THE DATA SUMMARIZED IN TABLE
13-A, THE EFFECT OF NOISE ON SPEEDED CONTINUOUS SPEECH

Source of Variation	Sum of Squares	Estimation of Variance
1. Speed-up	74,655	74,655
2. Noise	624	208
3. Interaction	360	120
4. Within	305	7.62

$$F_1 = \frac{74,655}{120} \quad 622.0; \quad P<.01$$

$$F_2 = \frac{208}{120} \quad 1.73; \quad P>.05$$

$$F_3 = \frac{120.0}{7.62} \quad 15.74; \quad P<.01$$

Table 16

ANALYSIS OF VARIANCE OF THE DATA SUMMARIZED IN TABLE
13-B, THE EFFECT OF NOISE ON SPEEDED CONTINUOUS SPEECH

Source of Variation	Sum of Squares	Estimation of Variance
1. Speed-up	17,256	8,628
2. Noise	14,095	4,698
3. Interaction	1,297	216
4. Within	3,656	60.93

$$F_1 = \frac{8,628}{216} \quad 39.94; \quad P<.01$$

$$F_2 = \frac{4,689}{2.6} \quad 21.75; \quad P<.01$$

$$F_3 = \frac{216}{60.93} \quad 3.54; \quad P<.01$$

The results of the analysis of variance of the data summarized
in Table 14-B are presented in Table 16. From this table it can be
seen that the overall effect of both speed-up and noise on intelligibility is statistically significant beyond the 1 per cent level of confidence. The interaction effect of noise and speed-up on intelligibility
was also found to be significant beyond the 1 per cent level.

Discussion of Results: When the data, which were broken
down into Tables 14-A and -B, are recombined, as indicated in Table 12, and plotted in the graph in Figure 5 the following generalizations may be drawn.

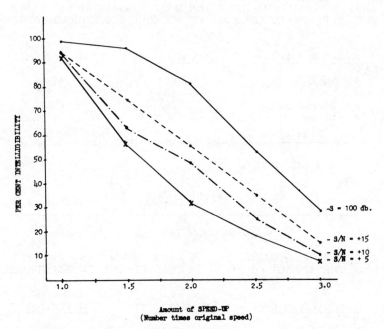

Figure 5. Relationship between intelligibility and amount of speed-up, with signal-noise ratios of the parameters.

The effect of speed-up is to reduce the intelligibility of the speech material under all S/N conditions used in this experiment. In general, the greater the speed-up, the greater the loss in intelligibility. The effects are not completely uniform, however. (As pointed out above, the interaction is statistically significant.) At low S/N ratios, the effect of increasing the speed-up is greater at the lower speed-up rates, at higher S/N ratios, this differential decreases until, when speech is presented without noise, the effect of increasing the speed-up is actually greater at higher speed-up rates. This could be interpreted as follows: when no noise is present, chopping is relatively ineffective until fairly large amounts are chopped out, possibly because of the excess cues normally present in speech. However, at low S/N ratios, where the excess cues have been already largely eliminated, chopping immediately has a large effect.

Noise, in the amounts used in this experiment, reduces intelligibility significantly on the average for speed-up rates of 1.5, 2.0, and 2.3. The higher the noise level, the lower the intelligibility, though the effects are not completely uniform, as shown by the significant interaction in Table 14-B. The effects on speech at a rate

of 2. 7 follow the same trend but are smaller in magnitude, while
the effects on normal speech show no such regular trend.   (These
last facts make the significant interaction in Table 14-A understandable.)

Effect of Prior Familiarization with Message

It was noted during the earlier experiments that the experimenter and his assistants, who had heard the speech material at its
normal speed, were able to understand the material when presented
subsequently at a highly speeded rate.   As a result of this observation an experiment was designed to test the effect of previous familiarization with non-speeded speech material on the intelligibility of
the same material when subsequently speeded up.

Statistical Design: Twenty-four subjects were used, six subjects being assigned to each of four experimental conditions (see Table 17).   Two conditions of speed, 2. 0 and 2. 7 times the original
speed, and two conditions of familiarization, two and four trials,
were used.   Apparatus and Procedure: The familiarization sentences
were the Harvard SI Test Sentences used in previous experiments.
The speeded test sentences were these same sentences chopped in the
same manner.

In the two familiarization conditions the sentences were presented as follows: in the two-trial familiarization condition the set
of 20 sentences was presented to the subjects twice, but each set of
20 was given in random order; and in the four-trial familiarization
condition the set of 20 sentences was given to the subjects four
times, but each set of 20 was given in random order.   (The order
was randomized in order to minimize the effects of serial learning.)
The subjects were first given one of the familiarization conditions
and then were presented the sentences speeded up to either 2. 0 or
2. 7 times the speed of the familiarization sentences.   The test sentences were presented to the subjects with the same apparatus and
under the same experimental conditions used previously.

Results: The results obtained from the experiment are presented in Table 17 and are shown graphically in Figure 6.

Since there was no statistically significant difference between
the data for two and four familiarization trials, the two-trial familiarization data will be used for comparison with the intelligibility
scores obtained from the speech material without previous familiarization.   Table 18 is a summary presentation of such a comparison.

A t-test was made for each of the speed-up rates on the differences in the intelligibility scores obtained with and without previous familiarization.   The results of the statistical analysis are
presented in Table 19.   The differences obtained between the intelligibility scores at both the speed-up of 2. 0 and 2. 7 were found to be
statistically significant at the 1 per cent level of confidence.

Table 17

TABULATION OF THE RESULTS OF THE EFFECT
OF FAMILIARIZATION UPON THE INTELLIGIBILITY
OF SPEEDED SPEECH

Number Familiarization Trials

			2		4
		Subject	Intelligibility	Subject	Intelligibility
		1	100%	1	100%
		2	94	2	99
		3	99	3	100
Amount of Speed-Up (Number Times Original Speed)	2.0	4	99	4	99
		5	95	5	100
		6	97	6	98
		Total	584.0	Total	596.0
		Mean	97.3%	Mean	99.25%
		S.D.	2.2	S.D.	.91
		Subject	Intelligibility	Subject	Intelligibility
		1	89%	1	90%
		2	90	2	93
		3	100	3	98
	2.7	4	100	4	95
		5	90	5	90
		6	90	6	95
		Total	559.0	Total	561.0
		Mean	93.1%	Mean	93.5%
		S.D.	4.8	S.D.	2.88

Discussion of Results: It is clear from the data presented in Tables 18 and 19 and in the graph in Figure 6 that previous familiarization with the test material before it is presented in a speeded condition increases the intelligibility of the speeded speech greatly. With no previous familiarization, speech which had been speeded to twice its original speed gave a mean intelligibility of 75.5 per cent, but with two previous familiarization trials the mean intelligibility was 97.3 per cent. At a speed of 2.7 times the original speed, the mean intelligibility without familiarization was 36.67 per cent, with familiarization the intelligibility scores obtained had a mean of 93.1 per cent.

In order to check whether the subjects were memorizing the sentences during the familiarization trials, understanding one word,

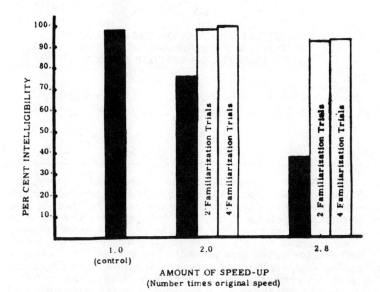

Figure 6.   The relationship between intelligibility and speed-up when
subjects have had previous familiarization with the speech material.
The solid bars represent the results obtained without previous familiarization.   The white bars represent the results found with two and
four familiarization trials.

Table 18

COMPARISON OF THE INTELLIGIBILITY OF THE
SPEEDED SPEECH MATERIAL, WITH AND WITHOUT PREVIOUS
FAMILIARIZATION WITH THE MATERIAL

Amount of Speed-Up (Number Times Original Speed)		No Previous Familiarization	(Two Trials) Previous Familiarization
	2.0	Total - 453 Mean - 75.5 S.D. - 4.92	Total - 584 Mean - 97.3 S.D. - 2.2
	2.8	Total - 220 Mean - 36.67 S.D. - 4.85	Total - 559 Mean - 93.1 S.D. - 4.8

Table 19

STATISTICAL ANALYSIS OF THE EFFECT
OF PREVIOUS FAMILIARIZATION ON THE
INTELLIGIBILITY OF SPEEDED SPEECH

Speed-up (Number of times original speed)	Computed "t"	Level of Significance
2. 0	9. 41	. 01
2. 7	18. 68	. 01

and then filling in the remainder of the material from memory, an
additional experiment was designed. In this experiment the subjects
were familiarized with the material as previously; but then, in place
of hearing the speeded sentence, they were presented with one of the
five key words from each sentence. The word with which the subject was presented was selected by checking the original responses
of the subjects who had been presented with the speeded sentences at
a speed-up of 2. 7 without previous familiarization. The subjects in
this present experiment then were presented randomly one correct
word response per sentence. If the original subject made only one
correct response in a particular sentence, the subject in the familiarization experiment was presented that word and asked to fill in
the remainder of the sentence, if the original subject made more
than one correct word response, then one word was randomly selected from these responses and then presented to the subject in the
presently described familiarization study. Since there were six subjects used in the original experiment without any previous familiarization, and this study was designed so that six subjects would be
used, each of the new subjects was randomly assigned a correct response of one of the original six subjects. The subjects then attempted to fill in from the word as much of the sentence as they
could from memory. The subjects presented with one key word obtained a much lower score than those presented with the speeded sentences. However, it is worth noting that the subjects in the present
experiment were able to fill in a considerable number of words as a
result of their two familiarization trials. The results obtained from
this experiment are compared with the results of the previous experiment (in which the subjects were presented the speeded-up sentences)
in Table 20.

The level of significance of the mean difference was tested
and it was found that the difference was significant beyond the 1 per
cent level of confidence.

From the combined results of the experiments on the effect
of familiarization on the intelligibility of speeded speech it can be
said that previous familiarization with the material before it is
speeded up serves to increase markedly the intelligibility of the
speech when subsequently speeded up. Also it can be said that this

Table 20

COMPARISON OF RESULTS OBTAINED FROM
FAMILIARIZATION UNDER TWO DIFFERENT TEST CONDITIONS

Subject	Intelligibility	Subject	Intelligibility
1	89%	1	57%
2	90	2	60
3	100	3	67
4	100	4	63
5	90	5	61
6	90	6	83
Total	559	Total	391
Mean	93.1%	Mean	65.17%
S.D.	4.8	S.D.	8.53

is not due to memorizing the sentences and being able to fill in each
sentence from one key word.   The effects of familiarization in raising the intelligibility of speeded speech may be due to getting several
key words and filling in the rest (these processes may be correlated
in a given person); or the subject may be able after familiarization
to utilize small cues in the speech which previously were uninterpretable.   The experiment on sentence reproduction from a single key
word after familiarization would indicate that "fill-in" from key words
is probably part of the process.

Effect of Slowing Down Chopped Speech with an Accompanying Frequency Shift:

Steinberg ["Effects of Distortion on Speech and Music"] slowed
down normal (unspeeded) speech by mechanically reducing the speed
of the rotation of the record discs and found that when the record
was slowed down to eight-tenths of its original speed, intelligibility
dropped to approximately 80 per cent.   The experiment about to be
described was performed to determine the effect of slowing down
"chopped" (speeded) speech by similarly reducing the speed of the
speech record, i.e., by spreading the remaining portions of the
"chopped" speech elements out over a longer period of time with an
accompanying frequency shift.   It is conceivable that even "chopped"
speech elements if spread out over a longer period of time might
give better intelligibility ... sufficient to overcome the effects of frequency distortion.

Statistical Design: The experiment was designed for t-tests
of the significance of the differences between the intelligibility scores
obtained with "chop-splice" speeded speech material before and after
it had been slowed down.   A control tape (no speed-up) and four
"chop-splice" speed-up tapes (with speed-up rates of 1.5, 2.0, 2.3
and 2.7) were each slowed down to seven-tenths and also eight-tenths
of their original speed, giving a total of ten experimental conditions.

Table 21

INTELLIGIBILITY SCORES OF SLOWED DOWN SPEEDED SPEECH

Slowdown Factor of 0.8

Subject	Control	Speed-Up 1.5	Speed-Up 2.0	Speed-Up 2.3	Speed-Up 2.7
1	100	84	88	66	39
2	96	85	84	75	29
3	94	88	84	64	28
4	97	76	86	75	32
5	97	83	83	67	25
6	94	80	87	67	24
Total	578	496	512	416	177
Mean	96.33	82.67	85.33	69.33	29.51
S.D.	.92	1.71	.80	1.91	2.23

Slowdown Factor of 0.7

Subject	Control	Speed-Up 1.5	Speed-Up 2.0	Speed-Up 2.3	Speed-Up 2.7
1	79	69	78	46	23
2	75	63	84	41	20
3	90	75	76	58	22
4	85	70	74	44	17
5	88	77	69	65	19
6	87	70	75	70	23
Total	504	424	456	324	124
Mean	84.00	70.64	76.00	54.00	20.67
S.D.	5.29	4.49	4.51	10.80	2.21

Original Speed-Up Without Slowdown

Subject	Control	Speed-Up 1.5	Speed-Up 2.0	Speed-Up 2.3	Speed-Up 2.7
1	100	97	65	76	35
2	97	90	75	61	30
3	97	95	78	61	33
4	98	91	77	49	36
5	96	93	80	61	43
6	99	86	78	55	43
Total	587	552	453	363	220
Mean	97.83	92.00	75.5	60.5	36.67
S.D.	1.27	3.56	4.92	8.2	4.85

Table 22

RESULTS OF THE T-TESTS ON THE DIFFERENCES BETWEEN
THE DATA OBTAINED FROM SPEEDED SPEECH
WITH AND WITHOUT SUBSEQUENT SLOWDOWN

Slowdown Factor of 0.8

Original Speed-Up (Number of times original speed)	Computed "t"	Level of Significance
Control	6.76	.01
1.5	5.27	.01
2.0	3.49	.01
2.3	2.62	.05
2.7	3.01	.02

Slowdown Factor of 0.7

Original Speed-Up (Number of times original speed)	Computed "t"	df	Level of Significance
Control	5.09	10	1%
1.5	5.46	10	1%
2.0	.17	10	--
2.3	1.52	10	--
2.7	6.72	10	1%

Six subjects were used in each of these conditions, making a total of 60 subjects (see Table 21).

Apparatus and Procedure: The "chop-splice" speeded speech material consisted of sentences which had been used in a previous experiment. The slowing down of the speech material in the abbreviated records was accomplished by mechanically reducing the speed of the record tape past the magnetic pick-up of the playback recorder.

Results and Discussion: The results obtained from the ten conditions are shown in Table 21 and are plotted in the graph in Figure 6. T-tests were made of the significance of the differences between the intelligibility scores obtained from speeded speech with and without subsequent slowdown; the results are presented in Table 22. The most striking finding from the experiment is that slowing down the speeded speech had so little effect on intelligibility. However, some changes did occur. It can be seen from Tables 21 and 22 and the graph in Figure 7 that when the "chopped" speech was slowed down, in some cases the intelligibility decreased and in other instances it increased. For the control (no speed-up) and the speed-up of 1.5 the intelligibility scores decreased significantly when the speed of the tapes was multiplied by a factor of eight-tenths or seven-tenths. When the speed of the speech material which was originally speeded up to 2.0 and 2.33 was multiplied by a factor of eight-tenths, the intelligibility scores increased significantly; however, when they were multiplied by a factor of seven-tenths, there

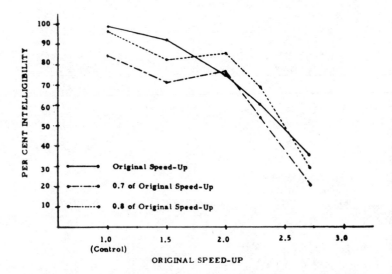

Figure 7. Relationship between intelligibility and amount of speed-up, with subsequent slowdown. The solid line is a plot of the results obtained when continuous speech is speeded up. The broken line represents the results obtained when the original speed of the speech was multiplied by a factor of 0.7. The dotted line is a plot of the results obtained when the speeded speech was multiplied by a factor of 0.8.

were no significant changes in the resulting intelligibility. The speech material which had been originally speeded up to 2.7 times its original speed decreased significantly in intelligibility when its speed was subsequently multiplied by a factor of either seven-tenths or eight-tenths.

It has been pointed out previously that the intelligibility of "normal" speech decreases with lowering of frequency. In the present experiments, in order to slow down the speeded speech to eight-tenths its original speed, the speed of the record was multiplied by eight-tenths; thus all frequencies in the speech were multiplied by a factor of eight-tenths. It would be expected, then, that the intelligibility of the control records would drop. In the case where the speech was originally speeded up to 1.5 times the original and then showed down, the decrease in intelligibility may be due to the fact that frequency shift caused by slowing the tape down mechanically had a greater effect in lowering the intelligibility than any enhancing effect that may have resulted from spreading the "chopped" speech elements out over a longer period of time. However, spreading these "damaged" elements out may in some cases have further distorted them, thus acting with the frequency shift to lower the intelligibility further.

From the graph in Figure 7 it can be seen that the curves plotted from the "slow-down" results closely parallel one another. Also the points on these curves for either the speed-up of 1. 5 or 2. 0 do not appear to be in line with the trend of the rest of the curve. It is conceivable that these results may be due to the condition of the particular "chopped" tapes used. The 1. 5 speed-up tape may have been "chopped" in such a way as to damage elements within its speech material so that when spread out, these elements became even more distorted, thus lowering the intelligibility. Also the 2. 0 speed-up tape may have been so "chopped" that its damaged elements, when spread out, became more intelligible; thus raising the overall intelligibility. How much the "slowed down" intelligibility is a function of the particular "chopped" tape used cannot be determined from these results, another tape would have to be "chopped" and used under the same experimental conditions to determine this adequately.

For the speech materials which had originally been speeded up to 2. 0 and 2. 3 times, the significant increase in intelligibility from the mechanical slowing down of the tapes indicates that the slowdown of the speech material probably enhanced the intelligibility to a greater extent than the accompanying frequency shift hindered it. However, the possibility of the nature of the "chopped" elements in the abbreviated record must be kept in mind here. The fact that there were no significant changes in intelligibility when the speed of the speech material was multiplied by a factor of seven-tenths may be attributable to a balancing out of these factors.

At a speed-up of 2. 7 the intelligibility of the speeded speech dropped significantly when slowed down by either of the slowdown factors. In addition to the factor of frequency shift, it is possible that at such a high speed-up, some "chopped" speech elements which were intelligible in their speed-up state (though damaged) became further distorted and unintelligible when spread out by slowdown, thus the words which contained them became less intelligible.

AN ANALYSIS TO DETERMINE THE CAUSES FOR LOWERED INTELLIGIBILITY OF SPEEDED SPONDAIC WORDS

Although the previous experiments throw some light on the reasons for decrease in intelligibility of speeded speech, as well as providing information for practical importance for the use of speeded speech, it seemed important to investigate further and in more detail the reasons for the decrease in intelligibility. To this end a study was carried out on speeded-up spondaic words. This study in-

volved analyzing the errors made by the original subjects and analyzing the separate speech sounds in these speeded-up words. From
these data it was felt that it would be possible to determine the nature of the errors made, and to disclose whether an explanation of
these errors could be found in the goodness of the separate sounds
of the "chopped" words.

The analysis in the section is broken down into three parts:
an analysis of the errors made by the original subjects on certain
speeded up spondaic words; an auditory analysis of the speech sounds
in certain spondaic words after they had been "chopped"; and an attempt to relate these two analyses.

Analysis of Errors Made By Original Subjects: Procedure:
The errors analyzed were those made on spondaic words which had
been speeded up to 4.0 times their original speed (chop ratio of
three centimeters removed and one centimeter left in). This speed-
up was chosen because it was one of those where a considerable
number of errors was made. In the original experiments intelligibility was measured in terms of total number of words correct. To
supplement the information from a count of words correct, each of
the words in the test material was broken down into its phonetic elements. The original recorded responses of the subjects were then
listened to and each phonetic element in the word (whether the word
response was correct or not) was scored for accuracy. By thus
breaking down the responses of a subject into speech elements and
scoring each element separately, it was possible to obtain a finer
measure of correct responses.

Results: Even though the intelligibility scores of the original
subjects ranged from 38 per cent to 44 per cent at this speed, the
subjects did not get the same words correct. Only three words out
of the total of 50 were correct for all six subjects. The results of
the phonetic analysis of the responses of the subjects are tabulated
in Table 23. The average number of correct phonetic elements per
word for the subjects was 3.32 (S.D. of 1.11). An idea of the low
consistency of the subjects is obtained when it is seen that the average number of correct responses in common for the subjects was
1.97 (S.D. of 1.21).

Discussion of Results: The fact that the subjects did not all
make the same mistakes (even though the total scores for the subjects were very close) indicates that variables within the individual
are important in addition to the specific ways in which the words
are damaged by the "chop-splice" technique. Such within-individual
variables are possibly understandable in terms of differential familiarity with the words, individual differences in attention to the various words in the list, or misleading "sets" on the part of the subjects.

Auditory Analysis of "Chopped" Spondaic Words: Further analysis was desired to reveal the nature of the damage caused in the
speech pattern when abbreviated by the "chop-splice" technique. A

Table 23

AVERAGE NUMBER OF SPEECH ELEMENTS
PER WORD CORRECT

Test Word	Average Number Correct Elements	Average Number Correct Elements in Common*
DOORWAY	4.0	2.1
AIRPLANE	3.4	1.9
PLAYGROUND	4.2	2.4
CHURCHBELL	1.8	0.9
HARDWARE	2.2	1.0
EYEBROW	2.8	0.9
EARTHQUAKE	1.2	0.5
RAILROAD	3.7	2.1
ARMCHAIR	3.7	2.5
SHIPWRECK	3.2	2.1
BLACKBOARD	2.8	1.7
BIRTHDAY	3.6	2.0
BACKBONE	2.3	0.9
BLOODHOUND	4.5	3.8
SCHOOLHOUSE	5.2	4.5
COWBOY	2.8	1.3
WILDCAT	1.8	0.5
LOOKOUT	4.4	3.0
COUGHDROP	2.2	0.9
NORTHWEST	5.0	4.2
RAINBOW	1.3	0.4
WHITEWASH	4.0	2.7
ICEBOX	3.4	1.4
FIREFLY	1.8	0.5
DOORSTEP	3.5	2.3
SIDEWALK	5.0	4.0
MOUSETRAP	3.5	2.2
DUGOUT	4.0	2.1
BEEHIVE	2.8	1.4
SCARECROW	2.8	1.0
FOOTSTOOL	1.5	0.3
LIGHTBULB	3.3	1.8
JACKKNIFE	5.3	4.9
ICEBERG	4.6	2.8
SCHOOLBOY	3.4	1.5
BLACKOUT	3.4	1.5
COOKBOOK	5.0	4.0
FAREWELL	2.8	1.0

*The responses of each subject were analyzed to determine the number of speech elements (per word) which was correct. The correct speech element of each subject was compared with those of each of the other subjects to determine the responses in common.

Table 24

SCALE USED TO RATE SPEECH SOUNDS IN SPONDAIC WORDS

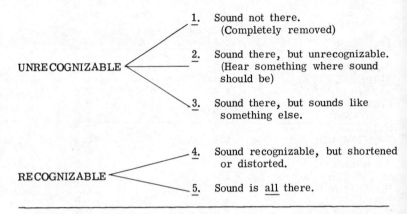

UNRECOGNIZABLE

1. Sound not there.
   (Completely removed)

2. Sound there, but unrecognizable.
   (Hear something where sound should be)

3. Sound there, but sounds like something else.

RECOGNIZABLE

4. Sound recognizable, but shortened or distorted.

5. Sound is all there.

means was needed whereby the "chopped" words could be analyzed element by element to determine the extent of the damage which had resulted from the chopping. One method would be to determine physically how much of each sound was present: this would be quite difficult without an elaborate high-speed recording and analyzing apparatus. Examination of a sound-film track of the words indicated that only the power of the speech was observable and that such an examination would be inadequate to analyze the damage to the separate speech elements.

It seemed possible that an auditory analysis could be used in which judges rated the "goodness" of each sound in the words; this was therefore tried. A possible limitation of such an analysis is that the rating of each sound may not be independent. How severe a limitation this is, however, can be determined with the data from the analysis. An auditory analysis appears to have an advantage over a visual analysis in that it indicates how the speech elements actually sound. It is possible that considerable damage may be done physically to an element without the subjective sound being basically changed.

Procedure: Two graduate students in speech, who had had previous experience with phonetic analysis, acted as judges. The speech materials used were the spondaic words which had been used previously in the experiments on speeded-up discrete words. Each word appeared twice in the list of words to be judged; once "chopped" at a ratio of one centimeter removed and two centimeters left in (speed-up of 1.5) and again at a ratio of three centimeters removed and one centimeter left in (speed-up of 4.0). In order to make the analysis less time-consuming, only those words were used on which the original subjects had made at least one error. These two chop

rates were used to see to what extent differences in intelligibility
for these rates might be reflected in differential damage to the sound
elements of the words.   A list containing all of these chopped words
in random order was made up for presentation to the judges.

For a given judging session, each word in the list was presented to the judge five times in succession in order that the judge
might have a good chance to listen carefully for the particular sound
he was judging.   On the first day, the judges rated only the first
element in each word; on the second day, they rated the second; and
so on, until all elements had been rated.

The judges received preliminary practice for an hour a day
for seven days with 24 words which were not used in the experiment
proper.   During this period the scale used in rating the sounds was
improved upon and checks were made on the agreement between the
judges, and between ratings of the same judge from day to day.
Throughout the practice period the judges discussed their ratings;
following the practice period, they were not allowed to discuss or
compare their ratings.   During the preliminary practice period the
rating scale shown in Table 24 was worked out.

Results: The results discussed below refer to the complete
list of words rated, i. e. , including both speed-up rates of 1. 5 and
4. 0.   Better than 80 per cent of the ratings of the judges were in
agreement.   A chi-square test indicated that the agreement was highly significant statistically.

The following correlations were calculated to determine the
degree to which the judges were able to rate sounds within the word
independently.   The correlation between ratings of vowels in a word
with ratings of consonants in the word was found to be -. 16.   (When
computed separately for those words with a speed-up of 4. 0 it was
found to be . 23.)   The correlation between ratings of vowels in a
syllable with ratings of consonants in the syllable was -. 12.   The
correlation between the rating of each vowel on a word with the consonant following it was found to be -. 01.   These extremely low correlations indicate that the judges were rating each sound independently
of the other sounds in the word.

The "chopping" used severely damaged only a small per cent
of the sounds.   Only 20 sounds, out of a possible 422, received a
rating of three or less.   An assumption, which seems reasonable,
is that when listening carefully for one particular sound, "fill-in"
would not operate to create a sound which was missing.   That such
"fill-in" probably is not operating is borne out by the fact that judges
agree well as to the ratings of slight or no damage, which is scarcely possible if simple "fill-in" were taking place.   However, regardless of any "fill-in," the results can be taken as a perfectly straightforward report of how each element sounded to the judges.

Despite the fact that "chopping" severely damaged only a small
percentage of sounds, the average ratings for the words which were

Table 25

AVERAGE RATING OF SPEECH SOUNDS
IN SPEEDED SPONDAIC WORDS

Word	Average Rating (Speed-up of 1.5)	Average Rating (Speed-up of 4.0)
DOORWAY	5.0	4.0
AIRPLANE	5.0	4.1
PLAYGROUND	4.4	4.1
CHURCHBELL	5.0	3.6
HARDWARE	4.8	4.2
EYEBROW	5.0	4.5
EARTHQUAKE	4.8	4.0
RAILROAD	4.8	4.0
ARMCHAIR	5.0	4.2
SHIPWRECK	4.9	3.9
BLACKBOARD	4.8	4.0
BIRTHDAY	4.7	4.6
BACKBONE	4.7	3.9
BLOODHOUND	5.0	4.2
SCHOOLHOUSE	4.7	4.5
COWBOY	5.0	3.5
WILDCAT	4.2	3.9
LOOKOUT	4.7	4.5
COUGHDROP	4.8	3.9
NORTHWEST	4.7	4.4
RAINBOW	4.8	3.7
WHITEWASH	4.9	4.2
ICEBOX	4.9	3.9
FIREFLY	5.0	3.7
DOORSTEP	4.3	3.7
SIDEWALK	4.8	4.4
MOUSETRAP	4.9	4.2
DUGOUT	4.8	4.5
BEEHIVE	4.5	4.3
SCARECROW	5.0	3.7
FOOTSTOOL	5.0	3.7
LIGHTBULB	4.1	4.2
JACKKNIFE	4.6	4.4
ICEBERG	5.0	4.3
SCHOOLBOY	4.8	4.2
BLACKOUT	5.0	4.2
COOKBOOK	5.0	4.4
FAREWELL	5.0	3.9

speeded up to 1.5 times were higher for 37 out of 38 words than the ratings for those words which were speeded up 4.0 times (see Table 25). Again, the fact that this is no simple "halo" effect is indicated by the good agreement between the judges as to which sounds were harmed.

The difference between the average ratings of vowels per word and consonants per word was found to be significant at the 1 per cent level of confidence. This finding is understandable in terms of the greater power and duration of vowels; thus more of the vowel can be removed by "chop" and still leave enough vowel on the record to give an adequate sound to the listener.

Relation of the Auditory Analysis to the Response Errors: This section compares the ratings of the sounds in each word with the errors made by the original subjects. The comparisons are made between the errors and ratings on the speech recordings which were speeded up 4.0 times; the material with a speed-up of 4.0 was appropriate because there was a good range of errors made by the original subjects on these words to correlate with the ratings. Although the number of original subjects was small, the total number of responses made (211) was sizeable, thus allowing considerable data for analysis such as: the correlations between the average number of correct responses per syllable and the average ratings of: all sounds (consonants and vowels) per syllable; consonants per syllable; and vowels per syllable were found to be .51, .66, and .32 respectively.

The fact that the correlation for all the sounds (vowels and consonants combined) is lower than for consonants alone indicates the importance of the consonants in determining the intelligibility of sounds in a syllable. (Perhaps the generality of this conclusion is limited by the fact that the vowel sounds were not greatly damaged by the chopping in the present words.) Also, the differential prediction by consonants and vowels, as well as the size of the correlation coefficients, bears witness to the degree of sharpness of discrimination made by the judges, as shown by the following:

The correlations between the average number of correct responses per word and the average rating: per word; of consonants per word; and of vowels per word were found to be .76, .40, and .21, respectively.

A scatter diagram of the correlation between the average rating per word and the average number of correct responses per word was made to determine the nature of its trends; the results of the plot are presented in Figure 8; the trend appears to be linear. From the size of the correlation coefficient (+.76), it would appear that both vowel and consonant sounds are essential to intelligibility (or correct recognition) of word sounds. Perhaps the most striking thing is the accuracy of the prediction of the average number of sounds per word recognized by the subjects from the average rating of the sounds in the word. The correlations between the number of

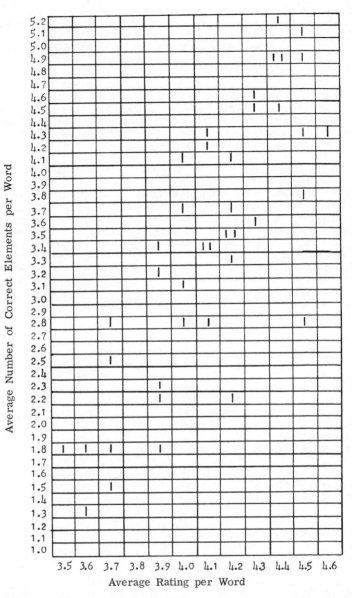

Figure 8.   Scatter diagram of the relationship between average rating per word and average number of correct elements per word.

subjects getting the word correct and the average rating: per word; of consonants per word; and of vowels per word were .47, .19, and .40, respectively.

The question immediately arises: why do vowels predict better than consonants, and almost as well as average rating per word? An hypothesis was made that the subjects were "filling in" the words from the vowels; and they were most successful in doing this when the vowels were good. This hypothesis was tested by an experiment in which a group of 11 subjects were presented only the vowel sounds from the spondaic words. The vowel sounds only of each of the stimulus spondaic words were recorded at their proper intervals in the word, e.g., only -a---a-- of baseball was recorded. These recorded vowel sounds were then presented to the subjects. The task of the subjects was to "fill in" consonant sounds to form words. The result of the experiment was that there was no appreciable "fill-in" by subjects. (The average number of "fill-ins" per subject was less than one out of the possible 38 words.) The hypothesis probably must be modified to state: with vowel sounds present, and with consonant sounds (which help to define the vowels) no more severely damaged than they were in these experiments, some "fill-in" probably does take place.

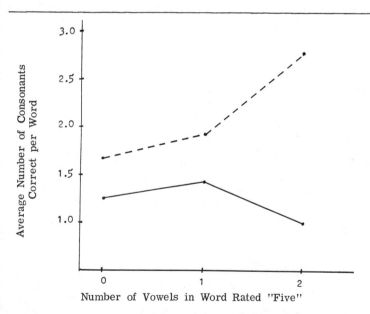

Figure 9. The relationship between average number of consonant sounds correct per word and the number of vowels in the word rated "five." The dotted line is a plot of the relation for responses of all subjects; the solid line is a plot of the relation for the responses of the subjects missing the word.

The next question which arises is: why shouldn't prediction from ratings of vowels to number of sounds correctly interpreted (+.21) be as good as for number of words correct (+.40)? It appears possible that there is some poor "fill-in" going on. Data on this point are furnished in Figure 9 which shows the relationship between the average number of consonants correct per word and the number of vowels in the word receiving ratings of "five." The solid line is a plot of this function for responses of the original subjects scored wrong in terms of correct words, and the dotted line is the plot for all responses. From these graphs it appears that two good vowels sometimes cause the subjects to make more consonant errors. A check was made of the "goodness" of the ratings of the consonants for zero, one, and two ratings of "five" in a word, and it was found that there was actually a slight increase in the average ratings of consonants with an increase in the number of ratings of "five" in a word. Thus, we have a situation where, even though the consonants are getting better, and the number of consonants heard correctly by most of the subjects is increasing, some subjects on these same words get fewer consonants in response to words with two vowels rated "five." The erroneous consonants would have a relatively greater weighting than the correct vowels on the total speech sounds (since there are more consonants in a word); but when words only are counted, a correct word counts equally with an incorrect word. Hence it is understandable that the prediction from vowels to number of sounds heard correctly is not as good as for number of words correct.

Further data on the hypothesis that incorrect "fill-in" was occurring were obtained from analysis of the incorrect word responses of the original subjects. The complete (but incorrect) word responses which had both vowel responses correct but certain consonants wrong were examined. The average number of incorrect consonants (prorated for a three-consonant word) for these words is plotted as a function of number of vowels rated "five" in Figure 10. Again we find clear evidence of an increase in the number of consonant errors with the words for which both vowels were rated "five." (It must be remembered that this analysis is of incorrect word responses only.) These results point more clearly to the fact that the increase in consonant errors for incorrect words, when both vowels are rated "five," is a faulty "fill-in" process rather than some other process such as blocking, which would cause omission errors.

The fact that the size of the correlation coefficient for predicting average number of sounds correct in a word (+.76) is larger than that for predicting average number of words correct is possibly a reflection of the grossness of the latter criterion when there are only six subjects used. The trend of prediction for words correct was examined for non-linearity, but none was apparent. However, a plot of the average number of words correct versus number of ratings of "four" or less per word indicated a non-linearity for small amounts of damage (Figure 11). This would indicate that damage to one or two elements impairs audibility of the word somewhat, but a really marked drop in intelligibility only follows damage to several

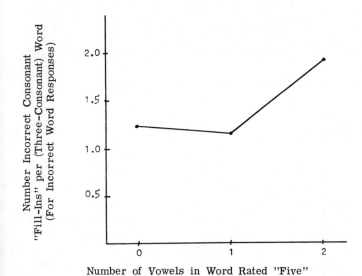

Figure 10. The relationship between the average number of incorrect consonant "fill-ins" (per three-consonant word) for incorrect word responses and the number of vowels in word rated "five."

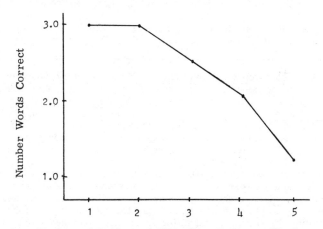

Figure 11. Relationship between number of words correct for subjects and the number ratings of "four" or less per word.

elements.   But this may be due to generally small damage in the
present experiments; for a plot of the number of words correct as
a function of the number of sounds in a word with a rating of "three"
or less (see Figure 12) shows a pronounced drop in intelligibility
when even one sound has severe damage, as indicated by a rating of
"three" or less.

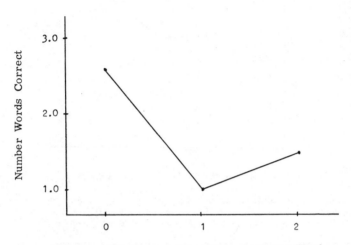

Number of Ratings of "Three" or Less per Word

Figure 12.   Relationship between number of words correct for subjects and number of ratings of "three" or less per word.

Discussion of Some Implications of the Auditory Analysis:
One of the most important hypotheses concerning which the auditory
analysis provides data is the following: briefness of presentation of
"chopped" word sounds is the primary cause of lowered intelligibility.
The results of the auditory analysis showed that the sounds were almost all rated intelligible by the judges: i. e. , the judges gave ratings of "four" or "five" to 94 per cent of the sounds, when given the
correct word, and several presentations of the speeded word.   These
results contrast with the relatively small number of sounds reported
correctly when the speeded speech was presented once to the original subjects.   One of the judges who was available after the auditory
analysis was tested with unfamiliar speeded speech to determine if
his intelligibility score would differ from those obtained from naive
subjects.   His intelligibility score was found to be within one standard deviation of the mean of the other subjects' scores.   This is
taken as evidence in support of the hypothesis.

There are several objections which may be raised to the rele-
vance of this evidence to the hypothesis.   First, it might be said

that since the judges know the word they "fill in" the sounds. This objection is answered, however, by the fact that from the data sim- ple "fill-in" does not appear to be taking place. There are precise differential (and independent) ratings of sounds in the words, and the judges agree on these differential ratings.

Second, it might be said that even if there is no simple "fill- in" taking place, there is a complex perception taking place which is peculiar to the judging situation--i.e., the rating results have noth- ing to do with the presentation situation with the original subjects. This objection may be answered by the fact that predictions are rath- er precise from the rating situation to the situation where speeded speech is presented to naive subjects; sounds which are most intelli- gible by ratings make syllables or words intelligible. The most reasonable interpretation would seem to be that briefness of presen- tation is operating to cause this different, but proportional relation.

Further evidence in support of the hypothesis comes from the work on interrupted speech reported by Miller and Licklider [B283]. They report that after several presentations of the "chopped" words to the same subject the intelligibility increased. This increase in intelligibility occurred even though the subjects were never told the correct words.

The question might be raised as to whether the auditory ana- lysis indicates the goodness of the physical sounds. The purpose of the auditory analysis was to measure the psychological sounds of the words in their context. This has an advantage over a physical ana- lysis in the sense that partially damaged sound may psychologically be intelligible. If there are context effects, it is important that they be measured--e.g., if a consonant defines a vowel in a word, then this should be measured. Obviously there are advantages which a physical analysis would have as well; but the facilities and time did not permit doing both types of analyses in a single study. It is probable that the auditory analysis does have a close relation to a physical analysis, but this must be proved by further experimenta- tion. The present auditory analysis serves to demonstrate the dif- ferent effect which different rates of "chopping" have upon the sounds of the spondaic words, as well as the differential effects upon the sounds within a word of a given "chopping" rate.

Perhaps the most interesting finding is the relationship be- tween the judged goodness of the sounds and the success with which the sounds, or words with which they belonged, were recognized by the original subjects. It is especially significant that this analysis indicated that the perception of words in the speeded condition is not a simple one, involving as it does good and bad "fill-in."

DISCUSSION

Practical Considerations: Specific Characteristics of the Present Experiments:

Speech Articulation: The speech materials used in the present experiments were of better articulation than that found in average conversation. The voice of the speaker was of good quality (without apparent dialect), and great care was taken that every sound in each word was articulated correctly. Also considerable pains were taken to insure good quality in the recordings. Thus, the character of the speech material used in the present experiments must be borne in mind when attempting to apply the results to other situations. It should, however, be noted that the practical use of highly speeded speech would be limited to situations where standardized or "canned" messages only are employed. Good articulation of such messages would be one aspect of their construction.

Speech Rate: The original recordings of the speech material were made with the speaker talking at an average rate of 174 words per minute. This rate is above that of 150 w.p.m., which has been reported as average conversation rate.

Type of Speed-up Used: With the "chop-splice" technique used in the present experiments, it was found impractical to work with segments smaller than 1.5 centimeters in length due to the difficulty of splicing these small segments back together. Earlier experiments indicated that intelligibility was a function of the size of the "chops" made; these results showed that with 50 per cent of the speech pattern removed intelligibility increased as the size of the "chop" was made smaller. It is conceivable, then, that if some means were developed whereby the size of the "chops" could be made relatively small (e.g., one millimeter or less), and made more frequently, the intelligibility for a specific speed-up might be even higher than that obtained in the present experiments. The particular sizes of "chops" removed must therefore be kept in mind when attempting to generalize the present results. Practical Implications of Variables Investigated: The practical implications of results obtained with certain of the variables will be briefly discussed here, particularly as they bear upon aviation communication.

Rate of Presentation: It was pointed out in the introductory section of this report that slowness was an important deficiency involved in aviation voice communication. The implications of the experimental results reported here, therefore, are clear. It appears that the human listener can interpret speech in a much shorter time than that consumed in normal conversation. It follows that time of transmission and presentation could be cut down considerably without reducing message intelligibility to too great an extent. Any time saved in this way would be of tremendous aid in clearing the over-saturated radio channels used. However, the amount of "safety factor" desired, which would be a function of the undesirable consequences of errors, would undoubtedly enter into the decision as to what speed to use.   Whether or not an operator who is engaged in one or more tasks while listening would find speeded speech as intelligible as these results indicate requires experimental investigation.

Intensity: Only slight differences were found between intelligibility scores for speeded speech presented to subjects at intensities of 44 and 100 decibels above threshold.   The results did show that the higher the rate of speed the more detrimental was the effect of a high (100 db) intensity.   Although the differences were slight the results do indicate that with rapid rates of presentation of speeded speech intensity is a variable which must be considered.

Noise: An important feature of all voice communication in aviation operations is noise.   The experiments designed to determine the effect of noise on the intelligibility of speeded speech disclosed that high intensities (90, 95, and 100 db above threshold) of noise of the aircraft type in general decreased the intelligibility of speeded speech more than that of normal (unspeeded) speech.   For "chopped" speeded speech to be used at high rates of speed in aviation communication, efforts would have to be taken to eliminate all noise possible.

Familiarization: The standard messages used in the Air Force (for particular flying conditions) are relatively few in number and pilots are comparatively familiar with these messages.   The present experiments on familiarization indicate that previous familiarity with the speech material greatly increases the intelligibility of speeded speech.   This finding implies that for aviation communications, where the pilot is familiar with the messages, speech may be speeded up to a high degree without serious losses in intelligibility.

Theoretical Considerations:

Abbreviation of the Speech Pattern as a Type of Distortion: Previous experiments which were performed to determine the effect of various distortions on intelligibility have indicated that speech could be seriously distorted without large losses in intelligibility.   In particular the work of Miller and Licklider showed that normal speech contains more cues than are necessary for adequate intelligibility. In speeding up speech by the "chop-splice" technique the number of speech cues is greatly reduced; yet speech remains intelligible until well over 50 per cent of the record is removed.   These results further support the hypothesis drawn from the earlier experiments on distortion, that speech normally contains more cues than are necessary for good intelligibility.

The Importance of Rate of Presentation for Intelligibility: In the following paragraphs two types of presentation rate will be discussed: words per minute and presentation rate of the speech elements in the word.   The implications of each of these will be discussed separately, for although they are highly correlated, they refer to slightly different aspects of the experimental situation.

Words Per Minute: Goldstein [B193] reported relatively small losses in comprehension for his material (standard paragraphs of reading comprehension material) when read at rates of 125 to 175 words per minute. These rates were not reported by Goldstein as optimal rates, however, due to the fact that he found large individual differences in his measures of comprehension--i. e. , the more intelligent subjects grasped more words at 325 words per minute than they did at 100 w. p. m.   At a rate of 285 w. p. m. Goldstein obtained intelligibility of approximately 80 per cent; at a rate of 325 w. p. m. the resulting intelligibility scores were less than 80 per cent.   In the present study large losses in intelligibility for short sentences were not obtained with the "chop-splice" technique at rate of 261 words per minute (speed-up rate of 1. 5) or 345 w. p. m. (speed-up of 2. 0).   It was not until a rate of 400 w. p. m. (speed-up of 2. 3) was used that intelligibility dropped below the 75 per cent level; mean intelligibility scores below the 50 per cent level were not obtained until a rate of 470 w. p. m. (speed-up of 2. 7) had been reached.

It will be recalled from an experiment described earlier in the present report that speeding up speech by increasing turntable speed, (causing an accompanying frequency shift) lowered intelligibility much more than did speeding up speech by the "chop-splice" technique.

The speed-up technique used in the present experiments apparently affords an efficient method for speeding speech.   But type of material as well as measure of intelligibility used must be considered in interpreting the results; for it should be recalled that the present experiments showed the differential effect on intelligibility of speeding words as against sentences.

Presentation Rate of Speech Elements: When speech is speeded up by the "chop-splice" technique, intelligibility is probably a function of both presentation rate and the amount of the speech record removed.   Obviously the "rate" of the speech in words per minute is increased; but there is a problem in determining whether decreases in intelligibility are caused primarily by the increase in rate of the remaining sounds or by removal of sounds.   To answer this question we need to know the loss of intelligibility caused by merely removing parts of words.

Miller and Licklider [B283] removed certain amounts of the speech pattern of monosyllabic words without an accompanying increase in presentation rate.   An experiment was performed by the writer using the "chop-splice" speed-up technique on 20 of the same words which Miller and Licklider used.   With the exception of the speed-up which accompanied the removal of portions of the speech material, the experimental conditions were maintained as nearly as possible identical with those used by Miller and Licklider.   The 20 words were chosen at random from Miller and Licklider's list.   Two experimental record tapes were prepared, one which had 62 per cent

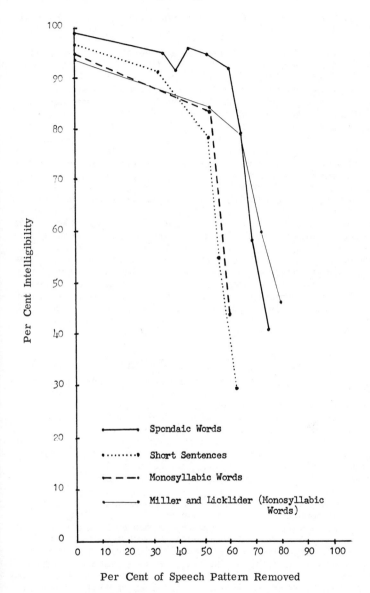

Figure 13.   Relationship between intelligibility and per cent of speech pattern removed.

of its speech material removed (speed-up of 2.7) and another which had 50 per cent of its speech material removed (speed-up of 2.0).

The results of this experiment are compared with those of Miller and Licklider in Figure 13. The Miller and Licklider results are so labeled while the "chop-splice" data are shown in the curve labeled <u>monosyllabic words.</u> When 50 per cent of the speech is removed there is no appreciable difference in the mean intelligibility scores for the two methods--i.e., with and without increase in presentation rate. The fact that there is no difference at this point may be attributable to a distortion which accompanied Miller and Licklider's "chopping," a distortion which was not noticeable in the present "chop-splice" technique. Miller and Licklider state that, due to this distortion, the talker sounded as though he were speaking in a "hoarse and raucous" voice. Such distortion may have balanced out any advantage which the non-speeded speech may have had over the speeded speech. Also it is possible that a speed-up of 2.0 times that of normal speech may not be a rate which is sufficient to cause a detrimental effect on intelligibility. When 62 per cent of the speech pattern is removed there is a striking difference between the mean intelligibility scores of the speeded and the non-speeded speech. Assuming that the remaining experimental conditions were equivalent for the two experiments, this difference must be attributable to the difference in presentation rate. It is, therefore, reasonable to conclude that rate of speech sounds (at least for the more rapid speed-up of 2.7) is an important variable affecting the intelligibility of "chop-splice" speeded speech.

The Role of Briefness of Presentation in Intelligibility: The results of the auditory analysis indicated that if "chopped" words (which were known to the judges beforehand) were presented to the judges several times, the individual sounds in the word appeared to be intelligible. However, the original subjects, who had only one brief presentation of the word, were able to perceive only a few of the sounds in the word. The difference between the two perceptions can be attributed to the fact that the judges were able to get a better "look" at the words and thus grasp more of the sounds, whereas the original subjects were able to get only one brief "look" at the words and thus were able to grasp only a few of the sounds.

From the graphs in Figure 12 a comparison can be made of the results obtained when short sentences and single monosyllabic words were speeded up. If it can be assumed that the key words in the sentences (four monosyllabic and one disyllabic word) are equivalent in difficulty to the single monosyllabic words used, then the difference in intelligibility of the two must be explained by some other variable. The difference between these two appears to be tied in with "briefness of presentation." In the short sentences a series of words, one immediately after another, is presented to the subject. The subject does not have time at the end of each word to review what he has heard or to "get set" for the next one. With the single words the subject is presented a word and is then given time to review for cues in what he has heard before the next word is presented to him. It is conceivable, then, that the intelligibility of the sentences is lower because the total time for presentation per word is more brief than that for the single words.

The Importance of Size of Chop Removed in Speeding Speech (Rate Held Constant): With the amount of the speech material held constant (e.g., 50 per cent) intelligibility is a function of the size of the "chop" removed. In general it might be expected that the smaller the "chop" the higher the resulting intelligibility. As the "chop" becomes smaller there is less chance of whole syllables or whole speech elements being removed; therefore, the intelligibility will not be lowered to the same extent as with large "chops."

The results of the work of Miller and Licklider [B293] reveal that intelligibility is not a regular function of the size of the "chop" removed (with the amount of the speech removed held constant). They report that intelligibility increases up to about 100 interruptions per second and that then there is a significant drop until approximately 2000 interruptions per second. At about 3000 interruptions per second the intelligibility again increases, until at 10,000 interruptions per second there is no significant difference between the intelligibility here and that obtained when all the speech pattern is present. This drop in intelligibility at 100 to 2000 interruptions per second is explained by Miller and Licklider by considering interruptions between 200 and 2000 per second as setting up square waves which modulate the speech carrier. The result of such modulation is a masking noise which interferes with the intelligibility of the speech. When the rate of interruption is less than 100 per second or more than 2000 per second the modulation does not produce a noise which interferes seriously with the speech frequencies.

If some means were devised for "chopping" speech and closing the gaps (as in the "chop-splice" technique) there is reason to believe that intelligibility would be a regular function of the size of the "chop" removed, since no such modulation would be set up as in the Miller and Licklider technique.

Interpretation of the Effect of Noise on Speeded Speech: The effect of noise on speech is to decrease the number of cues available. With unspeeded speech, which normally affords an excess of cues, the noise must remove a considerable proportion of the cues before intelligibility is affected. But when the number of cues is already reduced, as when speech is "chopped," the noise immediately begins to remove cues necessary for intelligibility. This is the interpretation given in the present report of the fact that noise has a greater effect on intelligibility of "chopped" speech than it does on normal speech.

Relative Importance of Various Cues in a Word for Intelligibility: The results of the auditory analysis imply that vowels are the most important cues in determining word intelligibility for the "chopped" speeded words of the present experiments. Apparently, with good vowel sounds in the word the subjects are able in many

cases to "fill in" the consonants, thus correctly interpreting the word.
In some cases, however, the subjects appear to "catch" two good
vowels, discard the consonant sounds, and "fill in" incorrect consonants, thus mistaking the identity of the word.

Possible Explanations of the Role of Familiarization: When
speech is "chopped" the number of cues is reduced. If enough of
these cues are removed the intelligibility of the speech drops significantly. If, however, the subjects are familiar with the speech material, the abbreviated speech is highly intelligible. This difference
in intelligibility for subjects who are familiar or unfamiliar with the
material may be explained by two processes. First, certain cues
in the speech pattern may have been reduced below "threshold" by
chopping. When the subjects become familiar with the speech material and are then presented with the "chopped" speech, the cues
which were formerly uninterpretable may now sound meaningful.
Second, the subjects may have learned the speech material, then
when presented the abbreviated material perceived enough cues to
"fill in" the rest of the material from memory. That part of the
process is one of "fill-in" was shown in one of the experiments previously described.

Interpretation of Individual Differences in Responses of Subjects: It has been pointed out that the subjects did not all make the
same mistakes on the speeded speech. Thus, it appears that individual differences are important. We have already stressed the fact
that various kinds of "fill-in" can occur. It is reasonable to suppose that this "fill-in" process might in many cases reflect individual
differences in familiarity with the material, or differences in aptitude
in this direction, as well as possible different individual "sets." In
addition, there are probably differences among individuals in attention to the various words, or elements of words in the list presented.

SUMMARY

The research reported in this dissertation is an extension of
research previously reported (in an M.A. thesis [B167]) on determining the intelligibility of spondaic words at various rates of speed-up.
The speed-up technique involved abbreviating the speech pattern by
removing certain portions of the speech record, and joining together
the remaining portions. Factors affecting intelligibility of speeded
speech were investigated in some detail. The effect of certain of
these factors can be summarized as follows: (1) Intelligibility of
speeded speech was found to be a function of the type of material
speeded up. Three types of speech material (spondaic words, monosyllabic words, and short sentences) were useful. Of these the intelligibility of spondaic words was the least affected by speed-up; the
intelligibility of the short sentences showed the greatest loss when
speeded up.

(2) Only slight differences in intelligibility were found at intensities of 44 and 100 decibels above threshold for speech speeded
up by various amounts. With higher speed-ups, it was found that

speech at 100 db had lower intelligibility than that at 44 db.   (3) Noise was found to have a detrimental effect upon the intelligibility of speeded speech.   The presence of noise always decreased the intelligibility at all speed-up rates, though the effect was not completely uniform.   (4) The intelligibility of speech which was speeded up with an accompanying frequency shift was found to be lower than that which was speeded up to the same degree without an accompanying frequency shift.   Also speech which had been speeded up by the method of abbreviating the speech pattern and then slowed down with an accompanying frequency shift showed slight but various changes in intelligibility.   The intelligibility of the lowest and the highest speeded-up material was decreased under conditions of slowdown, the intelligibility of the moderately speeded speech increased with subsequent slowdown.

Subjects who had been familiarized with the speech material before it was presented to them in a condition of speed-up were able to obtain much higher intelligibility scores than were those who had not had the previous familiarization.

In order to determine the nature of the errors made by the subjects, and to discover whether an explanation of these errors could be found in terms of the goodness of the separate sounds in the "chopped" words, a study was made of the speeded-up spondaic words. This study involved analyzing the errors made by the original subjects and also analyzing the separate speech sounds in these words. The results of the study were as follows: (1) Although the range of errors made by the subjects under any one speed-up condition was quite small, the subjects did not tend to make the same errors on the test material.   (2) Ratings by the judges of the goodness of the individual sounds in the speeded words indicated that only a relatively few sounds in the words were damaged (by "chopping") beyond recognition.

(3) In those words whose speech pattern had been most abbreviated the individual sounds were found by the judges to be more damaged than the sounds in those words which had been less abbreviated.   (4) Average ratings of the goodness of sounds in a word were found to agree quite closely with the average number of errors (in terms of individual sounds per word) made by the original subjects.   (5) The perception of speeded speech appears not to be a simple process.   The auditory analysis indicated that the vowel sounds were the most important cues present in the speech pattern for determining intelligibility of words.   In many cases the subjects were able to "fill in" the correct consonants from the presence of good vowel sounds alone.   In some cases, however, the subjects disregarded the consonant sounds in the word and "filled in" incorrect consonant sounds from the good vowel sounds present, thus missing the word.   On the other hand it appeared that a certain amount of consonant sounds was necessary to help define "good" vowels.

Chapter 4

TWO EARLY EXPLORATIONS

The first excerpt included in this chapter, by Miller and Licklider, is another of the "classic" studies in the field of speech compression which along with Goldstein and Garvey is cited very often in
subsequent writings. The purpose of the study here reported was to
determine the effect on intelligibility of interruptions (deletions from
a tape-recorded list of phonetically balanced words). It must be
noted that unlike the work reported by Garvey in his theses which
were excerpted in the two previous chapters, there was no attempt
to abut the remaining portion of the interrupted material. The interrupted message thus was perforce of the same time duration as
the uninterrupted message had been. In the first experiments reported, the interruptions were evidenced by periods of silence, but
in subsequent trials the spaces were filled with masking noise.

Miller and Licklider were concerned with investigating the effect on intelligibility of the number of interruptions and of the length
of these interruptions. It is obvious that the determination of firm
answers to these questions is of prime importance to the planner of
any kind of speech compression who contemplates the deletion of a
portion of the textual material which is to be shortened. The study
here reported was carefully performed and its findings have stood
the test of time. The research worker in the field of rate alteration of oral material will be well repaid for a careful examination of
this article.

The second excerpt in this chapter is taken from a 1956 University of Southern California thesis by Leo Goodman-Malamuth II.
This was the third of a series of theses reporting on investigations
of factors involved in "listenability" (a coined term parallel to the
term "readability") of an oral message. In the first thesis, Kenneth
A. Harwood [An Experimental Comparison of Listening Comprehensibility and Reading Comprehensibility, Los Angeles: USC, 1950] investigated the applicability of readability measures to the measurement of listenability. Francis A. Cartier, Jr., [An Experimental
Study of the Effect of Human Interest Factors in Listenability, Los
Angeles: USC, 1951] was concerned in the second thesis with the effect of human interest, particularly the use of personal words, as
designated by the Flesch Readability Formula, on listenability. The
third and last of this series of theses was the one which is excerpted
here.

The matter investigated, using the same material and the
same subjects as were used in the two preceding theses, was the

effect of rate on listenability.   The rate in this study was determined
by the speaker.   The method followed in securing rapidly spoken passages at a constant rate in this study was one that required great
care and precision.

INTELLIGIBILITY OF INTERRUPTED SPEECH

George A. Miller, J. C. R. Licklider

Studies of frequency and amplitude distortion have made it
evident that undistorted speech waves contain more information than
is necessary for intelligibility.   Because they do it is often possible
to economize on the band width or on the peak-power capacity of a
speech-transmission system.   It is also possible to economize in the
time domain without sacrificing performance.   One of the simplest
ways to save time is to turn the speech off at intervals so the system can be used for another transmission.   Effects of such interruptions upon intelligibility, as determined in a series of articulation
tests, are described in this paper.

A. INTERRUPTED SPEECH IN QUIET

The kind of interruption used in these studies is equivalent to
100 per cent amplitude modulation by a train of rectangular pulses.

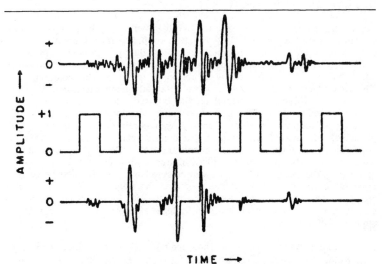

TIME ⟶

Figure 1.   Multiplying the continuous speech wave (top line) by the
square wave (middle line) produces the interrupted speech wave (bottom line).

Periodic interruptions are illustrated in Figure 1. The undistorted speech wave at the top of Figure 1 is multiplied by the modulating wave to produce the interrupted speech wave at the bottom of the figure. The basic variables are: (1) the number of interruptions per second, the frequency of interruption; (2) the proportion of the time the speech is on, the speech-time fraction; and (3) the degree of regularity of the interruptions.

The speech materials used in the articulation tests were the phonetically balanced ("PB") lists of monosyllabic words published by Egan. They were recorded phonographically by two talkers and reproduced for the articulation tests by an equalized playback. A crew of five listeners (male college students with normal hearing) was used, and each datum point is based upon the results of at least two 50-word tests, one with each talker. The electronic switch used to produce the interruptions was the one described by G. A. Miller and W. G. Taylor ["The Perception of Repeated Bursts of Noise," J. of Acoustical Soc. of Amer. 20:171-82, 1948]. When it turned the signal off it in fact reduced the level approximately 80 db. With that much attenuation, no speech sounds could be heard during the interruptions. The listeners heard the speech through Permoflux dynamic receivers PDR-8. The frequency-response characteristic of the entire system (earphones terminating in a 6-cc coupler) was essentially uniform from 200 to 7000 c.p.s. This characteristic has been published by J. C. R. Licklider ["The Influence of Interaural Phase Relations upon the Masking of Speech by White Noise," J. of Acoustical Soc. of Amer. 20:150-59, 1948].

Regularly Spaced Interruptions

Consider first the results obtained with regularly spaced interruptions and a speech-time fraction of 0.5. The frequency of interruption was varied between 0.1 and 10,000 per second. In Figure 2 the percentage of the words heard correctly is plotted on the ordinate, and the frequency of interruption is given on the abscissa. The three curves of Figure 2 were obtained under slightly different conditions. Curve 1 is based on the tests conducted at the beginning of the experiments. The listeners had never before served as subjects in articulation tests. Curve 2 was obtained after a few days' practice. Note that the scores are consistently higher. At this point the frequency-response characteristic of the phonograph playback was equalized. (In the preliminary tests--curves 1 and 2--the system had a response that de-emphasized the low frequency components of the speech.) Curve 3 shows the results obtained after the response was equalized. Here the dip of 460 interruptions per second is greater, and intelligibility is less affected at the lower frequencies of interruption.

The general shapes of the three functions are approximately the same, and about what we should expect on the basis of an analysis of the experimental conditions. If the frequency of interruption is low enough, the articulation score must be equal to the product of

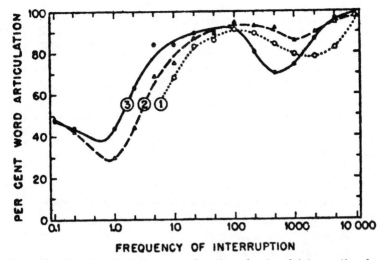

FREQUENCY OF INTERRUPTION

Figure 2. Word articulation as a function of rate of interruption for a speech-time fraction of 0.5. Curve (1) was obtained with naive listeners, (2) with the same listeners after a few days practice, (3) again with the same listeners, but with a system having more uniform frequency-response characteristics.

the speech-time fraction (here 0.5) and the articulation score for un-interrupted speech (here almost 100 per cent). With the speech on five seconds, then off five seconds, the listeners heard half of the words correctly. At the other extreme, if the frequency of interruption is high enough, the words must be just as intelligible as if they were not interrupted at all. The very rapid oscillations between on and off were not transduced by the earphones, but even if they had been transduced, the mechanical transmission system in the middle ear would have acted as a low pass filter to eliminate the interruptions and restore the speech wave essentially to its original form.

Between the very low and the very high frequencies of interruption the functions pass through a minimum, a maximum, then another minimum. The first minimum occurs in the neighborhood of one interruption per second. It is reasonable to expect intelligibility to be low when the duration of the "on" period is approximately equal to the duration of one word. The entire word can be heard correctly only if the "on-time" coincides rather exactly with the occurrence of the word. The word is likely to be missed if either its initial or its final phoneme is chopped off. However, as the listeners grow more familiar with the word lists they become better able to recognize the mutilated words. In curve 3, which was obtained after the listeners had considerable experience, the minimum had almost disappeared.

The maximum between 10 and 100 interruptions per second is also attributable to the temporal characteristics of the spoken words. The average duration of a word in these tests was 0.6 second. Five interruptions per second would, on the average, give the listeners three "looks" at each word. For the majority of the words this is enough to ensure a glimpse of every phoneme. It appears that one glimpse per phoneme is sufficient. Since, according to this interpretation, the durations of the phonemes are important in determining the articulation scores over the range from 1 to 10 interruptions per second, an attempt was made to measure the durations. Cathode-ray oscillograms were made of the recorded words, and from them the durations of the initial consonants, the vowels, the final consonants and the entire words were measured to the nearest 0.01 second. The results are shown in Figure 3. The durations are

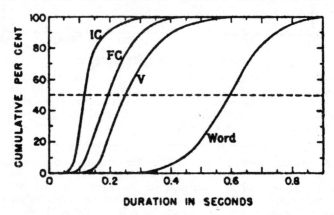

Figure 3. Durations of speech sounds in the monosyllabic words used in the articulation tests. Initial consonants (IC) were shortest, final consonants (FC) next, and vowels (V) were longest. The average word lasted about 0.6 second.

somewhat longer than would be obtained for conversational speech. Even with no time allowed for spaces between words, the median duration of 0.6 second corresponds to only 100 words per minute. Since conversational rates average around 130 words per minute, including pauses and polysyllabic words, it appears that the two talkers pronounced the words slowly and carefully when they made the records. If they had used normal conversational rates, the word articulation scores probably would have reached their maximum at a slightly higher rate of interruption.

An incidental but related observation concerns the effect of an interrupted sidetone on a talker's normal rate of speaking. If slowly interrupted speech is fed back at a high intensity to the talker's own ears, there is a strong tendency to slow down. At one interruption per second, the talker tries to drawl out his words until each speech sound is heard at least once. At somewhat higher rates of interruption, he tends to synchronize his vowels with multiples of the frequency of interruption. (Our attention was called to this last point by J. M. Stroud, who suggests that our articulation scores might have been slightly higher had we used "live" talkers and side-tone monitoring.)

Intelligibility remains high until the frequency of interruption reaches 100 per second, but between 200 and 2000 per second there is a slight, though significant, deterioration. Consider the speech as a carrier modulated by a 1000-cycle square wave. Each component in the speech spectrum will have sidebands spaced at 1000-cycle intervals on either side of it, and these sidebands will constitute a noisy masking signal to interfere with intelligibility. Apparently such sidebands are not a serious consideration when the modulating frequency is less than 100 per second. When the frequency is greater than 3000 interruptions per second, on the other hand, the sidebands do not seriously overlap the range of speech frequencies, and intelligibility is high.

It is possible to account in the manner just outlined for the various inflections in the functions of Figure 2 when the interruptions are regular and the speech-time fraction is 0.5. Does the picture change when different speech-time fractions are employed? The answer is given by the set of functions shown in Figure 4. These

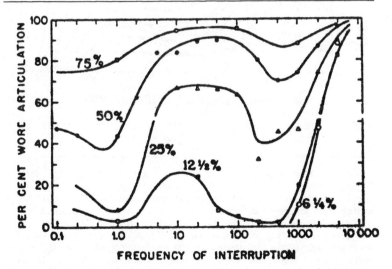

Figure 4. Word articulation as a function of frequency of interruption, with speech-time fraction as the parameter. The interruptions were spaced regularly in time.

functions were obtained with speech-time fractions ranging from
0.063 to 0.75 and with periodic interruptions. These functions follow roughly similar courses. However, as the speech-time decreases, the maxima grow lower and narrower. Fewer words get
through between gaps, and interference due to modulation products
become more serious.

Irregularly Spaced Interruptions

The data we have just examined are represented in another
way in Figure 5: the speech-time fraction is plotted against the frequency of interruption. The resulting curves are equal-articulation

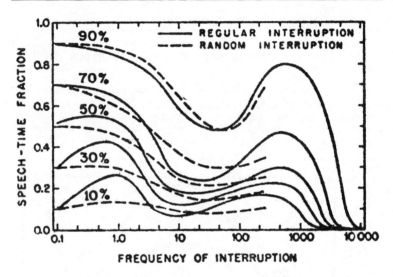

Figure 5. Equal-articulation contours obtained with regularly spaced
and with randomly spaced interruptions of speech.

contours. The solid curves of Figure 5 are based upon the data of
Figure 4 and hold for regularly spaced interruptions. The dashed
curves of Figure 5 are not irregular interruptions. The electronic
switch was arranged in such a way that it could be triggered on and
off by pulses derived from two noise generators. Every time the
randomly fluctuating voltage of one of the noises rose past a predetermined amplitude the switch turned on and stayed on until the other
noise voltage rose past its predetermined amplitude level. By varying the two levels at which the switch would trigger it was possible
to produce random interruptions at various rates and speech-time
fractions. Because the triggering was random, however, it was not
possible to tell exactly what the frequency and speech-time fraction

were going to be until the test was completed.   It was necessary to run the test and then see what had happened.   The average frequency of interruption during the test was determined with the aid of an electronic counter, and the average speech-time fraction was determined from the time integral of the triggering voltage.   Once these values were determined, the articulation score could be indicated at the proper point on a graph like that of Figure 5.   From these points the dashed curves of Figure 5 were obtained.

The functions for random interruption turn out to be straighter than the functions for regular interruption.   This result is to be expected because random interruption gives rise in some parts of the test to frequencies of interruption that are higher than average and in other parts to frequencies of interruption that are lower than average.   Similarly, a range of speech-time fractions is involved in every test.   The effect is to smooth out the variations in the curves, just as a running average smooths out fluctuations in a column of numbers.   These results are displayed in still a third manner in Figure 6.   The word articulation score is plotted against the speech-

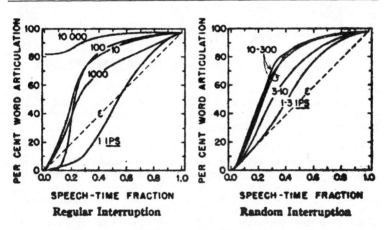

Figure 6.   Word articulation as a function of the speech-time fraction, with frequency of interruption as the parameter, for both regularly spaced and randomly spaced interruptions.

time fraction, with the rate of interruption as the parameter, for both regular and irregular interruption.   At nearly all points the articulation score lies above the speech-time fraction.

Gradual Modulation, Periodic Inversion, and Double Talk

A few tests were conducted with regularly spaced interruptions that were gradual rather than abrupt.   The modulating voltage took various proportions of the time to rise from zero to one and to return. The results of these tests are shown in Figure 7, where the articulation score is plotted as a function of the percentage of the

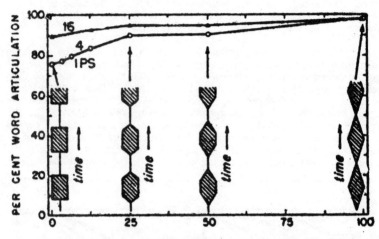

Figure 7. Effects of reducing the abruptness with which the speech is turned on and off. Gradual transition from off to on and back produces less interference than abrupt transition if the speech is "half-way on" for the same fraction of the time.

time occupied by the build-up and decay of the speech burst. These data were obtained with regular interruptions four and 16 times per second and, figuring the speech to be "on" whenever it is more than half-way on, with a speech-time fraction of 0.5. Changing from abrupt to gradual modulation improved both the quality and the intelligibility of the interrupted speech. Returning to abrupt modulation, a curious effect was obtained when, instead of turning the speech wave off, we simply turned it over. At low frequencies, periodic inversion of the speech wave form did not affect intelligibility, but as the frequency of inversion is increased a number of the speech sounds acquired a W-like character. The process of reversing polarity turned itself into "the pwowess of wewersing."

In a short series of tests, we examined the listeners' ability to hear two talkers at once. In some of the tests, the talkers' voices were interwoven as the electronic switch alternated between them 10 or 100 times per second. In other tests the talkers spoke together and their speech waves were superposed without switching. And, in still other tests for purposes of comparison, the talkers spoke singly. The results are summarized in Table 1. When both

Table 1

ARTICULATION SCORES OBTAINED WITH TWO TALKERS SPEAKING ALONE AND TOGETHER

| | Interruptions (or alternations) per second | | |
	None	10	100
Talker H alone	99. 8%	89. 0	97. 6
Talker L alone	98. 8	94. 6	98. 4
H and L together:			
H's words	64. 5	34. 3	32. 8
L's words	62. 1	58. 0	41. 9
Average	63. 3	46. 2	37. 4

voices were on continuously the listeners heard correctly more than half the words spoken by each talker. The total number of words heard correctly was greater (126) than when either talker spoke alone (99). When the talkers' voices alternated 10 times per second, the listeners got 92 words correct which is the same number of words they heard when one talker spoke alone. When the voices alternated 100 times per second, the listeners got fewer words correct (75) than when either talker spoke alone (98). Alternating the two voices does not reduce the interference between them: if two talkers are going to speak to a listener at the same time, no advantage can be gained by switching back and forth between the two voices. In the series of tests with two talkers only about two-thirds of the words that were heard correctly were attributed to the talker who had uttered them.

Applications

Interruptions that do not seriously impair intelligibility are of practical utility. Time-multiplex and pulse-code systems of speech transmission take advantage of the fact that intelligibility is not impaired by regular interruptions at a high frequency. These systems sample the fluctuating amplitude of the speech wave at very frequent intervals and the sample contains all the information that is carried by the original wave. (Shannon has shown that a signal confined to band width $\underline{W}$ can be described uniquely by $2\underline{W}$ samples per second.)

A related but quite different application would take advantage of the maximum between 10 and 100 interruptions per second in the curve relating intelligibility to interruption rate. In 1936 Marro, who repeated the earlier work of Poirson, suggested the use of two-way transmission in a single frequency channel by switching from transmit to receiver and back about 20 times per second. Switching would allow the transmitters at both ends of the link to operate in the same frequency channel without blocking the adjacent receivers. Recently the idea of infrasonic switching was porposed again by Montani, who made the statement, however, that--because of the persist-

ence of hearing--15 interruptions per second are inaudible.   We
agree that interruptions are inaudible, but only in the sense that little is heard during interruptions.   Despite 15 gaps per second, it is
easy to understand what is being said, but the talker sounds as
though he has a strange defect of phonation.   A very similar effect
is obtained by patting the lips lightly and rapidly while speaking.

B. SPEECH INTERRUPTED BY NOISE

We turn now to the situation in which speech is left on continuously but is heard in the presence of interrupted masking noise.
The speech is not intermittently attenuated--it is intermittently
masked.   The experiments already described must be duplicated to
explore the same variables--noise-time fraction, frequency and regularity of interruption--but now these apply to noise rather than to
speech.   To these three variables we must add a fourth, the signal-
to-noise ratio.   The signal-to-noise ratios to be given will refer to
the intervals during which the noise is on.   These ratios, which
will be stated in decibels, can be changed to averages for the entire
cycle by expressing the silent-time fraction in decibel notation and
subtracting it.   Thus, if the noise is on half the time, the silent-
time fraction is 0.5 or -3 db, and the signal-to-noise ratio averaged
over the cycle is 3 db higher than the signal-to-noise ratio measured
during a typical burst of noise.

The signal-to-noise ratios, measured during bursts of noise
and in the frequency band from 100 to 7000 c.p.s., were -18, -9,
0, and +9 db.   The average speech level was held constant at 90 db
re 0.0002 dyne/cm^2.   The tests with interrupted noise were run during the same sessions and with the same equipment and personnel as
the tests with interrupted speech that are summarized in Figures 4,
5, and 6.   Therefore the results to be discussed now can be compared directly with the results discussed in the preceding section.

Regularly Spaced Bursts of Noise

Figure 8 summarizes the results obtained with regular interruptions of the masking noise and a noise-time fraction of 0.5.   At
the lowest frequencies of interruption the articulation score behaves
in about the same way it does when the speech is interrupted by silence.   Consider first the function obtained with a signal-to-noise
ratio of -18 db.   When the noise is on it completely masks the
speech, so five seconds of speech and noise alternating regularly
with five seconds of speech alone gives an articulation score of approximately 50 per cent; all the words heard at all are heard correctly.   As the frequency of interruption is increased to 10 per second the articulation score rises (see lowermost curve of Figure 8
and curve 3 of Figure 2).   When there were 10 bursts of noise per
second the listeners were able to get several glimpses of every word
and to patch these glimpses together well enough to record three-
fourths of the test words correctly.

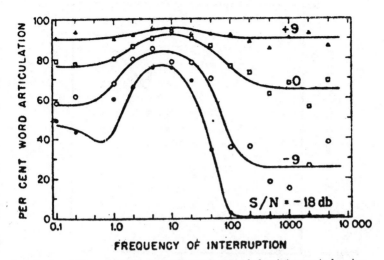

Figure 8.   The masking of continuous speech by interrupted noise.
Word articulation is plotted against the frequency of interruption of
the noise, with the speech-to-noise ratio in decibels as the parameter.   Noise-time fractions, 0.5.

When the slow bursts of noise do not drown out completely
the speech that occurs with them, the articulation score is higher
than the silent-time fraction.   In a test of 100 words, for example,
about 50 of the words will occur in the silent interval and will be
heard correctly.   The remaining 50 words are heard in the presence
of noise, and the articulation score for these masked words depends
upon the signal-to-noise ratio.   Figure 9 presents the results obtained when speech was masked by a continuous noise.   With Figure
9 it is possible to estimate what fraction of the masked words are
heard correctly.   For example, with a signal-to-noise ratio of 0 db
the listeners heard correctly 50 per cent of the masked words.   If
the noise is interrupted half the time and once every 10 seconds, the
listeners should get 50 per cent for the unmasked words plus half of
the masked words, or a total articulation score of approximately 75
per cent.   This method of estimation is relatively accurate for interruption frequencies below one per second.

At the other extreme of interruption frequency, also, the
masking produced by interrupted noise can be estimated from Figure
9.   When the noise is interrupted several hundred times each second
it is effectively continuous insofar as aural masking is concerned.
With a noise-time fraction of 0.5 the level of the noise averaged
over a full on-off cycle is 3 db lower than it would have been had
the noise been on all the time.   Thus the articulation score obtained
in the presence of a noise interrupted 1000 times a second and half
the total time is the same as the one obtained in the presence of a

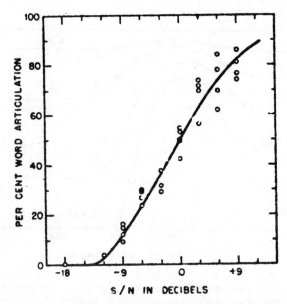

Figure 9. Word articulation for continuous speech heard in the presence of continuous noise, plotted as a function of the signal-to-noise ratio in decibels. The average level of the speech was held constant at approximately 90 db re 0.0002 dyne/cm^2.

---

continuous noise 3 db lower in intensity.

The range of interruption frequencies between 10 and 1000 per second remains to be discussed. This portion of the functions can be estimated with the aid of results obtained by G. A. Miller and W. R. Garner in their study, "The Masking of Tones by Repeated Bursts of Noise" [J. of Acoustical Soc. of Amer. 20:691-96, 1948]. Their results are summarized in a single function that relates the masking efficiency of an interrupted noise (ratio of masking by inter-rupted to masking by continuous noise) to the duration of the silent intervals. When the silent interval is shorter than three or four milliseconds--higher than about 150 interruptions per second at a noise-time fraction of 0.5--the interrupted noise is effectively con-tinuous. For lower frequencies the masking by interrupted noise is a proper fraction of the masking by continuous noise. Miller and Garner's results can be used to estimate the change in the masked threshold for tones, and from the new masked threshold the articula-tion score can be computed in the manner described by N. R. French and J. C. Steinberg ["Factors Governing the Intelligibility of Speech Sounds," J. of Acoustical Soc. of Amer. 19:90-119, 1947].

The effects of varying the noise-time fraction are summarized in Figure 10. Four rates of interruption were used--1, 10, 100 and

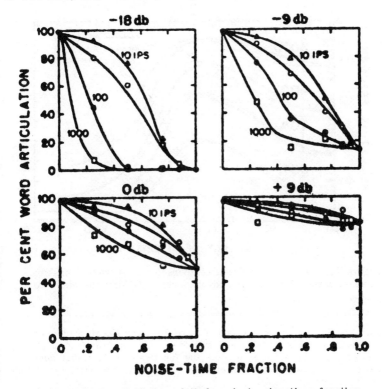

Figure 10. Word articulation plotted against noise-time fraction, with the frequency of interruption of the noise and the signal-to-noise ratio as parameters.

1000 per second. At all noise-time fractions and all signal-to-noise ratios, 10 bursts of noise per second produced the least interference and 1000 bursts of noise per second produced the most interference. Since the signal-to-noise ratios refer to the intervals during which the noise is on, the amount of interference of course increases with increasing noise-time fraction.

Irregularly Spaced Bursts of Noise

The effects of irregular interruption of the masking noise were explored at a signal-to-noise ratio of -9 db. The method for turning the noise on and off at random was the same as that described in the preceding section for turning speech on and off at random. The results are summarized in Figure 11, where the noise-time fraction is plotted against the frequency of interruption, with articulation score as the parameter. The solid functions represent the results obtained

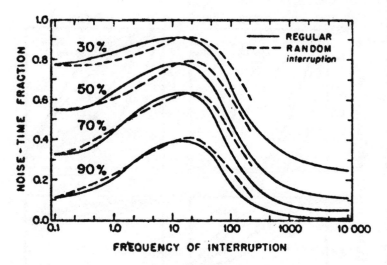

Figure 11. Equal-articulation contours obtained with a masking noise interrupted regularly and at random. Signal-to-noise ratio, -9 db.

with regular interruptions (see Figure 10), and the dashed functions represent the results obtained with irregular interruptions. The effect of irregularity is to smooth the functions slightly, but qualitatively the picture is quite similar for regularly and randomly interrupted masking noise.

SPEECH ALTERNATING WITH NOISE

The preceding sections have discussed the results obtained (1) when speech is interrupted by silence, and (2) when continuous speech is masked by an interrupted noise. A third class of tests explored the effects of alternating speech and noise. These tests are similar to (1), except that the silent intervals are filled with noise. They are similar to (2), except that the speech is not present when the masking noise is on. By comparing the results with (1) we obtain an estimate of how much the masking effect of a burst of noise "spills over" into temporally adjacent intervals. If the ear recovered immediately from the masking produced by a burst of noise, no effect would be observed when noise was introduced during the silent interval. By comparing the results with (2) we obtain an estimate of how much the speech during the bursts of noise contributes to intelligibility.

Results of Articulation Tests

The articulation scores obtained when speech alternated with noise are shown in Figure 12. The speech-time fraction was 0.50, the frequency of interruption was varied from 0.1 to 10,000 per second, and the signal-to-noise ratio was varied from -18 to +9 db.

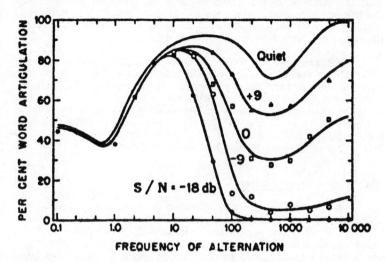

FREQUENCY OF ALTERNATION

Figure 12. Word articulation as a function of the frequency of alternation between speech and noise, with signal-to-noise ratio in decibels as the parameter.

The top curve in Figure 12 has been taken from Figure 4 and represents the scores obtained when no noise is introduced into the intervals between successive bursts of speech. So long as the frequency of alternation is below 4.6 per second the introduction of noise during the "no-speech" intervals has practically no effect upon the articulation scores. With intervals longer than about 0.1 second the alternation between speech and noise is not different from the alternation between speech and silence. The recovery time of the auditory system is negligible (for the noise levels used) in comparison to intervals of 0.1 second or longer.

When the frequency of alternation is increased to or beyond 215 per second, the noise masks the speech with which it alternates just as effectively as if both speech and noise were on at the same time. Thus, although the decay of the masking effect is rapid enough that the intelligibility of a 100-millisecond burst of speech is not impaired by the noise preceding and following it, the decay is not instantaneous. At 215 alternations per second between speech and noise intervals of equal length, the intervals are 2.3 milliseconds

long. During a speech interval of that duration the auditory system
does not recover sufficiently to derive any information at all from
the speech wave. As an immediate example we can take 100 alternations per second, which gives intervals of speech and of noise each
five milliseconds long. In this instance a surround of noise 18 db
more intense than the speech lowers the articulation score from 90
to 4 per cent (see Figure 12). From Figure 9 we find that this
shift is equivalent to that produced by a change of 24 db (12 to -12
db) in signal-to-noise ratio. Hence the "spill-over" into temporally
adjacent regions must be about 24 db greater with five-millesecond
intervals than with 100-millisecond intervals.

The principal difference between alternating speech and noise
and masking speech with interrupted noise appears in the region from
200 to 2000 interruptions per second. In that region unintelligible
components arising from the modulation of the speech by the inter-
rupter contribute significantly to the masking. We have the dip in
the quiet curve of Figure 12 plus the "spill-over" masking due to the
noise. About 2000 per second the functions approach the values indicated for continuous speech and noise in Figure 9.

The "Picket Fence" Effect

An interesting effect is observed if noise is introduced into
the gaps between bursts of speech when the speech is interrupted
about 10 to 15 times per second. Without the noise the talker's
voice sounds hoarse and raucous. The speech is intelligible, but
the interruptions are quite evident. When noise is introduced between the bursts of speech, the on and off transients are assimilated
into the noise and, when the noise is somewhat more intense than the
speech, the speech begins to sound continuous and uninterrupted. It
is much like seeing a landscape through a picket fence--the pickets
interrupt the view at regular intervals, but the landscape is perceived as continuing behind the pickets. The same effect can be obtained with pure tones. An interrupted tone will sound quite pure
and continuous if the intervals between the bursts of tone are filled
with a sufficiently intense white noise. When interrupted speech is
made to sound continuous by "masking the silent intervals," the listener feels that the speech is certainly more natural and probably
more intelligible. As Figure 12 shows, however, no actual improvement in intelligibility was obtained by adding noise.

EFFECTS OF RATE OF SPEAKING UPON LISTENABILITY

Leo Goodman-Malamuth II

The general purpose of this study was to investigate one major component of oral presentation, speaking rate, and its possible

effect upon the understanding of heard materials of various levels of measured difficulty. More specifically the problem of this study was as follows: given (a) seven language samples ranging from "very easy" to "very difficult" as predicted by a readability formula, (b) oral presentation of each of the foregoing samples at the rates of 125, 150, 175, and 200 words per minute, and (c) groups of listeners tested and scored upon their ability to recall information from the language samples, 1. What effects do different rates have upon the listenability scores when the data for all seven levels of difficulty are combined? 2. Do any of the rates produce significantly higher or lower scores on any of the language samples in comparison with any of the other language samples? 3. Do the data indicate that there is an optimal rate of oral presentation? 4. To what degree do the levels of difficulty as predicted by a readability formula correspond with levels of difficulty established by the obtained listenability scores at different rates of oral presentation?

Review of the Literature

In 1950 Harwood reported an investigation of 240 tenth-grade students from the secondary schools of Compton, California. Seven matched selections equated for levels of difficulty by Flesch formulation, each 300 words in length, were presented for reading in mimeographed booklet form and orally at a controlled rate of 150 words per minute by means of tape recording. Subsequent to each presentation, either oral or visual, subjects answered 15 five-part multiple-choice questions for each of the seven selections. Conclusions indicated that the series of language samples were only insignificantly more comprehensible when presented for reading than when presented for listening [K. A. Harwood, An Experimental Comparison of Listening Comprehensibility with Reading Comprehensibility, Ph.D. dissertation, Los Angeles: USC 1950].

Cartier in 1951 reported an investigation of 300 tenth-grade students from the Compton secondary schools, designed to determine the effects of variance of the "human interest" factor on listenability. Seven selected language samples, each 300 words in length, were equated by Flesch's five-step formula for "human interest." Three groups of seven recorded language samples having measured "human interest" levels of 15, 30, and 50, were presented orally at a controlled rate of 150 words per minute. Subjects were objectively tested with 15-item, five-part multiple-choice type tests subsequent to each listening sample. Conclusions indicated that, in general, varying the "human interest" factor by one or two steps according to the Flesch five-step scale had no significant effect on the listenability of the language samples, as measured by audience comprehension [F. A. Cartier, An Experimental Comparison of Human Interest Factors on Listenability, Ph.D. dissertation, Los Angeles: USC, 1951].

Techniques and Procedure

The development of the experiment was undertaken in four phases: (1) preparation of the test materials, (2) examination and selection of the subjects, (3) testing of the subjects, and (4) analysis of the raw data. This was one of three concurrent studies using basically the same materials, the same subjects, and the same testing procedures. Each experimenter varied the presentation according to his particular problem and study.

Preparation of materials: The assumption that various speaking rates might affect the listenability of materials at various levels of difficulty prompted the investigation of measured levels of difficulty at controlled speaking rates. Before language samples could be written, certain criteria were established. These were: 1. the language samples should be as informative and unemotional as possible; 2. the language samples should be of generally equal interest to both sexes; 3. the language samples should not be readily identifiable in time or place, e.g., specific events of news report occurrences; 4. the possibility of the language samples having been heard by the subjects should be kept to a minimum; 5. the language samples should approximate the type of material that would be heard over radio or through loud-speaker systems; and 6. each language sample should contain a complete story or theme within its continuity.

Complying with the criteria set forth, journals, magazines, and radio news features were perused for materials that approximately met all requirements. Seven examples were found and adjusted for content, continuity, and levels of difficulty. It was decided to keep all language samples used within this study of equal length. Preliminary experimentation with lengths of language samples and rates of oral presentation indicated that in the time allotted for each oral presentation and subsequent testing all language samples should be 300 words in length. (See Table 1.)

In order to equate the selected language samples for various levels of predicted difficulty, an acceptable standard was necessary. J. S. Chall and H. E. Dial presented evidence in 1948 to indicate that readability formulae did have some direct relationship in predicting listenability ["Predicting Listener Understanding and Interest in Newscasts," Educat. Research Bull. 27:141-53, 1948]. The correlation between predicted readability of news stories and their listenability as measured by immediate recall was +.72. This evidence was based upon the first Flesch Readability Formula [Marks of Readable Style; New York: Columbia Univ. Bureau of Publications, 1943].

Harwood's study, using a later Flesch formula, confirmed the applicability of a readability formula for predicting listenability [B211]. Examination of the data indicated that the ease rank as predicted by the new Flesch formula for readability and the ease rank of the same language samples as indicated by the mean comprehension scores of his listeners corresponded closely. Therefore, evidence indicated that the newer Flesch "Yardstick" ["A New Readability Yardstick,"

Table 1

CHARACTERISTICS OF THE LANGUAGE SAMPLES

Story Number	Story Title	Readability	Reading-ease Score	Human Interest Score*
I	Power	Easy	85.22	30.29
II	Suzanne	Standard	65.04	30.29
III	Instructor	Difficult	39.90	30.29
IV	Middletown	Very Difficult	15.08	30.29
V	DDT	Fairly Difficult	54.97	30.29
VI	North Pole	Fairly Easy	75.02	30.29
VII	Ice Cream	Very Easy	95.11	30.29

*Because of the length of the language sample, it was impossible to formulate a true HI mid-point of 30.00. The same was true of RE. The result closest to any mid-point was used in all cases.

Total No. of Words	No. of Sentences	No. of Syllables	No. of Personal Words
300	23	385	25
300	19	446	25
300	15	520	25
300	9	560	25
300	17	475	25
300	21	416	25
300	25	353	25

J. of Applied Psych. 32:221-33, 1948] for predicting readability was probably the best available formula for equating and scaling the language samples for measured levels of readability.

Four rates were chosen, each being separated by steps of 25 words per minute. The slowest rate chosen was 125 words per minute, or 15 words per minute below the minimum of 140 words per minute; 150 words per minute, or ten words above the minimum of 140 words per minute and 16 words below the 50th percentile of 166 words per minute; 175 words per minute, or nine words per minute above the Franke 50th percentile and ten words per minute below the upper limit of 185 words per minute; and 200 words per minute, or 15 words per minute above the upper rate limit of 185 words per minute. Each story sample was recorded at the four rates of speaking by a male speaker who had been judged by a group of graduate students of speech to be an "average" trained speaker. To assure proper timing for the speaker and a control for consistent timing, all language samples were divided into time intervals. (See Table 2.)

Table 2

RECORDED LISTENING TIME OF STORIES

Story	Oral Rate in Words Per Minute	Seconds per Time Check Interval	Total Recorded Listening Time
I - VII	125	18"	2' 24"
I - VII	150	15"	2' 0"
I - VII	175	12.75"	1' 42"
I - VII	200	11.25"	1' 30"

Construction of test materials: Upon completion of the recorded listening materials, it was necessary to construct the test
forms. Because of the amount of recorded material to be presented
and the limits of time operable during a test session, and since it
was recognized that the greater the number of items contained within
a test, the greater the degree of reliability, it was necessary to construct as many questions as possible for each listening sample. With
a two-minute limit for each test, 15 questions were found to be the
maximum feasible number. With reliability again the aim, it was
required that the factor of chance, in correctly responding to the
questions, should be as low as practicable. Each question was designed as a multiple-choice question with five possible responses.
The tests followed the general construction practice of (1) randomiz-
ing correct answers, (2) making incorrect answers reasonably attractive, (3) avoiding tricks of language, interpretation, and reasoning,
(4) avoiding catch questions, and (5) making the questions and responses brief.

Subjects: 487 subjects were drawn from the tenth grade of
the Union secondary school system of Compton, a residential suburb
of Los Angeles which may be classified as a city of middle social
rank and average urbanization. The subjects were randomly divided
into four listening groups, each group hearing one specific rate of
presentation. In general, the examination of the subjects by mean
scores indicated that general homogeneity did not exist among the
random samples. The groups manifested certain differences in age,
I. Q., and reading comprehension grade placement as indicated by an
analysis of variance implying heterogeneous group qualities. Two of
the four groups, A and B, did not differ significantly ($t_{.05}$) in age,
I. Q., and reading comprehension grade placement, while one group,
group D, differed significantly ($t_{.05}$) from each of two other groups
in one or more attributes of age, I. Q., and reading comprehension
grade placement.

Table 3

MEAN CORRECTED LISTENABILITY SCORES AND STANDARD
ERRORS OF THE MEAN FOR EACH STORY AT EACH RATE

Story	Predicted RE	Rate	Mean	Mean S.E.	N
VII	95	125	8.8325	.372	106
		150	10.3646	.261	120
	Very Easy	175	9.3844	.304	132
		200	9.1570	.281	129
I	85	125	8.6085	.430	106
		150	9.7917	.312	120
	Easy	175	9.2330	.300	132
		200	8.4981	.312	129
VI	75	125	7.8892	.405	106
		150	9.3542	.318	120
	Fairly	175	8.3049	.358	132
	Easy	200	7.9942	.310	129
II	65	125	7.2288	.389	106
		150	8.9583	.343	120
	Standard	175	8.6648	.290	132
		200	8.1880	.325	129
V	55	125	5.9552	.364	106
		150	8.1875	.308	120
	Fairly	175	7.0170	.302	132
	Difficult	200	5.9399	.292	129
III	40	125	3.7028	.294	106
		150	5.5000	.337	120
	Difficult	175	4.6402	.300	132
		200	4.0234	.263	129
IV	15	125	4.5000	.357	106
		150	6.1458	.346	120
	Very	175	5.3598	.306	132
	Difficult	200	5.0000	.293	129

Table 4

COMBINED MEAN LISTENABILITY SCORES OF SEVEN
STORIES AT FOUR RATES OF PRESENTATION

	Group A 200 WPM	Group B 175 WPM	Group F 150 WPM	Group D 125 WPM
Combined Mean Listenability Scores	6.97	7.51	8.33	6.68

Presentation and Interpretation of the Data

        To facilitate subsequent analysis the data were first compiled
as shown in Table 3.   The first problem was to determine what effect different rates have upon the listenability scores when the data
for all seven levels of difficulty are combined.   The combined listenability scores of the seven stories at four rates of presentation,
as shown in Table 4, indicated that for three of the four rates listenability tended to decrease as the rate of presentation was increased.
Listenability was also observed to have decreased as the rate was
decreased from a rate of 150 wpm to a rate of 125 wpm.   (See Figure 1.)

        The significance of the decrease in listenability with an in-
crease in rate for the three fastest rates as shown in Table 5, indicated that 150 wpm was very significantly superior to 175 wpm (t =

Table 5

MEAN, DIFFERENCE OF THE MEAN, AND T-RATIOS OF
LISTENABILITY SCORES AT FOUR RATES OF PRESENTATION

Group	Rate	Mean	dm 150	dm 175	dm 200	T-ratio 150	T-ratio 175	T-ratio 200	t.01
D	125	6.68	1.65	.84	.30	8.30	4.10	1.50	2.60
F	150	8.33		.81	.35		4.50	7.44	
B	175	7.51			.54			2.97	
A	200	6.97							

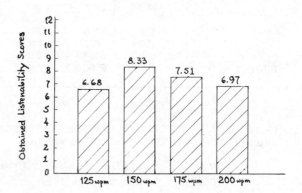

Figure 1.   Distribution of obtained listenability scores at four rates
of oral presentation.

4.50), and 200 wpm (t = 7.44) in obtaining a high listenability score; also, 175 wpm was significantly superior to 200 wpm (t = 2.97). As shown in Table 5, 125 wpm presented the lowest obtained listenability; 150 wpm was very significantly superior to 125 wpm (t = 8.30), and 175 wpm was significantly superior to 125 wpm (t = 4.10). No significant difference appeared between 125 wpm and 200 wpm. The foregoing description of the differences between the rates of presentation and the obtained listenability scores at each rate indicated a dropping off of obtained listenability in both directions from the mode (150 wpm). It would appear from this that listenability scores are adversely affected by rates that are either too fast or too slow.

Total Effects of Rate upon Listenability

1. For three of the fastest rates of presentation, obtained listenability decreased as the rate of presentation increased; 150 wpm was very significantly superior to 175 and 200 wpm in obtaining a high listenability score; 175 wpm was significantly superior to 200 wpm.
2. Listenability was observed to have decreased as the rate of presentation decreased from 150 wpm to a rate of 125 wpm.
3. It appeared that listenability is adversely affected by rates of oral presentation that are either too fast or too slow.

Effects upon Listenability at Different Levels of Language Difficulty

4. Of the seven levels of difficulty tested, RE = 55 (fairly difficult) was found to be the optimal level of language difficulty at which to best observe the effects at the four different speaking rates.
5. One hundred fifty words per minute was significantly better than 125 wpm at all levels of language difficulty.
6. The direction of the remaining differences between the rates of presentation at the various levels of language difficulty was in all cases in the proper direction despite the fact that these remaining differences were not all statistically significant.

Optimal Rate of Oral Presentation

7. For informative material of mixed levels of difficulty as measured by a formula for the predictability as used within the experimental design, presented in an expository style by an unseen speaker using radio or recording facilities, 150 wpm will produce a high degree of listenability.
8. Within the limits of the study, the data indicated that an optimal rate of oral presentation would probably fall between 145 and 160 wpm.

Readability as a Predictor of Listenability

9. Flesch's formula for predicting readability cannot be used to predict listenability at the two most difficult levels (RE = 15 and 40).
10. The use of predicted readability within the limits and under the conditions studied herein might be used as a gross predictor of listenability if the accuracy of plus or minus one rank of listenability within a total range of the first five ranks is desired.

Chapter 5

GRANT FAIRBANKS, 1

The two articles in this chapter present striking evidence of the versatility of that remarkable man, Grant Fairbanks, who found himself equally at home in a theoretical discussion and in the development of an engineered device to put theory into practice. The first excerpt is a preliminary description of a speech compressor which was subsequently patented in U.S. Patent No. 2,866,650 [B102]. At about the same time that "cut and splice" was being investigated at the University of Virginia by Garvey and others, Fairbanks and his associates had hit upon the same concept at the University of Illinois. They found, as Garvey had, that the interruption of speech could result in a time-saving procedure when the uninterrupted portions of the textual material were abutted. The amount of meticulous measurement and labor involved in this procedure was, except for demonstrating the resulting effect, such as to finally foreclose any practical application of the resulting speech.

Fairbanks and his associates reasoned that the same process which was so extremely time consuming when done manually could be done just as effectively and with great speed electronically and mechanically. The result of this reasoning was the development of the first speech compressor, the prototype of which is still at the University of Illinois. Subsequent inventions have refined the process of speech compression but up until very recently, no radical innovations have appeared. Most of the inventions, for example those of Springer [B389-393], were modifications rather than departures from the Fairbanks invention. In very recent days several substantial variations have been developed. The present situation has been catalogued by E. Foulke ["Compressors--Actual and Imminent," CRCR Newsletter 6(5):1-4, 1972] and is discussed in Chapter 15 of this book. The description in this excerpt of the theory underlying the speech compressor is of particular interest to the research worker in this field as it is still a substantially valid one even after almost two decades.

In the second article Fairbanks examines with care and discrimination the various models that have been offered of the bio-acoustical systems involved in speech. It seems logical that anyone concerned with the modification of the rate of speech must first have a thorough understanding of the nature of the process that he seeks to modify. This article is an invaluable source of ideas and an excellent analysis of previous thinking for one who wishes to acquire such an understanding.

171

METHOD FOR TIME OR FREQUENCY
COMPRESSION-EXPANSION OF SPEECH

Grant Fairbanks, W. L. Everitt, R. P. Jaeger

The purposes of this paper are to outline a method for compression and expansion of speech, to describe the device employed
in the method, and to demonstrate by means of recordings the results of the method at this experimental stage. Until comparatively
recently we had not been aware of the fact that several approaches
to the problem similar to ours had previously been made by other
experimenters. We have now learned that our method, although developed independently, resembles in certain features of theory and
details the earlier work of French and Zinn [B148], Gabrilovitch
[B166], Haase, Gabor [B161] Vilbig [B426], and, perhaps, others.

Fundamentally, the process depends upon the fact that the
duration of the average speech element or phoneme of live connected
speech, such as ah or s or r, exceeds the minimum duration necessary for perception by a listener, or exceeds the minimum time necessary for sampling the essential phonemic qualities of the speech
element in question. This minimum duration has been the object of
a psychophysical study by Peterson [B323] and of theoretical calculation by Gemelli and Pastori. The excess duration may be referred
to as temporal redundancy, which term we suggest as a useful specification at the experimental level when spoken language is in question. The dimensions of the problem are clearly not only those of
engineering, but also those of psychophysics. In this paper we confine ourselves to the method. A psychophysical program is in progress and its results will be reported separately.

For purposes of explanation assume two different phonemes,
A and B, which are of equal duration and joined without interruption
as shown (Figure 1). Assume that A' and B' are valid samples of
A and B, and that each is of adequate duration for perception. Assume that samples A' and B' are extracted from A and B and abutted
in time as shown without discontinuity, and that A - A' and B - B'
are discarded. If, now, A', B' is reproduced, the time will be
shorter than the original A, B, but the phonemes should be percepta-
ble.

When this proposition was advanced several years ago by the
first author it was validated for connected speech by cutting and
splicing magnetic tape at arbitrary points, without regard to the
phonemes. It was discovered that substantially more than 50 per
cent of the total time of connected speech could be discarded by this
means without destroying intelligibility. That is, A - A' could exceed A'. At about the same time, Garvey and Henneman [B171] independently used the same cutting-and-splicing method to compress
isolated words and found similar results. In the case of expansion,
assume that phonemes A and B are caused to be repeated, as in the
middle portion. If A, A, B, B is reproduced, the time will be longer

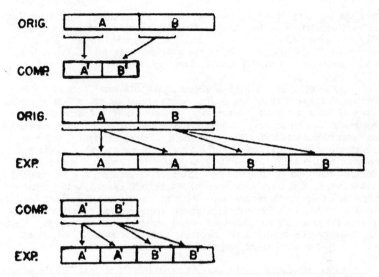

Figure 1. Theory of time compression and expansion by sampling.

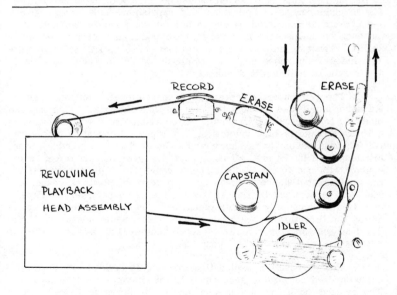

Figure 2. Sketch of apparatus.

and the auditory effect, given the above assumptions, should be that
of prolongation of A and of B. Finally, assume that A and B are
first compressed to A' and B', and then expanded to A', A', B', B'
as shown at the bottom. Here the original time for A and B has
been restored. A and B have been reconstructed from A' and B'.

Figure 2 shows a photograph of the essential part of an experimental model of a device for compression or expansion along the
lines of such a theory. Basically, the device is a continuous loop
magnetic tape recorder, mounted at the bottom of the rack containing
the other components. The tape loop, approximately 12 feet long,
rises along the right edge of the rack to a pulley under slight spring
tension at the top. Its pathway is shown by arrows. Entering the
device, the tape is directed by means of rollers over a Magnecord
erase head, and then over a fixed Magnecord record head where the
input is temporarily recorded. Passing over another roller, the tape
then descends to a revolving playback head assembly enclosed in a
mu-metal box, where signal recorded on the loop is scanned. Next
the tape passes to the drive capstan, around a roller, and, finally,
over a Brush permanent magnet erase head.

The revolving head assembly consists of a brass drum with
four Brush playback heads equally spaced around its periphery. The
output of the heads is taken off by means of a slipring-brush unit.
The circumferences of both drum and capstan are 7.64 inches. Drum
and capstan are mounted on shafts supported in sleeve bearings at
the back of the panel. Massive flywheels are also mounted on the
shafts. The two units are driven by twin 1/15 hp DC Bodine motors
with independent speed controls by means of GR Variacs. Speeds
are measured with a GR Strobotac.

The remaining components are conventional. An independent
Magnecorder PT6-A is used for storage and playback. This has been
modified for continuously variable speed reduction and furnished about
a 15-to-1 range of tape velocities. In Figure 3 operation of the revolving head assembly is shown at the left. The four playback heads
are identified by letters. The tape passes over the drum and is in
contact with one-fourth of its circumference, or a distance equal to
the peripheral distance between any two adjacent playback heads.
The tape is retained by flanges around the drum periphery. Tape
direction is constantly counter-clockwise. In the compression application the direction of drum rotation is also counter-clockwise. Under load the top tape velocity is approximately 190 in/sec. The top
peripheral drum velocity is about 225 in/sec.

For purposes of explanation the tape is divided into hypothetical numbered segments, each equal to the distance between heads.
The relative positions of tape and heads are shown as representative
times. The diagram shows 50 per cent time compression as an example. In Part I segment 1 is shown at t_0 when it first comes into
contact with the drum. At this time it is intercepted by head A,
which is moving in the same direction. If the drum were stationary,
reproduction would be one-for-one. If its velocity were equal to the

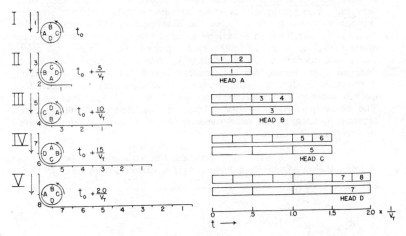

Figure 3.   Compression process.

tape, no signal would be reproduced.   Between times I and II, however, head $\underline{A}$ moves through one-fourth of a revolution.   During the
same interval tape segments 1 and 2 pass the 9 o'clock point where
head A was at t_0.   As a result, head $\underline{A}$ reproduces segment 1 during that interval.   The effective tape velocity is $V_T - V_H$.   In the
example diagrammed V_H equals $V_T/2$ which equals the effective velocity.   Therefore, the frequencies of segment 1 as reproduced by
head $\underline{A}$ are divided by two.

At time II head $\underline{A}$ is at 6 o'clock and head $\underline{B}$ is at 9 o'clock,
while segment 2 lies between them in contact with the drum.   Head
$\underline{A}$ is about to leave the drum, while head $\underline{B}$ is about to begin reproducing segment 3.   Accordingly, although there is no discontinuity,
segment 2 is not reproduced by any head.   The remaining diagrams
show how the process continues, the odd-numbered segments being
reproduced at reduced frequency and the even-numbered segments being discarded.   It is evident that various durations of either reproduced or discarded segments can be realized by varying the absolute
and relative velocities of tape and head, and that a range of sampling
frequencies and compression ratios can thus be produced.

The output of the device with respect to time is diagrammed
at the right.   Between I and II, for example, segment 1 is reproduced by head $\underline{A}$ in the time necessary for both segments 1 and 2 to
pass a point.   Head B then reproduces segment 3, etc.   The final
yield is segments, $1, \overline{3}, 5, 7$.   When these segments are stored at a
given speed and then reproduced at an appropriately higher speed,
their original frequencies are restored and the elapsed time is
shortened.

With respect to duration the odd-numbered segments are
termed sampling intervals; the even-numbered segments discard intervals. The reciprocal of their summed durations is the sampling
frequency. One hundred times the discard interval divided by the
sum of the two intervals will be termed the compression percentage.
Since sampling is periodic the ratio applies also to the total message
time, and describes the percentage by which that total time has been
reduced. Assuming that the process results in intelligible speech,
it becomes evident that the processed message may be transmitted
over a system with smaller bandwidth than originally necessary.
The capacity of a conventional transmission link for handling simultaneous messages will be a function of the amount of compression,
or frequency division.

Figure 4 is a similar diagram for expansion. Here the drum
bearing the playback head revolves in a direction opposite to that of

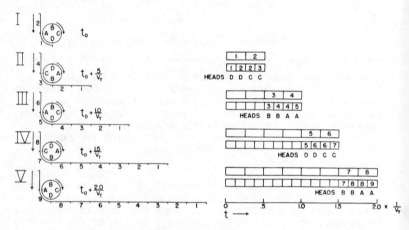

Figure 4.   Expansion process.

the tape. The illustrative example shows the condition when these
velocities are equal. The effective velocity is equal to their sum.
At t_0 shown at I, segment 1 is in contact with the drum between
heads A and D. During the next interval head D, as it moves from
6 o'clock to 9 o'clock, will reproduce both segments 1 and 2 and
then leave the tape. At that time it will be replaced by head C,
which has moved to the 6 o'clock position to intercept the tape at the
beginning of segment 2, and which will reproduce segments 2 and 3
during its sweep. The result, shown in Figure 5, is that between
times I and II, while segments 1 and 2 are passing the 6 o'clock
point, segments 1, 2, 2, 3 are reproduced. The rest of the figure
shows how this process continues. Since the effective tape velocity
has been increased by the opposite movement of head and tape, fre-

quency multiplication has been incurred. The original frequencies
are restored by reproducing the processed message in an appropriately longer time. One hundred times the amount of time thus added by the original time in the <u>expansion</u> <u>percentage.</u> In the diagram
this equals 100 per cent.

Figure 5 summarizes the various stages in compression.
The comparative times and frequencies are indicated at the bottom.

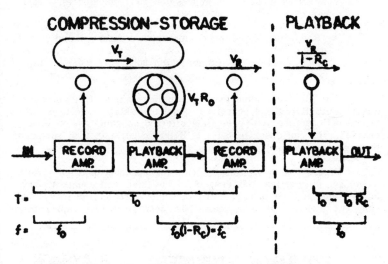

Figure 5.   Method of time compression.

In an original time T_0 and with original frequencies f_0, the input is
recorded on the loop at the velocity V_T and scanned by the revolving
head unit moving in a positive direction $V_T R_C$. This yields the compressed frequency f_C shown at the bottom. Simultaneously the compressed signal is stored at a recording tape velocity which will be
taken as V_R. This recording is reproduced at a later time at the
higher tape velocity shown by the relative time indicated, and with
f_0 restored. The following recordings will illustrate this. [Editor's
note: Even though one cannot share the recordings as the live audience did, I have left the descriptions in as they may be of interest.]

In this and the other recordings you will "hear" repetitions of
a semi-nonsense test sentence which provides a rigorous test of the
system. The sentence contains one and only one example of every
American phoneme with exception of the unstressed neutral vowel as
in the first syllable of the word <u>away,</u> which occurs three times.

"Recording 1. Compression. Original message: We has-
ten the boy off my garage path to show which edge young

owls could view. Frequency division 1.25. No time compression. Sampling frequency 10: (sentence). Time compression 20%: (sentence). Test out. "

Next you will "hear" the perceptual effects of various degrees of compression.

"Recording 2. Time compression series. Sampling frequency 10. Compression 10%: (sentence). Compression 30%: (sentence). Compression 50%: (sentence). Test out. "

"Recording 3. Time compression series. Sampling frequency 20. Compression 50%: (sentence). Compression 70%: (sentence). Compression 90%: (sentence). Test out. "

You will have noted that the smaller values of compression affect intelligibility and perceived speed of talking very little. Although both factors are perceptibly affected as compression is increased, you can observe that intelligibility persists with surprisingly large compression percentages.

Figure 6 is a similar diagram for speech expansion. Head movement is negative with respect to the tape, and equals $V_T R_E$. In the original time the original frequencies are multiplied by one plus R_E, yielding f_E as stored. The message is then reproduced at

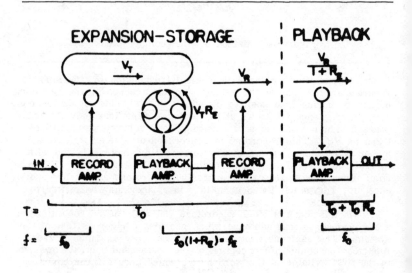

Figure 6.   Method of time expansion.

the lower velocity shown, f_0 being restored with the time expansion. The next recording illustrates the three stages.

>"Recording 4. Expansion. Original message: (sentence). Frequency multiplication 1.2. No time expansion. Sampling frequency 10: (sentence). Time expansion 20%: (sentence). Test out."

We will now illustrate the perceptual effects of expansion. The expansion percentage will be progressively increased.

>"Recording 5. Expansion series. Sampling frequency 10. Expansion 10%: (sentence). Expansion 30%: (sentence). Expansion 50%: (sentence). Test out."

>"Recording 6. Expansion series. Sampling frequency 33.3. Expansion 50%: (sentence). Expansion 70%: (sentence). Expansion 90%: (sentence). Test out."

Note that small percentages did not affect the perceived speed of talking very much, and that the details of speech became more readily heard as expansion increased. Toward the end you may have heard an echo-like sound. This occurs when the interval repeated exceeds the duration of one phoneme. This is a size limitation in our experimental model and not a limitation of the method.

Figure 7 shows a system which involves the following: (1) compression, (2) transmission of the compressed message, (3) expansion of the compressed message. The steps are carried on simultaneously with two units. A transmission link, undiagrammed, is

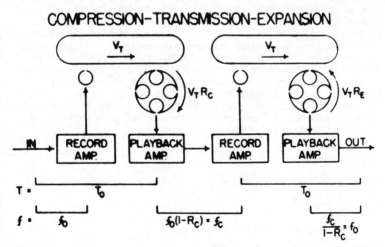

Figure 7.   Method of frequency compression-transmission-expansion.

inserted between the two at the arrow. Velocities, times and frequencies are labeled. The process is illustrated in the next recordings. First you will hear the original message. Then you will hear the transmitted message with frequency division. Finally you will hear the message as received after reconstruction by means of expansion and corresponding frequency multiplication. Eighty per cent of the message was discarded before transmission and the final message as you hear it was reconstructed from the 20 per cent fragment that remained. To help you appreciate the last point we will also "play" at the end a recording which the original frequencies are restored by accelerated playback without time expansion.

We present this next recording with some hesitation and we hope you will not be disappointed. It was made on an experimental model of the device. Its main purpose is to validate the theory and demonstrate potential feasibility. (You will "hear" considerable noise and distortion. Some of this can be eliminated fairly readily, but part of it is inherent in the method and will need to be counteracted.) The important thing, however, is that the final output is intelligible at all when bandwidth reduction is by a factor of five and compression is 80 per cent.

> "Recording 7. Compression-transmission-expansion.
> Original message: (sentence). Transmitted message.
> Original time. Frequency division 5. Sampling frequency
> 60: (sentence). Restored message. Original time. Frequency multiplication 5. Sampling frequency 16: (sentence). Time compression 80% (sentence). Test out. "

Apart from its theoretical interest, the method appears to have several practical applications. For one thing, the smaller compression and expansion ratios should be useful in the programming of rebroadcast speeches in radio, since they furnish "tailor-made" time without the audience's knowledge. A saving of 10 minutes per hour is completely realistic. Conversely, and we advance this suggestion with diffidence, thinking of commercials, more intelligence can be communicated to an audience in a given amount of time. Straightforward compression by larger amounts should be useful wherever high-speed communication is crucial, as in certain military situations. Expansion should facilitate branches of study such as experimental phonetics and linguistics where auditory analysis is important. Finally, of course, the method gives promise as an approach to the long-standing problem of bandwidth reduction.

SYSTEMATIC RESEARCH IN EXPERIMENTAL PHONETICS:
A THEORY OF THE SPEECH MECHANISM AS A SERVOSYSTEM

Grant Fairbanks

Experimental phonetics is the study of the biological action
known as speaking which produces the acoustical time-series known
as speech. Numerous biological systems are involved in this action,
but it is possible to consider them collectively as a single, larger,
bio-acoustical system which is a proper object of study as such. It
is this system, the speaking system, as a system, that I propose to
discuss. While it is impractical to cite all my sources here, I want
to mention my reliance upon the writings of MacColl*, Wiener*, and
Trimmer* in the fields of control theory and cybernetics, and to
make special acknowledgement of the personal influences of Seashore,
Tiffin and Travis, who originally aroused my interest in the speaking
system almost 20 years ago.

By way of review I will first call attention to, without discussion, five diagrams of communication systems. Figure 1 is from
Scripture**, Figure 2 from Shannon**, Figure 3 from Davis**, and
Figure 4 from Peterson**. Figure 5 shows E. A. Bott's unpublished
speaker-listener causal series, which has been passed on by word of
mouth. As nearly as I can determine, it must have been formulated
about 1930, antedating the four others. The diagram, which shows
only structural elements, does not attempt to do justice to the complete statement.

Figure 6 shows an extension of the Bott scheme to a two-way
speaker-listener system. Note that the brain of Speaker 1, B_1 at
the left, is the source of Message L, M_1k and also the destination
of M_2, with B_2 serving analogous functions. Note also that each
speaker is equipped with a transmitter and a receiver. Reflect that
a given receiver, such as E_1, is operative at all times, even when
its related transmitter, S_1, is producing a signal intended for the
independent receiver, E_2. M_1, in the form that it issues from S_1
under orders from B_1, is simultaneously relayed back to B_1 through
E_1. In short, Speaker 1 hears himself as he talks. In Figure 7
we divide the diagram down the middle, make certain adaptations,
and arrive at a more complete diagram of the situation at the time

---

*L. A. MacColl, A Fundamental Theory of Servomechanisms, New
York: Nostrand, 1945; N. Wiener, Cybernetics, New York: Wiley,
1948; J. D. Trimmer, "The Basis for a Science of Instrumentology,"
Science 118:461-65, 1953.
**E. W. Scripture, "Der Mechanismus der Sprachsysteme," Zeit-
schrift für Experimental-Phonetik 1:85-90, 1931; C. E. Shannon and
W. Weaver, The Mathematical Theory of Communication, Urbana:
Univ. of Illinois, 1949; H. Davis, "Auditory Communication," J. of
Speech and Hearing Disorders 16:3-8, 1951; G. E. Peterson, "Basic
Physical Systems for Communication Between Two Individuals," J. of
Speech and Hearing Disorders 18:116-20, 1953.

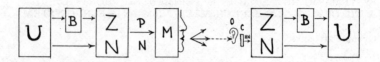

Figure 1. Diagram of the speech system. U, das Unbewusste [the unconscious]; B, Bewusstsein [the conscious]; ZN, Zentralnervensystem [Central nervous system]; O, Ohr [ear]; C, Endorgan im Ohr [terminal organ in the ear]; HN, Hörnerv [auditory nerve]. From Scripture**.

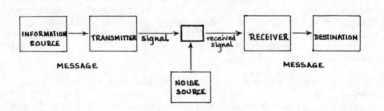

Figure 2. Schematic diagram of a general communication system. From Shannon**.

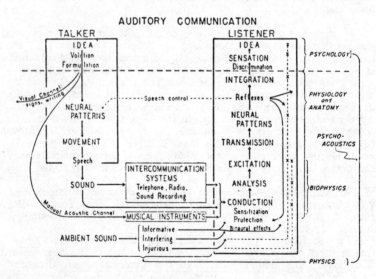

Figure 3. Diagram of the process of auditory communication. From Davis**.

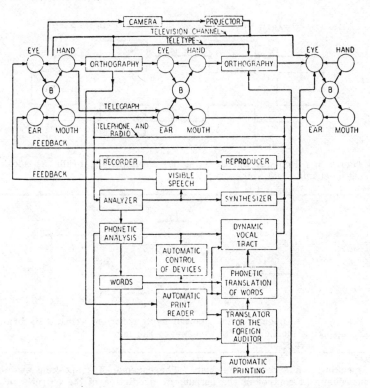

Figure 4. Fundamental systems in communication technology. From Peterson**.

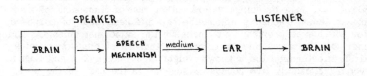

Figure 5. Structures of the speaker-listener causal series. After E. A. Bott.

S_1 is transmitting.

The return of M_1 to B_1 has often been referred to in such words as auditory monitoring, and interpreted as a sort of "checking up" on what the speaking apparatus has produced. There is nothing wrong with this view of matters as far as it goes, but it seems to me that it misemphasizes the significance of self-hearing during

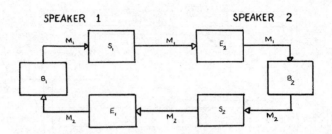

Figure 6. Two-way speaker-listener system. B, brain; S, speaking mechanism; M, message; E, ear.

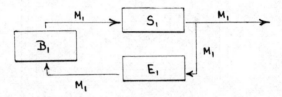

Figure 7. Elements of the control system for speaking. B, brain; S, speaking mechanism; M, message; E, ear.

speaking. It stresses the past. The essence of a speaking system, however, is control of the output, or prediction of the output's future. In this kind of system the significance of data about the past is that they are used for prediction of the future.

The "monitoring" interpretation also suggests that the ear is a receiver in a listening system rather than a component of a speaking system. Theorists emphasize two different kinds of purposes for which measurements are made by the same instruments. Trimmer (*) illustrates this by comparing the use of the same scales, first to determine the unknown weight of a watermelon and then to weigh out exactly five pounds of sugar. In the case of the watermelon, the purpose was estimation of weight; in the case of the sugar it was control of weight. In Figure 7, E_1 and B_1 are measuring M_1 for purposes of control. In Figure 6 they are measuring M_2 for purposes of estimation. When I say a word and you repeat it, your hearing apparatus measures my word for purposes of estimation and then your word (the same word) for purposes of control. When we are referring to the control functions of the auditory signal, I suggest auditory feedback as the term of choice.

The speaking system does not seem to be what is called an open cycle control system. In open cycle control the device that produces the output is controlled by some quantity that is independent of the output. Devices such as alarm clocks, in which an event is controlled by time, are familiar examples. The speech synthesizers that I have seen employ this form of control. A deaf child, while being taught to speak by a deaf therapist who pursues the method of phonetic placement with a tongue blade, is almost entirely under open cycle control.

A closed cycle system, or servosystem, on the other hand, employs feedback of the output to the place of control, comparison of the output to the input, and such manipulation of the output-producing device as will cause the output to have the same functional form as the input. The system performs its task when, by these means, it produces an output that is equal to the input times a constant. Examples of such systems are the heating plants of our homes and the homeostatic mechanisms of our bodies. It seems evident that the speaking system has at least the rudiments of a servosystem. In Figure 8 we explore this further with the model shown in the block diagram. If we start with the effector unit, shown at

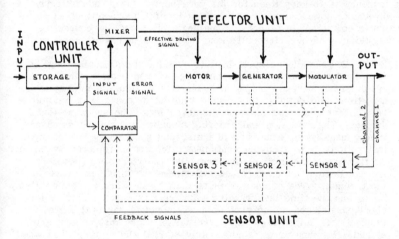

Figure 8.   Model of a closed cycle control system for speaking.

the top, we observe a motor, a generator and a modulator connected as shown. These are the respiratory, vibratory and resonation-articulatory structures, respectively. (The model deliberately simplifies. If it were more elaborate, the generator, for instance, would be shown as a multi-unit device capable of producing various types of inputs for the modulator, and in part located physically within the latter.) The output is shown by the heavy arrow at the right. The heavy lines and arrows at the top symbolize the effector's motor innervation.

The sensor unit at the bottom is so labelled to emphasize its control function. (If its function were estimation, it would be called a receiver.) Sensor 1 is the primary component for output take-off, the ear. The output is conducted to sensor 1 over two separate channels, representing the acoustic pathways to the ear through the air and through the body tissues. Sensor 2 and sensor 3 symbolize the tactile and proprioceptive end-organs. These supply data about the mechanical operation of the effector, but not directly about its output. Although correlated with the output data taken off through sensor 1, these data are comparatively fragmentary. The sensor unit relays its data to the controller unit in the form of feedback signals.

The controller is an automatic device that issues specific orders to the effector. It does not originate the message, but receives its instructions from a separate unit not shown. We are concerned here with a speaking system and assume an input, although plausible extensions along these same lines may be made to a model of a language system which also originates messages. The anatomical analogy is less definite here than for the effector and sensor, and my tendency is to keep it so for the time being. This indefiniteness does not, however, restrain us from fruitful discussion of an automatic controller in terms of functional units, and, of course, we should remind ourselves all along that this is a model, not a replica.

While a closed cycle heating system, for example, may be required only to maintain a constant pre-set temperature, the speaking system must vary its output as a function of time, according to instructions laid down at the input. The output consists of qualitatively different units that must be displayed in a time sequence that is unique. The selection and ordering of units are carried on in advance, usually for a number of units, and represent a set of input instructions. As speaking continues, each set is replaced by another. As the first component of the controller therefore, we provide a storage device, which receives and stores the input and gives off an input signal. The number of units that it can store is comparatively small and the time that it will retain them is short. This is the short persistence memory of what we intend to say next. We may think of this device as a tape recorder in which instructions are stored. Its tape drive is alternately started and stopped, and when the tape is stationary a given unit of instruction is repeatedly reproduced by a moving scanning head.

A stored unit of instruction, or input, corresponds to a unit of output. Each such unit furnishes what is termed a control point, sometimes called set point. The control points are the unit goals of the output. The input signal corresponding to a control point goes simultaneously from the storage component to the controller's other two components, a comparator and a mixer. The comparator also receives the feedback signals, as stated earlier. With the input and feedback signals it performs a calculation, essentially subtraction, in which it determines the difference between the two. At any given time it thus yields a measure of the amount by which the control point has not yet been reached by the output, or a measure of the non-accomplishment of the control point. This measure is termed the error signal. In the act of speaking, the error signal, at the time in question, is the amount by which the intended speech unit, then displayed in the storage device, has not yet been produced by the effector.

The error signal will equal zero when the control point has been achieved by the effector. At such a time as it does not equal zero, the error signal provides data which cause the effector to modify its operation in such a manner as to bring the error signal closer to zero. It continues with time to modify the operation of the effector progressively so that the error signal approaches and finally reaches zero. To bring this about the error signal is continuously fed into the mixer, the function of which is to combine error signal and input signal into the effective driving signal. The latter furnishes specific instructions to the effector. It alters the effector's operation, causing its output, relayed back to the comparator in the form of feedback signal, more nearly to equal the input signal and thus reduce the error signal. The reduced error signal is then fed into the mixer, modifies the effective driving signal accordingly, and so on around the loop until the error signal equals zero.

At such a time the first unit has been completed and the system is ready for new instruction. The information that that is the state of the system is given, we repeat, by the fact of zero error signal. In the model you will note that the error signal is fed into the storage component as well as into the mixer. In the storage component, however, it acts in simple all-or-none fashion to trigger display of the next control point when it equals zero, or to retain a given control point when it does not equal zero. In the tape recorder that we imagined earlier as the storage device, it would start and stop the tape drive.

This triggering device has an important refinement of that basic operation. Since the time constants of the live speaking system are relatively long in comparison to the durations of steady states in the output, analogous time constants are assumed for the model. This being the case, the system would have a low ceiling on its rate of output, if advancement of instructions were permitted only at times of zero error signal. The comparator includes, therefore, a predicting device. By plotting the error signal as a function of time during production of a given unit, this device continuously predicts by extrapolation the future time at which the error signal will equal zero. Thus advancement of the storage component to the next control point is not necessarily delayed until the actual moment when a condition of zero error signal obtains. It may be triggered in advance of that time by an amount, let us say, equal to the relevant time constants. By this means, over suitable channels, a new input can be started on its way toward the effector before the previous control point has been reached so that it will arrive there at an appropriate anticipated time.

It may have been observed that, when the model starts operation from the inactive state, the effective driving signal is not at the outset modified by the error signal, there being as yet no error signal. Under such conditions the output is uncontrolled for an amount of time equal to the time constant of the entire system. This is inherent in a feedback-controlled system unless the time constant is negligible. In the live system it is suggested either that the excitation of the effector is highly generalized, resulting in an initial output that is undifferentiated until it comes under control, or that the effector's operation during this initial period is mediated by subtle programing of sequences not dependent upon sensory feedbacks.

The system has another important undiagramed characteristic. In the mixer the rate of change of the effective driving signal is caused to vary with the magnitude of the error signal. When the error signal is large, as at the start of a unit, the corrective change is rapid. It becomes progressively slower as the error signal is reduced. An advantage of this feature is reduction of overshoot. Numerous times we have used the term unit in the sense of unit of control. Such a control unit should not be identified with any of the conventional units such as the phoneme, the syllable, the word, or the word group. There is no time to develop this idea for the live speaking system beyond saying, first, that it is not theoretically necessary that the unit of control be any presently identified phonetic unit, and, second, that we have evidence from several experiments suggesting that it is something else. It might be ventured tentatively that the unit of control is a semiperiodic, relatively long, articulatory cycle, with a correlated cycle of output. It is more satisfactory at present, however, merely to propose the existence of a hypothetical unit of speech control, as yet unspecified and unnamed, whose characteristics are dimly coming to be seen.

The idea of building a mechanical model of the speaking system that we have discussed is appealing. Comparatively simple effector and sensor components which can process recognizable speech signals are within the art. We hope shortly to begin construction of a simple controller, based on a relay network, that works on paper. Although to validate the theory it is not necessary that the machine talk, it seems possible that a first approximation to connected speech can be realized.

One evident feature of the model, as well as of the live system, is that it contains many components in a complicated arrangement and readily becomes disordered. One type of disorder is part failure. In that case, unless the part can be replaced or repaired, the change in output must either be compensated or tolerated. A part disorder is also a system disorder. The model can be caused to repeat, prolong and hesitate by several different manipulations, one of which is feedback delay. By manipulations that are revealingly similar it can be caused to make other kinds of mistakes, such as substitutions, distortions and omissions. All such disorders are demonstrably caused by component deficiencies. In the model organic and functional are one.

Since the dynamic events of connected speech have become
conveniently accessible through the X-ray motion picture and the
acoustic spectrogram, students of speech perception have been giving considerable attention to the psychophysical significance of spectral changes in the speech signal.   Although this subject is outside
the scope of the present paper, a brief comment seems worthwhile.
Phoneticians have long recognized that the elements of speech are
not produced in step-wise fashion like the notes of a piano, but by
continuous modulation as a function of time.   Certain of the elements,
such as the diphthongs, involve characteristic changes during their
durations, losing their entities if they do not so change.   Other elements, such as the vowels, may be prolonged, indefinitely in the
steady state and change is not considered to be a defining feature.
During production of elements of the latter type in connected speech,
however, changes occur.   Movements to and from articulatory positions result in acoustic transitions to and from steady states in the
output.

In the model we have seen how a transition is used for purposes of control and prediction.   From it is derived a changing error signal.   The model's objective is to reduce this error signal to
zero, and at such a time as that has been accomplished the control
point will have been reached.   In the case of the production of elements of speech that involve steady states, the control points and
error signals correspond, respectively, to steady states and acoustic
transitions in the output.   It is to be emphasized that the steady
states are the primary objectives, the targets.   The transitions are
useful incidents on the way to the targets.   The roles of both are
probably very analogous when the dynamic speech output is perceived
by an independent listener.

Chapter 6

GRANT FAIRBANKS, 2

The three excerpts in this chapter are taken from articles written by Grant Fairbanks and two of his doctoral students, Newman Guttman and Murray Miron. Guttman is now with Bell Telephone Laboratories and Miron is a professor at Syracuse University. The latter contributed an article which appears in Part II of this work. These three articles from the March 1957 issue of the Journal of Speech and Hearing Disorders are frequently cited in the literature.

In the first article the effect of varying degrees of compression on comprehension is examined. The material used was a 1500-word passage on "weather" presented in a non-technical manner. The investigation here reported demonstrated that three variables affected comprehension: degree of compression, listener aptitude, and message effectiveness. The second article is a report on a study of the relative effectiveness of presenting a message once at its original rate compared to presenting it twice after it has been compressed so that it is presented in half of the initial time period. In the third article an experiment in which a substantial amount of explanatory material was added to a compressed message is reported on. The important issue here was to determine whether such an augmented, compressed message would result in better comprehension than the original message without compression or augmentation. All three items deserve careful study and consideration.

EFFECTS OF TIME COMPRESSION UPON
THE COMPREHENSION OF CONNECTED SPEECH

Grant Fairbanks, Newman Guttman, Murray S. Miron

This article reports an experimental investigation of the relationship between comprehension of the factual details of extended spoken messages and the rate at which they were heard. The matters of greatest interest were the variation of comprehension as a function of rate and the efficiency of comprehension, the amount per listening time. In addition, the interactions of rate, content difficulty, and listener aptitude were explored.

Control of message time, or of listening rate, was accomplished by means of the device for automatic time-frequency compres-

sion-expansion described by Fairbanks, Everitt and Jaeger [B105].
When used for time compression as in the present experiment, the
device displays recorded material in less than the original time without essential alteration of the other dimensions of the signal. In a
sample of speech, the time base is unselectively and uniformly compressed throughout with the time proportions of the signal units undisturbed. The essentials of the phonetic units, vocal pitch, stress,
etc., are preserved. The amount of compression, which may conveniently be thought of as a percentage of the original time, is variable and a given message may be presented to listeners at a variety
of rates. In the experiment, for example, a message which was
originally spoken at 141 words per minute was compressed by selected amounts. The largest of these was 70 per cent, which yielded
a listening rate of 470 wpm.

Auditory comprehension and speaking rate have been studied
separately many times, but investigations of their interrelationships
have not been numerous and the data are not extensive. No evidence
of association was found by Miller [B279], who studied classroom
lectures delivered at comparatively slow rates. Harwood [B211] and
Nelson [B296], both of whom included moderately fast rates among
their conditions, reported that the effect of rate was discernible, but
not significant. At fast rates, Goldstein [B193] obtained significant
reduction of comprehension. In considering the results of these experiments, however, it is important to observe that the objective in
each instance was to study the effect of the rate of the total speaker-
listener situation, and that the independent variable, appropriately,
was speaking rate. It is well known that live variations of speaking
rate are accompanied by correlated non-rate changes which are large,
systematic, and obviously important in the complete, live speaker-
listener system. Examples of such accompaniments are the deterioration of articulation and the disproportionate reduction of pause time
which ensue as speaking rate is increased. Variations of the kind
were not at issue in the present investigation: it has been a study
of listening rate.

Experimental Materials

The basic stimulus materials were two technical messages on
the subject of meteorology. One was concerned with meteorological
instruments and the other with weather forecasting in support of flying. They were written for this special purpose and consisted of
straightforward expositions of factual information, including descriptions of instruments, definitions of concepts, explanations of procedures, etc. Attempts were made to present content in which pre-
knowledge would be small, dependence upon background information
and skills (e. g. technical terminology and mathematics) minimal,
and levels of abstraction low. The messages were relatively long,
1554 and 1573 words, respectively. They bore close general similarity to classroom lectures, or to speeches such as a technical expert might prepare for presentation to a motivated lay audience.

The messages were read for original uncompressed tape recordings by an experienced, mature, male speaker who was paced at a target rate of 140 wpm by light flashes at one-minute intervals. This rate was selected on the basis of the data available in the literature, the results of a pilot experiment with another message, and a number of measurements made while the speaker practiced. The obtained rate was 141 wpm for each message, the total times being 11.04 and 11.18 minutes, respectively. The overall impression was that of a rate unquestionably close to the central tendency which would be expected for skilled speakers reading to communicate the content in question. The master recordings were made on Magnecord PT6 equipment at 15 ips, with an Altec M11 microphone system.

Comprehension was sampled by means of two tests, each consisting of 30 five-alternative multiple-choice items confined to the factual content. An attempt was made to provide a substantial range in difficulty among the items. A further goal, for each test considered individually, was to construct it so that the mean score of unselected subjects would approximate chance without the message and a point midway between chance and perfect score immediately after having heard the message, i.e., 20 and 60 per cent correct, respectively. The final tests were achieved after a series of trial presentations and revisions, which involved carrying six different recorded messages and their tests through all stages, and selecting the two best message-test units. At the last preliminary presentation, to 49 subjects, these two units yielded mean scores of 59 and 62 per cent, Kuder-Richardson reliability coefficients of .77 and .81, and a pooled reliability coefficient of .87. When the tests were administered without the messages to other subjects, the mean scores were 23 and 18 per cent.

An additional consideration in test construction was provision for treatment of message-test difficulty. After various attempts to separate content difficulty from item difficulty it was decided, in view of the purposes of the experiment, to manage the two factors jointly and empirically in terms of the increment in comprehension produced by the message, or the message effectiveness. It was proposed to estimate the message effectiveness of each content item, the particular portion of the message corresponding to a given test item, as the difference between the percentage of correct responses to the test item when message-test and test-only conditions were administered to independent groups of unselected subjects. This method seemed warranted since the intention was not to deal with individual items, but to provide a rough means of stratification so that the tests could be sub-scored. As will appear below, five Message Effectiveness Levels (MELs) were specified in this manner, each with 12 items distributed through the two message-test units.

Experimental Procedure

The plan involved assignment of independent groups of subjects to five message-test conditions corresponding to time compressions of 0, 30, 50, 60, and 70 per cent, and an additional test-only, or 100 per cent compression, condition. All subjects were young adult, male trainees at Chanute Air Force Base not engaged in weather training. Thirty-six were assigned to each of the message-test conditions, 44 to the test-only condition. Each group was composed of four equal subgroups formed according to Stanine levels on the Technical Specialist Aptitude Index of the Airman Classification Battery. Stanines Five through Eight from the upper part of the distribution, with aptitude increasing in that order, were represented by random selection from available men for the various conditions. The plan further involved determination of the five MELs from the 0 and 100 per cent conditions, as described above, and an analysis of variance with the four 30-70 per cent conditions. The analysis was of a mixed factorial type, Compression by Stanine by MEL.

At each session which entailed message presentation the procedures were as follows: standardized, extemporaneous instruction; a two-minute sample of a similar message appropriately compressed (considered to cover adaptation to the particular rate); first message; first test; second message; second test. Message-test order was counterbalanced for each group and sub-group, and similar counterbalancing was employed with the test-only condition. Except where specified below, the 60-item yield from the two tests was pooled for each subject. Testing time was not limited. Experimental sessions were conducted in a typical classroom located at Chanute Air Force Base. Ambient noise was appreciable, but not objectionably high or variable. Presentation was bilateral over Permoflux PDR-10 earphones with 1505 cushions. Twenty-four such headsets were arranged in a distribution system and fed by the Magnecord equipment through a matching transformer. The level was comfortable for listening and approximately equal by VU meter for all conditions. The various compressed versions of the messages were prepared in advance by methods described elsewhere [B105] and it is necessary to note here only that a discard interval of 0.02 sec. was arbitrarily selected. Since the process involves periodic time sampling, the discard interval, or the segment between successive sampling intervals, should be short in relation to significant units of the signal. Although the optimum interval for connected speech is not known as yet, the value chosen was sufficiently short to avoid impairment of intelligibility by fragmentation of words.

General Effects of Time Compression

Table 1 presents the mean number of items correct for the six conditions. The scores at 0 and 100 per cent compression represent 63.8 and 20.7 per cent, respectively, of the 60 items, close to the range mentioned above as a target for the materials. This range, 25.9 in terms of items correct, is a useful estimate of the

Table 1

MEAN NUMBER OF ITEMS CORRECT
AT THE VARIOUS EXPERIMENTAL CONDITIONS: 60 TOTAL ITEMS

% Compression	Rate	Mean
0	141	38.3
30	201	35.9
50	282	34.8
60	353	26.8
70	470	15.7
100		12.4

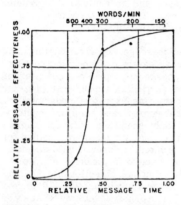

Figure 1. Variation of relative message effectiveness with relative message time. Upper scale: rate in words/minute.

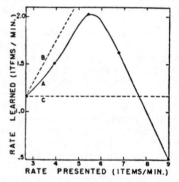

Figure 2. Variation of rate learned with rate presented. A, experimental. B, items correct unchanged by reduction of message time. C, items correct proportional to message time.

effectiveness of the message under the most favorable condition, and is taken as 1.0 for purposes of the ordinate in Figure 1, which shows relative message effectiveness as a function of relative message time. The latter is the decimal fraction of the original message time remaining after compression. Corresponding values of rate in wpm are shown along the top edge of the figure. The curve is seen to be typically sigmoid, with major inflection between 30 and 50 per cent of the original message time. The message was 50 per cent effective when the relative message time was approximately 40 per cent of the original, rate being higher than 350 wpm. At 50 per cent compression, with a rate of 282 wpm, the reduction in message effectiveness was small. In this condition the costs in time of the large amount learned and the small amount not learned were equal.

The negatively accelerated portion of the curve of Figure 1 may be interpreted as a reduction in message efficiency, or in learning per time. This view led to the re-plotting of the data shown in Figure 2, where the coordinates are rate learned and rate presented, both given in items per minute. The ordinate will be recognized as the reciprocal of the mean amount of message time per correct item; the abscissa is expressed in terms of the rate of item presentation, that is, the rate at which the content corresponding to the 60 test items was presented. The points show ordinate values for the five message-test conditions.

The slope of the broken line B is that which would obtain if there were no reduction in amount of learning as message rate was increased, while C would be the case if number of items correct were found to be directly proportional to message time. The empirical curve, A, is seen to be higher than C over much of the range (the 30, 50 and 60 per cent compression conditions), and to be fairly close to B at the left, where it reaches its maximum at the 50 per cent condition. Thus message efficiency, as measured by the amount of factual comprehension per stimulus time, increased up to a message rate of 282 wpm, at which rate the reduction in absolute amount of comprehension was not large (Figure 1).

It seems reasonable to suggest that, for learning of this type, the original message as recorded was relatively inefficient. If the original message is representative of expository lectures on factual topics, as it is believed to be both in content and delivery, then the implications for training procedures are direct, namely, that when message rate is slowed beyond a certain point the increment in learning becomes relatively costly in time, and that the cost should be weighed in terms of the objectives of the learning.

In the present experiment both messages were displayed to the subjects in the 50 per cent condition in the mean time used for one message in the uncompressed condition, or 11.11 minutes. In the 50 per cent condition that amount of time yielded an increment of 34.8 - 12.4 = 22.4 in mean number of items correct (Table 1); in the uncompressed condition the same amount of time yielded a mean of (38.3 - 12.4)/2 = 13.0 items correct. Thus, if the standard of learning were set by the amount effected by the two messages in the 50 per cent condition, then the use of the same time to display one message at one-half the rate would be little more than one-half as efficient. In short, the data appear to justify the conclusion that acceleration of message presentation beyond rates ordinarily practiced effects a given amount of learning of the type in question in less time, or a greater amount of learning in a given time.

Message Order and Serial Position

Since, as has been explained, the plan of the experiment involved pooling results from the two messages and subscoring according to variations in message effectiveness among the test items, the

general effects of order of messages and of serial position of content
within messages were studied.   The experiment was not designed to
investigate either effect; study of them was for the purpose of supporting the intended procedures.   It will be recalled that precaution-
ary counterbalancing of order was practiced.   When the two messages
were scored separately for the various conditions, no evidence of
order effect was found.   Special attention was given to the large compression conditions with the idea that experience with the ultrarapid
rate during the first message might have placed the second message
in a more favorable position.   If such a situation in fact obtains, the
present measures were not sensitive to it.

In writing the messages no attempt was made to control the
frequency of occurrence of the portions of the content to be sampled,
and the portions also were allowed to vary in "difficulty" without regard to place of occurrence within the messages.   However, the
planned procedure of subscoring the results according to variations
in response would have been open to question had such variations
been significantly associated with serial position.   Study of this possibility also gave negative results.   Representative findings are presented in Figure 3.   The abscissa is percentage of the total message
time for the condition in question, the locations of content portions
within that time being shown along the top by item number.   The latter points were determined by measuring the cumulative time for
presentation of the content measured by the first six, the first 12,
etc., items in the two messages and computing the mean.   For example, the content corresponding to the first six items was presented
in slightly less than 20 per cent of the total message time.

It will be noted that the occurrence of sampled content was
not completely periodic and that the density was reduced in the last
one-fifth of the message particularly, where one-fourth of the time
was used to present one-fifth of the content items.   For a given point
on the abscissa, the ordinate is the mean number of items correct
per message.   Curves are plotted for the various message rates; the
test-only curve has been added as a control since neither message
time nor position within message was a factor.   Given periodic occurrence and equal difficulty of items, a straight line from zero to
maximum would have been expected in the absence of positional effects.   Deviations will be seen to be attributable largely to the lower
item density in the last part of the message and to the test-only
variations.   It was concluded that serial position might be disregarded
since, as will be shown below, effects were small in comparison to
those of the groups of specific items formed in subscoring.   It is of
interest to observe the similarities of the shapes of the five message-
test curves in Figure 3 to each other and to the curve for the test-
only condition; interaction of compression and serial position was
clearly small.

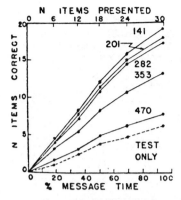

Figure 3.   Cumulative number of items correct during message at various experimental conditions, rates labelled in words / minute.   Broken line, reference curve for test-only condition.

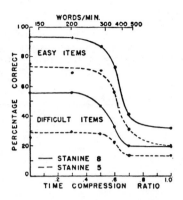

Figure 4.   Mean percentage of items correct for the various experimental conditions.   Stanine sub-groups five and eight; easy and difficult items.

Aptitude of Listeners and MEL

Figure 4 shows the general dimensions of the combined effects of compression, Stanine and difficulty upon comprehension.   The ordinate is percentage of items correct; compression increases to the right along the abscissa, the compression ratio being the percentage of compression divided by 100.   For purposes of this illustrative graph, the 60 test items were arranged in descending order on the basis of number of correct responses in the uncompressed condition. The highest ranking 12 items have been designated in Figure 4 as "Easy" and the lowest 12 as "Difficult."   The solid and broken lines show mean scores for the Stanine Eight and Five subgroups.   The outstanding features are the large overall effects of all three factors, and the similarities in the shapes of the four curves as inflected by time compression.

The mean scores expressed in percentage correct for the five stanine subgroups at each of the six experimental conditions are shown in Table 2.   The progressions are as would be expected from the pairs of stanine curves in Figure 4, except for a few minor reversals.   The distribution of items according to message effectiveness, estimates as described above from the results of the uncompressed and test-only conditions, was entered to yield five graduated subsets of 12 items each, referred to herein as MELs.   Table 3 presents the mean percentage correct at each MEL for the two conditions mentioned, which will be observed to be negatively correlated, and the set of mean differences, which range roughly from 20 to 70 per cent.   In preparation for the statistical analysis the responses of

Table 2

MEAN PERCENTAGE CORRECT
FOR STANINE SUBGROUPS AND TOTAL GROUPS
AT THE VARIOUS EXPERIMENTAL CONDITIONS

	Stanine				
% Compression	5	6	7	8	Total
0	50.6	61.7	69.8	73.2	63.8
30	50.4	50.6	61.1	77.2	59.8
50	50.2	53.9	59.8	68.2	58.0
60	40.0	39.1	50.0	49.1	44.6
70	23.9	25.0	24.1	31.5	26.1
100	16.5	19.8	20.5	26.1	20.7

Table 3

MEAN PERCENTAGE CORRECT
AT UNCOMPRESSED AND TEST-ONLY CONDITIONS
AND MEAN DIFFERENCE BETWEEN CONDITIONS FOR FIVE MELS

	% Items Correct		
MEL	Uncom-pressed	Test-Only	Mean Difference
1	79.6	10.8	68.8
2	71.3	20.6	50.7
3	60.9	19.1	41.8
4	59.5	25.2	34.3
5	47.7	27.8	19.9

Table 4

MEAN MESSAGE EFFECTIVENESS
AT VARIOUS EXPERIMENTAL CONDITIONS FOR FIVE MELS

	MEL				
% Compression	1	2	3	4	5
0	68.8	50.7	41.8	34.3	19.8
30	58.1	45.7	36.9	35.7	18.9
50	58.4	47.8	34.8	30.6	14.8
60	41.9	31.7	23.4	19.3	2.8
70	11.2	8.0	6.7	4.0	-3.1
100	0	0	0	0	0

each subject were subscored for the five MELs and each subscore was adjusted by subtracting therefrom the appropriate mean score from the test-only condition; this procedure may be thought of as correcting for pre-knowledge and test item difficulty at each MEL. The means of these adjusted scores expressed in percentage correct are presented in Table 4. It will be seen that the sets of five means decrease progressively in all message-test conditions, and that the same is generally true from condition to condition within MEL.

The results of the analysis of variance are summarized in Table 5. This analysis estimated the effects of compression, Stanine and MEL, and their interactions, employed the adjusted response

Table 5

SUMMARY OF ANALYSIS OF VARIANCE;
COMPRESSION, STANINE, MEL.

	df	ms	F
Between Subjects			
Compression (C)	3	628.80	79.09*
Stanine (S)	3	135.91	17.10*
C x S	9	12.59	1.58
Error (b)	128	7.95	
Within Subjects			
MEL (M)	4	335.62	149.83*
M x C	12	14.14	6.31*
M x S	12	2.51	1.12
M x C x S	36	3.10	1.38
Error (W)	512	2.24	
Total	719		

*<.001

scores as measures, and was confined to the 30, 50, 60 and 70 per cent message-test conditions. As will be seen in Table 5, all three F's for the main effects are large and significant beyond the 0.1 per cent level; the evidence for interaction is negative except for MEL by Compression.

The nonsignificance of interactions involving Stanine should be interpreted with due regard to the restricted range of levels in the present experiment. Study of the means of Table 2 discloses that the differences between Stanine levels decrease with increasing compression, although small differences obtain, as would be expected, even in the test-only condition. However, if the test-only mean is

200   Time-Compressed Speech

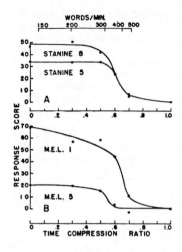

Figure 5. Mean response score
(obtained percentage correct minus test-only percentage) for the
various experimental conditions.
A, Stanine subgroups five and
eight. B, Message Effectiveness
Levels 1 and 5.

subtracted from the remaining
means in each column to explore
the differential effect of the message as if "pre-knowledge" were
equal, the result is as illustrated
in Figure 5A, which shows curves
for the extreme Stanine subgroups.
Figure 5B illustrates the necessity of specifying MEL in a statement about the effects of large
time compressions.

Summary

A pair of independent message-test units, each consisting of
an extended exposition of technical
information and a corresponding
test of factual comprehension,
were developed. The messages
were read by an experienced speaker at 141 wpm, recorded, and compressed automatically in time by
various amounts. Independent
groups of subjects, all Air Force
trainees, were assigned to five
experimental conditions which represented a series of compressions
ranging from 0 to 70 per cent, and to a sixth test-only condition in
which no message was presented. Listener aptitude was controlled
by forming equal subgroups for each condition at four different levels.
The effect of message-test difficulty was assessed by subscoring the
results of the tests according to five message effectiveness levels
which were based upon differences in response to test items in the
0 per cent compression condition and the test-only condition.

The curve of comprehension as a function of message time
was characteristically sigmoid. Response was approximately 50 per
cent of maximum when message time was 40 per cent (60 per cent
compression, 353 wpm). When message time was 50 per cent (282
wpm), the response was slightly less than 90 per cent and efficiency,
response per time, was maximal. Analysis of variance indicated
that time compression, listener aptitude and message effectiveness
all affect factual comprehension significantly, and afforded evidence
that interaction of time compression and message effectiveness in the
expected direction is significant.

AUDITORY COMPREHENSION
OF REPEATED HIGH-SPEED MESSAGES

Grant Fairbanks, Newman Guttman, Murray S. Miron

The experiment here reported is related to a general investigation of the effects of time compression upon the comprehension of connected spoken messages [B109]. In the basic experiment two relatively long technical messages were read by an experienced speaker at a representative rate. These original readings were recorded, compressed in time by selected amounts, and presented to groups of subjects. Comprehension of factual details was tested. The technique for compression was automatic and operated upon the original recording only in the time dimension [B105], so that the various versions of the message differed in total listening time, or reciprocally, in listening rate. Variation of comprehension was significant.

It was found that listeners could tolerate substantial amounts of compression before reduction of comprehension became excessive. For example, subjects who heard the messages with 50 per cent compression at a rate of 282 words per minute yielded a mean score which was approximately 90 per cent of that for subjects who heard the original versions at 141 wpm. If the amount of comprehension of a double-rate message adequately satisfied the requirements of a given communication situation, then 50 per cent of the original message time obviously becomes available for double-rate presentation of a second message which had an original length equal to that of the first message. If it should be desired, however, to increase the comprehension of one message, the finding suggests that this might be done, without exceeding the original speaking time for the message, by means of a special arrangement; this would consist of a compressed version of the message plus reinforcing material added in some manner within the time "saved." It is with such a proposition that the present experiment was concerned.

Among various arrangements the case chosen for experimentation was double presentation of the complete message. The most important of the reasons for making this choice was that it was considered possible that the comprehension (not the intelligibility) of extended material presented at a fast rate might be so close to ceiling at the rate in question that it might not be susceptible to improvement by additional stimulation at fast rate. Another factor in selection was that complete verbatim repetition of a recording avoids all questions of content and speaking effectiveness, while use of the complete message as the unit of repetition is a limiting case of "dovetailed" repetition versions (e.g., word - word, sentence - sentence). It should also be noted that complete double presentation in this form would not be thought to be a powerful method of increasing comprehension and constitutes a strong test of the basic proposition for that reason.

Procedure

The experiment was performed in conjunction with the main
investigation and the procedural details have already been described
[B109]. Data were used from two of the single-presentation conditions in that investigation, namely, those involving 0 and 50 per cent
compression. Two comparable double-presentation conditions were
added. For single presentation the routine was: Message A, test;
Message B, test. For double presentation it was: Message A,
Message A, test; Message B, Message B, test. In the latter conditions the instructions included the information that the message
would be repeated and a pause of three seconds was inserted between repetitions to mark the break. Thirty-six Air Force trainees
were assigned to each of the four conditions. Each main group consisted of four subgroups of nine subjects each, representing Stanines
Five through Eight and affording levels of listener aptitude. As in
the main experiment, the tests were subscored for five Message Effectiveness Levels (MELs) to assess the effect of message-test difficulty. The design of the experiment envisioned an analysis of variance of the mixed factorial type. Number of Presentations by Compression by Stanine by MEL, following the pattern of the main study,
although only the first two and their first-order interaction were of
particular concern.

Table 1

MEAN PERCENTAGE CORRECT
FOR TOTAL GROUPS, STANINE SUBGROUPS AND MELs
(Single and double message presentation at 50% and 0% compression;
T equals original message time; single presentation data from basic
experiment [B109].)

| | 50% Compression | | 0% Compression | |
	Single (T/2)	Double (T)	Single (T)	Double (2T)
Total	58.0	65.4	63.8	67.6
Stanine				
Five	50.2	60.6	50.6	49.3
Six	53.9	62.8	61.7	75.7
Seven	59.8	71.1	69.8	68.7
Eight	68.2	67.0	73.2	76.9
MEL				
1	69.2	78.0	79.6	78.9
2	68.5	74.1	71.3	74.5
3	53.9	62.0	60.9	66.7
4	55.8	66.2	59.5	65.5
5	42.6	46.5	47.7	52.6

Results

Table 1 shows mean scores expressed in percentage correct. The means in the row designated "Total," each based on the scores of 36 subjects on the 60-item test, are of main interest. The third value, that for uncompressed single presentation in a relative message time T, serves as a reference to which the other means may be compared. It will be observed that the effect of double presentation was in the expected direction at both compressions, and that in the two conditions where stimulus time equaled T, single 0 per cent and double 50 per cent, the latter had a small advantage. The results of the analysis of variance were straightforward and will not be presented in detail. The effect of number of presentations, tested with the between-subjects error, was found to be significant; F was 6.98, with 1 and 128 degrees of freedom. Neither compression nor t'ie interaction of number of presentations and compression was significant. As would be expected from the basic experiment, the effects of stanine and MEL were both significant. All tests of the numerous interactions failed. Since the evidence supports and at no point controverts the general proposition advanced above, it is concluded that such a possibility for increasing auditory comprehension of a given content in a given time merits further study.

AUDITORY COMPREHENSION IN RELATION TO LISTENING RATE AND SELECTIVE VERBAL REDUNDANCY

Grant Fairbanks, Newman Guttman, Murray S. Miron

In a previous investigation of the effects of listening rate upon comprehension of connected speech [B109], two long technical messages were read at 141 words per minute, recorded, and compressed instrumentally in time [B105] by amounts which varied progressively over a suitable range. Factual comprehension, as measured by tests after presentation, was found to vary inversely and significantly with listening rate, but not linearly. At 201 and 282 wpm, corresponding to time compressions of 30 and 50 per cent, respectively, of the original speaking time, the decrement in comprehension was small in comparison to the reduction in listening time. This suggested that the time "saved" might be used to add reinforcing material to the compressed message within the time of the original message, and that some such arrangement might produce an increase in comprehension. Accordingly, a second experiment [B108] was performed to explore one possibility for the use of 50 per cent compression in this manner. Subjects heard the complete message twice in succession and the results were positive.

The present experiment was arranged to examine a less radical case, in which the extra time assumed to be available is smaller, the use thereof is selective, and the rate is within the range at-

tainable by a skilled live speaker. The experiment was planned
around the 30 per cent versions of the messages, and that percentage
of the original time was used for manipulation of message redundancy. The general idea was to regard time compression as a reduction of "temporal redundancy" and to trade this reduction for an increase in the "verbal redundancy. " Specifically, the verbal additions
consisted of blocks of words concentrated at selected points in the
text.   These blocks related to specific items of the test in a manner
that will be explained. The effect of such additions upon comprehension of portions of the content which were not so augmented was also
a matter of interest. It was decided to divide the items, 60 in all,
into two equal groups of approximately equal message-test difficulty,
or message effectiveness, in order to provide comparable sets.   In
addition, it was decided to confine the additions to restatements,
paraphrases, etc. , of the selected portions, avoiding exact repetition
on the one hand and distinctly new content on the other. In short,
the intention was to augment the presentations of certain facts in the
message by using more words to do so, and to follow a procedure
similar to that which a speaker might adopt if he were revising a
speech to emphasize certain specific points which he considered important.   It will be noted, however, that the additions were not confined to portions of the message at which it was least effective prior
to augmentation.

Procedure

        The general plan for the stimulus materials is shown in Table
1.   The augmented version of the message (long version) contained
the complete, unaltered, original message (short version), and expanded both the words and the time of the latter by 43 per cent.
The message time of the long version when compressed by 30 per
cent equalled that of the uncompressed short version.   From Table
1 it will be seen that the latter differed from the uncompressed long
version in words and time, but not in rate; that it differed from the
compressed short version in time and rate, but not in words; that it
differed from the compressed long version in words and rate, but
not in time.

        In preparing the long version it was decided, as has been
mentioned, to augment the content corresponding to 30 of the 60 items
in the combined test of the two messages.   These will be termed experimental items; the remainder, identical in both versions, will be
termed control items.   Equal numbers of both types were selected
from both messages.   The two sets of items were approximately
matched by pairing and both were representative of the range of response.   Each of the five Message Effectiveness Levels, as defined
by the basic experiment [B109], contributed six items to each set.
Data from the uncompressed condition of the basic experiment were
subscored for the 30 experimental and 30 control items; the respective means were 18. 03 and 20. 25 items correct per subject.   Corresponding means for the test-only condition (test administered, but no
message presented) were 5. 43 and 6. 99, so that the respective differ-

Table 1

WORDS, TIME AND RATE
AT THE FOUR EXPERIMENTAL CONDITIONS
RELATIVE TO THE UNCOMPRESSED ORIGINAL MESSAGE
(Long version contains short version plus inserted blocks of content.)

	Short Version	Long Version
0% Compression		
Words	1.0	1.43
Time	1.0	1.43
Rate	1.0	1.0
30% Compression		
Words	1.0	1.43
Time	.7	1.0
Rate	1.43	1.43

ences, estimates of message effectiveness, were 12.60 and 13.26.
In order to compare the sets of items with respect to degree of association between test items and content, the uncompressed message-
test and test-only conditions were intercorrelated separately, using
items as N and number of correct responses as the measure. The
obtained coefficients were low and approximately equal; .23 and .22
for experimental and control items, respectively.

An attempt was made to compare the relative number of words
devoted to the experimental and control content in the two versions.
In general, this involved identifying the content which supported each
item. Study of the problem revealed that item density was so high
and relatively constant that virtually none of the message could be
said to be unrelated to the test. Since all items were factual, however, the location of the specific content corresponding to each could
be readily determined, and afforded a basis for comparison of experimental and control items on the assumption that the remainder of the
text supported the two sets of items equally. The specific content
was defined as the minimum continuous portion of the text consisting
of whole sentences which, if isolated, would supply the correct answer to the test item, subject to the qualification that said portion
include the antecedent of any pronoun. The mean lengths of these
specific content sections for the experimental and control items were
29 and 26 words, respectively. Four pairs of experimental and control items overlapped by a total of 95 words. For purposes of assessing the division of the total messages between the two sets of
items, this overlap was equally divided, as was the remainder of the
text outside the specific content sections. The 3127 words of the two
basic messages thus were estimated to be divided 1625 and 1502, 52
and 48 per cent, between the experimental and control content, respectively, or with mean amounts of 54 and 50 words per item. The
subjective impressions were that the latter values are good approxi-

mations to the general length of the content supporting comprehension
of the average item, and to the difference between experimental and
control items.

In preparing the long version, the augmentation of the short
version by 43 per cent amounted to adding 1358 words, or 45 words
per experimental item. The total addition was satisfied exactly, as
were the different 43 per cent additions to the two messages required by their slightly different lengths. No attempt was made to
equate the lengths of the augmentations of specific experimental items,
which ranged from 25 to 64 words, although minor adjustments were
made to satisfy the total requirements. The 4485 words of the long
version were estimated as dividing 2754 and 1731, or 61 and 39 per
cent, between experimental and control content. Thus, the long version provided 92 and 58 mean words per experimental and control
item, respectively, in comparison to the 54 and 50 words in the
short version. For these estimates the augmentations were regarded
as adding only to the experimental content, except in the instances of
overlap mentioned above, where equal division again was practiced.

Each of the 30 augmentations was a section of content designed
to be inserted as a block into the short version and fit smoothly into
the text. The location of each was immediately after the basic content section for the item in question defined as described above.
Twenty-three augmentations consisted of two sentences, six of three,
and one of one. The general orientation during preparation of each
augmentation was to increase comprehension as much as possible by
a brief addition which included at least one paraphrase or restatement of the content, but which in no case involved complete repetition of the wording of either content section or test item. It is to
be stressed that each augmentation was viewed as a natural-sounding
portion of the long message which did not signal its existence in any
particular way. The intention, in other words, was to produce a resultant which also could be regarded as a reference message, in
comparison to which the original message was a briefer version from
which 30 redundant blocks of content had been excised.

The augmentations were prepared in spoken form by having
them recorded separately and splicing them into the original recordings. This procedure was considered more likely to provide good
experimental control than the other two possibilities, namely, having
the long version recorded and either excising the augmentations to
produce a new original, or comparing it to the independently recorded original. With the complete augmented text before him, the
speaker listened repeatedly to his original recording before and after
the point of insertion, re-reading the original in concert in an attempt to duplicate his previously used rate, intonation, etc., and
then read the augmentation. The recorded augmentation was immediately cued in with the original, played, monitored, and either accepted or rejected. The 30 augmentations were then spliced into the
original and the transitions judged in the continuous message. Certain augmentations were re-recorded, substituted and checked again.
Finally, minor adjustments of the total durations were made to meet

the requirements mentioned above. These involved only a few seconds altogether and were readily distributed through the pauses at points of insertion.

Given the long version in recorded form, the procedure followed in all respects that previously described [B109]. All subjects were trainees at Chanute Air Force Base and technical aptitude (Stanine level) was equalized between groups. Presentation of recordings was over a headset distribution system of excellent quality in a conventional classroom. Each message was followed immediately by its test, time for the latter not being limited. Two separate experiments were performed. For reasons that will be explained, the first experiment was not considered to be unequivocal. A second experiment was carried out under improved conditions and its results analyzed.

Results

First Experiment: The original plan was to administer the long version under the same conditions as previously used in the basic experiment with the short version [B109], and to incorporate data from the two experiments into a single analysis. In addition to 0 and 30 per cent compression conditions, which were the basis for construction of the long version, a 50 per cent condition was added as a matter of interest, for a total of six conditions. Unfortunately for this economical plan, the weather which prevailed on the days of the experiment happened to be unusually hot and humid, extremely uncomfortable for the subjects in contrast to the favorable conditions for the first experiment.

Table 2 shows the means for the six conditions, each subtest being based on 30 items. If the four subtest means within each of the three compression conditions are examined, it will be observed that the highest value is invariably that for the experimental content in the long version, as would be expected. When the three pairs of means for control content are compared, the value is lower in the long version in all cases, but it was felt that the reduction might be a reflection of the uncomfortable conditions under which the long version was presented and that it could not be attributed confidently to the stimulus materials. The impression that discomfort might have confounded the experiment was reinforced by the fact that the experimenters had expected a net increase in response to the long version, since they considered that the augmentations had improved the original message.

Several other explanations were advanced, among them the possibility that augmentation had reduced the message-test reliability. For the uncompressed short version the Kuder-Richardson reliability coefficient was .87, as previously reported [B109]. For the 0, 30 and 50 per cent compressions of the long version, coefficients derived from the new data were .87, .82 and .90, respectively, which seemed to be satisfactory. Consideration was also given to the pos-

Table 2

MEAN NUMBER OF ITEMS CORRECT
UNDER SIX EXPERIMENTAL CONDITIONS
(Independent groups of 36 subjects; data for short version from basic experiment [B109].)

	Short Version	Long Version
0% Compression		
Experimental	18.03	21.53
Control	20.25	17.69
Total	38.28	39.22
30% Compression		
Experimental	16.94	21.67
Control	18.94	18.14
Total	35.89	39.81
50% Compression		
Experimental	16.81	18.09
Control	18.00	15.17
Total	34.81	33.26

Table 3

MEAN NUMBER OF ITEMS CORRECT AND MEAN MESSAGE
EFFECTIVENESS (SEE TEXT) FOR 30 EXPERIMENTAL, 30 CONTROL
AND 60 TOTAL ITEMS UNDER FOUR EXPERIMENTAL CONDITIONS
(Four independent groups of 38 subjects each.)

	Mean Items Correct		Mean Message Effectiveness	
	Short Version	Long Version	Short Version	Long Version
0% Compression				
Experimental	19.00	21.21	14.00	16.21
Control	20.37	17.32	13.10	10.05
Total	39.37	38.53	27.10	26.26
30% Compression				
Experimental	18.42	20.16	13.42	15.16
Control	19.21	16.53	11.94	9.26
Total	37.63	36.69	25.36	24.42

sibility that relative item difficulty had been upset by the augmentations. Since no attempt had been made to insure augmentations that were equally effective, this would be likely for the experimental items, but whether or not it would also be true of the control items was the issue. The intercorrelation of response (subjects correct) to the control items in the short and long versions, essentially an estimate of item reliability, was . 81; for the experimental items it was . 73. All in all, it seemed advisable to repeat the experiment under conditions that would permit more confident interpretation.

Second Experiment: The new plan involved only four stimulus conditions, namely, the short and long versions each at 0 and at 30 per cent compression; it was decided to eliminate 50 per cent conditions on the grounds that the 30 per cent conditions seemed adequately representative. All subjects were drawn from Stanine Seven, independent groups of 38 each being assigned at random to the four conditions. A single message order was used exclusively. Experimental sessions with subgroups were distributed at various hours over three days, essentially counterbalancing the conditions. Environment was good throughout.

The means are presented in the left section of Table 3 and comparison with the data of Table 2 will show that the two experiments yielded results that were essentially identical, namely, small differences between total means for the four stimulus conditions and consistent interaction within compression as described above. Apparently the misgivings about the effects of weather upon the first experiment had not been warranted, but the confirmation is reassuring.

The first step in analysis was to consider the variance of total response in the four main conditions. Analysis corresponded to the double-entry arrangement of Table 1 and tested the effects of message version, compression, and version-by-compression interaction against the within-groups error with 148 degrees of freedom. All three tests failed by wide margins. Interpretation of this finding is approached with suitable diffidence, but confidence is increased by the extreme care which characterized the procedure, the high reliability of measurement, and the significant internal responses which are discussed below. With mean total response approximately constant across the four conditions, the variation in efficiency is remarkable. For example, in the extreme case, the uncompressed presentation of the long version utilized 43 per cent more words and 104 per cent more time than the short version displayed with 30 per cent compression.

An analysis of the version by type of item interaction appeared to be an appropriate test of the significance of the observed internal variations, and it was considered sufficient to handle the two compression levels in parallel as separate problems. The results are summarized in Table 4. Both interaction Fs are large and significant beyond the 0. 1 per cent level, and the F for type of items is likewise significant at both compressions. Attention was then directed to

the differences between the specific subtest means within compression
level shown in the left section of Table 3, which were tested by t.
Since the two values for type of items within a given version were
based upon the same 38 subjects, the within-subjects errors of Table 4 were used for the experimental-control differences; conventional
t's were computed for the four between-versions-within-items differences, each derived from two groups of 38 subjects each.

Table 4

SUMMARY OF ANALYSES OF VARIANCE
AT TWO COMPRESSION LEVELS; VERSION x TYPE OF ITEM

	df	0% Compression		30% Compression	
		ms	F	ms	F
Between Subjects					
Version (V)	1	6.73		8.52	
Error (b)	74	27.43		36.12	
Within Subjects					
Type of Item (I)	1	63.18	13.59*	79.60	14.11*
V x I	1	257.93	55.47*	260.79	46.24*
Error (w)	74	4.65		5.64	
Total	151				

*$p < .001$

Within the short version, the difference between the experimental and control content in favor of the latter, obtained for both
presentations, confirms the difference already mentioned above in the
description of the procedure. At 0 per cent compression it was
found to be significant at the 1 per cent level, but failed to meet the
5 per cent requirement at 30 per cent compression. The reversed
and larger differences between experimental and control content in
the long version are significant beyond the 0.1 level at both values
of compression. For the experimental content the increase from
short to long version is significant at the 1 per cent level with uncompressed presentation, at the 5 per cent level with 30 per cent
compression. The decrease for the control content is significant beyond the 0.1 per cent level at both compressions. In terms of number of correct responses to items in the long version in comparison
to the short version, 21 of the 30 experimental items increased,
while 23 of the 30 control items decreased. Therefore, it may be
asserted with considerable confidence that augmentation of the experimental content sharply differentiated it from the control content, but
that the differentiation took the form of an absolute sum of positive
and negative changes, respectively, of approximately equal amounts.

Special interest attaches to the lower relative response to the control content. It has been noted above that the experimental and control items were not exactly matched, according to scores in the basic experiment and in estimated words per item in the text. The data from the basic experiment were re-examined and 15 carefully matched pairs of experimental and control items extracted, three from each Message Effectiveness Level. The respective mean scores were 2.97 and 2.91 items correct in the test-only condition, 9.54 and 9.56 in the uncompressed original condition, and the mean numbers of words in specific content sections of the text were 31.7 and 30.4. The comparable long version was that administered to the 36 subjects across four stanines in the first experiment; there the scores were 10.67 and 8.03. In the same condition the remaining 15 experimental and control pairs, less exactly matched, with means of 8.49 and 10.69 for the short version, yielded means of 10.86 and 9.66, respectively.

The results for the control content were also studied for possible differential effects related to relative message effectiveness, or message-test difficulty. The intercorrelation of response to control items in the uncompressed short and long versions was repeated with the new data for the second experiment; the coefficient was .86. The scatter was inspected and various subsets formed according to scores in both versions with uniformly negative results. For example, the 15 highest ranking control items in the short version yielded a mean score per subject of 12.45 in comparison to 7.92 for the lowest 15 items. The same two sets of items incurred respective mean reductions of 1.45 and 1.60 in the long version. This unselectivity with respect to message-test difficulty suggests that the potent factor in reduction of response was relative verbal redundancy, a possibility that should be studied in a future experiment. Various other subsets of control items were formed according to location within message, length in words, proximity to experimental items, etc., likewise with no positive indication. The depressed score for the control content in the long version appears to have been a fairly uniform effect across the items.

In the long version the difference between responses to experimental and control content was in the same direction as the difference in quantity of the content, as has been observed. The design of the experiment assumed that the experimental and control content would be approximately equal in the short version, and it was noted above that the word count showed this division to have been approximately realized; that is, the estimate for experimental content was 52 per cent. If the experimental content of the short version had been exactly 50 per cent, and if all augmentation, 43 per cent of the total short version, had been added to it exclusively, the experimental content would have constituted 65 per cent of the long version. The word count showed that 61 per cent is probably a closer estimate, as also has been stated.

The mean scores were converted to estimated message effectiveness by subtraction of the means for the Stanine Seven subjects in the test-only condition of the basic experiment, following previous procedures [B109]. These means were 5.00, 7.27 and 12.27 for experimental, control and total items, respectively. The converted means are shown in the right section of Table 3. Calculation will show that the experimental component was 62 per cent of the total message effectiveness in the long version at both compressions. Similarly, for the first experiment, with data based on Stanines Five through Eight, the corresponding test-only means are 5.43, 6.99 and 12.42. For the long version at 0, 30 and 50 per cent compression (Table 2) the experimental components were 60, 59 and 61 per cent, respectively, of the totals. Reciprocally, prediction of the experimental component as 61 per cent (the estimated percentage of experimental words) of the total message effectiveness for the five conditions in the first and second experiments yielded a maximum difference of .47 item from the obtained mean. Since five independent groups were involved, the compactness of the percentages and predictions is provocative.

It is interesting that substantial selective increases in redundancy, which increased response to the selected portions of the message, were accompanied by decreased response to other portions and by no change in the total response. The present study was not designed to explain this finding, although a few speculations may be useful. First, however, there is the possibility that some unintended factor, or combination of factors, in the experimental materials and situation placed a ceiling on response which was approached by both the short and the long versions of the message. Such factors might reside in the verbal message, acoustic message, instructions, test, environmental conditions, length of stimulus period in time or words, characteristics of subjects, etc. This explanation seems unlikely. In a long and careful scrutiny of the experimental details and results, no basis for a ceiling effect could be discerned. On the other hand, there is positive evidence of significant sensitivity of response to variations of the stimulus, from the previous experiments which used the short version and the same test [B108, B109], and also from the exploratory work during preparation of materials, in which sensitivity of the test was one criterion.

If the experiment may be assumed to have been satisfactory from the above point of view, considerable interest attaches to the fact that, although the long version was not a "better" message than the short version in the experimental situation, it read and sounded as if it were, as was stated earlier. That impression was distinct, was formed prior to the experiment, and was confirmed by critics other than the experimenters. The suggestion is strong that it was based largely upon improved ease of comprehension of the facts in the redundant experimental content. It may be, then, that the redundancy of the experimental content during display of the long version invited a degree of listener participation in the communication act which was inappropriate to the more terse control content, i.e., behavior analogous to an elevation of threshold. Although standardized instructions were used in all conditions, it is worth noting that subjects were allowed to seek their own levels of effort. Cooperation

was generally excellent, but no special motivation was attempted, and
it is possible that the long version commanded less effort than the
short version by virtue of the stimulus itself.   Along the same general line of reasoning, it may be that listeners come through experience to associate redundancy with importance, and that the relative
redundancies of the two sets of content items operated as signals in
the long version.   A different possibility is that the response to the
experimental portions of the long version actively inhibited the response to the control portions in a conventional sense.   In this regard it should be observed that item density was high in the message,
one sampled fact per 75 words, or about two facts per minute with
no compression, and that the relationships between consecutive blocks
of content were typical of those found in coherent messages.

The realism of the experimental situation is believed to justify
an observation regarding application to live situations.   Although the
findings do not permit a sure explanation of the mechanisms, they
imply that the common practice of singling out certain points in a
speech for redundant treatment may be effective at such points, but
that its accompaniment may be an absolute, as well as a relative reduction of effectiveness at other points.

Summary

A recorded technical message, read at 141 wpm, together with
an accompanying test of factual comprehension, were available from
a previous experiment, which furnished data used to construct a se-
lectively augmented version of the message.   The 60-test items were
divided into matched pairs according to message-test difficulty, and
the pairs split to yield two approximately equal sets.   For one set
the corresponding content of the message (control content) remained
unaltered.   For the other set the content relating to each item (experimental content) was augmented by a smoothly continuous, non-
repetitive restatement of the sampled fact which was inserted as a
block into the basic test.   The augmented version was prepared in
recorded form by splicing recordings of the augmentations, read at
141 wpm with suitable vocal continuity by the original speaker, into
a copy of the original recorded message, so that the resulting long
version contained the short version.   By design, the recorded augmentations, which represented a total addition of 43 per cent to the
short version in both number of words and message time, constituted
30 per cent of the words and time of the long version.   Both recorded versions then were subjected to 30 per cent automatic time
compression with rate increasing to 201 wpm, for a total of four recordings, two versions times two compressions of 0 and 30 per cent.
In comparison to the uncompressed short version, the compressed
long version presented 43 per cent more words in no greater time.

The experiment consisted of presentation of the four recordings to independent groups of subjects, and analysis of test results
in relation to version, compression, and type of item.   Because of
of uncertainty about the environment at the time of first performance

the experiment was repeated with improved control; the results of the two experiments differed in no essential way. Appropriate analyses of variance were performed with data from the second experiment. No evidence of significant variation in the total responses to the four different recordings was found, but the experimental and control components of the response changed significantly from version to version within rate. Augmentation of the experimental content resulted in a significant increase in response which was accompanied by an approximately equal, unselective, significant decrease in response to the control content. Such internal changes obtained equally at both messages rates, and their relative amounts corresponded closely to the changes in the proportions of the number of words in the two sections of the content.

Chapter 7

GRANT FAIRBANKS, 3

The excerpt in this chapter is taken from a taped transcript of a series of lectures delivered by Fairbanks during a seminar at the University of Florida in June, 1963, one year before his untimely death. The content of this excerpt, in sharp contrast to most other writing and speaking by Fairbanks, is at an informal level. We find here an attempt to present comprehensively and understandably a summary of the work done by Fairbanks and his associates in relation to compressed speech. Included in this summary are the studies involved in doctoral theses sponsored by Fairbanks. Excerpts from three such theses are found in the following chapters.

EFFECTS OF TIME COMPRESSION AND EXPANSION OF SPEECH

Grant Fairbanks

I will try to disclose some of the unusual aspects of this kind of compression-expansion program. Not the technological, instrumental aspects; they have been published. The basic article on method was published in 1954 in the Transactions of the IRE Professional Group on Audio under the names of Fairbanks, Everitt and Jaeger [B105]. There is some material that is unpublished and I want to touch on that, attempting to indicate some of the unique or special features of the method. Very early, as a student, when I began to be aware that there were such things as speech sounds, that they had duration and so on, and that people had ears and vocal systems and what not, it became clear, as it is to most people, that the ear plus brain of a listener is a faster system than the brain plus vocal system of a talker. There is a disparity between the time constants of these two systems.

During World War II, when for a time I was a technical assistant to Charles Bray at the National Research Council, we were asked to make a survey of voice communication problems in the Air Force, then the Army Air Force. At that time my later colleague, Bill Everitt, was Chief of the Operations Group in the Office of the Chief Signal Officer. His main psychologist was Don Lewis, the expert on quantitative methods, who had been my colleague at Iowa. Lewis and I, then, surveyed Flight Training Commands for the Army Air Force. On the basis of this survey the Air Force decided to

establish a research laboratory at Waco, Texas.   John Black, James
Curtis, and Paul Moore were identified with this later in various
ways, to name the persons whom I recall at the moment that are involved in this seminar.

Lewis and I wrote our report; we concluded, of course, that
communications were very bad in the Air Force, and they were indeed bad.   The gear was bad, and the procedures were bad.   One of
the main things we reported was that although time is often of the essence in aircraft operations, nonetheless, the main problem in communications was with the talker, not the listener--the talker's articulation in particular.   We concluded that one of the main sins in articulation was too fast a rate, and so we recommended that, in spite
of the fact that rate was of the essence, we slow the talkers down.
Then we said that until some sort of device could be interposed between the talker and the listener to take advantage of the speed at
which the listener could take in the material, operations would have
to put up with a comparatively slow rate to provide for good articulation.   You soon reach your ceiling in articulation as you accelerate,
as you well know.

This stuck with me until I got to fooling around at Illinois,
about 1950, with a library of tapes of speech sounds.   I had a bunch
of continuant sounds, vowels and consonants, each on a little bit of
tape.   I began to splice samples of these together and make synthetic
words.   I found that I was able to do fairly well and it sounded kind
of like speech.   And then I began to wonder how short these segments could be, and I began to abbreviate them until I got them
down much shorter than average.   Then I got into the notion of time
sampling, and the idea that one could enter a speech signal at random, and with periodic time sampling could effect a compression that
was not selective, but instead would bear some fractional relation to
the total time.

Now, we'll try to zero in on this problem.   You all recognize
what we have in Figure 1.   We have a spectrogram, and, as you
know, the coordinates are frequency and time, and the energy is
roughly proportional to the density of the bars.   This probably displays something very like what a listener hears as time goes on.
He has a kind of delay circuit in his system that permits him to perform these kinds of analyses and to get out the spectral content.   But
actually the top row shows the way that the signal is delivered to the
tympanic membrane, as one thing follows another.   This is part of
an oscillogram of a vowel.   It is periodic, as you can readily see,
and its fundamental frequency is given by the reciprocal of the repeated periods that are readily apparent.   You can also see that the
wave has a fairly rich, harmonic content because of its complexity.
The ear operates on this kind of signal.   The top figure comes first
and the rest of it follows in order.   Now, in the middle section of
the graph the oscillograph is moving at a slower speed, and here we
see word and syllable envelopes.   The reason that I want to show
this is that these various syllables, although not as regular as the
waves in the oscillogram, have their own rates too, and these will

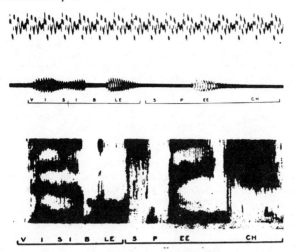

Figure 1. Speech spectrogram.

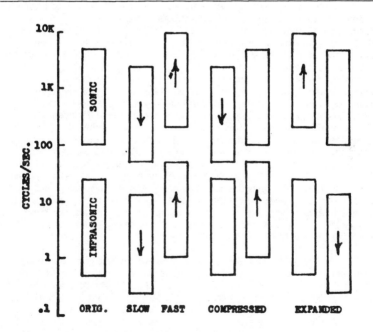

Figure 2. Diagramatic representation of problem of compression.

occur so many per second although they are only quasi-periodic. Essentially our problem is to operate on the time/frequency display and to extract time samples in some automatic fashion. The problem, then, is really one of time compression, that is, to accelerate rate without altering frequency. I show in Figure 2 a diagram of the main problem. The ordinate displays frequency in cycles per second, and you'll note that it is logarithmic, starting with one and proceeding upward by a factor of ten. At the lower part of the ordinate are the infrasonic ranges, that is, the rate and quasi-periodic events, the event frequencies, and at the upper portion are the sonic frequencies roughly restricted to the range shown by the boxes of the diagram. These sonic frequencies define the quasi-periodic events of the lower portion of the diagram. Our problem is to speed up the rate of the infrasonic frequencies without changing the rate of the sonic frequencies. Now if we take a recording and simply play it slowed by a factor of two, we're going to halve both the sonic and infrasonic frequencies. We're going to divide these frequencies by half, and we're going to divide the rate by half. Both of them will be slowed because they are both displayed as a function of time. On the other hand, if we play this material at a faster rate, we're going to multiply both the event rate and the internal frequencies as well.

Now in compressed speech, our method of time sampling provides for doing either one of two things. First, leaving the event frequencies alone, which you'll see are like the originals, we can divide the internal frequencies down and decrease the distance between the upper end of the event frequency and the lower end of the internal frequencies. Or, in the time compression example, we can speed up the event frequency but keep the range of the internal frequencies the same as in the original. In the case of frequency expansion, we're increasing the distance between the upper end of the event frequencies and the lower end of the internal frequencies. We're multiplying the internal frequencies up, leaving the event frequencies alone, or in time expansion, the time application, we will slow the rate of the event without altering the internal frequencies. We do this in a manner roughly shown in Figure 3 for the 50 per cent case. From original segments A and B, we extract as a sample A and B. We will discard the sample A-A and B-B, and we will abut interval A and interval B so that the net result is that we have sampled A and we have sampled B, reproduced in half the time. In expansion we take A and repeat it, and we take B and repeat it, thus doubling the duration of A and B.

In the last example of the figure we first compress A and B and then we repeat A and B, restoring the original frequency and the original duration. Now for this we would probably find it useful to supply a little notation. First of all, we will define one of these A or B segments as an interval and we'll call this interval in our notation P_S; the sampling period, which in turn is the reciprocal of the sampling frequency, we'll call F_S. Now, instead of using the 2-to-1 example, I'm going to use a 4-to-1 example. We will consider this P_S to be composed of four units; the first portion of this four-unit P_S interval we will extract and retain. This in our notation will show

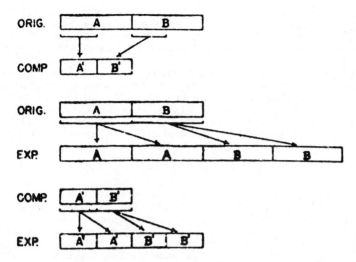

Figure 3. Diagramatic representation of speech compression and expansion.

---

as I_s, the sampling interval. The remainder of P_s we're going to discard. In our notation we'll show this as I_d, this discard interval; then $I_d + I_s = P_s$ as is obvious. Now the sampling, or the compression ratio, R_c, is defined as I_d/P_s. It will also be obvious then that the sampling frequency previously defined as $F_s = 1/P_s$ is the rate at which we enter the signal. However, in the time compression case, where we enter the signal at $1/P_s$ and subsequently play it fast to restore the original frequencies, we are going to elevate F_s to a higher frequency that we call the interruption frequency F_i, which is defined as $1/I_s$ in our notation.

Now there are various aspects to this particular kind of a program. I want to list them first, and then I want to comment on each of them. First, there is the matter of the effect on intelligibility. Second, there is the problem of learning or comprehension. I will want to talk a bit about learning and comprehension as affected by these matters. Third, obviously if you play something fast you increase its rate. If you play it slowly you decrease its rate. I want to talk about the perceived rate in relation to these things. Then I want to describe an experiment on the estimation of the temporal redundancy of language using this particular technique. I want to go into expanded speech and do some demonstration and, finally, I want to talk about a technique where we first compress, then transmit, and then expand back up into the original.

I'd like to review briefly the study of Fairbanks and Kodman, published in 1957 [B104], having to do with intelligibility. Some of this material was used as part of Kodman's Ph.D. dissertation at

Illinois. We have a list of 50 PB words. One of the standard PB word lists was picked at random; one speaker spoke them. The median duration of the words was .60 second with a range of .3675 second. There were eight sophisticated observers. That is, they had no hearing loss, they had superior speech discrimination by test, and they were trained in phonetic notation. Before the first administration of this 50-word vocabulary, they were thoroughly familiarized with the vocabulary in a training task where the stimulus was degraded. Administration was by PDR-10 headsets. Various compression ratios, R_e, and I_d values were chosen. As I_d becomes large, progressive fragmentation of the word occurs, of course. We wanted to cover the range from small I_d to large I_d intervals.

Thus, in Figure 4 we see the first order results of word intelligibility in percentage plotted along the ordinate vs. the compression ratio along the abscissa, with I_d as the parameter. I_d, you will note, is .01 second, .04, .08, .16, and .24. Obviously as compression ratio is increased and as the duration of the words is shortened, intelligibility is going to fall off. But it is equally clear from the figure that intelligibility remains quite high out to a surprisingly large amount of time compression. I'll go into that in a later experiment, and I think in a better way. We estimated that the temporal redundancy was of the order of 70 per cent in these PB words. You understand now that this was in a closed set of 50 words with the observers familiar with the set. You'll also observe that intelligibility varies as a function of the size of I_d, with the larger values of I_d, shown in the lower part of the figure, producing the least intelligibility. You'll recognize that the maximum intelligibility was less perfect when I_d became quite long.

Now in Figure 5 we are plotting work intelligibility vs. the size of the sampling interval. The curves are the five curves that you saw in the preceding figure, but reversed and displayed along the abscissa. Now you'll notice that as the sampling interval increases, that is to say as the compression percentage decreases, each of these curves begins to rise. The lines in the horizontal plane connect equal time compression. For instance, the lowest curve is that for 90 per cent compression and the next highest that for 80 per cent, etc. Now an interesting thing about this is that when I_d is .16 or .24, the curves become asymptotic, indicating that intelligibility will never reach 100 per cent. That is to say that when the discard intervals are sufficiently long, regardless of how small we make the compression, we are always going to be leaving out something that will prevent the intelligibility from being optimal. For the case for which R_e equals .5, that is, where I_d equals I_s, we should expect the curve of intelligibility to become asymptotic at the point of 50 per cent word intelligibility. For the average word of this experiment, this asymptote should occur with an I_s of .3 since this would yield a P_s of .3 and together they would produce a sampling period of .6, which is the mean duration of the words in the list. You may wonder why, in the case of 90 per cent compression, the curve is so sharply double-inflected. What's going on here is that in the fast play we said that the interruption frequency, as the listener hears it,

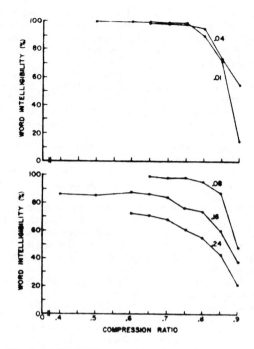

Figure 4.   Word intelligibility as a function of compression ratio.

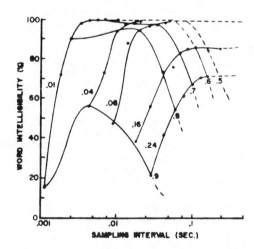

Figure 5.   Word intelligibility as a function of length of the sampling interval.

is the reciprocal of the sampling interval. This means that the interruption frequency is equal to approximately 900 cycles at the shorter sampling intervals. Accordingly, these interruptions are getting up into the audible spectrum, and are artifactually interfering with the intelligibility.

Figure 6 is what I call, rather facetiously, a nonsensory discrimination function. At the conclusion of this experiment these eight observers had each been presented with this word list about 90 times. They knew it backwards and forwards, or in any other random order. As a matter of fact, a number of years later one of them, George Kurtzrock, sat down just for kicks and wrote 44 of the words on a piece of paper--so they really knew the words. When we got through with this experiment, these young phoneticians were presented with a pencil and paper fragmentation task. The original PB items were randomly fragmented into parts. For example, if the original word was of the CVC form it might have been presented as CV, VC, CC or any of the eight possible deletions of the original letters including complete deletion. Each of the original items was thus represented by an orthographic fragment. We then shuffled up the fragments, gave them to the subjects, and had them turn the cards over one at a time and guess the word from the fragment. In other words, now they were getting portions of the words, and our interest was to see the percentage of the total vocabulary that they would get on this basis. The figure displays the percentage of identification of the list of stimulus fragments vs. the percentage of the word that was presented on the card. You'll note that this is a sigmoid curve and that about 50 per cent identification corresponds roughly with 50 per cent of the individual word. This is, I think, rather interesting, particularly if you consider a transformation of it in Figure 7.

Here we have a plot along a normal probability ordinate shown on the left. These are the same empirical points from the previous figure. We'll make the arbitrary assumption here that the range is ± 2.5 standard deviations. Now we plot the word intelligibility values appropriately here against the percentage of the word, as in the previous figure. But now we employ a Z notation metric, where zero equals the median, and the distance between any two intelligibility values is expressed as the ratio of the difference between the median value and the obtained value relative to the obtained standard deviation. Now I suggest to you that this is getting pretty lawful. When you are dealing with fragments of words in this particular manner, you're beginning to be able to get at something that might be thought of as a kind of transfer function from word intelligibility to a portion of phonemes perceived; and attribute which is basic to these data and our general approach to the problems of intelligibility.

Also in the realm of rate, I shall now refer to the Ph.D. thesis of Kurtzrock [B248] who was interested in time frequency and time frequency distortion and their effects on intelligibility. The plan of the experiment is shown in Figure 8. The left-hand ordinate of this figure is relative frequency logarithmically scaled. If the event frequency in question were 100, the lowest value of the ordinate

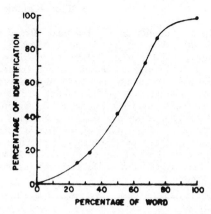

Figure 6.   Percentage of word needed for word identification.

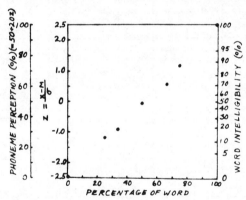

Figure 7.   Percentage of word heard in relation to word intelligibility and to phoneme perception.

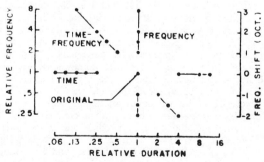

Figure 8.   Diagramatic presentation of problem dealt with in Kurtz-rock dissertation.

would correspond to a frequency of 25, the next 50 and so on to the uppermost value of 800. The original value is shown as the center-most dot of the figure, and the problem was to multiply the frequencies and to divide the frequencies. In this demonstration we wished to abbreviate the duration frequency as shown along the abscissa, to expand the frequency constant along the left-hand ordinate, and to abbreviate the duration and to multiply the frequency reciprocally as in fast play, and to divide the frequency and to accompany it with time expansion as in slow play. Each point of the figure represents a particular combination of these parameters and provides a graphic representation of the conditions of the experiment. Now for this experiment and for others I have devised a rather interesting word list, which is shown in Figure 9.

	-p	-t	-d	-m	-r	-s	-b	-n	-l	-z
p-			e	a	ɛ	ʊ		ɔ		
t-	e					ɔ		ɪ	o	i
d-	ɪ			u		ɔ		ɛ		o
m-		i	u		ʊ	æ	a			
r-		ʊ	ɛ	o		ɪ				e
s-	u		æ	i				o		ɔ
w-	i	a			ɔ		ɛ		ʊ	
v-		o		ɪ		e		æ	i	
ʃ-	a		ʊ		ɪ				æ	u
dʒ-		ɛ			a	u	æ		e	

Figure 9. Construction of a word list.

I wanted to construct a list that had 50 words in it, and it had to be a CVC kind of list--a single initial consonant, a single final consonant, a single vowel or nucleus in the middle of a CVC model. Now across the top the post-vocalic consonants, are shown that were used; along the side, the pre-vocalic consonants, and the cell entries are the vowels, there being ten of the common American vowels-- those with a low formant two and those with a high formant two. First of all, all entries are real words, they're not nonsense. As a matter of fact, 42 of the 50 occur in the highest-frequency category of the Thorndike-Lorge list. It is also a condition that in no row and in no column will there be more than one vowel entry. Now, there are five occurrences of each of the ten pre-vocalic consonants, five occurrences of each of the ten vowels, and five occurrences of each of the ten post-vocalic consonants, so you see that the end product is a rather precise kind of vocabulary. This particular design means, then, that each consonant-vowel combination, each vowel-consonant combination, and each consonant-consonant combination is unique. Given the identification of a consonant or a vowel, or a post-vocalic consonant in a given word, the chance probability of correctly identifying the entire word is .2, there being five occurrences of each. On the other hand, being given two elements of the word, you should get 100 per cent because each one of these is unique, and if you know the set, you know what the third element is. This provided a very interesting training situation because, in fact, the subjects were trained in this vocabulary and the method of testing. We trained to the level of 100 per cent identification on randomized two-element fragments of the original list.

In Figure 10 we can see the main effects of the experiment. Word intelligibility is plotted along the ordinate in percentage and

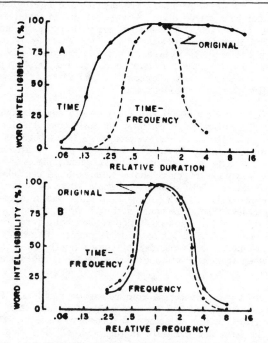

Figure 10. Intelligibility related to relative duration and frequency.

relative duration along the abscissa increasing toward the right. The original version of the vocabulary is indicated in each of the curves, 100 per cent correct identification for a relative duration of 1. Now if we decrease the relative duration, time constant, our intelligibility falls off smoothly to the left. If we increase the relative duration, frequency constant, intelligibility continues to be high and perfect.

The final point of expansion, by a factor of 12, begins to dip down a
little bit because when you get expansions of this magnitude, the
speech takes on a sort of unreality and it no longer sounds like
speech.   It should be observed that the abscissa of this plot is scaled
logarithmically.   The range summarized by the plot is very wide.
This demonstrates the great elasticity of the time domain in speech.
The dotted curve of the upper figure summarizes the results obtained
from fast and slow play.   That is, values to the left of the original
value are for fast play with duration decreasing and frequency going
up, and values to the right are for slow play with duration increasing and frequency going down.   Note that for these latter values the
intelligibility falls off much more rapidly.   Obviously, then, the difference between these two curves demonstrates very graphically the
importance of frequency distortion in the signal.   In the lower figure,
the abscissa now is relative frequency.   Frequency is then increasing
toward the right; our original is up here at the top repeated from the
upper figure.   As we multiply the frequencies the intelligibility falls
off as the right-hand curve displays.   As we divide them, time constant, it falls to the left.   The dashed curve displays the data for
time-frequency distortion superimposed on the curve of frequency distortion.   You can note the difference between frequency division,
time constant, and frequency division accompanied by slow play.   The
difference is small, but it is discernible, and these differences are
in the direction that you would expect.

I wish I had time to go into the phonetic analysis and attempts
to predict intelligibility given phoneme identification, but let me just
note the fact that significant differences were found between the specific consonants, vowels, and pre-vocalic and post-vocalic consonants
in the list.   The data showed that when frequency distortion was in
question, the vowels were much more vulnerable to degradation than
were the consonants.   The consonants would stand up a lot better under frequency distortion.   When time distortion was in question the
reverse was true.   The consonants suffered more in their intelligibility than did the vowels.   Vowels with low formants were more intelligible than those with high formants in frequency distortion.   Finally,
voiceless consonants were considerably more intelligible than voiced
consonants when frequency distortion was present.   So much for the
rate problem.

Now let's get on with the comprehension problem.   I'm referring now to work published by Fairbanks, Guttman, and Miron in
1957 [B107, B108, B109], a series of three experiments.   I'm going
to refer to the first and the third in that series.   For this particular
problem, we were interested first of all in establishing some materials that could be used for the measurement of comprehension, so we
devised two technical messages.   They had to do with meteorology;
they were highly factual.   There was reference to numbers, to historical dates, the design of instruments for meteorological observa-
tions, and so on; in short, they were highly technical messages.
One of them was 1,554 words long, and the other was 1,573 words
long.   Both messages were read by a skilled talker at the rate of
141 words per minute, the target being 140.   The talker was paced

with one-minute light flashes, and that means that each of the messages was a little bit longer than 11 minutes. That means we're
dealing with fairly long periods of content.

The technique was to present one message, then test it, then
present the second message and test it. So, message, test, message, test was the general administrative situation. We devised a
30-item test for each of these messages which originally started out
as a 50-item test, then was reduced to a 40-item test and then to a
30-item test. It was a five-alternative multiple-choice form of test.
By item analysis procedures and the Kuder-Richardson Reliability
formula, R was .87 and 98 subjects hearing the message with any
distortion, which we regarded as a highly acceptable standard of reliability. This demonstrates, incidentally, that it is possible to devise a test of auditory comprehension with high reliability and strong
face validity.

These messages were subjected to a series of compressions;
first there was the uncompressed version which we will refer to as
0 per cent compression, 30 per cent compression, 50, 60, 70 per
cent, and then there was the test without having heard the message,
comparable to 100 per cent compression. We wanted to test a priori
information, and we picked meteorology, incidentally, because there
isn't very much popular information about the kind of technical detail
that we are getting at here. That is, it isn't commonly available to
the kind of subjects we employed. Thirty-six subjects were used in
each of the compression conditions, except for the test situation, 100
per cent compression, in which 44 were used. The subjects were
airmen and were controlled with respect to stanine. The subjects
were run in groups and were presented the message through PDR-10
headsets. The discard interval was .02 second for all compressions,
an interval you will recall which produces high over-all intelligibility.
We did not want intelligibility to be a question. Now, for instance,
in the case of 50 per cent compression I_d would be .02; I_s would
also be .02; P_s would be .04. The sampling rate would be 25 cycles,
and the interruption frequency would be 50 cycles.

Now, in Figure 11 we see the general effect upon comprehension when all the data are pooled. Our ordinate now is relative message effectiveness for the people who had no message but took the
test. Their obtained score was 20.7 per cent for a five-alternate
multiple-choice test. You can see that this is very close to the assumed a priori probability. The maximum of those who had the complete message uncompressed, which is shown at the top of the ordinate as 1, corresponds to a score mean of 63.8 per cent. The intermediate ordinate values are expressed relative to the difference
between the maximum and minimum scores, 63.8 and 20.7. Thus,
this is what the message added to the pre-knowledge of the subjects.
The abscissa indicates message time. You'll note that it is linear.
The upper abscissa indicates the corresponding rates in words per
minute, and you'll observe that at times these rates get very high
indeed, 500 words per minute for the maximum compression condition. You'll notice that as the rate decreases, message effectiveness

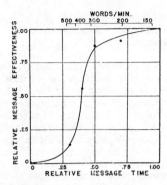

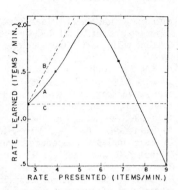

Figure 11. Relationship between
time of message and its intelligibility.

Figure 12. Message efficiency
in terms of rate.

increases; but you'll also notice that out of 300 words per minute we
don't lose much. As a matter of fact, the analysis showed that we
were unable to show evidence that the 300 wpm rate and the intermediate point did not differ significantly from the original, uncompressed, message effectiveness.

Figure 12 shows the same data plotted in the sense of message efficiency. Here the ordinate is the rate at which the tested
items were learned in terms of items presented per minute, there
being 60 total items for the two messages. The rate at which the
items were presented is shown along the abscissa, and this of course
increases to the right in terms of items per minute, the rightmost
point being the fastest compression case, and the leftmost being the
uncompressed case. If the rate of learning depended strictly on the
duration, that is, if the rate of learning were proportional to the
duration of the message, we would have line C because the rate
would stay the same irrespective of how we presented it. However,
if the rate of learning stayed constant in spite of acceleration, we
would have line B--that is to say, line B would describe the ideal
case where compression or acceleration of rate had no effect whatso-
ever. The A curve is, of course, the empirical function, and it
shows that for compressions of 0, 30, and 50 per cent, the A curve
is fairly close to the B curve. In short, the evidence suggests that
for factual comprehension of technical material, rates up to about
twice normal will pay their way in terms of increasing efficiency.
Beyond the 50 per cent compression point we fall off in efficiency.
In short, this suggests that if efficiency is what you're after, you can
present twice as much material in a given time, or we could present
the two messages in the time of one and we would not lose too much
in factual comprehension.

The next experiment that I want to refer to was rather interesting in its results. We took as the model the 30 per cent; of

course you have a net time of 70 per cent of the original. You're saving 30 per cent of the time. The obvious question is what do you do with that 30 per cent. Do you go out and have coffee, or what do you do with it? We decided that we were going to use this to do a study on selective verbal redundancy. Now the 30 per cent compression ratio permits us to put at the same rate of speech 43 per cent more words into that time saved; this is, the ratio of discarded to retained material, 30/70. Thus, with 30 per cent compression we would produce a message that had 43 per cent more words in it, but was equal to the original obtained time. You'll remember that in these two messages we had a 60-item test, a 30-item test on each of the two. We took 30 of the items from the representative message effectiveness levels and considered them to be control items. We took the remaining 30 items and considered them as experimental items. For the experimental items we went into the messages and identified the portions of the content that supported the factual information called for in each of the test items. We then divided up the 43 per cent of the words that we added, and we augmented the statement about each one of these content sections by reaffirming, by repeating in some cases to paraphrase or saying them in different ways. In other words, we added to the explanation about these experimental items, so that we then had 30 control items that were left unchanged, as in the material that I reported before, and we had 30 experimental items that had a total of 43 per cent added information. Thus we had what we will call a short version and a long version. We have a short version, the original message, and the long version with 43 per cent more words in it. Remember that we used 0 per cent compression with the original message, and a 30 per cent compression condition for the augmented version, and vice versa.

Now I think I'll skip a little bit. The bottom portion of Figure 13 shows the plan of the experiment. The zero point divides the message up into the control items at the bottom, and the experimental items at the top. This is just sort of a schematic of the experiment. Half the words are controlled; half the words are experimental; half the time is controlled; half the time is experimental in the uncompressed case. The dashed boxes indicate the long-version messages. We leave the controlled item alone, but we augment the experimental items by 43 per cent, both in words and in time in the uncompressed case shown on the left. On the right is shown the case of the time compression where we have the original message in 70 per cent of the original time and the augmented message in 100 per cent of the original time. The results are shown schematically at the top, and the things that we can see here are fairly obvious. The controlled and the experimental items match fairly well, that is, they are about equally learnable in the short version of the message. In the long version we have produced an increase in the comprehension of the experimental items, but we have a corresponding decrease in the comprehension of the controlled items. For 30 per cent compression the short version still produces about the same total comprehension as the uncompressed case, but the augmented message under compression again shows an increase of comprehension on the experimental items at the expense of the control items. We augment the compre-

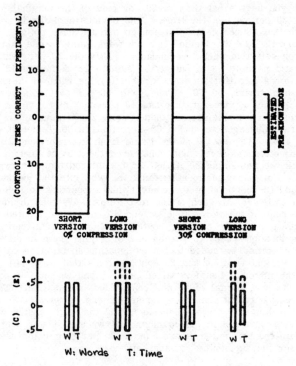

Figure 13. Diagramatic representation of experiments in learning efficiency of various message types.

hension of the experimental items, but we reduce the comprehension of the controlled items.

Now this is certainly an interesting result. First of all let me tell you the result of the statistical treatment. The difference between versions, the augmented and the unaugmented, was not significant. The difference between compressions was not significant. The items-by-version interaction was significant beyond the .001 level. That is, if you are talking about the controlled or the experimental items, you have to specify what version you are referring to --the short or the long. The difference between item classes, the controlled items vs. experimental items, was also significant. In other words, this audience of subjects was behaving much as a sponge would. A sponge doesn't care what kind of fluid it mops up, but it can only take so much, and thus these subjects apparently are operating rather like that. They are fairly well saturated. You can improve these items by increasing their redundancy, but you do it at the expense of taking away from the comprehension of the other items. This is a salutary piece of information, and it behooves us all to

note it well. It means that the more I say about a particular thing
now, the more you'll understand that thing, but at the expense of
something else that I devote less time to.

Now I want to go into the business of rate. I'd like to refer
here to the Ph. D. thesis of Hutton [B229], done under my direction
at Illinois, which had to do with the psychophysical aspects of rate,
partly in the compressed and expanded realm. Estimation of rate,
duration, and preference were the objects of concern in this problem.
A superior speaker produced numerous versions of the well-known
Rainbow Passage. An attempt was made to produce the passage at
widely varying rates, and from this range of rates to select a number of versions limited by one that was as short as 9. 6 seconds, and
one that was as long as 35. 3 seconds, where our long time average for
a large sample of speakers is 17. 2 seconds. Out of this range,
eight versions of the passage were picked to produce a geometric series in duration such that each one was 20 per cent longer in duration than the preceding one. Then the plan was to compress and expand these eight versions by 10 and 20 per cent. Thus, the passage
of a given duration could be expanded by 20 per cent in order to
make its duration like the one that had been originally produced next
higher. By expanding it 10 per cent in duration we would put it mid-
way between two of the original versions. The ordinate of Figure
14 shows the duration of the eight original readings. Phonation is
shown in the hashed bars at the bottom, and you'll see the familiar
phenomenon that has been insufficiently studied, in my estimation;
that is, as the total duration increases and the rate slows down, the

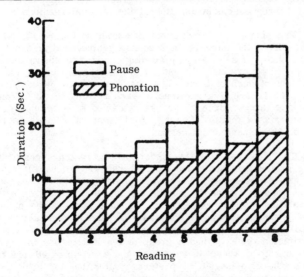

Figure 14.   Diagramatic presentation of problem in Hutton's thesis.

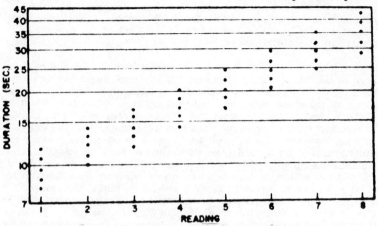

Figure 15.   Plan of Hutton's experiment.

proportion of phonation time to total time becomes smaller, or conversely, it becomes higher as rate increases.   A speaker with good
articulation was a condition of this experiment.   A speaker who is
interested in good articulation will speed up by taking it primarily
out of the pauses.   Sure he'll abbreviate his speech sounds, but there
comes a point where he cannot abbreviate them any longer and maintain good articulation so most of the time that he takes will come
out of the pauses.   This figure also graphically displays the regularity of the progression in duration of the original readings.

The plan of the experiment is shown in Figure 15, where the
ordinate shows the duration in seconds, geometrically, and the eight
readings that you saw in the preceding figure are shown along the
abscissa.   The original, 10 and 20 per cent compressed and expanded versions of each of these eight are represented by the plotted
points.   There are five versions of each reading in all.   You can
readily see that we have a successive series of overlapping durations.
There are, as a matter of fact, 19 different rate levels as represented in the experimental design.

The observers for this experiment were ten sophisticated listeners, graduate students and instructors, who were well practiced
in the art of observing.   They were given samples of these versions
taken at random out of the middle of the set of the 40 different versions to illustrate the extremes of the ends of the scale of duration
and rate, and to show what the scale of rates they would be hearing
were to be.   In addition to this group that judged rate and duration,
and estimated them we had a group of ten instructors who judged the
preferred rate of these 40 versions, and a group of 40 undergraduate
students who also judged the preferred rate; that is, made estimates
of the degree to which they preferred the rate and also estimated the
over-all effectiveness of the sample.   These latter two groups, the

ten instructors and the 40 undergraduates, did not differ significantly
so consequently the two groups were pooled for an N of 50 for the
rate preference judgments.

I'm not going to talk about the rate preferences, I'm going to
talk only about the estimate. The procedure was that these were ad-
ministrated to these people in random order and duration estimates
taken. They were given a graphic scale in time units ranging from
0 seconds up to 60 seconds; with various markers along for each
second, and their mode of judgment was for each passage reading.
They would make a mark as to what they judged the duration to have
been on this linear rating scale. The rate scale ranged from 1 to
9, 1 being slow, 9 being fast. They were told that the units of the
scale were equally separated, and, as I said, they were given examples of readings of the passages in both cases so they would know
about what range of durations and rates they could expect. Analysis
was made of these data for both the original and processed versions;
that is, the compressed and expanded versions vs. the original ones
that came out of the mouths of the talkers. The rate and duration
estimates of these did not differ significantly. Consequently, they
were pooled with respect to their duration, and so the figures that I
will show you now pertain to these 19 rate levels that were in common. In other words, the compressed and uncompressed messages
of equal duration were pooled.

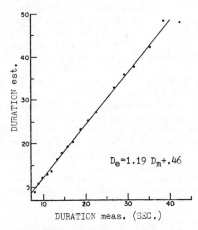

Figure 16. Message duration
compared to estimated duration.

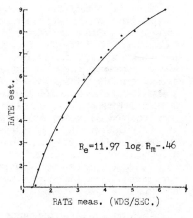

Figure 17. Message rate compared to estimated rate.

Figure 16 shows estimated durations ranging from ten seconds
at the bottom of the ordinate to 50 at the top vs. measured duration
along the abscissa. The 19 points are for the 19 rate levels, or
duration of rectilinearity. In other words, the observers are pretty

good judges of periods of time in this particular kind of task. Now Figure 17 shows estimated rate vs. measured rate. Note that the measured rate is in words per second with rate increasing toward the right. This is again logarithmic, the curve having been fitted by the least square criterion. The equation says that the estimated rate, the ordinate, is well approximated by 11.97 times the logarithm of the measured rate minus .46. In other words, given the rate in words per second, we may take roughly 12 times the logarithm of that rate in words per second and arrive at a nine-point scale value less .5 of what the estimated rate will be. A handy transformation to have.

I want to tell you about some of the preliminary considerations that guided an experiment I did shortly before I left Illinois. The actual experiment is very compact in its reporting, but I think it is a rather standardized sort of procedure that might be commended to your attention as an approach to other such estimates in realms other than that of temporal redundancy. In brief, the problem was to trade flat thermal noise for time. We have a lot of data on the estimation of temporal redundancies; some of it is pretty old, and some of it is pretty good. For instance, we know that the temporal redundancy or duration of a vowel in connected speech is far beyond the needed requirement. This is intrinsic to the nature of vowels so we might well ignore the steady states of vowels that are very long. In one of the technically very fine studies of Parmenter and Trevino, in 1935, oscillographic measurements of consonant and vowel durations were made. These investigators were sophisticated in picking the limits of the sound, and their mean vowel is about 120 milliseconds long in contrast to their mean consonant, which is about 80 milliseconds long, a difference factor of about 1.5. The data were collected from an extended sample of connected readings performed by one subject, but very well done. House and I, [B224] in a study of the effect of consonant environments in disyllabic nonsense syllables, the second syllable being stressed, found the mean duration for six stressed vowels to be 200 milliseconds, or roughly 1/5 of a second. Gordon Peterson, in 1939 [B323], did a study on the minimum duration required for vowel recognition and found the value to be as low as five milliseconds. From these studies we come out with an average representative value of about five milliseconds for duration up to a respectable maximum as high as 200 milliseconds. We realize now that the a priori guessing probability of the Peterson study is very high so that the minimum value derived from that study has to be viewed in that sense.

Vowels are not the place to look for temporal redundancy. I was interested in looking at consonants. For this reason, I developed the Rhyme Test with which some of you are familiar. The Rhyme Test was developed at this time because we felt that considerable information could be gleaned from a study of rather briskly spoken consonants in which the normal consonant-vowel transient effects were retained. The test thus constituted a representative situation for an estimation of the temporal redundancy of consonants. We also wanted, as much as possible, to eliminate some of the non-acoustic, nonphonemic, non-auditory sorts of things that we were referring to in the last hour, such features as word length, word familiarity, and so forth. Among these latter effects must be included the effect of the open or closed character of the vocabulary. This is a factor that probably contributes 20 to 25 per cent to the mid-range intelligibility score. That is, a closed set with known vocabulary in the mid-range contributes extensively to any obtained intelligibility score.

Now if we reduce these kinds of effects we should be able to make a more refined estimate of the pure consonant effect. We're going to expect, from what we know of previous data, to have a rather large temporal redundancy for words; we don't know yet about consonants. We did know that when the signal-to-noise ratio exceeds approximately 15 db, the maximum identification score of the Rhyme Test is not increased. So in trading noise for time we were working at values lower than 15 db, we thought. Also, from some of the pilot work at a signal-to-noise ratio of 15 db, we discovered very swiftly that compressing these words to 50 per cent of their original time did not degrade the intelligibility. Of course we know that from previous studies, but such might not have been obtained for the Rhyme Test, in which consonant and consonant-vowel transitions were in question

Clearly, it would be unrewarding to attempt to determine temporal redundancy at any point along the maximum-identification asymptote of 100 per cent intelligibility. The problem becomes much more difficult because of the very slow slope of the intelligibility function near maximum. You don't know, really, how to evaluate redundancy. On the other hand, where the function is fairly steep in the 50 per cent correct-identification range, we have a manageable value that is representative, reproducible, within the range, and much more useful for our purposes. Essentially our problem then was to discover that combination of the duration of words and noise that would yield 50 per cent correct identification. Our goal then was to trap this result within the experimental conditions. It took quite a bit of pilot work and quite a lot of preliminary experimentation before we decided on the exact values that it would be useful to use.

In Figure 18 you see the plan of the experiment. The left ordinate of the figure represents the percentage of the word that remains after compression. For instance, the top row would be the uncompressed version. At the lowest value, 17.5 per cent of the average word remained in the highest compression condition of 82.5 per cent, a very heavy compression indeed. The four compression values of the experiment were, then, 0, 50, 78.5, and 82.5 per cent.

Now to each of these was assigned a random form of the Rhyme Test. The Rhyme Test is a 50-word test using a limited number of identical stems with a fixed stimulus vocabulary. A form was assigned to each of these compressions. In all of these compressions I_d was 15 milliseconds. This means that the sampling frequency increased as a function of the amount of compression. Six signal-to-noise ratios were chosen, ranging from -9 up to 15, and

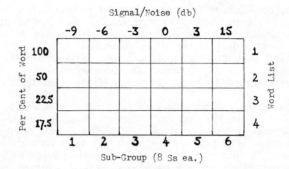

Figure 18.   Diagram of experiment in temporal redundancy.

---

are represented by the columns of the figure.   To each of these a
subgroup of eight observers was assigned.   The order of events at
the time of the experiment, which was administered over headsets in
half subgroup sections, four subjects at a time, was a constant signal-to-noise ratio for each subgroup across the compressed versions
in descending order.   This was preceded by training in a fifth random form of the Rhyme Test administered with a signal-to-noise ratio of 3 db, under which condition the obtained identification is approximately 75 per cent.   The signal level was about 65 db sensation
level; thermal noise was adjusted relative to the median vowel of the
list.   There were no carrier phrases used in this study; all words
were spoken in isolation.

In summary, then, we have 24 noise-by stimulus-duration combinations.   In each of these 24, the mean will be based on 400 re-
sponses--eight subjects times 50 words.   Our expectation will be that
when the compression is large and the signal-to-noise ratio is low,
we'll have low intelligibility.   When the compression is small and the
signal-to-noise ratio is high, high intelligibility should obtain.   We
seek the 50 per cent intelligibility point, that is our criterion, so we
will expect to find it by interpolation.   It will take fairly good noise
or compression to degrade intelligibility to 50 per cent, but hopefully
we will be able to trap the value by this set of combinations in the
matrix.

Figure 19 shows identification of the word, the word intelligibility, on the ordinate vs. the signal-to-noise ratio along the abscissa
with percentage word retained as the parameter.   You'll remember
that the subgroups of subjects were assigned by signal-to-noise ratio.
Thus, each column of plotted points corresponds to the values of one
subgroup; the lines are drawn across subgroups by compression.
You'll notice that when we compress to 17.5 per cent of the original
word we get the lowest intelligibility values, from 22.5 per cent at
-9 S/N to 60 at 15 S/N.   Some of you will have noted that the 50
per cent compression version up at the top end is higher than the 100
per cent version.   This is not because compression improves intelli-

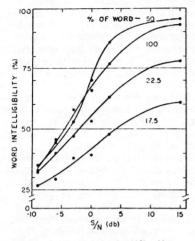

Figure 19. Word identification
in relation to signal-to-noise ratio and degree of compression.

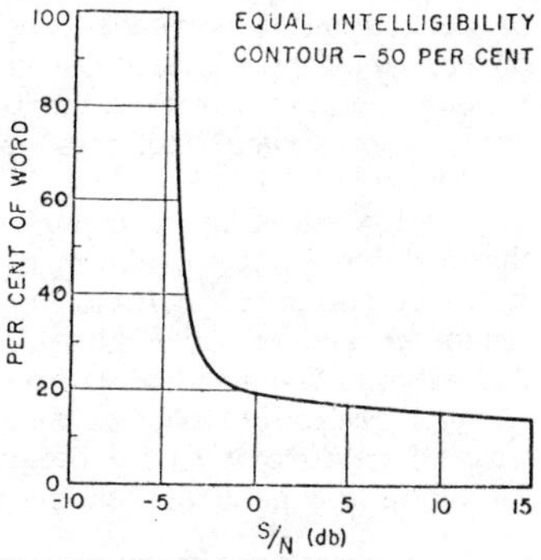

Figure 20.   Intelligibility of 50
per cent in relation to signal-to-
noise ratio and degree of compression.

gibility.   This is because different word lists were assigned to these
different compression values, and it merely means that toward the
high end this particular form of the Rhyme Test yielded higher intelligibility than the others.   Our problem is the specification of these
combinations of the experimental conditions which produce an intelligibility value represented by the 50 per cent horizontal of the graph.
So our problem is one of interpolation.

Figure 20 will show the results.   In this figure you see the
50 per cent equal intelligibility contour.   The ordinate is the percentage of the word that remains after experimental manipulation.   The
abscissa is signal-to-noise ratio, and you'll observe that at approximately -4.5 db the uncompressed version yields 50 per cent intelligibility.   You'll also notice that with increasing compression the curve
descends almost vertically, until you get to approximately 75 per cent
compression, and then you turn the corner and begin to require increasing signal strengths.   Now we're about where we want to get.
We drop fairly straight in duration to about 25 per cent of the duration of the original word.   This value occurs roughly at the signal-
to-noise ratio of -2.5 db.   We therefore proposed that where this
corner is turned, we could specify the value exactly by some treatment combination, but it is not neccessary that we do so.   We proposed that the treatment condition producing this sharp corner of the
function is the condition that will provide us with an estimate of the
temporal redundancy.   On that basis, I estimate that the temporal
redundancy of the consonants and the consonant-vowel transition elements of the language are of the order of 75 per cent.   Cautiously

stated, this means that when the noise level is such as to yield 50
per cent intelligibility with a normal signal, the duration can be reduced about 75 per cent before a substantial decrease in the noise
or a substantial increase in signal strength is necessary to maintain
50 per cent intelligibility. In concluding a review of this experiment,
I would remind you that the temporal redundancy of vowels is very,
very much larger than this, probably in the order of 25 to 1.

    I would like to report one final experiment in this program
that relates to the problem of compressing a message, transmitting
it in its compressed form, and then reconstructing the message at
the other end of the channel. This experiment is a little difficult to
describe. The general purpose will be to pass a signal through a
channel of limited bandwidths. After limiting the channel in this way,
we will restore it to its original bandwidth at the other end. Figure
21 shows the general scheme of the process. Time is displayed
along the abscissa, frequency
along the ordinate. The lines
are quite arbitrary. They're
designed to show some of the
changes in formants to be expected in connected speech. For
instance, the first line of the
lower figure could represent a
change in the fundamental. The
next line might be formant 1,
the next formant 2, and so on.
In compression you will remember that we periodically extract
a piece and throw the next piece
away. The diagram assumes
that compression is 50 per cent.
That is, the discard and the
sampling intervals are equal. If
in the original message, sche-
matized by the lower figure, we
take the first half of the first
formant, for instance, and divide
it by two, and stretch it in time
by two so that the frequencies
are halved, we would have something like that displayed in the
middle figure. In other words,
we now would have a sampled
and divided version in the origi-

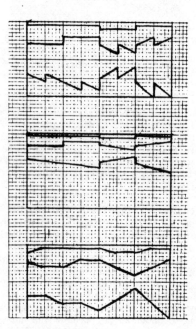

Figure 21. Schematic representation of bandwidth compression.

nal time. We now have the signal displayed in half the bandwidth, but it's in the same time.
At the receiver we have only half
of the original material. But we can use the material that we have
saved, and from it reconstruct the original message. Obviously the
discard interval has to be appropriately short so that we don't irre-
trievably throw away material. The upper figure schematizes the

reconstruction which might be made from the sampled transmission. The reconstruction is accomplished by the simple expedient of repeating the small segments of the material which were preserved in the transmission. This expanded reconstruction is then reproduced at higher speed in order to restore the original bandwidth and the original total time. I have purposely shown the reconstruction of the upper figure as being rather hashed up, a situation to be expected when restoration is based upon so little of the original signal.

Now the experiment.

In this experiment I used five PB lists. One talker rendered these lists with average effort, unmetered at a sound-pressure level of about 79 db. A carrier phrase, used for each word, turned out to be rather successful, and I commend it to you: "Copy --------- in a line." Both carrier and word were spoken quite briskly. You notice that the test word is bounded in the carrier phrase by essentially the same phoneme on both ends, so that the influences attributable to context should not be very strong. The sound-pressure range of the 250 words was 8 db and the list with highest median sound pressure was only 9/10 of a db higher than the median of the list with lowest sound pressure.

The plan of the experiment is shown in Figure 22. The flow arrows represent the treatment conditions for two independent groups of observers. The speech was first passed through the compression

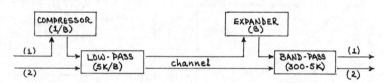

Figure 22. Diagramatic representation of experiment in reconstituting compressed words to original length.

device for Group 1, then through a 5 KC low-pass filter, and expander, and finally a .3 to 5 KC band-pass filter. For Group 2 the signal was not processed in this manner; it was simply transmitted directly into the channel, cropped at the upper end by the low-pass filter, passed through the channel, and presented to the band-pass filter at the other end. Both filters had 36 db per octave slopes.

Essentially, our problem is to compare the performances of the two groups. But first it is essential that we define a couple of units. I think that everything is clear with the exception of the symbol B. B is the band-width-reduction factor, the amount by which the signal is divided in compression or multiplied in expansion. It is also equal to the reciprocal of $1 - R_e$, namely $1/1 - R_e$ (R_e being the compression ratio). In the uncompressed case, B has the value of 1 and the channel bandwidth is 5K/1, and that was the value of the low-pass filter across the channel. In the second instance B was 2, the value of the low-pass filter was 2,500, in the third case it was 4, with a low-pass filter of 1,250, for B = 6 the filter was 833, and the final case, where B = 8, the filter was 625, for a total of five different channel bandwidths. In Group 1 we're going to divide the frequency so that it will duck under the upper limit of the channel bandwidth. In this case the sampling frequency that was used was 20 cycles for compression, and 90 cycles for expansion. One PB list was assigned to each of these five conditions. The procedure was as follows: In each of groups 1 and 2 there were 20 subjects. They were divided into five subgroups of four subjects each, according to a Latin Square design, in which five different orders of presentation of the B value conditions were employed, one order for each subgroup. The constraints of such a design are that in any given row or column of the Latin Square, one, and only one, of the five experimental conditions will appear. Each experimental condition is thus presented to each subject only once. Each subject heard each word only once, and he heard all the words from the five lists of vocabulary. The words were presented at about 65 db sensation level calculated on the basis of the median word, the response was written down, the administration was by means of headsets in subgroups of four. The design was used for both groups.

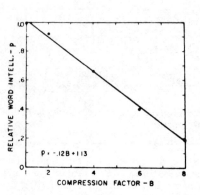

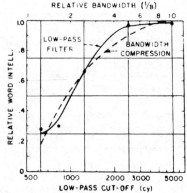

Figure 23. Relationship between compression factor and probability of word intelligibility.

Figure 24. Variance in intelligibility as a factor of low-pass filter cut-off.

Figure 23 is a plot of the probability of word intelligibility vs. the compression factor B, the amount by which the signal was divided or by which the channel was cropped. The plot summarizes the data obtained from Group 1. As you see, the empirical points are well fitted by a straight line of .12 B slope. These data suggest that factor B, in this particular use, is essentially an infrasonic high-pass filter system. That is, the cutoff frequency of this infrasonic filter is proportional to the value of B, and we see that intelligibility falls as the cutoff frequency rises in this infrasonic range. The reason I say this is that we are getting longer and longer values of I_d, so that we are starting to throw away significant chunks of the speech. The other reason I say this is that we're rolling the lower end of these frequencies off the bottom of the system as we divide them on down, and once we roll them off the bottom of the system we don't get them back. So essentially, the data show the effect of a high-pass filter operating at very low frequencies, even though the channel is limited by a low-pass filter.

The unbroken line of Figure 24 will show how intelligibility varies as a function of the low-pass filter cutoff. Across the top of the figure are the frequency values resulting from the division process that correspond to the bandwidths employed. The solid curve is similar to the old work that the Bell Laboratory has reported and that Hirsh and his followers did on the effect of filtering on word intelligibility. You'll notice that the curve rises in a fairly familiar way at about 1,000 cycles, yielding intelligibility of 50 per cent. Those of you who are familiar with this kind of function will recognize that some of these scores are somewhat higher than are often found with low-pass filter systems. The reason for these higher values is that it was a condition of the experiment that the level be raised on up to the original level for each filtering condition. If you'll study the old orthotelephonic response curves you will realize that as they lower the frequency of the low-pass filter, the total strength of the signal also decreases as the energy is cut out. In this experiment we equalized the signal level because we wanted to simulate a system in which such a condition would be assumed. It might be argued, in fact, that this is the way to study the effects of filtering on speech. At any rate, the shape of the function is typical.

The broken line of Figure 24 is derived from the previous figure but converted now to frequency. From the proximity of the two curves, it seems that we're doing about the same things in these two systems. The one is a low-pass system and the other is essentially a high-pass system. In the compression reconstruction the highs are not lost; we divide them down and they pass under the upper end of the low-pass filter and then come on back up at the other end. Now there are a lot of interesting things that one can say about this. First of all, we know that the intelligibility lost from these two different kinds of effects is not additive. In other words, if we put a signal through a low-pass filter and we lose 25 per cent of the word, the sum of these is not the proper statistic to express how they would operate if jointly employed. Not only do we think that they are theoretically independent but the empirical data obtained from many compression studies in which material was cropped from 2,000 cycles low-pass up to 10,000 cycles low-pass also show the effect. If the two effects were independent, it follows that cascading the two should produce a probability of item identification for the

over-all system which would be approximately equal to the product
of the probability of the low-pass system times the probability of the
bandwidth compression. This gives us something to test, and we
would propose to construct an experiment based on the proposition
that the effects of these two methods of compressing the signal are
not additive, but multiplicative.

We'll start with a low-pass filter, and in developing this illustration B will be equal to four; I'll just assume the frequencies
will be divided by four. The highest value of the low-pass filter
will again be 5,000 cycles because that seems to be useful bandwidth
for intelligibility. We're going to divide this by B, the bandwidth
factor, which is to say we're going to multiply it by the reciprocal
of B, and if we do this, filter will yield an output that has an upper
limit of 1,250 cycles when B = 4. In the previous work in which
we transmitted this signal through the low-pass filter for Group 2 at
1,250 cycles, the obtained intelligibility was 66 per cent. The obtained intelligibility for Group 1 exposed to the bandwidth-compres-
sion condition when B = 4 was .66 as well, as you will recall. Now,
if our theorem holds that the net probability of the combined system
is the product of the probabilities of the two separate systems, then
we should expect a net probability of approximately .44 when B = 4.
For every combination of the first study in which the systems were
independent, this kind of prediction was made for the combined systems.

Figure 25 displays the predicted intelligibility function for the
combined system. Now you'll notice several interesting things about
this combined system. First of all, we reduce its slope. The original slopes of the separate system are about 25 per cent per octave.
We now have a slope that is of the order of 50 per cent per octave.
The second interesting thing is, if we were to use 1,000 cycles as
our arbitrary channel bandwidth, we would find that instead of getting
50 per cent intelligibility out of a 1,000-cycle bandwidth channel, we
would get something closer to 80 per cent intelligibility out of that
same channel in the combined system. If we want to use our familiar criteria of 50 per cent intelligibility, the curve for the combined
system predicts that we will find that instead of needing about 1,000
cycles of bandwidth, we will only need about 350 cycles of bandwidth.
If we come up higher to a useful value of intelligibility such as 75
per cent, we will find 75 per cent intelligibility at a bandwidth of approximately 750 cycles instead of at a bandwidth of 1,400 cycles in
the separate systems. I haven't completed the experiment, so we
don't have the empirical validation, but the theory is the important
thing. That is, the idea that if we operate on the signal in a combined way with modes that are truly independent, then the loss will
not be additive but, instead, will be derived from some function of
the product of the separate probabilities. This is the basic proposition. As I started out by saying, at this moment I am less intereste
in the factual results than I am in some of the conceptions of the experimental attacks, valid or invalid, right or wrong, fruitful or un-
fruitful. This is dirty, hard-nosed research in the laboratory.

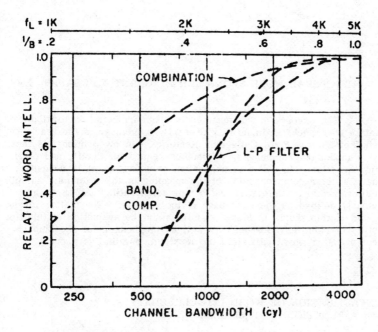

Figure 25. Diagramatic representation of bandwidth compression combined with time compression.

Chapter 8

DOCTORAL WORK SPONSORED BY GRANT FAIRBANKS, 1

The excerpt in this chapter is taken from the doctoral dissertation of Francis Kodman Jr., presently a member of the teaching
staff of Murray State College in Kentucky. In my opinion this thesis
is a model of preciseness, meticulous regard for detail, and clarity
in exposition. In order to understand this passage it is necessary to
have a clear comprehension of the meaning of three terms: sampling
interval, discard interval, and compression ratio. All three are
clearly defined on the first page of the excerpt. The matter investigated in this thesis is highly significant in the evaluation of intelligibility of compressed speech as well as in planning for the kind of
compression which will yield the maximum intelligible product.

INVESTIGATION OF WORD INTELLIGIBILITY
AS A FUNCTION OF TIME COMPRESSION

Francis Kodman, Jr.

In a comparatively recent and extensive study of the intelligibility of interrupted speech, Miller and Licklider [B283] found that
considerable amounts of the speech signal could be removed without
appreciably affecting intelligibility. Their method did not alter the
total elapsed time of speech, but reduced the total duration of the
signal presented to observers. The percentage of the reduction was
the total time that the signal was interrupted divided by the total
time of the signal. More recently, Fairbanks, Everitt and Jaeger
[B105] have described and demonstrated an automatic device which
compresses the duration of speech by periodically sampling the signal
and abutting the retained segments without discontinuity. Effectively
this is like the periodic interruption technique employed by Miller and
Licklider, but without the pauses between the samples.

In this method the sampling interval (I_S) is the duration of the
sample and the discard interval (I_d) is the duration of the discarded
portion, the sum of the two being termed the sampling period (T_S).
The proportion of the signal discarded is the compression ratio (R_c)
defined as I_d/T_S, and 100 times this ratio is referred to as the
compression percentage. The frequency of sampling of the original
signal is called the sampling frequency (f_S) and equals $1/T_S$. The
interruption frequency (f_i), the frequency at which f_S is reproduced at

the final stage of the process, equals $1/I_S$. It is the particular purpose of the present experiment to explore the relationships between word intelligibility and automatic time compression by varying the compression ratio at each of a number of selected values of discard and sampling intervals.

The fundamental premise of time compression applied to speech has been described by Fairbanks et al. as dependent "upon the fact that the duration of the average speech element ... of live connected speech ... exceeds the minimum duration necessary for sampling the essential phonemic qualities of the speech element in question" [B105]. Goldstein [B193], in a study of reading comprehension as a function of rate, reported that the speaker he used could not read satisfactorily above 285 words per minute and that he was unable to investigate the upper limits of fast speech even with an additional recorded speed-up. Making an allowance for time spent in pause, the average duration of each sound at his speaker's fastest rate was approximately .05 sec. On the other hand, a listener is able to identify a vowel in less than .01 sec., according to the work of G. E. Peterson ["Systematic Research in Experimental Phonetics: 4. The Evaluation of Speech Signals," Journal of Speech and Hearing Disorders 19:158-68, 1954].

During the early stages of work on time compression, Fairbanks showed informally by periodically cutting and splicing magnetic tape that more than 50 per cent of the signal could be discarded without destroying intelligibility. Using the same technique, Garvey [B167, B168, B169] and Garvey and Henneman [B171] also investigated intelligibility in a group of formal experiments, finding similar results for spondaic words. It was reported, for example, that 50 per cent of each word could be removed with a loss of approximately 15 per cent intelligibility. Earlier the effect of shortening signal time by the process of speeded playback was studied by Fletcher [B114] and Steinberg who reported that intelligibility began to drop below 80 per cent when the ratio of speed-up was approximately 1.5. It will be noted that the latter method, unlike the present one, involved multiplication of all the signal frequencies as well as shortening of the listening time.

Plan of the Experiment

The general plan was to select a representative set of compression ratios at each of several discard intervals, process the same group of words under each of these conditions, and present each of the processed versions of the words to the same group of trained observers. The 36 experimental conditions that were selected are shown in Table 1, where it can be seen that compression ratios ranged from .4 to .9 and discard intervals from .01 to .24 second. Table 2 shows the corresponding sampling intervals, sampling periods, sampling frequencies and interruption frequencies. Study of the values will show the manner and range of variation in each variable. The compression ratio was extended to .9 at all five values of I_d,

Table 1

TIME COMPRESSION RATIOS AND DISCARD INTERVALS
USED IN THE EXPERIMENT

Compression Ratio	Discard Interval (sec.)				
	.01	.04	.08	.16	.24
.40				x	
.45					
.50	x			x	
.55					
.60	x			x	x
.65	x	x	x	x	x
.70	x	x	x	x	x
.75	x	x	x	x	x
.80	x	x	x	x	x
.85	x	x	x	x	x
.90	x	x	x	x	x

exploration having shown that intelligibility was low but appreciable
at this compression. Each lower limit was selected to yield a percentage of intelligibility at the expected maximum for the discard interval in question. These limits varied as shown and also were selected on the basis of exploration. The spacing of the intermediate
values of R_c was likewise determined by preliminary trial. The results indicated that these choices were generally satisfactory, although more values of R_c were used than necessary, and values in
excess of .9 would have been useful at some of the discard intervals.

Basic Materials

The 50 words used were from the well-known PB-50 series.
This series was constructed to approximate the following characteristics: monosyllabic structure, equal average difficulty, equal range of
difficulty, equal phonetic composition, a composition representative of
English speech and words in common usage. In general construction
these words are distributed as follows:

	N
Consonant-Vowel	4
Vowel-Consonant	4
Consonant-Vowel-Consonant	25
Consonant-Vowel-Consonant Cluster	9
Consonant Cluster-Vowel-Consonant	7
Consonant Cluster-Vowel-Consonant Cluster	1

An uncompressed master tape recording was made of the words as
spoken by a mature adult male with superior articulation who speaks
the General American dialect natively and habitually.

Table 2

SAMPLING INTERVALS (sec.), SAMPLING PERIODS (sec.), SAM-
PLING FREQUENCIES (cps) AND INTERRUPTION FREQUENCIES (cps)
CORRESPONDING TO THE COMPRESSION RATIOS AND DISCARD
RATIOS USED

R_c	Discard Interval .01 Sec.				Discard Interval .04 Sec.			
	I_s	T_s	f_s	f_i	I_s	T_s	f_s	f_i
.50	.010	.020	50.0	100				
.60	.007	.017	60.0	150				
.65	.005	.015	65.0	186	.022	.062	16.3	46.4
.70	.004	.014	70.0	233	.017	.057	17.5	58.3
.75	.003	.013	75.0	300	.013	.053	18.75	75.0
.80	.0025	.0125	80.0	400	.010	.050	20.0	100.0
.85	.0018	.0118	85.0	567	.007	.047	21.25	142.0
.90	.0011	.0111	90.0	900	.004	.044	22.5	225.0

R_c	Discard Interval .08 Sec.				Discard Interval .16 Sec.			
	I_s	T_s	f_s	f_i	I_s	T_s	f_s	f_i
.40					.240	.400	2.50	4.17
.50					.160	.320	3.13	6.25
.60					.107	.267	3.75	9.38
.65	.043	.123	8.13	23.2	.086	.246	4.06	11.6
.70	.034	.114	8.75	29.2	.069	.229	4.38	14.6
.75	.027	.107	9.38	37.5	.053	.213	4.69	18.8
.80	.020	.100	10.0	50.0	.040	.200	5.00	25.0
.85	.014	.094	10.6	70.0	.028	.188	5.31	35.4
.90	.009	.089	11.3	113.0	.018	.178	5.63	56.3

R_c	Discard Interval .24 Sec.			
	I_s	T_s	f_s	f_i
.60	.160	.400	2.50	6.25
.65	.129	.369	2.71	7.74
.70	.103	.343	2.92	9.72
.75	.080	.320	3.13	12.5
.80	.060	.300	3.33	16.7
.85	.042	.282	3.54	23.6
.90	.027	.267	3.75	37.5

Observers

Eight young adults were selected from among the available observers. All were advanced graduate students with previous experience as observers, who had normal hearing. Since the primary task was concerned with speech, the master recording of the word list was administered under laboratory conditions as a supra-threshold discrimination test at a sensation level of approximately 80 decibels, the criterion of acceptance as an observer being 100 per cent identification.

The data were collected in 12 experimental sessions distributed over six weeks. One discard interval was completed at a time in the order: .01 (initial), .04, .08, .16, .01 (repeated) and .24 sec. The tests were scored after each discard interval was completed and the results used to determine the next set of values. It is not believed that the consequent regularity of order for all subjects seriously disturbed the results. For each discard interval two sessions were held. At the first one the versions were presented in order of progressively increasing compression (descension toward the word intelligibility threshold); at the second the order was reversed (ascension toward threshold). Earphones were rotated systematically.

The observers were seated in tablet armchairs facing away from each other and tested four at a time. Responses were written and listening was binaural. At each session the observers were rested between compression versions. Prior to the first experimental session the following instructions were read.

> Listen carefully to each word. Each will be preceded by
> a carrier phrase as in the previous discrimination test.
> If you hear only part of the word (i. e., a vowel or conso-
> nant) write down what you hear. Do not go back and fill
> in any of the blank spaces. There is a three-second pause
> between each word. Follow the numbers on the scoring
> sheet. Begin when the red light flashes.

Training of the Observers

Since the same test list and the same observers were used in all experimental conditions, a pre-experimental training period was employed. Immediately prior to the first experimental session, the observers were given a typed list of the words in the same random order as on the master tape and instructed to familiarize themselves with the spelling and pronunciation of each word. They were then instructed to read the list silently word by word as they listened simultaneously to three non-experimental versions of the list at .1, .2 and .3 compression ratios, amounts of compression which had no effect whatever on percentage of intelligibility. Since the observers also had heard the list presented without compression during the screening procedure, they thus had four presentations of the recorded words prior to the first experimental tape, during three of which they

also observed the written list.   Following this they then recorded responses to the first .01 discard interval versions in order of increasing compression.   As will be reported below, it was not until
R_c reached .75 that intelligibility was affected.   Therefore, the observers heard the words with perfect intelligibility an additional four
times.   This comprised a total of eight times prior to invasion of
intelligibility by compression.   During the course of the experiment
the number of exposures to the list progressively increased.   The
following table shows the number prior to the start of each division
of the experiment.

.01 (initial	4
.04	20
.08	32
.16	44
.01 (repeated)	62
.24	78

The results of the first .01 series were analyzed at the time and
used as exploratory data.   Although these results will be presented
below, serious study was confined to the data collected for the repeated .01 series, since the number of exposures prior to the latter
was more comparable to those for the longer discard intervals.

Measurement of the Stimulus Materials

For purposes of interpretation of the results four measurements were made of each of the 50 words on the master (uncompressed) tape recording.   The results of these measurements are discussed below.   Duration measurements were made to the nearest .01
second from oscillograms made on locally constructed apparatus and
confirmed by spectograms.   The relative sound pressure of the vowel
of each word was measured to the nearest decibel by means of a
high-speed level recorder.   Inspection of the graphic records showed
that the maximum level was reached midway in the duration of each
word, which, together with the results of previous investigations, indicated that the vowel was being measured.   The number of "phonetic
units" was determined for each word from phonetic transcriptions
(see Table 3), but a variation from conventional practice was employed because of the manner in which the counts were to be used in
this particular study.   The variation consisted of counting each diphthong and affricate as contributing one and one-half units.   The de-
sire was to describe the "length" of each word in terms of the number of units, and it seemed unsatisfactory to weight [ʃ], [æ], [dʒ]
and [ɑʊ], for example, equally when the purpose of the count was to
assist interpretation of word identifications at near-threshold durations.   The procedure is arbitrary and is not necessarily applicable
to other circumstances.

The final measure had to do with the complex of factors that
are involved in the reconstruction or synthesis of a complete word
from knowledge of a fragment of it.   The situation which made the

Table 3. CHARACTERISTICS OF THE TEST WORDS

	Word	Tran-scription	Duration (sec)	Relative Pressure	Vowel (db)	Phonetic Units (N)	Inference Level (%)
1.	as	æz	.61	6		2.0	56
2.	badge	bædʒ	.63	7		3.5	88
3.	best	bɛst	.49	4		4.0	81
4.	bog	bɔg	.61	5		3.0	81
5.	chart	tʃɑrt	.62	5		4.5	88
6.	cloth	klɔθ	.72	5		4.0	81
7.	clothes	klouðz	.64	2		5.5	94
8.	cob	kab	.59	5		3.0	62
9.	crib	krɪb	.51	3		4.0	94
10.	dad	dæd	.59	7		3.0	88
11.	deep	dip	.51	5		3.0	69
12.	eat	it	.36	2		2.0	50
13.	eyes	ɑɪz	.62	3		2.5	69
14.	fall	fɔl	.71	4		3.0	88
15.	fee	fi	.58	4		2.0	62
16.	flick	flɪk	.60	3		4.0	81
17.	flop	flap	.51	3		4.0	75
18.	forge	fɔrdʒ	.71	3		4.5	69
19.	fowl	faul	.59	3		3.5	69
20.	gage	geidʒ	.68	9		4.0	75
21.	gap	gæp	.57	6		3.0	62
22.	grope	group	.57	3		4.5	94
23.	hitch	hɪtʃ	.50	1		3.5	88
24.	hull	hʌl	.53	2		3.0	62
25.	jag	dʒæg	.73	7		3.5	69
26.	kept	kɛpt	.72	3		4.0	88
27.	leg	leg	.54	6		3.0	94
28.	mash	mæʃ	.67	7		3.0	94
29.	nigh	nɑɪ	.61	4		2.5	62
30.	ode	oud	.58	6		2.5	69
31.	prig	prɪg	.55	7		4.0	75
32.	prime	prɑɪm	.59	2		4.5	88
33.	pun	pʌn	.45	2		3.0	88
34.	pus	pʌs	.48	2		3.0	44
35.	raise	reɪz	.72	5		3.5	50
36.	ray	reɪ	.60	3		2.5	69
37.	reap	rip	.40	3		3.0	75
38.	rooms	rumz	.66	4		4.0	94
39.	rough	rʌf	.54	5		3.0	88
40.	scan	skæn	.75	5		4.0	75
41.	shank	ʃæŋk	.64	5		4.0	62
42.	slouch	slɑutʃ	.71	3		5.0	81
43.	sup	sʌp	.48	5		3.0	88
44.	thigh	θɑɪ	.68	5		2.5	56
45.	thus	ðʌs	.49	3		3.0	50
46.	tongue	tʌŋ	.49	2		3.0	62
47.	wait	weɪt	.52	4		3.5	88
48.	wasp	wɔsp	.58	3		4.0	62
49.	wife	wɑɪf	.52	4		3.5	75
50.	writ	rɪt	.55	4		3.0	88

measure possible was the over-learning of items in the list by the observers.   By the end of the experiment each observer had heard the list 92 times under conditions in which he was concentrating on identifying the words.   During 89 of these times he also wrote each intelligible word.   Each observer, then, was undoubtedly very famil- iar with these particular 50 words by the end of the experiment. Data for this measure were collected after the psychophysical pro- cedures had been completed.   Each word was "fragmented" into eight versions.   With the understanding that <u>vowel</u> includes diphthongs, and <u>consonant</u>, consonant clusters, the fragments were:

	Examples
1. Entire word	<u>buk</u>
2. Initial consonant	<u>b</u>
3. Vowel	<u>u</u>
4. Final consonant	<u>k</u>
5. Initial consonant-vowel	<u>bu</u>
6. Initial consonant-final consonant	<u>bk</u>
7. Vowel-final consonant	<u>uk</u>
8. Entire word absent	<u> </u>

The versions were typed individually on 3 x 5 cards in pho- netic notation as shown in the above examples.   No information ap- peared on the card to indicate the position of the symbols in the word.   The resulting 400 versions were randomly assigned to eight sets of 50 cards each, each set containing one version of each word and the cards in each set being randomly ordered.   The cards were then presented to each observer individually.   He was oriented gen- erally and then formally instructed as follows:

> In the auditory experiment sometimes you heard the whole word and sometimes only a segment of the word.   In this part of the experiment you will have the identical situation shown by phonetic symbols.   You will be given a set of 50 cards; each representing a stimulus word.   Your task is to identify the word.   Work at your own speed.

> Let us suppose that the word <u>book</u> is the stimulus.   This word could appear in the following ways: <u>buk</u>, <u>b</u>, <u>u</u>, <u>bu</u>, <u>uk</u>, <u>k</u>, <u>bk</u>, <u>___</u>.

> Each set of cards has the same 50 words you have been listening to in the auditory experiment.   Select the first card from the set.   Imagine you hear what is on the card. Try to identify the word correctly from the information on the card just as you have been doing in the auditory ex- periment.

It will be seen that a variety of scoring options were available and the results of some of them are reported below.

RESULTS

Word Intelligibility as Function of Time Compression and Discard Interval

The major findings are presented in Table 4 which shows the mean intelligibility for the 36 experimental conditions. (The corresponding standard deviations are shown in Table 5, the calculations being confined to those distributions in which the mean was sufficiently lower than 100 per cent to be meaningful.) It will be observed in Table 4, columns two and three, that parallel values are reported

Table 4

MEAN PERCENTAGES OF WORD INTELLIGIBILITY AT VARIOUS TIME COMPRESSION RATIOS AND DISCARD INTERVALS

Compression Ratio	Discard Interval (sec.)					
	.01*	.01**	.04	.08	.16	.24
.40					85.75	
.50	100.00	100.00			84.62	
.60	100.00	100.00			86.62	71.50
.65	99.62	100.00	98.75	98.50	85.62	71.12
.70	98.35	99.25	98.00	97.88	83.88	68.25
.75	91.88	98.62	98.00	97.75	75.62	60.88
.80	72.38	90.12	93.75	95.12	74.38	54.75
.85	35.25	72.12	72.75	88.12	55.75	41.50
.90	2.50	15.38	55.5	47.38	37.75	21.12

*Initial.   **Repeated.

for both of the .01 discard interval series. The first of these was used for exploratory purposes and the discussions are confined to the second, or repeated, series for reasons stated previously. Comparison of the pairs of values for these two series will show that the second value is uniformly higher over the range of discrimination, as would be expected from the fact that the subjects had been exposed to the list 58 times between the two. At .80 and .85 compression, where the differences are large, their direction and magnitude are consistent with the findings of Egan regarding the effect of practice. The close similarity of the means for the initial .85 and repeated .80 compression ratios gives an idea of the difference in threshold attributable to practice and increased familiarity.

In the means of Table 4 the results of the ascending and descending orders for each discard interval are combined. This procedure was considered justifiable when separate scoring of the results for the initial .01 series resulted in the following percentages of intelligibility.

Compression Ratio	Compression Increasing	Compression Decreasing
.65	100.00	99.25
.70	99.00	97.70
.75	94.50	89.25
.80	77.25	67.50
.85	42.75	27.75
.90	3.50	1.50

The directions of the differences are uniform as would be expected. Separate treatment of the two orders throughout the analysis was deemed unnecessary, and pooling improved the estimates. The initial .01 series was used to estimate listener reliability. Reliability coefficients were computed for four compression conditions spanning the range of intelligibility from 98 to 35 per cent. The method of computation was an estimation of reliability coefficients using an analysis of variance technique. The coefficients were as follows:

R_c	% Intelligibility	r
.70	98.35	.97
.75	91.88	.92
.80	72.38	.92
.85	35.25	.85

The means presented in Table 4 have been displayed graphically in Figure 1, in which mean intelligibility is plotted as a function of compression ratio with separate curves for the discard intervals. It is understood that here, and in the other figures presented below, the intelligibility values for the second administration of the .01 series were used. It can be seen in Figure 1 that intelligibility decreased as R_c increased for all five curves. There is a tendency for the steepness of the intelligibility function to vary with the size of the discard interval. For the .01, .04 and .08 discard conditions, intelligibility does not become substantially smaller than 100 per cent until R_c exceeds .8, but for the .16 and .24 discard intervals, intelligibility at no time reaches 100 per cent at the conditions considered. In the case of the .16 discard interval, the long plateau is at approximately 85 per cent intelligibility, while for the .24 discard interval the highest value reached is about 70 per cent. Although it does not seem permissible to conclude that the maximum values for intelligibility were reached in the last two instances, it is believed that they will not become much larger until the compression percentage becomes very small. The .16 discard interval approaches and the .24 discard interval exceeds the mean duration of the sounds in the list as reported below. Thus entire sounds may be discarded under these two conditions often enough to keep intelligibility from reaching 100 per cent.

It is to be regretted that compression ratios sufficiently large to continue the downward inflections of the curves were not used. It can only be said that the amount of time compression that can be

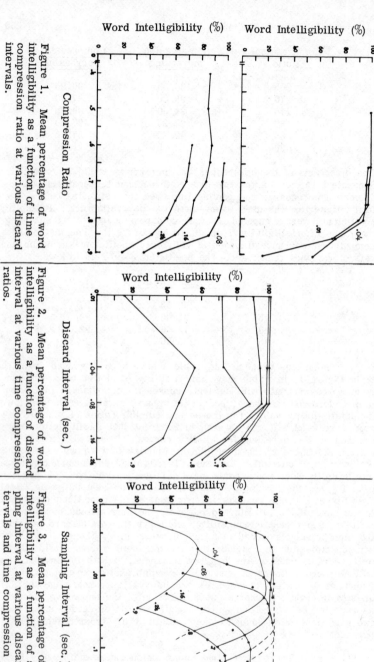

Word Intelligibility (%)

Word Intelligibility (%)

Compression Ratio

Figure 1. Mean percentage of word intelligibility as a function of time compression ratio at various discard intervals.

Word Intelligibility (%)

Discard Interval (sec.)

Figure 2. Mean percentage of word intelligibility as a function of discard interval at various time compression ratios.

Word Intelligibility (%)

Sampling Interval (sec.)

Figure 3. Mean percentage of word intelligibility as a function of sampling interval at various discard intervals and time compression ratios.

tolerated without destruction of intelligibility was underestimated substantially. The means of Table 4 have been re-plotted in Figure 2 in order to make the interaction between compression and discard interval more clear. In this figure percentage of word intelligibility has been plotted against discard interval displayed logarithmically, with separate curves for the various compression ratios.

At the top of Figure 2 it can be seen that the curves for compressions smaller than .8 are essentially parallel, do not differ much from each other, and descend in the expected order. For this group of curves it is seen that intelligibility remains close to 100 per cent at the small discard intervals, falling off steadily above .08.

The three curves with the highest compression ratios are somewhat different. Here, compression constant, intelligibility first rises and then falls as discard interval increases. The differences in the shapes of the upper and lower curves may be attributable to the interruption frequency. At the smaller discard intervals the frequency of interruption is getting sufficiently high that it is beginning to intrude into the significant range of the speech spectrum. It is seen in Table 2 that f_i for the three largest compressions of the .01 series was 400, 567, and 900 per second, respectively. Subjectively the impression was that the interruption frequency was noticeable only at the higher compressions and only when the discard interval was .01 sec.

Effects of Various Time Compression Ratios, Discard Intervals and Sampling Intervals upon Word Intelligibility

In Figure 3 the 36 means from Table 4 are plotted as a function of sampling interval, the experimental values being shown by the dots. The abscissa value for each point may be seen in Table 2. For example, the point in the lower left corner of Figure 3 is located at .0011 sec., this being the value of I_s which, combined with .01 sec. discard interval, produces a compression ratio of .90. The ascending curves have been smoothed through the experimental points for the five discard intervals and intersecting curves connect corresponding compression ratios. The lines are unbroken within the range of experimental values, while the dashed lines suggest a few possible extrapolations.

The curve for a given discard interval may be thought of as showing the change of word intelligibility as R_c decreases, or as the percentage of the signal retained increases from left to right. Essentially this is a re-plotting of Figure 1 with reversed and transformed abscissa. Again it is seen that intelligibility increased rapidly to 100 per cent for the three smaller discard intervals. These extrapolations are believed to be warranted on the basis of the exploratory runs and the obvious 100 per cent intelligibility of the .3 and .2 compression series which were used in the training of the observers. The extrapolations of the .16 and .24 curves at approximately 85 and 70 per cent, respectively, were made with less certainty.

The intersecting curves connecting points of equal time compression are analogous to the curves of Figure 2, but progressively displaced to the right as time compression decreases. Where these curves bend down at the right they have been extended beyond the data. It is predicted that they will level off and remain parallel to the base-line after I_S becomes sufficiently large, and that such plateaus will be at ordinate values at which the percentage of intelligibility is equal to 100 minus the compression percentage. Along the abscissa it is predicted that each plateau should be reached at a value of I_S that bears a relationship to the durations of the units (e.g., words) in question. This should vary systematically with the amount of compression. In the case of the present words, for example, the median duration was approximately .6 sec. When the curve for the .5 compression ratio, in which I_S and I_d are equal by definition, reaches this point on the abscissa, the intelligibility ratio also should be .5 and should not decrease further with larger sampling and discard intervals. It should not, however, increase, since the same percentage of the signal will be discarded.

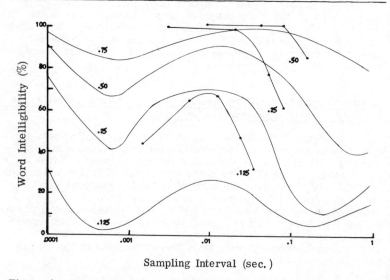

Sampling Interval (sec.)

Figure 4. Mean percentage of intelligibility as a function of sampling interval for representative retained portions of the signal. Lighter lines adapted from Miller and Licklider [B283].

Three similar curves of equal compression are shown in Figure 4. The upper two were taken directly from Figure 3, while the lower curve was obtained by interpolation. The labels show the values of $1 - R_C$. The four curves shown in lighter line are from the work of Miller and Licklider [B283]. Although that study did not involve time compression, one variable was the "speech-time fraction, " the percentage of signal presented to the subject, analogous to $1 - R_C$ of the present study. Another variable was the frequency of interruption which is analogous to the reciprocal of the sampling interval in the present study. The data of Miller and Licklider were converted to the present units for purposes of Figure 4.

The two sets of curves have certain obvious similarities, such as the location of the peak in the lowest pair of curves. It will also be noted that corresponding curves are inflected downward similarly at the right. It will be observed that in all four of the Miller-Licklider curves the percentage of intelligibility is approaching the speech-time fraction at the long sampling intervals. At the short sampling intervals, just as in the case of the present study, the percentage of intelligibility exceeds the speech-time fraction. An interesting aspect of the comparison is the uniformly higher location of the curves of the present study. With due regard to the differences in apparatus and method, it is suggested that this can be attributed to the elimination or reduction of modulation by the frequency of interruption during compression as compared to the flip-flop interruption technique.

Equal Intelligibility Contours

In Figure 5 smoothed equal intelligibility contours within the range of the experimental values are presented. In the upper portion $1 - R_C$ is plotted versus I_d and in the lower portion versus I_S. The dots show the data of Table 6. The values of R_C were obtained by interpolation into the means of Table 4 to determine the value which would yield the intelligibility in question. The corresponding sampling intervals were calculated therefrom. The values of R_C in Table 6 might be visualized as obtained by drawing horizontal lines across Figure 1 and reading the abscissa at the intersections. The 70 per cent contours for both upper and lower curves are probably illustrative of the general character of the functions. The typical curve appears to drop slowly to a minimum at a discard interval of about .1 sec., and a sampling interval of about .01 sec. Above these points a given intelligibility requires a progressively increasing percentage of the signal.

Extrapolations of the curves can be envisioned along lines discussed above. At larger values of I_d and I_S the curves should ultimately reach plateaus at levels of $1 - R_C$ corresponding to their respective percentages of intelligibility; at smaller values they should lower slightly. In general terms the levels of the curves at the left show the amount of time compression that can be tolerated. The percentage of intelligibility is approximately five times greater than the percentage of the original signal's duration. The curves of Figure 1 show that the lowest contour for 100 per cent intelligibility would not be far from the .3 level if it were drawn. It is suggested, therefore, that the temporal redundancy of speech, as sampled by words for this experiment and subject to the special conditions of this experiment, may be estimated at approximately 70 per cent.

Table 5

STANDARD DEVIATIONS OF WORD INTELLIGIBILITY AT VARIOUS TIME COMPRESSION RATIOS AND DISCARD INTERVALS

Compression Ratio	Discard Interval (sec.)					
	.01*	.01**	.04	.08	.16	.24
.40					20.18	
.50					20.90	
.60					19.35	28.22
.65					17.64	30.54
.70	10.63				18.94	35.46
.75	14.47	14.61	10.07		24.39	33.26
.80	24.14	25.26	24.73	8.58	27.18	31.90
.85		22.60	24.41	13.48	29.16	26.18
.90				24.43	29.52	20.70

*Initial. **Repeated.

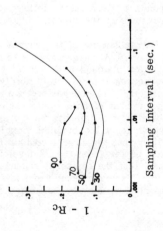

Figure 5. Equal intelligibility contours (see text).

Relationships between Intelligibilities of Individual Words and Certain
Word Characteristics

It is the general purpose of this section to inquire into the
interrelationships between intelligibility, time compression and other
objective characteristics of the test words. Since compression essentially shortens the duration of the individual words and reduces
their intelligibility thereby, one question that arises is whether or
not words of longer duration tolerate more compression than shorter
words₊ Further, it might be expected that to a certain extent one
could "trade" intensity and duration. If two words equal in duration,
but differing in vowel pressure, were presented, the one with the
higher pressure might be expected to be more intelligible.

The bases for such exploration were the measurements of the
individual words which have been described. The results of these
measurements were given in Table 5 for each of the 50 words, together with a transcription of each word as spoken for the master
tape. The cumulative frequency distributions for each measure are
shown in Figure 6, the four graphs having a common ordinate, namely, percentage of the total words. Study of Figure 6A will show that
duration ranged from .36 to .75 sec. with a median of approximately
.6 sec. The distribution is seen to be reasonably normal. The
mean duration per phoneme was .18 sec. These values are some-

---

Table 6

TIME COMPRESSION RATIOS, SAMPLING AND DISCARD INTERVALS
FOR FOUR EQUAL INTELLIGIBILITY CONTOURS

Discard Interval	% Word Intelligibility			
	30	50	70	90
.01 R_c	.89	.87	.85	.80
I_s	.0012	.0015	.0015	.0025
.04 R_c			.86	.81
I_s			.007	.009
.08 R_c		.90	.87	.84
I_s		.009	.012	.015
.16 R_c		.87	.81	
I_s		.024	.038	
.24 R_c	.88	.82	.67	
I_s	.033	.053	.118	

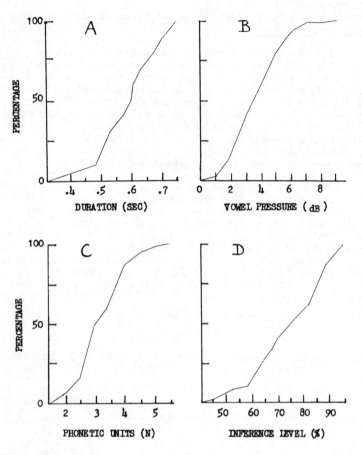

Figure 6.   Cumulative frequency distributions of four word characteristics.

what in excess of those obtained for connected speech, but are almost identical to those reported by Miller and Licklider [B283] for similar spoken monosyllables. In producing the list the talker apparently spoke the words quite deliberately, more so than is habitual for him in connected speech. It is probable that in connected material these same words would approximate a mean duration about onehalf as long.

It will be recalled that the master list was recorded under conditions in which the speaker monitored his output visually and attempted to approximate constancy from word to word, although without special effort to enforce this requirement rigidly. From Figure

6B it can be seen that the obtained vowel pressures were distributed fairly normally over an eight decibel range. Study of the phonetic transcriptions in Table 3 will show that the 50 words included a total of 36 vowels, 14 diphthongs and 110 consonants, or an average of 3.2 sounds per word. The individual word values given in column four are for the number of phonetic units, employing the variation described above in which a weight of one and one-half units was given to each diphthong and affricate. The distribution of these values is shown graphically in Figure 6C. There it may be seen that the 50 words ranged from 2.0 to 5.5 units with a median of three units and approximate a normal distribution. The mean is 3.4 units, very close to that for the conventional count.

It will be recalled that the observers were presented with phonetically transcribed fragments of the words and instructed to proceed with an identification task according to procedures that have been detailed above. For each of the 50 words the stimuli consisted of eight versions ranging from the whole word down to a blank card. Since the words varied in length (e. g. , from eat to clothes), each of the 400 versions was expressed in terms of the percentage of the conventional phonetic elements which the word contained. These percentages were then grouped as shown in the first column in Table 7.

Table 7

MEAN PERCENTAGES OF WORD IDENTIFICATION CORRESPONDING
TO MEAN PERCENTAGES OF THE WORDS PRESENTED

% Word	N Versions	Mean % Word	Mean % Identification
0	58	0	0
20-25	33	24. 9	12. 9
33-40	77	33. 0	18. 7
50	64	50. 0	42. 4
60-67	77	66. 8	72. 7
75-80	33	75. 2	87. 5
100	58	100. 0	99. 4

Their distribution is shown in the second column. The zero and 100 per cent fragments number 58 for the reason that in each of the eight consonant-vowel and vowel-consonant words, two versions were identical. The third column of Table 7 shows the mean percentage of the word for each of the seven step intervals, and the corresponding mean percentages of identification are given in the final column. These appear in Figure 7, where a smoothed curve has been drawn by inspection through the experimental points.

In Figure 7 it will be noted that the function closely resembles a classical probability curve, and it is suggested that it probably does

Table 8

DURATIONS OF WORDS EQUATED IN INTELLIGIBILITY AT THREE LEVELS

	Intelligibility (%)				Intelligibility (%)		
	25	50	75		25	50	75
1. as	.07	.08	.08	26. kept	.08	.09	.10
2. badge	.04	.08	.09	27. leg	.07	.08	.10
3. best	.06	.08	.11	28. mash	.05	.08	.10
4. bog	.07	.08	.11	29. nigh	.07	.08	.09
5. chart	.04	.07	.09	30. ode	.06	.07	.08
6. cloth	.08	.09	.10	31. prig	.06	.07	.08
7. clothes	.05	.08	.09	32. prime	.06	.07	.08
8. cob	.07	.08	.09	33. pun	.06	.07	.08
9. crib	.05	.06	.07	34. pus	.06	.06	.07
10. dad	.07	.08	.09	35. raise	.02	.04	.07
11. deep	.07	.08	.10	36. ray	.07	.08	.09
12. eat	.04	.05	.05	37. reap	.05	.05	.06
13. eyes	.03	.06	.08	38. rooms	.08	.09	.10
14. fall	.10	.15	.17	39. rough	.06	.07	.08
15. fee	.06	.07	.08	40. scan	.03	.06	.08
16. flick	.06	.07	.08	41. shank	.08	.10	.12
17. flop	.06	.07	.08	42. slouch	.08	.09	.10
18. forge	.10	.10	.12	43. sup	.02	.03	.04
19. fowl	.08	.10	.12	44. thigh	.10	.12	.13
20. gage	.08	.09	.10	45. thus	.09	.11	.12
21. gap	.07	.09	.11	46. tongue	.06	.06	.07
22. grope	.07	.08	.10	47. wait	.06	.08	.09
23. hitch	.02	.04	.06	48. wasp	.02	.04	.06
24. hull	.08	.09	.10	49. wife	.05	.06	.07
25. jag	.08	.10	.12	50. writ	.06	.07	.08

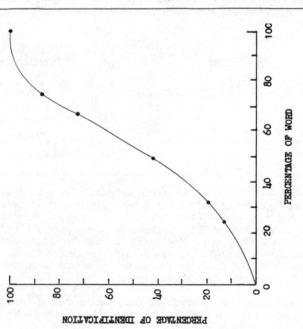

Figure 7. Mean percentage of word identification as a function of the mean percentage of the word presented.

not depart far from a display of the general relationship between word identification and the relative amount of a verbal stimulus that is perceived. It bears a close resemblance, for instance, to the typical function of the percentage of identification of monosyllables versus sensation level. The latter experimental condition may be considered as "fragmentizing" the stimulus by attenuation, and such acoustic fragmentation has a plausible relationship to phonetic fragmentation visually presented. The variable of special interest in this study, duration, also shows a similar function for identical material as has been seen. In other words, all three parameters exhibit a basic functional similarity. Although this direction of thought is of considerable interest and shows promise as an experimental approach, it is outside the scope of the present experiment and digresses from the main focus of interest.

Using the data shown in Figure 7, an attempt was made to find a single measure of this characteristic of the words for purposes of interpreting the primary results. It was regarded as desirable that the measure, in addition to discriminating between words, cover an extended range between, but not including zero and 100 per cent, and be plausibly related to such fragmentation of the words that might be incurred in compression.

On the basis of the above considerations and study of the results it was decided to give special attention to those versions of each word in which the initial or final consonant or consonant cluster had been discarded. In these versions the remaining fragments would be approximately two-thirds of the word. From the auditory point of view, it would appear likely that the consonants would become imperceptible sooner under acoustic fragmentation on grounds of their typically shorter duration and lower intensity. For each word these two versions were pooled and the mean percentage of identification calculated. The 50 words ranged in identification from 44 to 94 per cent, with a mean and median of 75 per cent. In terms of Figure 7 these versions are to be found in the upper portion of the curve in a region of approximate rectilinearity. For purposes of convenience the percentage of identification of a word from fragments presented under these conditions has been referred to as its inference level. The individual inference levels of the 50 words are shown in Table 3 and the distribution in Figure 6D.

With intelligibility varying as a function of duration, it is of interest to investigate the intelligibility variation between words of a given duration, or conversely, the variation in duration when words are equally intelligible. In the latter instance, it seems appropriate to inquire if the durational order of the words varies as intelligibility is altered. Three levels of intelligibility were selected, namely, 25, 50, and 75 per cent. At these levels data for the .01 series were entered for each word by interpolation to determine the corresponding compression ratios and the resultant word durations. At the three levels, the mean durations were .062, .077 and .091 sec. for the 25, 50, and 75 per cent levels, respectively. The latter two values might be interpreted as duration thresholds. The individual values appear in Table 8.

The durational orders at the three levels were interrelated by computing product-moment correlation coefficients with the following results:

	r
25 - 50%	.88
50 - 75%	.96
25 - 75%	.79

Over a wide range of intelligibility the words were ordered very much alike with respect to compressed duration, suggesting the existence of non-durational attributes which preserve the rank order. The data also indicated that study of interrelationships could be pursued at various possible points over a comparatively wide range of intelligibility and duration.

One method of investigation of the relationship between intelligibility and duration might have been to select a particular compression ratio such as .8, at which each word would be .2 times its original duration. Such a method, however, would not have taken full advantage of the durational control possible through the method, since the words, although shortened, would have their ordinal durations preserved with a restricted range. Procedures were followed which had the effect of stretching the relative range by a factor of two. Thus the longest word (.75 sec.), which was 2.08 times the shortest word (.36 sec.), was studied under conditions when it was 4.16 times the shortest word. This relationship obtained under conditions when the longest word was compressed .8 and the shortest .9. For each of the remaining words, that duration between these two values was determined which would preserve the original relative position. The compression yielding this duration for each word was computed and the corresponding percentage of intelligibility determined by interpolation into the .01 intelligibility data. The range of compressions between .8 and .9 provided optimum intelligibility discrimination among the 50 words without significant skewing toward either extreme of intelligibility. The results of these adjustments may be viewed as predicting the intelligibility of the individual words as they would have been had the durations of the words been distributed proportionately over twice as wide a range originally, and then compressed by a constant and large compression ratio such as to distribute their intelligibilities across a wide range.

The word intelligibility and duration values resulting from this adjustment procedure together with the data for the remaining three variables as reported in Table 3 were used as the basis for the product-moment correlation coefficients shown in Table 9. The correlation between intelligibility and duration is seen to be substantial. The remaining coefficients in the top row are smaller and only one, that for vowel pressure, is significantly greater than zero, but they suggest that the intelligibility of the words in this experiment tended to be partially determined by non-duration factors. This is particularly interesting in view of the deliberate attempt to limit vowel pressure variation at the time of recording, and in view of the restriction of the number of phonetic units implicit in the use of monosyllabic words.

Table 9

ZERO-ORDER CORRELATION COEFFICIENTS* BETWEEN WORD
INTELLIGIBILITY AND WORD CHARACTERISTICS

	Duration	Vowel Pressure	Phonetic Units	Inference Level
Word Intelligibility	.56	.29	.23	.21
Duration		.42	.31	.10
Vowel Pressure			-.14	.14
Phonetic Units				.50

*r, df 48: 1%, .36; 5%, .28

The remaining portion of Table 9 shows the interrelationships
between the four basic word characteristics. The positive correlation between duration and vowel pressure would be expected from the
results of numerous earlier studies; the correlation of .31 between
duration and phonetic units is likewise plausible; the coefficient of
.50 between phonetic units and inference level suggests that these
two variables tend in part to measure the same thing as far as word
intelligibility is concerned.

The partial correlation coefficients presented in Table 10 were
calculated largely because of interest in the possibility that the relationship between intelligibility and duration might be altered if vowel
pressure, phonetic units and inference level were held constant. It
will be observed that the coefficients in the top row of Table 10 do
not differ substantially from the zero-order coefficient of .56 between
intelligibility and duration. It is of passing interest to observe in
the balance of Table 10 that several of the relationships between intelligibility and factors other than duration tended to be lowered
when other factors are held constant.

Table 11 presents the results of first-order multiple correlation coefficients, and shows the relationships between word intelligibility and the combined effects of the various possible pairs of word
characteristics. The top row of coefficients shows no substantial
rise in the basic relationship between intelligibility and duration when
any of the other three factors is combined with duration. It is of
interest, however, to observe that the combined effect of vowel pressure and phonetic units, for which the coefficient is .40, is significantly positive. These two characteristics alone, as shown in the
top row of Table 9, correlated .29 and .23, respectively, with intelligibility. This suggests the possibility that the word intelligibility
results of this experiment may have been partially determined by the
relatively small changes in relative vowel pressure and number of
phonetic units acting in combination.

As a final step a five-variable coefficient was computed be-

Table 10

FIRST ORDER PARTIAL CORRELATION COEFFICIENTS* BETWEEN
WORD INTELLIGIBILITY (VARIABLE 1) AND VARIABLE 2 WITH
VARIABLE 3 CONSTANT

		Variable 3		
Variable 2	Duration	Vowel Pressure	Phonetic Units	Inference Level
Duration		.50	.53	.55
Vowel Pressure	.28		.33	.30
Phonetic Units	.07	.29		.15
Inference Level	.19	.18	.11	

*r, df 47: 1%, .36; 5%, .28

tween word intelligibility and the four word characteristics in combination. The resulting coefficient was .58, significant beyond the 1
per cent level, and again it will be observed that the basic relationship between intelligibility and duration that obtained in this experiment was not significantly changed. This, of course, is hardly surprising considering the conditions of the study, and it clearly does
not permit any conclusion about the relative importance of the variables in question as determinants of word intelligibility generally.
However, the powerful role of duration in intelligibility, shown by
the large general effects of time compression, is confirmed by the
above findings at the level of individual words.

SUMMARY

In an investigation of the effects of time compression upon intelligibility, recorded monosyllabic words were subjected to a number
of different conditions of compression and presented for identification
to a group of trained observers, with the following major findings:

1. Intelligibility varied inversely as a function of time compression, or in direct relation to the proportion of the signal remaining after time compression.
2. Intelligibility varied with the duration of the discard and
sampling intervals, decreasing progressively as such intervals became long in relation to the durations of the signal units.
3. Within the range of values considered, the percentage of
intelligibility invariably exceeded the percentage of the signal remaining after time compression.
4. When the discard and sampling intervals were short the
percentage of intelligibility was approximately five times as great as
the percentage of the signal remaining.
5. When the discard and sampling intervals were long the

Table 11

FIRST-ORDER MULTIPLE CORRELATION COEFFICIENTS* BETWEEN
WORD INTELLIGIBILITY (VARIABLE 1) AND COMBINATIONS
OF VARIABLES 2 AND 3

Variable 2	Vowel Pressure	Variable 3 Phonetic Units	Inference Level
Duration	.56	.56	.58
Vowel Pressure		.40	.34
Phonetic Units			.25

*$\underline{r}$, $\underline{df}$ 47: 1%, .42; 5%, .346

relative excess decreased, and the percentage of intelligibility appeared to become increasingly dependent upon the proportion of subword units sampled.

　　6.　The minimum percentage of the signal's duration necessary for 100 per cent intelligibility was estimated to be 30, and the temporal redundancy of the signal, under the specific conditions of this experiment, to be 70 per cent.

　　7.　The intelligibilities of individual words were strongly related to their durations. They were also related to certain combinations of non-durational attributes, although the latter were restricted in range by the conditions of the experiment.

　　8.　Under conditions in which the possibilities of correct identification were restricted to a known number of well-known alternatives, the non-auditory identification of words was directly related to the proportion of the total word perceived, the function being S-shaped.

Chapter 9

DOCTORAL WORK SPONSORED BY GRANT FAIRBANKS, 2

The second doctoral dissertation written under the direction of Professor Fairbanks at the University of Illinois was written by Charles Lee Hutton, Jr., and is excerpted in this chapter. This thesis bears the same stigmata that other Fairbanks' sponsored theses do. It is carefully planned, executed with precision and reported with exactness and clarity. The excerpt speaks for itself and I will not, therefore, dwell on its contents other than to note that it is concerned with rate and its psychophysical aspects. Spoken passages at their original rates, compressed, and expanded were employed to determine estimates of rate and preferences for rate from both trained and untrained listeners.

PSYCHOPHYSICAL STUDY OF SPEECH RATE

Charles Lee Hutton, Jr.

Speech rate has been measured and controlled many times in experimental investigations, is often an object of special attention in teaching and clinical situations, and is mentioned in almost every textbook of speech. As far as can be determined, however, the fundamental functional relationship between measured rate and rate as it is perceived by a listener has not been investigated, and it is probably not unjust to suggest that the assumption of a simple one-to-one relationship between the two is commonly made by workers in the field.

Specified time intervals filled with speech are commonplace in everyday life. There are, for example, the 50-minute lecture, the 15-minute newscast, and the 60-second radio commercial. Although time estimates, such as "He talked for about 10 minutes," are often heard, neither the ability of a listener to make a judgment of this kind, nor the nature of the relationship between such judgments of time and the physical times in question have, as far as can be discovered, been studied. Judgments of time intervals were investigated long ago by experimental psychologists, but a search of the literature has not revealed experiments on the estimated durations of speech samples.

The present investigation has represented an attempt to explore certain aspects of the psychophysics of the time factor in speech somewhat more directly. Specifically, it has been concerned with perceived rate and perceived duration on the one hand in relation to measured rate and duration on the other, and with preferred rate as a function of measured or estimated rate. In addition, the recent development of a device for time compression and expansion of speech has made it possible to examine the possibility that recorded speech samples might be improved aesthetically by compression or expansion, and to study the effects of holding certain temporal characteristics constant while varying others.

Procedure

The general plan of the experiment was to select from a large number of recorded readings of the same prose passage a representative series of samples over a widely varying range of speech rates; to add to these samples versions of each, compressed and expanded in time; to present the total series of recordings to observers for judgments of various types; to make acoustical measurements of the recordings; to study the relationships between the judgments and the acoustical measurements.

Eight readings were selected with durations which approximated a geometric progression by a factor of 1.2. The corresponding rates ranged from 94 to 344 words per minute, more than spanning the range ordinarily encountered. These will be referred to as the original readings, or simply as $\underline{O}$. The results of this selection and further processing are shown below in Table 1. Each of the original readings was compressed to equal the duration of the reading below it (i.e., $D_C = D_O/1.2$), and expanded to equal the duration of the reading above it (i.e., $D_C = 1.2\ D_O$). In addition, each reading was also compressed between each two adjacent original readings. These various versions will be referred to as C20, E20, C10, and E10, respectively.

Measurements of the Stimulus Materials

The articulation of the eight original readings was carefully studied sound by sound and the numbers of words, syllables, and phonemes counted. The readings were then inter-compared and differences noted. Graphic recordings of the relative sound pressure of the eight original readings were made on a high speed level recorder with a 0-50 db potentiometer set for stylus speed and for 10mm/sec. paper speed. The peaks were identified and counted, fluctuations of less than 5db being ignored, and measured to the nearest decibel. Oscillograms made on a locally constructed oscillograph, which duplicates in principle that described by Cowna were divided into 0.05 second intervals and measured. The number of pause and phonation intervals for each reading was tabulated. Preliminary measurements of total duration of the 40 processed versions were made to the nearest 0.1 second from the graphic recordings noted above.

Table 1

DURATIONAL MEASURES OF THE 40 PROCESSED VERSIONS
IN SECONDS

Reading	Compression-Expansion Level				
	C20	C10	0	E10	E20
1	8.0	8.8	9.6	10.6	11.6
2	10.0	10.9	12.1	13.2	14.2
3	11.9	13.1	14.3	15.8	16.9
4	14.1	15.7	17.1	18.7	20.5
5	16.9	18.8	20.3	22.6	24.7
6	20.7	22.4	24.3	26.8	29.4
7	24.4	26.7	29.3	31.8	35.3
8	28.8	31.9	35.3	38.9	42.6
Mean	16.8	18.5	20.3	22.3	24.4

Observers

Three independent groups of observers were assembled.
Trained Group A consisted of 10 experienced observers. It included
eight male and two female advanced graduate students and staff members. This group made estimations of rate and duration. Because
it was felt desirable to assemble a group with special skill in evaluating speech, Trained Group B, consisting of 10 males from the staff
of speech instructors, was assembled. These members were chosen
on the basis of training and experience in speech, interest in the
problem, and presumed ability to rate reliably. Judgments of rate
preference were made by this group.

Since it was a matter of incidental interest to discover whether or not untrained observers differ in their rate preferences from
trained observers, a group of 20 males and 20 female undergraduate
students was formed. Members of this Untrained Group were not experienced in evaluation of speech and made judgments of rate preference only. Trained Group B and the Untrained Group were pooled to
form a Combined Group of 50 observers.

The 40 processed versions in their random order were reproduced for scaling purposes in a sound-treated room. Two to five
observers at a time were seated in tablet armchairs, approximately
eight feet in front of the loud speaker. A comfortable level well
above threshold was determined in a preliminary trial and gain settings were held constant thereafter. In regard to the matter of these
rather arbitrarily controlled equalizations of frequency response, both
here and at the time of processing, it should be stated that the stage
of development of the compression-expansion apparatus did not permit
more precise specification. The procedures described degraded all

the versions, of course, but the resulting quality was not sub-standard in the opinion of several experts. In addition, members of Trained Group A and other sophisticated observers who participated in preliminary judgments were carefully questioned as to the possible effect that variations among the versions might have upon their judgments. Although all reported that variations could be heard, no observer considered them either obtrusive or confounding.

In connection with each of the various judgment procedures special attention was given to instruction of the observers. All the basic instructions were written in advance and read aloud formally.

Estimates of Rate

Trained Group A made estimations of the rate of each of the 40 processed versions on a nine-point graphic rating scale with equidistant points, a compressed version of which is reproduced below.

1	2	3	4	5	6	7	8	9
SLOW								FAST

The general orientation of the observers was to listen to each version as a whole and, during the pause that followed, to enter a mark in the appropriate space. The 40 recordings were presented in four subgroups of 10 each.

Estimates of Duration

The same group of observers, Trained Group A, participated in making the duration estimates. A 60-second time scale was used as follows:

```
0        10        20        30        40        50        60
1....1.... 1....1.... 1 ....1.... 1 ....1.... 1 ....1.... 1....1....1
```

The range, it will be noted, extended both above and below the 8.0 sec. and 42.6 sec. extreme durations among the versions. The 40 randomized versions were presented as before.

Judgments of Rate Preference and General Effectiveness

Both types of judgments were made by Trained Group B, while the Untrained Group judged rate preference only. A nine-point scale similar to that for estimating rate was used for both judgments. Its lower portion is reproduced below.

	Inferior	Very Poor	Poor	Below Average	Average
	1	2	3	4	5

Above the four numbers not shown appeared the terms Above Average, Good, Very Good, and Superior, respectively. Half of the observers from Trained Group B judged rate preference first and the other half judged general effectiveness first.

RESULTS

Non-Durational Characteristics of the Stimulus Materials

The primary purpose of studying the non-durational characteristics of the original readings was to determine the degree to which the readings were essentially constant in such respects, so that evaluation of the rate factor could be made without extensive equivocation. Before discussing these measures it is interesting to note that most observers would probably agree that the basic speech habits of the subject are satisfactory. This observation is supported by the fact that Reading 5, which employed a rate normal for the subject, received a mean rating of 6.9 in general effectiveness from the group of speech instructors. It will be recalled that the nine-point scale was defined in this case as ranging "from inferior to superior as you have heard the oral reading of people of various degrees of skill and ability during your life." As will be shown below, the judgments of general effectiveness and rate preference were very similar, suggesting that the variations in general effectiveness could be attributed chiefly to rate.

Table 2

NON-DURATIONAL MEASUREMENTS
OF THE EIGHT ORIGINAL READINGS

Reading	Phonemes Correct (N)	Median Relative Sound Pressure (db)	Median Fundamental Frequency	
			Cycles/Sec.	Tones re 16.35
1	180	.45	86.1	14.38
2	184	.60	87.1	14.48
3	185	.85	87.5	14.52
4	185	1.72	86.8	14.45
5	185	2.35	86.9	14.46
6	185	2.28	83.8	14.15
7	185	0.0	79.9	13.73
8	185	.35	82.0	13.97

The results of the non-durational measurements of the original readings are shown in Table 2.   Readings 3 through 8 provided the full complement of 185 accurately articulated phonemes.   These six readings covered the range of 94 to 231 words per minute.   Four errors of omission and one error of distortion occurred in Reading 1, the most rapid reading, and one error of omission occurred in Reading 2.   The rate of Reading 1 was 344 wpm, more than double the most preferred rate of 163 wpm, and the errors which occurred were of the types which might be expected as a consequence of such extremely fast rates.   The total range of 94 to 344 wpm encompassed by the readings is substantially greater than any previously reported in the literature.   Darley [B73] reported a range of 129 to 222 wpm for 200 college students reading comparable material.

Measurements of Duration and Rate

Seven measures of duration for each of the eight readings are graphed in Figures 1, 2, 3.   The relationships between total speaking time, total phonation time, and total pause time are illustrated in Figure 1.   There it can be seen that total time and pause time

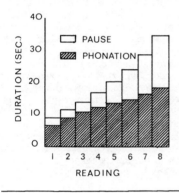

Figure 1.   Division of the total durations of the original readings into phonation and pause.

increased by progressively larger amounts from Reading 1 to 8, while phonation time increased by a relatively constant amount.   Geometric progression by a factor of 1.2 was a condition of the experiment for total time.   Pause time also increased in a geometric progression, the factor being approximately 1.3.   On the other hand, phonation time increased arithmetically in step-wise fashion by approximately two seconds per reading.   The ratios of these time relationships are plotted in the left graph of Figure 2.   It will be seen that the progression of the two ratios is fairly linear from Reading 2 on.   The change spans the range from approximately 80/20 division to 50/50.   It will be seen that a progressively larger proportion of the total time was spent in pause as the total time increased.   The phonation and pause ratios, approximately .7 and .3, respectively, for Readings 4 and 5, are consistent with values previously reported

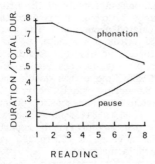 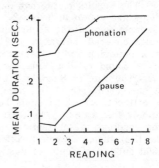

Figure 2.   Ratios of total phonation and pause durations to the total speaking time (left graph); mean durations of phonations and pauses (right graph).

by a number of experimenters for normal rates of speech.

Mean durations of phonations and pauses are plotted by readings in the right graph of Figure 2.   It will be observed that the mean duration of phonations increased from .287 sec. to .409 sec. for Readings 1 through 5, but remained relatively constant thereafter. The increase in mean duration of phonations between Readings 2 and 3 was greater than the total increase of all other readings.   The mean duration of pauses increased from .079 sec. to .373 sec., but it will be noted that the curve is steeper than that for phonations and has no plateau.   The pause and phonation values for Readings 4 and 5 are similar to those previously reported.   The two graphs in Figure 2 show that Readings 1 and 2 did not differ greatly in the internal aspects of duration, and this may indicate a limit beyond which such aspects of speech cannot be modified.   Of these four measures it should be noted that only the mean duration of pauses for Readings 1 and 2 approached the resolving power of the technique of measurement, which was approximately .03 sec.

Figure 3 presents four representative pairs of frequency distributions of durations of phonations and pauses in the solid and dashed lines, respectively.   The progressive increase in the area under the curves is apparent.   It will be seen that the number of short pauses remained relatively constant, but that the number of short phonations decreased slightly as Reading 1 were less than .15 sec.   Casual listening to this reading gave the impression of virtually continuous phonation, apart from one or two between-phrase pauses.

The numbers of articulatory units for the original readings are given in the first three columns of Table 3 and displayed graphically in Figure 4.   Their constancy is apparent.   The remaining two columns of Table 3 show the numbers of phonations and intensity peaks. The plot of these values in Figure 4 shows that phonations and peaks tended to increase in number as the total duration increased.   The

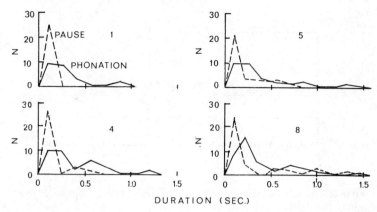

Figure 3. Representative distributions of the durations of phonations (solid line) and pauses (broken line). Readings 1, 4, 5 and 8.

Table 3

NUMBERS OF UNITS IN THE EIGHT ORIGINAL READINGS

Reading	Words	Syllables	Phonemes	Phonations	Intensity Peaks
1	55	76	181	26	34
2	55	76	184	32	37
3	55	76	185	29	38
4	55	76	185	33	40
5	55	76	185	33	44
6	55	76	185	37	50
7	55	76	185	40	56
8	55	76	185	45	58

increase in number is more regular for intensity peaks than for phonations. Figure 4, then, shows that the number of "symbolic" units of speech remained constant as duration increased, while the number of "vocal" units increased. Only at the extremely slow rate of 94 wpm did the number of "vocal" units approach that of any of the "symbolic" units.

Values for measures of rate are plotted for the eight readings in Figure 5. It is seen that four of the different rates, namely, words, peaks, and phonations during total speaking time, and words during phonation time, decreased as duration increased. The rate of phonations and peaks during phonation time decreased for about the first half of the readings, but remained relatively constant thereafter, and it is apparent that these would not furnish a listener information

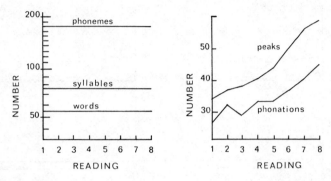

Figure 4. Numbers of "symbolic" units and "vocal" units for the original readings.

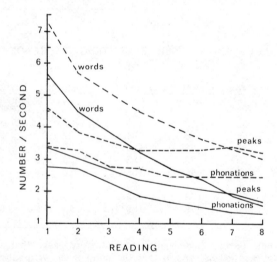

Figure 5. Rate of words, intensity peaks, and phonations in number per second. Solid line, during total speaking time; broken line, during phonation only.

for discriminating between rates on the slower half of a rate scale. There were differences in the rate of decrease from Readings 1 to 8; word rate was nearly twice as fast as peak and phonation rate in Reading 1, but the three rates were almost equal in Reading 8. It can be seen in Figure 5 that the curve of word rate had the sharpest decline, while the peak and phonation rates declined in approximately the same proportion. Since word rate during total speaking time showed the greatest change and the most regular decrease as a function of duration, it appears to be a promising physical measure of rate as a prospective correlation of estimated rate, a relationship that will be considered below.

It was mentioned above that word, peak and phonation rates were very similar at the longest duration. That is, at 94 wpm in Reading 8 there was approximately one intensity peak per phonation per average word. It was also noted that only at this very slow rate did the number of peaks and phonations approach that of any of the "symbolic" units.

Judgments of Rate, Duration, Rate Preference, General Effectiveness

Tables 4 through 7 present the results of the judgment procedures for the 40 versions of the passage, five for each of the eight original readings. Attention is first directed to the means for the original readings, shown in the third columns of the tables. The mean rate preferences for the Combined Group of observers are presented in Table 6. The trained and the untrained groups had mean ratings for the 40 versions of 4.18 and 3.91, respectively. The difference was tested by means of t, which was 1.00, with 2.01 being required at the 5 per cent level for 48 df. The variances of the two groups were also examined. The F ratio was 1.30, the variance of the trained group being the larger of the two, which fails to meet the requirement of 2.13 at the 5 per cent level for 9 and 39 df. It was believed that pooling was justified. The rates of Readings 4 and 5 were 193 and 163 wpm, respectively, and the latter reading, with the higher mean rating, was also the highest ranking version among the total of 40, as study of Table 6 will show. The rate for Reading 5 compares favorably with mean rates of 166 and 167 wpm, respectively, reported for six superior male speakers on the same test passage and for 200 college students on a 300 word passage with comparable syllabic structure.

Inspection of Table 6 shows that the more extreme versions provided by compression and expansion were rated as being very close to Inferior. Thus the fact that none of the extreme original versions was rated Inferior can be explained on the basis that the observers were presented with even more extreme rates. The question remains as to why none of the mid-range rates were judged as being Superior, since the rates for several versions corresponded closely to values previously reported for normal and superior speakers, and since the normal rate range was spanned. The probable explanation is that individual differences between the rates preferred by observers were large enough to hold down the largest mean. The mean ratings of general effectiveness of speech for the original readings are presented in column three of Table 7.

(cont. on p. 280)

Table 4

MEAN ESTIMATED RATES FOR THE 40 VERSIONS
OF THE ORIGINAL READINGS
(Scale 1 - 9; 10 Observers, Trained Group A)

Reading	Compression-Expansion Level				
	C20	C10	0	E10	E20
1	9.0	9.0	8.5	8.0	7.9
2	8.6	8.0	7.6	7.4	6.7
3	7.9	7.0	7.1	6.5	6.0
4	6.5	5.7	5.2	5.1	4.8
5	6.1	5.1	5.1	3.8	3.4
6	4.4	4.4	3.7	2.5	2.3
7	3.6	3.7	3.3	2.5	1.7
8	3.0	2.5	1.9	1.1	1.0
Mean	6.14	5.68	5.30	4.61	4.22

Table 5

MEAN ESTIMATED DURATION FOR THE 40 VERSIONS
OF THE ORIGINAL READINGS
(0 - 60 seconds; 10 Observers, Trained Group A)

Reading	Compression-Expansion Level				
	C20	C10	0	E10	E20
1	8.9	10.9	11.4	13.5	13.7
2	12.7	12.1	15.0	15.0	20.7
3	11.7	17.3	14.6	18.7	19.8
4	18.1	19.8	23.0	22.4	25.6
5	17.7	23.6	24.7	26.9	35.1
6	25.4	27.0	30.0	34.9	38.6
7	31.3	30.5	34.0	39.8	42.4
8	34.6	35.9	41.6	48.2	48.0
Mean	20.05	22.14	24.29	27.42	30.49

Table 6

MEAN RATE PREFERENCE FOR THE 40 VERSIONS OF THE ORIGINAL READINGS

Reading	Compression-Expansion Level				
	C20	C10	0	E10	E20
1	1.1	1.3	1.8	2.4	2.0
2	1.6	2.7	3.1	3.7	4.6
3	1.8	4.5	4.2	4.9	5.9
4	6.1	7.1	7.1	7.0	6.3
5	6.4	7.3	7.6	5.8	4.3
6	6.8	6.3	4.6	3.0	3.0
7	4.7	4.7	4.4	2.7	1.8
8	4.5	3.4	2.1	1.3	1.4
Mean	4.12	4.66	4.36	3.85	3.66

Table 7

MEAN GENERAL EFFECTIVENESS RATINGS FOR THE 40 VERSIONS OF THE ORIGINAL READINGS

Reading	Compression-Expansion Level				
	C20	C10	0	E10	E20
1	1.2	1.4	1.8	2.2	1.7
2	1.8	2.6	2.6	3.0	3.3
3	2.4	3.9	4.5	4.9	5.0
4	5.3	6.0	6.2	5.9	4.9
5	4.9	7.0	6.9	6.0	4.4
6	6.9	6.5	4.5	3.9	3.2
7	5.4	4.6	4.3	3.2	2.7
8	4.5	3.8	2.5	2.3	2.3
Mean	4.05	4.48	4.16	3.92	3.44

Analysis of Estimated Rate

The purpose of this section is to consider the relationships between rate as estimated by the observers and selected measurements of rate. The mean estimated rates for the complete set of 40 versions (Table 4) were plotted against all of the measured rates. As will be explained in detail in a following section, the 40 versions of estimated rate were then examined for differences that could be attributed to type of version. On the basis of negative findings, the 40 versions were grouped into the 19 rate levels, thus improving the stability of the judgment means, the similar plottings made. An additional rate measure, the number of phonation-pause cycles per second was also considered, but found to be so erratic that, although promising theoretically, it was rejected.

The graphs of estimated rate as a function of measured rate showed that, of the various possibilities, the curve for words per second during the total speaking time had the most regular progression, the smallest amount of dispersion, and the greatest amount of change over all. The values are listed in columns one and two of Table 8 and plotted in Figure 6. It will be noted that the shape of the curve suggests the existence of a logarithmic relationship, a familiar finding in psychophysics, and a plot of estimated rate versus the logarithm of measured rate was found to approximate a straight line. Accordingly, a curve was fitted by the method of least squares and the resulting equation was:

$$R_e = 11.97 \log R_m - .46 \qquad\qquad (1)$$

where R_e is estimated rate on the 1 to 9 rating scale and R_m is measured rate in wps. The curve is shown in Figure 6 and is seen to fit the experimental points satisfactorily. It is concluded that perceived rate may be predicted with considerable confidence by means of Equation 1. For practical purposes, the two constants might be conveniently rounded to 12 and .5, respectively.

Analysis of Estimated Duration

The mean estimated and measured durations are given in the right portion of Table 8 for each of the 19 rate levels. The decision to group the versions by rate levels was made after intercomparisons showed no evidence that estimated duration depended significantly upon type of version. In the case of duration, however, an additional judgmental procedure was arranged before the psychophysical analysis was pursued. It will be recalled that the basic procedure for judging duration was estimation along a zero- to 60-second graphic scale without specification of the shortest and longest durations, and that Trained Group A was used. A special group of observers from among those available was formed, consisting of six from Trained Group A and one from Trained Group B. These observers repeated the duration estimates, but this time the shortest and longest of the 40 versions were played prior to the judgment series, and their ex-

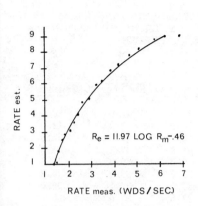

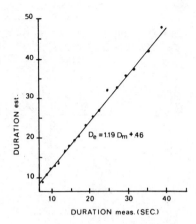

Figure 6.   Mean estimated rate (scale 1-9) as a function of mean measured rate (words/sec.) for the 19 rate levels.   The curve is a plot of the equation shown.

Figure 7.   Mean estimated duration (scale 0-60 sec.) as a function of mean measured duration (sec.) for the 19 rate levels. The line is a plot of the equation shown.

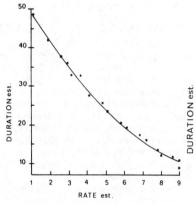

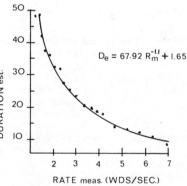

Figure 8.   Mean estimated duration (scale 0-60 sec.) as a function of mean estimated rate (scale 1-9) for the 19 rate levels.   The curve was drawn by inspection.

Figure 9.   Mean estimated duration (scale 0-60 sec.) as a function of mean measured rate (words/sec.) for the 19 rate levels.   The curve is a plot of the equation shown.

Table 8

MEAN ESTIMATED RATE (1-9), MEASURED RATE (words/sec.),
ESTIMATED DURATION (0-60 sec.), MEASURED DURATION (sec.)
FOR THE 19 RATE LEVELS

Rate Level	Rate Measured	Rate Estimated*	Duration Measured	Duration Estimated*	Estimated**
1	1.30	1.0	42.6	48.0	42.1
2	1.42	1.1	38.9	48.2	42.0
3	1.57	1.8	35.3	42.0	36.6
4	1.72	2.5	31.8	37.8	34.3
5	1.86	2.9	29.2	35.7	31.9
6	2.06	3.1	26.8	32.7	29.2
7	2.25	3.6	24.5	32.1	26.0
8	2.44	4.1	22.5	27.0	23.8
9	2.68	4.8	20.5	25.2	22.1
10	2.93	5.1	18.8	23.0	19.4
11	3.24	5.8	17.0	20.2	18.6
12	3.49	6.1	15.8	19.2	17.8
13	3.87	6.8	14.2	17.8	15.6
14	4.18	7.2	13.2	16.2	14.6
15	4.63	7.8	11.9	13.8	12.6
16	5.12	8.0	10.8	12.8	12.5
17	5.62	8.6	9.8	12.0	10.7
18	6.25	9.0	8.8	10.9	8.7
19	6.86	9.0	8.0	8.9	8.1

*10 Observers, Trained Group A.   **7 Observers; see text.

_____

act durations, 8.0 and 42.6 sec., were stated and marked on the
scale. The difference between the two procedures, then, was in the
scale, which was "open-ended" in the first instance and "anchored"
in the second. Both sets of estimates are presented in Table 8.
Point-by-point study of these data will show identical ranks, with the
exception of the second rate level, and differences in the expected
direction. Careful study of the results, for rate levels and for the
40 versions, and comparisons of the estimates of the six observers
common to both procedures showed no evidence that the difference
altered the shape of the function. Since the open-ended scale has
more face validity and was used with a larger number of observers,
it was therefore decided to use that set of judgments. In other words,
the original plan of the experiment was not changed.

Estimated duration was plotted against measured duration with
the result shown in Figure 7, the points being for the 19 rate levels
noted above. It will be seen that the function is essentially linear
and that duration was consistently overestimated. The equation for
the line of best fit, solved by the method of least squares, was:

$$D_e = 1.19 \ D_m + .46, \tag{2}$$

where D_e is estimated duration, a value smaller than 60 sec., and D_m is measured duration. This equation is shown by the straight line in Figure 7. In summary, the data show that estimated duration was linear function of measured duration, and that the average speech sample sounded about 20 per cent longer than it actually was.

This relationship should not, however, be interpreted as indicating that estimates of duration are based upon physical duration per se. In the present instance it was thought possible that the formation of a duration estimate might be based upon the observer's sub-vocal empathic responses to the speech stimuli, referred to his own experiences with the familiar act of speaking, and that the perception of rate might be fundamental. It has already been shown, in discussion of Figure 8, that estimates of duration and rate were found to be closely related. In order to demonstrate this relationship further estimated duration has been plotted against estimated rate for the 19 rate levels in Figure 8, where it is seen that the relationship is high and curvilinear.

The relationship between estimated duration and measured rate was pursued with each of the various rate measures. Again, as for estimated rate, the most satisfactory measure was found to be words per second during the total speaking time. Figure 9 is a plot of estimated duration versus this rate measure for the 19 rate levels, the values being those of columns one and four in Table 8. The relationship is seen to be hyperbolic in fcrm. A re-plotting of the same data with logarithmic coordinates yielded approximately a straight line, and solution by the method of least square resulted in the following equation:

$$D_e = 67.92 \ R_m^{-1.1} + 1.65, \tag{3}$$

where D_e is estimated duration on a 0-60 second scale and R_m is measured rate in wps. The curve of this equation in Figure 9 appears to represent the experimental data adequately. Equation 3 indicates that estimated duration is proportional, approximately, to the reciprocal of measured rate, or to the mean duration per word, including pause time, a relationship which would be expected from the foregoing analysis of rate and duration.

Analysis of Rate Preference

In the earlier discussion of the judgments of the eight original readings it was observed that estimated rate and preferred rate appear to be related. In the upper left portion of Figure 10 rate preference is plotted as a function of estimated rate, and it will be observed that rate preference peaked at an estimated rate close to the midpoint of the latter's scale. For slower and faster estimated rates, the curve is quite rectilinear. In other words, the placement of a given reading along a rate preference scale appears to be a linear

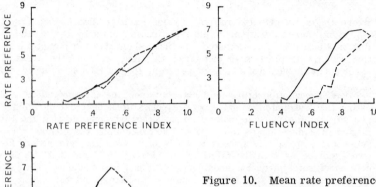

Figure 10. Mean rate preference ratings (scale 1-9) versus the variables indicated (see text) for the 19 rate levels. Rates slower than most preferred rate, solid line; faster, broken line.

function of the difference between the estimated rate for that reading and the estimated rate most preferred. This observation led to the thought that a useful Rate Preference Index, patterned somewhat after the earlier Articulation Fluency Index developed by Fairbanks and Guttman, might be tentatively proposed which would express rate preference as a quantity smaller than 1.0 by means of the following expression:

$$I = 1 - \frac{|5.1 - R_e|}{5.1} \qquad (4)$$

where 5.1 is the mean estimated rate of the most preferred rate level and R_e is the estimated rate of a given reading on a 1 to 9 scale. It is seen that the absolute difference is expressed as a fraction of 5.1 and subtracted from 1.0. Since the range of R_e was one to nine, the index range is .196 to 1.0, the latter value obtaining when $R_e = 5.1$.

In the upper left graph of Figure 10 the preference means are plotted against the index, the solid line pertaining to slow rate and the broken line to fast rate. Apart from a few irregularities, probably attributable to chance, the measure seems to be very satisfactory at all of the rate levels. For practical use, in order to exclude subjective factors completely, R_e would be predicted from measured rate by means of Equation 1, so that the index would have the following form:

$$I = 1 - \frac{|5.1 - (11.97 \log R_m - .46)|}{5.1} \qquad (4a)$$

It is pointed out that the application of the Rate Preference Index is restricted to performances in which the subjective effect of rate is not conditioned by non-durational factors, such as articulation, for example, which was essentially constant in the present experiment.

The Articulatory Fluency Index is:

$$I = \frac{W_c^2}{W_t^2} \cdot \frac{D_n}{D_n + |D_n - D_o|}$$

where W_c is the number of correct words, W_t is the total number of words, D_n is a reference duration and D_o is the obtained duration. In the case of the Rainbow Passage W_t is 55 words, and D_n is taken as 17.2 sec., the median duration of 122 young adult males reading the passage with special instructions. When applied to readings which varied in the degree of disturbance caused by delayed auditory feedback, this index correlated -.92 with reliable ratings of severity of disturbance; when applied to undisturbed readings, it correlated .72 with ratings of general effectiveness. The index was applied to the present data with the results plotted as a function of the index in the upper right portion of Figure 10. It will be seen that the Articulatory Fluency Index curve is similar in general shape to that for the Rate Preference Index immediately above, but that it is not as closely related to rate preference. Inspection of the curve, for instance, shows that the most preferred rate and the maximum value of the Articulatory Fluency Index were one rate level apart, causing the fast portion of the curve (broken line) to be displaced to the right. This finding was not unexpected. Since the number of correct words in the present experiment equalled the total number of words, except for the rate levels which included versions of Readings 1 and 2, duration was the factor of heaviest weight and the generally high level of articulation restricted the range at the lower end. In addition, the value of D_n, 17.2 sec., is shorter than the mean duration of the most preferred rate level in the present experiment, which is 18.8 sec.

Effects of Time Compression and Expansion

It will be recalled that the basic plan of the experiment involved five compression-expansion versions of each of the eight original readings, the durations of the 40 versions being shown in Table 1 [page 270]. In that table the column means show the systematic changes in total speaking time among the five version types. Since number of words was constant, division of 55 by each value yields the mean rate in wps. At the bottom of Table 4 corresponding mean estimated rates are shown. It will be remembered that in this situation reading is effectively held constant and total speaking time varied.

The plan of the experiment also made it possible to compare different readings while holding total speaking time constant, i.e., to make comparisons within the 19 rate levels as exhibited in Figure 1. Such comparisons can be made by studying the diagonal entries of

Table 9. DURATIONAL MEASURES OF THE EIGHT ORIGINAL READINGS

Reading	Total Speaking Time (sec.)	Dur. (sec.)	Phonation		Dur. (sec.)	Pause	
			Dur./Tot.	Dur./N		Dur./Tot.	Dur./N
1	9.6	7.5	.780	.287	2.1	.220	.081
2	12.1	9.5	.786	.298	2.6	.214	.079
3	14.3	10.6	.739	.365	3.7	.261	.129
4	17.1	12.2	.720	.371	4.9	.280	.145
5	20.3	13.5	.667	.409	6.8	.333	.205
6	24.3	15.2	.626	.411	9.1	.374	.245
7	29.3	16.4	.563	.411	12.9	.437	.320
8	35.3	18.4	.523	.410	16.9	.477	.373

Table 10. MEASURES OF RATE OF THE EIGHT ORIGINAL READINGS IN NUMBER PER SECOND

Reading	Words		Peaks		Phonations	
	Total Time	Phonation Only	Total Time	Phonation Only	Total Time	Phonation Only
1	5.73	7.34	3.54	4.53	2.71	3.47
2	4.54	5.79	3.06	3.90	2.64	3.37
3	3.85	5.19	2.68	3.58	2.03	2.74
4	3.22	4.51	2.34	3.28	1.93	2.70
5	2.71	4.07	2.17	3.26	1.63	2.44
6	2.27	3.62	2.06	3.29	1.52	2.43
7	1.88	3.35	1.91	3.42	1.36	2.44
8	1.56	2.99	1.64	3.15	1.28	2.45

columns one, three, and five in Table 4 from left to right. For example, the C20 version of Reading 3, the original version of Reading 2, and the E20 version of Reading 1 were equated in total speaking time as a condition of the procedure. A similar examination of columns two and four permits direct comparison of the C10 and E10 versions. As has been mentioned in a previous section, no differences in estimated rate were found that could be attributed to type of version. The mean estimated rates for the C20 versions of Readings 3 through 8, the original versions of Readings 2 through 7, and the E 20 versions of Readings 1 through 6, which have comparable durations, were found to be 5.2, 5.3, and 5.2, respectively. The means for the C10 versions of Readings 2 through 8 and the E10 versions of Readings 1 through 7 were 5.2 and 5.1.

The absence of difference in the rate estimates of the various readings, total speaking time constant, is interesting, since it suggests that internal changes, such as the rate during phonation, phonation and pause ratios, etc., did not affect the estimations of rate. Examination of Tables 9 and 10 will show that the differences in the values of the reported measurements between any three readings, as would obtain in a comparison of C20, 0, and E20, which had equal total speaking times, are quite large. From both approaches, then, the evidence is clear that estimates of rate were more closely dependent upon rate during the total speaking time than upon rate during phonation, within the limits of change in both effected in this study. The graph of the mean duration estimates for the five types of versions, readings pooled, is displayed in Figure 11, where it is seen that estimates of duration increased as total speaking time increased. As has been noted above, there were no systematic differences in the duration estimates of versions within the same rate level. Twelve out of 25 times the compressed and original versions were estimated as being longer than the expanded versions. The mean duration estimates for pooled readings, measured duration constant, were 23.1, 23.6, and 25.6 sec., respectively, for the six comparable C20, 0, and E20 versions, while the values for the seven comparable C10 and E10 versions were 23.7 and 24.5 sec., indicating a slight tendency for expanded versions to be estimated as longer than the others.

Inspection of the mean rate preference values of the 40 versions given in Table 6 indicates large systematic differences between the five versions of the same reading. Detailed examination of versions within the same rate level also showed systematic differences in rate preference, with the compressed and original versions being preferred over the expanded versions 20 out of 25 times. As would be expected, these differences were not large when compared to the within-reading differences noted above. Application of the sign test showed this division to be significant at the 1 per cent level. Mean rate preferences with readings pooled so as to hold measured rate constant were: 5.0, 5.2, and 4.3 for comparable C20, 0, and E20 versions respectively; 5.1 and 4.2 for comparable C10 and E10 versions. Mean rate preference values for all compressions and all expansion by readings are presented in Table 11, and graphed in Figure

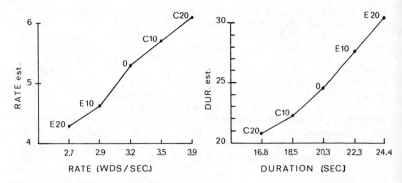

Figure 11. Mean estimated rate (scale 1-9) versus mean measured rate (words/sec.) and mean estimated duration (scale 0-60 sec.) versus mean measured duration (sec.) for the five types of time compression-expansion versions.

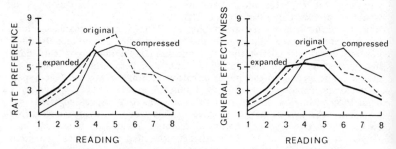

Figure 12. Effects of time compression and expansion in improving or degrading the original readings.

12. This group of curves shows that expansion of the three fastest readings toward the most preferred rate increased the ratings while compression of the same readings had the opposite effect. For the four slowest readings the expected reversals may be seen. It can also be observed that compression resulted in greater improvement than expansion. That these shifts were in some cases substantial is demonstrated by the change exhibited by Reading 6, which covered one-third of the scale range, going from Poor to Good. Other readings followed a similar pattern.

Differences in ratings of general effectiveness of speech within the same reading can be seen in Table 7 [page 279]. These mean ratings were also examined for systematic differences within rate levels, and the compressed or original versions were found to be superior to the expanded versions 21 out of 25 times, a division significant at the 1 per cent level. The mean ratings of general effectiveness for types of versions with comparable measured rates, as

Table 11

MEAN RATE PREFERENCE AND GENERAL EFFECTIVENESS
RATINGS FOR THE COMPRESSED AND EXPANDED
VERSIONS OF THE ORIGINAL READINGS

Reading	Rate Preference		General Effectiveness	
	Compressed	Expanded	Compressed	Expanded
1	1.2	2.2	1.3	2.0
2	2.1	4.2	2.2	3.2
3	3.1	5.4	3.2	5.0
4	6.6	6.7	5.6	5.4
5	6.8	5.0	6.0	5.2
6	6.6	3.0	6.7	3.6
7	4.7	6.3	5.0	3.0
8	3.9	1.3	4.2	2.3

above, were: 4.9, 4.8, and 3.8 for the C20, 0, and E20 versions, respectively; 4.9 and 4.2 for the C10 and E10 versions. The pooled mean ratings of all compressions and all expansions are given in Table 11 and graphed in the right portion of Figure 12. It is readily seen that the same relationships obtained for ratings of general effectiveness as obtained for rate preference. That is, slow readings were improved by compression, fast readings were improved by expansion, but to a lesser extent, and the readings in the middle of the range were degraded by either type of processing. It is interesting to note in Figure 12 that compression of Reading 6, for instance, improved its general effectiveness to a level comparable to that of the original version of Reading 5. The size of this change, more than two scale points, is approximately one-fourth of the total scale range.

Summary and Conclusions

An experimental procedure was arranged to permit investigation of the functional relationships between the perceived and measured rates and durations of speech samples, preferred speech rates, and the perceptual effects of time compression and expansion of speech. Appropriate stimulus materials were prepared, measured and presented to groups of observers for judgments of various types, and the relationships between measurements and judgments were analyzed. Within the limitations of the experiment, the following were the major findings:

1. Estimated rate was found to be a logarithmic function of measured rate in words per second during the total speaking time. This measure of rate exhibited the best relationship to estimated rate among seven rate measures considered.

2. Estimated duration was related linearly to measured total

duration, and was approximately 1.2 times the latter within the range considered.

3. Since it appeared unlikely that duration estimates were based directly on physical duration, the relationship between estimated duration and measured rate was explored, with the finding that estimated duration was proportional to the reciprocal of rate in words per second during the total speaking time.

4. Equations were derived from the above mentioned data for predicting estimated rate from measured duration, and estimated duration from measured rate.

5. The judged appropriateness of the rate of a given speech sample was found to be an inverse linear function of the difference between the estimated rate of the sample and the estimated rate most preferred. An objective expression of this relationship in the form of an index was proposed and applied to the data.

6. Speech performances with inappropriately slow or fast rates were found to be substantially improved by automatic time compression or expansion toward the most preferred rate level. When rate was changed by time compression or expansion, estimated rate and duration changed correspondingly in appropriate directions and amounts.

Chapter 10

DOCTORAL WORK SPONSORED BY GRANT FAIRBANKS, 3

The third and last of three doctoral dissertations sponsored by Dr. Fairbanks to be excerpted here was written at the University of Illinois by George H. Kurtzrock in 1956. The author is now on the staff of the University of Florida. Kurtzrock's work was in large part a follow-up and expansion of the work previously done by Kodman and Hutton. It is interesting to note that Kurtzrock served as a subject in the experiments reported by Kodman.

The study here excerpted dealt with intelligibility and the effects on intelligibility of extremely high compression and expansion as well as of frequency distortion in the forms of both multiplication and division. It is one of the hallmarks of theses approved by Fairbanks that although at first glance they appear very complex, complicated, and difficult to read, as one progresses through the text, the facts determined and the discussion of their significance fall into place logically and, it seems, almost inevitably. The statement just made is certainly true of the study by Kurtzrock. The issues discussed and investigated here are fundamental and need to be understood by any serious student of the process of changing the rate of oral communication.

EFFECTS OF TIME AND FREQUENCY DISTORTION UPON WORD INTELLIGIBILITY

George H. Kurtzrock

Most of the previous psychophysical investigations of word intelligibility have been concerned with the effects of sensation level, signal-to-noise ratio and frequency response. Recently the apparatus devised by Fairbanks, Everitt and Jaeger has permitted control over the time dimension (time distortion) and supplied a technique for the experiment of Kodman [B246], who investigated the intelligibility of words as a function of compressed duration. Garvey [B167, B168, B169] by the method of cutting and re-splicing magnetic tape, performed similar experiments. A partial objective of the present study has been to increase the information regarding the same relationship and to extend it into the region of time expansion.

The automatic method in question also provides for compression or expansion of frequency without altering original time, since its first stage divides or multiplies the signal frequencies. As far as can be determined, the effects of this type of frequency distortion upon intelligibility have not been investigated and constitute a second main area of interest in the present study. An earlier study of the effects of frequency shift has been reported by Fletcher [B114], but the method, subtraction or addition of frequency, displaced the intact spectrum downward or upward along the scale with accompanying destruction of harmonic relationships.

Fletcher also reported the effects upon intelligibility of varying time and frequency conjointly by varying the speed with which a recording is reproduced. This method of controlling the stimulus causes its duration and frequency to change reciprocally, an effect referred to herein as time-frequency distortion, and is a third major condition of the study. The inclusion of this condition provides for direct comparisons with other conditions for purposes of assessing relative effects. It was of particular interest to explore the effects upon the phonetic characteristics of the words and to compare these with respect to the possible differential influence of the form of distortion.

Plan of the Experiment

The general plan of the experiment was to select sets of stimulus values appropriate to the various types of distortion, process the same word list under each of these conditions, and present the processed versions to a group of observers. For each of the three major types of distortions, versions in both directions from the original were produced for a total of six conditions: time compression and expansion, frequency constant; frequency division and multiplication, duration constant; slow and fast play, duration and frequency varying reciprocally. Figure 1 shows how the various stimulus values related to the original undistorted version in duration and frequency. Relative duration is shown along the abscissa with relative frequency given along the ordinate. The latter is also shown as frequency shift in octaves at the right. The stimulus values were selected on the basis of extensive preliminary study and with knowledge of the results previously obtained by Kodman and Fletcher. They were chosen to provide for the inflection of the intelligibility curves for each condition with a minimum of values. Even with this economy there were a total of 16,800 judgments.

It can be seen in Figure 1 that points along the horizontal line, with frequency constant, specify the values of time distortion. For time compression, shown on the left, the values ranged from .063 to .25 times the original duration, and for time expansion, shown on the right, the original duration was multiplied by values from 4.0 to 11.3. Frequency distortion is shown by the vertical line, along which duration is constant. For frequency division, shown at the bottom, it will be seen that the stimulus values ranged from .25 to .50 times the original frequency, or downward frequency shifts as

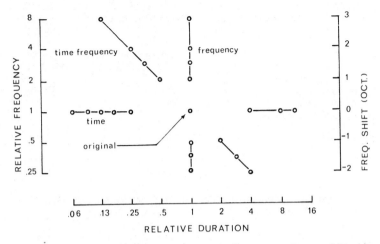

Figure 1. Frequencies and durations of stimulus values relative to original stimulus words.

---

large as two octaves. The values for frequency multiplication, seen at the top, ranged from 2.0 to 8.0 times the original frequency, or upward frequency shifts as large as three octaves. Time-frequency distortion is displayed along the diagonal line, illustrating the reciprocal effect on duration and frequency. Stimulus values for slow play, lower right, ranged downward from .50 to .25 times the original frequency and upward from 2.0 to 4.0 times the original duration. For fast play, shown at the upper left, the values ranged from 2.0 to 8.0 times the original frequency and from .50 to .125 times the original duration.

Table 1 shows the plan in terms of the distortion factors employed for each condition. It will be seen that the distortion factor of 4.0 was common to all conditions, and that the four conditions involving frequency distortion had three factors in common, namely, 2.0, 2.83, and 4.0, thus providing for various direct comparisons between conditions. As will be shown below (Results), detailed analysis was restricted to certain of the stimulus values. These values are indicated by x in Table 1.

Basic Materials

The words used were 50 consonant-vowel-consonant monosyllables constructed according to the phonemic design shown in Table 2. The structure of each word is shown by entry of its vowel symbol at the intersection of its initial consonant row and its final consonant column. As study of the table will show, 10 initial consonants, 10 vowels, and 10 final consonants were each used five times. For ex-

Table 1

DISTORTION FACTORS OF THE VARIOUS STIMULUS VALUES
FOR EACH EXPERIMENTAL CONDITION; (x used for analysis)

	Distortion Factor							
	1.00	2.00	2.83	4.00	5.66	8.00	11.3	16.0
Time Compression	x			x	x	x	x	x
Time Expansion	x			x		x	x	
Frequency Division	x	x	x	x				
Frequency Multiplication	x	x	x	x		x		
Slow Play	x	x	x	x				
Fast Play	x	x	x	x		x		

Table 2

PHONEMIC CONSTRUCTION OF THE 50 STIMULUS WORDS

Initial Consonant	Final Consonant									
	/t/	/p/	/s/	/d/	/m/	/r/	/n/	/z/	/b/	/l/
/t/		e	ɔ				ɪ	i		o
/p/		ʊ	e	ɑ	ɛ	ɔ				
/s/		u		æ	i			o	ɔ	
/d/		ɪ			u		ɛ	o	ɔ	
/m/	i		æ	u		ʊ			ɑ	
/r/	ʊ			ɛ	o			e	ɪ	
/v/	o		e		ɪ		æ			i
/w/	ɑ	i				ɔ			ɛ	ʊ
/ʃ/		ɑ		ʊ		ɪ		u		æ
/dʒ/	ɛ	u			ɑ				æ	e

Table 3

DISTRIBUTION OF THE FREQUENCY OF OCCURRENCE
OF THE 50 STIMULUS WORDS ACCORDING TO THORNDIKE

Thousand	No. of Words	Cumulative Total
1	12	12
2	8	20
3	10	30
4	5	35
5	3	38
6	4	42
7	1	43
8	0	43
9	2	45
10	2	47
11	1	48
Unlisted [jab, vim]	2	50

ample, the five words with initial /t/ were <u>tape</u>, <u>toss</u>, <u>tin</u>, <u>tease</u>, <u>toll</u>; with final /t/, <u>meet</u>, <u>root</u>, <u>vote</u>, <u>watt</u>, <u>jet</u>; and with /u/, <u>soup</u>, <u>doom</u>, <u>mood</u>, <u>shoes</u>, <u>juice</u>. The 50 words are listed below in Table 4 where they are ordered in vowel groups.

The C-C combination of every word in the list is unique, as shown by the fact of no more than one vowel entry. Similarly, all CV- and -VC transitions are also unique, as shown by no duplicate vowel entries in any row or column. Although six elements are common to both sets of 10 initial and final consonants, there are, furthermore, no symmetrical words (e. g. , <u>tot</u>). Thus each word differs from every other word in at least two elements and from all but four words in all three elements. Inspection of the rows and columns of Table 2 will show that for all initial and final consonant word groups the front-back vowel distribution is 2-3 or 3-2, except for initial /v/ where there are four front vowels and one back vowel.

The 10 different vowels employed included equal representation of front, /i/, /ɪ/, /e/, /ɛ/, /æ/, and back, /ɑ/, /ɔ/, /o/, /ʊ/, /u/, types. Two of these vowels, /e/ and /o/, are commonly diphthongized and were so articulated here. Study of the 14 different consonants in Table 2 will show adequate coverage of the range of features such as voicing, manner of articulation, and place of articulation. Considered as a whole, the consonant frequencies by types in the list are probably not seriously different from the total occurrences of consonants in the language. For example, the total consonants recorded by N. R. French, C. W. Carter, and W. Koenig ["The Words and Sounds of Telephone Conversations," <u>Bell System Tech. J.</u> 9:290-324, 1930] divided approximately 35-65 per cent in the voiceless-voiced feature; in the present list the division is also 35-65 per cent. Fifty-five per cent of the consonant occurrences in the list are of types ordinarily classified as "continuants," whereas the remainder are glides, stops and affricates (referred to herein for convenience as "dynamic"). In the language the division was 58-42 per cent for the sample studied by French, Carter and Koenig.

The distribution of the frequency of occurrence of the 50 stimulus words according to E. L. Thorndike [<u>The Teacher's Word Book of 30,000 Words</u>. N.Y.: Columbia Univ. <u>Bur. of Pub. , 1944</u>] is shown in Table 3. It can be seen that 42 of the words occur in the first 6000 most frequent words, and that 48 occur in the first 11,000. Although not listed by Thorndike, <u>jab</u> and <u>vim</u>, the remaining words, must certainly be considered familiar in modern colloquial speech. It may be noted here that analysis of the results revealed no systematic relationship between relative frequency of occurrence and intelligibility. In any case, the procedure described here was such as to minimize the possibility. A master tape recording of the 50 stimulus words, arranged in random order, was made by a mature adult male with superior articulation and considerable speaking experience, who speaks the General American dialect natively and habitually. Recording was done in a conventional two-room laboratory where the speaker was comfortably seated in a sound-treated room with his lips

approximately six inches from the microphone. Although control of
articulation was the primary object, the speaker was also instructed
to attempt to hold the intensity, duration and fundamental frequency
approximately constant for all words. No carrier phrase or auditory
alerting signal was recorded, the speaker speaking the words at 4.5
sec. intervals paced by a light flash. The articulation of each element of each word was determined to be in accordance with the phonemic design described above as judged by three trained phoneticians.
Careful attention was given to such words as root, moor, shear and
pair, which commonly have alternative pronunciations.

    The duration, to the nearest .001 sec., and the mean funda-
mental frequency in c.p.s. for each word were measured from oscillograms. Relative sound pressures were measured to the nearest
0.5 decibel by means of a high-speed level recorder. The results
for the three measures for each word are presented in Table 4. As
can be seen at the bottom of the table, the mean duration of the 50
stimulus words was .610 sec., which is close to the median duration
for similar words reported by Kodman [B246] and Miller and Licklider [B283]. The standard deviation of the distribution was .064
sec., with a range from .480 sec. for tape to .731 sec. for wool.
This represents a somewhat smaller dispersion than the recorded
words of Kodman, whose range was from .36 to .75 sec. The mean
relative sound pressure was 1.9 db above the smallest value (for rib
and tin), and the range was 4.0 db with a standard deviation of 1.04
db. It is of interest that this small range was attained without metering, but with the speaker attempting to maintain equal effort.
Kodman's recorded words had a range of nine decibels with metering,
and the same speaker was used in both experiments. As indicated
at the bottom of Table 4, the mean fundamental frequency of the
words was 107 c.p.s., with a range from 94 c.p.s. for several
words to 132 c.p.s. for soup. The standard deviation was 7.9 c.p.s.
These measures are within the range of fundamental frequencies reported for the connected speech of adult males by numerous investigators.

    Inasmuch as the above three variables are dominated by the
vowels of the words, means for the five words in each vowel group
are shown in Table 5. It can be seen that the range for duration
was .044 sec., for relative sound pressure, 1.4 db, and for mean
fundamental frequency, 10 c.p.s. These ranges are much smaller
than and do not follow the systematic patterns reported by other investigators [B28,B224] [G. A. Fairbanks, A. S. House and E. L.
Stevens, "An Experimental Study of Vowel Intensities," J. of the
Acoustical Soc. of Amer. 22:457-59, 1950]. Thus, the speaker's attempt to equate these variables may be considered to have been successful.

Preparation and Presentation of Stimulus Materials

    The original recording was processed in each of the conditions
at the stimulus values indicated in Table 1. The first step was to

Table 4.   DURATION, RELATIVE SOUND PRESSURE AND MEAN
FUNDAMENTAL FREQUENCY OF THE ORIGINAL STIMULUS WORDS
(Words Grouped by Vowel)

	Duration(sec.)	Sound Pressure(db re min.)	Fund. Freq. (cps)
meet	.551	2.0	110
seem	.673	3.5	106
tease	.625	2.5	114
veal	.614	1.0	118
weep	.541	1.0	114
dip	.590	1.0	111
rib	.549	0.0	103
shear	.708	3.5	105
tin	.541	0.0	101
vim	.691	1.5	99
jail	.576	1.0	99
paid	.556	0.5	100
raise	.707	3.5	98
tape	.480	1.0	108
vase	.625	1.0	117
den	.599	2.0	103
jet	.541	1.5	111
pair	.567	3.0	109
red	.636	2.0	106
web	.576	1.5	113
jab	.629	1.5	102
mass	.579	0.5	106
sad	.650	1.0	104
shall	.591	2.0	100
van	.716	1.5	100
jar	.668	3.5	94
mob	.649	2.0	102
palm	.668	3.5	94
shop	.575	1.0	115
watt	.535	3.0	107
daub	.637	2.0	109
pawn	.692	2.0	108
saws	.613	2.0	94
toss	.540	1.5	111
war	.657	3.0	99
doze	.650	3.0	103
roam	.665	1.5	97
sown	.699	2.0	99
toll	.568	1.0	100
vote	.527	2.5	119
moor	.628	3.0	109
puss	.483	0.5	118
root	.483	0.5	115
should	.655	1.0	114
wool	.731	3.0	103
doom	.665	3.0	97
juice	.588	3.0	118
mood	.623	4.0	103
shoes	.645	2.0	110
soup	.564	1.0	132
Mean	.610	1.9	107
S.D.	.064	1.0	8

Table 5

MEAN DURATION, RELATIVE SOUND PRESSURE
AND FUNDAMENTAL FREQUENCY
OF THE FIVE WORDS IN EACH VOWEL GROUP

	Duration (sec.)	Sound Pressure (db re min.)	Fund. Freq. (c.p.s.)
/i/	.601	2.0	112
/ɪ/	.616	1.2	104
/e/	.589	1.4	104
/ɛ/	.584	2.0	108
/æ/	.633	1.3	102
/ɑ/	.619	2.6	102
/ɔ/	.628	2.1	104
/o/	.622	2.0	104
/ʊ/	.596	1.6	112
/u/	.617	2.6	112

re-record the original tape using an SKL variable electronic filter, Model 302, to provide a 300 to 8000 cycle pass band with 36 db/octave cutoffs. Use of the 300 cycle high-pass filter is conventional in the compression-expansion process to reduce noise, and the 8000 cycle low-pass filter was used to provide tonal balance. The standard Magnecord system of pre- and post-emphasis for the M-90 yielded an essentially flat frequency response throughout the range in question. This filtered version of the original was used as the signal source for all of the various versions.

The stimulus values for time compression, time expansion, frequency division and frequency multiplication were processed according to procedures outlined elsewhere [B167]. A discard interval of .03 sec. was employed. The time-frequency distortion conditions namely slow and fast play, were produced by playing the source slower or faster than recorded according to the various speeds specified above. Extensive calibration studies showed that the time-frequency compression-expansion process imposes a positive slope of approximately six db/octave over a range of 30-16,000 c.p.s. This was accepted without compensation for all stimulus values. For the undistorted, slow play and fast play versions the same rising characteristic was imposed by processing them through the compression device, but without compression or expansion (i.e., with revolving heads motionless).

For convenience in presentation, each of the distorted versions was re-recorded at a constant speed, and additional filtering was imposed with the following effect. In the time distortion conditions, the 300 to 8000 cycle pass band with 18 db/octave cutoffs served to increase the amount of filtering to 54 db/octave. The effect on the frequency distortion conditions was to limit the frequency range pro-

portional to the amount of distortion. For example, in frequency
division or slow play by a distortion factor of 2.0, in which all of
the source frequencies were divided in half, or transposed to a 150-
4000 cycle range, this filtering reduced the effective range to a 300-
4000 cycle pass band. The effect was similar in frequency multiplication and fast play except that the high end of the range was limited. During presentation to the observers, the 300-8000 cycle pass
band with 18 db/octave cutoffs was again imposed. Thus the total
filtering for the time distortion conditions was 72 db/octave at both
ends of the range. For frequency distortion by division or slow
play, the total filtering amounted to 36 db/octave at the low end of
the range and 72 db/octave at the high end. For frequency distortion by multiplication or fast play, the total filtering was 72 db/oc-
tave at the low end and 36 db/octave at the high end of the range.

Each of the 28 experimental tapes was administered at approximately 75 db above the normal threshold for 1000 c.p.s. A 1000
cycle tone of known voltage was spliced at the beginning of each version, and the playback gain control was adjusted to produce the required level. The output of the tape recorder was fed through a
matching transformer to three pairs of Permoflux PDR-10 earphones
connected in parallel and fitted with Type 1505 ear cushions. According to voltage calibrations, these earphones had an essentially
flat frequency response from 100 to 7000 c.p.s. The final step in
the preparation of the experimental tapes was to arrange the words
into a different random order for each of 22 stimulus values (the
same order was used for all presentations of the undistorted version).
Each version was cut into individual words and these were spliced
together in random order with a blank piece of tape proportional to
4.5 sec. separating them. The 50 words in each tape were divided
into five equal groups identified as Part One, etc., and undistorted
part designations were spliced in.

Observers

Six young adult males were selected from the available observers. All were advanced graduate students in speech who had
normal hearing acuity bilaterally for pure tones from 250 to 8000
c.p.s. as determined by tests on a Microtone ADC, Model 53C, audiometer. Inasmuch as the primary task involved speech, suprathres-
hold speech discrimination tests were given. Each observer scored
100 per cent on a recorded PB list administered at approximately
75 db above threshold. An additional criterion was that each observer be familiar with phonetic notation. Eleven training sessions distributed over a period of two weeks were conducted in order to familiarize the observers with the vocabulary prior to the experimental
sessions. The first session consisted of two presentations of the undistorted original tape recording. The observers first wrote their
responses in orthography and then listened to the words while watch-
ing a card upon which the words were printed in order. This having
been completed, the general construction of the list was explained
along lines similar to the description above. It was pointed out, for

example, that any word could be correctly identified given two of its three elements, etc. Alternative pronunciations, as mentioned above, were discussed and attention was called to those employed in the recordings.

Each of the remaining 10 training sessions consisted of two presentations of the undistorted version as above, except that thermal noise was mixed with the first presentation to increase the difficulty of identification and insure attention. At the end of each of these sessions a word-fragment test was given to measure the increasing familiarity with the 50-word vocabulary. This test consisted of a randomized order of the words with only two elements given for each word. For example, the three possible fragments of the word paid were /pe-/, /p-d/ and /-ed/. The particular fragment used for each word in each test was chosen at random. Observers were asked to supply the missing element and to write the word on an answer sheet in orthography.

By the end of the training sessions all observers had scored 100 per cent on the word-fragment tests at least twice. Each observer had heard the undistorted version of the word list a total of 22 times, and the 100 per cent scores on the word-fragment tests indicated that they knew the vocabulary. Additional evidence of this fact was provided by each observer scoring 100 per cent on a word-fragment test given immediately after the last experimental session. One week following the last experimental session, without warning, each observer was asked to reconstruct the list by writing the 50 words from memory. Two observers offered all 50 words; the remaining four were able to produce, 49, 47, 45 and 39 words, respectively.

Procedure with Observers

The observers were divided into two groups of three, and the data collected in six experimental sessions for each group. Each session consisted of two distortion conditions separated by a rest period. No more than one session was held on a single day, and one week intervened between the first three sessions and the last three. In an attempt to counterbalance order effects, the following procedure was employed. The first three sessions included all six conditions, with the stimulus values being presented in order of progressively increasing distortion (descension toward threshold). Group one received the conditions in the following order: frequency division, frequency multiplication, time compression, time expansion, slow play, fast play. Group two received them in reverse order. The last three sessions also included all six conditions, with the stimulus values being presented in order of progressively decreasing distortion (ascension toward threshold). Group one received the conditions in the order of frequency multiplication, frequency division, time expansion, time compression, fast play, slow play. Group two received them in reverse order.

Table 6

PERCENTAGES OF WORD INTELLIGIBILITY
FOR THE VARIOUS STIMULUS VALUES.
ENTRIES FOR SLOW AND FAST PLAY REPEATED.

Relative Duration	Time Distortion — Compression	Time-Frequency Distortion — Fast Play
.063	5.7	
.088	16.5	
.125	42.3	0.7
.250	85.0	10.5
.350		50.2
.500		86.3
1.000	100.0	100.0

	Expansion	Slow Play
1.00	100.0	100.0
2.00		43.0
2.83		22.7
4.00	100.0	14.8
8.00	96.5	
11.31	92.8	

Relative Frequency	Frequency Distortion — Division	Time-Frequency Distortion — Slow Play
.25	13.8	14.8
.35	16.5	22.7
.50	32.8	43.0
1.00	100.0	100.0

	Multiplication	Fast Play
1.00	100.0	100.0
2.00	90.5	86.3
2.83	65.2	50.2
4.00	17.7	10.5
8.00	5.7	0.7

Earphones were rotated systematically by ears and conditions. Observers were seated in the sound-treated room facing away from each other, and responses were written in conventional orthography on suitably prepared answer sheets. The observers were instructed to guess when uncertain, to write word fragments in phonetic notation in instances of partial identification, and to respond with a dash when nothing intelligible was heard, but to make no changes in or additions to any responses after hearing any later stimulus. At the beginning of each condition the observers were informed as to the mode of distortion, were requested to listen carefully, and were given a brief resumé of the specific instructions.

General Effects of Time, Frequency and Time-Frequency Distortion

The percentages of word intelligibility for the various values of relative duration and relative frequency within each of the six conditions are shown in Table 6. Each entry is the percentage of correct responses among 600 judgments, the 50-word list having been presented to six observers twice for each stimulus value. Study of the results of the descending and ascending presentations showed differences in the expected directions and thus no need for treating them separately. The results for slow and fast play are repeated in Table 6 in order to facilitate direct comparisons of the time-frequency distortion data with the corresponding data for time and frequency distortion. At the top they are arranged according to relative duration and at the bottom according to relative frequency. Correlation coefficients were calculated between the results for the descending and ascending presentations of a single representative stimulus value for each condition, with the exception of expansion, which was not included because the effects upon intelligibility were too small. The 50 words were used as items with the number of correct responses as the measure, the maximum value being six (subjects). The stimulus value which yielded a combined descension-ascension mean nearest to 50 per cent was chosen as representative of each condition. Although the obtained coefficients, shown in Table 7, are probably attenuated by the small range, all of them are significant and provide evidence of satisfactory reliability.

Table 7

PRODUCT-MOMENT CORRELATION COEFFICIENTS BETWEEN THE RESULTS FOR REPRESENTATIVE STIMULUS VALUES REPEATED IN ASCENDING AND DESCENDING SERIES

	r
Compression	.80
Division	.74
Multiplication	.82
Slow Play	.65
Fast Play	.50

The means for the values of time distortion, frequency constant, shown in Table 6 are displayed graphically in the solid line of Figure 2A, with time compression at the left and time expansion at

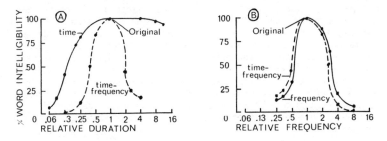

Figure 2. Percentage of word intelligibility as a function of relative duration, A, and relative frequency, B

the right. It can be seen that the curve rises in the characteristic form of a discrimination curve to 100 per cent, has a relatively long plateau, and ends with a slight downward inflection at large values of expansion. The time compression curve is inflected similarly to the curves presented by Kodman, with intelligibility decreasing as a function of increasing time compression. The mean intelligibility for the middle four stimulus values (indicated by x in Table 1) was 54.1 per cent. This may be compared to the mean of 50.5 per cent for comparable time compression values in Kodman's exploratory series in which observers had a similar amount of practice in identifying compressed words.

Inspection of the data will show that 50 per cent intelligibility was obtained at a relative duration of approximately .14. Since the mean duration for words in the list was .61 sec., this reduction would yield a mean word duration of .084 sec., with the longest word .102 sec. These durations are comparable to those of single elements in connected speech as reported by numerous investigators. A possible way of estimating the approximate durations of words which would be 50 per cent intelligible to naive listeners confronted with an unknown vocabulary is suggested by comparison of the data from Kodman's exploratory and experimental series. The comparison shows that, in the mid-ranges of intelligibility, practice with the vocabulary and the form of distortion may be estimated as increasing intelligibility approximately 25 per cent. Thus, although not definitive, it is possible to estimate 50 per cent intelligibility for a naive listener on the basis of the relative duration which yielded 75 per cent in the present study. This level was obtained at a relative duration of approximately .19 or a mean word duration of about .114 sec. The latter value is also within the range for single elements.

The significance of the slight decrease in intelligibility at

large time expansions is uncertain. At the time the stimulus materials were being prepared, distortion factors beyond those used were
not considered interpretable because of noise and frequency distortion.
Although the slight decrement might have been caused by the above
factors, subsequent improvement in the processing technique, which
has permitted the processing of factors as large as 32 without unduly
increasing noise, has led to a more plausible explanation. Informal
listening to time expansions of this magnitude revealed that the elements of the words are intelligible, but that factors such as the
lengthened transitions, the unfamiliar display of dynamic consonants
and the demands upon the memory span tend to make word identification appreciably more difficult. Thus it is possible that the slight
inflection of the curve is a true indication of a decrement produced
by time expansion. Since the obtained effect upon intelligibility was
so small, however, further analysis of the time expansion data was
not performed.

        In general, the data show that the range of high intelligibility
is wide, and it is clear that live speech, although shown to provide
excess duration, is closer to the short than to the long end for listeners. The intelligibility curve for time-frequency distortion is
shown by the broken line in Figure 2A, plotted as a function of relative duration. It will be noted that the steepness of the intelligibility
function is increased for this mode of distortion. For fast play,
shown at the left, 50 per cent intelligibility was obtained, for a relative duration of .35 at which speed frequency was 2.83 times the
original. Fifty per cent intelligibility was not obtained for any of the
stimulus values used in slow play, shown at the right, but it is estimated to have required a relative duration of slightly less than 2.0,
the original duration and a correspondingly lower relative frequency.
The shape of the curve as a whole is generally similar to that shown
by Fletcher [B114], for distortion by the same method.

        The relative importance of frequency can be seen by compar-
ing the broken curve with the solid curve in Figure 2A. For example, if a tape recording made at 7.5 i.p.s. were played at 15 i.p.s.,
relative duration would be .50 and relative frequency would be 2.0.
Inspection of the broken curve will show that the obtained decrement
in intelligibility was approximately 15 per cent. When, however, the
original frequencies were restored, as in time compression by a distortion factor of 2.0, intelligibility would be 100 per cent. Similarly,
if the recording were played four times as fast as the storage speed
relative duration would be .25 and relative frequency 4.0 times the
original. At this point, the obtained decrement in intelligibility was
approximately 90 per cent, but when the frequencies were restored,
as in time compression by a factor of 4.0, the decrement was only
15 per cent. On the other hand, if the 7.5 i.p.s. tape recording
were played at 3.75 i.p.s., as for slow play by a factor of 2.0, the
decrement shown is greater than 50 per cent, and restoration of the
frequencies would eliminate it. Playing the recording at 1.875 i.p.s.
or .25 times the storage speed, reduced intelligibility by 85 per cent.
Again, restoration of the original frequencies eliminated the decrement. Thus the difference between the ordinates of the time and fre-

quency curves at any point along the abscissa may be taken as a measure of the effect of dividing or multiplying the frequency by the amount in question. The importance of frequency is not surprising since a major characteristic of the speech signal is the location of energy with respect to frequency. These data emphasize the view that the absolute locations of component frequencies are important, inasmuch as the relative locations were preserved in the experiment. On the basis of these data, it is evident that with frequency constant, time is very elastic, but with frequency varying reciprocally, the time elasticity is easily overcome.

The intelligibility curve for frequency distortion is shown by the solid line of Figure 2B, with frequency division at the left and frequency multiplication at the right. The intelligibility function is seen to be relatively steep, and the curve appears to be generally symmetrical. Examination and comparison of the values in Table 6, however, reveal that, distortion factors equal, intelligibility is greater for frequency multiplication than for frequency division. The magnitude of this difference can be gauged by comparing ordinate values for the three common distortion factors and by inspection of the means shown in the top row of Table 8, where the common factors have been pooled. This difference was found to be significant beyond the 1 per cent level as shown by the large F for frequency in Table 9. Fletcher observed this phenomenon for frequency distortion by the method of addition or subtraction also, and reported that "the data indicate that shifting the speech frequencies downward produces a more serious deterioration than by producing the same upward shift." He also reported that "decreasing the speed has a greater effect than increasing the speed" in regard to the similar effect noted for time-frequency distortion by slow and fast play. Although the present study was not designed to permit a definitive explanation of the source of the difference, it is suggested that the pitch discriminations which are basic to speech identification may be better preserved with upward shifts of the spectrum than with downward shifts.

The time-frequency curve, shown by the broken line in Figure 2B, is a reversed version of the broken curve in Figure 2A, oriented with respect to frequency. Slow play is shown at the left and fast play at the right. If the two curves in Figure 2B are compared, it can be seen that, distortion factors equal, intelligibility for slow play slightly exceeded that for frequency division, but that intelligibility for fast play was less than for frequency multiplication by a corresponding factor. This is perhaps more readily apparent by intercomparison of the two pairs of means in Table 8. The statistical significance of this interaction was tested by the triple-classification analysis of variance summarized in Table 9. The F of interest is that for the first order interaction between duration and frequency (D x F), which is seen to have been significant beyond the 1 per cent level.

Taken as a whole, the foregoing data indicate that the duration of a word is a very elastic dimension as far as intelligibility is

Table 8.   MEAN PERCENTAGE OF WORD INTELLIGIBILITY IN
FOUR CONDITIONS INVOLVING FREQUENCY DISTORTION.   (Data
Restricted to Common Distortion Factors)   [x in Table 1]

Duration		Frequency	
		Lowered	Raised
		(Division)	(Multiplication)
Unaltered	Mean	21.1	57.8
	S.D.	15.8	14.1
		(Slow Play)	(Fast Play)
Altered	Mean	26.8	49.0
	S.D.	15.3	12.5

Table 9.   SUMMARY OF ANALYSIS OF VARIANCE OF FOUR CONDI-
TIONS INVOLVING FREQUENCY DISTORTION.   (Duration x Frequency
[as in Table 8] x Words [50].)

	df	MS	F	F.99
Duration (D)	1	14.58		
Frequency (F)	1	5618.00	267.40**	7.19
Words (W)	49	73.33	3.49**	1.96
D x F	1	343.22	39.54*	7.19
D x W	49	5.12		
F x W	49	21.01	2.42*	1.96
D x F x W	49	8.68		

*Error term = $MS_{D \times F \times W}$.   **Error term = $MS_{F \times W}$.

Table 10.   SUMMARY OF ANALYSIS OF VARIANCE OF STIMULUS
WORDS AND FIVE EXPERIMENTAL CONDITIONS.   (Time Expansion
Excluded.)

	df	MS	F	F.99
Conditions	4	104.06	23.12	3.41
Words	49	14.33	3.18	1.62
Residual	196	4.5		

Table 11.   INTERCORRELATIONS OF ADJACENT STIMULUS VALUES
FOR EACH EXPERIMENTAL CONDITION.   (See text for notation.)

	Between Values:		
	1 & 2	2 & 3	3 & 4
Compression	.48	.40	.52
Division	.52	.66	
Multiplication	.49	.38	
Slow Play	.65	.53	
Fast Play	.37	.56	

concerned, that intelligibility is considerably more sensitive to frequency distortion in the form of division or multiplication than to
time distortion by similar factors, that when time and frequency distortion are both present, as in slow play with accompanying frequency division or in fast play with accompanying frequency multiplication,
intelligibility is dominated by frequency distortion, although the effect
of duration remains discernible and significant, and, finally, that intelligibility is more resistive to frequency multiplication than to frequency division.

Intercorrelations of Distortion Conditions

In order to test the significance of the observation that, with
the exception of time expansion, all stimulus values yielded wide
ranges of intelligibility for various words, the analysis of variance
summarized in Table 10 was performed.   The stimulus value, regardless of its size, which yielded an intelligibility nearest to 50 per
cent was used to sample each condition.   Analysis was after the manner of a matched groups design with five conditions by 50 words, the
entry for each word being the number of correct responses, 0-12,
for the condition in question.   The significant F of 3.18 for words
confirms the observed difference, and is interpreted as indicating
that additional analysis of the nature of the differences would be
meaningful.   Such analysis is also supported in a more limited form
by the significant F for words shown in Table 9.

Product-moment correlation coefficients between adjacent stimulus values within each of the five conditions are shown in Table 11.
The stimulus values indicated by x in Table 1 were referred to for
convenience as 1, 2, 3, 4 in order of increasing distortion because
they were not the same for all conditions.   For example, the r of
.48 seen at the top of the first column, indicates the relationship between words for distortion factors of 4.0 and 5.66 in the time compression condition.   The r at the bottom of the second column was
obtained between distortion factors of 2.83 and 4.0 for fast play.
All of the coefficients are significant, indicating that, within conditions, words tended to be ordered similarly as the general level of
intelligibility was varied by the amount of distortion.   These results
lend support to the procedure of pooling the data for the stimulus
values indicated by x in Table 1 for each condition in order to en-
hance stability.

The extent of the correlation between different forms of distortion also was estimated by computing correlation coefficients,
again using words as items.   For this purpose the results for each
condition were pooled as described above for each word and are
shown in Table 12, where they are expressed in terms of mean percentage of intelligibility.   The table also includes the data for time
expansion for the sake of completeness.   Each entry is the percentage of correct responses among 48 total judgments for time compression (four stimulus values) and among 36 total judgments for all other
conditions (three stimulus values each).

Table 12. MEAN PERCENTAGES OF INTELLIGIBILITY OF THE
STIMULUS WORDS IN THE VARIOUS EXPERIMENTAL CONDITIONS.
(Stimulus values indicated x̄ in Table 1 have been pooled for all con-
ditions; expansion data from factors 4. 0, 8. 0 and 11. 3 have been added.)

	Comp.	Exp.	Div.	Mult.	Slow	Fast
meet	64. 6	97. 2	8. 3	66. 7	19. 4	52. 8
seem	68. 7	97. 2	11. 1	63. 9	16. 7	27. 8
tease	37. 4	94. 4	16. 7	69. 4	30. 6	69. 4
veal	58. 3	100. 0	5. 6	44. 4	11. 1	55. 6
weep	37. 4	100. 0	11. 1	61. 1	11. 1	41. 7
dip	35. 4	94. 4	30. 6	41. 7	33. 3	50. 0
rib	37. 4	97. 2	5. 6	38. 9	11. 1	41. 7
shear	77. 1	97. 2	5. 6	55. 6	11. 1	55. 6
tin	43. 7	97. 2	22. 2	61. 1	41. 7	47. 2
vim	54. 2	100. 0	3. 0	44. 4	8. 3	33. 3
jail	47. 9	97. 2	13. 9	50. 0	30. 6	30. 6
paid	37. 4	88. 9	16. 7	55. 6	30. 6	38. 9
raise	39. 6	100. 0	25. 0	75. 0	19. 4	58. 3
tape	37. 4	97. 2	22. 2	69. 4	38. 9	50. 0
vase	41. 7	100. 0	11. 1	50. 0	11. 1	41. 7
den	39. 6	100. 0	16. 7	52. 8	38. 9	44. 4
jet	68. 7	86. 1	16. 7	55. 6	38. 9	38. 9
pair	77. 1	94. 4	5. 6	50. 0	11. 1	44. 4
red	43. 7	100. 0	25. 0	52. 8	25. 0	52. 8
web	45. 8	100. 0	22. 2	30. 6	16. 7	50. 0
jab	50. 0	100. 0	27. 8	36. 1	36. 1	33. 3
mass	75. 0	94. 4	41. 7	77. 8	38. 9	69. 4
sad	39. 6	91. 7	19. 4	69. 4	27. 8	47. 2
shall	72. 9	94. 4	16. 7	38. 9	13. 9	33. 3
van	43. 7	100. 0	13. 9	55. 6	22. 2	33. 3
jar	64. 6	100. 0	13. 9	61. 1	25. 0	47. 2
mob	56. 2	100. 0	5. 6	44. 4	5. 6	27. 8
palm	33. 3	69. 4	5. 6	16. 7	8. 3	22. 2
shop	66. 7	94. 4	44. 4	52. 8	38. 9	50. 0
watt	83. 3	100. 0	11. 1	75. 0	25. 0	52. 8
daub	50. 0	100. 0	19. 4	55. 6	19. 4	55. 6
pawn	39. 6	100. 0	8. 3	50. 0	36. 1	44. 4
saws	58. 3	86. 1	22. 2	63. 9	30. 6	47. 2
toss	47. 9	100. 0	11. 1	75. 0	33. 3	61. 1
war	79. 2	100. 0	13. 9	72. 2	8. 3	61. 1
doze	70. 8	100. 0	61. 1	63. 9	58. 3	75. 0
roam	52. 1	100. 0	0. 0	58. 3	13. 9	38. 9
sown	66. 7	94. 4	25. 0	58. 3	13. 9	44. 4
toll	41. 7	97. 2	22. 2	52. 8	30. 6	61. 1
vote	52. 1	100. 0	27. 8	72. 2	41. 7	72. 2
moor	52. 1	97. 2	16. 7	66. 7	16. 7	50. 0
puss	41. 7	100. 0	86. 1	75. 0	80. 6	72. 2
root	56. 2	88. 9	22. 2	47. 2	0. 0	44. 4
should	50. 0	100. 0	47. 2	77. 8	41. 7	61. 1
wool	58. 3	88. 9	13. 9	36. 1	22. 2	36. 1
doom	68. 7	100. 0	16. 7	61. 1	25. 0	58. 3
juice	50. 0	94. 4	38. 9	61. 1	41. 7	55. 6
mood	47. 9	97. 2	33. 3	61. 1	38. 9	47. 2
shoes	58. 3	100. 0	33. 3	80. 6	38. 9	66. 7
soup	83. 3	94. 4	38. 9	83. 3	52. 8	55. 6

The intercorrelation coefficients are shown in Table 13.   It will be seen that the six coefficients between the various frequency and time-frequency conditions, shown in triangular arrangement at the right, are all substantial.   Of particular interest are the .81 and

Table 13

INTERCORRELATIONS OF EXPERIMENTAL CONDITIONS

	Comp.	Div.	Mult.	Slow
Division	.02			
Multiplication	.26	.40		
Slow Play	-.07	.81	.47	
Fast Play	.14	.58	.66	.53

.66 between frequency and time-frequency conditions which have directions and magnitudes of frequency shift in common.   In general, these six coefficients indicate the presence of significant common effects of frequency distortion, whether division or multiplication and with or without accompanying time distortion.   It should be noted, however, that the relationships are not perfect, as evidenced by the significant interaction between frequency distortion and words (F x W) shown in Table 9 above, and also by certain data presented below.   The coefficients in the first column of Table 13, which are between time compression and the conditions involving frequency distortion, suggest that the relationship between the effects of time distortion and frequency distortion are different.   In this instance the four values are small, and none is significantly greater than zero.   In other words, when intelligibility is attenuated by time distortion, the words appear to be ordered differently than they are when intelligibility is attenuated by frequency distortion.   Since the stimuli, as described above, were prepared under conditions which limited the range of non-phonetic acoustical characteristics and held familiarity of words constant, this finding is interpreted to mean that the two different modes of distortion operated differently upon specific phonetic elements, a type of analysis which was pursued as described below.

Effects of Word Characteristics in Different Distortion Conditions

As has already been explained, steps were taken to equate word familiarity by selecting words that were high in frequency of occurrence and by requiring observers to participate in an extensive training procedure.   In view of the directions of interest, and since Black has reported [B28] that "word intelligibilities are not independent of the Thorndike ratings of the words," it was desirable to hold this factor constant.   As a check against the possibility that it was present in spite of the precautions, words were grouped according to the Thorndike ratings as in Table 3 and mean percentages of intelligibility computed for each group in the various conditions.   Inspection of the means showed no discernible trends, as would be expected from the procedure, and it was felt that this factor could be disregarded. It will also be recalled that the ranges of duration, relative sound pressure and mean fundamental frequency were intentionally limited. The actual values of these variables have been reviewed in the procedure. To explore the possibility of relationships, however, correlation coefficients between the three sets of measures and word intelligibility in the time compression condition were computed. This involved data on the mean intelligibility of words shown in the first column of Table 12 and the duration, relative sound pressure and mean fundamental frequency data from Table 4. The coefficients were .08, .17 and .06, respectively. Whereas these data are clearly not to be interpreted as indicative of an absence of relationships between intelligibility and non-phonetic word characteristics, they may be regarded as justifying the planned restriction of the analysis in the present experiment to phonetic factors.

The purposes of the phonetic analysis were exploratory and descriptive rather than definitive. It was undertaken and should be interpreted with a realization of the limitations of the data. For example, the results must be qualified in terms of the obvious fact that the articulatory practices of the speaker who was used as the source cannot be regarded as representative in the sense that the 30 different phonetic elements were all equally well articulated or that they varied according to the central tendency of the population. A second limitation relates to the character of the stimulus words. Although the list was carefully constructed to represent different types of phonetic elements and to insure that words representing them were equally numerous, thus attempting to take full advantage of all 150 articulatory occurrences, it could not be exhaustive. Even with the restriction to the C-V-C elements employed, this would have required 1000 syllable combinations. Because of the limitation in number, conventional analyses of interactions between elements could not be performed. Regardless of the above, it was believed that analyses of phonetic factors could be pursued to some advantage, and that the results thereof, if interpreted conservatively, would at least indicate trends and suggest useful hypotheses for more exhaustive experimentation.

The first step was to group the words according to common initial consonants, vowels, and final consonants. Tables 14, 15 and 16 present the mean percentages of intelligibility for the three groupings. Each of these means was based on 240 total judgments for time compression and on 180 total judgments for the other four conditions. Analyses of variance of initial consonants, vowels and final consonants, summaries of which are shown in Tables 17, 18 and 19, respectively, indicate that significant differences exist between the three groupings in all five conditions, supporting analyses of differences between phonetic classes.

In view of the limitations already described, and because differences between means for initial consonants, vowels and final consonants are zero by definition, the relative intelligibility of elements

(cont. on p. 313)

Table 14

MEAN PERCENTAGES OF INTELLIGIBILITY
FOR WORDS GROUPED BY INITIAL CONSONANT

	Comp.	Div.	Mult.	Slow	Fast
/t/	41.7	18.9	65.6	35.0	57.8
/p/	45.8	24.4	49.4	33.3	44.4
/s/	63.3	23.3	67.8	28.3	44.4
/d/	52.9	28.9	55.0	35.0	56.7
/m/	59.2	21.1	63.3	23.9	49.4
/r/	45.8	15.6	54.4	13.9	47.2
/v/	50.0	12.2	53.3	18.9	47.2
/w/	60.8	14.4	55.0	16.7	48.3
/ʃ/	65.0	29.4	61.1	28.9	53.3
/dʒ/	56.3	22.2	52.8	34.4	41.1

Table 15

MEAN PERCENTAGES OF INTELLIGIBILITY
FOR WORDS GROUPED BY VOWEL

	Comp.	Div.	Mult.	Slow	Fast
/i/	53.3	10.6	61.1	17.8	49.4
/ɪ/	49.6	13.3	48.3	21.1	45.6
/e/	40.8	17.7	60.0	26.1	43.9
/ɛ/	55.0	17.2	48.3	26.1	46.1
/æ/	56.3	23.9	55.6	27.8	43.3
/ɑ/	60.8	16.1	50.0	20.6	40.0
/ɔ/	55.0	15.0	63.3	25.6	53.9
/o/	56.7	27.2	61.1	31.7	58.3
/ʊ/	51.7	37.2	60.6	32.2	52.8
/u/	61.7	32.2	69.4	39.4	56.7

Table 16

MEAN PERCENTAGES OF INTELLIGIBILITY
FOR WORDS GROUPED BY FINAL CONSONANT

	Comp.	Div.	Mult.	Slow	Fast
/t/	65.0	17.2	63.3	25.0	52.2
/p/	52.1	29.4	61.7	35.0	49.4
/s/	51.3	37.8	67.8	41.1	60.0
/d/	43.8	28.3	63.3	32.8	49.4
/m/	55.4	7.2	48.9	14.4	36.1
/r/	70.0	11.1	61.1	14.4	51.7
/n/	46.7	17.2	55.6	30.6	42.8
/z/	52.9	31.7	70.6	35.6	63.3
/b/	47.9	16.1	41.1	17.8	41.7
/l/	55.8	14.4	44.4	21.7	43.3

Table 17. SUMMARY OF ANALYSES OF VARIANCE OF INITIAL CONSONANTS

	df	MS	F*
Compression			
Consonants	9	62.84	3.54
Subjects	5	337.64	19.03
Residual	45	17.74	
Division			
Consonants	9	18.39	2.38
Subjects	5	272.38	35.28
Residual	45	7.72	
Multiplication			
Consonants	9	20.59	3.58
Subjects	5	221.06	38.45
Residual	45	5.75	
Slow Play			
Consonants	9	34.96	3.64
Subjects	5	428.82	44.67
Residual	45	9.60	
Fast Play			
Consonants	9	15.92	2.20
Subjects	5	167.96	23.23
Residual	45	7.23	

*F, df 9 & 45, 1%: 2.84; 5%: 2.10. F, df 5 & 45, 1%: 3.46.

Table 18. SUMMARY OF ANALYSES OF VARIANCE OF VOWELS

	df	MS	F*
Compression			
Vowels	9	33.97	3.57
Subjects	5	337.64	35.50
Residual	45	9.51	
Division			
Vowels	9	41.31	4.08
Subjects	5	272.38	26.92
Residual	45	10.12	
Multiplication			
Vowels	9	26.73	3.12
Subjects	5	221.06	25.82
Residual	45	8.56	
Slow Play			
Vowels	9	22.14	2.61
Subjects	5	428.82	50.57
Residual	45	8.48	
Fast Play			
Vowels	9	20.62	2.90
Subjects	5	167.96	23.66
Residual	45	7.10	

*F, df 9 & 45, 1%: 2.84; 5% 2.10. F, df 5 & 45, 1%: 3.46.

Table 19

SUMMARY OF ANALYSES OF VARIANCE OF FINAL CONSONANTS

	df	MS	F*
Compression			
Consonants	9	63.00	5.57
Subjects	5	337.64	29.85
Residual	45	11.31	29.85
Division			
Consonants	9	52.20	6.54
Subjects	5	272.38	34.13
Residual	45	7.98	
Multiplication			
Consonants	9	53.44	13.43
Subjects	5	221.06	55.54
Residual	45	3.98	
Slow Play			
Consonants	9	48.89	7.57
Subjects	5	428.82	66.38
Residual	45	6.46	
Fast Play			
Consonants	9	38.10	4.69
Subjects	5	167.96	20.66
Residual	45	8.13	

*F, df 9 & 45, 1%: 2.84; 5%: 2.10.   F, df 5 & 45, 1%: 3.46.

classified by position was pursued by a method which utilized analysis of the error responses. It will be recalled that observers were instructed to make a partial response when unable to identify the complete word. Such responses, together with the remaining incorrect responses which involved complete words, were studied from the standpoint of the correct C-, V and -C fragmentary identifications. The single representative stimulus value closest to 50 per cent intelligibility was employed for each condition as before. Observers were credited with only one correct response per element per word even when the same response was made in both the descending and ascending series. The sums of these responses for C-, V and -C are shown in Table 20. Attention is directed to the shape of the distributions, since the actual numbers are not directly comparable for all conditions. It will be seen that χ^2 was significant for all conditions. In the four conditions involving frequency distortion, the vowel was less intelligible than either the initial or final consonant, which suggests that the vowel formants were more seriously disturbed by this mode of distortion than were the basic correlatives of consonant intelligibility. The situation is different, however, in time compression. In this instance, the vowel was the most intelligible element of the three, which can probably be attributed in part to the relatively longer durations of vowels. In regard to initial and final consonants, there was no interpretable differentiation in the conditions where frequency was disturbed. Under this method of scoring, how-

Table 20

NUMBERS OF CORRECTLY IDENTIFIED PHONETIC ELEMENTS OF
WORDS IN INCORRECT RESPONSES AND CORRESPONDING CHI-
SQUARES. DATA RESTRICTED TO ONE REPRESENTATIVE STIM-
ULUS VALUE PER CONDITION.

	C-	-V-	-C	χ^2
Compression	27	58	48	11. 31
Division	50	15	69	33. 57
Multiplication	35	15	35	9. 43
Slow Play	59	10	48	33. 90
Fast Play	38	22	50	10. 76

ever, final consonants were more intelligible than initial consonants
in time compression, and it is possible that under conditions of reduced word duration, the final consonant is in a more favorable position for identification because it ends the stimulus.

Attention was then directed to the differences between classes
of phonetic elements. In the case of vowels the 10 elements were
grouped, first, according to the frequency of Formant One and, again,
according to the frequency of Formant Two. The divisions within
each group were "high" and "low" according to the usual findings and
were made at arbitrary points along a presumed frequency continuum.
Specifically, the grouping was as follows:

Formant One	Vowel	Position
Low	/i ɪ e o ʊ u/	Close
High	/ɛ æ ɑ ɔ/	Open
Formant Two		
Low	/u ʊ o ɔ ɑ/	Back
High	/æ ɛ e ɪ ɪ/	Front

The more familiar organogenetic terminology is shown at the right.
Consideration was given to separate analysis or omission of the two
diphthongs, but when study of the data (e. g. , as in Table 15) showed
no differences attributable to their diphthongal character and since it
was desired to include all words in the analysis, the decision was
reached to include them among the vowels as shown.

The mean intelligibility of words in each vowel class is shown
in Table 21. Differences between classes are also shown, and the
matched groups t was used to test significance, the results being
shown by asterisks. With respect to Formant One a tendency for the
low class to be more intelligible will be noted for conditions other
than time compression, but the difference was significant only in fast
play. Differences in favor of low formant vowels are seen also in
the Formant Two groups, four of the five being significant.

Initial and final consonants were grouped according to the

Table 21

DIFFERENCES BETWEEN MEAN PERCENTAGES OF INTELLIGIBILITY FOR VOWEL CLASSES

	Formant One		Formant Two	
Compression				
	Low	52. 3	Low	57. 2
	High	56. 8	High	51. 0
	Diff.	-4. 5	Diff.	6. 2**
Division				
	Low	23. 1	Low	25. 6
	High	18. 1	High	16. 6
	Diff.	5. 0	Diff.	9. 0*
Multiplication				
	Low	60. 1	Low	60. 9
	High	54. 3	High	54. 7
	Diff.	5. 8	Diff.	6. 2*
Slow Play				
	Low	28. 1	Low	29. 9
	High	25. 0	High	23. 8
	Diff.	3. 1	Diff.	6. 1
Fast Play				
	Low	51. 1	Low	52. 3
	High	45. 8	High	45. 7
	Diff.	5. 3*	Diff.	6. 6*

**Sign. at 1%.   *Sign. at 5%.

---

features of voicing, manner of articulation and place of articulation. Thus dichotomous groupings of all words into voiced or voiceless, continuant or dynamic, and labial or lingual were made first, by initial consonant and, again, by final consonant. The mean percentages of intelligibility for words so grouped are shown in Tables 22 and 23, respectively. Inspection of the voicing feature will show that with the exception of the initial consonant in time compression, all of the differences are in favor of voiceless consonants. It is of interest to note that there were significant differences in all four conditions involving frequency distortion in the case of the final consonant, and that a significant difference obtained in slow play for the initial consonant.

The differences between continuant and dynamic consonants were small and mixed among the conditions. Significant differences were obtained only in the case of the initial consonant in slow play, where dynamic consonants were more intelligible than continuants. In a special case of the manner of articulation feature, an analysis of variance of six initial voiced consonants differing in manner of articulation was performed for each of the five conditions. This analysis is summarized in Table 24. Significant differences were found for the frequency division and slow play conditions. It will be recalled that these conditions produced the highest correlation coefficient between words.

Table 22. DIFFERENCES BETWEEN MEAN PERCENTAGES OF IN-
TELLIGIBILITY FOR INITIAL CONSONANT CLASSES [**Sign. at 1%]

	Voicing		Manner		Place	
Compression						
Voiceless	54.0	Continuant	56.7	Lingual	54.2
Voiced	54.2	Dynamic	51.5	Labial	54.0
Difference	-.2	Difference	5.2	Difference	.2
Division						
Voiceless	24.0	Continuant	20.3	Lingual	23.1
Voiced	19.1	Dynamic	21.8	Labial	18.1
Difference	4.9	Difference	-1.5	Difference	5.0
Multiplication						
Voiceless	61.0	Continuant	60.0	Lingual	59.4
Voiced	55.7	Dynamic	55.6	Labial	55.3
Difference	6.3	Difference	4.4	Difference	4.1
Slow Play						
Voiceless	31.4	Continuant	22.8	Lingual	29.3
Voiced	23.8	Dynamic	30.9	Labial	23.2
Difference	7.6**	Difference	-8.1**	Difference	6.1
Fast Play						
Voiceless	50.0	Continuant	48.3	Lingual	50.1
Voiced	48.3	Dynamic	49.7	Labial	47.4
Difference	1.7	Difference	-1.4	Difference	2.7

Table 23. DIFFERENCES BETWEEN MEAN PERCENTAGES OF IN-
TELLIGIBILITY FOR FINAL CONSONANT CLASSES [**Sign. at 1%.
*Sign. at 5%.]

	Voicing		Manner		Place	
Compression						
Voiceless	56.1	Continuant	55.3	Lingual	55.0
Voiced	53.2	Dynamic	52.2	Labial	51.8
Difference	2.9	Difference	3.1	Difference	3.2
Division						
Voiceless	28.2	Continuant	19.9	Lingual	22.5
Voiced	18.0	Dynamic	22.8	Labial	17.6
Difference	10.2**	Difference	-2.9	Difference	4.9
Multiplication						
Voiceless	64.3	Continuant	58.1	Lingual	60.9
Voiced	55.0	Dynamic	57.4	Labial	50.6
Difference	9.3**	Difference	.7	Difference	10.3*
Slow Play						
Voiceless	33.7	Continuant	26.3	Lingual	28.7
Voiced	23.9	Dynamic	27.6	Labial	22.4
Difference	9.8**	Difference	-1.3	Difference	6.3
Fast Play						
Voiceless	53.9	Continuant	49.5	Lingual	51.8
Voiced	46.9	Dynamic	48.2	Labial	42.4
Difference	7.0*	Difference	1.3	Difference	9.4*

Table 24

SUMMARY OF ANALYSES OF VARIANCE OF SIX INITIAL VOICED CONSONANTS DIFFERING IN MANNER OF ARTICULATION

	df	MS	F*
Compression			
Consonants	5	31.14	1.63
Subjects	5	139.06	7.26
Residual	25	19.16	
Division			
Consonants	5	24.78	3.22
Subjects	5	130.64	16.97
Residual	25	7.70	
Multiplication			
Consonants	5	8.08	1.31
Subjects	5	152.88	24.70
Residual	25	6.19	
Slow Play			
Consonants	5	44.50	4.39
Subjects	5	272.90	26.94
Residual	25	10.13	
Fast Play			
Consonants	5	13.54	2.45
Subjects	5	145.80	26.37
Residual	25	5.53	

*F, df 5 & 25, 1%: 3.86; 5%: 2.60.

Examination of the place feature in Tables 22 and 23 will show that words containing either initial or final lingual consonants were more intelligible than those with labials. The direction of the difference is the same for all conditions, but the differences were significant only in the case of frequency multiplication and fast play. It is interesting that these two conditions both involve frequency multiplication. In general, this analysis of the effects of word characteristics in the different distortion conditions indicates that, within the limitations discussed above, there are differences between initial consonants, vowels and final consonants in all conditions, that vowels are more affected by frequency distortion than consonants but less affected by time compression, that classes of vowels having low formants are more intelligible than those with high formants, that voiceless consonants tend to be more intelligible than voiced consonants, and that lingual consonants tend to be more intelligible than labials. Most of the significant differences between phonetic classes were found in the conditions involving frequency distortion.

Effects of Phonetic Structure of Words

        In the preceding section the method of study involved the
specification of only one phonetic characteristic at a time without
study of interactions, a procedure which was essentially a regroup-
ing of the same words for exploration of the influence in question.
As has been explained above, the inability to study the phonetic interactions conventionally was a limitation of the materials. Unquestionably, however, the combination of phonetic elements into words
creates stimuli which become unique as combinations, and this kind
of interaction is of more than ordinary interest because of the CV-
or -VC transitions which are added as the combinations are formed.
As stated above, the procedure of the preceding section was to specify one element of each word. For example, in one comparison the
word soup was grouped with other words that had voiceless initial
consonants, in another instance with other words having a low Formant Two vowel, and in the third instance with other words having
dynamic final consonants. Soup, however, also belongs to the class
of words which have in common a voiceless initial consonant, a low
Formant Two vowel and a dynamic final consonant. Such specification of combinations, as the number of features is increased, may
involve several levels which increase in specificity toward the statement, for example, that soup is a word composed of /s/-, -/u/-
and -/p/, and even further. In addition to the level of specification,
numerous combinations of specifications may be made such as would
differentiate soup from loop, soup from seep, soup from soon, etc.
Obviously, the number of possible combinations becomes very large
and their study impractical. In fact, the 50 stimulus words used
here represent 50 such combinations.

        In view of the necessary limitations, it was decided to re-
strict the description of each word in a given comparison to dichotomous specification of each element, as for instance, classification of
the initial consonant as either voiced or voiceless. It was also decided to limit the number of possible combinations to be tested by
letting the trial combinations be guided by the results of the comparisons of classes described above. Finally, it was decided to confine
the analysis to time compression, frequency division and frequency
multiplication, since these conditions as shown by the general analysis, appeared to be representative of the effects of the different
forms of distortion.

        Table 25 presents the results for the specification of one dis-
tinctive feature of each of the three elements. The first row in each
of the three sections pertains to specification of the voicing of the
initial consonant, the openness of the vowel and the voicing of the
final consonant. For convenience in exposition the organo-genetic
terminology has been used in describing vowel classes. In this first
case, in the time compression condition, the C-V-C combination
voiced-open-voiceless was compared to the voiceless-close-voiced
combination, the data reported above for the phonetic classes having
suggested the possibility that the first combination might be more intelligible than the second. Study of Table 25 will show that similar

Table 25

DEGREE OF ASSOCIATION BETWEEN WORD INTELLIGIBILITY AND SPECIFICATION OF ONE PHONETIC ATTRIBUTE OF EACH WORD ELEMENT, AS SHOWN BY CONTINGENCY COEFFICIENTS

C-	-V-	-C	X^{2*}	$\underline{C}^{**}$
Compression				
Voiced	Open	Voiceless	.03	.025
Continuant	Open	Continuant	3.92	.270
Lingual	Open	Lingual	.03	.025
Voiced	Back	Voiceless	5.13	.305
Continuant	Back	Continuant	8.68	.385
Lingual	Back	Lingual	.80	.125
Division				
Voiceless	Close	Voiceless	3.90	.269
Dynamic	Close	Dynamic	2.98	.237
Lingual	Close	Lingual	.83	.128
Voiceless	Back	Voiceless	7.97	.371
Dynamic	Back	Dynamic	2.16	.203
Lingual	Back	Lingual	2.85	.232
Multiplication				
Voiceless	Close	Voiceless	2.80	.230
Continuant	Close	Continuant	2.26	.207
Lingual	Close	Lingual	3.91	.269
Voiceless	Back	Voiceless	1.98	.195
Continuant	Back	Continuant	.94	.136
Lingual	Back	Lingual	3.57	.258

$*X^2$, df 1, 1%: 6.64; 5%: 3.84.   **Cmax: .707.

manner of articulation and place of articulation specifications of consonants were tested for each of the two types of vowel specifications, open-close and front-back. It will be immediately obvious that all words in the list do not fall into the two categories thus far described. In the case of the first specification for time compression in Table 25, for example, the word <u>vim</u> would be excluded from both categories. All words meet at least two of the specifications in either one category or the other, however, and admission to a given category was made on this basis. It will be readily appreciated that had the more refined categories been added, the number of entries would have become meaninglessly small. In summary, one category was formed of those words which met two or three of the specifications and another category of those words which met one or none of the specifications, i.e., which met two or three of the opposite specifications.

For each condition separately, the 50 words were dichotomized on the basis of intelligibility. They were arranged in descending rank order according to values presented in Table 12, and the division was made between the ranks of 25 and 26. Simple 2 x 2, intelligibility-by-combination, contingency tables were formed, of which the following from the time compression condition will be illustrative.

	Intelligibility:		
	Low	High	
Continuant-Back-Continuant	11	21	32
Dynamic-Front-Dynamic	14	4	18
	25	25	50

The degree of association was estimated by computing contingency coefficients, and these are shown in Table 25 together with the values of X^2 upon which they were based. The significance of the latter may be evaluated by comparison with the tabled requirements shown, and the magnitude of C may in part be assessed by comparison to the maximum value it can attain in a 2 x 2 case, namely, .707. Although the interpretation of C is limited, it may be useful to note, since the total number was 50 and the contingency table was 2 x 2 in all instances in the present study, that the values of C when X^2 is significant at the 5 per cent and 1 per cent levels are .267 and .342, respectively.

If the values of X^2 are examined it will be observed that most of them fail of significance, whereas others meet the requirement. This suggests that there are in some cases differences between the intelligibilities of words which are related to the particular combinations of which they are composed. Although no value of C is very large relative to the maximum, two of them are substantial. One way of viewing these data is to consider the specification as "predicting" word intelligibility. For example, on the basis of Table 25 it might be predicted that in time compression words which met two or three of the requirements for the continuant-back-continuant specification would be relatively high in intelligibility. Thirty-two of the 50 words meet the requirement, but only five do so in all respects. These five are moor, roam, shoes, saws and sown, and all occur in the higher intelligibility group. Identification of the 10 highest ranking words on the basis of the intelligibility values in the first column of Table 12 reveals that eight of them fit this specification, namely, soup, war, shear, mass, shall, doze, seem and doom. Conversely, it would be predicted that words of the dynamic-front-dynamic type would have low intelligibility. The 10 lowest ranking words again include eight words of this form, namely, dip, paid, tape, rib, weep, tease, sad and den. The other substantial relationship, the voiceless-back-voiceless vs voiced-front-voiced dichotomy for frequency division, is also of interest. In this case, puss, should, shop, soup, juice and shoes are found among the highest 10, and meet, veal, rib, shear, pair, mob, vim and roam among the 10 at the bottom of the order.

As has been mentioned the combinations specified were not exhaustive and did not attempt to test association in such combinations as, for example, the voicing of the initial consonant and the manner of the final consonant. Guided, however, by study of some of the larger differences between means, a number of these were explored,

I. Doctoral Work, 3 (Kurtzrock)

of which one showed a stronger relationship than any presented in Table 25. This was in the condition of frequency division and involved a lingual-back-voiceless vs oral-front-voiced dichotomy. In this instance X^2 was 9.43 and $\bar{C}$ was .398.

In a similar manner an attempt was made to explore the effect of combinations in which two features were considered for each element in each word. For example, in the preceding section vowels were categorized as close or open in one treatment and as front or back in another. For the purposes of the present treatment it was desired to specify vowel class as close front, close back, open front or open back, or the four cells in an open-close by front-back contingency table. In the case of consonants, where voicing, manner and place are considered, there would be three such combinations, namely, voicing and manner, voicing and place, and manner and place. The following illustrative arrangement shows the categories for voicing by manner for the initial consonant.

	Continuant	Dynamic	
Voiceless	10	10	20
Voiced	15	15	30
	25	25	50

The entries in the four cells show the number of words in the stimulus list which had initial consonants as specified. Whereas the preceding analysis may be thought of as having specified only the row or the column, the present design was to specify both, or to allow the influence of interaction between the two features to be exerted. It will be appreciated, however, that if all possible combinations of four categories of C-, V and -C were employed, the numbers would become unmanageable and the number of words representing a given combination would, in the present study, become meaninglessly small. They would almost amount to naming individual words in many cases. A method of decreasing the number of combinations and thereby increasing the number of available words was found by combining the four categories for each element into two. As has been pointed out, this had already been done, in a sense, in the one-feature specification of the previous section (e. g. , voiceless dynamic and voiceless continuant consonants are both members of the voiceless class), so that what was added was diagonal pooling of cells in a 2 x 2 table. In the above example of initial consonants, this meant forming one category which included the 10 words with voiceless continuant consonants and the 15 with voiced dynamic consonants, and another category which included the remainder of the words. Although at first glance this might not appear to be very meaningful, it is possible that among continuant consonants, for instance, voiceless members might have higher intelligibilities than voiced members, but that the reverse might be true among dynamic consonants. It will be recognized that this method of two-feature specification implies one such dichotomy for vowels, in which only the open-close and front-back dimensions were considered in the present study, but three for the consonants. In other words, the structure of a word might be speci-

Table 26

DEGREE OF ASSOCIATION BETWEEN WORD INTELLIGIBILITY AND SPECIFICATION OF TWO PHONETIC ATTRIBUTES OF EACH WORD ELEMENT, AS SHOWN BY CONTINGENCY COEFFICIENTS

C-	-V-	-C	X^2*	C**
Compression				
Voiceless Continuant or Voiced Dynamic	Close Back or Open Back	Voiceless Dynamic or Voiced Continuant	6.65	.343
Voiceless Lingual or Voiced Labial	Close Back or Open Back	Voiceless Lingual or Voiced Labial	4.16	.277
Lingual Continuant or Labial Continuant	Close Back or Open Back	Lingual Continuant or Labial Continuant	8.68	.385
Division				
Voiceless Continuant or Voiced Dynamic	Close Back or Open Front	Voiceless Continuant or Voiceless Dynamic	7.78	.367
Voiceless Lingual or Voiceless Labial	Close Back or Open Front	Voiceless Lingual or Voiceless Labial	9.63	.402
Lingual Continuant or Lingual Dynamic	Close Back or Open Front	Lingual Dynamic or Labial Dynamic	15.63	.488
Multiplication				
Voiceless Continuant or Voiceless Dynamic	Close Back or Open Back	Voiceless Continuant or Voiceless Dynamic	1.98	.195
Voiceless Lingual or Voiced Labial	Close Back or Open Back	Voiceless Lingual or Voiceless Labial	7.94	.370
Lingual Continuant or Labial Continuant	Close Back or Open Back	Lingual Continuant or Lingual Dynamic	2.42	.215

*X^2 df 1, 1%: 6.64; 5%: 3.84.   **Cmax: .707.

fied in nine different ways, three types of two-feature specification for initial consonants, one for the vowel, and three for the final consonant, if only the diagonal case is considered.

Representative results from such procedures are presented in Table 26. The data shown are limited in two ways. First, only combinations of consonant specification which involve the same feature in both initial and final consonants are presented. Thus the first row of Table 26 considers the case of specifying voicing-manner in both initial and final consonants, whereas the combinations of voicing-manner initial specification and manner-place final specification are not included. The second restriction of the data presented has been made by showing only the case for each element in which the most powerful dichotomy among the row, column and diagonal specifications was tested. The effect of these restrictions is to show some data in Table 26 which are identical to those presented in Table 25. For example, the first specification for frequency multiplication is equivalent to the voiceless-back-voiceless type tested in the preceding section, and represents a case where two-feature specification was no improvement over one-feature specification.

The results presented in Table 26 may be thought of as summarizing tests of the hypothesis that words which have a specified structure do not differ in intelligibility from words which do not. In other words, in the case of the first row in the time compression condition, the division is into categories of words which either do or do not have two or three of the following characteristics: a voiceless continuant or a voiced dynamic initial consonant; an open back or a close back vowel; a voiceless dynamic or a voiced continuant final consonant. In this case it will be noted that χ^2 was significant beyond the 1 per cent level and that $\underline{C}$ was .343. Reference to Table 25 will show that this two-feature specification was an improvement over most of the one-feature specifications, even though the vowel specification was equivalent to using only one feature. This "improvement of intelligibility prediction" by specifying two features for each element instead of one is a general observation which may be made by comparing the size of $\underline{C}$ in Tables 25 and 26. Although study of the specific specifications presented shows that this is not the case with all specifications of three elements simultaneously, inspection of Table 26 will support the observation that, in these results at least, the particular combination of elements specified seems to be as powerful as the number of features specified for each element. For example, the highest $\underline{C}$ in Table 26 is .488 for the third case in the frequency division condition. The specification shown amounts to a combination of lingual initial consonant, open front or close back vowel, and dynamic final consonant. It will be observed that two features are specified only in the case of the vowel, whereas different features are specified for the initial and final consonants. In this instance 24 words have two or three of the specified elements, and, of these, 18 were in the higher intelligibility category. Twenty-one of the 26 words which did not meet this requirement were in the lower intelligibility group.

Exploration was also carried out in regard to the degree of association with intelligibility when all three features of the initial and final consonants, voicing, manner and place, were specified. The dichotomies were arrived at by means of 2 x 2 x 2, three dimensional tables. Not all possible dichotomies or combinations thereof were considered, but it is believed that the experience with the one- and two-feature specifications prevented promising dichotomies from being overlooked. The results of these procedures will not be presented in detail for the reason that they were largely negative. In the conditions of frequency division and multiplication no instance was found in which the previous coefficients were increased. For time compression, however, where the maximum value of $\underline{C}$ was .385 in the one-feature, continuant-dynamic consonant dichotomy and was not increased by the two-feature combinations (Table 26), the admission of the third consonant feature raised the value to .481. The CVC combination found to be associated with high intelligibility had specifications which may be summarized as follows: voiced, (but not also lingual continuant) or voiceless lingual continuant initial consonant; back vowel; continuant (but not also voiceless lingual) or voiceless lingual dynamic final consonant. It is interesting to observe that, with the exceptions noted for consonants, the specified combination here is also basically simple, namely, voiced-back-continuant. The importance of the exceptions, which are made possible by the utilization of three features, is evidenced by comparison with the obtained value of $\underline{C}$ in the simple one-feature, voiced-back-continuant vs voiceless-front-dynamic dichotomy. For that case $\underline{C}$ was .161.

In general, the data of this section, taken in conjunction with the findings of the previous section with regard to the means for phonetic classes, indicate that the intelligibility of a given word is probably based not only upon the intelligibilities of the classes of the individual elements of which it is composed, but also upon the particular combinations which these classes form, and that in some instances the particular sub-class exerts discernible influence. Interest also attaches to these findings because they suggest that prediction of degree of intelligibility by means of relatively simple phonetic specification may be applicable to other forms of distortion as well.

Summary and Conclusions

For the purpose of investigating the effects of time, frequency and time-frequency distortion upon word intelligibility, representative versions of a recorded sample of monosyllabic words were prepared and presented to a group of observers for identification. The phonetic structure of the materials permitted study of both general and specific effects. The major findings were as follows:

1. Intelligibility was unaffected over a wide range of time distortion. Fifty per cent intelligibility was obtained when the words had been reduced to approximately one-seventh of their original durations. Expansion of duration beyond 11 times the original had slight effect.

2. Intelligibility was considerably more sensitive to frequency distortion in the form of division or multiplication than to time distortion by comparable amounts.

3. When time and frequency were distorted reciprocally the intelligibility decrement was dominated by frequency distortion, although the effect of duration remained appreciable and significant.

4. Frequency multiplication had less effect upon intelligibility than frequency division by comparable amounts.

5. Individual words were ordered similarly in intelligibility as the amount of a given type of distortion was varied, but differently in the time distortion and frequency distortion conditions. There was a positive, but not perfect, relationship between the order of words in frequency division and multiplication.

6. Significant differences in intelligibility were obtained between words grouped according to specific initial consonants, vowels and final consonants in all conditions except time expansion, where the reduction in intelligibility was too slight to warrant analysis.

7. On the basis of the number of correct elements in error responses, vowels were found to be less intelligible than consonants in the conditions involving frequency distortion, but more intelligible

than consonants in the time compression condition.

8. Differences between words grouped by various phonetic classes were generally small and were more often significant in the conditions of frequency distortion than in time compression. Certain trends were noted. Back vowels were more intelligible than front vowels in all conditions. Open vowels tended to be more intelligible than close vowels in time compression but less intelligible in the other conditions. Voiceless consonants, whether initial or final, were more intelligible than voiced consonants in the frequency distortion conditions. Continuant consonants tended to be more intelligible than dynamic consonants in time compression. Lingual consonants were more intelligible than labial consonants in all conditions.

9. Combinations of classes and sub-classes of phonetic elements, such as are formed in words, were found to vary in degree of association with intelligibility, certain combinations being significantly associated.

Chapter 11

THEORY OF COMMUNICATION, 1

The author of the basic article excerpted in this and the next chapter is an eminent scholar, inventor, and scientist. Since granting me permission to use this material, Professor Gabor has been awarded the Nobel Prize in physics for his work with holography. Dr. Gabor is professor emeritus and senior research fellow at the Imperial College of Science and Technology, London, England as well as a staff scientist at CBS Laboratories in Stamford, Connecticut. He is a fantastically productive writer. It is a great honor to be permitted to reproduce major portions of his article on "Theory of Communication" in this anthology.

During the process of preparing the textual material of this work I have had some serious misgivings concerning the wisdom of including excerpts from this article in the anthology. The article, while it seems to me to be basic to the thinking concerning the theory of speech compression as a communicating device, is difficult to read without at least some background in both calculus and physics. Many of the readers of this compendium will not possess such a background and to them the reading of this article is not recommended. Nevertheless, I decided to include the material in this and in the following chapter on the theory that it contributes to the completeness of the presentation. After all, few people will read this anthology through starting at the beginning and continuing to the last page. Most users, it is my judgment, will be looking for information that will be specifically useful to their unique individual needs.

The finest tribute that can be paid to any piece of writing is extensive use. In four libraries in the New York area, this article, long and difficult as it may be, has been used so often that the pages are too worn for photocopying. Obviously, many readers have found this article worth studying. The material in this chapter consists of the development of basic concepts essential to the proper understanding of Parts 2 and 3 which are excerpted together in chapter 12.

THEORY OF COMMUNICATION

D. Gabor

Preface

The purpose of these three studies is an inquiry into the essence of the "information" conveyed by channels of communication, and the application of the results of this inquiry to the practical problem of optimum utilization of frequency bands. In Part 1, a new method of analyzing signals is presented in which time and frequency play symmetrical parts, and which contains "time analysis" and "frequency analysis" as special cases. It is shown that the information conveyed by a frequency band in a given time-interval can be analyzed in various ways into the same number of elementary "quanta of information," each quantum conveying one numerical datum.

In Part 2, this method is applied to the analysis of hearing sensations. It is shown on the basis of existing experimental material that in the band between 60 and 1000 c. p. s. the human ear can discriminate very nearly every second datum of information, and that this efficiency of nearly 50 per cent is independent of the duration of the signals in a remarkably wide interval. This fact, which cannot be explained by any mechanism in the inner ear, suggests a new phenomenon in nerve conduction. At frequencies above 1000 c. p. s. the efficiency of discrimination falls off sharply, proving that sound reproductions which are far from faithful may be perceived by the ear as perfect, and that "condensed" methods of transmission and reproduction with improved waveband economy are possible in principle. In Part 3, suggestions are discussed for compressed transmission and reproduction of speech or music, and the first experimental results obtained with one of these methods are described.

Part 1.   THE ANALYSIS OF INFORMATION

Summary

Hitherto communication theory was based on two alternative methods of signal analysis. One is the description of the signal as a function of time; the other is Fourier analysis. Both are idealizations, as the first method operates with sharply defined instants of time, the second with infinite wave-trains of rigorously defined frequencies. But our everyday experiences—especially our auditory sensations—insist on a description in terms of both time and frequency. In the present paper this point of view is developed in quantitative language. Signals are represented in two dimensions, with time and frequency as co-ordinates. Such two-dimensional representations can be called "information diagrams," as areas in them are proportional to the number of independent data which they can convey. This is a consequence of the fact that the frequency of a signal which

is not of infinite duration can be defined only with a certain inaccuracy, which is inversely proportional to the duration, and vice
versa. This "uncertainty relation" suggests a new method of description, intermediate between the two extremes of time analysis
and spectral analysis. There are certain "elementary signals"
which occupy the smallest possible area in the information diagram.
They are harmonic oscillations modulated by a "probability pulse."
Each elementary signal can be considered as conveying exactly one
datum, or one "quantum of information." Any signal can be expanded in terms of these by a process which includes time analysis and
Fourier analysis as extreme cases.

These new methods of analysis, which involve some of the
mathematical apparatus of quantum theory, are illustrated by application to some problems of transmission theory, such as direct generation of single sidebands, signals transmitted in minimum time
through emitted frequency channels, frequency modulation and time-
division multiplex telephony.

(1) Introduction

The purpose of this study is to present a method, with some
new features, for the analysis of information and its transmission
by speech, telegraphy, telephony, radio or television. While this
first part deals mainly with the fundamentals, it will be followed by
applications to practical problems, in particular to the problem of
the best utilization of frequency channels.

The principle that the transmission of a certain amount of information per unit time requires a certain minimum waveband width
dawned gradually upon communication engineers during the third dec-
ade of this century. Similarly, as the principle of conservation of
energy emerged from the slowly hardening conviction of the impossibility of a perpetuum mobile, this fundamental principle of communication engineering arose from the refutation of ingenious attempts to
break the as yet unformulated law. When in 1922 John R. Carson
["Notes on the Theory of Modulation," Proc. of Inst. of Radio Engineers 10:57-64, 1922] disproved the claim that frequency modulation could economize some of the bandwidth required by amplitude-
modulation methods, he added that all such schemes "are believed to
involve a fundamental fallacy." This conviction was soon cast into a
more solid shape when, in 1924, H. Nyquist ["Certain Factors Affecting Telegraph Speed," Bell System Tech. J. 3:324-46, 1924] and
K. Küpfmüller ["Transient Phenomena in Wave Filters," Elektrische
Nachrichten-Technik 1:141-52, 1924] independently discovered an important special form of the principle, by proving that the number of
telegraph signals which can be transmitted over any line is directly
proportional to its waveband width. In 1928 R. V. L. Hartley
["Transmission of Information," Bell System Tech. J. 7:535-63,
1928] generalized this and other results, partly by inductive reasoning, and concluded that "the total amount of information which may
be transmitted ... is proportional to the product of frequency range

which is transmitted and the time which is available for the transmission. "

Even before it was announced in its general form, an application was made of the new principle, which remains to this day
probably its most important practical achievement.   In 1927, F.
Gray, J. W. Horton and C. R. Mathes ["The Production and Utilization of Television Signals," Bell System Tech. J. 6:560-603, 1927]
gave the first full theoretical discussion of the influence of waveband
restriction on the quality of television pictures, and were able to fix
the minimum waveband requirements in advance, long before the
first high-definition system was realized.   In fact, in this as in
later discussions of the problem, the special Nyquist-Küpfmüller result appears to have been used, rather than Hartley's general but
somewhat vague formulation.

The general principle was immediately accepted and recognized as a fundamental law of communication theory, as may be seen
from its discussion by F. Lüschen ["Modern Communication Systems," J. of Inst. of Elec. Engineers 71:776, 1932] before this Institution.   Yet it appears that hitherto the mathematical basis of the
principle has not been clearly recognized.   Nor have certain practical conclusions been drawn, which are suggested by a more rigorous
formulation.

(2) Transmission of Data

Let us imagine that the message to be transmitted is given
in the form of a time function $s(t)$, where s stands for "signal."
Unless specially stated, s will be assumed to be of the nature of a
voltage, current, field strength, air pressure, or any other "linear"
quantity, so that power and energy are proportional to its square.
We assume that the function $s(t)$ is given in some time interval
$t_2-t_1 = \tau$, as illustrated in Figure 1.1.   Evidently this message contains an infinity of data.   We can divide τ into, say, N sub-intervals,
and define, for instance, the average ordinate in each sub-interval
as a "datum."   If there is no limit to the sub-division, there is no
limit to the number of data which could be transmitted in an absolutely faithful reproduction

As this is impossible, let us see whether it is possible to
transmit faithfully at least a finite number N of data.   Evidently
there is an infinite number of possibilities for specifying the curve
$s(t)$ in the interval τ approximately by N data.   Without knowing the
specific purpose of the transmission it is impossible to decide which
is the most economical system of selection and specification.   Yet,
certain methods will recommend themselves by reason of their analytical simplicity.   One of these, division into equal sub-intervals,
has been already mentioned.   Another method is to replace the curve
$s(t)$ in the interval τ by a polynomial of order N, to fit it as
closely as possible to $s(t)$ by the method of least squares, and to
take the coefficients of the polynomial as data.   It is known that this

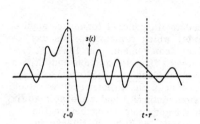

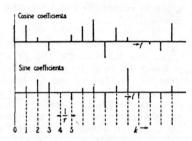

Figure 1.1. Signal as a func-   Figure 1.2. Fourier spectrum of
tion of time.   signal in an interval τ.

---

method is equivalent to specifying the polynomial in such a way that
its first N "moments" M_1 shall be equal to those of $s(t)$:--

$$M_0 = \int_0^T s\,dt \quad M_1 = \int_0^T ts\,dt \quad M_2 = \int_0^T t^2 s\,dt \ldots M_{N-1} = \int_0^T t^{N-1} s\,dt$$

Instead of the coefficients of the polynomial, we can also consider
these moments as the specified data.

A method closely related to this is the following. Expand
$s(t)$, instead of in powers of time, in terms of a set of N functions
$\phi_k(t)$, orthogonal in the interval $0 < t < \tau$, and consider as data the N
coefficients of expansion. It is known that this is equivalent to fitting the expansion to $s(t)$ by the method of least squares. How
close the fit will be, and how well it will suit the practical purpose,
depends on the set of functions selected.

One class of orthogonal functions, the simple harmonic functions sine and cosine, have always played a preferred part in communication theory. Let us now develop the curve $s(t)$ in the interval τ into a Fourier series. This gives an infinite sequence of
spectral lines, as shown in Figure 1.2, starting with zero frequency,
all equally spaced by a frequency $1/\tau$. Two data are associated
with each frequency, the coefficients of the sine and cosine terms in
the expansion. In a frequency range $(f_2 - f_1)$ there are therefore
$(f_2 - f_1)\tau$ lines, representing $2(f_2 - f_1)\tau$ data, that is exactly two data
per unit time and unit frequency range. This, in fact, proves the
fundamental principle of communication.

In whatever ways we select N data to specify the signal in the
interval τ, we cannot transmit more than a number $2(f_2 - f_1)\tau$
of these data, or of their independent combinations by means of
the $2(f_2 - f_1)\tau$ independent Fourier coefficients.

In spite of the extreme simplicity of this proof, it leaves a
feeling of dissatisfaction. Though the proof shows clearly that the
principle in question is based on a simple mathematical identity, it
does not reveal this identity in a tangible form. Besides it leaves
some questions unanswered: What are the effects of a physical filter? How far are we allowed to subdivide the waveband or the time

interval? What modifications would arise by departing from the rigid prescription of absolute independence of the data and allowing a limited amount of mutual interference? It therefore appears worthwhile to approach the problem afresh in another way, which will take considerably more space, but which, in addition to physical insight, gives an answer to the questions which have been left open.

(2.1) Time and Frequency

The greatest part of the theory of communication has been built up on the basis of Fourier's reciprocal integral relations:

$$s(t) = \int_{-\infty}^{\infty} S(f)e^{2\pi jft}df \qquad S(f) = \int_{-\infty}^{\infty} s(t)e^{-2\pi jft}dt \quad \ldots \ldots \quad (1.1)$$

where $s(t)$ and $S(f)$ are a pair of Fourier transforms. We will refer to $S(f)$ also as the "spectrum" of $s(t)$. Though mathematically this theorem is beyond reproach, even experts could not at times conceal an uneasy feeling when it came to the physical interpretation of results obtained by the Fourier method. After having for the first time obtained the spectrum of a frequency-modulated sine wave, Carson wrote [see page 328]: "The foregoing solutions, though unquestionably mathematically correct, are somewhat difficult to reconcile with our physical intuitions, and our physical concepts of such 'variable-frequency' mechanisms as, for example, the siren."

The reason is that the Fourier-integral method considers phenomena in an infinite interval, sub specie aeternitatis, and this is very far from our everyday point of view. Fourier's theorem makes of description in time and description by the spectrum, two mutually exclusive methods. If the term "frequency" is used in the strict mathematical sense which applies only to infinite wave-trains, a "changing frequency" becomes a contradiction in terms, as it is a statement involving both time and frequency.

The terminology of physics has never completely adapted itself to this rigorous mathematical definition of "frequency." In optics, in radio engineering and in acoustics the word has retained much of its everyday meaning, which is in better agreement with what Carson called "our physical intuitions." For instance, speech and music have for us a definite "time pattern," as well as a frequency pattern. It is possible to leave the time pattern unchanged, and double what we generally call "frequencies" by playing a musical piece on the piano an octave higher, or conversely it can be played in the same key, but in different time. Evidently both views have their limitations, and they are complementary rather than mutually exclusive. But it appears that hitherto the fixing of the limit was largely left to common sense. It is one of the main objects of this paper to show that there are also adequate mathematical methods available for this purpose.

Let us now tentatively adopt the view that both time and frequency are legitimate references for describing a signal and illustrate this, as in Figure 1.3, by taking them as orthogonal co-ordi-

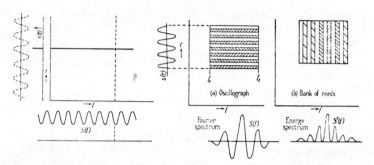

Figure 1.3. Unit impulse (delta function) and infinite sine wave in time/frequency diagram.

Figure 1.4. Time/frequency diagram of the response of physical instruments to a finite sine wave.

nates. In this diagram a harmonic oscillation is represented by a vertical line. Its frequency is exactly defined, while its epoch is entirely undefined. A sudden surge or "delta function" (also called "unit impulse function"), on the other hand, has a sharply defined epoch, but its energy is uniformly distributed over the whole frequency spectrum. This signal is therefore represented by a horizontal line. But how are we to represent other signals, for instance a sine wave of finite duration?

In order to give this question a precise meaning we must consider the physical effects which can be produced by the signal. The physical meaning of the $s(t)$ curve, shown at the left of Figure 1.4 is that this is the response of an ideal oscillograph which has a uniform response over the whole infinite frequency range. The interpretation of the Fourier spectrum, shown at the bottom of the same figure, is somewhat less simple. It could be obtained by an infinite number of heterodyne receivers, each of which is tuned to a sharp frequency, and connected with an indicating instrument of infinite time-constant. To simplify matters we take instead a bank of reeds, or other resonators, each tuned to a narrow waveband, with equally spaced resonant frequencies. It is known that such an instrument gives only an analysis of the energy spectrum, as it cannot distinguish phases, but this will be sufficient for the purpose of discussion. Let us compare this instrument with a real oscillograph, which responds only to a certain range of frequencies $(f_2 - f_1)$. For simplicity it has been assumed in Figure 1.4 that the bank of reeds extends over the same range, and that the time-constant of the reeds is about equal to the duration of the signal.

We know that any instrument, or combination of instruments, cannot obtain more than at most $2(f_2 - f_1)\tau$ independent data from the area $(f_2 - f_1)\tau$ in the diagram. But instead of rigorously independent data, which can be obtained in general only by calculation from the instrument readings, it will be more convenient for the moment to consider "practically" independent data, which can be obtained by direct readings. For any resonator, oscillograph or reed, a damping time can be defined, after which oscillations have decayed by, say, 10 db. Similarly one can define a tuning width as, say, the number of cycles off resonance at which the response falls off by 10 db. It is well known that in all types of resonators there is a relation between these two of the form:

Decay time x Tuning width = Number of the order one.

This means that for every type of resonator a characteristic rectangle of about unit area can be defined in the time/frequency diagram, which corresponds to one "practically" independent reading of the instrument. In order to obtain their number, we must divide up the (time x frequency) area into such rectangles. This is illustrated in Figures 1.4(a) and 1.4(b). In the case of the oscillograph the rectangles are broad horizontally and narrow vertically, for the tuned reeds the reverse. The amplitude of the readings is indicated by shading of different density. Negative amplitudes are indicated by shading of opposite inclination. We will return later to the question of a suitable convention for measuring these amplitudes.

Without going into details, it is now evident that physical instruments analyze the time-frequency diagram into rectangles which have shapes dependent on the nature of the instrument and areas of the order unity, but not less than one-half. The number of these rectangles in any region is the number of independent data which the instrument can obtain from the signal, i.e., proportional to the amount of information. This justifies calling the diagram from now on the "diagram of information."

We may now ask what it is that prevents any instrument from analyzing the information area with an accuracy of less than a half unit. The ultimate reason for this is evident. We have made of a function of one variable--time or frequency--a function of two variables--time and frequency. This might be considered a somewhat artificial process, but it must be remembered that it corresponds very closely to our subjective interpretation of aural sensations. Indeed, Figure 1.4(b) could be considered as a rough plan of analysis by the ear; rather rough, as the ear is too complicated an instrument to be replaced by a bank of tuned reeds, yet much closer than either the oscillogram or the Fourier spectrum. But as a result of this doubling of variables we have the strange feature that, although we can carry out the analysis with any degree of accuracy in the time direction or in the frequency direction, we cannot carry it out simultaneously in both beyond a certain limit. This strange character is probably the reason why the familiar subjective pattern of our aural sensations and their mathematical interpretation have hitherto differed so widely. In fact the mathematical apparatus adequate for treating this diagram in a quantitative way has become available only fairly recently to physicists, thanks to the development of quantum theory.

The linkage between the uncertainties in the definitions of "time" and "frequency" has never passed entirely unnoticed by physicists. It is the key to the problem of the "coherence length" of wave-trains, which was thoroughly discussed by Sommerfeld in 1914. But these problems came into the focus of physical interest only with the discovery of wave mechanics, and especially by the formulation of Heisenberg's principle of indeterminacy in 1927. This discovery led to a great simplification in the mathematical apparatus of quantum theory, which was recast in a form of which use will be made in the present paper.

The essence of this method--due to a considerable part to W. Pauli--is a re-definition of all observable physical quantities in such a form that the physical uncertainty relations which obtain between them appear as direct consequences of a mathematical identity.

$$\Delta t \, \Delta f \simeq 1 \quad . \quad . \quad . \quad . \quad . \tag{1.2}$$

Δt and Δf are here the uncertainties inherent in the definitions of the epoch t and the frequency f of an oscillation. The identity (1.2) states that t and f cannot be simultaneously defined in an exact way, but only with a latitude of the order one in the product of uncertainties.

Though this interpretation of Heisenberg's principle is now widely known, especially thanks to popular expositions of quantum theory, it appears that the identity (1.2) itself has received less attention than it deserves. Following a suggestion by the theoretical physicist A. Landé, in 1931 G. W. Stewart brought the relation to the notice of acousticians, in a short note--to which we shall return in Part 2--but apparently without much response. In communication theory the intimate connection of the identity (1.2) with the fundamental principle of transmission appears to have passed unnoticed. Perhaps it is not unnecessary to point out that it is not intended to explain the transmission of information by means of quantum theory. This could hardly be called an explanation. The foregoing references are merely an acknowledgment to the theory which has supplied us with an important part of the mathematical methods.

(3) The Complex Signal

In order to apply the simple and elegant formalism of quantum mechanics, it will be convenient first to express the signal amplitude $s(t)$ in a somewhat different form.

It has long been recognized that operations with the complex exponential $e^{j\omega t}$ --often called cos ωt --have distinct advantages over operations with sine or cosine functions. There are two ways of introducing the complex exponential. One is to write

$$\cos \omega t = \tfrac{1}{2}(e^{j\omega t} + e^{-j\omega t}) \quad \sin \omega t = \tfrac{1}{2j}(e^{j\omega t} - e^{-j\omega t}) \, . \, . \tag{1.3}$$

This means that the harmonic functions are replaced by the resultant of two complex vectors, rotating in opposite directions. The other way is to put

$$\cos \omega t = \mathcal{R}(e^{j\omega t}) \quad \sin \omega t = -\mathcal{R}(je^{j\omega t}) \, . \, . \tag{1.4}$$

In this method the harmonic functions are replaced by the real part of a single rotating vector. Both methods have great advantages against operation with real harmonic functions. Their relative merits depend on the problem to which they are applied. In modulation problems, for instance, the advantage is with the first method. On the other hand, the formalism of quantum mechanics favors the second method, which we are now going to follow. This means that we replace a real signal of the form

$$s(t) = a \cos \omega t + b \sin \omega t \quad \ldots \quad \ldots \quad (1.5)$$

by a complex time function

$$\psi(t) = s(t) + j\sigma(t) = (a - jb)e^{j\omega t} \quad \ldots \quad \ldots \quad (1.6)$$

which is formed by adding to the real signal $s(t)$ an imaginary signal $j\sigma(t)$. The function $\sigma(t)$ is formed from $s(t)$ by replacing cos ωt by sin ωt and sin ωt by -cos ωt. The function $\sigma(t)$ has a simple significance. It represents the signal in quadrature to $s(t)$ which, added to it, transforms the oscillating into a rotating vector. If, for instance, $s(t)$ is applied to two opposite poles of a four-pole armature, $\sigma(t)$ has to be applied to the other pair in order to produce a rotating field.

If $s(t)$ is not a simple harmonic function, the process by which $\psi(t)$ has been obtained can be readily generalized. We have only to express $s(t)$ in the form of a real Fourier integral, replace every cosine in it by $e^{j\omega t}$, and every sine by $-je^{j\omega t}$. This process becomes very simple if, instead of sine and cosine Fourier integrals, the complex (cisoidal) Fourier integrals are used according to equation (1.1). In this case the passage from $s(t)$ to $\psi(t)$ is equivalent to the instruction: Suppress the amplitudes belonging to negative frequencies, and multiply the amplitudes of positive frequencies by two. This can be readily understood by comparing equations (1.3) and (1.4).

Though the Fourier transform of $\psi(t)$ is thus immediately obtained from the Fourier transform of $s(t)$, to obtain $\psi(t)$ itself requires an integration. It can be easily verified that the signal $\sigma(t)$ associated with $s(t)$ is given by the integral

$$\sigma(t) = \frac{1}{\pi} \int_{-\infty}^{\infty} s(\tau) \frac{d\tau}{\tau - t} \quad \ldots \quad \ldots \quad (1.7)$$

This is an improper integral, and is to be understood as an abbreviation of the following limit

$$\int_{-\infty}^{\infty} = \lim_{\varepsilon = 0} \left[\int_{-\infty}^{t-\varepsilon} + \int_{t+\varepsilon}^{\infty} \right]$$

which is called "Cauchy's principal value" of an improper integral. To verify equation (1.7) it is sufficient to show that it converts cos ωt into sin ωt and sin ωt into -cos ωt. Conversely, $s(t)$ can be expressed by $\sigma(t)$ as follows:--

$$s(t) = -\frac{1}{\pi} \int_{-\infty}^{\infty} \sigma(\tau) \frac{d\tau}{\tau - t} \quad \ldots \quad \ldots \quad (1.8)$$

Associated functions $s(t)$ and $\sigma(t)$ which satisfy the reciprocal relations (1.7) and (1.8) are known as a pair of "Hilbert transforms."

Pairs of signals in quadrature with one another can be generated by taking an analytical function $f(z)$ of the complex variable $z = x + jy$, which can be expressed in the form $f(z) = u(x,y) + jv(x,y)$. Provided that there are no poles at one side of the x-axis (and if certain other singularities are excluded), $u(x,0)$ and $v(x,0)$ will be in quadrature. The function e^{jz} is an example which gives $u(x,0) = \cos x$ and $v(x,0) = \sin x$. It follows that, as the real axis is in no way distinguished in the theory of analytical functions of a complex variable, we can draw any straight line in the complex plane which leaves all the poles at one side, and the values of the two conjugate functions along this line will give a pair of functions in quadrature.

An example of two functions in quadrature is shown in Figure 1.5. In spite of their very different forms they contain the same

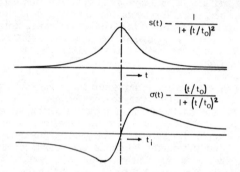

Figure 1.5.   Example of signals in quadrature.

spectral components. If these functions were to represent amplitudes of sound waves, the ear could not distinguish one from the other. A mechanical device for generating the associated signal $\sigma(t)$ to a given signal $s(t)$ is described in Appendix 9.2, which contains also a discussion of the problem of single-sideband generation.

(4) Exact Formulation of the Uncertainty Relation

By means of the complex signal $\psi(t)$ it is now easy to frame the uncertainty relation in a quantitative manner, using the formalism of quantum mechanics. In order to emphasize the analogy, the same symbol ψ has been chosen for the complex signal as is used in that theory for the "wave" or "probability" amplitudes. $\psi(t)$ is the time description of the signal. We can associate with this its frequency description by means of its Fourier transform $\phi(f)$, which will also be called the "spectrum" of $\psi(t)$. The two descriptions are connected by the reciprocal Fourier relations

$$\psi(t) = \int_{-\infty}^{\infty} \phi(f) e^{2\pi jft} df \quad \dots \dots \dots \dots \dots \quad (1.9)$$

$$\phi(f) = \int_{-\infty}^{\infty} \psi(t) e^{-2\pi jft} dt \quad \dots \dots \quad (1.10)$$

In order to emphasize the symmetry, the first integral has been also written with limits $-\infty$ and ∞, although we have specified $\psi(t)$ in such a way that $\phi(f)=0$ for negative frequencies; hence we could have taken zero as the lower limit. As in the following, all integrals will be taken in the limits $-\infty$ to ∞, the limits will not be indicated in the formulae.

In Section 1 several methods have been discussed for specifying a signal by an infinite set of denumerable (countable) data. One of these was specification by moments, M_0, M_1.... This method, with some modifications, will be the best suited for quantitative discussion. The first modification is that it will be more convenient to introduce instead of $s(t)$ the following "weight function":--

$$\psi^*(t)\psi(t) = [s(t)]^2 + [\sigma(t)]^2 \quad . \quad . \quad . \quad . \quad (1.11)$$

The asterisk denotes the conjugate complex value. The new weight function is therefore the square of the absolute value of ψ. This can be considered as the "power" of the signal, and will be referred to by this name in what follows. A second convenient modification is that, instead of with the moments themselves, we shall operate with their values divided by M_0, i. e. with the following quotients:--

$$\bar{t} = \frac{\int \psi^* t \psi dt}{\int \psi^* \psi dt} \quad \overline{t^2} = \frac{\int \psi^* t^2 \psi dt}{\int \psi^* \psi dt} \cdots \overline{t^n} = \frac{\int \psi^* t^n \psi dt}{\int \psi^* \psi dt} \quad (1.12)$$

These are the mean values of the "epoch" t of the signal of orders 1, 2... .... The factor t^n has been placed between the two amplitude factors to emphasize the symmetry of the formulas with later ones. By a theorem of Stieltjes if all mean values are known, the weight function $\psi^*\psi = |\psi|^2$ is also determined, apart from a constant factor. The signal ψ itself is determined only as regards absolute value; its phase remains arbitrary. This makes the method particularly suitable, for instance, for acoustical problems. In others, where the phase is observable, it will not be difficult to supplement the specification, as will be shown later.

Similarly we define mean frequencies f^n of the signal as follows:--

$$\bar{f} = \frac{\int \phi^* f \phi df}{\int \phi^* \phi df} \quad \overline{f^2} = \frac{\int \phi^* f^2 \phi df}{\int \phi^* \phi df} \cdots \overline{f^n} = \frac{\int \phi^* f^n \phi df}{\int \phi^* \phi df} \quad . \quad . \quad (1.13)$$

It now becomes evident why we had to introduce a complex signal in the previous Section. If we had operated with the real signal $s(t)$ instead, the weight function would have been even, and the mean frequency f always zero. This is one of the points on which physical feeling and the usual Fourier methods are not in perfect agreement. But we could eliminate the negative frequencies, only at the price of introducing a complex signal.

As by equations (1.9) and (1.10), ψ and ϕ mutually determine one another, it must be possible to express the mean frequencies by ψ and, conversely, the mean epochs by ϕ. This can be done indeed very simply by means of the following elegant reciprocal relations:--

$$\int \psi^* \psi dt = \int \phi^* \phi df \quad . \quad . \quad . \quad . \quad . \quad (1.14)$$

$$\int \phi^* f^n \phi \, df = \left(\frac{1}{2\pi j}\right)^n \int \psi^* \frac{d^n}{dt^n} \psi \, dt \quad . \quad . \quad (1.15)$$

$$\int \psi^* t^n \psi \, dt = \left(\frac{-1}{2\pi j}\right)^n \int \phi^* \frac{d^n}{df^n} \phi \, df \quad . \quad . \quad (1.16)$$

The first of these, (1.14), is well known as the "Fourier energy theorem" [Rayleigh, 1889]. The other relations can be derived from the identity

$$\int \psi_1(t) \psi_2(t) \, dt = \int \phi_1(f) \phi_2(-f) \, df \quad . \quad . \quad (1.17)$$

by partial integration, assuming that ψ, ϕ and all their derivatives vanish at infinity.

These very useful reciprocal relations can be summed up in the following simple instructions. When it is desired to express one of the mean values (1.12) by integrals over frequency, replace ψ by ϕ, and the quantity t by the operator $-\frac{1}{2\pi j} \frac{d}{df}$. This can be called "translation from time language into frequency language." Conversely, when doing the inverse translation, replace ϕ by ψ and the frequency f by the operator $\frac{1}{2\pi j} \frac{d}{dt}$. This corresponds to the somewhat mysterious rule of quantum mechanics: Replace in classical equations the momentum p_x by the operator $\frac{h}{2\pi j} \frac{\partial}{\partial x}$ where x is the co-ordinate conjugate to the momentum p_x. Actually it is no more mysterious than Heaviside's instruction: "Replace the operator d/dt by p," which has long been familiar to electrical engineers.

Applying the rule
$$\bar{f} := \frac{1}{2\pi j} \frac{\int \psi^* \frac{d}{dt} \psi \, dt}{\int \psi^* \psi \, dt} \quad . \quad . \quad . \quad (1.18)$$

to a simple cisoidal function $\psi = \text{cis } 2\pi f_0 t$, we obtain the value f_0 for the mean frequency $\bar{f}$, and similarly $\bar{f}^n = f_0^n$. The mean epochs $\bar{t}^n$, on the other hand, are zero for odd powers, and infinite for even powers $n > 1$. The cisoidal function is to be considered as a limiting case, as the theory is correctly applicable only to signals of finite duration, and with frequency spectra which do not extend to infinity, a condition which is fulfilled by all real, physical signals.

These definitions and rules enable us to formulate the uncertainty relation quantitatively. Let us consider a finite signal, such as is shown, for example, in Figure 1.6. Let us first fix the mean epoch and the mean frequency of the signal, by means of equations (1.12) and (1.13) or (1.18). These, however, do not count as data, as in a continuous transmission there will be some signal strength at any instant, and at any frequency. We consider $\bar{t}$ and $\bar{f}$ as references, not as data. The first two data will be therefore determined by the mean-square values of epoch and frequency, i.e.,

$$\bar{f}^2 = \frac{\int \phi^* f^2 \phi \, df}{\int \phi^* \phi \, df} = -\frac{1}{(2\pi)^2} \frac{\int \psi^* \frac{d^2}{dt^2} \psi \, dt}{\int \psi^* \psi \, dt} = \frac{1}{(2\pi)^2} \frac{\int \frac{d\psi^*}{dt} \frac{d\psi}{dt} \, dt}{\int \psi^* \psi \, dt} \qquad \bar{t}^2 = \frac{\int \psi^* t^2 \psi \, dt}{\int \psi^* \psi \, dt} \quad . \quad . \quad (1.19)$$

$$\qquad (1.20)$$

The second of these has been first translated into "time language," as explained, and transformed by partial integration to put its essentially positive character into evidence.

It may be noted that $\bar{t}^2$ and $\bar{f}^2$, and in general all mean values of even order, remain unaltered if the real signal $s(t)$ or its associate, $\sigma(t)$, is substituted in the place of $\psi(t) = s(t) + j\sigma(t)$. Hence in the following we could again use the real instead of the complex signal, but ψ will be retained in order to simplify some of the analytical expressions and to emphasize the similarity with the formulas of quantum mechanics.

We now define what will be called "the effective duration" Δt and the "effective frequency width" Δf of a signal by the following equations

$$\Delta t = [2\pi \overline{(t-\bar{t})^2}]^{\frac{1}{2}} \quad \ldots \ldots \ldots \quad (1.21)$$
$$\Delta f = [2\pi \overline{(f-\bar{f})^2}]^{\frac{1}{2}} \quad \ldots \ldots \ldots \quad (1.22)$$

In words, the effective duration is defined as $\sqrt{(2\pi)}$ times the r. m. s. deviation of the signal from the mean epoch t, and the effective frequency width similarly as $\sqrt{(2\pi)}$ times the r. m. s. deviation from f. The choice of the numerical factor $\sqrt{(2\pi)}$ will be justified later.

Using the identities
$$\overline{(t-\bar{t})^2} = \bar{t}^2 - (\bar{t})^2 \qquad \overline{(f-\bar{f})^2} = \bar{f}^2 - (\bar{f})^2$$
Δt and Δf can be expressed by means of (1.19) and (1.20). The expressions are greatly simplified if the origin of the time scale is shifted to $\bar{t}$, and the origin of the frequency scale to $\bar{f}$. Both transformations are effected by introducing a new time scale.

$$\tau = t - \bar{t} \quad \ldots \ldots \quad (1.23)$$

and a new signal amplitude

$$\Psi(\tau) = \psi(t) e^{-2\pi j \bar{f} \tau} \quad \ldots \quad (1.24)$$

Expressing t and ψ by the new quantities τ and Ψ, it is found that, apart from a numerical factor 2π, $(\Delta t)^2$ and $(\Delta f)^2$ assume the same form as equations (1.19) and (1.20) for $\bar{t}^2$ and $\bar{f}^2$. Multiplying the two equations we obtain

$$(\Delta t \Delta f)^2 = \frac{1}{4}\left[4 \frac{\int \Psi^* \tau^2 \Psi d\tau \int \frac{d\Psi^*}{d\tau}\frac{d\Psi}{d\tau}dt}{[\int \Psi^* \Psi d\tau]^2}\right] \quad . \quad (1.25)$$

But, by a mathematical identity, a form of the "Schwarz inequality" due to Weyl and Pauli, the expression in brackets is always larger than unity for any function Ψ for which the integrals exist. We obtain, therefore, the uncertainty relation in the rigorous form

$$\Delta t \Delta f \geqslant \tfrac{1}{2} \quad \ldots \ldots \quad (1.26)$$

This is the mathematical identity which is at the root of the fundamental principle of communication. We see that the r. m. s. duration of a signal, and its r. m. s. frequency-width define a minimum area in the information diagram. How large we assume this minimum area depends on the convention for the numerical factor. By choosing it as $\sqrt{(2\pi)} = 2.506$ we have made the number of elementary areas in any large rectangular region of the information diagram equal to the number of independent data which that region can transmit, according to the result obtained in Section 1.

Relation (1.26) is symmetrical in time and frequency, and it suggests that a new representation of signals might be found in which t and f played interchangeable parts. Moreover, it suggests that it might be possible to give a more concrete interpretation to the information diagram by dividing it up into "cells" of size one half, and associating each cell with an "elementary signal" which transmitted exactly one datum of information. This program will be carried out in the next Section.

(5) The Elementary Signal

The mathematical developments up to this point have run rather closely on the lines of quantum mechanics. In fact our results could have been formally obtained by replacing a co-ordinate x by t, the momentum p by f, and Planck's constant h by unity. But now the ways part, as questions arise in the theory of information which are rather different from those which quantum theory sets out to answer.

The first problem arises directly from the inequality (1.26). What is the shape of the signal for which the product $\Delta t \Delta f$ actually assumes the smallest possible value, i.e., for which the inequality turns into an equality? The derivation of this signal form is not given here; only the result, which is very simple, will be given: The signal which occupies the minimum area $\Delta t \Delta f = \frac{1}{2}$ is the modulation product of a harmonic oscillation of any frequency with a pulse of the form of a probability function. In complex form

$$\psi(t) = e^{-\alpha^2(t-t_o)^2} \text{ cis} (2\pi f_o t + \phi) \quad . \quad . \quad (1.27)$$

α, t_0, f_o and ϕ are constants, which can be interpreted as the "sharpness" of the pulse, the epoch of its peak, and the frequency and phase constant of the modulating oscillation. The constant α is connected with Δt and Δf by the relations

$$\Delta t = \sqrt{\left(\frac{\pi}{2}\right)}\frac{1}{\alpha} \qquad\qquad \Delta f = \frac{1}{\sqrt{(2\pi)}}\alpha$$

As might be expected from the symmetrical form of the condition from which it has been derived, the spectrum is of the same analytical form

$$\phi(f) = e^{-\left(\frac{\pi}{\alpha}\right)^2(f-f_o)^2} \text{ cis} \left[-2\pi t_o(f-f_o) + \phi\right] \quad . \quad . \quad (1.28)$$

The envelopes of both the signal and its spectrum, or their absolute values, have the shape of probability curves, as illustrated in Figure 1.6. Their sharpnesses are reciprocal.

Because of its self-reciprocal character, the probability signal has always played an important part in the theory of Fourier transforms. In three recent papers, F. F. Roberts and J. C. Simmonds have called attention to some of its analytical advantages ["Some Properties of a Special Type of Electrical Pulse," Philosophical Magazine 34:822-27, 1943; "Further Properties of Recurrent Exponential and Probability Function Pulse Wave-forms," Ibid. 35:459-70, 1944; "The Physical Realizability of Electrical Networks Having Prescribed Characteristics," Ibid. 35:778-83, 1944]. But its minimum property does not appear to have been recognized. It is this property which makes the modulated probability pulse the natural basis on which to build up an analysis of signals in which both time

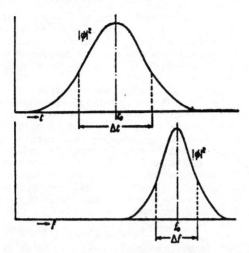

Figure 1.6. Envelope of the elementary signal.

and frequency are recognized as references. It may be proposed, therefore, to call a pulse according to equation (1.27) an <u>elementary signal</u>. In the information diagram it may be represented by a rectangle with sides Δt and Δf, and area one-half, centering on the point (t_o, f_o). It will be shown below that any signal can be expanded into elementary signals in such a way that their representative rectangles cover the whole time-frequency area, as indicated in Figure 1.7. Their amplitudes can be indicated by a number written into the rectangle, or by shading. Each of these areas, with its associated datum, represents, as it were, one elementary quantum

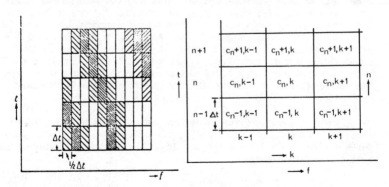

Figure 1.7. Representation of signal by logons.

Figure 1.8. Representation of signal by a matrix of complex amplitudes.

of information, and it is proposed to call it a <u>logon</u>. Expansion into elementary signals is a process of which <u>Fourier</u> analysis and
time description are special cases. The first is obtained at $\alpha = 0$,
in which case the elementary signal becomes a sine wave of infinite
length; the second at $\alpha \to \infty$, when it passes into a "delta function."

    It will be convenient to explain the expansion into elementary
signals in two steps. The first step leads to elementary areas of
size unity, with two associated data, but it is simpler and more
symmetrical than the second step, which takes us to the limit of
sub-division. This first step corresponds to division of the information area by a network of lines with distances Δt and $1/\Delta t$ respectively, as illustrated in Figure 1.8. The elementary areas have
suffixes n in the time direction, and k in the frequency direction.
The center lines (horizontally) may be at $t_n = n\Delta t$, assuming for
convenience that we measure time from the "zero"-th of these lines.
The expansion is given by the following formula

$$\psi(t) = \sum_{-\infty}^{\infty} {}_n \sum_{-\infty}^{\infty} {}_k \, c_{nk} \, exp - \pi \frac{(t - n\Delta t)^2}{2(\Delta t)^2} \, cis \, (2\pi kt/\Delta t) \, . \, . \, (1.29)$$

The matrix of the complex coefficients c_{nk} represents the signal in
a symmetrical way, as it is easy to see that if the expansion exists
we arrive--apart from a constant factor--at the same coefficients if
we expand $\phi(f)$ instead of $\psi(t)$.

    As the elementary signals in (1.29) are not orthogonal, the
coefficients c_{nk} are best obtained by successive approximations. In
the first approximation we consider each horizontal strip with suffix
n by itself, and expand the function $\psi(t)$ as if the other strips did
not exist, in the interval $(t_n - \frac{1}{2}\Delta t)$ to $(t_n + \frac{1}{2}\Delta t)$ by putting

$$\psi(t) \, exp \, \pi \frac{(t - n\Delta t)^2}{2(\Delta t)^2} = \sum_0^{\infty} {}_k \, c_{nk} \, cis(2\pi kt/\Delta t)$$

In this formula the exponential function, which is independent of k,
has been brought over to the left. We have now a known function on
the left, and a Fourier series on the right, which by known methods
gives immediately the first approximation for the coefficients c_{nk}.
This represents $\psi(t)$ correctly in the intervals for which the series
are valid, but not outside them. If the first approximations are added up with summation indices n, there will be a certain error due
to their overlap. A second approximation can be obtained by subtracting this error from $\psi(t)$ in equation (1.29) and repeating the
procedure. It can be expected to converge rapidly, as the exponential factor decays so fast that only neighboring strips n influence
each other perceptibly.

    This expansion gives ultimately one complex number c_{nk} for
every two elementary areas of size one-half. The real and imaginary
parts can be interpreted as giving the amplitudes of the following two
real elementary signals

$$\begin{matrix} s_c(t) \\ s_s(t) \end{matrix} = exp \, -\alpha^2(t - t_0)^2 \begin{matrix} cos \\ sin \end{matrix} 2\pi f_0(t - t_0) \, . \, (1.30)$$

where $\alpha^2 = \frac{1}{2}\pi/(\Delta t)^2$. These can be called the "cosine-type" and
"sine-type" elementary signals. They are illustrated in Figure 1.9.
We can use them to obtain a real expansion, allocating one datum to

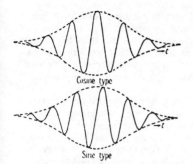

Cosine type

Sine type

Figure 1.9. Real parts of elementary signal.

$-a_{50}$	b_{50}	a_{51}	b_{51}	a_{52}	b_{52}
$-a_{40}$	b_{40}	a_{41}	b_{41}	a_{42}	b_{42}
$-a_{30}$	b_{30}	a_{31}	b_{31}	a_{32}	b_{32}
$-a_{20}$	b_{20}	a_{21}	b_{21}	a_{22}	b_{22}
$-a_{10}$	b_{10}	a_{11}	b_{11}	a_{12}	b_{12}

t

Δt

Δt

$|\tfrac{1}{2}\Delta t|\tfrac{1}{2}\Delta t|$ $\longrightarrow f$

Figure 1.10. Expansion of arbitrary signal in cosine-type and sine-type elementary signals.

---

every cell of one-half area. But it may be noted that this will have to be necessarily a more special and less symmetrical expansion than the previous one, as the transform of a cosine-type elementary signal, for example, will not in general be of the same type. As always in communication theory, a description by complex numbers is formally simpler than by real data.

We now divide up the information plane as shown in Figure 1.10 into cells of size one-half, measuring Δt in the time, and $\frac{1}{2}\Delta t$ in the frequency, direction. Starting from the line of zero frequency, we allocate to these areas in every strip alternately a cosine-type and a sine-type elementary signal. Evidently we must start with a cosine signal at $f = 0$, as the sine-type signal would be zero. This leads us to the following expansion of the real signal $s(t)$:--

$$s(t) = \sum_{-\infty}^{\infty} n \exp -\pi \frac{(t - n\Delta t)^2}{2(\Delta t)^2} \sum_{0}^{\infty} k \left[a_{nk} \cos 2\pi k(t - n\Delta t)/\Delta t \right.$$
$$\left. + b_{nk} \sin 2\pi (k + \tfrac{1}{2})(t - n\Delta t)/\Delta t \right] \quad \dots \quad (1.31)$$

In order to find the coefficients a_{nk} and b_{nk} we can carry out the same process of approximation as explained in connection with expansion (1.30), but with a difference. At the first step we arrive at an equation of a form

$$f_n(x) = \sum_{0}^{\infty} k\, a_{nk} \cos kx + b_{nk} \sin (k + \tfrac{1}{2})x$$

with the abbreviations $x = 2\pi(t - n\Delta t)/\Delta t$, and $f(x) = s(t) \exp \tfrac{1}{2}\pi(t - n\Delta t)^2 / (\Delta t)^2$. But the trigonometric series on the right is not a Fourier series. It is of a somewhat unusual type, in which the sine terms have frequencies mid-way between the cosine terms. It will be necessary to show briefly that this series can be used also for the representation of arbitrary functions. First we separate the even and odd parts on both sides of the equation, by putting

$$\tfrac{1}{2}\left[f_n(x) + f_n(-x) \right] = \sum_{0}^{\infty} k\, a_{nk} \cos kx$$

$$\tfrac{1}{2}\left[f_n(x) - f_n(-x) \right] = \sum_{0}^{\infty} k\, b_{nk} \sin (k + \tfrac{1}{2})x$$

The first is a Fourier series, but not the second. We have seen, however, in Section 3, how all the frequencies contained in a function can be raised by a constant amount by means of a process which involves calculating the function in quadrature with it. Applying this operation to both sides of the last equation we can add $\frac{1}{2}$ to $k + \frac{1}{2}$, and obtain the ordinary Fourier sine series, which enables the coefficients to be calculated.

The expansion into logons is, in general, a rather inconvenient process, as the elementary signals are not orthogonal. If only approximate results are required, it may be permitted to neglect the effect of their interference. This becomes plausible if we consider that an elementary signal has 76.8 per cent of its energy inside the band Δt or Δf, and only 11.6 per cent on either side. Approximately correct physical analysis could be carried out by means of a bank of resonators with resonance curves of probability shape. It can be shown that if the energy collected by a resonator tuned to $\bar{f}$ is taken as 100 per cent, the resonators on the right and left of it, tuned to $\bar{f} + \Delta f$ and $\bar{f} - \Delta f$, would collect only 65 per cent each. Roberts and Simmonds [see page 340] have given consideration to the problem of realizing circuits with responses of probability shape.

Though the overlapping of the elementary signals may be of small practical consequence, it raises a question of considerable theoretical interest. The principle of causality requires that any quantity at an epoch t can depend only on data belonging to epochs earlier than t. But we have seen that we could not carry out the expansion into elementary signals exactly without taking into consideration also the "overlap of the future." In fact, strict causality exists only in the "time language"; as soon as we use frequency as an additional reference the sort of uncertainty occurs which in modern physics has often been called the "breakdown of causality." But rigorous time-analysis is possible only with ideal oscillographs, not with any real physical instrument; hence strict causality never applies in practice. A limitation of this concept ought not to cause difficulties to electrical engineers who are used to the Fourier integral, i.e., to an entirely non-causal method of description.

(6) Signals Transmitted in Minimum Time

The elementary signals which have been discussed in the last Section assure the best utilization of the information area in the sense that they possess the smallest product of effective duration by effective frequency width. It follows that, if we prescribe the effective width Δf of a frequency channel, the signal transmitted through it in minimum time will have an envelope

$$\Psi(t) = \exp - (2\pi)(\Delta f)^2 (t - \bar{t})^2 \quad . \quad . \quad . \quad (1.32)$$

and, apart from a cisoidal factor, a Fourier transform

$$\Phi(f) = \exp - \frac{\pi}{2} \left(\frac{f - \bar{f}}{\Delta f} \right)^2 \quad . \quad . \quad . \quad . \quad (1.33)$$

But the problem which most frequently arises in practice is somewhat different. Not the effective spectral width is prescribed, but the total width; i. e., a frequency band $(f_2 - f_1)$ is given, outside which the spectral amplitude must be zero. What is the signal shape which can be transmitted through this channel in the shortest effective time, and what is its effective duration? Mathematically the problem can be reduced to finding the spectrum $\phi(f)$ of a signal which makes

$$\Delta t = \frac{1}{(2\pi)^2} \int_{f_1}^{f_2} \frac{d\phi^*}{df} \frac{d\phi}{df} df \Big/ \int_{f_1}^{f_2} \phi^*\phi\, df \quad \ldots \quad (1.34)$$

a minimum, with the condition that $\phi(f)$ is zero outside the range $f_1 - f_2$. But this is equivalent to the condition that $\phi(f)$ vanishes at the limits f_1 and f_2. Otherwise, if $\psi(f)$ had a finite value at the limits but vanished outside, the discontinuity at the limits would make the numerator of equation (1.34) divergent. (This is the converse of the well-known fact that a signal with an abrupt break contains frequencies up to infinity, which decay only hyperbolically, not fast enough to make f^2 finite.)

The problem is one of the calculus of variations, and is solved in Appendix 8.4, where it is shown that the signals transmitted in minimum time must be among the solutions of a differential equation

$$\frac{d^2\phi}{df^2} + \Lambda\,\phi = 0 \quad \ldots \quad \ldots \quad (1.35)$$

where Λ is an undetermined constant. But the possible values of Λ are defined by the auxiliary condition that $\phi(f)$ must vanish at the limits of the waveband. Hence all admissible solutions are of the form

$$\phi(f) = \sin k\pi \frac{f - f_1}{f_2 - f_1} \quad \ldots \quad \ldots \quad (1.36)$$

where k is an integer. We can call this the kth characteristic function of transmission through an ideal band-pass filter. Its effective duration is

$$\Delta t = \sqrt{\left(\frac{\pi}{2}\right)} \frac{k}{f_2 - f_1} \quad \ldots \quad (1.37)$$

and its effective frequency width is

$$\Delta f = (f_2 - f_1) \Big/ \left(\frac{\pi}{6} - \frac{1}{\pi k^2}\right) \quad \ldots \quad (1.38)$$

The shortest duration Δt belongs to $k = 1$, i. e., to the fundamental characteristic function, which is illustrated in Figure 1.11. The product $\Delta t \Delta f$ is also smallest for $k = 1$; its value is 0.571. Though this is not much more than the absolute minimum, 0.5, the transmission channel is poorly utilized, as the effective frequency width is only 0.456 of $(f_2 - f_1)$. Practice has found a way to overcome this difficulty by means of asymmetric, vestigial or single-sideband transmission. In these methods the spectrum is cut off at or near the center more or less abruptly. This produces a "splash," a spreading out of the signal in time, but this effect is compensated in the reception, when the other sideband is reconstituted and added to the received signal.

The advantages of a signal of sine shape, as shown in Figure 1.11, have already been noticed, as it were, empirically by Wheeler and Loughren in their thorough study of television images. As in television the signals transmitted represent light intensities, i. e.,

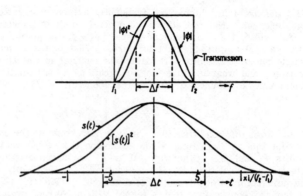

Figure 1.11.   Spectrum of signal which can be transmitted in minimum time through an ideal band-pass filter, and the signal itself.

___

energies--our definitions must be applied here with a modification.
Either the square root of the light intensity must be substituted for
ψ, or the square root of the Fourier transform of the signal for
ϕ.   The practical difference between these two possible definitions
becomes very small in minimum problems.   If we adopt the second,
we obtain the same "cosine-squared" law for the optimum spectral
distribution of energy which Wheeler and Loughren have considered
as the "most attractive compromise."

Figure 1.11 shows also the signal $s(t)$ which is transmitted
in minimum time by a band-pass filter.   It can be seen that it differs in shape very little indeed from its spectrum.   It may be noted
that the total time interval in which the signal is appreciably different from zero is $2/(f_2 - f_1)$.

It can be seen from Figure 1.11, that the optimum signal
utilizes the edges of the waveband--in single-sideband television, the
upper edge--rather poorly.   But this is made even worse in television, by the convention of making the electromagnetic amplitudes
proportional to the light intensities, so that the electromagnetic energy spectrum in the optimum case has the shape of a $\cos^4$ curve.
This means that the higher frequencies will be easily drowned by at-
mospherics.   Conditions can be improved by "compression-expansion"
methods, in which, for example, the square root of the light intensity is transmitted, and squared in the receiver.

(7) Discussion of Communication Problems
by Means of the Information Diagram

As the foregoing explanations might appear somewhat abstract,
it appears appropriate to return to the information diagram and to
demonstrate its usefulness by means of a few examples.   Let us take

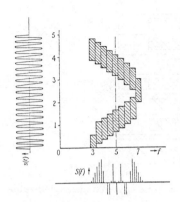

Figure 1.12. Three representations of frequency modulation.

frequency modulation as a first example. Figure 1.12 contains three different illustrations of the same slowly modulated carrier: the time representation, the spectrum and its picture in the information diagram. It can be seen that the third illustration corresponds very closely to our familiar idea of a variable frequency. The only departure from the naive representation that its pictorial representation would be an undulating curve is that the curve has to be thick and blurred. But it appears preferable not to show the blurring, not only because it is difficult to draw, but also because it might give rise to the idea that the picture could be replaced by a definite density distribution. Instead we have represented it by logons of area one-half. The shape of the rectangles, i.e., the ratio $\Delta t / \Delta f$, is entirely arbitrary and depends on the conventions of the analysis. If Δt is taken equal to the damping time of, say, a bank of reeds, the picture gives an approximate description of the response of the instrument. It gives also a rough picture of our aural impression of a siren. How this rough picture can be perfected will be shown in Part 2.

A second example is time-division multiplex telephony, a problem which almost forces on us the simultaneous consideration of time and frequency. W. R. Bennett ["Time-Division Multiplex Systems," Bell System Tech. J. 20:199, 1941] has discussed it very thoroughly by an irreproachable method, but, as is often the case with results obtained by Fourier analysis, the physical origin of the results remains somewhat obscure. An attempt will now be made to give them a simple interpretation. In time-division multiplex telephony, synchronized switches at both ends of a line connect the line in cyclic alternation to a number N of channels. Let f_s be the switching frequency, i.e., the number of contacts made per second. What is the optimum switching frequency if N conversations, each occupying a frequency band w are to be transmitted without loss of information and without crosstalk--i.e. mutual interference between channels--and what is the total frequency-band requirement W ?

The information diagram is shown in Figure 1.13. The frequency band W is sub-divided in the time direction into rectangles of a duration $1/f_s$, i.e., f_s rectangles per sec. If these are to transmit independent data they cannot transmit less than one datum at a time. But one datum, or logon, at a time is also the optimum, as otherwise the receivers would have to discriminate between two or more data in the short time of contact, and distribute them some-

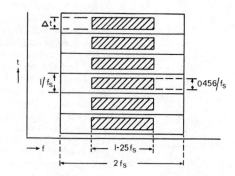

Figure 1.13.   Information diagram of time-division multiplex-tele-
phony system.

how over the long waiting time between two contacts.   Hence, if no
information is to be lost, the number of contacts per second must
be equal to the data of N conversations each of width w, i.e.,
$f_s = 2Nw$.   This is also Bennett's result.

      We now consider the condition of crosstalk.   This is the ex-
act counterpart of the problem of minimum transmission time in a
fixed-frequency channel, considered in the last Section, except that
time and frequency are interchanged.   Thus we can say at once that
the optimum signal form will be the sine shape of Figure 1.11, and
the frequency requirement will be very nearly $2f_s$.   The characteristic rectangle $\Delta t \Delta f$ of this signal is shown in every switching period, with the dimensions as obtained in the last Section.   The total
frequency band requirement becomes $W = 2f_s = 4Nw$.   This can be
at once halved by single-sideband transmission, i.e., transmitting
only one-half of W.   But even this does not represent the limit of
economy, as the signal is symmetrical not only in frequency, but
also in time.   In the case of the example treated in the previous
Section this was of no use, as the epoch of the signal was unknown.
But in time-division multiplex the epoch of each signal is accurately
known: hence it must be possible to halve the waveband once more
and reduce W to the minimum requirement $W = Nw$.   An ingenious,
though rather complicated, method of achieving this, by means of
special filters associated with the receiving channels, has been described by Bennett [see page 347].

(8) Appendices

(8.1) Analysis in Terms of Other Than Simple Periodic Functions

      The discussion in Section 1 suggests a question: Why are we
doing our analysis in terms of sine waves, and why do we limit our
communication channels by fixed frequencies?   Why not choose other

orthogonal functions? In fact we could have taken, for example, the orthogonalized Bessel functions

$$\sqrt{(t)}\, J_n(r_k t/\tau)$$

as the basis of expansion. J_n is a Bessel function of fixed but arbitrary order n; r_k is the kth root of $J_n(x)=0$; k is the expansion index. These functions are orthogonal in the interval $0 < t < \tau$. The factors r_k/τ have the dimension of a frequency. We could now think of limiting the transmission channel by two "Bessel frequencies," say μ_1 and μ_2. Here the first difference arises. The number of spectral lines between these limits will be the number of the roots of $J_n(x)=0$ between the limits $\mu_1\tau$ and $\mu_2\tau$. But this number is not proportional to τ. Hence a Bessel channel, or a channel based on any function other than simple harmonic functions, would not transmit the same amount of information in equal time intervals.

In principle it would be possible to construct circuits which transmitted without distortion any member of a selected set of orthogonal functions. But only harmonic functions satisfy linear differential equations in which time does not figure explicitly; hence these are the only ones which can be transmitted by circuits built up of constant elements. Every other system requires variable circuit components, and as there will be a distinguished epoch of time it will also require some sort of synchronization between transmitter and receiver. In competition with fixed-waveband systems any such method will have the disadvantage that wider wavebands will be required to avoid interference with other transmissions. Though this disadvantage--as in the case of frequency modulation-- might be outweighed by other advantages, investigation of such systems is outside the scope of the present study, which is mainly devoted to the problem of waveband economy.

(8.2) Mechanical Generation of Associated Signals, and the Problem of Direct Production of Single Sidebands

In order to gain a more vivid picture of signals in quadrature than the mathematical explanations of Section 3 can convey, it may be useful to discuss a method of generating them mechanically. It is obvious from equations (1.7) and (1.8) that, in order to generate the signal $\sigma(t)$ associated with a given signal $s(t)$, it is necessary to know not only the past but also the future. Though formally the whole future is involved, the "relevant future" in transmission problems is usually only a fraction of a second. This means that we can produce $\sigma(t)$ with sufficient accuracy if we convert, say, 0.1 second of the future into the past; in other words, if we delay the transmission of $s(t)$ by about this interval. Figure 1.14 shows a device which might accomplish this.

The light of a lamp, the intensity of which is modulated by the signal $s(t)$ is thrown through a slit on a transparent rotating drum, coated with phosphorescent powder. The drum therefore

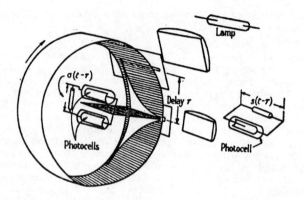

Figure 1.14. Device for mechanical generation of a signal in quadrature with a given signal.

carries a record of the signal with it, which decays slowly. After turning through a certain angle the record passes a slit, and here the light is picked up by a photocell, which transmits $s(t)$ with a delay corresponding to the angle. On the inside of the drum two hyperbolically-shaped apertures are arranged at both sides of the slit opposite to the first photocell. The light from the two hyperbolic windows is collected by two photocells, which are connected in opposition. By comparing this arrangement with equation (1.7) it is easy to see that the difference of the two photocell currents will be proportional to the function in quadrature with $s(t)$.

The complex signal has been discussed at some length as it helps one to understand certain problems of communication engineering. One of these is the problem of single-sideband transmission. It is well known that it is not possible to produce a single sideband directly. The method employed is to produce both sidebands and to suppress one. Equation (1.7) explains the reason. Direct single-sideband production involves knowledge of the future. The conventional modulation methods always add and subtract frequencies simultaneously. With mechanisms like the one shown in Figure 1.14 it becomes possible to add or subtract them. This means forming the following expression

$$\mathcal{R}\left[\psi(t)\exp j\omega_c t\right] = s(t)\cos \omega_c t - \sigma(t)\sin \omega_c t$$

where ω_c is the angular carrier frequency. By substituting a harmonic oscillation for $s(t)$ it is easy to verify that ω_c has been added to every frequency present in the signal. Direct production of single sidebands involves, therefore, the following operations: modulate the signal with the carrier wave, and subtract from the product the modulation product of the signal in quadrature with the carrier wave in quadrature. It is not, of course, suggested that this might become a practical method; the intention was merely to throw some light on the root of a well-known impossibility.

(8. 3) The Schwarz Inequality and Elementary Signals

The inequality

$$(\int \Psi^* \Psi d\tau)^2 \leqslant 4 (\int \Psi^* \tau^2 \Psi d\tau) \left(\int \frac{d\Psi^*}{d\tau} \frac{d\Psi}{d\tau} d\tau \right) \quad (1.39)$$

is valid for any real or complex function Ψ which is continuous and differentiable and vanishes at the integration limits. The following is a modification of a proof given by H. Weyl. If a_1, b_1 are two sets of n real or complex numbers, a theorem due to H. A. Schwarz states that

$$|a_1 b_1 + \ldots + a_n b_n|^2 \leqslant (a_1 a^*_1 + \ldots + a_n a^*_n)(b_1 b^*_1 + \ldots + b_n b^*_n) . \quad (1.40)$$

If a's and b's are all real numbers, this can be interpreted as expressing the fact that the cosine of the angle of two vectors with components $a_1 \ldots a_n$ and $b_1 \ldots b_n$ in an n-dimensional Euclidian space is smaller than unity. This can be easily understood, as in a Euclidian space of any number of dimensions a two-dimensional plane can be made to pass through any two vectors issuing from the origin; hence the angle between them has the same significance as in plane geometry. Equation (1.40) is a generalization of this for "Hermitian" space, in which the components or co-ordinates of the vectors are themselves complex numbers.

By a passage to the limit the sums in (1.40) may be replaced by integrals, so that

$$\sum a_1 b_1 \rightarrow \int f(\tau) g(\tau) d\tau$$

and similarly for the other two sums. The real variable τ now takes the place of the summation index. The Schwarz inequality now becomes

$$|\int f g d\tau|^2 \leqslant (\int f f^* d\tau)(\int g g^* d\tau) . \quad \ldots \ldots \quad (1.41)$$

This remains valid if we replace f and g by their conjugates

$$|\int f^* g^* d\tau|^2 \leqslant (\int f f^* d\tau)(\int g g^* d\tau) \quad \ldots \ldots \quad (1.42)$$

Adding (1.41) and (1.42) we obtain

$$2(\int f f^* d\tau)(\int g g^* d\tau) \geqslant |\int f g d\tau|^2 + |\int f^* g^* d\tau|^2 \geqslant \tfrac{1}{2} [\int (fg + f^* g^*) d\tau]^2 . \quad (1.43)$$

The second part of this inequality states the fact that the sum of the absolute squares of two conjugate complex numbers is never less than half the square of their sums. We now put

$$f = \tau \Psi \qquad g = \frac{d\Psi^*}{d\tau} \quad \ldots \ldots \ldots \quad (1.44)$$

Substitution in (1.43) gives

$$4(\int f f^* d\tau)(\int g g^* d\tau) \geqslant \left[\int \left(\Psi \frac{d\Psi^*}{d\tau} + \Psi^* \frac{d\Psi}{d\tau} \right) \tau d\tau \right]^2 . \quad \ldots \quad (1.45)$$

The right-hand side can be transformed by partial integration into

$$\int \left(\Psi \frac{d\Psi^*}{d\tau} + \Psi^* \frac{d\Psi}{d\tau} \right) \tau d\tau = \int \tau \frac{d}{d\tau} (\Psi^* \Psi) d\tau = -\int \Psi^* \Psi d\tau \quad (1.46)$$

where it has been assumed that Ψ vanishes at the integration limits. Substituting this in (1.45) we obtain the inequality (1.39).

In order to obtain the elementary signals we must investigate when this inequality changes into an equality. From the geometrical interpretation of Schwarz's inequality (1.40), it can be concluded at once that the equality sign will obtain if, and only if, the two vectors a, b have the same direction, i.e., $b_1 = C a_1$. In Hermitian space the direction is not changed by multiplication by a complex number, hence C need not be real.

This condition can be applied also to the inequality (1.39), but with a difference. (1.39) will become an equation only if both the conditions (1.41) and (1.42) become equalities; i.e., if the following two equations are fulfilled

$$f = Cg \qquad f^* = C'g^* \quad \cdots \cdots \quad (1.47)$$

where C and C' are real or complex constants. But these two equations are compatible if, and only if,

$$C' = C^* \quad \cdots \quad (1.48)$$

in which case the two equations (1.47) become identical. On substituting f and g from (1.44) they give the two equivalent equations

$$\frac{d\psi^*}{d\tau} = C\tau\Psi \qquad \frac{d\Psi}{d\tau} = C^*\tau\Psi^* \quad \cdots \quad (1.49)$$

From either of these we can eliminate Ψ or its conjugate Ψ^* and are led to the second-order differential equation

$$\frac{d}{d\tau}\left(\frac{1}{\tau}\frac{d\Psi}{d\tau}\right) = CC^*\tau\Psi \quad \cdots \quad (1.50)$$

Multiplying both sides by $(d\Psi/d\tau)/\tau$, this becomes integrable and gives

$$\left(\frac{1}{\tau}\frac{d\Psi}{d\tau}\right)^2 = CC^*\Psi^2 + \text{const.} \quad \cdots \cdots \quad (1.51)$$

But the constant is zero, as at infinity both Ψ and $d\Psi/d\tau$ must vanish. We thus obtain the first-order equation

$$\frac{d\Psi}{d\tau} = \pm (CC^*)^{\frac{1}{2}}\tau\Psi \quad \cdots \quad (1.52)$$

with the solution (apart from a constant factor)

$$\Psi = \exp\pm\tfrac{1}{2}|C|\tau^2 \quad \cdots \quad (1.53)$$

Of the two signs we can retain only the negative one, as otherwise the signal would not vanish at infinity. Putting $\tfrac{1}{2}|C| = \alpha^2$ we obtain the envelope of the elementary signal. The signal ψ itself results from this by multiplying by cis $2\pi\bar{f}(t - \bar{t})$ and is discussed in Section 5.

It will be useful to sketch briefly the difference between the analysis based on elementary signals and the method of wave mechanics. In the foregoing we have answered the question: What functions Ψ make the product $\Delta f \Delta t$ assume its smallest possible value, i.e., one-half? The question posed by wave mechanics is more general: What functions Ψ makes $\Delta f \Delta t$ a minimum, while fulfilling the condition of vanishing at infinity? This is a problem of the calculus of variations, which leads, instead of to equation (1.50), to a more general equation, called the "wave equation of the harmonic oscillator":--

$$\frac{d^2\Psi}{d\tau^2} + (\lambda - \alpha^2\tau^2)\Psi = 0$$

where λ and α are real constants. This equation, which contains (1.50) as a special case, has solutions which are finite everywhere and vanish at infinity only if

$$\lambda = \alpha(2n + 1)$$

where n is a positive integer. These "proper" or "characteristic" solutions of the wave equation are (apart from a constant factor)

$$\Psi_n = e^{-\frac{1}{2}\omega^2\tau^2}\frac{d^n}{d\tau^n}e^{-\alpha^2\tau^2}$$

They are known as orthogonal Hermite functions and form the basis of wave mechanical analysis of the problem of the linear oscillator. They share with the probability function--which can be considered as the Hermite function of zero order--the property that their Fourier transforms are of identical type. The product $\Delta f\Delta t$ for the nth Hermite function is

$$\Delta t\Delta f = \frac{1}{2}(2n+1)$$

That is to say that the Hermite functions occupy in the information diagram areas of size $\frac{1}{2}, \frac{3}{2}, \frac{5}{2}\ldots$. Because of their orthogonality Hermite functions readily lend themselves to the expansion of arbitrary signals; hence their importance in wave mechanics. But they are less suitable for the analysis of continuously emitted signals, as they presuppose a distinguished epoch of time $t=0$ and they do not permit the sub-division of the information area into non-overlapping elementary cells.

(8.4) Signals Transmitted in Minimum Time Through a Given Frequency Channel

It will be convenient to use "frequency language," i.e., to express the signal by its Fourier transform $\phi(f)$. The problem is to make the effective duration Δt of a signal a minimum, with the condition that $\phi(f)=0$ outside an interval f_1-f_2. Thus:--

$$\Delta t = \frac{1}{(2\pi)^2 M_0}\int_{f_1}^{f_2}\frac{d\phi^*}{df}\frac{d\phi}{df}df \quad \ldots \quad (1.54)$$

must be a minimum, where

$$M_0 = \int_{f_1}^{f_2}\phi^*\phi df$$

This is equivalent to making the numerator in (1.54) a minimum with the auxiliary condition $M_0 = $ constant, and this in turn can be formulated by Lagrange's method in the form

$$\delta\int\left(\frac{d\phi^*}{df}\frac{d\phi}{df}+\Lambda\phi^*\phi\right)df=0 \quad (1.55)$$

where Λ is an undetermined multiplier. The variation of the first term is

$$\delta\int\frac{d\phi^*}{df}\frac{d\phi}{df}df = \int\left(\frac{d\phi^*}{df}\delta\frac{d\phi}{df}+\frac{d\phi}{df}\delta\frac{d\phi^*}{df}\right)df =$$

$$\int\left(\frac{d\phi^*}{df}\frac{d\delta\phi}{df}+\frac{d\phi}{df}\frac{d\delta\phi^*}{df}\right)df=\left[\frac{d\phi^*}{df}\delta\phi+\frac{d\phi}{df}\delta\phi^*\right]_{f_1}^{f_2}-\int\left(\frac{d^2\phi^*}{df^2}\delta\phi+\frac{d^2\phi}{df^2}\delta\phi^*\right)df \quad (1.56)$$

But at the limits ϕ must vanish, as it is zero outside the interval and must be continuous at the limit, as otherwise the integral (1.54) would not converge. Hence we have here $\delta\phi=\delta\phi^*=0$, and the first term vanishes. The variation of the second term in (1.55) is

$$\Lambda\int(\phi^*\delta\phi + \phi\delta\phi^*)df \quad \ldots \quad \ldots \quad (1.57)$$

The condition (1.55) thus gives

$$\int\left[\left(\frac{d^2\phi^*}{df^2}+\Lambda\phi^*\right)\delta\phi + \left(\frac{d^2\phi}{df^2}+\Lambda\phi\right)\delta\phi^*\right]df = 0 \quad . \quad (1.58)$$

and this can be identically fulfilled for arbitrary variations $\delta\phi$ if, and only if,

$$\frac{d^2\phi}{df^2} + \Lambda.\phi = 0 \qquad \ldots \ldots \ldots (1.59)$$

This is the differential equation which has to be satisfied by the signal transmitted in minimum time. Its solution is discussed in Section 6.

Chapter 12

THEORY OF COMMUNICATION, 2

The excerpted material in this chapter comprises the second and third parts of the article by Professor Denis Gabor and supplements the material in the first part which was excerpted in the previous chapter. In Part 2 the method described in the previous chapter is applied to the analysis of hearing sensations. In Part 3 suggestions for compressed transmission and reproduction of speech or music are discussed and the first experimental results obtained with one of these methods are described.

THEORY OF COMMUNICATION, 2

Part 2. THE ANALYSIS OF HEARING

Summary

The methods developed in Part 1 are applied to the analysis of hearing sensations, in particular to experiments by Shower and Biddulph, and by Bürck, Kotowski and Lichte on the discrimination of frequency and time by the human ear. It is shown that experiments of widely different character lead to well defined threshold "areas of discrimination" in the information diagram. At the best, in the interval 60 to 1000 c.p.s. the human ear can discriminate very nearly every second datum of information; i.e., the ear is almost as perfect as any instrument can be which is not responsive to phase. Over the whole auditory range the efficiency is much less than 50 per cent, as the discrimination falls off sharply at higher frequencies. The threshold area of discrimination appears to be independent of the duration of the signals between about 20 and 250 milliseconds. This remarkably wide interval cannot be explained by any mechanism in the inner ear, but may be explained by a new hypothetical effect in nerve conduction, i.e., the mutual influence of adjacent nerve fibres.

(1) Analysis of Hearing

In relation to the ear, two rather distinct questions will have to be answered. The first is: How many logons must be transmitted per second for intelligible speech? The second is the corre-

sponding question for the reproduction of speech or music which the
ear cannot distinguish from the original.   A precise answer to the
first question will not be attempted, but some important data must
be mentioned.   Ordinarily it is assumed that the full range between
about 100 and 3000 c. p. s. is necessary for satisfactory speech transmission.   But Homer Dudley's ingenious speech-analyzing and syn-
thetizing machine, the Vocoder ["Re-making Speech," J. of Acoustical Soc. of Amer. 11:169-77, 1939] has achieved the transmission
of intelligible speech by means of 11 channels of 25 c. p. s. each,
275 c. p. s. in all.   This means a condensation, or compression,
ratio of about 10.   Another datum is an estimate by Küpfmüller of
the product of time-interval by frequency-width required for the
transmission of a single letter in telephony, and in the best system
of telegraphy, as used in submarine cables.   The ratio is about 40.
This suggests that the Vocoder has probably almost reached the admissible limit of condensation.

The transmission which the ear would consider indistinguishable from the original presents a more exactly defined and intrin-
sically simpler problem, as none of the higher functions of intelligence come into play which make distorted speech intelligible.
G. W. Stewart in 1931 was the first to ask whether the limit of aural sensation is not given by an uncertainty relation, which he wrote
in the form $\Delta t \Delta f = 1$, without, however, defining Δt and Δf precisely.   He found the experimental material insufficient to decide
the question, though he concluded that there was some evidence of
agreement.   New experimental results, which have become available
since Stewart's note, and a more precise formulation of the question,
will allow us to give a more definite answer.

In section 5 of Part 1, methods were described for the expansion of an arbitrary signal into elementary signals, allocated to
cells of a lattice.   Figure 2.1 is an example of a somewhat different
method of analysis, in which the elementary areas have fixed shape
but no fixed position, and are shifted so as to give a good represen-

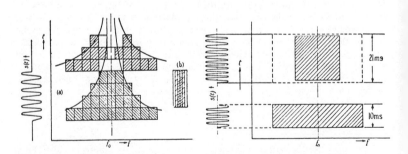

Figure 2.1.   Sine wave of finite   Figure 2.2.   Experiments of
length.   (a) Response of a bank of   Bürck, Kotowski and Lichte.
resonators.   (b) Approximate re-
sponse of the ear.

tation with a minimum number of elementary signals. We now must go a step further, and adjust not only the position but also the shape of the elementary areas to the signal, in such a way that it will be approximately represented by a minimum number of logons. This may be called "black-and-white" representation, and it is suggested that--within certain limits--it is rather close to our subjective interpretation of aural sensations. Figure 2.1 illustrates this. If a sine wave of finite duration strikes a series of resonators, say a bank of reeds, with a time-constant which is a fraction of the duration, their response will be approximately as shown by (a). But, as the ear hardly hears the two noises or "clicks" at the beginning and end of the tone, its sensations can be better described by Figure 2.1(b). We shall find later more evidence for what may be called the "adjustable time-constant" of the ear. It appears that, in general, the ear tends to simplify its sensations in a similar way to the eye, and the analogy becomes evident in the two-dimensional representation.

It will be shown below that there is good evidence for what may be called a "threshold information sensitivity" of the ear, i.e., a certain minimum area in the information diagram, which must be exceeded if the ear is to appreciate more than one datum. The usefulness of this concept depends on how far this threshold value will be independent of the shape of the area. We must therefore test it by analyzing experiments with tone signals of different duration.

It has been known for a long time (March 1871) that a very short sinusoidal oscillation will be perceived as a noise, but beyond a certain minimum duration as a tone of ascertainable pitch. The most recent and most accurate experiments on this subject have been carried out by W. Bürck, P. Kotowski and H. Lichte ["Development of Pitch Sensations," Elektrische Nachrichten-Technik 12: 326-33, 1935; "Audibility of Delays," Ibid. 12:355-62, 1935]. They found that both at 500 and 1000 c.p.s. the minimum duration after which the pitch could be correctly ascertained was about 10 milliseconds for the best observers. In a second series of experiments they doubled the intensity of the tone after a certain time, and measured the minimum duration necessary for hearing the step. For shorter intervals the stepped tone could not be distinguished from the one which started with double intensity.

These two series of tests enable us to estimate the threshold area for very short durations. Figure 2.2 explains the method for a frequency of 500 c.p.s. After 10 milliseconds the signal was just recognizable as a tone. But unless it lasted for at least 21 milliseconds, the ear was not ready to register a second datum, independent of and distinguishable from the first. We conclude, therefore, that the threshold area is determined by the frequency width of the first signal and the duration of the second. It is not necessary to approximate the chopped sine waves by elementary signals, as the ratio of the durations would remain the same. This was 2.1 for 500 c.p.s. and 3.0 for 1000 c.p.s. We conclude that in these regions it takes 2.1 and 3 elementary areas respectively to convey more than one datum to the ear.

Let us now consider another series of tests, the experiments of Shower and Biddulph on the pitch sensitivity of the ear. In these tests the frequency of a note was varied almost sinusoidally between a lower and an upper limit. The actual law of variation was not exactly sinusoidal, as the top of the wave was flattened and rather difficult to analyze in an expert manner. In the following approximate analysis we will replace it by sinusoidal frequency modulation with a total swing δf, equal to the maximum swing in the experiments. By this we are likely to commit an error in the sense of overrating the ear sensitivity, but this will give us a safe basis for estimating the chances of deceiving the ear. The modulation frequency in Shower and Biddulph's experiments was 2 c.p.s., and the sensation level was kept constant at 40 db above the threshold of audibility. Their results for the minimum variation δf at which the trill could be distinguished from a steady tone are as follows:--

f_0								
62.5	125	250	500	1 000	2 000	4 000	8 000	c.p.s.
$\delta f/f_0$								
0.043	0.025	0.012	0.005	0.003	0.0023	0.00225	0.0037	c.p.s.
δf								
2.7	3.1	2.9	2.5	3.0	4.6	9.0	29.5	c.p.s.

It will be seen that δf remains almost constant up to 1000 c.p.s.; from about 1000 c.p.s. it is the ratio $\delta f/f_0$ which is nearly constant.

We now replace the signals used in these experiments by two periodic sequences of elementary signals with frequencies $f_0 \pm \frac{1}{2}f_s$, staggered in relation to one another, so that pulses with higher and lower frequency alternate at intervals of 0.25 seconds. In order to approximate the actual signal as well as possible, we must use the available constants f_s and α (the "sharpness" of the elementary signals) so as to produce nearly the same spectrum.

It is well known [Gray, Horton, Mathes: see page 329] that the spectrum of a frequency-modulated wave with the mean frequency f_0, total swing δf and modulation frequency f_m can be expressed by the following series

$$\operatorname{cis}\left(2\pi f_0 t + \frac{\delta f}{2 f_m}\sin 2\pi f_m t\right) = \sum_{-\infty}^{\infty} J_n\left(\delta f/2 f_m\right)\operatorname{cis} 2\pi(f_0 + n f_m)t . . \quad (2.1)$$

J_n is the Bessel function of nth order. The amplitudes of the side lines, spaced by the repetition frequency, are therefore proportional to $J_n(\delta f/2 f_m)$. Their absolute values are shown at the bottom of Figure 2.3 for four tests of Shower and Biddulph. On the other hand, the absolute amplitudes of the side lines in the spectrum of the two alternating sequences of elementary signals are given by the following formulae

$$I_n = \exp -\left(\frac{\pi}{\alpha}\right)^2 (nf)^2 \; \frac{\cosh}{\sinh}\left(\frac{\pi}{\alpha}\right)^2 n f_m f_s . \quad (2.2)$$

The upper formula is valid for even, the lower for odd, orders n. With the help of equations (2.1) and (2.2) the available constants

α and f_s have been fitted so as to represent exactly the ratio of the first two side lines to the central one. The result is shown in Figure 2.3, in which the elementary signals are represented by

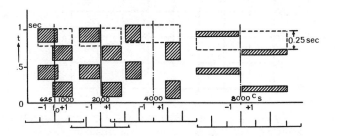

Figure 2.3. Experiments of Shower and Biddulph. The frequency-modulated signals are replaced by two alternating series of elementary signals which produce very nearly the same spectrum.

their rectangles of area one-half. The agreement of the spectra even for higher orders n is very good up to 2000 c.p.s., but less satisfactory at 4000 and 8000 c.p.s. But it would be useless to try better approximations, for example by adding one or two further sequences of elementary signals. More accurate information could be obtained only from experiments based on elementary signals. It may be hoped that such tests will be undertaken, especially as Roberts and Simmonds have suggested easy methods for producing such signals.

For a first orientation the results derived from the tests of Shower and Biddulph appear quite satisfactory. It can be seen from Figure 2.3 how rectangles can be constructed in the information diagram which mark the limit at which the ear can just begin to appreciate a second datum. In this case the meaning of the threshold is that the trill can just be distinguished from a steady tone. Measured in units of elementary areas of one-half, their values are as follows:--

Frequency	62.5-1 000	2 000	4 000	8 000 c.p.s.
(Threshold area)/0.5	2.34	2.88	3.92	6.9

The reciprocals of these figures can be considered as performance figures of the ear as compared with an ideal instrument. In fact, the performance figure of an ideal instrument would be unity, as it would begin to appreciate a second datum as soon as the minimum information area of one-half was exceeded by an amount, however small. The performance figure derived from the experiments of Shower and Biddulph between 62 and 8000 c.p.s. is shown in Figure 2.4. The diagram also contains two points derived from the experiments of Bürck, Kotowski and Lichte, which fit in as well as can be expected. It is very remarkable that up to about 1000 c.p.s.

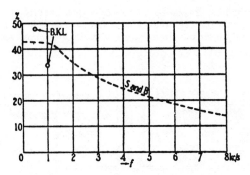

Figure 2.4. Performance figure of the ear. B.K.L. --Bürck, Kotowski and Lichte. S. and B. --Shower and Biddulph.

---

the performance figure is almost 50 per cent, which is the ideal for an instrument like the ear which cannot distinguish the phase of oscillations, i.e., rejects one-half of the data. At higher frequencies, however, the efficiency is much less.

The good fit of the figures obtained from the experiments of Bürck, Kotowski and Lichte, which were carried out with durations of 10 to 20 milliseconds, with those of Shower and Biddulph, in which the threshold area measured 250 milliseconds in the time direction, indicates two facts. One is that, at least up to about 1000 c.p.s., and for durations at least in the limits 20 to 250 milliseconds, the threshold information area is a characteristic of the ear. Evidently the performance figure must go to zero both for extremely short and extremely long elementary signals, but within these wide and very important limits it appears to have an almost constant value.

The other fact which arises from the first is that the ear appears to have a time constant adjustable at least between 20 and 250 milliseconds, and that the ear adjusts it to the content of the information which it receives. But there can be little doubt that, whatever resonators there are in the ear, they are very strongly damped, and that their decay time is of the order of 20 milliseconds or rather less. This is borne out by the experiments of Wegel and Lane on the amplitudes of the oscillations of the basilar membrane in the inner ear. A pure tone excites such a broad region to oscillations that R. S. Hunt ["Damping and Selectivity of the Inner Ear," J. of Acoustical Soc. of Amer. 14:50-57, 1942] who has recently made a thorough investigation of Wegel and Lane's data, infers from them a decay by 1 bel in only 2 cycles, i.e., in only 2 milliseconds at 1000 c.p.s.! Though this estimate might be too low, there can be no doubt that the decay time of the ear resonators cannot substantially exceed 10 milliseconds, and it is impossible to imagine that they would keep on vibrating for as much as a quarter of a second. Hence, even if the duration of a pure tone is considerably prolonged

beyond the 10 milliseconds approximately required for pitch perception, the ear resonators will still display the same broad distribution amplitude. This is illustrated in Figure 2.5. In order to explain the high pitch sensitivity of the ear, as shown, for example,
by the experiments of Shower and Biddulph, it is therefore necessary to assume a second mechanism which locates the center of the
resonance region with a precision increasing with the duration of
the stimulus. Its effect is indicated in Figure 2.5. The second
mechanism acts as if there were a second resonance curve, of a
non-mechanical nature, which after about 10 milliseconds detaches
itself from the mechanical resonance curve and continues to contract
until, after about 250 milliseconds, it covers only a few cycles per
second.

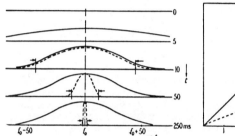

Figure 2.5.   The two mechanisms of pitch determination.

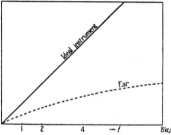

Figure 2.6.   Utilization of information area.

Both mechanisms are essential for our hearing. The first
by itself would probably enable us to understand speech, but only
the second makes it possible to appreciate music. One might be
tempted to locate this second function in the brain, but mechanisms
of nerve conduction can be imagined which might achieve the same
effect. Perhaps the simplest assumption is that the conduction of
stimuli in adjacent nerve fibers is to some extent unstable, so that
in an adjacent pair the more strongly stimulated fiber will gradually
suppress the conduction in its less excited neighbor. The available
evidence would not justify the suggestion that this is the actual mechanism; the intention is only to show that what manifests itself as the
"adjustable time-constant" of the ear is not necessarily a consequence
of some higher function of intelligence.

In the light of these results we can now approach the question
of a condensed transmission which entirely deceives the ear. The
performance figure as shown in Figure 2.4 appears to indicate that
considerable economy might be possible, especially in the range of
higher frequencies. This is brought into evidence even more clearly in Figure 2.6, which contains the integrals over frequency of the
performance figures for the ear and for an ideal instrument. Between zero and 8000 c.p.s., for instance, the maximum number of

data which the ear can appreciate is only about one quarter of the data which can be transmitted in a band of 8000 c. p. s. It is even likely that further investigations might substantially reduce this figure. It may be remembered that the experiments on which Figure 2. 6 is based have all been carried out with sharp or rather angular waveforms; it is not unlikely that the threshold was essentially determined by logons outside the area considered in our analysis. But it must also be remembered that the "adjustable time-constant" makes it very difficult to deceive the ear entirely. It will be shown in Part 3 that methods are possible which could deceive any non-ideal instrument with fixed time-constant. But the ear has the remarkable property that it can submit the material presented to it not only to one test, but, as it were, to several. Ultimately only direct tests can decide whether any such scheme will work satisfactorily.

Part 3.   FREQUENCY COMPRESSION AND EXPANSION

Summary

It is suggested that it may be possible to transmit speech and music in much narrower wavebands than was hitherto thought necessary, not by clipping the ends of the waveband, but by condensing the information. Two possibilities of more economical transmission are discussed. Both have in common that the original waveband is compressed in transmission and re-expanded to the original width in reception. In the first or "kinematical" method a temporary or permanent record is scanned by moving slits or their equivalents, which replace one another in continuous succession before a "window. " Mathematical analysis is simplest if the transmission of the window is graded according to a probability function. A simple harmonic oscillation is reproduced as a group of spectral lines with frequencies which have an approximately constant ratio to the original frequency. The average departure from the law of proportional conversion is in inverse ratio to the time interval in which the record passes before the window. Experiments carried out with simple apparatus indicate that speech can be compressed into a frequency band of 800 or even 500 c. p. s. without losing much of its intelligibility. There are various possibilities for utilizing frequency compression in telephony by means of the "kinematical" method. In a second method the compression and expansion are carried out electrically, without mechanical motion. This method consists essentially in using non-sinusoidal carriers, such as repeated probability pulses, and local oscillators producing waves of the same type. It is shown that one variety of the electrical method is mathematically equivalent to the kinematical method of frequency conversion.

(1) Introduction

High-fidelity reproduction of speech or music by current methods requires a waveband of about 8000 c. p. s. It has been shown in Part 1 that this band-width is sufficient for the transmission of 16000 exact and independent numerical data per second. This high figure naturally suggests the question whether all of this is really needed for the human ear to create an illusion of perfection. In Part 2 it was shown that, even in the frequency range in which it is most sensitive, the human ear can appreciate only one datum in two at the best, and not more than one in four as an average over the whole a. f. range. Moreover, it must be taken into consideration that, in the experiments which gave these limits of aural discrimination, attention was fixed on a very simple phenomenon. It appears highly probable that for complex sound patterns the discriminating power of the ear is very much less. This evidence suggests that methods of transmitting a reproducing sound may be found which are much more economical than those used at present, in which the original signal shape is carefully conserved through all the links of transmission or reproduction. In an economical method the information content must be condensed to a minimum before transmission or before recording, and the reconstruction need not take place before some stage in the receiver or reproducer. There is no need for the signal to be intelligible at any intermediate stage. Economical methods must therefore comprise some stage of "condensing" or "coding" and some stage of "expanding" or "decoding."

Homer Dudley's ingenious Vocoder [see page 356] which transmits intelligible speech through 11 channels of only 25 c. p. s. each, is a well-known example of such a system. It operates with a method of spectral analysis and synthesis. The spectrum of speech is roughly analyzed into 10 bands of 250 c. p. s. each, and the aggregate intensity in each band is transmitted through a separate channel of 25 c. p. s. The transmitted intensity is used for modulating a buzzer at the receiving end, which roughly reproduces the original spectrum. The 11th channel is used for transmitting the "pitch," which is, broadly speaking, the frequency of the vocal cords. The Vocoder in its present form has probably very nearly reached the limit of tolerable compression.

In this Part new methods will be discussed in which the coding of the message consists essentially in compression, i. e., in a proportional reduction of the original frequencies, and the decoding in expansion to the original range. It is evident that neither compression nor expansion can be exact if economy is to be effected. If, for instance, all frequencies were exactly halved, this would mean that it would take twice the time for transmitting the same message and there would be no saving. Compression and expansion --in general, "conversion"--of frequencies must be rather understood in an approximate sense. There will be unavoidable departures from the simple linear law, and hence there will be some unavoidable distortion. But, it appears that these can be kept within tolerable limits while still effecting appreciable waveband economy.

Two compression-expansion systems will be described. The first, which operates with mechanically moving parts, will be called the "kinematical" method, while the second does not require mechanical motion and will be called the "electrical" method. So far, experiments have been carried out only with the kinematical method, and for this reason it will occupy most of this Part.

(2) The Kinematical Method of Frequency Conversion

It will be convenient to explain this method by means of a particular example before generalizing the underlying principle. Assume that the message to be condensed or expanded is recorded as a sound track on a film. For simplicity, assume that the original signal is a simple harmonic oscillation, that is to say a frequency f_0 --to be called the "original frequency"--is produced if the record moves with standard speed v past a stationary slit. Imagine now that the slit itself is moving with some speed u, so that its speed relative to the film is $v-u$. The photocell behind the film now collects fluctuations of light of frequency

$$f_1 = \frac{v-u}{v} f_0 \quad . \quad . \quad (3.1)$$

This means that all frequencies in the record are converted in a constant ratio $(v-u)/v$. There is evidently no gain, as it would take the moving slit $v/(v-u)$ times longer to explore a certain length of the film than if it were stationary. But let us now imagine that the film moves across a fixed window, so that the moving slit is effective only during the time in which it traverses the window. In order to get a continuous record let a second slit appear at or before the instant at which the first slit moves out of the window, after which a third slit would appear, and so on. The device is still not practicable, as evidently every slit would produce a loud crack at the instant at which it appeared before the window and when it left it. But now assume that the window has continuously graded transmission, full in the middle and fading out at both sides to total opacity. In this arrangement the slits are faded in and out gradually, so that abrupt cracks can be avoided. This is the prototype of a kinematical frequency convertor, schematically illustrated in Figure 3.1, which will be investigated below. Though the nomenclature will be taken from this special example, the mathematical theory can be transferred bodily to any other realization of the same principle.

In Figure 3.1 the film is supposed to move in close contact with the slotted drum, but at different speed. A photocell collects the sum of the light transmitted by the individual slits and by the window. To obtain its response we must first write down the contribution of one slit and sum over the slits. All slits will be assumed to have negligible width. For simplicity let us measure all distances x from the middle of the window and all times t from the instant in which a slit, to be called the "zero"-th slit, passes through $x = 0$. The other slits will be distinguished by suffixes k, which increase in the direction in which the film is moving. Their position at the time t will be called x_k. The nomenclature is explained in Figure 3.2. Let v be the speed of the film, while the velocity of the slits will be called

$$u = (1-\kappa)v \quad . \quad . \quad . \quad (3.2)$$

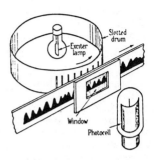

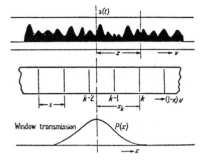

Figure 3.1 Frequency convertor with sound film.

Figure 3.2 Explanation of notations.

The reason for this notation is that equation (3.1) now simplifies to $f_1 = \kappa f_0$, i.e. κ has the meaning of a frequency-conversion ratio. If the spacing of two slits is s, the position of the kth slit at time t is given by

$$x_k = (1 - \kappa)vt + ks \quad \ldots \ldots \quad (3.3)$$

The record will be characterized by the signal $s_1(t)$ which it would produce if it were scanned in the ordinary way by a stationary slit in the position $x = 0$. Hence, if the window were fully transparent, the signal due to the kth slit at time t would be

$$s_1(t - x_k/v) = s_1(\kappa t - ks/v) \quad \ldots \ldots \quad (3.4)$$

The total reproduced signal, i.e., the light sum collected by the photocell, is obtained from this by multiplying by the transmission coefficient $P(x)$ of the window and summing over k.

In all the following calculations we will assume that this transmission follows a probability law. This law has unique properties in Fourier analysis and will immensely simplify our investigations. Other laws which appear equally simple a priori, and which may have even some practical advantages--such as triangular or trapezoidal windows--lead to expressions which are too complicated for anything but numerical discussion. Hence we assume

$$P(x) = \exp - (x/Ns)^2. \quad . \quad (3.5)$$

N is a number, to be called the "slit number," which characterizes the reproduction process. It is the number of slits in the length over which the transmission of the window falls from unity to $1/e$. The total length of the window in which the transmission exceeds 1 per cent is $4.3Ns$. Thus we can say broadly that the total number of slits simultaneously before the window is $4.3N$. The reproduced signal--i.e., the total light collected by the photocell--at time t, is

$$s(t) = \sum_{-\infty}^{\infty} k \, \exp - (x_k/Ns)^2 s_1(t - x_k/v) \quad . \quad (3.6)$$

This, in combination with equation (3.3), is a complete description
of the operation of the frequency convertor. It will now be illustrated in the special case in which s_1 is a simple harmonic oscillation

$$s_1(t) = e^{2\pi j f_0 t} = \text{cis } 2\pi f_0 t \quad . \quad . \quad . \quad . \quad (3.7)$$

The complex form will be used, with the understanding that the real
part constitutes the physical signal. Simple harmonic oscillations
are suitable for the analysis, as their spectrum will consist of a
few lines. But it may be mentioned that analysis in terms of the
elementary signals discussed in Part 1 (harmonic oscillations with
probability envelope) can be carried out almost equally simply, as
the reproduction of an elementary signal consists also in the sum of
a few elementary signals. This is carried out in Appendix 7.1, but
in the text only the more familiar method of Fourier analysis will
be employed.

Substituting the signal (3.7) in equation (3.6) and using equation (3.3), we obtain

$$s(t) = \sum_{-\infty}^{\infty} k \exp - \left[(1-\kappa)vt + ks\right]^2 / (Ns)^2 \text{ cis } 2\pi f_0 (\kappa t - ks/v) \quad (3.8)$$

The meaning of this somewhat complicated expression is explained
in Figure 3.3. Each slit, as it passes before the window, transforms the sine wave into an elementary signal. By adding up the
contributions of the individual slits we obtain for some frequencies
a very nearly faithful reproduction, i.e., an almost pure tone but
of different frequency from the original. For other frequencies we
obtain strong beats.

A more convenient and complete description of the frequency
conversion process is obtained by Fourier analysis. It will now be

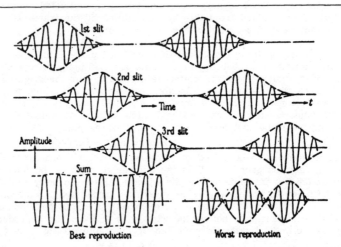

Figure 3.3. The contributions of individual slits and the resulting
light output.

convenient to measure distances in time intervals, and to introduce, instead of the slit spacing s, the time interval τ between the passage of two consecutive slits before a fixed point

$$\tau = s/(1-\kappa)\upsilon \ . \ . \ . \quad (3.9)$$

With this notation the Fourier transform, i. e., the spectrum of the signal $s(t)$, becomes, by known rules,

$$S(f) = \sqrt{(\pi)}\, N\tau \exp - (\pi N\tau)^2 \left(f - \kappa f_0\right)^2 \sum_{-\infty}^{\infty} k \ \text{cis} \ 2\pi k \tau (f - f_0) \quad (3.10a)$$

This expression allows of a simple interpretation. The second factor

$$\sum k \ \text{cis} \ 2\pi k \tau (f - f_0)$$

is the sum of an infinite number of complex vectors of unit length, with an angle of $2\pi\tau(f-f_0)$ between two consecutive vectors. This series, though not convergent, is summable, and its sum is zero for all values of f except those for which

$$\tau\left(f - f_0\right) = \text{an integer} \ . \ . \ . \quad (3.11)$$

Physically this means that the spectrum consists of sharp <u>lines</u> which differ from one another by multiples of $1/\tau$. In other words, the spectrum consists of all combination notes of the original frequency f_0 with the repetition frequency $1/\tau$.

The absolute sharpness of the spectral lines is a consequence of the assumption that the slits pass before the window at mathematically exact equal intervals. In each spectral line $S(f)$ is a "delta function," i. e., a sharp peak of infinite height but finite area. But as in what follows we shall always have to deal with line spectra, it is more convenient to re-interpret $S(f)$ as a function which is zero except at certain discrete values of f, where it assumes finite values, proportional to the amplitude of the spectral lines. In the same sense, we write the second factor of equation (3.10a) somewhat more simply as

$$\sum \ \text{cis} \ 2\pi k \tau (f - f_0) = \sum \delta \left(f - f_0 - k/\tau\right) \ . \quad (3.12)$$

and interpret this as a "selecting factor" which has zero value everywhere except for those values of f which fulfill condition (3.11), where it assumes the value unity (see Figure 3.4). Thus we write equation (3.10) as

$$S(f) = \exp - (\pi N\tau)^2 \left(f - \kappa f_0\right)^2 \sum \delta \left(f - f_0 - k/\tau\right) \ . \quad (3.10b)$$

Figure 3.4. The selection factor.

The first factor is independent of the summation index k and represents an attenuation function of probability shape, which has its maximum at $f = \kappa f_0$ i.e., at frequencies which have been converted in the correct ratio κ. The sharpness of this attenuation curve is reciprocal to the sharpness of the transmission curve of the window, measured in units of time. Thus, if the window were infinitely broad we should obtain exact conversion of all frequencies. But this would have the disadvantage that short signals occurring at some definite time would be reproduced at completely indefinite times (with an infinite number of repetitions). Conversely, if the window were infinitely short the attenuation would be zero and the frequencies scattered evenly over all possible values defined by equation (3.11). Thus we meet again the fundamental uncertainly relation between frequency and time (or rather, "epoch") which was discussed in some detail in Part 1. It follows immediately from previously obtained results that the probability window is ideal in the sense that it produces the smallest possible product of the linked uncertainties of frequency and epoch, as defined in Part 1. Nevertheless the probability window is not necessarily the best from a practical point of view. Some possible improvements will be discussed later.

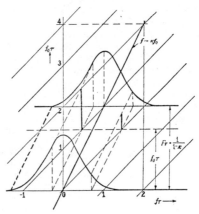

Figure 3.5.   Diagram of frequency compression. $N = \frac{1}{2}$; $\kappa = \frac{1}{2}$.

Equation (3.10a) or (3.10b) allows also a simple graphical interpretation, which is explained in Figure 3.5 in a numerical example. The original frequency f_0 is the ordinate; the reproduced frequencies f are the abscissae. Both are conveniently measured in units $1/\tau$, i.e., as multiples of the repetition frequency. All points (f, f_0) which satisfy condition (3.11) lie on lines at 45° to the two axes, and intersect the horizontal axis at integral values of $f\tau$. The attenuation curve

$$\exp - (\pi N \tau)^2 (f - \kappa f_0)^2$$

needs to be drawn only once, although in the Figure it has been done twice in order to give a clear visual impression of the way in which the amplitude is distributed over the (f, f_0) plane. The spectral lines are given by the heights of the attenuation curve above the points in which a line $f_0 =$ constant crosses the lines $(f - f_0)\tau =$ integer, as shown in an example. This Figure 3.5 shows the action of the frequency convertor at one glance. The correctly converted frequency $f = \kappa f_0$ appears in the reproduction only where a line $(f - f_0)\tau =$ an integer intersects the line $f = \kappa f_0$. This condition is always fulfilled for $f_0 = 0$, and for all frequencies which are multiples of

$$F = 1/\tau(1 - \kappa) \quad . \quad . \quad . \quad . \quad . \quad (3.13)$$

This may be called the length of the "cycle of reproduction," as the quality of reproduction varies cyclically with this period. If f_0 is an integral multiple of F the reproduction can be made almost perfect, as the side lines can be almost entirely suppressed if the slit number N is made sufficiently large. As can be seen in Figure 3.6, $N = 1$ is sufficient to achieve this. But this improvement in the reproduction of certain tones is made at the cost of others. If N is

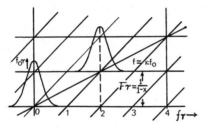

Figure 3.6. Diagram of frequency expansion. $N = 1$; $\kappa = 2$.

large, not only the side lines but almost all amplitudes near the middle of a cycle of reproduction will be supressed, i.e., certain notes will be missing. It is evident that a compromise must be struck between the purity of reproduction at the ends and at the middle of every cycle length F.

The effect of the slit number N on the quality of the reproduction is shown in Figure 3.7. Three cases are illustrated, all for an expansion ratio $\kappa = 2$, and for $N = 0.25$, 0.5 and 1. It may be recalled that the average number of slits before that part of the window in which the transmission exceeds 1 per cent is $4.3N$. In each case a full cycle of reproduction is shown, with ten equally-spaced original frequencies.

At the left, $N = 0.25$, Figure 3.7 shows the effect of too small slit numbers. The reproduction is very "noisy," no frequency being reproduced as an approximately pure tone. There is little difference between the spectra of frequencies near the middle or ends of the cycle; they are all of uniformly poor quality. At the right, $N = 1$, this Figure shows the effect of a too large number of slits

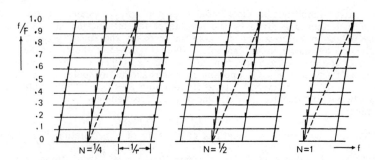

Figure 3.7.   Influence of slit number on quality of reproduction.
$$\mathcal{K} = 2$$

(cf. Figure 3.6).   The frequencies at the ends of the cycle are re-
rpoduced nearly ideally, as practically pure tones, but the frequencies in the middle of the cycle are almost entirely missing in the
reproduction.

        The best compromise appears to be $N = 0.5$, shown in the
middle of Figure 3.7.   The end frequencies are still reproduced as
almost pure tones, and the intensity falls of little towards the middle of the cycle.   (The intensity is obtained by squaring the amplitudes shown in the Figure and finding their sum.   It falls, in the
middle of the cycle, to 0.56 of the maximum.)   The spectra of the
intermediate tones consist mostly of only two lines; i.e., these
will be vibrating tones, vibrating with a beat frequency of $1/\tau$.
The beats are strongest in the middle, where the two spectral components have equal amplitudes.   It may appear at first sight that,
by reducing the beat frequency below any limit, the reproduction
could be made perfect to any desired degree.   But there are limits
to the increase of τ.   As N is fixed more or less at 0.4-0.5, τ
can be increased only by making the window longer.   The length of
the window may be now defined as the length of time T in which a
point of the film passes through the part of the window in which the
transmission exceeds 1 per cent.   This is

$$T = 4.3 N s / v = 4.3 N \tau (1 - \mathcal{K}) . \quad \cdots \quad (3.14)$$

Hence, for the optimum, $N = 0.5$

$$\tau = 0.47 T / (1 - \mathcal{K})$$

        If the time T is too long, the time resolution in the repro-
duction will be poor.   Determining the best compromise between
time resolution and frequency reproduction is a matter for experiment.   On general grounds one would expect that the window length
T must be kept below the limit at which the ear could begin to
separate the contribution of the two or more slits which are simultaneously before the window.   For speech the optimum of T is probably about 100 milliseconds; for music probably about 250 milliseconds.   With $\mathcal{K} = 2$ this would make the beat frequency 21 c.p.s. for
speech and about 8 for music.   It may be noted by comparing equa-

tions (3.13) and (3.14) that a simple reciprocity relation obtains between the cycle length F and the window length T, of the form

$$FT = 4.3 N \ . \ . \ . \quad (3.15)$$

With optimum choice of N the value of this is about 2. Thus for a window length of 100 milliseconds the optimally reproduced frequencies are spaced by about 20 c.p.s.; for $T = 250$ milliseconds by about 8 c.p.s. In the reproduction the spacing will be $\mathcal{K}$ times more.

The theory so far discussed was based on the assumption of a probability window, which not only has the advantage of mathematical simplicity, but also gives the most advantageous reciprocity relation between time resolution and frequency resolution. But the optimum number N was found to be only about 0.5, which means that there are on the average only about two slits before the window. This might produce a slight but noticeable noise in the optimally reproduced frequencies, in particular for $f_0 = 0$ (background). Hence it may be advantageous to depart somewhat from the probability shape in order to suppress the noise. Figure 3.8 shows window transmission shapes for two and three slits which produce no noise when passing before an even background, as the light sum in constant in any position. Though the mathematical theory of such win-

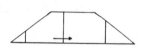 

Figure 3.8.   Window shapes with zero noise for two and three slits.

dows is very much more complicated, it is not to be expected that they would produce essentially different results from probability windows of comparable effective width.

(3) Distortion Resulting from Compression-Expansion Cycle

A full cycle of condensed transmission of the kind discussed consists in compression by a factor $\mathcal{K} < 1$, followed by expansion in the ratio $1/\mathcal{K}$. In general, if two conversion processes are applied in succession to a simple harmonic oscillation of frequency f_0, the resulting spectrum is given by

$$S(f) = \sum_{-\infty}^{\infty} k \sum_{-\infty}^{\infty} m \ \exp - \left\{ (\pi N_1 \tau_1)^2 [f_0(1 - \mathcal{K}_1) + k/\tau_1]^2 \right.$$

$$\left. + (\pi N_2 \tau_2)^2 [f - \mathcal{K}_2(f_0 + k/\tau_1)]^2 \right\} \delta(f - f_0 - k/\tau_1 - m/\tau_2) \ . \ . \ . \quad (3.16)$$

The derivation is given in Appendix 7.2. All data $N, \tau, \mathcal{K}$ of the first conversion have been given a suffix 1, those of the second conversion the suffix 2. k and m are summation indexes which run over all integral values.

The second factor is again a selection operator, which is zero for all values of f with the exception of those where

$$f = f_0 + k/\tau_1 + m/\tau_2 \quad . \quad . \quad . \quad . \quad (3.17)$$

This means that only those frequencies will appear in the spectrum which correspond to combination tones of the original frequency with one or the other or both of the repetition frequencies $1/\tau_1$ and $1/\tau_2$. These forms, in general, a double series, which in the particularly important practical examples to be considered reduces to a simple series.

In what follows we will consider only pairs of conversion processes which, on the average, reconstruct the original frequencies. The condition for this is

$$\mathcal{K}_1 \mathcal{K}_2 = \pm 1 \quad . \quad . \quad . \quad (3.18)$$

The ambiguity of sign expresses the fact that positive and negative frequencies are equivalent. But only the plus sign will be considered, and it will be assumed, moreover, that both $\mathcal{K}_1$ and $\mathcal{K}_2$ are positive. Negative conversion ratios are less advantageous, as for a given window length they require higher repetition frequencies [equation (3.14)]. The whole compression expansion cycle will be characterized by the compression ratio $\mathcal{K}$, $0 < \mathcal{K} < 1$, and the expansion ratio will be assumed as $1/\mathcal{K}$. To simplify the discussion it will be assumed that the window length T is the same in the transmitter and in the receiver. This corresponds to optimum conditions, as it will evidently be best to operate at both ends with the longest permissible T, which may have different values for speech and for music. This means--

$$T/4.3 = N_1 \tau_1 (1-\mathcal{K}) = N_2 \tau_2 (1-\mathcal{K})/\mathcal{K} \quad . \quad . \quad (3.19)$$

or--

$$\tau_1/\tau_2 = N_2/\mathcal{K} N_1 \quad . \quad . \quad . \quad . \quad . \quad . \quad (3.20)$$

A second simplifying assumption will be

$$\tau_1/\tau_2 = p = an\ integer \ . \quad (3.21)$$

This again is an assumption which is fulfilled in the most important practical cases. In the interest of optimum transmission the slit number will be used, in both the transmitter and the receiver, which gives the best results in simple conversion ($N = 0.4-0.65$), and if $\mathcal{K}$ is the reciprocal of an integer $1/2$, $1/3$, $1/4...$ the condition (3.21) will be fulfilled.

Mathematically this has the advantage that the double series of frequencies in the reproduced spectrum

$$k/\tau_1 + m/\tau_2$$

now becomes a simple series, with period $1/\tau_1$, as in simple conversion. We write

$$k/\tau_1 + m/\tau_2 = (k + pm)/\tau_1 = n/\tau_1 \quad . \quad . \quad (3.22)$$

so that the spectral lines are now characterized by the single suffix n, which can be called the "order number." As $S(f)$ will be different from zero for integer values of n, and for these only, we can now omit the selection operator δ in equation (3.16), on the understanding that we consider only integral values of n. Equation (3.17) now becomes

$$f = f_0 + n/\tau_1 \quad \ldots \ldots \quad (3.23)$$

Eliminating f by means of equation (3.23) and introducing the assumptions (3.20) and (3.21) into equation (3.16) we now obtain the simplified formula

$$S(f_0, n) = \sum\nolimits_k \exp - (\pi N_1)^2 \left\{ [f_0 \tau_1 (1-\kappa) + k]^2 + [f_0 \tau_1 (1-\kappa) + k - n\kappa]^2 \right\} \quad (3.24)$$

In this sum, however, not all integral values of k are included, but only those which are compatible with the given value of the order n. If there are two values k_0, m_0 which satisfy the equation

$$n = k_0 + m_0 p$$

all other values which satisfy it must be of the form

$$k = k_0 + \nu p \qquad m = m_0 - \nu$$

where ν is any integer. It will therefore be convenient to introduce ν as the summation index, and make the convention that k_0 is the smallest positive number in the sequence of k's. In other words, let k be the residue of n divided by p, or, in the notation of the elementary theory of numbers,

$$n \equiv k_0 \,(\mathrm{mod}\, p) \quad \ldots \quad (3.25)$$

As a further simplification we note that $S(f_0, n)$ is a periodic function of f_0, with a cycle length

$$F = \frac{p}{\tau_1 (1-\kappa)} = \frac{1}{\tau_2 (1-\kappa)} \quad . \quad (3.26)$$

and obtain

$$S(f_0, n) = \sum_{-\infty}^{\infty} \nu \, \exp - \left(\frac{\pi N_2}{\kappa}\right)^2 \left[\left(\frac{f_0}{F} + \frac{k_0}{p} + \nu\right)^2 + \left(\frac{f_0}{F} + \frac{k_0}{p} + \nu - \frac{n\kappa}{p}\right)^2 \right] \quad . \quad (3.27)$$

By rearranging the terms in the exponent this can be written, finally,

$$S(f_0, n) = \exp - \tfrac{1}{2}\left(\frac{\pi N_2}{p}\right)^2 n^2 \sum_{-\infty}^{\infty} \nu \, \exp - 2\left(\frac{\pi N_2}{\kappa}\right)^2 \left(\frac{f_0}{F} + \frac{k_0}{p} + \nu + \frac{n\kappa}{2p}\right)^2 \quad . \quad (3.28)$$

This formula lends itself well to graphical interpretation. In Figure 3.9 the ordinate is again the original frequency f_0, measured in units F, and the abscissae are the reproduced frequencies f. A line at $45°$ through the origin represents the correct reconversion law, $f = f_0$. This is the line of zero order, $n = 0$. Parallel to this we draw lines through all multiples of $1/\tau_1$ on the f-axis. These are the loci of all non-zero intensities. If we imagine the amplitude $S(f_0, n)$ as a surface above the (f_0, f) plane, this surface consists of a number of profiled planes, projecting above the lines $n =$ constant.

On the line $n = 0$ we have evidently a maximum of $S(f_0, 0)$ for every integral value of f_0/F. These may be called the "principal maxima." At the side lines of higher order there will also be maxima, but because of the probability function in front of the sum these will be smaller. We can draw lines connecting these

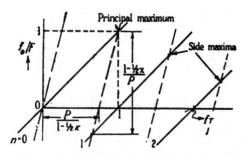

Figure 3.9.   Explanation of frequency-conversion diagrams.

---

maxima of different orders.   We obtain a set of straight lines connecting the points where

$$f_0/F + k_0/p - n\kappa/2p = \text{an integer} . \quad (3.29)$$

If the order n increases by one, by equation (3.24) k_0 also increases by unity and f_0/F changes by

$$-(1-\tfrac{1}{2}\kappa)/p . \quad . \quad . \quad . \quad (3.30)$$

as shown in Figure 3.9.   It can be shown from the geometry of Figure 3.9 that these lines will intersect the horizontal axis at multiples of

$$p/(1-\tfrac{1}{2}\kappa) \quad . \quad . \quad . \quad . \quad . \quad . \quad (3.31)$$

These lines, together with the lines n = integer, form a network with intersections at every maximum of the spectral function $S(f_0, n)$.

Along each line n = constant, the spectral amplitude is the same function of f_0/F, apart from the shift (3.30) and the factor

$$\exp\left[-\tfrac{1}{2}(\pi N_2/p)^2 n^2\right]$$

which varies with n but is a constant along each line.   Thus it is sufficient to compute the amplitude function once, for $n=0$, where the shift is zero and the exponential factor unity.   This function is

$$S(f_0, 0) = \sum \nu \, \exp - 2(\pi N_2/\kappa)^2 (f_0/F + \nu)^2 \quad (3.32)$$

This, as a function of f_0/F, is the sum of probability functions, recurring at unit distance.   It is shown in Appendix 7.3 that it can be reduced to a recognized transcendental function of analysis, the theta function θ_{00}.   Figure 3.10 shows this function for two values of the parameter N_2/κ.   In the cases which are of practical interest N_2/κ is equal to or larger than unity, and the probability functions become so sharp that their overlap is negligible, and (3.32) consists of recurring peaks of probability shape.

It is now possible to construct diagrams, which may be called frequency reconversion diagrams, which show the reproduced spectrum of any pure original tone in the same way as the previous simple conversion diagrams.   Figure 3.11 is a first example of such a

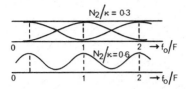

Figure 3.10.   The function $S(f_0, 0)$.

---

diagram, with $K = \frac{1}{2}$; i.e., the cycle consists in compression to one-half, followed by expansion to the original range. The slit numbers are assumed as $N_1 = N_2 = \frac{1}{2}$, which was previously found to represent the most advantageous compromise. The diagram can be considered as three-dimensional, with the profiles of the S-function at right angles to the (f_0, f) plane. The amplitudes are plotted in the direction f_0, so that the spectrum corresponding to any original frequency f_0 can be immediately constructed by drawing a horizontal line and plotting the heights of the S-function at the intersections with the lines of constant order.

This is carried out for a full cycle of reproduction in Figure 3.12, which may be compared with Figure 3.7 (central figure) illustrating the result of the expansion, starting from an undistorted record. It must be noted that τ in Figure 3.7 corresponds to T_2 in Figure 3.12, and as $T_1 = 2T_2$ the minimum interval between two frequencies in the spectrum in Figure 3.12 is half of that in Figure 3.7. If this is borne in mind, it can be seen immediately that the difference between the two cases is mainly that the two side-lines in Figure 3.7 have now split up into two lines each (with some insignificant satellites), and the center of gravity of these two lines follows very nearly the same course as in Figure 3.7. But it has been shown before that with $K = \frac{1}{2}$, $1/T_1$ can be made so small that the ear can hardly, if at all, distinguish between the two tones. ($1/T_1$ can be made about 7 to 10.5 c.p.s. for speech, and 4 c.p.s. for music.) Thus the practical difference between Figures 3.7 and 3.12 is almost negligible, and we can say that the distortions arise almost entirely in the expansion process.

Figure 3.13 is a reconversion diagram for a transmission cycle with $K = \frac{1}{4}$, with the same slit numbers as before. Figure 3.14 contains the reproduced spectra. This diagram approximates Figure 3.7 even more closely, as the separation in the doublets at either side of the correct reproduction has become even smaller as compared with the frequency interval between the doublets. Thus in this case the distortions arise even more exclusively in the expansion process. The only essential difference as compared with the case $K = \frac{1}{2}$ is quantitative. The beat frequency between the doublets is now about $4/T_1$, twice as large as before. If in Figuer 3.14 the doublets are imagined as merged into one, the lines connecting them will be almost vertical. Thus we can interpret the operation of the frequency reconvertor in a somewhat different way.

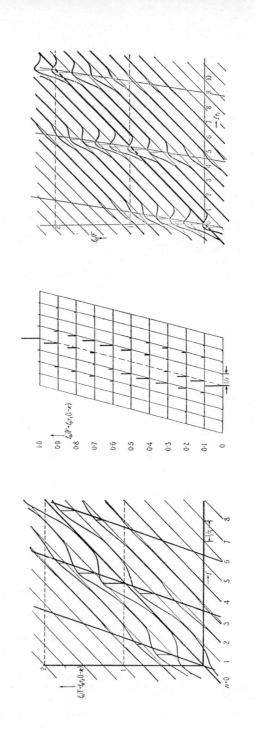

Figure 3.11. Frequency conversion diagram. $N_1 = N_2 = \frac{1}{2}$; $\kappa = \frac{1}{2}$

Figure 3.12. Re-expanded spectrum of ten frequencies (full cycle of reproduction). $N_1 = N_2 = \frac{1}{2}$; $\kappa = \frac{1}{2}$

Figure 3.13. Frequency conversion diagram. $N_1 = N_2 = \frac{1}{2}$; $\kappa = \frac{1}{4}$

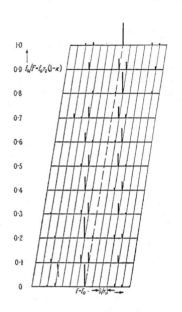

It acts very nearly like a musical instrument with a discrete set of frequencies, which tries to imitate speech or music as closely as possible with a limited number of tones. It is well known that if a vowel is sung into an open piano with the loud pedal depressed it will echo the vowel very clearly. The frequency reconvertor performs a similar imitation, but with the difference that its fixed frequencies are set at equal arithmetical, not geometrical, intervals. Hence the reproduction will tend to become more perfect at higher frequencies. At lower frequencies there must necessarily be departures from perfect reproduction. This becomes evident if it is remembered that the frequency convertor does not change the rhythm or "time-pattern" of speech or music. In frequency language this means that frequencies well below the audible range are reproduced almost with the original value, whatever the value of K.

Figure 3.14. Re-expanded spectrum of ten frequencies (full cycle of reproduction). $N_1 = N_2 = \frac{1}{2}$; $K = \frac{1}{4}$

Summing up, we can say that a frequency compressor and an expander operating in succession produce as close a reproduction of the original as is compatible with the uncertainty relation, and the limit is set almost entirely by the expansion, the errors introduced by the compression being relatively small.

(4) Provisional Report on Experimental Work

Theory can give a complete description of the operation of the frequency convertor either in time language, or in frequency language, or in the more general representation discussed in previous communications, but it does not enable us to draw conclusions on the quality of the reproduction. In order to subject the theory to a first rough test, a 16mm sound-film projector was converted by a few simple modifications into a frequency convertor. Figure 3.15a [p. 380] is a schematic illustration of the optical arrangement.

The usual single, stationary slit of the sound head was replaced by a slotted drum which rotated around an axis passing through the filament of the exciter lamp. The drum was of 0.005-inch steel tape, and the width of the slits was also about 0.005 inch.

The condenser lens was replaced by as large a lens as the fitting would take, with a free diameter of about one inch.   Immediately in front of the slotted drum a frame was arranged for the "window." In the case of films with variable-area sound tracks this film with graded transmission, produced by a photographic process or sprayed with an airbrush.   For variable-density films the window was cut out of black film or paper to the desired shape.   The window and the slits behind it were imaged on the film by the same microscope objective as used in ordinary operation, which reduced their image to about one-quarter.   Thus, allowing for optical errors, the effective slit-width was 0.0015 to 0.002 inch.   The maximum length, T, of the window that could be utilized was limited both by the diameter of the condenser lens and by the collecting system which guides the collected light to the photocell.   Measured on the film it was about six millimeters.   Sound-film moves at the standard speed of 183mm/sec.; thus the maximum T was about 32 milliseconds.   By running the film on the "silent" setting, at about 125mm/sec., this could be increased to about 48 m. sec.   The shortness of these times was a severe limitation of the apparatus.   The improvement between 32 and 48 milliseconds was so marked that it appears to confirm the expectation that the optimum T is considerably longer, probably 100 m. sec., perhaps even more.

The slotted drum had a stepped pulley attached to it which could be driven at different speeds by means of a spring belt from another stepped pulley attached to a sprocket of the projector.   By crossing the belt the motion could be reversed.   The following values of K were tried:--

$K = 0.25 \quad 0.33 \quad 0.42 \quad 1.5 \quad 1.75 \quad 2.0 \quad 3.0 \quad 3.33$

It became evident in the first experiments that the window length of 32 milliseconds was insufficient for the reproduction of music, hence the later tests were mostly restricted to the reproduction of speech.   The uneven rotation of the drum due to the elasticity of the spring belt was also much less objectionable with speech than with music.   Male speech remains completely intelligible with $K = 1.5$; i. e., if the frequencies are raised by 50 per cent, though a baritone changes into a high tenor.   The intelligibility falls appreciably with $K = 1.75$, when the voice changes into a mezzo-soprano, though even with $K = 2$ almost half of the words were intelligible.   This changes a baritone into a soprano.   Reduction by the available compression ratios of 0.42 or less, on the other hand, changed male speech into a deep growling, entirely unintelligible.

Such conversion experiments, in which the voice becomes unnatural by frequency transposition, do not, of course, give a test of intelligibility after reconversion to the original frequency range.   But two tests could be carried out immediately which allow a first rough estimate of these effects to be made.   One test was to run the sound film at "silent" speed, i.e., about $\frac{2}{3}$ standard speed, and apply expansion with $K = \frac{3}{2}$.   Speech restored in this way sounded almost entirely natural, and the intelligibility was appreciably better than if the record was run at $\frac{2}{3}$ speed before a stationary slit.   A second reconversion test is based on the fact that positive and negative frequencies are indistinguishable, so that $K = +1$ and $K = -1$ both reproduce the original frequencies of the record. But while +1 can be realized with a stationary slit, -1 means that the slits have to run in the same direction as the record, with double speed, so that the relative speed of the film against the slits is $-\nu$ instead of $+\nu$ -- i. e., the same in absolute value.

This experiment was tried with different slit numbers, $N = 0.5$, 0.75, 1, and 2. The beat frequencies $1/\tau$ were 60, 90, 120 and 240 c. p. s. $N = 0.5$ was easily the best, in full agreement with the theoretical expectations. It gave perfectly intelligible, though not quite natural, reproduction. The larger slit numbers produced strong "rrr" sounds, which decreased the intelligibility, but it is remarkable that even with a beat frequency of 240 c. p. s. about half the words were intelligible. It may be seen from equation (3.14) that the beat frequencies at $K = -1$ are the same as for $K = +3$. Thus this test corresponded roughly to a reconversion with $K = \frac{1}{3}$, at a window length of 32 milliseconds. As it appears highly probable that the best window length will be about three times as much, perhaps even more, it appears that ultimately even sevenfold compression and re-expansion can be realized without essential loss in intelligibility, though with noticeable distortion.

(5) Devices for Kinematical Frequency Conversion

So far the theory has been explained and illustrated only in the case of a sound film, i. e., with a permanent optical record, but evidently there are many more possibilities for realizing the underlying general principle. The essential features of the kinematical method are as follows. A permanent or temporary record moves past a fixed window with suitably graded attenuation, and inside this window the record is scanned by pick-ups which are themselves moving with some speed different from that of the record. Hence we can use any sort of record which persists long enough to pass across the window, and any sort of pick-up which does not damage the record. The last condition excludes gramophone records with needle pick-ups, but there are many more promising possibilities. Phosphorescence, wave motion and magnetization are well-known physical processes with "memory." The last of these is suitable for permanent as well as for temporary records, and will be discussed later. The first two are suitable for condensed transmission in communication channels.

Phosphorescent records can be used in very much the same way as the permanent optical records previously discussed. The film is replaced by a loop of film coated with phosphorescent material, or by a coated rotating drum. This is excited by a suitable recorder such as a variable light source or an oscillograph, after which it passes immediately into the window, where it is scanned by moving slits or their optical equivalents. The exponential decay of the phosphorescence can be compensated by a suitable exponential

wedge.   Behind the window the phosphorescence can be removed by
heating or by infra-red irradiation.   A similar apparatus can be
used at the receiving end.

Wave motion in fluids is an interesting substitute for a moving record.   It has been used in the Scophony system of television
in order to preserve the picture of a whole line for about 10^{-4} sec.
The Scophony trough contains a piezo-electric crystal at one end and
an absorber at the other.   The pressure waves running along the
trough produce difference in the refractive index of the liquid and
form an equivalent of a film running at extraordinary speed.   It is
well known that such a trough can also imitate a succession of running slits if the crystal is operated with a series of sharp pulses.
Thus a system of two Scophony troughs, in combination with a suitable optical system, appears to be a practicable form of frequency
convertor.   But it is not very suitable for the conversion of sound,
where the window width required is of the order of 0.1 second,
whereas Scophony troughs, unless they are made very large, con-
serve the record for only about 10^{-4} second.   They might perhaps
be suitable for compressed television transmission, if such a scheme
should prove practicable.   This subject, however, is outside the
scope of the present paper.

The most convenient method of condensed transmission will
probably use magnetic tape or wire recorders at both ends of the
communication channel.   Figure 3.15b shows the schematic arrangement.   A loop of the tape or wire runs continuously over two pulleys.   Before reaching the recorder the previous record is wiped

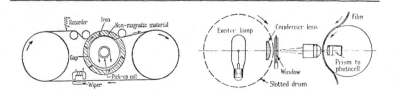

Figure 3.15a.   Frequency con-   Figure 3.15b.   Optical arrange-
vertor with magnetic tape.   ment in frequency convertor.

out, by demagnetization by saturation, or--as in some modern sys-
tems--by demagnetization with high frequency.   After passing under
the recording edge the tape runs over a wheel which has a number
of sharp, wedge-shaped iron spokes.   To avoid scraping, these are
embedded in non-magnetic material; friction may be prevented by
an oil film.   The spoked wheel rotates with some speed different
from that of the film, according to the κ of the conversion.   It
forms the equivalent of rotating slits in the film scanner.   The
equivalent of a window with graded transmission is formed by a suitably shaped magnetic gap between the annular wheel and a central
iron polepiece which carries the pick-up coil.   The current induced

in the pick-up coil is amplified and transmitted through the communication channel. At the receiving end the current is applied to the
recorder of a similar instrument, the only difference being that the
wheel rotates here with a different speed relative to the film. The
window length can be varied by changing the position of the two pulleys which determine the arc of contact, or--more advantageously--
by running the motor at different speeds. This may be necessary
if it is desired to transmit both speech and music under optimum
conditions. All systems of this kind necessarily produce a certain
delay between transmission and reception. The average delay cannot be less than the width T of one window, plus twice the time interval between the recorder and the near edge of the window. In
the transmission of speech this can probably be kept below 200 milliseconds.

The device shown in Figure 3.15b could be used also for long-
playing magnetic gramophones, dictaphones and the like. The only
change is that a permanent instead of a temporary record is used
and the "wiper" is eliminated. But it may be mentioned that in
gramophones, sound-film apparatus and the like, in which the aim
is as high a quality of reproduction as possible, and which must be
ready to reproduce speech or music without any change of adjustment, it does not appear practicable to apply compression to the
whole range of audible frequencies. In such cases it may be better
to divide the audio range into two parts, say 25 to 1500 and 1500 to
7500 c.p.s. A track may be provided for each, of which the first
is an ordinary record, whereas the second is compressed fourfold.
Thus with a double-track record it may be possible to reproduce a
waveband of 7500 c.p.s., at film speeds which would be normally
sufficient only for about 1500. This application may perhaps be of
interest in sub-standard sound-film projectors.

(6) Electrical Methods of Condensed Transmission

It may be surmised a priori that mechanical motion is not
an indispensable part of condensed transmission schemes. Mathematically speaking, the essence of the methods previously discussed
was to apply certain linear but time-dependent operators to an original signal $s_0(t)$, and it appears very likely that these can be produced also by suitable circuits. It will be shown that these, and
even more general operators, can be produced electrically if suitable signal generators are available. Mechanical motion in the
schemes previously described had the general function of producing
new frequencies from one given original frequency. Mathematical
analysis has shown that this consists essentially in the repeated addition of the "repetition frequencies" of the device to the original
frequency. But it is well known that addition and subtraction of frequencies can be produced without mechanical means, by the technique
of "mixing." Hence in order to devise an electrical equivalent of
the kinematical method we must search in the first place for a suitable method of modulation. Evidently modulation with other than
simple sine-wave carriers is necessary, as multiplication with a

simple carrier produces only a shifting and duplication of wavebands.

The other essential feature of the kinematical method was a permanent or temporary record, or more generally "memory" of some sort. Can ordinary electrical circuits have memory? The answer to this is that every tuned electrical system, i. e. , every system which has no unlimited flat response, has a sort of memory, because an instantaneous impulse has a certain aftereffect. A particularly interesting special case is a system with sharp resonance peaks which are at multiples of some fundamental frequency, approximating to the "selection factor" shown in Figure 3.4. Such a system would incessantly repeat the same waveform. If the damping were appreciable, the repetitions would become gradually less and less like the original. This repetition is something rather close to the everyday concept of memory.

It might appear that the simplest method of transmission with non-constant carrier frequency is modulation with a carrier of constant amplitude, but with a frequency which varies between two limits sinusoidally, or according to a saw-tooth curve. If the local oscillator of the receiver varies its frequency according to the same law, a signal similar to the original can be expected. This system is known as "re-entrant modulation." A certain amount of saving in frequency band may be obtained with this system without prohibitive distortions, if the transmission channel is made smaller than the total frequency sweep. But, though this system may be the simplest to realize, its mathematical treatment leads to considerable complications. Therefore the following investigation will be based on a system of modulation which may not be easy to realize, but which allows comparatively simple and general mathematical discussion. This will be achieved by making use once more of the unique properties of certain signal shapes with probability envelope.

We assume a carrier of the form

$$\sum_{-\infty}^{\infty} k \exp - \lambda (t - k\tau)^2 \ . \ . \ . \ (3.33)$$

If the constant λ is real and positive this represents a recurrent probability pulse. But the discussion is just as simple if we make the more general assumption that λ is a complex constant with a positive real part

$$\lambda = \alpha^2 + j\beta^2 \ . \ . \ . \ . \ . \ . \ (3.34)$$

The real part of (3.33) is, apart from a phase constant, the sum of pulses of the form

$$e^{-(\alpha t)^2} \cos (\beta t)^2 \ . \ . \ . \ . \ . \ (3.35)$$

An example of such a pulse is shown in Figure 3.16. It represents a sine-wave with a linearly-varying frequency, modulated by a probability pulse. An interesting feature of these waves is that by choosing the recurrent frequency conveniently their superposition can result in a waveshape which closely approximates a wave of constant amplitude with a frequency varying according to a saw-tooth curve; hence by suitable choice of the constants it is possible to cover "re-

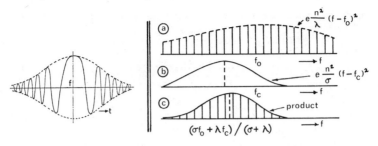

Figure 3.16.   Modulating pulse.   Figure 3.17.   Electrical frequency conversion.

---

entrant modulation" without its mathematical complications. The great advantage of the waveform (3.33) or (3.35) is that its Fourier transform is of the same type as the signal. This allows us to evade the danger of the formulae growing more and more complicated with every step of the analysis.

The signal $s_0(t)$ may again be a pure harmonic oscillation, which may be written in complex form as
$$s_0(t) = \operatorname{cis} 2\pi f_0 t \ . \ . \ . \quad (3.36)$$
Only the complex modulation product of (3.36) and (3.33) will be considered. It is well known that the real product can be obtained from this by adding to it the product with the sign of f_0 reversed, and adding to the sum its complex conjugate. But it will not be necessary to carry out this process in order to recognize the essential features of this method of transmission. The complex modulation product is
$$s_m(t) = \sum_{-\infty}^{\infty} k \, \exp\left[-\lambda\left(t - k\tau\right)^2 + 2\pi j f_0 t\right] \ . \ . \ . \ . \quad (3.37)$$
The Fourier transform of this is
$$S_m(f) = \sqrt{\left(\frac{\pi}{\lambda}\right)} \exp\left[-\frac{\pi^2}{\lambda}(f - f_0)^2 \sum_{-\infty}^{\infty} k \, \delta\left(f - f_0 - k/\tau\right)\right] \ . \ . \ . \ . \quad (3.38)$$
Thus by modulation with the carrier (3.33) the spectrum has been spread out according to a probability law on both sides of the original frequency, while the result of the recurrence is to split up the spectrum into sharp lines with constant frequency interval $1/\tau$.

We now assume that the modulated signal is passed through a filter with a transfer admittance
$$\exp - \pi^2 (f - f_c)^2 / \sigma \ . \ . \ . \quad (3.39)$$
where σ is a complex constant with positive real part. If σ is real this is a "probability filter." This filter transmission centers on f_c, but this will not be the center of the transmitted wave. As illustrated in Figure 3.17, the product of two probability functions is again a probability function, with a center somewhere between the center of the two factors. Hence the filtered spectrum $S(f)$ can

again be expressed in a mathematical form similar to (3.38) but
with changed constants:--

$$S(f) = \sqrt{\left(\frac{\pi}{\lambda}\right)} \exp\left[-\frac{\pi^2}{\sigma+\lambda}(f_0-f_c)^2\right]$$

$$\exp\left[-\pi^2\left(\frac{1}{\sigma}+\frac{1}{\lambda}\right)\left(f-\frac{\sigma f_0+\lambda f_c}{\sigma+\lambda}\right)^2\right] \sum_{-\infty}^{\infty} k\,\delta(f-f_0-k/\tau) \quad \cdot \quad \cdot \quad (3.40)$$

We write now

$$\sigma/(\sigma+\lambda) = \kappa \quad \cdots \quad \cdots \quad \cdots \quad (3.41)$$

and obtain the spectrum in the form

$$S(f) = \sqrt{\left(\frac{\pi}{\lambda}\right)} \exp\left[-\frac{\pi^2}{\lambda}(1-\kappa)(f_0-f_c)^2\right]$$

$$\exp\left\{-\frac{\pi^2}{\kappa\lambda}\left[f-\kappa f_0-(1-\kappa)f_c\right]^2\right\} \sum_{-\infty}^{\infty} k\,\delta(f-f_0-k/\tau) \quad \cdot \quad \cdot \quad \cdot \quad (3.42)$$

This is a formula very similar to that obtained in the case of kinematical compression, but with some differences, the most important
of which is that σ, λ and κ need not be real. It is interesting,
however, to consider the special case in which σ, λ and consequently also κ are real and positive. In this case, equation (3.42) differs
from equation (3.10a) or (3.10b) only in two points. One is that the
maximum of the amplitudes is not at $f=\kappa f_0$, but at $f=\kappa f_0+(1-\kappa)f_c$
i.e., the spectrum is not only compressed, but also shifted by a
certain constant amount, depending on the position of maximum filter transmission, f_c. The other new feature is the factor

$$\exp\left[-\pi^2(1-\kappa)(f_0-f_c)^2/\lambda\right] \quad \cdot \quad \cdot \quad \cdot \quad (3.43)$$

which is independent of f but dependent on the original frequency
f_0. Hence different frequencies are not reproduced with equal intensity. This effect can be reduced or eliminated by boosting the
original amplitudes in a ratio inverse to the factor (3.43) before
modulation.

We see now that by applying in succession the operations of
boosting, modulation with repeated probability pulses, and filtering,
we can produce by purely electrical means a compressed spectrum
identical to that obtainable by mechanical methods. But it is important to note that only compression can be achieved in this special
case, not expansion, as κ, given by equation (3.41), is necessarily
smaller than unity. By a rather complicated calculation, which may
be omitted, it can be shown that by a second modulation--in the re-
ceiver--with a modulating wave of the type (3.33), it is possible to
restore the original frequency, with very much the same distortions
as in kinematical reconversion. But it is essential that both λ and
σ should have imaginary components, i.e., both the modulating
pulses and the filter characteristic must be of the type as shown in
Figure 3.17. Simple probability pulses and probability filters can
achieve only part of the reconversion cycle. Hence the electrical
method is better described as "condensation-dilution" than as "compression-expansion." The transmitted signal spectrum is entirely
dissimilar to the original, as the spectrum corresponding to a single
original frequency is spread out over the whole transmitted range.

At the present stage it is impossible to overlook the possibilities of electrical methods of condensed transmission, which in principle appear almost unlimited. Progress is likely to be slow and difficult, as the mathematical treatment of pulses different from those considered here is liable to become excessively complicated, and experiments unguided by theory do not appear very promising. But the economy which may ultimately be achieved is likely to be large enough to encourage efforts in this direction.

(7) Appendices

(7.1) Response of Frequency Convertors to Elementary Signals

It has been shown in Parts 1 and 2 that signal analysis in terms of certain "elementary signals" has particular advantages, especially in problems of physiological acoustics. These elementary signals are simple harmonic oscillations, modulated with a probability pulse. Analysis in terms of these functions contains the representation of a signal as a time function $s(t)$ and as a frequency function $S(f)$ as limiting special cases. Elementary signals are also very suitable for describing the operation of a frequency convertor with a probability window, as a convertor reproduces any function of this type as the sum of functions of the same type.

The frequency convertor transforms an "original" signal $s_1(t)$ into

$$s(t) = \sum_{-\infty}^{\infty} {}_k \exp\left\{-\left(\frac{t+k\tau}{N\tau}\right)^2 s_1\left[\kappa t - (1-\kappa)k\tau\right]\right\} \quad . \; . \; (3.44)$$

This formula is obtained from equation (3.6) if x_k is substituted from equation (3.3) and the repetition interval τ from (3.9). Substitute for $s_1(t)$ a general elementary signal

$$s_1(t) = \exp - \frac{\epsilon^2(t-t_0)^2}{(N\tau)^2} \operatorname{cis} 2\pi f_0 (t-t_0) \; . \; . \; . \; . \; (3.45)$$

The dimensionless parameter ϵ characterizes the sharpness of the signal. In Part 1 the effective duration of a signal has been defined as $\sqrt{(2\pi)}$ times its r.m.s. duration. In the present case this is

$$(\Delta t)_1 = \sqrt{\frac{\pi}{2}} \frac{N\tau}{\epsilon} \; . \; . \; . \; . \; . \; . \; . \; . \; . \; (3.46)$$

The effective spectral width is, by the same definition,

$$(\Delta f)_1 = \frac{1}{\sqrt{(2\pi)}} \frac{\epsilon}{N\tau} \; . \; . \; . \; . \; (3.47)$$

The relation of the time interval $N\tau$ to the window width T is given by equation (3.14), which combined with (3.46) gives

$$\epsilon = \frac{0.41}{1-\kappa} \frac{T}{(\Delta t)_1} \; . \; . \; (3.48)$$

E.G., for $\kappa = 2 \epsilon$ (in absolute value) is 0.41 for signals with an effective duration equal to the window length. It is larger for sharper signals, smaller for longer ones.

Substitution of (3.45) is equation (3.44) gives

$$s(t) = \sum {}_k \exp\left[-\left(\frac{1}{N\tau}\right)^2 \left\{(t+k\tau)^2 + \epsilon^2[\kappa t - k(1-\kappa)\tau - t_0]^2\right\}\right]$$
$$\times \operatorname{cis} 2\pi f_0 \left[\kappa t - (1-\kappa)k\tau - t_0\right] \; . \; . \; (3.49)$$

This can be written in the simpler form

$$s(t) = \sum_k \exp\left[-\Omega^2(t-\beta_k)^2 + \gamma_k\right] \quad . \quad . \quad . \quad (3.50)$$

where the constants have the following values:--

$$\Omega^2 = (1+\epsilon^2 K^2)/(NT)^2$$

$$\beta_k = -\left\{kT - \epsilon^2 K\left[kT(1-K)+t_0\right] - j\pi f_0(NT)^2\right\}/(1+\epsilon^2 K^2)$$

$$\gamma_k = -\left\{(1+\epsilon^2 K^2)\beta_k^2 - (kT)^2 - \epsilon^2\left[(1-K)kT + t_0\right]\right\}/(NT)^2 - 2\pi j f_0\left[(1-K)kT + t_0\right] \quad . \quad (3.51)$$

The Fourier transform of the kth term of (3.50) is

$$\frac{\sqrt{\pi}}{\Omega} \exp\left[-\left(\frac{\pi f}{\Omega}\right)^2 - 2\pi j \beta_k f + \gamma_k\right] \quad . \quad . \quad (3.52)$$

Applying this to (3.50) a somewhat lengthy calculation leads to the following expression for the spectrum of the reproduced signal:--

$$S(f) = \frac{\sqrt{(\pi)}\, NT}{\sqrt{(1+\epsilon^2 K^2)}} \exp\left[-\frac{(\pi NT)^2}{1+\epsilon^2 K^2}(f-Kf_0)^2\right]$$

$$\times \operatorname{cis} \frac{2\pi}{1+\epsilon^2 K^2}(\epsilon^2 Kf - f_0)t_0$$

$$\times \sum_{-\infty}^{\infty}{}_k \exp\left[-\frac{\epsilon^2(kT+t_0)^2}{(1+\epsilon^2 K^2)(NT)^2}\right] \times \operatorname{cis} \frac{2\pi kT}{1+\epsilon^2 K^2}$$

$$\left\{\left[1 - \epsilon^2 K(1-K)\right]f - f_0\right\} \quad . \quad . \quad . \quad . \quad (3.53)$$

The first factor, in the first line, can be called the attenuation factor, the second the phase factor, and the third the spectral separation factor. If $\epsilon = 0$ and $t_0 = 0$, equation (3.53) simplifies to equation (3.10a) and (3.10b), discussed in the text. In this special case of infinite wave trains the separation factor becomes a "selection factor" and the spectrum becomes a line spectrum.

In the general case the attenuation factor has the effect that the effective spectral width of the reproduced signal becomes

$$\Delta f = \frac{1}{\sqrt{(2\pi)}} \frac{\sqrt{(1+\epsilon^2 K^2)}}{NT} \quad . \quad . \quad (3.54)$$

which is $\sqrt{(1+\epsilon^2 K^2)}/\epsilon$ times the original value (3.47). If ϵ is very large, i.e., if the signal is very sharp, this ratio approaches K, the conversion ratio. This means that with very short signals the spectral envelope is reproduced accurately, on a scale K times the original. The reproduced signal $s(t)$ itself consists of an accurate reproduction of the original, but on a time scale $1/K$ times extended, and of similar but weaker "echoes," produced by repeated passage of slits across the record of the short signal.

The opposite case arises if the signal is of long duration. Here the spectral width, which in the original is very small, is expanded to a value $1/\sqrt{(2\pi)}\, NT$, whereas the envelope of the reproduced signal $s(t)$ approaches the original very closely. This is the reason why the frequency convertor can reproduce without much distortion the articulation of speech or the time pattern of music.

(7. 2) Combination of Two Conversion Processes in Succession

      Consider the conversion as described by equation (3.10b) as a first operation on the frequency f_0, with suffix "1," which produces a certain spectrum S_i on an intermediate frequency scale f_i

$$S_i(f_i) = \exp\left[-(\pi N_1 T_1)^2(f_i - \kappa_1 f_0)^2\right]\sum_k \delta(f_i - f_0 - k/T_1) \quad . \quad . \quad (3.55)$$

This is different from zero only if

$$f_i = f_0 + k/T_1 \quad . \quad . \quad . \quad (3.56)$$

where k is any integer. Apply now a second similar operation, with suffix "2," to the result of the first operation. This splits every spectral line (3.56) into an infinity of equidistant lines given by

$$f = f_i + m/T_2 \quad . \quad . \quad . \quad . \quad (3.57)$$

Eliminating the intermediate frequency f_i from the two last equations, we see that non-zero amplitudes in the final spectrum will appear at

$$f = f_0 + k/T_1 + m/T_2 \quad . \quad . \quad . \quad . \quad (3.58)$$

The reduction of the spectrum to discrete lines can be conveniently expressed by the selection operator

$$\sum_m \sum_k \delta\left(f - f_0 - k/T_1 - m/T_2\right) \quad . \quad (3.59)$$

using again the "delta function," which is zero everywhere except at argument zero. We can now write the result of the two operations as follows:--

$$S(f) = \sum_m \sum_k \exp\left[-(\pi N_1 T_1)^2(f_i - \kappa_1 f_0)^2\right]$$

$$\times \exp\left[-(\pi N_2 T_2)^2(f - \kappa_2 f_i)^2\right] \times \delta\left(f - f_0 - k/T_1 - m/T_2\right) \quad . \quad . \quad . \quad (3.60)$$

Equation (3.16) is obtained from this by substituting the values of f_i and f from equations (3.56) and (3.57).

      Any spectral line as given by equation (3.58) can be characterized by two integers k_0 and m_0

$$f = f_0 + k_0/T_1 + m_0/T_2 \quad . \quad . \quad (3.61)$$

If T_1 and T_2 are incommensurable there will be no other integral values which satisfy this equation; hence only a single term of the sum (3.60) will contribute to the amplitude of this frequency. But if T_1 and T_2 are in a rational relation

$$T_1/T_2 = p/q \quad\quad\quad (3.62)$$

where p and q are relative primes, there will be an infinity of integer solutions of (3.61) of the form

$$k = k_0 + \nu_p$$
$$m = m_0 - \nu_q \quad\quad\quad (3.63)$$

where ν is any integer. But if the same window width is used in both conversion processes, and if the speed ratios are produced by toothed wheels, by equation (3.20) T_1/T_2 is bound to be rational. This means that the line spectrum (3.58) will repeat itself with a period

$$p/T_1 = q/T_2 \quad\quad\quad (3.64)$$

To avoid unessential complications the discussion in the text is restricted to the case $q = 1$.

(7.3) Reduction of the Recurrent Exponential Pulse to Theta Functions

In equation (3.28) for $S(f, n)$ introduce the following notations:--

$$2\left(\frac{\pi N_2}{\kappa}\right)^2 = \alpha^2; \quad \frac{n\kappa}{2p} =: \mu; \quad \frac{f_0}{F} + \frac{k_0}{p} = y \quad . \quad . \quad (3.65)$$

This enables us to write it in the form

$$S(f, n) = S(y, \mu) = e^{-\alpha^2\mu^2}\sum_\nu e^{-\alpha^2(y+\nu-\mu)^2} \quad . \quad (3.66)$$

The theta function θ_{00} as defined in analysis is

$$\theta_{00}(z, \tau) = \sum_{-\infty}^{\infty} e^{j\pi(\nu^2\tau + 2\nu z)} \quad . \quad . \quad . \quad (3.67)$$

or, with imaginary arguments,

$$\theta_{00}(jz, j\tau) = e^{\pi z^2/\tau}\sum_{-\infty}^{\infty} e^{-\pi\tau(\nu+z/\tau)^2}. \quad . \quad (3.68)$$

Now put $\pi\tau = \alpha^2; \quad z/\tau = y - \mu \quad . \quad . \quad . \quad . \quad . \quad . \quad (3.69)$

This gives

$$\theta_{00}\left[j\frac{\alpha^2}{\pi}(y-\mu), j\frac{\alpha^2}{\pi}\right] = e^{\alpha^2(y-\mu)^2}\sum_{-\infty}^{\infty} e^{-\alpha^2(\nu+y-\mu)^2} \quad . \quad . \quad . \quad (3.70)$$

Dividing this by equation (3.66) we obtain

$$S(y, \mu) = e^{-\alpha^2[(y-\mu)^2+\mu^2]}\,\theta_{00}\left[j\frac{\alpha^2}{\pi}(y-\mu), j\frac{\alpha}{\pi}\right] \quad . \quad . \quad (3.71)$$

and finally, substituting the original values for α, μ, and y,

$$S(f_0, n) = e^{-2\left(\frac{\pi N_2}{\kappa}\right)^2\left[\left(\frac{f_0}{F}+\frac{k_0}{p}-\frac{n\kappa}{2p}\right)^2+\left(\frac{n\kappa}{2p}\right)^2\right]}$$

$$\theta_{00}\left[j2\pi\left(\frac{N_2}{\kappa}\right)^2\left(\frac{f_0}{F}+\frac{k_0}{p}-\frac{n\kappa}{2p}\right), j2\pi\left(\frac{N_2}{\kappa}\right)^2\right] \quad . \quad . \quad (3.72)$$

Tables of theta functions may be found in Jahnke and Emde, Tables of Functions (New York: Dover Publications, 1945) and in other works.

Chapter 13

BACKGROUND INFORMATION

The material included in this chapter is not strictly speaking about compressed speech as such. The concepts presented, however, are those that must be fully grasped before a solid concept of the theory and practice of time-compressed speech can be mastered. Dr. J. M. Pickett, excerpts from whose article constitute the first portion of this chapter is professor of speech communication at Gallaudet College in Washington, D. C. The article here excerpted originally appeared in <u>American Annals of the Deaf</u> in 1968. The author was kind enough to revise it and bring it up to date especially for this anthology.

To those readers who have been trained in the field of speech or hearing the article may, I think, serve as a valuable review. To those who do not possess such training it seems to me that this readily understandable explanation of basic phonetics will be as invaluable as it was to me. Over and over again it will be impressed on the reader of this anthology that success in producing intelligible and comprehensible compressed material is dependent upon the respect which is paid to the preservation of the units of sound that are involved in the material being compressed. Professor Pickett brings to this anthology a valuable contribution concerning the nature of these sound patterns that must be preserved in compressing speech.

The late Dr. Gordon E. Peterson in his Louisiana State University doctoral thesis, excerpted in the second portion of this chapter, studied the minimum duration necessary for the recognition of vowel sounds. It hardly seems necessary to point out the importance of such a study in relation to the intelligibility and comprehensibility of compressed speech. Certainly knowledge of the minimum duration of any speech component sets the limits of the degree of compression that is possible without destroying intelligibility. It is very unfortunate that the original copy of Dr. Peterson's thesis is no longer available. The figures included in that work lent much to the meaningfulness of his work through their graphic representations. I would very much have liked to reproduce a number of those figures here. Since I had to work from a rather poor photocopy of portions of the thesis this was not possible.

The short excerpt from Dr. Barbara R. Zimmerman's Ohio University doctoral thesis describes still another approach to the determination of the minimum recognizable segment of a short syllable.

389

In a study such as Zimmerman's, for example, the experiment would have been much easier to carry out or to replicate with a device such as the one Ruth S. Day describes in an excerpt here from her thesis. Another excerpt will be presented at a later point in this anthology.

SOUND PATTERNS OF SPEECH

J. M. Pickett

The purpose of this paper is to provide a brief review of the acoustic patterns of the speech sounds. It is assumed that the reader is acquainted with general phonetics, that he does not need a review of how the various speech sounds are articulated, but that he may need a concise description of speech sound patterns. Speech articulation consists of a series of movements and states of the speech organs imposed upon the breath stream. The breath stream is modified by the articulatory movements so as to produce certain consistent patterns of speech sound. One type of sound is noise-like (aperiodic) and is produced by the turbulence in the breath stream as it passes through a small constriction in the vocal tract. Examples of noise-like speech sounds are the fricatives, s, sh, f, and the brief noise bursts after the stop consonants, p, t, and k. Another type of modification of the breath stream is due to the periodic opening and closing of the vocal cords when they are held together, adjusted for "voicing," and supplied with appropriate breath pressure. This articulation produces a pulsing or periodic source of sound distinctly different from the noise-like sound. Examples of periodic speech sounds are the vowels, the liquid and nasal consonants, and the voiced phases of stop and fricative consonants.

The consonant sounds of speech fall into one of two classes, they are either "voiced," i.e., closely associated with the periodic vocal cord motions, or they are "unvoiced," in which case a noise-like sound is usually produced. This phonetic distinction, voiced vs. unvoiced, carries a heavy load in speech communication [P. Denes, "On Statistics of Spoken English," J. of Acoustical Soc. of Amer. 35:892-904, 1963]. The noise sounds are mostly high in frequency because the mouth cavity in front of the constriction is small and reinforces the high frequencies of the turbulence. The voiced sounds have their main energy in the middle and low frequencies.

The manner of articulation is a second major distinction among consonant sounds. For example, the nasal consonant, n, differs from the stop, d, and the fricative, z, in that the velum (the nose-sealing flap) is dropped open during the n but is held tightly closed for those other consonants. The voiced sound during all these consonants contains frequency differences that signal the manner of articulation. These frequency differences are found in the low and middle range from 200 to 3000 c. p. s. If the sound in this range is distorted, the manner distinctions among consonants become difficult or impossible to perceive. This would mean difficulty in distinguishing among nasal, lateral, voiced stop, and voiced fricative when produced at the same place of articulation. These distinctions, as a group, are just as important as the voiced-unvoiced distinction.

A third type of distinction among consonants is the place of the consonant constriction; there are three major places of consonant articulatory constriction: front, middle, and back--e. g. , respectively, the stops, p̠, t̠, and k̠. The importance of this distinction is not as great, statistically, as that of the voicing and manner distinctions because of the preponderant occurrence of middle consonants. Distortion of the middle range of frequencies, 1000 to 3000 c. p. s. , will interfere with distinguishing middle and back consonants.

The different vowels of speech are distinguished mainly in the region 500 to 2500 c. p. s. As a class they convey only about one-third as much information as the consonants. The important frequency range for vowels is similar to that for the place distinctions among consonants, which distinctions are embodied mainly in frequency transitional changes in the adjacent vowels but to some extent also in the frequencies present in the noise-like phases.

The low frequencies of the vowel sounds contain information about the voicing and unvoicing of the adjacent consonants. The intense low-frequency region of vowel sound, at about 500 c. p. s. , is rather completely suppressed during all consonant intervals. The duration of this suppression is consistently short for voiced consonants and longer for unvoiced consonants. Normal listeners use this difference in duration of "vowel gap" as an important cue to hearing the voiced-unvoiced distinction (in addition to the noise-burst cue mentioned above). The shorter vowel gap for voiced consonants is due to the voicing conditions being maintained during the consonant constriction, i. e. , the vocal cords are held together and the air pressure above the vocal cords is relatively low. For the unvoiced consonants, on the other hand, the vocal cords are held apart during the consonant constriction and the air pressure above the vocal cords rises to the same pressure as that below the cords; thus, upon release of the unvoiced constriction, extra time is required for the conditions for voicing to be restored in order to produce the following vowel: the air pressure is lowered by bursting through the narrow early stages of the opening of the constriction and the vocal cords are brought back together to the voicing position. The noise-burst phases on release of unvoiced stop consonants last 20 to 60 milliseconds. Upon release of voiced stop consonants, there is only a very brief burst, if any, and vowel voicing starts almost immediately. Nasality of speech sound is needed during the nasal consonants. However, during other phases of speech, extreme nasality tends to obscure the normal frequency patterns of all the speech sounds.

Formants and Transitions

The voicing action of the vocal cords produces a source of buzz-like or periodic sound which then passes through the vocal tract to the air outside the speaker. The vocal tract changes the frequency composition of the buzz-like sound in special ways that relate closely to the different articulatory shapes of the vocal tract. We now wish to describe these important frequency patterns.

The original buzz-like sound produced by the vocal cord action has a low buzz frequency: about 100 pulses per second for men and 200 for women. However, the sharpness of each pulse of the buzz produces other sound components at frequencies above the basic buzz frequency. The shape over frequency of the intensities of the components is called the frequency spectrum. The frequency spectrum of the vocal cord buzz has a smooth downward slope in the contour of intensity as we go from low to high frequencies. The smoothness of this spectrum slope is modified by the resonant peaks in the transmission response of the vocal tract. These resonances are called formants; their locations in the frequency spectrum depend on the length and shape of the vocal tract. The length of the tract determines the overall frequency spacing between the peaks; in the relatively long vocal tract of an adult male, the formant peaks are spaced about 1000 c.p.s. apart, beginning with the first peak at 500 cycles. The formant frequency locations are proportionately higher for shorter vocal tracts; if the tract is half as long as the adult male tract, the average formant frequencies are all multiplied by two, if one-third as long, multiplied by three, and so on.

The resonant peaks are due to strong reinforcement of the buzz-sound frequency components in the region of each resonance. In the case of the lowest resonance at about 500 c.p.s., the 500-cycle component will be more intense than any other component, even stronger than the basic buzz frequency. The adult female vocal tract is, on the average, about 0.87 times the length of the adult male tract. The formant frequency locations are altered radically by the articulatory movements of the lips and tongue as they modify the shape of the vocal tract and open and close it. These changes are called formant transitions and, especially in the lowest three formants, they are important auditory cues for distinguishing the speech sounds. Further details on the rules for vowel formant frequencies are explained in K. Stevens and A. House ["An Acoustical Theory of Vowel Production and Some of Its Implications," J. of Speech & Hearing Research 4:303-20, 1961].

Similarly, if the sound source is the noise-like sound produced by a consonant constriction, the frequency spectrum of the noise will have resonant formant peaks determined by the shape of the vocal tract in front of the constriction [J. Heinz and K. Stevens, "On the Properties of Voiceless Fricative Consonants," J. of Acoustical Soc. of Amer. 33:589-96, 1961]. If the shape of the cavity in front of the constriction is in transition from one position to another, then frequency transitions in the cavity resonances take place which

furnish auditory cues as to the identity of the preceding and following sounds.

Articulatory Timing

The movement coordinations of speech articulation form a
complex system that is not as well understood as are the acoustic
patterns.   However, there are certain timing consistencies which
produce reliable duration cues for distinguishing classes of speech
sound.   First we should note that the syllables of speech occur at
an average rate of two to five syllables per second, depending on
the style of speaking.   The slow rate would be for careful, exag-
gerated enunciation while the fast rate would be for rapid, fluent,
but still clear, conversation.   Considering the stream of speech syllables to be a series of alternations between a relatively constricted
state of articulation (consonant) and a more open state (vowel), typical time durations can be assigned to the basic phases of alternation.   A typical open period is about 100 milliseconds, the closing
transition takes about 50 msec., the constricted period is about 100
msec., and the opening transition is about 50 msec.   The total cycle, open to closed and back just to open, would be 300 msec.;
this corresponds to a rate of 3.3 syllables per second, an average
rate of utterance.   In specifying the duration of a vowel phase, the
convention is to include the transitions, so a typical vowel duration
at this utterance rate would be 200 milliseconds.   Long stressed
vowels however would be longer and short unstressed vowels much
shorter.

At other rates of utterance the consonant constriction and
transition timing remain about the same and the rate changes are
produced more by vowel duration changes than by consonant changes.
If the rate of utterance becomes slower, the open periods (vowels)
lengthen while the transitional and constricted periods lengthen rather little.   Similarly, if the rate is very rapid, the vowels shorten
proportionately more than the consonants.

Voice Pitch and Stress

The voice pitch is the frequency of the opening and closing
cycle of the vocal cords.   This frequency varies under two main influences, the lung air pressure and the tension on the vocal cords.
With increasing pressure or lung effort the voice pitch frequency increases; with increasing vocal cord tension the pitch also increases.
Thus a stressed or emphasized part of an utterance, is produced by
a higher air pressure and vocal cord tension which causes a higher
pitch of the voiced sounds.   The vocal cord tension also raises or
lowers the pitch depending on the expressive intention of the talker
[P. Ladefoged, "Some Physiological Parameters in Speech," Language & Speech 6:109-19, 1963; P. Liberman, Intonation Perception
and Language, Cambridge, Mass.:   M. I. T. Press, 1967].   It should
be especially noted that the voice pitch is independent of the formant

Table 1

SPEECH SOUND CHARACTERISTICS

Frequency Regions, c. p. s. [Hz]

	Low 200-1000	Mid 1000-2000	High 2000-3000	Very High 3000 Hz and above
Periodic Sounds				
1 Vowels	u, ʊ, o, ɔ	ɑ, a, æ, ʌ, ɛ, e, ɪ, i	ə	
2 Formant transitions	p, b, w, m, f, v	t, d, y, n, s ʃ, z, ʒ, θ, ð	k, g, ŋ, r	
3 Nasal consonant murmurs	m, n, ŋ			
Aperiodic Sounds				
4 Stop bursts		p		t, k
5 Fricative sounds		f, h	ʃ	s, f, θ
Timing Features				
6 Vowel duration	Short: ʌ, ɛ, ɪ Long: u, o, ɔ, a, æ, e, i			
7 Voiced consonant gaps	50-100 msec.			
8 Unvoiced conso-nant gaps	100-200 msec.	Unvoiced noise: stops, short, 40 msec. fricatives, long, 100-200 msec.		
9 Formant transi-tion duration	w	Long: liquid & glide consonants, y r, l 75 msec. Short: all other consonants, 50 msec.		

pattern of the voiced sounds, the formant pattern being determined only by the length and shape of the vocal tract above the vocal cords.

Table 1 summarizes current acoustic knowledge about English speech sounds. It is based on a condensation of acoustic research results in speech analysis, speech synthesis, and speech perception. A number of arbitrary divisions and over-simplifications were made to arrive at a compact representation but it is hoped that the table will be useful as a broad schema. Basically speech sounds are pat-terns of sound energy which vary over frequency and over time. A major simplification for most of the table consists of representing speech sound energy to be either present or absent, in a given frequency region, and either on or off over certain time intervals. This is not true in actual speech but results of synthesis experiments and amplitude compression studies show that the listener perceiving speech is much more sensitive to frequency and time structure than to energy level structure. The following notes are explanations of how to interpret the table.

Use of Table. Each speech sound is entered in one or more of the four frequency columns and in one or more of three horizontal groups representing three classes of overall sound features namely, periodic, aperiodic, and timing features. Within each feature class there are further phonetic subdivisions. The table is meant to be used either as a means of roughly characterizing any given speech sound acoustically, or to locate those sounds having acoustically distinctive features in any of the four frequency regions. Some of the sounds may have acoustic energy in nearly all frequency regions but each sound is entered only in those cells where the acoustic features occur that are considered primarily responsible for its discrimination from other speech sounds.

Frequency Columns. The frequency ranges are for the adult male voice. Actually the mid-frequencies of the first three ranges correspond roughly to the first three resonant frequencies (formant frequencies) of the average adult male vocal tract for a neutral vowel, namely 500, 1500, and 2500 c.p.s. For adult females the ranges should be raised by about 15 per cent. For children the ranges should be multiplied by the inverse of the approximate ratio of the child's vocal tract length (from Adam's apple to lips) to that of the adult. For example, the adult male vocal tract is about 7 inches in length; for a child whose tract is half this length, the frequency ranges should be doubled.

Periodic, Buzz-like Sounds. The distinction periodic-vs-aperiodic is basic in speech because it corresponds to two distinctly different articulatory conditions for the origin of sound. Periodic sounds stem from periodic modulation of the breath stream by the action of the vocal cords. On the other hand, aperiodic sounds stem from random turbulence caused by a rush of air through a constriction of the vocal tract. The formant or resonance patterns of the sounds convey information as to the identity of both vowels and consonants.

Row 1. Within a frequency column the vowels are ordered from low (left) to high (right) frequencies, according to the second formant positions for the front vowels, / æ / through /i/, and according to the mean positions of the first two formants for the back vowels, /u/ through /ɑ/.

Row 2. The periodic sound features correlated with consonants are the transitions in the formant frequencies of the adjacent vowels, especially the transitions of the frequency of the second formant. The particular transition for a given consonant varies somewhat depending on the vowel but these

variations are largely encompassed by the broad frequency
categories of the table. It will be noted that the consonant transitions group according to place of constriction;
the low transitions occurring for front constrictions such
as for b, medium-frequency transitions for the middle constrictions, and the high-frequency transitions for back constrictions.

Row 3. The nasal consonants are characterized by strong low-frequency periodic sound (murmur) during the consonant clo-
sure. This feature helps differentiate the nasals as a
class from other voiced continuant consonants. Discrimination among nasal consonants is conveyed by the second
formant transitions of Row 2.

Aperiodic, Noise-like Sounds. The noise-like phases of
speech are produced by turbulence in the breath stream as it rushes through a constriction in the vocal tract. These constrictions
are the apical phases of articulation of the stop consonants and the
fricative consonants. When these consonants are unvoiced, their
noise phases are fairly intense. On the other hand when these consonants are accompanied by vocal cord action--i. e., when they are
voiced--the air flow rate is drastically reduced and thus the intensity of the turbulence is also reduced or even absent. The duration of the noise phase is longer for fricatives than for stops because the turbulence conditions are maintained over the interval corresponding to the occlusion interval of a stop consonant. Typical
fricative durations range 100 to 250 milliseconds. The stop bursts
occur during the short interval at the release of the occlusion while
the breath pressure built up during the occlusion rushes through the
narrow constriction in the early phase of the opening movement. A
typical duration for this burst is 50 milliseconds.

Rows 4 & 5. The stop and fricative consonant constrictions produce
sounds that have important frequency and durational differences. The frequency range and spectrum shapes of these
sounds are dependent on the place of the constriction and
the size of the oral cavity in front of the constriction.
Typical frequency range extents are shown for each sound
by lines across the columns.

Timing Features. The distinctive timing features of speech
can be considered in two classes: those of more or less arbitrary
linguistic origin, such as vowel duration characteristics of a language, and those which depend almost entirely on articulatory movement conditions and aerodynamic constraints.

Row 6. Vowel duration is long or short. Each of the different
vowels of a given language tends to have a typical mean
duration under controlled utterance conditions; style, rate,
and regional accent can introduce large deviations from the
average but this may be compensated by the listener so that
rough durational categories are useful to him for discriminating vowels.

Rows 7 & 8.   In fluent speech most consonants occur between vowels and thus the strong low-frequency vowel energy may
be considered as repeatedly interrupted or suppressed by
consonant constrictions.   A consonant-produced "gap" in
the vowel stream is long when the consonant is unvoiced
and short when it is a voiced consonant.   The unvoiced
stop consonants have brief release noises at middle and
high frequencies, as compared with the long noises of the
fricatives.

Row 9.   The glide and liquid consonants are articulated with a longer movement to and from the position for maximum consonant constriction and thus their associated vowel formant
transitions are more extensive and require more time than
for the other consonants.   The frequency regions of the
glide transitions are the same as the other corresponding
consonants produced at the labial and alveolar places of
articulation.

SIGNIFICANCE OF VARIOUS PORTIONS OF THE WAVELENGTH IN
THE MINIMUM DURATION NECESSARY FOR RECOGNITION OF VOW-
EL SOUNDS

Gordon E. Peterson

Experimental investigations concerning the shortest identifiable
speech sounds have only recently been undertaken.   The scientific implications of the problem of identifying short speech sounds are more
numerous than the purely practical ones.   At present the following problems appear to be the most significant.

1.   The Nature of the Function.   One of the first questions
which presents itself is that of the nature of the ability to recognize
short speech sounds.   Any test of this ability would first assume
that the individual had been well trained in the recognition of speech
sounds of normal duration and also in their indication, preferably in
phonetic script.   There remains, however, the question of the other
factors important in this ability to recognize short sounds: whether
it is chiefly physiological, or psychological; whether it is a native
ability, incapable of improvement, or whether training would promote better performance.

2.   Relationship to Phonetics and Vowel Theory.   Another
question is whether there is any correlation between ability to recognize short sounds and ability in general phonetics.   If such correlation should be found to exist, testing for aptitude in recognizing
short sounds might offer considerable information concerning basic
phonetic abilities.

Previous Investigations

A question of some standing is that of determining the duration of a tone necessary for the perception of its pitch. A survey
of attempts to estimate the minimum interval necessary for this perception has been presented by two Italian psychologists, A. Gemelli
and G. Pastori [L'Analise Elettro-Acustica del Linguaggio, Milan,
Italy: Vita e Pensiero, 1934]. According to these authors, Stefanini and Gradenigo concluded that only two complete vibrations are
necessary for the sensation of tonality; and Stefanini suggests that
one vibration may be adequate [Ibid.]. According to Abraham and
Bruehl, the minimum duration necessary for the perception of pitch
varies considerably with the pitch studied [Ibid.]. S. S. Stevens
and H. Davis, in their recent and commendable work Hearing [New
York: Wiley, 1938], report an investigation of this problem by
Bürck, Kotowski, and Lichte, and conclude, "The absolute time necessary for the identification of the pitch of a tone is smallest in
the middle range of frequencies, where it is approximately .01 seconds."

The first truly experimental approach to the problem was
made by Gray at Louisiana State University. In this study, several
series of short vowel sounds of varying periods of duration were
presented to a group of subjects for identification. The subjects
were asked to identify the sounds, and the duration of the sounds
was reduced until recognition became exceedingly difficult. It was
then assumed that the minimum duration necessary for the recognition of the given vowel had been approximately located. The question arises as to whether sudden sounds of such short duration will
give the same psychological impression as will sounds of normal
duration. Obviously the impression will not be exactly the same;
but so long as the sound is identifiable with the original from which
it came, it would appear that true recognition has occurred.

The Present Problem

With recognitions occurring on as little as .24 of one cycle,
the question arises as to whether one segment from a given cycle
is recognized with greater ease than is another. Gray reports that
when the interval of .01 was accidentally repeated in his study,
"somewhat different data were secured for the two identical intervals." This is a question which would have to be answered before
any successful attempt could be made to standardize tests for the
minimum duration necessary for the recognition of speech sounds.
It should further be pointed out that the investigation of nearly all
problems relating to the recognition of short sounds, as for example
the two problems proposed at the beginning of this paper, would require the standardization of such a test. The present investigation,
then, has the purpose of discovering whether facility in recognizing
short sounds does depend upon the particular portion of the wavelength presented. The proposed technique is similar to that developed by Gray: the duration of the sound is to be controlled by

switches placed in the speaker circuit of a public address system.

The identification of short segments as belonging to a given vowel will depend upon how much the segment, as heard, resembles that particular vowel. This probably depends chiefly upon the degree to which the acoustic spectrum of the short segment resembles the acoustic spectrum of the complete cycle of the vowel from which it came. It is probably true that considerable variation occurs in the harmonic content of segments taken from different portions of a particular cycle. It is quite conceivable that variations perhaps as great, occur in the harmonic content of two segments taken from approximately the same section of a given cycle, even though these segments have a large portion of their wave form in common. It is proposed in the present study to discover whether significant differences in the recognition of various segments do occur and to investigate the nature of these differences. There are two major requirements for such an investigation. First, a technique is necessary for obtaining short segments of equal duration from a given cycle and of presenting these segments to a group for the test of recognition. Second, a technique is necessary for recording each segment, and identifying the particular portion of the cycle from which each segment came.

Procedure

The subjects in the present investigation were, for the most part, students enrolled in a class in general phonetics taught at the university. Two faculty members and a few persons who had previously taken the course, having since done further work in phonetics, also served as subjects during the first session. The experiment was explained to the group and a preliminary training period was given at the regular class hour. A few sounds were photographed at this time as a final check against possible flaws in the procedure. A brief practice period, during which longer sounds were presented, was given. At this time, a master photograph of well over one wavelength was made of each vowel; the short curves taken thereafter were compared with these longer wave forms. The period was then progressively shortened until the interval desired for the present study was reached. At this short interval, several series of vowels were presented for recognition and simultaneously photographed.

Eight vowels were used, those tending toward diphthongization being avoided. The vowels were presented in series of nine, with one vowel repeated. One of the duplicate vowels used in each series was arbitrarily chosen as a "joker" and was not photographed. This was to reduce the possibility of guessing the correct symbols. The only explanation made to the subjects concerning the vowels was that they all occurred on the conventional diagram, and that / ə / was not used. This left a minimum of 15 sounds from which to choose. On this basis, if it is assumed that the subjects were entirely ignorant of the arrangement of the vowels in the series, then

1/15 is the probability of their having guessed any one symbol right, and 1/225 is the probability of their having guessed any two symbols correctly.

A second set of data was taken in an attempt to get more information on one or two particular vowels. This time, instead of producing the vowels over the microphone, phonograph recordings were employed. The voice used in making the record was the one used over the microphone. The vowels were viewed on the screen of the cathode-ray oscillograph, and the recording was made at a period during which the vowel showed a particularly steady wave form. The vowels were given in series of five and with no duplications /æ/ and /ɔ/ were photographed for later analysis, and the other three vowels were presented merely as "jokers." A total of 17 vowels was used, and 15 subjects served in the experiment.

Data

Some of the short segments agreed rather well with the master; but others did not. It should be remembered, however, that so far as was possible, the actual quality produced at the microphone was held constant. Wide variations in recognition appeared throughout the cycles. Certainly the difference between 0 recognitions and 17 recognitions in 19 indicates that one segment taken from the /æ/ cycle is more easily recognized than certain others. The percentage of recognitions of the vowel /ɑ/ was especially high. Here, again, the wave forms of many of the segments are not easily located in the master cycle. Throughout this study, however, it is assumed that the master wave form resembles fairly well the wave form from which any short segment was taken. To avoid inaccuracy, the position of each segment was determined by two individuals; each of the short segments was located in the only portion of the wavelength from which it could have come. Segments occurring at the extremities of the arbitrarily chosen wavelength are more easily recognized than the segment which appears near the center of the cycle. The recognition score of 17 for the vowels /ɑ/3 and /ɑ/4 near the beginning of the wavelength is especially significant.

Nearly all portions of the master wavelength are represented by the short segments of the vowel /ɔ/. Those segments near the arbitrarily chosen beginning of the wavelength were especially difficult to recognize; while other portions were recognized with considerable facility. For the most part, the segments shown for /u/ did not closely parallel the master wave form. The significant feature in this set was the fact that the segment at the end of the wavelength was recognized only four times, while the recognitions for the curves at the beginning of the wave form were consistently higher. It is obviously beyond the scope of this study to determine whether segments coming from one section of the cycle are generally recognized more easily than others. Such a study would demand a large quantity of data for each specific vowel.

The identification of a short segment as belonging to a given vowel obviously will depend upon how much the segment sounds like the given vowel. This probably depends chiefly upon the degree to which the acoustic spectrum of the given short segment resembles that of the complete cycle of the vowel. Considerable variation may occur in the harmonic content of two segments taken from approximately the same section of a given cycle, even though they have a large portion of their wave form in common. It is thus significant to consider the relationship between the distances separating various segments and the differences in the recognition of those segments.

This problem may be attacked by determining whether the distance separating each pair of segments is highly correlated with the difference in the recognitions of those segments. Correlations showed that the difference in the number of recognitions of any two segments has little relation to the distance separating those segments. Thus two segments may be very close together and one recognized with ease, the other with difficulty. On the other hand, two segments may lie at some distance from each other and yet be recognized with the same degree of facility.

Conclusions

From the data, four specific conclusions may be drawn.

1. This study verifies Gray's findings that significant recognitions may occur on only a small fraction of one complete vowel cycle.

2. For vowel sounds, definite differences occur in the facility with which various sections of a given wavelength are recognized. the fact that such variations exist will now have to be taken into consideration in any attempt to standardize tests of the minimum duration of vowel sounds necessary for recognition. It should further be pointed out that vowel sounds, as normally intoned by different individuals, vary in pitch and quality, and thus in wave form, so as to preclude any comprehensive statements concerning the segments generally most easily recognized.

3. Correlations show that the difference in the number of recognitions of say two segments will have little relation to the distance separating those segments.

4. As a result of the wide variations in the recognitions of the different segments presented, it follows that variation not only occurs in the facility with which various short sounds are recognized, but that it also occurs in the ability of different individuals to recognize short speech sounds.

SPEECH SEGMENTATION PROCEDURES

Barbara R. Zimmerman

Reference pulse. The CV syllables were recorded at 15
i. p. s. on magnetic recording tape (Scotch Type 311) on channel one
of the two channel tape recorder. A pulse was recorded immediately before the initiation of each of the 24 syllables on channel two.
The pulse served two purposes. (1) It was used to trigger an oscilloscope (Tektronix 502-A), permitting the photographing of the oscil-
loscopic displays of randomly selected segmented syllables. These
photographs were then examined by three staff members of the Ohio
University Department of Speech Pathology, Audiology, and Speech
Science to insure that no noise or distortion was introduced by the
segmentation. (2) The pulse served as a reference point in the
measurements necessary for segmenting the syllable. Because the
pulse was recorded preceding the original recorded syllables, each
time a syllable was re-recorded the distance between the pulse and
the initiation of the consonant remained constant. The original recorded syllables, each with an accompanying pulse, were then re-
recorded in a random manner to produce 30 sets of the 24 syllables.
This procedure allowed for an orderly arrangement of the stimuli necessary for the method of segmentation employed in the present
study.

Segmentation. The actual process of segmentation was accomplished in the following order. (1) Each of the 24 syllables and
their accompanying pulses were directly mixed and the combined
signal fed to a sound spectrograph (Kay Electric 6061-A). (2) Sona-
grams were made of each syllable and pulse. (3) It was determined
that 1mm measured on the Sonagram was equal to 7.6 milliseconds.
(4) The onset of the voicing bar was used as a reference point and
labeled "0" msec. point. (5) The time measurement to be removed
from the syllable was converted to millimeters and this distance recorded on the Sonagram. (6) The distance between the point of segmentation marked on the Sonagram in step 5 and the pulse could
then be established. (7) This distance was then converted to correspond to the same distance on the tape. (8) The pulse was located
on the tape and the portion to be removed was carefully marked.
(9) The final step was the removal of the iron oxide from the unwanted portion of the tape by dissolving it with an acetone base sol-
vent. To check the accuracy of the segmentation, the syllable was
again fed to the spectrograph and a new Sonagram made. In no case
was the inaccuracy greater than $\pm$ 2 msec. It is possible to be even
more precise by changing certain factors such as the tape speed during recording. However, greater accuracy was not deemed necessary for this study.

Experimental conditions. The procedure described was employed to establish 30 conditions of segmentation. To avoid confusion
concerning the amount of syllable removed in any specific condition,
arbitrary signs were attached to the measurements. Any measure-

Table 1

DESCRIPTION OF EXPERIMENTAL CONDITIONS

Condition	Segmented Boundaries	Division
1 (+ 100 msec)	Onset of C to + 100 msec	Control & rise time
2 (+ 50 msec)	Onset of C to + 50 msec	rise time
3 (+ 25 msec)	Onset of C to + 25 msec	rise time
4 (+ 0 msec)	Onset of C to 0 msec	rise time
5 (+ 25 msec)	Onset of C to - 25 msec	rise time
6 (- 50 msec)	Onset of C to - 50 msec	rise time
7 (- 75 msec)	Onset of C to - 75 msec	rise time
8 (- 100 msec)	Onset of C to - 100 msec	rise time
9 (- 125 msec)	Onset of C to - 125 msec	rise time
10 (- 150 msec)	Onset of C to - 150 msec	rise time
11 (- 175 msec)	Onset of C to - 175 msec	rise time
12 (- 200 msec)	Onset of C to - 200 msec	rise time
13 (- 200 msec)	+ 100 msec to - 200 msec	transitions
14 (- 175 msec)	+ 100 msec to - 175 msec	transitions
15 (- 150 msec)	+ 100 msec to - 150 msec	transitions
16 (- 125 msec)	+ 100 msec to - 125 msec	transitions
17 (- 100 msec)	+ 100 msec to - 100 msec	transitions
18 (- 75 msec)	+ 100 msec to - 75 msec	transitions
19 (- 50 msec)	+ 100 msec to - 50 msec	transitions
20 (- 25 msec)	+ 100 msec to - 25 msec	transitions
21 (0 msec)	+ 100 msec to 0 msec	transitions
22 (+ 25 msec)	+ 100 msec to + 25 msec	transitions
23 (+ 50 msec)	+ 100 msec to + 50 msec	transitions
24 (- 200 msec)	- 25 msec to - 200 msec	noise burst
25 (- 175 msec)	- 25 msec to - 175 msec	noise burst
26 (- 150 msec)	- 25 msec to - 150 msec	noise burst
27 (- 125 msec)	- 25 msec to - 125 msec	noise burst
28 (- 100 msec)	- 25 msec to - 100 msec	noise burst
29 (- 75 msec)	- 25 msec to - 75 msec	noise burst
30 (- 50 msec)	- 25 msec to - 50 msec	noise burst

(+ msec) indicates vocalic portion of syllable
(- msec) indicates fricative portion of syllable
(0 msec) indicates beginning of voicing bar
Arrow indicates the direction of segmentation

ment made to the left of 0 msec. point and affecting the consonant was labled "- msec." Any measurement made to the right of the 0 msec. point and affecting the vocalic portion of the syllable was labeled "+ msec." The conditions divided into three groups depending on the direction of segmentation. Table 1 offers a description of the conditions and shows the divisions.

Condition 1 served as a control condition to the extent that only the vowel was segmented to limit the duration of all the vocalic portions of the syllables to 100 msec. This condition also represented the first segmentation in the first group. The first division, 1-12, consisted of those conditions designed to investigate the importance of rise time in the perception of voiceless fricatives. Segmentation moved from the vocalic portion of the syllable toward the onset of the fricative in 25 msec. steps. All conditions in this category were designated by an arrow (⟶) under the number of milliseconds represented by the condition, i.e., Condition 5 (- 25). The second division contained those conditions designed to investigate the influence of vowel transitions. In conditions 13-23 the syllable was segmented in 25-msec. steps beginning at the initiation of the fricative and moving toward the vocalic portion. All millisecond points in this category are marked by the arrow (⟶).

The final division was designed to investigate the importance of the noise burst in the perception of the voiceless fricatives when the vowel transitions are removed and rise time is gradually diminished. To eliminate the vowel transitions, all the vocalic portions of the syllable and -25 msec. of the adjacent fricative were removed. The -25-msec. point was chosen as the constant point because spectrographic examinations did not reveal any transitions extending as far as this point; all fricatives had reached maximum amplitude before this point. After all syllables serving as stimuli in this division were prepared in the above manner, the process of segmentation began at the -200-msec. point (the initiation of the consonant) and moved in 25-msec. steps toward the -25-msec. point. This procedure allowed for the gradual diminishing of rise time leaving only the cue of the noise burst. All millisecond points in the final group were designated by the symbol (⟶ι).

DESCRIPTION OF A TAPE VIEWER

Ruth S. Day

For determining word-onset, practice with the 3-M Magnetic Tape Viewer was undertaken. This tape viewer is about the size and shape of a heavy pocket watch. Its face is glass, through which can be seen tiny particles, much like iron filings in solution. The bottom of the device is metal. As the viewer is passed over the recorded tape, a gentle tapping motion is applied. When the viewer is in contact with a magnetized segment (i.e., speech) the particles line up in a vertical pattern. These patterns differ with respect to the width of vertical lines, the distance between the lines, the clarity of line boundaries, and so on. The stops were quite easy to identify: there was a magnetized portion of about one-eighth inch, followed by an unmagnetized portion before the main body of the word itself. "Onset" was labeled at the beginning of the short portion.

Liquids were more difficult to identify: by moving the viewer back
and forth over the general onset region, it was impossible to tell
exactly where the word began. The fricatives presented even more
difficult problems.

When determining the onsets for items the following procedure was employed. The tape was mounted on a board perpendicu-
lar to a table; on the table, the distance of 15 inches was marked
off. Since the record speed for these "original" tapes was 15 i. p. s. ,
and since the inter-item interval was about 3. 5 seconds, three
lengths of 15 inches each (= 3 seconds) were transferred to the take-
up reel without examination by the viewer. Then the viewer was
placed on the tape, and passed along it, using a slight tapping motion. When the randomly arranged particles lined up in a vertical
pattern, onset was determined by a procedure akin to an ascending
and descending method of limits. First the viewer was passed carefully from the non-magnetized region to the point where the particles
began to line up. This point was noted. Then the procedure was
repeated, this time beginning from within the body of the word, and
moving outward until the pattern reverted to a random arrangement.
This point was also noted. These procedures were repeated several
times until the two points seemed fairly well determined and close
together, if at all possible. Then the mid-point of this interval was
marked on the back (non-magnetic portion) of the tape with an indeli-
ble marking pen. Two lengths of 15 inches each were then measured out, prior to word onset, and a mark made at that point. This
mark was two seconds before word onset. The ordinal number of
the item in the list was written next to this two-second mark. Future work should use more accurate methods. Computer techniques
for synchronizing dichotic inputs are now available at the Haskins
Laboratories and at Lincoln Laboratories.

Chapter 14

THE PROCESSING OF INFORMATION

Probably no other item in this anthology is so well known to so many people as the article by George A. Miller which, for all practical purposes is reproduced in full in this chapter. Thus far we have been more concerned with the message itself rather than with its receiver. We now shift our attention to the individual who is seeking to secure information from a message of one kind or another. Obviously, any kind of interference either in time or frequency, as we have seen from Kurtzrock's study, makes obtaining information more difficult. What Miller tells us in this article is therefore of great importance to the student of rate alteration of speech. The author is past president of the American Psychological Association and after years at Harvard University is now head of the Psychology Department at Rockefeller University in New York. He is widely known and admired for his penetrating analyses of communication problems in his extensive writing and speaking.

THE MAGICAL NUMBER SEVEN, PLUS OR MINUS TWO:
Some Limits on our Capacity for Processing Information

George A. Miller

My problem is that I have been persecuted by an integer. For seven years this number has followed me around, has intruded in my most private data, and has assaulted me from the pages of our most public journals. This number assumes a variety of disguises, being sometimes a little larger and sometimes a little smaller than usual, but never changing so much as to be unrecognizable. The persistence with which this number plagues me is far more than a random accident. There is, to quote a famous senator, a design behind it, some pattern governing its appearances. Either there really is something unusual about the number or else I am suffering from delusions of persecution.

I shall begin my case history by telling you about some experiments that tested how accurately people can assign numbers to the magnitudes of various aspects of a stimulus. In the traditional language of psychology these would be called experiments in absolute judgment. Historical accident, however, has decreed that they should have another name. We now call them experiments on the capacity

406

of people to transmit information. Since these experiments would
not have been done without the appearance of information theory on
the psychological scene, and since the results are analyzed in terms
of the concepts of information theory, I shall have to preface my
discussion with a few remarks about this theory.

Information Measurement

The "amount of information" is exactly the same concept that
we have talked about for years under the name of "variance." The
equations are different, but if we hold tight to the idea that anything
that increases the variance also increases the amount of information
we cannot go far astray. The advantages of this new way of talking
about variance are simple enough. Variance is always stated in
terms of the unit of measurement--inches, pounds, volts, etc. --
whereas the amount of information is a dimensionless quantity.
Since the information in a discrete statistical distribution does not
depend upon the unit of measurement, we can extend the concept to
situations where we have no metric and we would not ordinarily
think of using the variance. And it also enables us to compare results obtained in quite different experimental situations where it
would be meaningless to compare variances based on different met-
rics. So there are some good reasons for adopting the newer concept.

The similarity of variance and amount of information might
be explained this way: When we have a large variance, we are very
ignorant about what is going to happen. If we are very ignorant,
then when we make the observation it gives us a lot of information.
On the other hand, if the variance is very small, we know in advance how our observation must come out, so we get little information from making the observation.

If you will now imagine a communication system, you will
realize that there is a great deal of variability about what goes into
the system and also a great deal of variability about what comes out.
The input and the output can therefore be described in terms of their
variance (or their information). If it is a good communication system, however, there must be some systematic relation between what
goes in and what comes out. That is to say, the output will depend
upon the input, or will be correlated with the input. If we measure
this correlation, then we can say how much of the output variance
is attributable to the input and how much is due to random fluctuations or "noise" introduced by the system during transmission. So
we see that the measure of transmitted information is simply a measure of the input-output correlation.

There are two simple rules to follow. Whenever I refer to
"amount of information," you will understand "variance." And whenever I refer to "amount of transmitted information," you will understand "covariance" or "correlation." The situation can be described
graphically by two partially overlapping circles. Then the left circle

can be taken to represent the variance of the input, the right circle the variance of the output, and the overlap the covariance of input and output. I shall speak of the left circle as the amount of input information, the right circle as the amount of output information, and the overlap as the amount of transmitted information.

In the experiments on absolute judgment, the observer is considered to be a communication channel. Then the left circle would represent the amount of information in the stimuli, the right circle the amount of information in his responses, and the overlap the stimulus-response correlation as measured by the amount of transmitted information. The experimental problem is to increase the amount of input information and to measure the amount of transmitted information. If the observer's absolute judgments are quite accurate, then nearly all of the input information will be transmitted and will be recoverable from his responses. If he makes errors, then the transmitted information may be considerably less than the input. We expect that, as we increase the amount of input information, the observer will begin to make more and more errors; we can test the limits of accuracy of his absolute judgments. If the human observer is a reasonable kind of communication system, then when we increase the amount of input information the transmitted information will increase at first and will eventually level off at some asymptotic value. This asymptotic value we take to be the channel capacity of the observer: it represents the greatest amount of information that he can give us about the stimulus on the basis of an absolute judgment. The channel capacity is the upper limit on the extent to which the observer can match his responses to the stimuli we give him.

Now just a brief word about the bit and we can begin to look at some data. One bit of information is the amount of information that we need to make a decision between two equally likely alternatives. If we must decide whether a man is less than six feet tall or more than six feet tall and if we know that the chances are 50-50, then we need one bit of information. Notice that this unit of information does not refer in any way to the unit of length that we use --feet, inches, centimeters, etc. However you measure the man's height, we still need just one bit of information. Two bits of information enable us to decide among four equally likely alternatives. Three bits of information enable us to decide among eight equally likely alternatives. Four bits of information decide among 16 alternatives, five among 32, and so on. That is to say, if there are 32 equally likely alternatives, we must make five successive binary decisions, worth one bit each, before we know which alternative is correct. So the general rule is simple: every time the number of alternatives is increased by a factor of two, one bit of information is added.

There are two ways we might increase the amount of input information. We could increase the rate at which we give information to the observer, so that the amount of information per unit time would increase. Or we could ignore the time variable completely and increase the amount of input information by increasing the number of alternative stimuli. In the absolute judgment experiment we are interested in the second alternative. We give the observer as much time as he wants to make his response; we simply increase the number of alternative stimuli among which he must discriminate and look to see where confusions begin to occur. Confusions will appear near the point that we are calling his "channel capacity."

Absolute Judgments of Unidimensional Stimuli

Now let us consider what happens when we make absolute judgments of tones. I. Pollack ["The Information of Elementary Auditory Displays [I]," J. of Acoustical Soc. of Amer. 24:745-49, 1952; "----II," Ibid. 25:765-69, 1953] asked listeners to identify tones by assigning numerals to them. The tones were different with respect to frequency, and covered the range from 100 to 8000 c.p.s. in equal logarithmic steps. A tone was sounded and the listener responded by giving a numeral. After the listener had made his response he was told the correct identification of the tone. When only two or three tones were used the listeners never confused them. With four different tones confusions were quite rare, but with five or more tones confusions were frequent. With fourteen different tones the listeners made many mistakes.

These data are plotted in Figure 1. Along the bottom is the amount of input information in bits per stimulus. As the number of alternative tones was increased from two to 14, the input information increased from 1 to 3.8 bits. On the ordinate is plotted the amount of transmitted information. The amount of transmitted information behaves in much the way we would expect a communication channel to behave; the transmitted information increases linearly up to about 2 bits and then bends off toward an asymptote at about 2.5 bits. This value, 2.5 bits, therefore, is what we are calling the channel capacity of the listener for absolute judgments of pitch.

So now we have the number 2.5 bits. What does it mean? First, note that 2.5 bits corresponds to about six equally likely alternatives. The result means that we cannot pick more than six different pitches that the listener will never confuse. Or, stated slightly differently, no matter how many alternative tones we ask him to judge, the best we can expect him to do is to assign them to about six different classes without error. Or, again, if we know that there were N alternative stimuli, then his judgment enables us to narrow down the particular stimulus to one out of N/6.

Most people are surprised that the number is as small as six. Of course, there is evidence that a musically sophisticated person with absolute pitch can identify accurately any one of 50 or 60 different pitches. Fortunately, I do not have time to discuss these remarkable exceptions. I say it is fortunate because I do not know how to explain their superior performance. So I shall stick to the more pedestrian fact that most of us can identify about one out

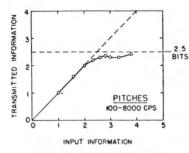

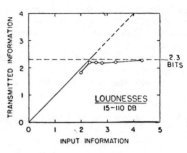

Figure 1. Data from Pollack [see text] on the amount of information that is transmitted by listeners who make absolute judgments of auditory pitch. As the amount of input information rises by increasing from two to 14 the number of different pitches to be judged, the amount of transmitted information approaches as its upper limit a channel capacity of about 2.5 bits per judgment.

Figure 2. Data from Garner [see text] on the channel capacity for absolute judgments of auditory loudness.

of only five or six pitches before we begin to get confused. It is interesting to consider that psychologists have been using seven-point rating scales for a long time, on the intuitive basis that trying to rate into finer categories does not really add much to the usefulness of the ratings. Pollack's results indicate that, at least for pitches, this intuition is fairly sound.

Next you can ask how reproducible this result is. Does it depend on the spacing of the tones or the various conditions of judgment? Pollack varied these conditions in a number of ways. The range of frequencies can be changed by a factor of about 20 without changing the amount of information transmitted more than a small percentage. Different groupings of the pitches decreased the transmission, but the loss was small. For example, if you can discriminate five high-pitched tones in one series and five low-pitched tones in another series, it is reasonable to expect that you could combine all ten into a single series and still tell them all apart without error. When you try it, however, it does not work. The channel capacity for pitch seems to be about six and that is the best you can do.

While we are on tones, let us look next at W. R. Garner's work on loudness ["An Informational Analysis of Absolute Judgments of Loudness," J. of Exper. Psychol. 46:373-80, 1953]. Garner's data for loudness are summarized in Figure 2. Garner went to some trouble to get the best possible spacing of his tones over the

intensity range from 15 to 110 db.   He used 4, 5, 6, 7, 10, and
20 different stimulus intensities.   The results shown in Figure 2
take into account the differences among subjects and the sequential
influence of the immediately preceding judgment.   Again we find that
there seems to be a limit: the channel capacity for absolute judgments of loudness is 2.3 bits, or about five perfectly discriminable
alternatives.   Since these two studies were done in different laboratories with slightly different techniques and methods of analysis, we
are not in a good position to argue whether five loudnesses is significantly different from six pitches.   Probably the difference is in
the right direction, and absolute judgments of pitch are slightly
more accurate than absolute judgments of loudness.   The important
point, however, is that the two answers are of the same order of
magnitude.

The experiment has also been done for taste intensities.   In
Figure 3 are the results obtained by J. G. Beebe-Center, M. S.
Rogers, and D. N. O'Connell ["Transmission of Information about
Sucrose and Saline Solutions Through the Sense of Taste," Amer. J.
of Psychol. 39:157-60, 1955] for absolute judgments of the concen-
tration of salt solutions.   The concentrations ranged from 0.3 to

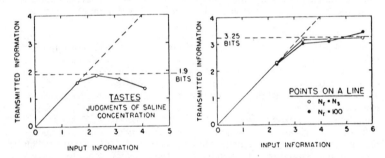

Figure 3.   Data from Beebe-
Center, Rogers, and O'Connell
[see text] on the channel capacity
for absolute judgments of saltiness.

Figure 4.   Data from Hake and
Garner [see text] on the channel
capacity for absolute judgments
of the position of a pointer in a
linear interval.

34.7 grams of NaCl per 100 cc. tap water in equal subjective steps.
They used 3, 5, 9, and 17 different concentrations.   The channel
capacity is 1.9 bits, which is about four distinct concentrations.
Thus taste intensities seem a little less distinctive than auditory
stimuli, but again the order of magnitude is not far off.

On the other hand, the channel capacity for judgments of visual position seems to be significantly larger.   H. W. Hake and
W. R. Garner ["The Effects of Presenting Various Numbers of Discrete Steps on Scale Reading Accuracy," J. of Exper. Psychol. 42:

358-66, 1951] asked observers to interpolate visually between two
scale markers. Their results are shown in Figure 4. They did
the experiment in two ways. In one version they let the observer
use any number between zero and 100 to describe the position, although they presented stimuli at only 5, 10, 20, or 50 different positions. The results with this unlimited response technique are
shown by the filled circles on the graph. In the other version the
observers were limited in their responses to reporting just those
stimulus values that were possible. That is to say, in the second
version the number of different responses that the observer could
make was exactly the same as the number of different stimuli that
the experimenter might present. The results with this limited response technique are shown by the open circles on the graph. The
two functions are so similar that it seems fair to conclude that the
number of responses available to the observer had nothing to do
with the channel capacity of 3.25 bits. The Hake-Garner experiment has been repeated by Coonan and Klemmer. Although they
have not yet published their results, they have given me permission
to say that they obtained channel capacities ranging from 3.2 bits
for very short exposures of the pointer position to 3.9 bits for longer exposures. These values are slightly higher than Hake and Garner's, so we must conclude that there are between 10 and 15 distinct positions along a linear interval. This is the largest channel
capacity that has been measured for any unidimensional variable.

At the present time these four experiments on absolute judgments of simple, unidimensional stimuli are all that have appeared
in the psychological journals. However, a great deal of work on
other stimulus variables has not yet appeared in the journals. For
example, C. W. Eriksen and H. W. Hake ["Absolute Judgments As
a Function of the Stimulus Range and the Number of Stimulus and
Response Categories," J. of Exper. Psychol. 49:323-32, 1955] have
found that the channel capacity for judging the sizes of squares is
2.2 bits, or about five categories, under a wide range of experimental conditions. In a separate experiment C. W. Eriksen ["Multidimensional Stimulus Differences and Accuracy of Discrimination,"
USAF, WADC Tech. Report No. 54-165, 1954] found 2.8 bits for
size, 3.1 bits for hue, and, 2.3 bits for brightness. Geldard has
measured the channel capacity for the skin by placing vibrators on
the chest region. A good observer can identify about four intensities, about five durations, and about seven locations.

One of the most active groups in this area has been the Air
Force Operational Applications Laboratory. Pollack has been kind
enough to furnish me with the results of their measurements for
several aspects of visual displays. They made measurements for
area and for the curvature, length, and direction of lines. In one
set of experiments they used a very short exposure of the stimulus
--1/40 second--and then they repeated the measurements with a five-
second exposure. For area they got 2.6 bits with the short exposure
and 2.7 bits with the long exposure. For the length of a line they
got about 2.6 bits with the short exposure and about 3.0 bits with the
long exposure. Direction, or angle of inclination, gave 2.8 bits for

the short exposure and 3.3 bits for the long exposure.   Curvature
was apparently harder to judge.   When the length of the arc was
constant, the result at the short exposure duration was 2.2 bits, but
when the length of the chord was constant, the result was only 1.6
bits.   This last value is the lowest that anyone has measured to
date.   I should add, however, that these values are apt to be slightly too low because the data from all subjects were pooled before the
transmitted information was computed.

Now let us see where we are.   First, the channel capacity
does seem to be a valid notion for describing human observers.
Second, the channel capacities measured for these unidimentional
variables range from 1.6 bits for curvature to 3.9 bits for positions
in an interval.   Although there is no question that the differences
among the variables are real and meaningful, the more impressive
fact to me is their considerable similarity.   If I take the best estimates I can get of the channel capacities for all the stimulus variables I have mentioned, the mean is 2.6 bits and the standard deviation is only 0.6 bit.   In terms of distinguishable alternatives, this
mean corresponds to about 6.5 categories, one standard deviation
includes from 4 to 10 categories, and the total range is from 3 to
15 categories.   Considering the wide variety of different variables
that have been studied, I find this to be a remarkably narrow range.
There seems to be some limitation built into us either by learning
or by the design of our nervous systems, a limit that keeps our
channel capacities in this general range.   On the basis of the present evidence it seems safe to say that we possess a finite and rather small capacity for making such unidimensional judgments and that
this capacity does not vary a great deal from one simple sensory attribute to another.

Absolute Judgments of Multi-Dimensional Stimuli

You may have noticed that I have been careful to say that this
magical number seven applies to one-dimensional judgments.   Everyday experience teaches us that we can identify accurately any one of
several hundred faces, any one of several thousand words, any one
of several thousand objects, etc.   The story certainly would not be
complete if we stopped at this point.   We must have some understanding of why the one-dimensional variables we judge in the laboratory give results so far out of line with what we do constantly in our
behavior outside the laboratory.   A possible explanation lies in the
number of independently variable attributes of the stimuli that are
being judged.   Objects, faces, words, and the like differ from one
another in many ways, whereas the simple stimuli we have considered thus far differ from one another in only one respect.

Fortunately, there are a few data on what happens when we
make absolute judgments of stimuli that differ from one another in
several ways.   Let us look first at the results E. T. Klemmer and
F. C. Frick have reported ["Assimilation of Information from Dot
and Matrix Patterns," J. of Exper. Psychol. 45:15-19, 1953] for the

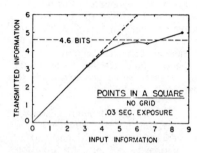

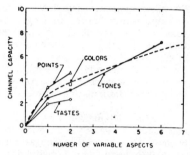

Figure 5. Data from Klemmer and Frick [see text] on the channel capacity for absolute judgments on the position of a dot in a square.

Figure 6. The general form of the relation between channel capacity and the number of independently variable attributes of the stimuli.

absolute judgment of the position of a dot in a square. In Figure 5 we see their results. Now the channel capacity seems to have increased to 4.6 bits, which means that people can identify accurately any one of 24 positions in the square. The position of a dot in a square is clearly a two-dimensional proposition. Both its horizontal and its vertical position must be identified. Thus it seems natural to compare the 4.6-bit capacity for a square with the 3.25-bit capacity for the position of a point in an interval. The point in the square requires two judgments of the interval type. If we have a capacity of 3.25 bits for estimating intervals and we do this twice, we should get 6.5 bits as our capacity for locating points in a square. Adding the second independent dimension gives us an increase from 3.25 to 4.6, but it falls short of the perfect addition that would give 6.5 bits.

Another example is provided by Beebe-Center, Rogers, and O'Connell [see page 411]. When they asked people to identify both the saltiness and the sweetness of solutions containing various concentrations of salt and sucrose, they found that the channel capacity was 2.3 bits. Since the capacity for salt alone was 1.9, we might expect about 3.8 bits if the two aspects of the compound stimuli were judged independently. As with spatial locations, the second dimension adds a little to the capacity but not as much as it conceivably might. A third example is provided by Pollack [see page 409], who asked listeners to judge both the loudness and the pitch of pure tones. Since pitch gives 2.5 bits and loudness gives 2.3 bits, we might hope to get as much as 4.8 bits for pitch and loudness together. Pollack obtained 3.1 bits, which again indicates that the second dimension augments the channel capacity but not so much as it might.

A fourth example can be drawn from the work of R. M. Halsey and A. Chapanis ["Chromaticity-Confusion Contours in a Complex Viewing Situation," J. of Optical Soc. of Amer. 44:442-54, 1954] on

confusions among colors of equal luminance. Although they did not
analyze their results in informational terms, they estimate that there
are about 11 to 15 identifiable colors, or, in our terms, about 3.6
bits. Since these colors varied in both hue and saturation, it is
probably correct to regard this as a two-dimensional judgment.   If
we compare this with Eriksen's 3.1 bits for hue (which is a ques-
tionable comparison to draw), we again have something less than
perfect addition when a second dimension is added.

It is still a long way, however, from these two-dimensional
examples to the multidimensional stimuli provided by faces, words,
etc.   To fill this gap we have only one experiment, an auditory
study done by I. Pollack and L. Ficks ["Information of Elementary
Multidimensional Auditory Displays," J. of Acoustical Soc. of Amer.
26:155-58, 1954].   They managed to get six different acoustic variables that they could change: frequency, intensity, rate of interruption, one-time fraction, total duration, and spatial location.   Each
one of these six variables could assume any one of five different
values, so altogether there were 5^6, or 15,625 different tones that
they could present.   The listeners made a separate rating for each
one of these six dimensions.   Under these conditions the transmitted
information was 7.2 bits, which corresponds to about 150 different
categories that could be absolutely identified without error.   Now we
are beginning to get up into the range that ordinary experience would
lead us to expect.

Suppose that we plot these data, fragmentary as they are, and
make a guess about how the channel capacity changes with the dimensionality of the stimuli.   The result is given in Figure 6.   In a
moment of considerable daring I sketched the dotted line to indicate
roughly the trend that the data seemed to be taking.   Clearly, the
addition of independently variable attributes to the stimulus increases
the channel capacity, but at a decreasing rate.   It is interesting to
note that the channel capacity is increased even when the several
variables are not independent.   Eriksen [see page 412] reports that,
when size, brightness, and hue all vary together in perfect correlation, the transmitted information is 4.1 bits as compared with an
average of about 2.7 bits when these attributes are varied one at a
time.   By confounding three attributes, Eriksen increased the dimensionality of the input without increasing the amount of input information; the result was an increase in channel capacity of about the
amount that the dotted function in Figure 6 would lead us to expect.

The point seems to be that, as we add more variables to the
display, we increase the total capacity, but we decrease the accuracy
for any particular variable.   In other words, we can make relatively
crude judgments of several things simultaneously.   We might argue
that in the course of evolution those organisms were most successful
that were responsive to the widest range of stimulus energies in their
environment.   In order to survive in a constantly fluctuating world,
it was better to have a little information about a lot of things than to
have a lot of information about a small segment of the environment.
If a compromise was necessary, the one we seem to have made is

clearly the more adaptive.

Pollack and Ficks's results are very strongly suggestive of
an argument that linguists and phoneticians have been making for
some time [R. Jakobson, C. G. M. Fant and M. Halle, Prelimi-
naries to Speech Analysis (Tech. Report No. 13), Cambridge, Mass.:
M.I.T. Press, 1965]. According to the linguistic analysis of the
sounds of human speech, there are about eight or ten dimensions--
the linguists call them distinctive features--that distinguish one phoneme from another. These distinctive features are usually binary,
or at most ternary, in nature. For example, a binary distinction
is made between vowels and consonants, a binary decision is made
between oral and nasal consonants, a ternary decision is made
among front, middle, and back phonemes, etc. This approach gives
us quite a different picture of speech perception than we might otherwise obtain from our studies of the speech spectrum and of the ear's
ability to discriminate relative differences among pure tones. I am
personally much interested in this new approach [G. A. Miller and
P. E. Nicely, "An Analysis of Perceptual Confusions Among Some
English Consonants," J. of Acoustical Soc. of Amer. 27:338-52,
1955] and I regret that there is not time to discuss it here.

It was probably with this linguistic theory in mind that Pollack and Ficks conducted a test on a set of tonal stimuli that varied
in eight dimensions, but required only a binary decision on each dimension. With these tones they measured the transmitted information at 6.9 bits, or about 120 recognizable kinds of sounds. It is
an intriguing question, as yet unexplored, whether one can go on
adding dimensions indefinitely in this way. In human speech there
is clearly a limit to the number of dimensions that we use. In this
instance, however, it is not known whether the limit is imposed by
the nature of the perceptual machinery that must recognize the
sounds or by the nature of the speech machinery that must produce
them. Somebody will have to do the experiment to find out. There
is a limit, however, at about eight or nine distinctive features in
every language that has been studied, and so when we talk, we must
resort to still another trick for increasing our channel capacity.
Language uses sequences of phonemes, so we make several judgments successively when we listen to words and sentences. That is
to say, we use both simultaneous and successive discriminations in
order to expand the rather rigid limits imposed by the inaccuracy of
our absolute judgments of simple magnitudes.

These multidimensional judgments are strongly reminiscent of
the abstraction experiment of O. Külpe ["Versuche über Abstraktion,"
Berichte über der I Kongress für Experimentele Psychologie p. 56-
68, 1904]. As you may remember, Külpe showed that observers report more accurately on an attribute for which they are set than on
attributes for which they are not set. For example, D. W. Chapman ["Relative Effects of Determinate and Indeterminate Aufgaben,"
Amer. J. of Psychol. 44:163-74, 1932] used three different attributes
and compared the results obtained when the observers were instructed
before the tachistoscopic presentation with the results obtained when

they were not told until after the presentation which one of the three attributes was to be reported.   When the instruction was given in advance, the judgments were more accurate.   When the instruction was given afterwards, the subjects presumably had to judge all three attributes in order to report on any one of them and the accuracy was correspondingly lower.   This is in complete accord with the results we have just been considering, where the accuracy of judgment on each attribute decreased as more dimensions were added.   The point is probably obvious, but I shall make it anyhow, that the abstraction experiments did not demonstrate that people can judge only one attribute at a time.   They merely showed what seems quite reasonable, that people are less accurate if they must judge more than one attribute simultaneously.

Subitizing

I cannot leave this general area without mentioning, however briefly, the experiments conducted at Mount Holyoke College on the discrimination of number.   In experiments by E. L. Kaufman, M. W. Lord, T. W. Reese, and J. Volkmann ["The Discrimination of Visual Number," Amer. J. of Psychol. 62:495-525, 1949] random patterns of dots were flashed on a screen for 0. 2 second.   Anywhere from one to more than 200 dots could appear in the pattern.   The subject's task was to report how many dots there were.   The first point to note is that on patterns containing up to five or six dots the subjects simply did not make errors.   The performance on these small numbers of dots was so different from the performance with more dots that it was given a special name.   Below seven the subjects were said to subitize; above seven they were said to estimate. This is, as you will recognize, what we once optimistically called "the span of attention."

This discontinuity at seven is, of course, suggestive. Is this the same basic process that limits our unidimensional judgments to about seven categories?   The generalization is tempting, but not sound in my opinion.   The data on number estimates have not been analyzed in informational terms; but on the basis of the published data I would guess that the subjects transmitted something more than four bits of information about the number of dots.   Using the same arguments as before, we would conclude that there are about 20 or 30 distinguishable categories of numerousness.   This is considerably more information than we would expect to get from a unidimensional display.   It is, as a matter of fact, very much like a two-dimensional display.   Although the dimensionality of the random dot patterns is not entirely clear, these results are in the same range as Klemmer and Frick's for their two-dimensional display of dots in a square.   Perhaps the two dimensions of numerousness are area and density.   When the subject can subitize, area and density may not be the significant variables, but when the subject must estimate perhaps they are significant.   In any event, the comparison is not so simple as it might seem at first thought.

This is one of the ways in which the magical number seven has persecuted me. Here we have two closely related kinds of experiments, both of which point to the significance of the number seven as a limit on our capacities. And yet when we examine the matter more closely, there seems to be a reasonable suspicion that it is nothing more than a coincidence.

The Span of Immediate Memory

Let me summarize the situation in this way. There is a clear and definite limit to the accuracy with which we can identify absolutely the magnitude of a unidimensional stimulus variable. I would propose to call this limit the span of absolute judgment, and I maintain that for unidimensional judgments this span is usually somewhere in the neighborhood of seven. We are not completely at the mercy of this limited span, however, because we have a variety of techniques for getting around it and increasing the accuracy of our judgments. The three most important of these devices are (a) to make relative rather than absolute judgments; or, if that is not possible, (b) to increase the number of dimensions along which the stimuli can differ; or (c) to arrange the task in such a way that we make a sequence of several absolute judgments in a row.

The study of relative judgments is one of the oldest topics in experimental psychology, and I will not pause to review it now. The second device, increasing the dimensionality, we have just considered. It seems that by adding more dimensions and requiring crude, binary, yes-no judgments on each attribute we can extend the span of absolute judgment from seven to at least 150. Judging from our everyday behavior, the limit is probably in the thousands, if indeed there is a limit. In my opinion, we cannot go on compounding dimensions indefinitely. I suspect that there is also a span of perceptual dimensionality and that this span is somewhere in the neighborhood of ten, but I must add at once that there is no objective evidence to support this suspicion. This is a question sadly needing experimental exploration.

Concerning the third device, the use of successive judgments, I have quite a bit to say because this device introduces memory as the handmaiden of discrimination. And, since mnemonic processes are at least as complex as are perceptual processes, we can anticipate that their interactions will not be easily disentangled. Suppose that we start by simply extending slightly the experimental procedure that we have been using. Up to this point we have presented a single stimulus and asked the observer to name it immediately thereafter. We can extend this procedure by requiring the observer to withhold his response until we have given him several stimuli in succession. At the end of the sequence of stimuli he then makes his response. We still have the same sort of input-output situation that is required for the measurement of transmitted information. But now we have passed from an experiment on absolute judgment to what is traditionally called an experiment on immediate memory.

Before we look at any data on this topic I feel I must give you a word of warning to help you avoid some obvious associations that can be confusing. Everybody knows that there is a finite span of immediate memory and that for a lot of different kinds of test materials this span is about seven items in length. I have just shown you that there is a span of absolute judgment that can distinguish about seven categories and that there is a span of attention that will encompass about six objects at a glance. What is more natural than to think that all three of these spans are different aspects of a single underlying process? That is a fundamental mistake, as I shall be at some pains to demonstrate. This mistake is one of the malicious persecutions that the magical number seven has subjected me to.

My mistake went something like this. We have seen that the invariant feature in the span of absolute judgment is the amount of information that the observer can transmit. There is a real operational similarity between the absolute judgment experiment and the immediate memory experiment. If immediate memory is like absolute judgment, then it should follow that the invariant feature in the span of immediate memory is also the amount of information that an observer can retain. If the amount of information in the span of immediate memory is a constant, then the span should be short when the individual items contain a lot of information and the span should be long when the items contain little information. For example, decimal digits are worth 3. 3 bits apiece. We can recall about seven of them, for a total of 23 bits of information. Isolated English words are worth about 10 bits apiece. If the total amount of information is to remain constant at 23 bits, then we should be able to remember only two or three words chosen at random. In this way I generated a theory about how the span of immediate memory should vary as a function of the amount of information per item in the test materials.

The measurements of memory span in the literature are suggestive on this question, but not definitive. And so it was necessary to do the experiment to see. J. R. M. Hayes ["Memory Span for Several Vocabularies As a Function of Vocabulary Size," M. I. T. Acoustics Lab., Qrtrly. Progress Report Jan. -June, 1952--ed. note: not verified] tried it out with five different kinds of test materials: binary digits, decimal digits, letters of the alphabet, letters plus decimal digits, and with 1000 monosyllabic words. The lists were read aloud at the rate of one item per second and the subjects had as much time as they needed to give their responses. A procedure described by R. S. Woodworth [Experimental Psychology, New York: Holt, 1938] was used to score the responses. The results are shown by the filled circles in Figure 7. Here the dotted line indicates what the span should have been if the amount of information in the span were constant. The solid curves represent the data. Hayes repeated the experiment using test vocabularies of different sizes but all containing only English monosyllables (open circles in Figure 7). This more homogeneous test material did not change the picture significantly. With binary items the span is about nine and, although it

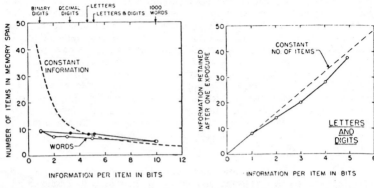

Figure 7.   Data from Hayes [see text] on the span of immediate memory plotted as a function of the amount of information per item in the test materials.

Figure 8.   Data from Pollack [see text] on the amount of information retained after one presentation plotted as a function of the amount of information per item in the test materials.

drops to about five with monosyllabic English words, the difference is far less than the hypothesis of constant information would require.

There is nothing wrong with Hayes's experiment, because I. Pollack ["The Assimilation of Sequentially Encoded Information," Amer. J. of Psychol. 66:421-35, 1953] repeated it much more elaborately and got essentially the same result.   Pollack took pains to measure the amount of information transmitted and did not rely on the traditional procedure for scoring the responses.   His results are plotted in Figure 8.   Here it is clear that the amount of information transmitted is not a constant, but increases almost linearly as the amount of information per item in the input is increased.

And so the outcome is perfectly clear.   In spite of the coincidence that the magical number seven appears in both places, the span of absolute judgment and the span of immediate memory are quite different kinds of limitations that are imposed on our ability to process information.   Absolute judgment is limited by the amount of information.   Immediate memory is limited by the number of items. In order to capture this distinction in somewhat picturesque terms, I have fallen into the custom of distinguishing between bits of information and chunks of information.   Then I can say that the number of bits of information is constant for absolute judgment and the number of chunks of information is constant for immediate memory. The span of immediate memory seems to be almost independent of the number of bits per chunk, at least over the range that has been examined to date.   The contrast of the terms bit and chunk also serves to highlight the fact that we are not very definite about what constitutes a chunk of information.   For example, the memory span

of five words that Hayes obtained when each word was drawn at random from a set of 1000 English monosyllables might just as appropriately have been called a memory span of 15 phonemes, since each
word had about three phonemes in it.   Intuitively, it is clear that
the subjects were recalling five words, not 15 phonemes, but the
logical distinction is not immediately apparent.   We are dealing here
with a process of organizing or grouping the input into familiar units
or chunks, and a great deal of learning has gone into the formation
of these familiar units.

Recoding

In order to speak more precisely, therefore, we must recognize the importance of grouping or organizing the input sequence into units or chunks.   Since the memory span is a fixed number of
chunks, we can increase the number of bits of information that it
contains simply by building larger and larger chunks, each chunk
containing more information than before.   A man just beginning to
learn radio-telegraphic code hears each dit and dah as a separate
chunk.   Soon he is able to organize these sounds into letters and
then he can deal with the letters as chunks.   Then the letters organize themselves as words, which are still larger chunks, and he
begins to hear whole phrases.   I do not mean that each step is a
discrete process, or that plateaus must appear in his learning curve,
for surely the levels of organization are achieved at different rates
and overlap each other during the learning process.   I am simply
pointing to the obvious fact that the dits and dahs are organized by
learning into patterns and that as these larger chunks emerge the
amount of message that the operator can remember increases correspondingly.   In the terms I am proposing to use, the operator learns
to increase the bits per chunk.   In the jargon of communication theory, this process would be called recoding.   The input is given in a
code that contains many chunks with few bits per chunk.   The operator recodes the input into another code that contains fewer chunks
with more bits per chunk.   There are many ways to do this recoding, but probably the simplest is to group the input events, apply a
new name to the group, and then remember the new name rather
than the original input events.

Since I am convinced that this process is a very general and
important one for psychology, I want to tell you about a demonstration experiment that should make perfectly explicit what I am talking
about.   This experiment was conducted by Sidney Smith and was reported by him before the Eastern Psychological Association in 1954.
Begin with the observed fact that people can repeat back eight decimal digits, but only nine binary digits.   Since there is a large discrepancy in the amount of information recalled in these two cases,
we suspect at once that a recoding procedure could be used to increase the span of immediate memory for binary digits.   In Table
1 a method for grouping and renaming is illustrated.   Along the top
is a sequence of 18 binary digits, far more than any subject was
able to recall after a single presentation.   In the next line these

Table 1

WAYS OF RECODING SEQUENCES OF BINARY DIGITS

Binary Digits (Bits)	1 0 1 0 0 0 1 0 0 1 1 1 0 0 1 1 1 0								
2:1 Chunks	10	10	00	10	01	11	00	11	10
Recoding	2	2	0	2	1	3	0	3	2
3:1 Chunks	101	000		100	111		001	110	
Recoding	5	0		4	7		1	6	
4:1 Chunks	1010		0010		0111		0011		10
Recoding	10		2		7		3		
5:1 Chunks	10100			01001			11001		110
Recoding	20			9			25		

same binary digits are grouped by pairs. Four possible pairs can occur: 00 is renamed 0, 01 is renamed 1, 10 is renamed 2, and 11 is renamed 3. That is to say, we recode from a base-two arithmetic to a base-four arithmetic. In the recoded sequence there are now just nine digits to remember, and this is almost within the span of immediate memory. In the next line the same sequence of binary digits is regrouped into chunks of three. There are eight possible sequences of three, so we give each sequence a new name between 0 and 7. Now we have recoded from a sequence of 18 binary digits into a sequence of 6 octal digits, and this is well within the span of immediate memory. In the last two lines the binary digits are grouped by fours and by fives and are given decimal-digit names from 0 to 15 and from 0 to 31.

It is reasonably obvious that this kind of recoding increases the bits per chunk, and packages the binary sequence into a form that can be retained within the span of immediate memory. So Smith assembled 20 subjects and measured their spans for binary and octal digits. The spans were 9 for binaries and 7 for octals. Then he gave each recoding scheme to five of the subjects. They studied the recoding until they said they understood it--for about 5 or 10 minutes. Then he tested their span for binary digits again while they tried to use the recoding schemes they had studied. The recoding schemes increased their span for binary digits in every case. But the increase was not as large as we had expected on the basis of their span for octal digits. Since the discrepancy increased as the recoding ratio increased, we reasoned that the few minutes the subjects had spent learning the recoding schemes had not been sufficient. Apparently the translation from one code to the other must be almost automatic or the subject will lose part of the next group while he is trying to remember the translation of the last group.

Since the 4:1 and 5:1 ratios require considerable study, Smith decided to imitate Ebbinghaus and do the experiment on himself. With Germanic patience he drilled himself on each recoding successively, and obtained the results shown in Figure 9. Here the data follow along rather nicely with the results you would predict on the

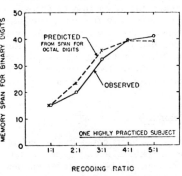

Figure 9. The span of immediate memory for binary digits is plotted as a function of the recoding procedure used. The predicted function is obtained by multiplying the span for octals by 2, 3 and 3.3 for recoding into base 4, base 8, and base 10 respectively.

basis of his span for octal digits. He could remember 12 octal digits. With the 2:1 recoding, these 12 chunks were worth 24 binary digits. With the 3:1 recoding they were worth 36 binary digits. With the 4:1 and 5:1 recodings, they were worth about 40 binary digits. It is a little dramatic to watch a person get 40 binary digits in a row and then repeat them back without error. However, if you think of this merely as a mnemonic trick for extending the memory span, you will miss the more important point that is implicit in nearly all such mnemonic devices. The point is that recoding is an extremely powerful tool for increasing the amount of information that we can deal with. In one form or another we use recoding constantly in our daily behavior.

In my opinion the most customary kind of recoding that we do all the time is to translate into a verbal code. When there is a story or an argument or an idea that we want to remember, we usually try to rephrase it "in our own words." When we witness some event we want to remember, we make a verbal description of the event and then remember our verbalization. Upon recall we recreate by secondary elaboration the details that seem consistent with the particular verbal recoding we happen to have made. The well-known experiment by L. Carmichael, H. P. Hogan, and A. A. Walter ["An Experimental Study of the Effect of Language on the Reproduction of Visually Perceived Form," J. of Exper. Psychol. 15:73-86, 1932] on the influence that names have on the recall of visual figures is one demonstration of the process.

The inaccuracy of the testimony of eyewitnesses is well known in legal psychology, but the distortions of testimony are not random --they follow naturally from the particular recoding that the witness

used, and the particular recoding he used depends upon his whole
life history. Our language is tremendously useful for repackaging
material into a few chunks rich in information. I suspect that im-
agery is a form of recoding, too, but images seem much harder to
get at operationally and to study experimentally than the more symbolic kinds of recoding. It seems probable that even memorization
can be studied in these terms. The process of memorizing may be
simply the formation of chunks, or groups of items that go together,
until there are few enough chunks so that we can recall all the
items. The work by W. A. Bousfield and B. H. Cohen ["The Occurrence of Clustering in the Recall of Randomly Arranged Words
of Different Frequencies-of-Usage," J. of General Psychol. 52:83-
95, 1955] on the occurrence of clustering in the recall of words is
especially interesting in this respect.

Summary

I have come to the end of the data that I wanted to present,
so I would like now to make some summarizing remarks. First,
the span of absolute judgment and the span of immediate memory im-
pose severe limitations on the amount of information that we are able
to receive, process, and remember. By organizing the stimulus input simultaneously into several dimensions and successively into a
sequence of chunks, we manage to break (or at least stretch) this informational bottleneck.

Second, the process of recoding is a very important one in
human psychology and deserves much more explicit attention than it
has received. In particular, the kind of linguistic recoding that people do seems to me to be the very lifeblood of the thought processes.
Recoding procedures are a constant concern to clinicians, social
psychologists, linguists, and anthropologists and yet, probably because recoding is less accessible to experimental manipulation than
nonsense syllables or T mazes, the traditional experimental psychologist has contributed little or nothing to their analysis. Nevertheless,
experimental techniques can be used, methods of recoding can be
specified, behavioral indicants can be found. And I anticipate that
we will find a very orderly set of relations describing what now
seems an uncharted wilderness of individual differences.

Third, the concepts and measures provided by the theory of
information provide a quantitative way of getting at some of these
questions. The theory provides us with a yardstick for calibrating
our stimulus materials and for measuring the performance of our
subjects. In the interests of communication I have suppressed the
technical details of information measurement and have tried to express the ideas in more familiar terms; I hope this paraphrase will
not lead you to think they are not useful in research. Informational
concepts have already proved valuable in the study of discrimination
and of language; they promise a great deal in the study of learning
and memory; and it has even been proposed that they can be useful
in the study of concept formation. A lot of questions that seemed

fruitless 20 or 30 years age may now be worth another look.   In
fact, I feel that my story here must stop just as it begins to get
really interesting.

And finally, what about the magical number seven?   What
about the seven wonders of the world, the seven seas, the seven
deadly sins, the seven daughters of Atlas in the Pleiades, the seven
ages of man, the seven levels of hell, the seven primary colors, the
seven notes of the musical scale, and the seven days of the week?
What about the seven-point rating scale, the seven categories for absolute judgment, the seven objects in the span of attention, and the
seven digits in the span of immediate memory?   For the present I
propose to withhold judgment.   Perhaps there is something deep and
profound behind all these sevens, something just calling out for us
to discover it.   But I suspect that it is only a pernicious, Pytha-
gorean coincidence.

Chapter 15

COMPRESSORS AND EXPANDERS

This chapter contains a number of descriptions of speech compressors. It is not complete but is representative. E. Foulke ["Compressors--Actual and Imminent," CRCR Newsletter 6(5):1-4, 1972] has given a brief description of compressors now available on the market as well as of newly developed compressors which have not yet been marketed. The first item is a description by H. Schiesser of the compressor invented by Springer (see his patents in Part IV of this Anthology). This has been the most widely used compressor as it was marketed for a number of years under various names. It is, however, no longer available, at least in the United States.

The original Fairbanks compressor (see his patent in Part IV of this Anthology) was originally marketed by the Kaye Electric Co. Notwithstanding the fact that the prototype, which is still at the University of Illinois, is able, with a little engineering prodding, to produce an excellent compression, Kaye was never able to produce a satisfactory product and only a few of their models are still in existence. Wayne Graham of Discerned Sound developed a compressor based on the Fairbanks invention which he calls the Whirling Dervish. This compressor is described in the second passage in this chapter by Professor Emerson Foulke of the University of Louisville. A rather unique variation of previous compressors has been developed, but not yet manufactured by Richard Koch. The third item in this chapter is a brief description of this piece of equipment.

It is utterly impossible to draw an absolute line that will separate time- compression and bandwidth or frequency compression. These volumes deal with time-compression and not at all with bandwidth compression as such. In the excerpts by M. R. Schroeder, B. F. Logan, and A. J. Prestigiacomo, all of whom are associated with the Bell Telephone Laboratories, a scheme is outlined whereby bandwidth compression is used for the sole purpose of changing the rate of the message. Hence this excerpt becomes appropriate at this point. The "harmonic compressor" described here had not been built at the time this paper was written but had only been simulated by computer. The plan for its construction was donated to the American Foundation for the Blind and has been developed by this organization as is related in the next excerpt.

John W. Breuel and Leo M. Levens, who are engaged in research activities at the American Foundation for the Blind, describe the actual operation of the harmonic compressor which was described in the previous excerpt. The actual compressor is now located at the University of Louisville. The last section in this chapter is an excerpt from a description by Compressed Time Incorporated of a newly-developed compressor which has not yet been manufactured.

DEVICE FOR TIME EXPANSION USED IN SOUND RECORDING

H. Schiesser

In Volume three, 1948, of <u>Funk and Ton</u> there was described a device for finding certain recorded sound elements on recorded tape. To do that, the tape was usually standing still and the play-back head was rotating. Gunka and Lippert have mentioned that this kind of device could be used not only for editing but also for sound analysis. Actually an article was found in American technical literature where a similar device was used for a tape recorder which was very similar to the German "Magnetophon." The magnetic tape recorder "Magnetophon-Special" produced by AEG used rotating heads. That recorder was developed at the beginning of the last war and manufactured on a large scale. In that recorder, the time expansion device was called a "Zeitdehner." The basic principles will be discussed further in this article.

Modulated recording media for different sound recording systems, such as disc, film or tape, never hold the recorded frequency by themselves. By measuring the distance between two maximum groove amplitudes, maximum opaque for film, or maximum magnetization of tape, we can determine the wave length. For the frequency, we have to know the velocity for the recording medium.

$$f = v/\lambda \tag{1}$$

Usually the velocity for recording medium remains the same in the recording and playback processes. Any unwanted change in velocity, caused by speed variation will cause variations in the reproduced sound pitch. By increasing the speed of recording medium carrying a recorded message, we can transmit the message more cheaply, because the time is reduced to use cable lines and the charge will be less. Furthermore, there will be a need to slow down recorded dictation for the typist. By slowing down the speed in the usual fashion, the intelligibility will be changed and it would result in a complete misunderstanding.

The velocity v in (1) represents the relative velocity between recording medium and recording or playback head element. Usually, the recording or playback head will not be in motion. Gunka and Lippert described a device where the recording medium stands still, and the playback head element moves. In general, it could be arranged that the recorded medium and the playback head element both

are in motion. Velocity for the recorded medium is V_t and for playback element V_a. Recording done by a relative velocity V will give
us the same pitch in playback at two different velocities for the recording medium, depending on the relative direction of motion between medium and playback head element.

$$V_t = V \div V_a \qquad (2)$$

As long as the pitch in playback is determined by the relative velocity between recording medium and playback head, the tempo by
which the recorded information can be reproduced is determined by
the velocity of the playback gap moving along the recording medium.

From a design standpoint, the playback gap striking area on
tape is determined and the tempo for reproduction depends upon the
speed of the recording medium. Expanded playback requires diminishing the velocity of recording medium V_t with respect to velocity
that was used in the recording process. To simplify the problem,
a stationary head was used in the recording process, equal to the
relative velocity between medium and recording device. The expansion factor will be

$$d = V / V_t \qquad (3)$$

The above-mentioned relation represents the ratio between the time
for recording and reproduction. For d smaller than 1, it appears
as a time compression. Figure 1 curves, where, by a chosen certain amount of compression or expression d, there can be found the
corresponding velocity for recording medium in playback and the two
velocities V_a for the playback head rotational motion, to get the same
pitch as it was recorded.

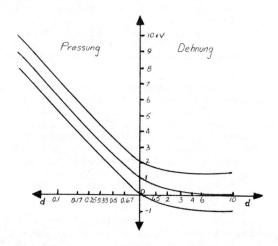

Figure 1. Velocity for recording medium V_t and the playback device
V_a as a multiple of velocity used by recording vs. compression expansion factor (d).

The resulting velocities will be multiples of the recording velocity V. Only in one special case $d = 1$, the motional velocity for the gap along the medium will be the same as the relative velocity between medium and playback device. And only in that case is it possible to have uninterrupted continuity in playback. It can be seen that a time compression in playback by keeping the original pitch, could be done only by partially sampling the recorded information from the tape. For time expansion we have partly to overlap the recorded information by our playback gap striking area or by introductory interruptions. By introducing interruptions or by repeated (overlapped) reproduction, the samples of the separate recorded signal elements and the interruptions should be short so as to avoid introducing too much discontinuity so as to be out of range where human hearing system distinguishes sound separations. That principle used here is similar to human optical inertial that is encountered in moving pictures.

The interrupted "take off" procedure is done periodically by using a rotating or oscillating scanning device. The disc recording is rather difficult, but it is easier in magnetic or photoelectric recording. The gap must move periodically along the recording medium at a velocity V_a and displacement h. At the end of determined displacement h, the gap must jump back to starting point and repeat the same procedure. By photoelectric recording, that motion can be reached by using a rotating spiral opening in the path of the light beam. For magnetic tape recording, it is more convenient to use a rotating device with many gaps distributed around a rotating drum. The wrap angle for tape around the playback head with a number of gaps, must be wider than $2\pi/n$ and there must be provisions that allow only one effective gap in contact with the tape in this sector.

Figure 2 represents the rotating head arrangement for AEG tape recorder. There are four independent heads mounted on a base. Every one is a closed ring head by Schuller with a proper gap and core made of high permeability material. Magnetic potential developed in the gap creates an EMF in the coil. The lead ends from

Figure 2. The basic principles of a rotating device, using four heads 90° apart and electric current commutator.

Figure 3. The basic principles of rotating playback head by using four playback gaps 90° apart and magnetic commutator.

coil are going to a collector lamination, and then from collector to
the input of playback amplifier.   By this collector arrangement,
after 90° rotational displacement of the gap, the point of pickup re-
turns to the beginning of the sector.   The very low current through
collector causes some troubles, and that is why a "magnetic switching" arrangement will be better.   (The induced voltage into the coil
is around 1 mv).

Figure 3 represents this so-called "magnetic switching" device basically.   This in rotational motion is only a cylinder made of
hi-μ material.   The cylinder or drum has four gaps distributed
evenly around this surface.   The magnetic flux lines come from the
effective gap through a part of the drum, and then by the shortest
path through a wide overlapped gap into the pole piece with the coil.
The playback effective gap displacement h will be the distance between two gaps.   For one playback element the distance that the effective gap strikes the medium is L. L is different from h, because the tape is in motion.

$$L = h \, v / v_a \qquad\qquad (4)$$

The sequence for separate "picking ups" for the two corresponding
spots on the tape will be e.

$$l = h \, v / v_a \, d \qquad\qquad (d = \text{compression-expansion factor})$$

For $d = 1$, $L = l$, indicating that the distance between two corresponding spots contacted by two sequentially following "picking-ups"
will be the length of the partial element on tape.   The playback will
follow with an uninterrupted continuity.   For d smaller than 1
(meaning time compression) there will be introduced dead spots between two played back elements.   For d larger than 1   (meaning
time expansion) there will be overlaps of played back elements;
every separate spot on tape gets reproduced d-times.

Figure 4 represents a time-displacement diagram.   The horizontal axis represents the displacement of the playback gap on the
recorded medium.   An example will be for $d = 4$, and $d = 0.5$, the
playback head is rotating in one direction for one diagram and in the
opposite direction for the other diagram.   The gap displacement h
is in both cases the same.   The projection of arrows on horizontal
direction will represent the length L by which the playback gap
strikes the tape.   The distance between the arrow points will represent 1.   The slope of the arrows is reversed proportional to the
velocity v_a of the playback device.   The slope of the center line of
arrows is revised proportional to the velocity v_t of the recording
medium.   As it can be seen from examples on B and D, the separate
elements get played back reversed since the motion of medium and
playback device are in the same direction.   That way we get larger
amounts of separate short elements by using an opposite motion for
the head and tape, there will be less separate elements, but longer.

The number of elements will be greater when d is smaller.
To get a better continuity for listening, the separate elements should
be many and small, and that is why for time compression it is necessary to have the same motional directions for both the medium

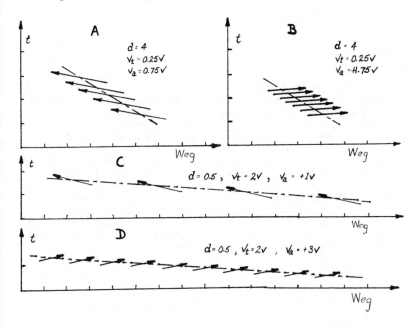

Figure 4. Time-displacement diagram for interrupted playback for $d = 4$ (expansion) and $d = 0.5$ (compression) for both velocities v_a for the playback device.

and the playback device. In that case, the separate elements get reproduced backwards, but that doesn't matter since the elements are small enough. A tape recorder with rotating head assembly for the most unfavorable condition in playback which was represented in Figure 4, diagram B, and uses a gap displacement $h = 2.5$ cm and recording tape speed of 75 cm/sec. The separate element length in playback is $L = 2$ cm. That corresponds to a 26.6 millisecond recording or it will be 1/8 syllable. That length of the separate element is short enough to give us a sufficient continuity in playback and the elements could be played back backwards without introducing noticeable distortions. By the above discussed example, 38 elements per second were played back with the listener having the impression of discontinuity. It is supposed that much greater expansion would not be necessary in general use. For special occasions where we have to use a much greater expansion, the tape speed has to be increased in recording.

THE WHIRLING DERVISH

Emerson Foulke (information furnished by Wayne Graham, of Discerned Sound)

The speech compressor known as the Whirling Dervish, represents a further development of the instrument originally built by Grant Fairbanks and his colleagues at the University of Illinois [B105]. Like the Fairbanks compressor, it makes use of a storage loop, on which is recorded the signal that is to be sampled for compression or expansion. The loop passes over an erase head, a record head, the sampling wheel on which four playback heads are mounted, and between the capstan and rubber pressure roller which control the speed of the loop. From this point, it enters a bin capable of holding 20 feet of loop, and emerges again to repeat the circuit. The loop is formed by splicing the ends of a piece of magnetic recording tape together. The use of a long loop reduces wear, and reduces noise by reducing the frequency with which the splice in the loop passes over the sampling wheel.

The sampling wheel is driven by a motor, the speed of which is continuously variable. The storage loop is driven by a motor of constant speed equipped with a pulley that has two diameters, permitting two operating speeds for the loop. The duration of the sample discarded by the compressor is a function of its loop speed and, if greater flexibility is required, the compressor can be supplied with a variable speed loop motor.

Mounted on the same shaft with the sampling wheel are two preamplifiers. The input of each preamplifier is connected to a pair of opposing heads on the sampling wheel. The outputs of the preamplifiers are mixed and removed from the rotating shaft through a brush and ring assembly. Noise is generated when brushes rub against rings, but the preamplifiers provide enough gain in signal level so that the signal-to-noise ratio is satisfactory, and brush noise is no longer a problem. Because the gain afforded by each preamplifier is adjustable, the output levels of the four heads on the sampling wheel can be equated. This is an important provision since, for satisfactory results, all of the samples in the compressed or expanded signal should be at the same signal level.

When speech is compressed or expanded by a compressor of the Fairbanks type, samples obtained from different locations in the original speech signal are abutted in time, and there may, as a result, be a considerable discontinuity in signal level at sample boundaries. To reduce the effect of this problem, the Graham compressor has been provided with switching circuitry which attenuates the output of each of the preamplifiers on the sampling wheel shaft in the period during which neither of the heads connected to its input is obtaining samples from the storage loop. At the instant a head makes contact with the storage loop, the attenuation applied to the output of its preamplifier is removed and applied to the output of the

other preamplifier, thus muting the signal level of the head which is
losing contact with the storage loop at that instant.   This switching
circuitry has been designed so that the head just making contact with
the storage loop is not switched on instantaneously.   Rather, its
signal rises to full strength gradually, and decays gradually as it
loses contact with the storage loop.   Thus, the abrupt discontinuities
in signal level that may occur at sample boundaries are smoothed.

Another desirable effect is achieved by the switching circuitry
just described.   The low frequency content of the signal recorded on
tape may excite a playback head which, though in close proximity to
the tape, is not in physical contact with it.   Thus, when samples
required for compressed or expanded speech are obtained by a sampling wheel, both the head preceding and the head following the head
in contact with the storage loop at any given instant may be in close
enough proximity to that loop to be excited by the low frequency content of the signal recorded on it, and this unwanted excitation will
appear as noise in the output signal.   Since, on the Graham compressor, the two heads that are adjacent to the head in contact with
the storage loop are connected to the preamplifier whose output is
attenuated at that time, they are not excited by proximity to the storage loop, and the noise they might contribute to the output signal is
thus eliminated.   The amount by which the outputs of the two preamplifiers are alternately attenuated is adjustable by a control on
the front panel of the compressor, identified as a smoothing control.

Operation of the Whirling Dervish requires a tape player, or
some other source, to generate the signal that is recorded on its
storage loop, and a tape recorder to copy the output signal.   To accomplish compression or expansion, it is necessary to change the
speed of either the input player or the output recorder.   The desired speed change can be accomplished incrementally, by the use of
pulleys with different diameters, or continuously with a variable
speed motor.   In terms of the final result, it makes no difference
whether the speed of the input player or the speed of the output recorder is varied.   If the speed of the output recorder is varied, the
tape to be compressed is played on the input player at the original
recording speed, and the output of the compressor, altered in pitch,
is recorded.   The resulting tape is played back at a speed that will
restore pitch to the proper value.   If the speed of the input player
is varied, it is set for the playback time that is desired after compression or expansion, and the compressor is adjusted to make the
required correction in pitch.   The advantage of this mode of operation is that the signal appearing at the output of the compressor is
properly adjusted in pitch and time for the desired amount of compression or expansion, and thus can be monitored more easily by
ear.   Also, if this signal is recorded, the resulting tape can be
played directly on a conventional tape player, without making a further adjustment in tape speed.

One configuration of equipment available from Discerned Sound
includes the Whirling Dervish, and an input tape player with continuously variable tape speed.   The control of the speed of this input

tape player and of the speed of the sampling wheel on the compressor has been coupled, so that the equipment may be adjusted for the desired amount of compression by turning a single knob on the front panel of the compressor.

THE AMBICHRON

Richard Koch

The AmBiChron is an all-electronic compressor. The experimental breadboard model provides for rate changes of about 25:1 and pitch changes of about three octaves; each is symmetrical about the 0 per cent point. In addition, pitch can be shifted up or down about one-and-one-half octaves in either direction. Rate and pitch are adjusted by separate controls, and combined changes of the two characteristics can be made for any values within the stated limits. Control settings can be changed at any time, and can pass through 0 per cent rate change and 0 per cent pitch change in either direction. In order to attain these ranges, each control consists of a continuous control and a range switch, with overlap from range to range of the switches.

Since the AmBiChron is designed for the compression of speech, the upper frequency limit of signals which it will process has been chosen to be about 5kHz (normalized to 0 per cent compression). Modifications to extend the frequency to well beyond the range of human hearing can readily be made. The AmBiChron uses a sampling technique akin to that of Fairbanks and Springer. At 0 per cent compression the maximum interval is 26.6 milliseconds, and this varies inversely with the degree of compression. In the breadboard model, the interval is variable down to nearly 1/20th of the maximum value, but early experiments have shown no great value for this flexibility. Being all-electronic, the AmBiChron is independent of the format of the recorded material with which it works. That is, the input can be provided by a tape recorder, a phonograph, or other playback device. And, if the AmBiChron is used in real time, solely to change pitch, the question of recording format is moot. This would be the case in such an application as correcting the pitch of a deep-sea diver's helium speech. When it is used for rate change, the only requirement on the associated recording or reproducing apparatus is that the transport rate be variable.

In general, compressors are used to change the time frame of speech that has already been recorded; this implies that the transport associated with the AmBiChron is a reproducer. The AmBiChron includes a low-frequency power amplifier, which delivers a variable-frequency AC output, to control the speed of the associated transport. Ideally, then, the transport should be driven by a synchronous motor but less expensive types of induction motors will also follow line-frequency changes; however, the latter may exhibit significant slip. The frequency of the power output of the AmBiChron is directly related to the degree of compression selected by the rate controls. Thus, in the ideal case, a single setting by the operator can suffice to provide the required compensation within the AmBiChron and speed change within the transport, for a desired compression. If the transport's motor does not follow exactly as desired, the operator can compensate by trimming the pitch control.

However, the AmBiChron is not limited to operating with transports having AC motors. The only requirement is that the transport speed be changeable, somehow. It is entirely feasible to set the compression control of the AmBiChron and the speed control of the transport separately. It is also possible to modify the AmBiChron so that an external signal will set its degree of compression. Such a modification is relatively minor, and provides control over compression by means of an external AC signal, instead of one generated within the AmBiChron. In this case, an AC tachometer in the transport can generate the required signal. Then, single-knob control of the transport's speed will automatically bring with it pitch-normalization of the compressed signal.

By another simple modification of the AmBiChron, it can be used to compress recordings at the same time that they are being duplicated in a speeded-up mode. For example, it is often the practice to duplicate a tape recorded at 3-3/4 i.p.s. by playing it back at 15 i.p.s. while the re-recording tape deck is also operated at 15 i.p.s. If it is desired simultaneously to compress the original tape by 25 per cent, the re-recorder can be run at 18-3/4 i.p.s., and an AmBiChron between playback deck and re-recorder can provide the required pitch normalization. In the special case where it is desired to make a compressed (or expanded) recording in a single pass, the AmBiChron can also be used. In this case, the recorder is slowed (or speeded) relative to its normal speed, during recording. At the same time, the AmBiChron shifts the pitch of the signal to be recorded downward (or upward). Then, when the recording is played back at its nominal speed, the desired degree of compression (or expansion) is obtained, and the pitch is normalized. In this mode of operation single-knob control over compression and transport speed is obtainable to the same extent as in the case of playback.

A proposed demonstration model of the AmBiChron, in addition to the basic controls for rate and pitch, will provide switches to select preset "normal" values of each; these are useful when only one of these parameters is to be adjusted. (The range of pitch adjustment will be slightly over one-and-one-half octaves, provided by a continuous control, without a range switch.) Two-position switches for input sensitivity and output level will be provided, and controls for input and output filters. The filters are simple RC devices, chosen to provide gradual high-frequency roll-offs without ringing, and having corner frequencies of about 5kHz. The demonstration

model will have a volume of less than one-half cubic foot, and a
size saving in future models is expected.   If a special model without the power amplifier were built, a volume decrease of about 30
per cent should be realized.

NEW METHODS FOR SPEECH ANALYSIS-SYNTHESIS AND BANDWIDTH COMPRESSION

M. R. Schroeder, B. F. Logan, A. J. Prestigiacomo

Harmonic Compressor

The principle of frequency division, applied to individual harmonic frequency components, for speech bandwidth reduction is not
new.   It has in fact been suggested by R. L. Miller several decades
ago.   The idea has been reinvented, in a different form, more recently (in 1957) by B. F. Logan.   However, in neither case has any
attempt at implementation been made.   The required circuitry
seemed prohibitive for the expected bandwidth reduction and computer simulation had not yet arrived.   Compared to vocoders, the harmonic compressor possesses the following advantages: There are no
pitch or voiced-unvoiced decision problems.   No multiplexing of channel signals is required.   The compressed signal has speech-like
characteristics on the reduced frequency scale and is therefore well
suited for transmission over speech circuits.   The relative phases
of the individual harmonic frequency components are preserved.   It
is anticipated that an important application of harmonic compressors
will be to the basebands of voice-excited vocoders thereby giving
further impetus to these vocoders and decision-free voice coding in
general.

The Analyzer

Figure 1 shows the block diagram of a harmonic compressor
which has been simulated on a digital computer (IBM 7090).   The
speech signal is applied to a bank of 50 bandpass filters A, each
60 c. p. s. wide and spaced 60 c. p. s. apart.   The frequency band
covered extends from approximately 240 to 3240 c. p. s.   The filters
are of a special computer-adapted type described below.   The frequency response of the entire filter bank (all filter outputs connected
together) is flat within a small fraction of a decibel and has a linear
phase.   Individual filters have a minimum attenuation in the rejection band of 23 db; the filter skirts are -12 db/octave.   The purpose
of filter bank A is to separate a voiced speech input into its individual harmonic frequency components.   Thus, the amplitude and phase
modulations of the filter outputs have narrow bandwidths corresponding to the syllabic rate rather than the fundamental frequency.   The
resolution into individual harmonics is believed to be important for

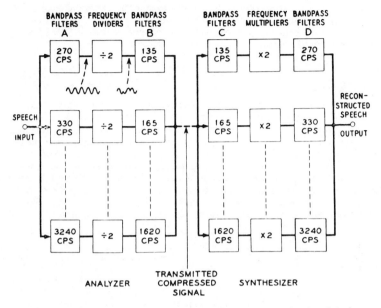

Figure 1.   Block diagram of a harmonic compressor simulated on a digital computer.

the proper functioning of the harmonic compressor.   With the present filters, a good harmonic separation is assured down to fundamental frequencies of approximately 60 c.p.s.

The outputs of filters A are applied to frequency dividers which divide the instantaneous frequencies of the narrow band signals by 2.   The resulting waveform at one divider output for a sinewave input is shown in Figure 1.   It consists of a sinewave with every other period inverted.   This signal contains a frequency component whose instantaneous frequency is one half of that of the input signal with an amplitude proportional to the input.   The filters of filter bank B removes the distortion components from the half-frequency signal.   The outputs of filters B are added together to form the compressed signal ready for transmission over a channel of one half bandwidth.

The Synthesizer

In the synthesizer (right half of Figure 1) the compressed signal is applied to a filter bank C covering the compressed frequency scale (120 to 1620 c.p.s.).   The individual filter bandwidths must be small enough to separate the compressed signal into individual harmonics of half the fundamental frequency.   The filter outputs are

connected to fullwave rectifiers which double the instantaneous frequencies, thereby regenerating the original harmonic frequencies.
Filter bank D removes the distortion products resulting from the
full-wave rectification.

Discussion

The harmonic compressor capitalizes on the quasi-periodic
nature of speech sounds. Figure 2 shows (schematically) harmonics
of the short-time amplitude spectrum of a monotone speech sound of
fundamental frequency f_0. Each harmonic has a certain bandwidth
which reflects the quasi-periodic nature of speech and is proportional to the syllabic rate. From experiments with spectrum vocoders
it is known that spectrum channel signals can be low-passed to about
20 c. p. s. for average syllabic rates. Therefore, the width of each
harmonic component can be limited to about 40 c. p. s. (The 3-db
bandwidth is probably considerably narrower than 40 c. p. s.)

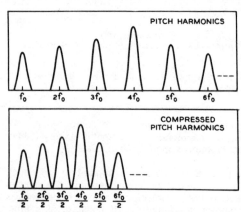

Figure 2.   Harmonics of the short-time amplitude spectrum of a
monotone speech sound of fundamental frequency f_0 shown schematically.

The spectrum of the analyzer output is also illustrated in Figure 2. The frequency gaps between the harmonics are reduced or
eliminated; but adjacent lines do not significantly overlap. For fundamental frequencies exceeding 80 c. p. s. and a line width less than
40 c. p. s., a 2:1 compression is possible with little distortion for
voiced speech sounds. For fundamental frequencies exceeding 160
c. p. s. a compression of 4:1 should be feasible for the same syllabic
rate (line width). The higher compression possible for higher fundamental frequencies reflects the fact that for a given syllabic rate
more fundamental periods are similar (a fact sometimes loosely and
ambiguously stated as "female speech has less information"). It is

difficult to predict what happens for compression ratios larger than the ratio of fundamental frequency to line width. The subjective effects of overlapping compressed harmonics are not known and difficult to predict. Experiments now in progress will establish the limits on the compression and demonstrate the resulting degradation if these limits are violated.

Subharmonic Distortion

If any of the filters in filter bank C passes two or more adjacent halved harmonics, the full-wave rectifier will generate frequencies which are multiples of half the fundamental frequency of the input speech signal. These "subharmonics" will appear in the output and, if sufficiently intense, constitute an audible distortion reminiscent of diplophonia. With the present filters, this occurs only for fundamental frequencies below 60 c.p.s. The subharmonic distortion has been observed on an earlier model of the harmonic compressor using wider filters.

Response of Harmonic Compressor to Noise and Unvoiced Sounds

Quasi-periodicity, the property of speech signals on which the harmonic compressor is based, is absent in noise and unvoiced sounds. Therefore, we must expect some sort of degradation for this class of speech sounds. The main distortion results form the frequency doubling in the synthesizer. The full-wave rectifiers double the phase modulation without changing the amplitude modulation of the narrow-band signals from filter bank C. After frequency doubling, these signals therefore no longer exhibit the relationship between amplitude and phase modulation appropriate for a band of Gaussian noise. The resulting sound is known to resemble burbling water. Burbles have also been observed in the harmonic compressor output for a steady Gaussian noise input. Fortunately, for short aperiodic speech sounds, the distortion is hardly noticeable.

The Harmonic Compressor as Syllabic Rate Compressor-Expander

The harmonic compressor analyzer and synthesizer preserve the correct relationship between fundamental and formant frequencies. Therefore, they can be used as a syllabic rate compressor and expander, respectively. The divided frequencies at the analyzer output can be restored to their original values by a speeded-up playback. By this process, syllabic rate of speech signals is doubled. The harmonic compressor synthesizer doubles all frequencies. They can be restored to their original values by a slowed-down playback thereby halving the syllabic rate. Our results indicate that syllabic rate doubling and halving can be performed by a 50-channel harmonic compressor with practically no audible "distortion." Surprisingly, the half-rate speech sounds quite natural (if rather "sleepy")--in spite of the fact that human talkers, when instructed to speak slowly, probably do not employ the uniform time stretching (particularly for stop and plosive speech sounds) realized by the machine.

Computer Simulation

The harmonic compressor described above was simulated on a large digital computer (IBM 7090) programmed by means of a "block diagram compiler" (BLØDI). The inventory of the BLØDI-compiler has been enriched by two items, one filter with a cosine impulse response (CØS) which is used in simulation the bandpass filters, and a frequency divider (HLF) required in the analyzer. The total number of blocks in the "shorthand" BLØDI-program is approximately 640. In unabbreviated BLØDI the total number of blocks would be about 3200. The programming effort in any computer language less sophisticated than BLØDI is prohibitive. The computation time for the combined analyzer and synthesizer with a total of 200 narrow bandpass filters (including input and output routines) is 530 times real time.

The CØS-block, the basic building block of the bandpass filters, is a recursive filter with a cosine impulse response. It requires only one multiplication per sample. To construct one bandpass filter, the outputs of two CØS-blocks with a frequency difference corresponding to the desired bandwidth are subtracted from each other and their impulse responses are truncated by a transversal filter after one beat cycle of the two chosen frequencies. For filter banks with constant bandwidth, the transversal filter is common to all filters. Thus, the total number of multiplications in the computer is only slightly more than two per sample time and bandpass filter.

The frequency division in the analyzer and the frequency multiplication in the synthesizer are nonlinear operations. Thus, in an analog implementation, nonbandlimited signals would be generated. The infinite sampling rate required for these nonbandlimited functions is not feasible in the computer. Therefore, distortions in the form of image frequency components (sidebands of the sampling rate and its multiples) occur in the computer. (The distortion could, in principle, be avoided by more complex computations. These, however, would no longer correspond to the analog circuit to be simulated.) The most practical solution appears to be the use of sufficiently high sampling rates to eliminate any subjective distortion. In a separate experiment, with half-wave rectifiers between two identical filters banks, it was found that for a speech bandwidth of 3.3 kc and 10-kc sampling, image frequency distortion is negligible for speech signals (but not for sinewaves!).

Conclusion

In informal listening, members of our Laboratories have ranked the remade speech quality of the harmonic compressor be-

tween that of an unmultiplexed voice-excited vocoder with a 700-
c. p. s. baseband and unprocessed speech of the same bandwidth.
Whether compression factors greater than 2:1 are feasible without
upsetting the above rank order is not yet known.   Following a suggestion by E. E. David, Jr. we are presently studying the application of harmonic compression to the baseband of a voice-excited vocoder.   Preliminary results indicate that a 2:1 compression is feasible with little additional degradation of the vocoded speech.   The
broader goal of this investigation is a "decision-free" vocoder not
relying on some uncoded portion of the speech spectrum at the synthesizer.

THE HARMONIC COMPRESSOR

John W. Breuel, Leo M. Levens

The publication of books and magazines is increasing rapidly.
Conversion of this material into recorded form is keeping pace.
There is great interest in reducing the bulk of this material in space
and time.   Our previous paper presented at last year's Audio Engineering Society Convention dealt with increasing the spatial density
of recordings.   This paper deals with an effort to increase the time
density by speech compression.   Speech compression refers to any
method of reducing the time required to transmit a spoken message.

The American Foundation for the Blind has been producing
Talking Book records for more than 35 years.   Many blind readers
of these books found the pace of normal speech too slow.   There
were several reasons.   Some people did not have the time to devote
to all the reading they wanted to do or were required to do.   The
slow reading rate caused some people to lose interest.   When the
45-rpm turntables became common these people found a partial solution.   They played the 33-1/3 rpm discs at 45 rpm.   Strangely comprehension did not suffer, interest was heightened, and more reading was accomplished.   The books for the blind programs have now
grown to the point where more than 60 hours of new recorded material is produced each working day.   It would be impossible for any
person to read more than a small fraction of this mass of material.
But many blind people derive their greatest pleasure from aural
reading.   It is their chief source of information.   Blind students
may use this method in place of or in addition to braille reading.
Add to this the time spent in listening to radio and television--yes
television--and you can see the need for accelerating aural reading.

The Foundation produced devices for increasing the speed of
tape and disc reproducers.   This provides a limited answer, but the
intelligibility of recorded speech is lost to most people at about 75
per cent overspeed, because of pitch distortion.   In 1954, Dr. Grant
Fairbanks of the University of Illinois, developed a method of speech

compression without pitch distortion. This method sampled speech in small segments, discarded some segments and eliminated the gaps. Additional compression capability was provided by this method but it presented some limitations. It was thought that a means of accomplishing rapid speed electronically would present significant technological advantages. These would be principally higher speed processing, improved speech quality, and simpler and more flexible operation and maintenance. In 1965, the Foundation asked Bell Laboratories whether it was possible to use vocoder techniques to speed up recorded speech without distorting it.

History and Theory

Previously Bell Laboratories' scientists had thought of the harmonic compressor while studying frequency compression as a possible means for reducing the transmission bandwidth required in voice communications. Drs. M. R. Schroeder and R. M. Golden of Bell Labs provided information on the harmonic compressor to suit the needs of the Foundation. The device was first simulated on a digital computer. The simulation proved the effectiveness of the design without requiring actual equipment to be built. The Engineering Division of the American Foundation for the Blind then undertook the development of the necessary circuitry and completed the system at the end of 1968.

The original system design is the result of combined efforts of the Bell Telephone Laboratories and American Foundation for the Blind staff members. Bell supplied the overall system block diagram and specifications for the filters. The Foundation provided the production engineering for the filters and the development and design of the electronic circuitry. The basic theory of the harmonic speech compressor has been previously described by Schroeder, Logan, and Prestigiacomo of Bell Telephone Laboratories. The harmonic compressor halves the frequencies of the individual harmonic frequency components, and from these half frequency components synthesizes a new signal. If the input signal was applied at twice normal rate, the new signal will approximate the speech of a person speaking at twice his normal rate but with his normal pitch.

System and Circuits

A block diagram of the complete harmonic compressor system is shown in Figure 1. A filter bank separates voiced speech into individual harmonic frequency components. The amplitude and phase modulations of the filter outputs have narrow bandwidths. These are proportional to the syllabic rate rather than to the fundamental frequency. The speech input is resolved into its separate harmonics. The filter bank should be capable of separating harmonic frequencies spaced as closely as 100 Hz. Each filter should have a minimum attenuation in the rejection band of 24 db. The filter skirts should slope at least 12 db per octave. The frequency response of the com-

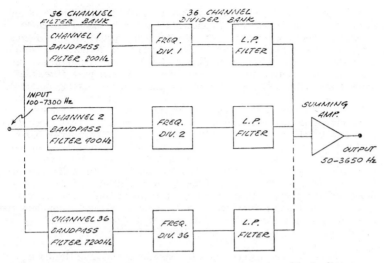

Figure 1. A. F. B. Harmonic compressor system block diagram.

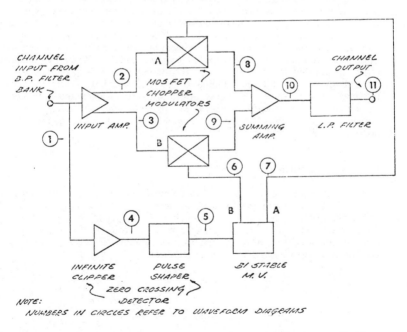

Figure 2. A. F. B. Harmonic compressor typical frequency divider channel block diagram.

bined filter band should be flat within 1 db and have a linear phase
response. The output of each individual filter is fed to its corresponding frequency divider. The divider must preserve the original
amplitude and phase relationship over a range of 70 db. The divider block diagram is shown in Figure 2. An input consisting of an
individual harmonic component from one of the bandpass filters is
applied simultaneously to an amplifier and a zero crossing detector.

Waveforms of the input and outputs are shown in Figure 3.
Zero crossings are detected by "infinite clipping." The clipped wave
is fed to a trigger pulse amplifier and shaper. The trigger pulse
controls the output of a bistable multivibrator. Trigger and multivibrator waveforms are shown in Figure 4. The multivibrator outputs are applied to the gates of two MOSFET chopper modulators in
opposite phases. The output of the audio amplifier is fed to the
drains of the chopper modulators in opposite phases. The outputs
of the two modulators are fed to a summing amplifier, combined and
filtered by a low pass filter to remove distortion. Modulator waveforms and output waveforms are shown in Figure 4.

Note that the output from the summing amplifier following the
modulators consists of a sine wave with every other period inverted.
This is a signal with a fundamental frequency one half that of the
input signal and with an amplitude and phase proportional to that input. The output filter removes the distortion components from a
half frequency signal. These consist mainly of the input signal now
seen as a second harmonic and the spikes caused by chopper transients. The outputs from all the channels are combined in a summing amplifier and fed to a tape or disc recorder. When the input
signal is applied at normal speed, the output signal is produced at
normal speed with all frequencies reduced to one-half. The recording may be reproduced at double speed with all frequencies returned
to normal. When the input signal is applied at double speed, the
output will be produced at double normal rate with all frequencies
normal.

Use and Capabilities

The Foundation will use the compressor as a research instrument and as a tool in the production of compressed talking books
and magazines. The system is capable of compressing music as
well as speech. The pitch of music may be lowered an octave by
similar techniques. Also speech expansion may be accomplished by
frequency multiplication instead of division.

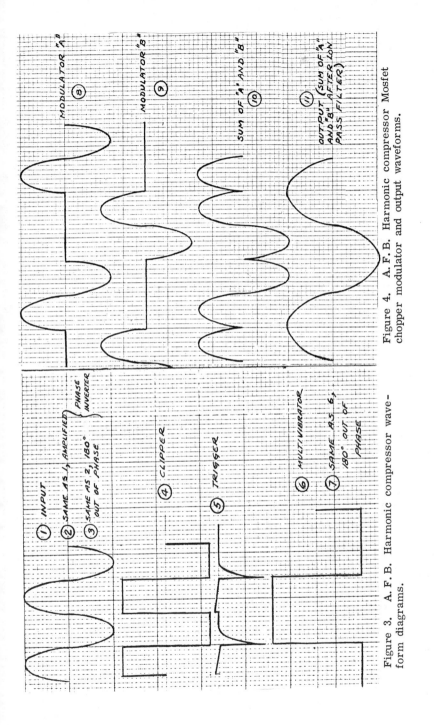

Figure 3. A.F.B. Harmonic compressor wave-form diagrams.

① INPUT
② SAME AS 1, AMPLIFIED } PHASE
③ SAME AS 2, 180° INVERTER OUT OF PHASE
④ CLIPPER
⑤ TRIGGER
⑥ MULTIVIBRATOR
⑦ SAME AS 6, 180° OUT OF PHASE

⑧ MODULATOR "A"
⑨ MODULATOR "B"
⑩ SUM OF "A" AND "B"
⑪ OUTPUT (SUM OF "A" AND "B" AFTER LOW PASS FILTER)

Figure 4. A.F.B. Harmonic compressor Mosfet chopper modulator and output waveforms.

DESCRIPTION OF TIME-COMPRESSED INFORMATIONAL COMMU-
NICATION AND OF THE SPEECH COMPRESSOR DEVELOPED BY
COMPRESSED TIME INCORPORATED

Compressed Time, Inc.

Definitions

Informational Communication. Although, broadly, all communication is intended to transmit information, we reserve this term
for the situation in which the communicator purposefully attempts to
transfer specific knowledge, subject matter, or facts to the receiver.

Time Compression. This is the condition wherein an existing informational communication such as a tape recording is presented to the receiver at a rate of information flow greater than the rate
of information flow at which it was originally produced. The essential characteristics of the informational communication, other than
its relation to the time dimension, remain unchanged by the compression process.

The Compression Process

The goal of time compression is to decrease the playback
time of a recorded informational communication without altering the
pitch characteristics or rhythm of the voice. Time compression is
accomplished by taking systematic samples in time of the recorded
communication and playing them back, in proper sequence, with no
time gaps between them. These samples are called Sampling Intervals, and the spaces between them are called Discard Intervals.

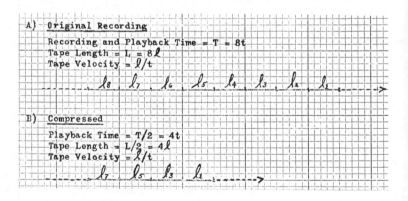

Figure 1. 2x compression by cutting and splicing.

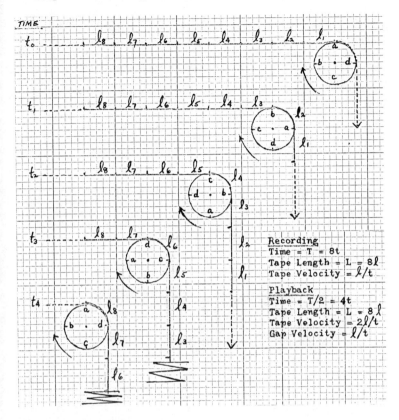

Figure 2.   Four-gap rotary head sampling tape played back at 2x.

Compressed speech is intelligible and natural when the Discard Interval is less than 40 milliseconds but greater than 10 msec. The process can be understood most easily by considering the case of a 2x rate increase since, at this rate, the Sampling Interval is of the same duration as the Discard Interval. Figure 1A shows a portion of a tape recording of length L= 8l. Let us cut this length L into eight equal segments and, by a mechanical splicing process, reassemble alternate segments as shown in Figure 1B. We now have a portion of tape of length L/2 which, when played back at the rate at which it was recorded, will present the recorded communication in half the time it took to record, that is, in T/2=4t. At rates of increase less than 2x, the Sampling Interval will be longer than the Discard Interval; at rates greater than 2x the Sampling Interval will be shorter than the Discard Interval.

Cutting and Splicing is obviously impractical, but the procedure is analogous to the sampling carried out by a rotating, multi-gap head. This is illustrated in Figure 2. Again, we will consider the case of a 2x rate increase and a portion of tape of length L which was recorded in time $T = 8t$. The four-cap rotary head and tape depicted in Figure 2 are moving in such a way that the playback tape velocity minus the gap velocity equals the original recording tape velocity (assuming a stationary recording head). In the time interval between t_0 and t_1, gap "a" reads tape segment 1_1. At time t_1, gap "a" moves away from the tape and stops reading; simultaneously, gap "b" begins to read segment 1_3. Segment 1_2 has never been in contact with a gap and, hence, is never read. Segments 1_1, 1_3, 1_5, 1_7 are Sampling Intervals; segments 1_2, 1_4, 1_6, 1_8 are Discard Intervals.

Rotary head speech compressors are of two general types. The rotary head may either sample directly from magnetic recording tape, or it may sample from a loop of magnetic recording material to which the signal has been transferred from the original recording medium. The latter arrangement allows the use of any recording medium as an input source.

The CTI Speech Compressor

The photograph shows the demonstration prototype of the CTI speech compressor. It is designed for standard cassette input; the output may be heard either through the self-contained loudspeaker or through earphones. The rectangular object on the right hand side is a cassette deck which is synchronously attached to the loop and head assembly located under the cover on the left side of the machine. The large knob at front and center is the variable rate control. Turning this knob provides continuously variable rate control from normal to 2.5x normal. The lever on the left, above the name plate turns the machine on and off and engages the friction drive system. The three knobs on the far right, directly in front of the cassette deck are the base, treble, and volume controls.

The friction drive system, which synchronizes the loop and rotary head assembly with the input source, can be adapted to any input source including optical sound tracks and disk recordings. A patent covering this system has been applied for. The rotary head employed in the CTI compressor is unique in two important respects: it can be produced at a cost well below that of heads of any other design, and it can be made with a smaller intergap distance than is possible with any other design. The intergap distance and the loop velocity determine the duration of the discard interval and, hence, the intelligibility and naturalness of the compressed speech. A patent covering the design of the head has been applied for.

Chapter 16

INTELLIGIBILITY AND TIME COMPRESSION EXAMINED

The three excerpts in the final chapter of Part One involve
fundamental problems that are associated with effective time compression procedures. The first describes experimental investigation
by R. G. Klumpp and J. C. Webster of the maximum compression
that will allow comprehension by untrained personnel. The work in
this experiment was performed at the Navy Electronics Center Laboratory at San Diego. The reported findings have not been negated
by subsequent investigations.

The material in the second excerpt is drawn largely from
Frances F. Pezzullo's master's thesis, completed under the direction of Sanford E. Gerber at the University of California's Santa
Barbara campus. Professor Gerber has written extensively on the
subject of dichotic listening and has engaged in research on this subject alone and jointly with Robert J. Scott (whose patent related to
this matter may be found in Part IV [number 19]). The present paper is concerned with determining the maximum amount of compression that is possible without destroying the intelligibility of the message.

The final selection in this chapter, by David H. Beetle, Jr.
and William D. Chapman, is concerned with a use of time-compression or expansion which is peculiar to a situation where it becomes
desirable to adjust the length of a word in time to a pre-designated
arbitrary and fixed time slot. The most common example of the
practical application of this procedure is the use of a computer for
the purpose of giving oral information in spoken language. Such use
is applicable, for example, to intercept a telephone call to a discon-
nected number and so forth. Another example is the use of a computer to give oral stock market quotations. This problem was previously dealt with by Rew [B354] in 1962. The procedure described
here was previously discussed by Chapman, the second author [B33],
in 1966.

INTELLIGIBILITY OF TIME-COMPRESSED SPEECH

R. G. Klumpp, J. C. Webster

Our work on message storage devices [Webster & L. Sharpe, "Improvement of Message Reception from 'Sequencing' Competing Messages," J. of Acoustical Soc. of Amer. 27:1194-98, 1955] has shown that, in a situation where several overlapping or rapidly sequenced voice messages come to a person, he performs better (fewer errors, fewer requests for message repeats, less time to complete a given problem) if he can store messages and listen to them when he is ready to process them. If a message is stored, even momentarily, it is ipso facto delayed and even though a man's overall performance is better and he handles problems faster with the aid of a storage device, the concept of delay is not easily accepted. One way of reducing delay in a message storage device is to listen to the stored messages in less time than it took to say them in the first place, i.e., speed up the speech.

There are two general methods of speeding up (time compressing) a recorded sample of speech: by increasing the speed of playback which raises all frequencies by an amount equal to the ratio of speedup, and by sampling in short segments and re-assembling a portion of the segments [B168] which does not shift the frequencies. The first method requires only an increase in playback shaft rotation rate, which can readily be accomplished by simple mechanical or electronic means. The second method, although possessing many advantages, requires relatively complex equipment [B105] with possible attendant disadvantages in a service communication system.

The experimental portion of this paper will be confined to results based on simple speedup with associated frequency shift. In the discussion of results, comparisons will be made to the results of the no-frequency-shift speedup. Simple frequency-shift-speedup is not new. Fletcher [B114] found articulation (intelligibility) scores for nonsense syllables recorded on phonograph disks for speeds of rotation from 1/2 to 1-1/2 of normal. He noted that "Changes of speed less than 10 per cent produce very little effect. For greater changes the articulation falls off rapidly. Decreasing the speed has a greater effect than increasing the speed."

The work reported by Fletcher was limited to difficult speech materials heard in the quiet over a relatively broad-band system. This study was designed to ascertain the effects of simple speedup on different types of speech materials over a narrow-band, noisy communication system. The study consists of four sub-experiments designed to determine the effects of simple speedup on speech intelligibility as influenced by differences among (1) talkers, (2) speech-to-noise ratios, (3) speech materials, and (4) listeners. These experiments will be referred to as experiments I through IV, respectively.

Procedure and Equipment

        The general procedure in these experiments was to record
speech materials on one track of a magnetic tape recorder and
thermal noise on the second track.   On playback the two tracks were
mixed electrically to get desired S/N ratios.   By means of a variable frequency power supply and a synchronous motor, the playback
speed of the tape recorder was varied in the ratio of from 0.75 to
2.00 as compared to the original recording speed.   Signals were
presented via PRD-8 earphones in a quiet room.   Speech level was
held constant at 80 db re 0.0002 d/cm^2.   For all experiments the
frequency response of the playback system was restricted to a 200-
to 2000-c.p.s. bandwidth with 10-db down points at 150 and 3500
c.p.s.   This was done to simulate a practical system in which
speedup might be used.

        Five types of speech materials were employed in the tests:
(1) two phonetically balanced (PB) word lists, (2) one list of 100
"R" words [both the PB and R lists are from J. P. Egan, Laryngoscope 58, 955, 1948--also found in L. L. Beranek, Acoustic Measurements, New York: Wiley, 1949, chap. XVII; the R lists are 100
words "made to resemble one another as closely as possible--in
which 15 vowels and diphthongs are represented by six words each;
the different consonant sounds are distributed among these 90 words
and the remaining 10 words are used to sample some of the compound consonants"], (3) one list of 100 two-digit numbers (pronounced
as, "two five, zero nine"), (4) one list of 20 five-syllable flight
phrases [C. Walker & J. W. Black, The Intrinsic Intensity of Oral
Phrases, Surgical Project NM 001 064, U.S. Naval School of Aviation Medicine: Bureau of Medicine. --Ed.:   this reference not veri-
fied] ("Speed is kept constant"), and (5) one list of 25 phrases similar to those sent over aircraft carrier flight deck communications
systems.

        Experiment I was run to train the listening crew, and to pick
out the most and least intelligible talkers from a crew of five.
Talkers and listeners were members of the U.S. Navy Electronics
Laboratory.   Five experienced listeners with normal or near normal
hearing were used.   The three male talkers were experienced talkers and had a General American accent.   The two female talkers
were not experienced and had a tinge of Southern drawl (accent).
PB lists were presented with a speech-to-noise (S/N) ratio of 7 db
as measured in the restricted bank with a VU meter.   For normal
speed playback an overall average score of 64 per cent was obtained
for the five talkers.   For playback in 0.67 of the original time
(speedup by a factor of 1.5) an overall average of 30 per cent was
obtained.   The most intelligible talker, male, produced scores of
71 and 45 per cent, while the least intelligible talker, female, produced scores of 55 and 23 per cent.   Only the materials recorded
by these two talkers were used for Experiments II and III.

        Figure 1 shows the results of Experiment II, which considered
the effect of speedup of S/N ratios of 30 and 7 db on the intelligibil-

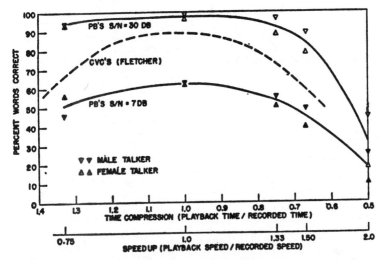

Figure 1.   Per cent PB words correct at different speedup ratios for two S/N ratios. Each datum point is based on 250 words (50 words x five listeners).   For comparison the data of Fletcher using CV, VC, and CVC syllables is shown as the dotted curve.

ity of PB words.   The listening order was from slow to fast (speed-up ratio of 0.75 to 2.0) for the male talker at the 30 db S/N, then at 7 db, and then slow to fast, female talker, 30 db, then 7 db. The female talker scores (1) exceed the male talker scores when the speech is slowed down, (2) equal the male scores at normal speeds, and (3) fall off rapidly at higher speedups.   This may well be because of the 150 to 3500 c.p.s. effective passband of the play-back system.   At speeds slower than normal the male talker's funda-mental voice frequency is shifted out of the passband; this is not so for the female talker.   For speeds higher than normal more of the female talker's higher partials than the male's higher partials are shifted out of the passband.   The point of practical value is that at a speedup ratio of 1.5, intelligibility of PB words drops between 14 and 17 per cent, depending upon S/N.

Table 1 shows the results of Experiment III which considered the effects of speedup ratios of 1.0 and 1.5 on four different types of materials; PB words, digits, flight phrases, and R lists at the 7 db S/N ratio and using both the male and the female talker.   The things to note are that (1) the digits are more intelligible than the phrases and in fact remain 95 per cent intelligible at a speedup ratio of 1.5, (2) phrases are 40 per cent more intelligible than learned PB words, and (3) learned PB words are about 25 per cent more in-telligible than "R" words heard for the first time.

Table 1

PERCENT DIGITS OR WORDS CORRECT
FOR FOUR SPEECH MATERIALS
At a S/N Ratio of 7 db At Normal Speed and At a Speedup of 1.5
(Time Compression of 0.67)

Speech material	Percent correct Time comp. 1.0	Time comp. 0.67	Diff.
Digits	98	95	3
Phrases	94	89	5
PB's	71	49	22
"R" Words	48	25	23

Note: Five listeners and one male and one female talker were used.
Each percentage is based on:
　　　Digits, (0,1,2,...9)(10)(2 talkers)(5 listeners)=1000.
　　　Phrases, (20 phrases)(3.95 words/phrase)(2 talkers)(5 listen-
　　　　　ers)=790.
　　　PB's, (50 words)(2 talkers)(5 listeners)=500.
　　　"R" Words, (100 words)(2 talkers)(5 listeners)=1000.

For Experiment IV only the male talker was used.   The purpose was to find the effect of speedup ratios of 1.0 and 1.5 under
more realistic conditions, namely, U.S.N. fleet personnel using
U.S.N. soundpowered phone equipment [Phrases were recorded using
a standard soundpowered microphone with the talker located in 100
db of ambient jet aircraft noise; playback was over the same restricted bandwidth system used in experiments I, II and III; S/N ratio was approximately 20 db] and simple phrases containing words
familiar to these listeners.   These phrases were cast in the form of
an address, a sender identification, the words "we need," a digit,
and the name of an item used on the flight deck, for example:
"Ready Room One, Flight Deck, we need six goggles."   Twenty-five
phrases comprised a test.   In each test ten stations were used five
times each as either the called or calling station, while the digits
1 to 10 and 25 different items were assigned at random.

Table 2 shows the results of this experiment.   Note that the
call signs (to and from) and digits are quite intelligible; it is the
items that suffer from speedup.   If all incorrect elements occurred
in the same message(s), the message score could equal the item
score.   If all element errors occurred in different messages, the
message score could be as low as 93.7 per cent (for 1.0) and 88.0
per cent (for 1.5).   The actual message score is somewhat closer
to this minimum score than to the maximum (item) score, indicating
that the errors tend to be independent of each other, i.e., they don't
occur in the same message.

Table 2

PERCENT ELEMENTS IN MESSAGES AND MESSAGES CORRECT
FOR SPEEDUP RATIOS OF 1.0 AND 1.5

| | | Percent correct | |
Speech material	Time comp. 1.0	Time comp. 0.67	Diff.
Address (To)	99.0	97.5	1.5
Sender (From)	99.2	98.5	0.7
Digit	99.9	99.5	0.4
Item	95.6	92.5	3.1
Av of above elements	98.4	97.0	1.4
Complete message	94.5	89.5	5.0

Note: Listeners were 12 Navy sound-powered phone operators.
One male talker was used. Each element percentage is based on
600 responses.

Discussion

The practical application of these results is that a speedup
of 1.5 (time-compression of 2/3) can be advantageously utilized in
routine message passing. Recorded messages can be played back
one and a half times faster, even with resultant frequency shifts,
and still maintain basic intelligibilities of roughly 90 per cent (Table 2). U.S.N. enlisted men with no experience in test taking, but
much experience in passing messages, scored as high as experienced laboratory personnel. The laboratory listeners with but a few
hours of listening to speeded speech dropped from 62 to only 45 per
cent (at 1.5 speedup) on difficult speech material (PB's) at an unfavorable S/N ratio of 7 db.

One must be circumspect in comparing these results to those
of other investigators because of differences in talkers, listeners,
choice of test words, psychological testing methods, etc. Kurtzrock
and Fairbanks show CVC monosyllabic scores of 85 per cent for
speedups of 2.0 allowing frequency shift and almost 90 per cent using the complex equipments which produce speedup but avoid frequency shift. Results on this more complex technique show that
spondaic words (words having two equally accented syllables: "baseball," "railroad," etc.) maintain better than 95 per cent intelligibility at speedups of 2.0. Comprehension of connected speech is retained for time compressions up to 0.5 (speedup of 2.0) at least until the I.Q. of the listener or the difficulty of the subject matter
becomes limiting [B109]. These studies suggest that it is not the
brain of the listener that is overloaded by the speech speedup. The
limit is apparently set by the ability of the ear to decode the frequency shifted patterns and not by the speedup per se. Even with

frequency shift plus speedup, a listener can be pushed 50 per cent faster than normal in comprehending messages with but a relatively small sacrifice of intelligibility.

LIMITS OF SPEECH TIME COMPRESSION

Sanford E. Gerber, Frances F. Pezzullo

The sampling method of speech time compression depends upon the discard of information. The sampling method of Garvey or Fairbanks is well known to the readers of this volume, who need only to be reminded that a signal time-compressed in this way contains only alternate segments of the original recording. With such a system it is possible to achieve any amount of compression that might be desired along the continuum from zero (no compression) to 100 per cent (which would delete the entire signal). In 1965, Scott developed a digital computer method of simulating the Fairbanks technique [B382]. Furthermore, he assumed that, given the Fairbanks method of compression, the loss of intelligibility due to increased compression was probably due to the discard of information. He therefore developed a system utilizing a hybrid computer whereby that information was restored. The system devised was called dichotic speech time compression and recorded the restored information on a second tape track to be presented to one ear while the first track (identical to that devised by Fairbanks) was presented to the other ear.

In the past, experiments comparing diotic and dichotic listening have failed to resolve the issue of whether the loss of intelligibility attendant upon time compression is due to the loss of information (that which has been discarded) or due to the rate at which the information is presented, therefore indicating a limitation within the auditory mechanism to process the signal. As speech is compressed in time, one of the primary perceptual effects is due to the acceleration of the rate at which the speech occurs. Several studies have measured the comprehension of speech as a function of the rate at which words were presented. Given these studies collectively, the relationship of comprehension to word rate slowly decreases from a normal uncompressed word rate of approximately 125 words per minute until a word rate of approximately 275 words per minute is reached, after which comprehension decreases sharply. It is important to recognize, however, that given an increase in the amount of compression, comprehension declines more rapidly than intelligibility. Intelligibility is much less affected than comprehension as a function of increased time compression. This finding would seem to suggest that as speech is compressed in time, factors in addition to intelligibility and comprehension are at work within the auditory perceptual mechanism.

Gerber and Scott [B178] demonstrated that an auditory signal presented dichotically at a compression ratio of 3:1 was more intelligible than a diotic signal presented at the same amount of compression. These findings indicated that, at least up to a compression ratio of 3:1, the intelligibility factor was solely a function of information lost or discarded rather than a function of the speed at which the signal was presented. In that paper [i.e., B178] Gerber and Scott raised the question of what causes the loss of intelligibility due to the compression of time. Is a loss of intelligibility due solely to a loss of information due to the discarding of information in the sampling method? Or, is the loss of intelligibility due to the press of time upon the auditory processing system? That is to say, if intelligibility fails at some compression ratio, is the failure due to excessive demands put upon the auditory processing system or is the failure due entirely to the loss of information?

The Dichotic Method

Before we can attempt to answer this question, we must first describe how dichotic speech time compression may be achieved. Recall that the sampling method of speech time compression depends upon the sampling of some of the speech information and the discarding of the rest of the speech information. Recall that if we have 50 per cent time compression (2:1), then we have retained half of the information in the original uncompressed speech signal and we have discarded half of the information in the original uncompressed speech signal. If the amount of compression is less than 50 per cent, then we have retained more than half of the original information; if the compression is more than 50 per cent, then we have discarded more than half of the information. To illustrate dichotic speech time compression it is easiest to talk about only 50 per cent. To achieve 50 per cent speech time compression by a time sampling method one elects a sampling interval. The optimum interval is probably 40 milliseconds. To accomplish 50 per cent speech time compression would require then retaining 40 milliseconds of the original speech signal, discarding the next 40 msec., retaining the next 40 msec., etc. Recall also that the effect of the sampling method is to abut the retained segments to each other and to lose the discarded segments entirely. Scott's [B382] idea was that it is not necessary to lose the discarded segments. Instead he pointed out that we could also retain the discarded segments and play them to one ear while the other ear heard the segments which would normally have been retained. When the compression is 50 per cent the effect then is that half of the information is presented to one ear and the other half is presented to the other ear. Saving time occurs insofar as the segments overlap 50 per cent with respect to each other. This is achieved, using a 40 millisecond discard interval, by delaying the onset of the signal 20 msec., then segment 1 begins in one ear. Twenty milliseconds after the beginning of segment 1, segment 2 begins in the other ear. Each segment is 40 msec. long. Of course, it is necessary to listen to this kind of dichotic compression with earphones. Listening to it in a sound field presents a very peculiar sort of echo effect even though the signals have nothing in common when the compression ratio is 2:1. When the compression ratio is less than 50 per cent, less than 2:1, then the two signals do indeed contain some common information. Similarly, if the compression is more than 2:1--that is, greater than 50 per cent--then some information is still not recovered in either ear since we only have two ears.

Is it useful to compress speech in the time domain dichotically? This question was addressed by Gerber [B197, B199] and by Gerber and Scott [B178]. In 1968, Gerber reported a study [B174] designed to compare the intelligibility of Scott's method of compression, restoring the discarded segments and listening dichotically, with the method described by Fairbanks. A hybrid computer system was used to prepare the dichotic materials for this study which consisted of Fairbanks' own recordings of the Rhyme Test words [B101]. For the study he used compression ratios of 2:1 (50 per cent), 3:2 (33 per cent), and 4:3 (25 per cent), and discard intervals of 30, 40, and 50 milliseconds. The results were compared as to rate of compression, method of presentation (diotic vs. dichotic), and discard interval. He found that for all of his subjects the dichotic signals were more intelligible than their diotic counterparts, although differences between the means of 2:1 with a discard interval of 40 milliseconds, 3:2 with a discard interval of 30 msec. and 4:3 with a discard interval of 40 msec. were not found to be significant. But it was found that on the average dichotic signals were more intelligible than diotic signals with the aggregate of dichotic signals being 97.69 per cent intelligible and the aggregate of diotic signals being 93.31 per cent. There were no significant differences in considering the compression ratio with respect to the method of presentation. However, with respect to discard intervals Gerber found a significant difference only between the 50 millisecond discard and the others; that is, a 50 msec. discard interval produced speech which was less intelligible than that produced with either a 30 or a 40 msec. discard interval at any compression ratio or method of presentation. However, a significant difference was found between dichotic and diotic presentations when the discard interval was 50 milliseconds. In this case the dichotic presentation was significantly superior. There were two important conclusions of this study. One was that significant improvement in intelligibility will not be found when the compression ratio is less than 2:1. The second important conclusion was the dichotic presentation as recommended by Scott [B382, B383] was preferable to diotic presentation.

Foulke and Wirth [B147] reported a similar study in which they used compression ratios of 47, 44, 41, 39 and 37 per cent, all with a discard interval of 40 milliseconds. They did not find a significant interaction between the method of presentation (diotic vs. dichotic) and amount of compression, but they did find significant differences with regard to the compression ratio in favor of dichotic speech when the ratio was 47 per cent. However, they felt this finding could have been due to uncontrolled factors in the experiment and was probably without experimental significance. Notice that this observation is in contrast to that of Gerber's [B179] observation. On the other hand, Foulke and Wirth considered that their study was not directly comparable to Gerber's since none of the words was reproduced in less than 50 per cent of the original production time. They concluded that the differences may have been due to sampling accidents. They also felt that the differences reported by Gerber were too small to be of any practical significance.

Later, Gerber reported a study that was designed to determine if the improved intelligibility of dichotic over diotic speech time compression was due to the dichotimizing of the signal or to the presentation of the dichotic signal dichotically (one signal in one ear and one signal in the other ear). This study showed that indeed it is necessary to listen to dichotic speech time compression dichotically. That is to say, if one listens to both signals with both ears, the intelligibility is poorer than if one listens to one signal with one ear and the other signal with the other ear. Remember that all of the original information is contained in a dichotic signal up to compressions of 50 per cent (compression ratio of 2:1). Therefore, Gerber concluded that--because the intelligibility scores of a dichotic signal were significantly higher, given a dichotic listening arrangement--the loss of intelligibility (at least up to a compression ratio of 2:1) inherent in speeded speech was "due to the loss of information and not due to any excessive rate demands upon the perceptual processor. "

At ratios greater than 2:1 are the intelligibility losses indeed due to a loss of information or are they due to an overload on the perceptual process? Gerber and Scott [B178] at the second Louisville conference reported a study designed to determine the cause of intelligibility losses at a compression ratio of 3:1. Bear in mind that a compression ratio of 3:1, according to the Fairbanks method of compression, only one-third of the original information is presented to the listener; while if we use a dichotic means of speech time compression, two-thirds of the original information is present. In this experiment Fairbanks' Rhyme Test was again used with compression and dichotimization again being effected by a hybrid computer system. Three different presentations, dichotic, diotic and time-restored, were used with a discard interval of 40 milliseconds. It is to be pointed out that, at any compression ratio, time restoration involves repeating of the segments in the diotic presentation. However, above a compression ratio of 2:1 it is impossible to recover all of the information lost by compression even by dichotimizing the signal. Results showed that intelligibility scores using dichotic presentation at a compression ratio of 3:1 were significantly better than either diotic or time-restored at the same ratio. This fact lent further support to the "information lost" concept but conclusive evidence was still not available. The question remained: is the loss of intelligibility due to the compression of speech in time--a function of the loss of information--or to excessive demands being put upon our auditory rate processing ability? In the study reported in this chapter it was hoped that the problem would be resolved conclusively one way or the other.

The Problem

Gerber and Scott [B178] demonstrated that a dichotic signal was more intelligible than a diotic one, both at 3:1, indicating that the intelligibility factor was a function of information lost. The purpose of the present investigation was to determine, given a compression ratio of 4:1, if the same thing held true.

Because of the nature of diotic and dichotic speech time compression, a 4:1 dichotic signal would contain the same amount of information as a signal that has been compressed at a ratio of 2:1 and presented diotically. Therefore, if intelligibility losses in time compressed speech are in fact a function of the discarded information, then the intelligibility of the two signals, 4:1 dichotic and 2:1 diotic, should be approximately equal. But if intelligibility losses are due to rate of presentation, thereby indicating a temporal limit in auditory perceptual ability, then 4:1 dichotic might prove too fast a rate to be processed auditively. If the signal were presented diotically at a compression ratio of 4:1 and proved less intelligible than that presented dichotically at a compression ratio of 4:1, then further support would be provided for the hypothesis suggested by Gerber and Scott's research on 3:1 compression that losses are due to information discarded rather than to the speed of presentation of the stimulus material. The hypothesis of the present study was that 4:1 diotic would be less intelligible than 4:1 dichotic, which would approximate intelligibility of speech compressed 2:1 diotic. If this hypothesis proved to be true, then we would demonstrate that losses of intelligibility are due to losses of information and not to the press of time. Data relevant to this hypothesis were gathered by Pezzullo [B329] and are reported below.

Procedures

The subjects in this experiment were one male and 14 female adults ranging in age from 22 to 59 years. It was determined that age was not a significant parameter. Selection was based upon the subject's awareness of any hearing loss or pre-existing ear pathology. Those subjects in which pathology was found were excluded from the study. The experiment was conducted in an audiological laboratory which was relatively free of ambient noise. As many as four subjects were seated at a table wearing matched telephonics TDH-39 earphones in MX-41/AR cushions attached to an Ampex model 350AG recording system with output by means of a MacIntosh 225 amplifier. The length of the prepared tapes required three different listening sessions of approximately 45 minutes for each subject.

Dichotic speech time compression was created for the study by the use of a hybrid computer system similar to that described by S. E. Gerber ["Scientific Computation in Speech Research," Computer Studies in Humanities & Verbal Behav. 2:91-7, 1969]. A PDP-7 digital computer, manufactured by the Digital Equipment Corporation of Maynard, Massachusetts, was on-line with the analog portion of the hybrid system, an EAI-8800 made by Electronic Associates, Inc. , of Long Branch, New Jersey. Fairbanks' recordings of the Rhyme Test words were the stimulus material used for this study. The recordings of the Rhyme Tests were input from the tape play-back via the analog computer interface to the analog-to-digital converter which put the digitized speech onto magnetic tape. Then, under operator control, the computer time-compressed the digitized speech and wrote this version onto another magnetic tape. When the compression process had been completed, the compressed digital tape was output via the digital-to-analog converter onto audio tape. In this way all 250 items of the Fairbanks' recordings were compressed and dichotimized. Two master tapes were compressed in the above manner. Both tapes represented a discard interval of 40 milliseconds but one was compressed to a ratio of 2:1 and dichotimized while the other was compressed to a ratio of 4:1 and dichotimized.

Three different listening conditions were prepared from the compressed master tapes: 4:1 dichotic, 4:1 diotic and 2:1 diotic. To control for learning, the order of presentation of the three different conditions was randomized within certain limits: no single listening condition or Rhyme Test was allowed to follow itself. Because the compressed tapes produced by the computer were dichotimized and because it was necessary to reorder the tests and to present a 2:1 dichotic and a 4:1 diotic condition, it was necessary to re-record from the master tapes. For the 4:1 dichotic listening condition it was only necessary to record in the desired order the contents of the master tape onto the test tape. To create the 2:1 and 4:1 diotic conditions it was necessary to copy only one channel of the master tape onto both channels of the test tape. The master tapes were recorded from a Sony TC-200 tape recording system. The resulting test tapes contained all 250 items of the Fairbanks' Rhyme Test, randomized as to order of the test and the listening conditions (each condition contained a complete series of tests) and recorded with a period of ten seconds between the start of one word and the start of the following word. The order of presentation of the tapes was controlled such that one-third of the subjects heard tape 1 first, one-third heard tape 2 and one-third heard tape 3 first. The subjects were presented with lists of all the words contained in the Rhyme Test in blocks of six. They were asked to cross out each of the words heard. It has been observed that right and left earphone placement does not make any decided difference in intelligibility and therefore no specific instructions were given in reference to earphone placements.

Results

A single factor analysis of variance using the percentage of correct scores from the 2:1 compression with diotic listening, the 4:1 compression with dichotic listening, and the 4:1 compression with diotic listening indicated that there were significant differences beyond the 1 per cent level among the scores of the three listening conditions. In order to determine where the differences lay, and between which scores, a two-tailed t test was conducted. The mean per cent correct for the three different listening conditions were as follows: 4:1 diotic, 81.92 per cent; 4:1 dichotic, 81.38; and 2:1 diotic, 90.04 per cent. The value of t for the 4:1 diotic and 4:1 dichotic listening conditions did not indicate a significant source of variation. The value of t for the 4:1 diotic and 2:1 diotic presentations was significant in favor of the 2:1 diotic presentation at the 1 per cent level, as was t for the 4:1 dichotic and 2:1 diotic conditions. That is, the differences between 2:1 and 4:1 dichotic were significant at the 1 per cent level, whereas the differences between 4:1 dichotic and 4:1 diotic were not significant.

In terms of the intelligibility of the three different listening conditions the 2:1 diotic signal was significantly more intelligible than both the 4:1 diotic and the 4:1 dichotic signal presentations. The mean score for the 4:1 diotic signal was not significantly superior to the 4:1 dichotic signal. Therefore, in ranking the three conditions as to intelligibility the 2:1 diotic signal was the most intelligible with the 4:1 diotic and 4:1 dichotic signals being approximately equal to one another and less intelligible than the 2:1 diotic presentation.

Conclusions and Implications

The results of the present investigation indicated that a compressed 2:1 signal presented diotically was significantly more intelligible than a compressed 4:1 signal presented diotically. These results could be interpreted in one of two ways: because of the rate, compression at 4:1 leads to an inability within the auditory system to process the signal; or, the loss of information inherent in the 4:1 diotic presentation would be responsible for the significant difference.

In comparing 4:1 dichotic with 4:1 diotic compression scores, the results did not yield a statistically significant difference. This fact indicated that, given a compression ratio of 4:1, intelligibility losses were probably due to a failure of the auditory system to process the signal at the 4:1 compression ratio because of the seemingly excessive compression.

Results also showed that 2:1 diotic compression was significantly better at the 1 per cent level of confidence than 4:1 dichotic compression, although the information quantity of the two presentations was the same. This result, in conjunction with the 4:1 dichotic by 4:1 diotic result, provided conclusive evidence that a compression ratio of 4:1 is indeed too fast for the information presented to be processed auditively.

Gerber and Scott [B178] showed that, up to a compression ratio of 3:1, a dichotic signal was more intelligible than its diotic counterpart. The present investigation showed that, at a compression ratio of 4:1, a dichotic signal was not more intelligible than its diotic counterpart and indeed was significantly less intelligible than a 2:1 diotic signal, both signals containing essentially the same amount of information.   It was therefore the general conclusion, given the results of this study, that the greater the amount of compression in time, the greater the intelligibility loss of the speeded signal, which is due to an inherent inability of the human auditory mechanism to process the speeded signal because of the press of time placed upon that mechanism.   The reduced intelligibility is not due to a loss of information as a result of the compression.   In other words, it appears that a compression ratio of 3:1 (the signal being one-third the duration of the original signal) is not too fast a rate to be processed, but 4:1 is too fast and therefore intelligibility scores suffer.   If one examines Figure 1, one can see an increasing advantage of dichotic compression up to a ratio of approximately

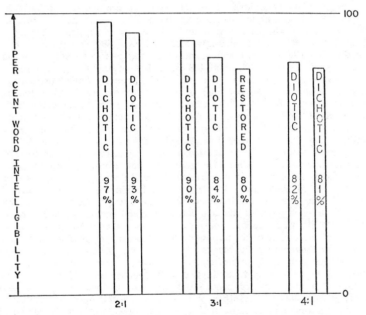

Figure 1.   The effect of dichotic compression on intelligibility.

3:1 compression but at 4:1 compression the dichotic advantage is apparently lost, indicating that at this point the factor of the press of time is operating rather than the factor of the amount of information presented being the decaying factor.

It would appear that at some yet to be determined point between 67 and 75 per cent compression, dichotic listening loses its

464   Time-Compressed Speech

advantage over diotic listening because of the rate of presentation
of the material, thereby making these conditions approximately equal
as to intelligibility. As the compressed dichotic signal contains
more information than the compressed diotic signal (given the same
rate of compression), and up to a ratio of at least 3:1 is more intelligible, it would be interesting to determine at what point between
67 and 75 per cent compression the rate becomes too fast to maintain the dichotic advantage. If this were resolved, then we could
determine at what point along the compression continuum dichotic
presentation of speeded speech remains superior to the diotic presentation and thereby utilize that yet-to-be-determined compression
ratio to its best advantage in the fields of education, science and
technology.

Epilogue

     Further consideration of our several studies and of the data
reported herein had led us to consider some additional possibilities.
We are now of the impression that our use of Fairbanks' Rhyme
Test has led us to misleadingly high scores. We remind our reader that the Rhyme Test represents a closed response set, whereas
a test such as the traditional PB word list or the CNC word list
represents an essentially open set. We currently have the feeling
that an open response set may lead to lower scores than a closed
response set. If this is the case, then our conclusions relevant to
the limit of time compression for intelligibility may be based upon
misleadingly high data. We are presently reconsidering some of our
data, using the CNC word list [B326] rather than the Rhyme Test
word list. Moreover, an additional consideration has come to mind.
In all of our later studies, including the one reported herein, we
have fixed the compression ratio at 40 milliseconds. A number of
studies [B174, B104] have led to the conclusion that discard intervals
much longer than 40 milliseconds are excessive. Certainly our own
data have shown that a discard interval of 50 msec. renders poorer
intelligibility than discard intervals of either 40 or 30 msec. What
we have not considered, however, would be the effects of discard
intervals longer than 50 msec. It is not our purpose in the present
paper to consider the significance of a value of 50 milliseconds but
there is some reason to believe that it represents a kind of "magic
number" in the auditory processing system and there is a real possibility that the intelligibility of time compressed speech when the
discard interval is greater than 50 msec. may, in fact, be superior
to the intelligibility when the discard interval is set precisely at 50
msec. This subject is currently under investigation along with the
factor of test materials.

     In essence, however, the issue has been to resolve the mat-
ter of there being an excessive rate of auditory processing time regardless of the amount of information. The data of the present study
suggests that four times the normal rate is too much, whereas the
data of previous studies has suggested that three times the normal
rate is not too much. Again it needs to be stressed that what we

are measuring here is intelligibility and not comprehension, and that intelligibility is more resistant to degradation as a function of time compression than is comprehension. In any case we would tentatively suggest that quadrupling the rate of speech is excessive.

FLEXIBLE ANALOG TIME COMPRESSION OF SHORT UTTERANCES

David H. Beetle, Jr., William D. Chapman

A technique for decreasing the duration of spoken words or short phrases is of practical interest in relation to vocabulary preparation for computer speech output devices. The IBM 7770 Audio Response Unit stores its vocabulary of words and subphrase elements in analog form on the tracks of a magnetic drum. The drum completes one revolution every 500 milliseconds and, thus, reads out a word or a subphrase element completely in this time. Response messages are compiled by sequentially selecting appropriate tracks or a silence interval for successive 500-millisecond intervals until the message is complete. Generating the vocabulary to be stored on the drum involves recording on an analog tape the list of necessary words and phrases uttered by a trained speaker, compressing words when necessary to fit the 483 milliseconds of available recording time on the drum tacks (17 milliseconds for track switching), and recording these compressed words on the drum in synchronism with the fixed time slot.

Originally, this vocabulary generation was done by digitizing the output of the analog master tape, feeding the digitized signal into a computer, and generating under program control a digital tape of compressed words written in 483-millisecond records. The output of each record of this digital tape was converted back to analog form and recorded on the proper track of the drum. For this purpose, the digital tape was started by a "ready" signal from the drum, thus synchronizing the drum and tape properly.

Two major drawbacks were found with this analog-digital-analog vocabulary preparation method. First, the signal quality was degraded by the two conversions, A-D and D-A. Second, the time compression was periodic and linear in the sense that each portion of the word was reduced in length by the same percentage. The advantage of nonlinear or selective time compression for vocabulary preparation will be discussed in Section III. Neither of these drawbacks was inherent to the processing methods used, and each could be corrected for a price. The first drawback can be avoided by using a higher sampling rate and more bits per sample at the cost of increased processing time. The second drawback, however, can be cured, within the limitations of the present state of the art, only by using a human operator to interact with the computer compression process, and immediately judge aurally the results of his interaction.   Hardware, software, and processing time costs would be greatly increased if these techniques had been used.

Of course, it would have been desirable if a process could be designed which would overcome inexpensively and practically the aforementioned drawbacks, still adequately perform the task of time compression, and have the ability to synchronize with the drum for recording.   The subject of this paper is the device that was designed as the key to achieving these goals.   This device was named SPACELOOP (SPeech Analog Compressing and Editing LOOP).   Section I gives a brief description of SPACELOOP and describes its method of operation.   Section II is concerned with the key design features of the device that were necessary to achieve acceptable quality and accuracy.   Section III discusses selective time compression and gives some qualitative rules for proper compression, and Section IV mentions possible uses of this device in other areas of speech study.

I. Physical and Operational Description

Mechanically, SPACELOOP consists of a 100-inch magnetic tape loop, a three-speed drive assembly, and 10 magnetic heads. Two of the heads, one erase and one record playback, are mounted to operate on the upper track of the quarter-inch tape and are used for timing information.   The remaining eight heads operate on the lower, or audio, track.   Six are used for playback alone, one for both recording and playback, and one for erase.   The seven audio heads used for playback are mounted on sliders on a 20-inch track, such that they can be moved and positioned at various points on the track.

Electrically, SPACELOOP consists of the circuitry for performing the obvious functions of erasing and recording, as well as playing back the signal from the loop using the playback heads, one by one, in a controllable sequence.   In addition, circuitry is included to operate a drive idler solenoid, thus starting the loop at the proper time to synchronize it with the drum of the Audio Response Unit.   Operationally, the seven movable playback heads are the key to the function of time compression and the electrically operated idler is the key to the function of synchronizing the compressed word on the tape loop with the drum time slot, an operation that we call "time-slotting."

Time Compression.   After a word or phrase has been recorded on the loop in a normal manner, it may be reproduced by amplifying the signal from any one of the seven playback heads.   The heads all read the same signal, but at different times, the delay being proportional to the distance between the heads.   In Figure 1, the playback heads are numbered 1 through 7, beginning with the head which the signal passes last.   In the case of time compression, the system is initiated by reproducing from head 1 until a point in the utterance is reached where the beginning of a deletion is desired.

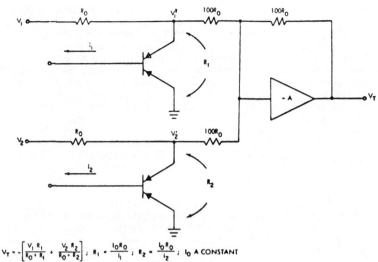

$$V_T = -\left[\frac{V_1 R_1}{R_0 + R_1} + \frac{V_2 R_2}{R_0 + R_2}\right] ; \quad R_1 = \frac{I_0 R_0}{i_1} ; \quad R_2 = \frac{I_0 R_0}{i_2} ; \quad I_0 \text{ A CONSTANT}$$

ASSUME THAT $V_1 = V_2 \triangleq V$

IT CAN BE SHOWN THAT IF ;

$\quad i_1\ i_2 = i_0^2$, OR EQUIVALENTLY IF $\ln i_1 + \ln i_2 = 2 \ln I_0$

$\quad$ THEN V_T IS ALWAYS EQUAL TO $-V$

IT CAN BE FURTHER SHOWN THAT IF;

$\quad \ln i_1 = e_0 + e(t), \ln i_2 = e_0 - e(t);$ DEFINED SUCH THAT $i_1\ i_2 = $ CONSTANT

THEN $\dfrac{V_1'}{V_1} = \dfrac{1}{1 + \exp[e(t)]}$ AND $\dfrac{V_2'}{V_2} = \dfrac{1}{1 + \exp[-e(t)]}$ ARE THE RESULTING ATTENUATIONS

AS AN EXAMPLE

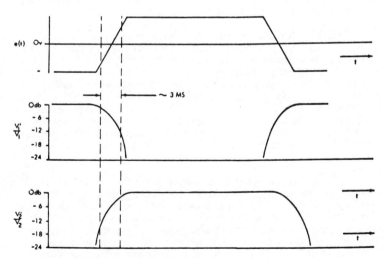

Figure 1. Simplified cross-fading circuit and control signals.

At this point, the reproduce amplifier is switched rapidly from head 1 to head 2, thereby deleting the portion of the utterance between those two heads at the instant of switching. The deleted portion consists of the signal which has already passed head 2, but has not yet reached head 1. Reproduction continues from head 2 until the beginning of a second deletion is desired, when the reproduce amplifier is switched rapidly from head 2 to head 3, thereby deleting the portion of the utterance between those two heads. The process is repeated until the desired number of deletions has taken place, and the last head to be connected reproduces the remainder of the utterance. Time expansion is performed in a similar manner, but by sequencing the heads in reverse numerical order, resulting in intervals of repeated signal.

There are two parameters associated with each deletion: the point in time where the deletion interval is to begin, and the duration of the deletion interval. The beginning of the desired dele tion interval is set by controlling the elapsed time from a reference point on the timing track to the initiation of the head switching operation. The length of the deletion interval is adjusted by varying the spacing between the playback heads. The operator thus has sufficient control over the compression process to use selective non-periodic deletions to determine the most appropriate way to shorten the utterance. Further, he has immediate aural feedback from the output, and thus can instantly evaluate the effects of the compression. If this method does, indeed, work without degrading signal quality substantially, it affords a means for time compression which eliminates the two drawbacks of the original analog-digital-analog method of vocabulary preparation described at the beginning of this paper. The design features necessary for obtaining acceptable signal quality are discussed in Section II.

Time-Slotting. Another operation necessary for vocabulary preparation is that of time-slotting. Time-slotting is the process of recording the compressed utterance on the drum in proper relation to the 483-millisecond recording space actually available. Synchronization of two movable media must be accomplished by cueing the position of one medium, and starting it in response to a "start" signal from the second medium. Since the drum is a large mass device, the method chosen was to cue the tape loop containing the utterance to a known position (after all the compression controls are set properly), and then to start it precisely and rapidly with a signal from the drum.

In practice, a delay is employed after the "start of time slot" signal from the drum to compensate for finite operating time of the loop capstan idler. The delay time is set to synchronize the beginning of the utterance on the loop with the next "start of time slot" signal on the drum when the drum recording operation is initiated. An additional adjustable delay is provided to enable the operator to center a short word in the time slot. Further delay intervals, in multiples of 500 milliseconds, are also provided to delay the initiation of drum recording until the beginning of the later revolutions of the drum. This is done so that the operator may record the second, or later, half-second segment of a long word or phrase in the drum time-slot.

II. Design Features

Mechanical. The most important mechanical feature of SPACELOOP is the array of movable playback heads. Seven heads form this array and thus allow up to six deletions to be taken from the audio signal, a number which has proved sufficient to allow natural sounding compression for most words. These heads are mounted on aluminum sliders that may be freely moved along a 20-inch aluminum track and then locked in place by a thumbscrew. The distance between adjacent heads and the velocity of the tape determine the duration of the deletion interval. Analogously, the maximum total deletion time is fixed by the length of the track, the minimum individual deletion times by the distance between the gaps of two adjacent heads positioned as close as possible to each other, and the total recording time by the total loop length. The aluminum sliders were designed to be narrower than the heads, so that the minimum head spacing is determined by the head dimensions alone.

The length of the loop is 100 inches, the highest loop speed is 100 inches per second, and the track length is 20 inches. Thus, the maximum total deletion time equals one-fifth of the total loop length, or 200 milliseconds at this loop speed. For the worst case, this would allow shortening a 683-msec. word to 483 msec. In order to handle phrases that are to occupy more than one time slot on the drum, two additional loop speeds of 50 and 25 inches per second were provided, with corresponding loop rotation times of two and four seconds. Here, the maximum total deletion time is scaled upward proportionately. Each of the heads is 0.7 inch wide, making the minimum deletion at 100 inches per second equal to seven milliseconds. In addition, note that a distance of one inch between head gaps at this speed corresponds to 10 msec., allowing the use of a rule marked in tenths of an inch to be conveniently used for time calibration. Another reason for choosing the one-second loop rotation time was to have a portion of the loop unrecorded, about 30 per cent in this case, to allow time to switch the playback amplifier back to the first head before the word is repeated.

The second most important mechanical feature of SPACELOOP is the solenoid-operated drive idler, which pinches the tape against the capstan to provide loop motion. It is important to maintain consistency in the time lapse between the application of an electrical signal to the solenoid and the attainment of proper speed by the loop. Any inconsistency will directly affect the position of the word in the drum time-slot. The electrical and mechanical time constants of the solenoid and solenoid linkage determine the largest part of this time lapse, and were found to be highly consistant. The remainder of the time lapse is determined by the time required to overcome the inertia of the idler and the loop. This portion depends on the mass of the idlers and tape loop, the available friction between the idler and the capstan, and the friction between the tape loop and the various tape guides. These factors could be extremely variable. The eight main tape guides in SPACELOOP, where the tape is bent at 90 degrees, use ball bearing idlers and produce very little friction. They do add inertia, but the acceleration time needed to overcome this was found to be negligible due to the small mass and short radius involved. The remaining tape guides are polished to reduce friction. The main idler is driven continuously, either by the main capstan when the tape is in motion, or by a dummy capstan when the solenoid is deactivated and the tape is at rest. Thus, no time is wasted in accelerating the capstan idler. As a result of these factors, the starting time of SPACELOOP is consistent to within one millisecond, even though 45 msec. are required to accelerate the tape to a constant velocity.

The remaining mechanical design of SPACELOOP follows standard practice. A three-speed synchronous motor is used to ensure accurate and consistent speed at three tape velocities. The aluminum sliders each contain two tape guides designed to produce a 15-degree tape wrap around the head gap. The remaining tape guides were placed such that a 100-inch loop would fit into the available space, a movable guide was included to allow easy tape threading, and a spring-loaded tension arm was included to ensure proper tape tension. It should be mentioned in connection with the mechanical design that either a heat tape splicer or video splicing tape is required for manufacturing the loop. The use of ordinary splicing tape results in the gradual separation of the tape splice due to constant tension, and the splicing adhesive is deposited on contact surfaces, resulting in dirt collection and tape wear.

Electronic Design. The two most important electronic design aspects of SPACELOOP are the circuits which control the switching operation between playback head signals, and the circuits which allow the operator to control where in the utterance a deletion is to be made.

Playback Signal Control. Ideally, the switching operation should not introduce noise or distortion in the output signal and should minimize sharp transients generated by rapidly switching between two different signals. The transients were minimized by following the practice of cross-fading the head signals.

This is the practice of gradually increasing the amplitude of the signal from the second head, while simultaneously decreasing the amplitude of the signal from the first head. An ideal condition was hypothesized for which the outputs of the first and second heads were equal-amplitude in-phase sine waves. The cross-fading circuitry was then designed such that the output of the playback amplifier would remain instantaneously equal to the input sinusoid throughout the cross-fading operation. In specific detail, as was shown in Figure 1, the output of each of the heads is fed into a separate voltage divider. The output of each voltage divider is then fed into a high-impedance input-summing network which feeds the remainder of the playback amplifier. Signal amplitude control is accomplished by using a variable resistance device as the shunt leg of each voltage divider. This device is a symmetrical transistor which has the following properties: (1) a small-signal collector-to-emitter resistance which is inversely proportional to base current; (2) a constant, nearly zero, open-circuit collector-to-emitter offset voltage over the required range of base current; and (3) linear resistance characteristic for small collector-to-emitter signals, thus providing low distortion.

Under the assumption of equal input voltages, it can be shown that, to achieve a constant output cross-fade, the product of the base currents must remain constant and equal to the square of the current required to adjust either divider such that the signal is attenuated by one-half. This is equivalent to specifying that the sum of natural logarithms of the base currents must be constant. An equal-amplitude cross-fade is accomplished by equating the logarithm of each base current to a voltage time function. This is realized by a simple circuit, which generates and takes the logarithm of opposite phase trapezoidal voltage functions, each with the same average voltage. This was shown more clearly in Figure 1. The cross-fade duration was chosen to be approximately three milliseconds.

In order to avoid duplicating the cross-fading circuits for each adjacent pair of heads, additional switching is required. This is accomplished, as shown in Figure 2, by providing two audio channels, labeled Channel A and Channel B, and sequentially switching the proper heads to the proper channel. Heads 1, 3, 5, and 7 may be switched to Channel A, and heads 2, 4, and 6 may be switched to Channel B. Initially, head 1 is connected to Channel A and head 2 to Channel B; also, initially, the output of Channel A passes through the cross-fading circuitry unattenuated, while the output of Channel B is completely attenuated. After the first cross-fading operation, the reverse condition exists, and the signal from head 2, connected to Channel B, is passed to the output amplifier, while the signal from head 1 is completely attenuated by the cross-fading circuitry. At this time, we can switch the input to Channel A from head 1 to head 3 without affecting the output; as a result, relatively noisy switches may be used. After the next cross-fading operation, the output from head 3, connected to Channel A, is passed to the output amplifier, and Channel B is completely attenuated. Similarly at this time, the input to Channel B is switched from head 2 to head 4 without affecting the output, preparing for the third deletion. Reed relays are used for switching the heads. Their fast operation and ability to be driven easily by transistor circuitry make them attractive for this purpose.

Proper equalization also plays an important part in reducing noise introduced by the cross-fading operation. A constant current recording characteristic is used in SPACELOOP and, thus, an integration or falling frequency characteristic is needed in the playback circuitry to return to a flat overall frequency response. The sym-

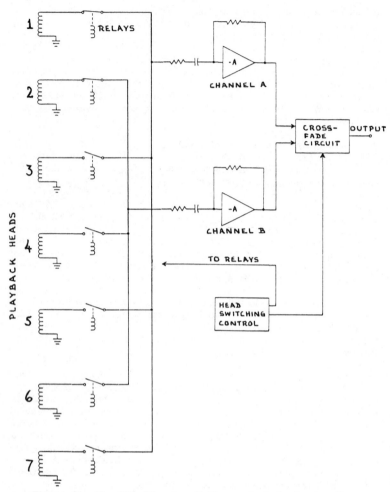

Figure 2.   Simplified head-switching and playback circuit.

metrical transistors used in the cross-fading circuit are not perfectly symmetrical and, therefore, have a small offset voltage which
varies as the base current varies.   This characteristic produces
low-frequency noise below 500 Hz during the cross-fading operation.
If the integration or equalization were placed after the cross-fading
circuit, its frequency characteristic would tend to emphasize this
noise.   Therefore, the equalization is placed in each channel amplifier before their output signals are fed to the cross-fade circuit.
The head inductance is used as the equalization impedance.   The remaining audio circuitry follows standard practice and therefore will

not be described here.   Next, the logic and timing circuitry associated with the head switching operation will be described.

Deletion Initiation Control.   As pointed out earlier, to control the compression process the operator most be able to adjust
two parameters accurately: the length of a deletion, and the beginning point of the deletion.   As was shown earlier, the first parameter is controlled by adjusting the distance between adjacent heads.
To control the second parameter, both an accurate time reference
related to some portion of the word, and a controllable accurate delay from this time reference are necessary.   A useful reference
time would be the start of the word.   Although the start of the word
is relatively easy to locate grossly, it is difficult to maintain a re-
peatable measurement to a fraction of a pitch period tolerance each
time the tape loop completes a revolution.   In SPACELOOP, this
problem was surmounted by using a start-of-word detector only once,
and placing an accurately detectable time reference mark on the
second track of the tape loop in a fixed relationship with this event.
The reference mark is no more accurate than the start-of-word detector; however, once recorded, it provides a consistent time reference for further operations.   The timing reference is recorded on
the timing track by a pulse of current passing through the head associated with that track.   The recorded signal is read out as a voltage doublet which is accurately detectable.   This same time reference is also used for hand-cueing the loop in preparation for recording onto the drum time-slot.   If, now, an accurate adjustable time
delay is used to reference the portion of the word where a deletion
is desired, then this deletion will be made consistently at the same
point in the word for subsequent rotations of the tape loop.

An accurate, consistent, linear voltage ramp is the key to
providing the time delay function.   The ramp is started by the timing marker at the point where the initial indication of the start-of-
word was given.   Ten-turn potentiometers are used to provide adjustable voltages which are compared with the ramp voltage.   When
the ramp voltage equals a potentiometer voltage, a pulse is generated which initiates the cross-fading process.   After a delay sufficient to ensure the completion of cross-fading, the relays connect
the next head to the unused channel.   Six potentiometers are used,
one each to indicate the desired beginning of the six available deletion intervals.   A seventh potentiometer is supplied to provide a
calibrated oscilloscope synchronizing pulse.   Since the most commonly used tape speed is one revolution per second, the digital potentiometer knobs are calibrated directly in milliseconds from start-
of-word.

The slope of the voltage ramp is $1/100$ volt per millisecond.
Considerable care was taken to reset the ramp accurately to the
same starting point before each sweep, and to ensure ramp linearity
to the same tolerance as that of the potentiometers.   Other electronic and operational features follow essentially standard practice and
will not be discussed here.

III. Selective Compression Applied to Vocabulary Preparation

The principal advantage of SPACELOOP over previous time-compression methods lies in its ability to compress a word in a selective manner. Selective compression implies that some portions of the word are shortened by a greater percentage than are others. As will be discussed, selective compression allows the duration of a word to be shortened while changing only slightly the pace or perceptual utterance speed of the word.

Applications. In the recording process, the words are uttered in a metronomed cadence with a slightly rising pitch contour in order to make their duration relatively brief and the utterance pace uniform. Ideally, the words would be stored in this form with naturally varying lengths, requiring random access to synthesize messages by sequencing varying length words. However, because the IBM 7770 contains synchronous word storage with a fixed time-slot of minimal length, this is not possible. Thus, about 15 to 20 per cent of the words uttered as described must be time compressed to fit the 483-millisecond time slot. The primary purpose of SPACELOOP is to perform this compression. The secondary objective in time compression is to minimize the change in pace of compressed words, thereby forming a message that has few annoying pace changes. Although the resulting message is unavoidably cadenced due to the fixed time-slot length, it should at least sound as if it could have been uttered by a speaker with uniform pace in the given sequence of words.

During the preparation of vocabularies for the IBM 7770, some experience has been gained concerning the portions of words that appear to have the least influence on pace and may, therefore, be deleted without unduly increasing the pace. From this experience, we have generated a set of guidelines for segment deletion so that words may be processed by a relatively inexperienced operator in very little time. At the present writing, rigorous tests with listening panels and a variety of operators have not been conducted to confirm the broad utility of these guidelines and, consequently, they are offered here merely as qualitative suggestions for points of interest in further quantitative research.

As a general rule, segments may be more easily taken from steady-state portions than from dynamic portions of a word. Segments may be easily taken from the continuant portions of consonants, and voiceless portions affect pace less than voiced portions. The steady-state parts of vowels appear to have considerable influence on pace, especially when the vowels occur medially in the word. In certain instances, segments have been successfully deleted from long vowels in word final position. It is important in these cases to remove at least approximately an integral number of pitch periods during voiced portions. Although the cross-fading operation successfully smooths waveform discontinuities, the phase modulation resulting from the removal of fractional pitch periods is still audible.

Nasal consonants yield to segment deletion in initial and me-
dial positions of words, but not in final position.   Here, the problem is more one of phoneme modification than of pace change.
Voiceless fricatives, particularly in initial and final position may be
shortened extensively; voiced fricatives may be shortened to a lesser extent.   The stop portion of both voiced and voiceless plosives
may be reduced by as much as one-half wherever it occurs.   There
appears to be no tendency toward phoneme modification when such
large segments are deleted.   Final aspiration or schwa release of
voiced stops in final position may be removed completely.

Minimal experience has been gained in removing small portions of semivowels when they occur following vowels, but it appears
that about 10 to 20 per cent may be removed either from the semi-
vowel itself or from the transition between it and adjacent vowel.
Employing just the preceding guidelines, it has been possible to compress certain words by as much as 30 per cent to fit the 483-milli-
second time-slot without changing the pace of utterance.   Typically,
15 to 20 words in a 100-word vocabulary are naturally longer than
483 msec. using the controls on speaking format described earlier.
In two or three instances, the words are lengthy polysyllabics and
do not yield to compression techniques without pace change; these
words are relegated to two or more time slots on the drum.

IV. Conclusion

The purpose of this paper has been to describe a device
which is an interesting tool for selective time compression of words
and short phrases.   Both the major design aspects of the device and
guidelines for its use in preparation of vocabularies for a computer
audio response device have been described.   This paper has not
dealt with the myriad of problems concerning the speech quality of
messages where the words typically occupy a fixed time-slot.   Likewise, we have not compared messages without time-compressed
words (the words occupying multiple time-slots wherever necessary)
to messages where the words were produced by the techniques previously described.

In addition to its use for vocabulary preparation, SPACE LOOP
could be employed in the preparation of data for perceptual tests
where practically any aspect of the time dimension plays an important role in the experiment.   It would be useful as a processing tool
for fundamental studies in the physical segmentation of speech, for
aiding in determining the contribution of a particular time segment
toward the perception of a phoneme, and also, possibly, for investigating the proper duration of segments for synthesized speech.   The
flexibility of SPACE LOOP makes its use a distinct advantage over
tape splicing techniques employed by many researchers over the
years in studies of speech perception where the time dimension alone
is being modified.

Part II

RESEARCH

In this part of the Anthology there are presented excerpts from about 40 research studies. The research represented here is highly selective and the selection is necessarily subjective to a considerable extent. It is certain that no one else would have selected these identical studies but, on balance, it appears to me to be a representative selection both from the standpoint of quality and from the standpoint of representing the various research interests in the field of time-compressed speech.

In reading this section it is important that one determine for himself the quality of the research. One needs to ask himself several questions concerning each item read: (1) What evidence is there to support the findings and conclusions? (2) Is this evidence convincing? If not, is this due to inadequate procedures? (3) What was the nature of the material used? (This becomes of prime importance to the prospective researcher who needs to determine whether the material used is comparable to the material he proposes to use. This is also important in the consideration of the next two questions.) (4) What is the nature quantitatively and qualitatively of the subjects used? (5) What other variables exist in the plan of the study? (6) What limitations can be found in the study?

In some cases the reader may feel that the material excerpted does not furnish all the answers he needs in a particular study that is of special interest to him. In that event it is strongly urged that the reader avail himself of the original from which the portion reproduced here was excerpted. Microfilms of the doctoral theses from which material was excerpted may be obtained from University Microfilms of Ann Arbor, Michigan, at a nominal cost. Photocopies are also available from that source but are generally quite expensive. Articles specially written for this anthology are reproduced in full. When articles in this collection are based on master's theses, it is generally, but not always, possible to secure the original document on inter-library loan.

Chapter 1

REVIEWS OF RESEARCH

In this chapter three reviews of research are presented.
The first, by Foulke and Sticht, is the most comprehensive review
available. Professor Emerson Foulke of the Psychology Department
at the University of Louisville, where he heads the Perceptual Alternatives Laboratory, is without any question the foremost personality in the field of time-compressed speech. He has performed
much experimental work, has written and spoken on this subject to
an extent that is unique and not exceeded by anyone else, and has
carried on as a clearing house for information concerning all phases
of the subject. Dr. Thomas A. Sticht, formerly associated with
Foulke at Louisville, is now with HumRRO, a division of American
University at Monterey, California. He too has done extensive work
in investigating many phases of compressed speech. A review of
research by two such highly qualified experts is a particularly felic-
itous event.

Following the first review is one that is much briefer and
less comprehensive in scope; I have written it with the intent of sup-
plementing the first item rather than duplicating any portions of it.
The concluding item by Dr. John T. Tschantz is a fine example of
a review of the literature on one specific phase of time-compressed
speech.

REVIEW OF RESEARCH ON TIME-COMPRESSED SPEECH

Emerson Foulke, Thomas G. Sticht

Accelerated speech is speech in which the word rate has been
increased. Increasing the word rate reduces the time required for
a given message. Therefore, accelerated speech is often referred
to as time-compressed, or simply, compressed speech. If speech,
when accelerated, remains comprehensible, the savings in time
should be an important consideration in these situations in which extensive reliance is placed upon aural communication. The expression of interest in time-compressed speech came originally from
communication services where limited channels for communication
are available, and a great deal of information must be transmitted.
Obviously, more messages can be sent through a given channel if
the time per message is reduced. Recently, there has also been an

interest in the use of time-compressed speech in order to make available to blind people a reading rate that compares more favorably with the visual reading rate. This paper is concerned with the communication problems produced by those operations that must be performed upon speech in order to compress it in time. First, the various techniques for accelerating speech are described, and then the methods which have been used for the evaluation of the intelligibility and the comprehensibility of time-compressed speech are discussed. There follows a comparison of the different methods of accelerating speech with respect to intelligibility and comprehension. Attention is next focused on those characteristics of the listener, such as age and intelligence, that may have a bearing upon the comprehension of accelerated speech. Finally, an hypothesis is formulated to account for the effects of acceleration on the comprehension of speech, and directions for future research are suggested.

METHODS FOR ACCELERATING SPEECH

Speaking Rapidly

Within limits, word rate is under the control of the speaker (Caleare & Lazzaroni [B48], deQuires [B81], Enç & Stolurew F1*, Fergen [B112], Goldstein [B193], Harwood [B211], Nelson [B297]). This method has the virtue of simplicity and requires no special apparatus. However, speaking at a rate that is faster than normal introduces undesired changes in vocal inflection and fluctuations in rate, and a relatively low upper limit makes the method generally unsuitable.

Speed Changing Method

The word rate of recorded speech may be changed simply by reproducing it at a different tape or record speed than the one used during the recording. If the playback speed is slower than the recording speed, the word rate is decreased and the speech is expanded in time. If the playback speed is increased, the word rate is increased and the speech is compressed in time. Changing word rate in this manner is, technically speaking, quite easy. With relatively simple and inexpensive modification, the speed of many tape and record reproducers may be made continuously variable. However, when speech is accelerated in this manner, there is a shift in the frequency components of the voice signal that is proportional to the change in tape or record speed. For instance, if the speed is doubled, the component frequencies will be doubled, and overall vocal pitch will be raised one octave. Speech, the rate of which has been altered by this method, has been examined in several experiments (Fletcher [B114], p. 293-294], Foulke [B115], Garvey [B170], Klumpp & Webster [B244], McLain [B273]).

---

*For the notes--"F" numbers--see end of this article.

Sampling Method

In 1950, Miller & Licklider demonstrated the redundancy in speech by deleting segments of the speech signal. This was accomplished by a switching arrangement that permitted the speech signal to be turned off periodically. They found that so long as these interruptions occurred more than ten times per second, the interrupted speech was easily understood. Intelligibility of monosyllabic words did not drop below 90 per cent until half of the speech signal had been discarded. Thus, it appeared that a large portion of the speech signal could be discarded without a serious disruption of communication. Garvey [B170], taking cognizance of these results, reasoned that if the gaps in a message that had been periodically interrupted were closed, the result should be time-compressed intelligible speech without distortion in vocal pitch. To test this notion, he prepared a tape on which speech had been recorded by periodically cutting out short segments of tape, and by splicing the free ends of the retained tape together again. Reproduction of this tape achieved the desired effect. Garvey's method was, of course, too cumbersome for any but research purposes. However, the success of the general approach having been shown, an efficient technique for accomplishing it was not long to follow.

In 1954, Fairbanks, Everitt, & Jaeger published a description of an electromechanical apparatus which makes possible the time-compressed or expanded reproduction of recorded tape. Since that time, other similar equipment has been made commercially available. A description by Foulke [B118] of the device used in his research characterizes the electromechanical approach in sampling speech. "The device we use to compress speech is the Tempo-Regulator, manufactured by Telefonbau und Normalzeit, Frankfurt-am-Main, Germany. The Tempo-Regulator samples recorded tape in the following manner. The tape passes over the curved surface of a cylinder and wraps around the cylinder enough to make contact with one-quarter of its circumference. Four tape reproducing heads are spaced equally around the circumference of the cylinder. When this cylinder is stationary, and the tape is moving at the same speed at which it moved during recording (15 inches per second), it makes contact with one of the reproducing heads and the signal is reproduced as recorded. When the Tempo-Regulator is adjusted for some amount of compression, the speed of the tape increases and the cylinder begins to rotate in the direction of tape motion. As the speed of the tape is increased, the rotational speed of the cylinder is increased so that the speed of the tape relative to the surface of the cylinder is held constant at 15 i. p. s. Under these conditions, each of the four heads, in turn, makes and then loses contact with the tape. Each head reproduces, as recorded, the material on the portion of the tape with which it makes contact. When the cylinder is so positioned that one head is just losing contact with the tape while the preceeding head is just making contact with the tape, the segment of tape that is wrapped around the cylinder between these two heads never makes contact with a reproducing head and is therefore not reproduced. The segment of the tape that is eliminated from the reproduction in this manner is always the same length, one-quarter of the circumference of the cylinder. The amount of speech compression depends upon the number of such eliminations per unit time, and this, in turn, depends upon the tape and cylinder speed. Speech may be expanded by reversing the direction of rotation of the cylinder and moving the tape across the cylinder at a slower speed than was used during recording. " The apparatus described by Fairbanks et al. makes use of the principle just described. However, it differs in that tape speed and cylinder speed are independently variable, making it possible to vary the temporal value of the discarded portions of the message. A detailed description of the means by which such variation is accomplished, is beyond the scope of the present paper. Those interested in such a description are referred to the article by Fairbanks, Everitt, & Jaeger [B105].

A computer may also be used to compress speech by the sampling method (Scott [B382]). In this approach, speech that has been transduced to electrical form--e. g. , the output of a microphone or tape reproducing head--is temporally segmented by an analog-to-digital converter and these segments are stored in the computer. Then, the computer samples these segments according to a sampling rule for which it has been programmed, e. g. discard every third segment. The sample thus constructed is supplied to the input of a digital-to-analog converter and the signal at the output of this converter, compressed in time, is appropriate for transduction to acoustical form again.

Two variables that have an important bearing on the character of the time-compressed speech signal are the temporal value of the discarded and retained portions of speech, and the rule according to which speech is sampled. In devices like the Tempo-Regulator and its successor, the Eltro Information Rate Changer, the temporal values of retained portions of speech is variable, but the temporal value of discarded portions is fixed by the distance between playback heads along the surface of the rotating cylinder that samples the tape to be compressed, and is not variable. Using the Fairbanks scheme, the temporal value of both the retained and the discarded portions is variable. Using the computer, the temporal value of both portions is variable over a wide range of values.

Electromechanical compressors, like the Tempo-Regulator or the Fairbanks apparatus, are unselective with respect to the parts of a message that are discarded. Portions are discarded on a periodic basis and may occur anywhere within or between words, and it is quite unlikely that a given message, subjected to consecutive compressions, would be sampled in the same way. If sampling is accomplished manually, as Garvey did, some selectivity is possible. Though Garvey sampled on a periodic basis, he was careful to insure that the onset of each word coincided with the first segment of tape to be discarded in sampling that word. Diehl, White & Burk [B83], using Garvey's manual method, compressed speech to some extent by removing the time between words. With use of the computer, it is feasible to use a great variety of sampling rules. For instance, a program might be written according to which the temporal intervals between words were discarded and the time filled by a given word was periodically sampled with the restriction that no consonantal sounds could be discarded.

From what has just been said, it would appear that the computer, because of its flexibility, offers the most satisfactory method for the time compression or expansion of speech. This may ultimately prove to be the case. However, at present, computer time is too expensive to justify the employment of a computer in this capacity for any but research purposes.

EVALUATION METHODS USED

Some Procedural Problems

There is no common practice in specifying amount of compression to which a listening selection has been subjected. This lack of uniformity can result in confusion, especially when the results of different studies are compared. The problem has been discussed by Bellamy [B20].

The amount of compression may be specified by the fraction, expressed as a per cent, of the time originally required for the production of a message, that is saved by reproducing that message at a faster word rate (30 per cent compression means that 30 per cent of the original time has been saved), or the compliment of that fraction, expressed as a per cent, may be used to indicate the fraction of the original time remaining after compression. Alternatively, specification may be made in terms of the acceleration of the original word rate, tape speed, or record speed, (an acceleration of 1.5 means that the word rate after compression is 1.5 times the word rate before compression). In comparing these indices, it must be remembered that the relationship between them is not linear. For instance, whereas an increase in acceleration from 1.1 to 1.2 corresponds to an increase in the per cent of compression from 9 to 17 per cent, an increase in acceleration from 1.9 to 2.0 corresponds to a change in the per cent of compression from 47 to 50 per cent. A problem common to both indices is that they do not indicate directly the word rate of compressed speech. The final word rates of two listening selections compressed or accelerated by the same amount will depend upon the original or uncompressed word rates, and may differ considerably. Although initial word rates ranging from 125 to 175 w.p.m. have been used in these experiments exploring the relationship between word rate and comprehension (Nelson [B297], Harwood [B211], Diehl et al. [B83], Fairbanks, Guttman & Miron [B109], Foulke, Amster, Nolan & Bixler F2), the general conclusion to be drawn from these studies is that comprehension is only moderately affected by increasing word rate until a word rate of approximately 275 or 280 w.p.m. is reached, and that comprehension begins to decline rapidly at about this word rate, regardless of the initial or uncompressed word rate. Also, in an experiment by Foulke (unpublished data), a listening selection was read at three different rates, (149, 164.6 and 195.7 w. p. m.) by a professional reader. These renditions were then compressed to a final word rate of 275 w. p. m., and each rendition was presented to one of the three comparable groups of listeners. Upon hearing the selections, listeners were tested for comprehension, and the resulting distributions of test scores were not significantly different.

Thus, in describing compressed speech, specification in terms of word rate appears to be necessary, and it is probably sufficient. Word rate is probably the most meaningful dimension in terms of the cognitive and perceptual processes of the listener. Johnson, Darley & Spriestersbach (F3, p. 202-203) have summarized research supporting the conclusion that the perception of rate of speaking corresponds directly to the oral reading rate in words per minute.

For certain purposes, such as the measurement of intelligibility, single words are compressed, and it is of course meaningless to speak of the word rate of a single word. In these cases, specification must be stated in terms of compression or acceleration.

If compressed speech is to be specified in terms of percentage of compression or acceleration ratio, the word rate of the original production must be determined and reported. There is no "normal" word rate that can safely be assumed since there is considerable variability in the published estimates of normal word rate. Part of this variability is undoubtedly due to the difference between spontaneous conversational word rate and oral reading word rate. Nichols & Stevens (F4) found a conversational speaking rate of 125 w. p. m. while Johnson et al., (F3, p. 220), found a median oral reading rate of 176.5 w. p. m. and Foulke (unpublished research) found a mean oral reading rate of 174 w. p. m. The oral reading rate is the word rate that is relevant to the issue under discussion, since, in most cases, the speech that is compressed is recorded oral reading. However, there is considerable variability in the speaking rates of professional oral readers. In the unpublished study just mentioned, Foulke found a standard deviation of 23.53 words. There is confusion regarding the various terms used for compressed speech. Examples are compressed speech, accelerated speech, speeded speech, and rapid speech. These terms are used discriminately by others. The Library of Congress (F5) has suggested that the term "compressed speech" be reserved for speech that has been accelerated by the sampling method, while the term "rapid speech" should be reserved for speech that has been accelerated by increasing the playback speed of a recording. In the opinion of the authors, however, the term "compressed speech" should more appropriately be regarded as a term referring to recorded speech which is reproduced in less than the original time regardless of the method used.

Measurement of Intelligibility

Two general approaches have been employed in the evaluation of time-compressed speech: tests of the ability to repeat brief messages accurately, and tests of the comprehension of listening selections. Brief message reproduction is taken as an index of the intelligibility of time-compressed speech. A procedure typical of this approach is one in which single words are compressed in time by some amount and presented, one at a time, to a listener. The listener's task is to reproduce these words, orally or in writing, and the intelligibility score is the percentage of correctly identified words. This procedure is sometimes referred to as an articulation test (Miller [B279, p. 60]). Disjunctive reaction time (R-T) may also be taken as an index of intelligibility (Foulke F6). The underlying rationale in this case is that in the disjunctive R-T experiment, reduced intelligibility means reduced discriminability. It has been shown that as stimuli are made more similar and hence less discriminable, choice reaction time is increased, (Woodworth & Schlosberg F7, p. 33). The procedure, under this approach, is to acquaint the subject with a list of words (e. g. , three of them) and then to present them to him one at a time in random order for identification. The subject indicates his choice with a discriminative response (for instance, pressing the appropriate one of several response keys). The subject can then be scored for reaction time and accuracy. The experiment is performed with words that have been compressed in time by several amounts and changes in reaction time and/or accuracy are regarded as indicative of changes in intelligibility. The reaction time method may be more sensitive than other methods since a change in the amount of compression may produce a change in the reaction time to words that are discriminated without error.

Calearo & Lazzaroni [B48] report the use of a method familiar to those in clinical audiology in order to detect the effects of compression. The minimum intensity required for words to be intelligible is determined for words at several levels of compression. Threshold intensity is defined as that intensity at which some percent of a list of words (e. g. , 50 per cent) are correctly identified. If a change in the compression of a list of words is accompanied by a change in threshold intensity for that list, it is concluded that time compression has altered intelligibility.

Tests of Comprehension

The other common approach in evaluating the effects of the acceleration of speech is one in which the listener first hears a listening selection at some accelerated word rate and then is tested for knowledge of the facts and implications of that selection. Any kind of test may be used, but researchers have, in general, preferred objective tests of specifiable reliability. The multiple choice test has been a frequent choice. Many researchers (Enç & Stolurow F1, Foulke [B118], Voor & Miller [B428]) have used published tests such as the listening sub-test of the Sequential Tests of Educational Progress, which consists of listening selections covering a broad content area and multiple choice questions concerning these selections. Such tests have the advantage of good technical specifications, including normative data. However, in some cases, these tests have not been well adapted to the researcher's needs, and he has undertaken the construction of his own tests (Foulke et al F2, Foulke [B117], McLain [B273], Orr & Friedman F8). Wood [B449], dealt with the problems inherent in assessing the listening comprehension of young children by scoring their responses to imperative statements, compressed in time by various amounts, such as "buzz like a bee."

Some measures of listening comprehension may be more sensitive than others. Bellamy [B20], in comparing the performance of a blind and a sighted group with respect to the ability to comprehend accelerated listening selections, used both a multiple choice test and an interview technique and reported that the interview technique revealed a difference in favor of the blind group, not detected by the multiple choice test. Friedman, Orr, Freedel & Norris (F9) used short answer and essay tests of the comprehension of accelerated speech and found no discernable trends in performance as a function of practice in listening to such speech. A multiple choice test, on the other hand, revealed considerable improvement. They also found a lack of correlation between the results of short answer and essay tests. Perhaps the superiority of a recognition test over a recall test in detecting differences in the comprehension of accelerated speech is a consequence of the retrieval problems arising from the incomplete encoding of stimulus material in partially learned tasks. Robinson (F10) offers evidence in support of the view that memory involves encoding of information in such a way as to make retrieval possible. An incompletely encoded message might be released by stimuli in a recognition test but unretrievable in a recall task.

The two general approaches just presented have tended to yield different results. Increasing the amount of time compression appears to have a smaller influence on intelligibility (Garvey [B170]) than on comprehension (Foulke et al. F2). The diversity of procedures used in the study of accelerated speech argues for a generous measure of caution in comparing the results of different experiments. But the consistency of findings, in spite of such diversity, lends credence to the relationship just mentioned. The lack of complete agreement in the results produced by the two approaches in evaluating the effects of time compression may be more than an artifact of the method used. It may be that such disagreement is a reflection of differences in the mediating processes underlying the behaviors on which the two kinds of scores depend. If so, thorough evaluation will, of course, require both approaches. This thesis will be developed more fully in a later section of this paper (see A TWO-PROCESS HYPOTHESIS).

FACTORS AFFECTING INTELLIGIBILITY

Factors that have been shown to have an effect upon the intelligibility of time-compressed speech can be divided into two general classes. One class includes stimulus variables associated with the context in which the signal to be identified is presented, and characteristics of the signal itself. The second class includes organizmic variables, such as the listener's age, sex, intelligence and prior experience with stimulus material. In this section, the research relating to the characteristics of this signal and to the listener's familiarity with stimulus words is reviewed.

Characteristics of the Signal

(1) Method of Compression

The intelligibility of time-compressed words depends upon the method used for compression. When the speed changing method is used, a compression in time of approximately 33 per cent, results in a loss in intelligibility of 40 per cent or more (Fletcher [B114], Garvey [B170], Klumpp & Webster [B244]). On the other hand, Garvey [B170] found only a 10 per cent loss in the intelligibility of words compressed 60 per cent in time by his manual sampling method, and a 50 per cent loss in intelligibility at 75 per cent. Kurtzrock [B248], using an electromechanical sampling method, found 50 per cent intelligibility for monosyllabic words presented at a compression of 85 per cent. Using a similar method and similar materials, Fairbanks & Kodman [B104] obtained 50 per cent intelligibility at a compression of 87 per cent.

Compression by either method increases the rate at which the discriminable elements of speech occur. However, whereas vocal pitch is unaffected by the sampling method, it is elevated by the speed changing method. The difference in the intelligibility of words compressed by the two methods is probably due to the distortion in vocal pitch, since this is the factor that is not common to the two methods.

(2) Intelligibility and Sampling Rule

The sampling period of speech that is to be compressed in time by the sampling method is the interval between the onsets of consecutive retained portions of the message. Compression is accomplished by discarding part of this interval. It is the ratio of the retained to the discarded portions of sampling periods that determines the amount of compression. If ten milliseconds of a 20-millisecond sampling period, or 30 msec. of a 60-msec. sampling period are retained, the result is the same--50 per cent compression. For any given sampling period, changing the ratio of retained to discarded portions changes the amount of compression.

When the sampling method is used, the effect that a given

amount of compression will have on the intelligibility of words depends upon the duration of the discarded portion of the sampling
period, and hence upon the duration of the sampling period itself.
The duration of the discarded portion of the sampling period must
be short relative to the durations of the speech sounds to be sampled. If it is not, a speech sound may fall entirely within the discarded portion of a sampling period and in which case it would not
be sampled at all. With spondaic words compressed to 50 per cent
of their original durations, Garvey [B170], using discard intervals
of 40 milliseconds, 60 msec., 80 msec. and 100 msec., found corresponding intelligibility scores of 95.33 per cent, 95.67 per cent,
95 per cent, and 85.67 per cent. In a two-factor experiment in
which five discard intervals and eight compressions were represented, Fairbanks & Kodman [B104] also found a substantial loss in intelligibility when the duration of the discard interval exceeded 80
msec. This was true at all eight compressions.

The intelligibility of a word may be degraded if the word is
sampled too frequently. Speech that is compressed in time by the
sampling method consists of a succession of abutted samples of the
original speech. If the transitions from sample to sample in this
succession occur with sufficient frequency, the result is an audible
tone with definite pitch. If the sampling rate is high enough, the
pitch of this tone will intrude into the speech spectrum and mask
some speech frequencies. Fairbanks & Kodman [B104], using a discard interval of 10 msec., found 90 per cent intelligibility for words
compressed to 20 per cent of their original durations. When this
discard interval was changed to 40 msec., they found 94 per cent
intelligibility. When a 10-msec. discard interval is used to compress speech to 20 per cent of its original time, the retained samples are 2.5 msec. in duration and they occur at a rate of 400 per
second. The 400-cycle tone corresponding to this rate is well within the speech spectrum and might be expected to interfere with intelligibility. If, on the other hand, a 40-msec. discard interval is
used in compressing speech to 20 per cent of its original duration,
the retained samples are 10 msec., in length and they occur at a
rate of 100 per second. The audible tone of corresponding frequency
is below the speech spectrum in this case, and there should be little
interference.

Cramer (F11) reports that when subjects use earphones to
listen to speech that has been compressed in time by the sampling
method, delaying the signal to one earphone by 7.5 msec. improves
intelligibility. This delay provides what Cramer has called "binaural redundancy." If, as Garvey [B169] suggests, it is the briefness of highly compressed speech sounds that makes them unintelligible, "binaural redundancy" may increase the effective duration of
such sounds. Scott [B382] reports a favorable result when subjects
use one earphone to listen to the normally retained samples of time-
compressed speech and the other earphone to listen, at the same
time, to the normally discarded samples of time-compressed speech.
He refers to such speech as "dichotic speech." As yet, there are
no data on which to base a comparison of "dichotic speech" and conventional sampled speech.

(3) Intelligibility and Rate of Occurrence of Speech Sounds

Garvey [B170] compared the intelligibility of words compressed in time by the sampling method with the intelligibility reported by Miller & Licklider [B283] for words that had been interrupted periodically. Garvey's words and Miller & Licklider's words were treated alike in that portions of sampling periods were discarded. However, the retained samples of Garvey's words were abutted to produce time-compressed speech, while the retained samples of Miller & Licklider's words were not abutted and the resulting speech, though interrupted, was not compressed in time. There was no difference between the intelligibility of time-compressed words and interrupted words when 50 per cent of each word was discarded. However, when 62 per cent of each word was discarded, interrupted words were 40 per cent more intelligible than time-compressed words. Since the two groups of words were alike with respect to the amount of speech information that had been discarded, the poorer intelligibility of the time-compressed words when 62 per cent of the speech information was discarded was probably due to the accelerated rate of occurrence of speech sounds.

(4) Intelligibility and Word Structure

Kurtzrock [B248] found that compression by the speed changing method degraded the intelligibility of vowel sounds more than consonantal sounds, and that compression by the sampling method degraded consonantal sounds more than vowel sounds. Garvey's subjects [B169] rated the vowel sounds in words that had been compressed in time by the sampling method higher in "goodness" than consonantal sounds. In a study in which the number of phonemes in a word was varied from three to nine, Henry [B217] found that increasing the number of phonemes improved the intelligibility of words that had been compressed in time by the sampling method. In a similar vein, Klumpp & Webster [B244] found short phrases compressed in time by the speed changing method to be more intelligible than single words. The findings of Henry and of Klumpp & Webster are probably explained by the cues the subjects can derive from the contexts of multiphonemic words and short phrases.

Characteristics of the Organism

(1) Intelligibility and Prior Experience

Using the sampling method, Fairbanks & Kodman [B104] found a group of highly compressed words to be more intelligible than a group of the interrupted words of Miller & Licklider when the two groups were equated with respect to the amount of speech information that was discarded. However, the subjects of Fairbanks & Kodman had received extensive familiarization with the words to be identified before tests were made, whereas the subjects of Miller & Licklider were relatively naive. Miller & Licklider [B283], using interrupted words, and Garvey [B169], using words compressed in time by the sampling method, found that repeated exposure to such words improved their intelligibility.

If a group of listeners agree that a particular speech sound in a word that has been compressed in time by the sampling method is unrecognizable, it may fairly be concluded that the difficulty lies with the signal itself. However, Garvey found that subjects disagreed about the speech sounds that were rendered unintelligible by compression of the words in which they occurred. Garvey explained this finding in terms of the differential experience of subjects with respect to the words in question. In this connection, Henry [B217] found words which occur with greater frequency in general language, as indicated by the Lorge-Thorndike count, to be more intelligible.

(2) Intelligibility and Anatomical Damage

The intelligibility of time-compressed speech is influenced by hearing capacity. Calearo & Lazzaroni [B48], using subjects with normal hearing, determined the intensity required for threshold intelligibility of short sentences presented at 140, 250, and 350 w. p. m. With each increase in word rate, a 10-db increase in intensity was required in order to maintain threshold intelligibility. When elderly patients with presbycusis and patients with temporal lobe tumors were given the same test, increases in word rate were accompanied by much greater losses in intelligibility. In a test of patients with hearing losses due to peripherial damage, deQuiros [B81] found intelligibility thresholds resembling those of Calearo's normal subjects at 140 and 250 w. p. m. , but an elevated threshold at 350 w. p. m. Thus, it appears that the extent to which the intelligibility of time-compressed speech is influenced by loss of hearing capacity depends upon the kind of underlying anatomical damage.

COMPREHENSION OF TIME-COMPRESSED SPEECH

As in the case of intelligibility, the comprehension of time-compressed speech is influenced by factors relating to the listener and to the stimulus. Factors relating to the listener include such variables as age, sex, and intelligence. Stimulus factors include such variables as the amount and method of compression, and the characteristics of an oral reader's voice. Of course, to the extent that comprehension of connected discourse depends upon the intelligibility of individual words, variables affecting word intelligibility will also affect comprehension.

Stimulus Variables

(1) Comprehension and Amount of Time Compression

When speech is compressed in time, the principle effect is the acceleration of the rate at which words occur. There are several studies in which comprehension rate has been varied through a

relatively limited range.   Therefore, in order to gain an impression
of the influence of this variable, it is necessary to combine the results of several studies.

Within the range from 126 to 172 w. p. m. , Diehl et al. [B84]
found listening comprehension to be unaffected by changes in word
rate.   In the range from 125 to 225 w. p. m. , Nelson [B297] and
Harwood [B211] found a slight but insignificant loss in comprehension as word rate was increased.   Fairbanks et al. [B109] found little difference in the comprehension of listening selections presented
at 141, 201, and 282 w. p. m.   Thereafter, comprehension, as indicated by percentage of test questions correctly answered, declined
from 58 per cent correct at 282 w. p. m. to 26 per cent at 470
w. p. m.   Foulke et al. (F12), using both technical and literary listening selections, found comprehension to be only slightly affected by
increases in word rate up to 275 w. p. m.   However, in the range
from 275 to 375 w. p. m. , they found an accelerated decrease in comprehension as word rate was increased.   Foulke & Sticht (F13), using the STEP Listening Test Form 1A, found a decrease in comprehension of 6 per cent between 225 and 325 w. p. m. , and a decrease
in comprehension of 14 per cent between 325 and 425 w. p. m.   The
three studies just cited are in agreement regarding the finding that
there is a change in the rate at which comprehension declines as
word rate is increased.   A similar relationship has also been found
in many other studies in which the determination of the influence of
word rate upon comprehension was not the primary objective (Foulke
[B129]).

The relationship revealed from the studies reviewed in this
section is one in which comprehension, as indicated by test scores,
decreases as word rate or the amount of compression is increased.
However, outcome measures based upon test performance alone do
not take into account the learning time that is saved when speech is
presented at an accelerated word rate.   Such an allowance may be
made by dividing the comprehension score by the time required to
present the message.   This index of learning efficiency expresses
the amount of learning per unit time.   Using such an index, Fairbanks et al. [B109], Enç & Stolurow (F1), and Foulke et al. (F12)
found that learning efficiency increased as word rate was increased
up to approximately 280 w. p. m. , and remained constant with further
increases in word rate.   Thus, although one who listens to a selection presented at 325 w. p. m. may not be able to demonstrate as
much comprehension as one who listens at a normal rate, he may
be learning more per unit time.   Using the same logic, Enç &
Stolurow (F1) have computed an index of the efficiency of retention.

The word rate at which a listening selection is presented apparently has no special effect on the rate at which forgetting occurs.
Enç & Stolurow (F1), Friedman, Orr, Freedel & Norris (F9), and
Foulke [B129] have performed studies in which tests of the comprehension of listening selections presented at several word rates have
been made after several retention intervals.   In general, these studies support the conclusion that differences in the course of forgetting

are due to differences in original learning. Of course, as has already been shown, the amount of original learning is a function of the word rate at which a listening selection is presented.

(2) Comprehension and Method of Compression

McLain [B273] and Foulke (F12), using subjects who were naive with respect to compressed speech and unaccustomed to reading by listening, compared the comprehension of speech compressed by the sampling method with the comprehension of speech compressed by the speed changing method. In both instances, a slight but statistically significant advantage was found for the sampling method. However, in a similar experiment in which blind school children, who were accustomed to reading by listening, served as subjects, Foulke [B115] found no statistically significant difference in favor of either method. The conclusion suggested by the research just cited is that the relative superiority of the sampling method is slight, and that this superiority may be erased by experience in reading by listening. However, there are not enough data to provide firm support for any conclusions. In the studies mentioned here, all subjects have been naive with respect to time-compressed speech of any kind, the subjects have had only brief exposures to time-compressed listening selections, and tests have been made in a limited range of word rates. There can be little disagreement among listeners about which kind of compressed speech results in a more agreeable listening experience. Whereas compression by the speed changing method results in serious distortions of vocal quality that renders the speaker's voice unrecognizable, compression by the sampling method preserves vocal quality so that, even at very fast word rates, a listener can often identify a speaker with whose voice he is familiar.

The issue at stake is important for both practical and theoretical reasons. Practically speaking, the equipment required for the compression of speech by the speed changing method is readily available and cheap enough so that individual ownership of compressors is feasible. On the other hand, the equipment required for the time compression of speech by the sampling method is scarce and very expensive. If it is not possible to demonstrate an obvious advantage with respect to comprehension, for speech compressed by the sampling method, the mere fact that the product of the sampling method is more pleasing to hear may not be sufficient to justify the added expense it entails.

From a more theoretical point of view, the finding that the obvious superiority of the sampling method, when the comparison is based on the intelligibility of single words, cannot be demonstrated when the comparison is based on the comprehension of connected discourse, is quite interesting. It suggests that some other factor, such as the rate at which words occur, is relatively more important than the intelligibility of single words in determining the comprehension of time-compressed speech. This suggestion, if substantiated experimentally, has important implications. The intelligibility of a single compressed word should be, in large part, a function of the signal quality of the equipment used in compressing it. If, beyond a certain point, the intelligibility of single words becomes relatively unimportant, then little gain can be expected from efforts directed at further refinement of speech compression equipment. Attention will be directed more appropriately to a consideration of the perceptual and cognitive processes of the listener who must contend with accelerated speech.

(3) Nature of Material to be Comprehended

The way in which the level of difficulty of a listening selection and the word rate at which it is presented interact to produce a given comprehension score may depend upon the formula used for estimating difficulty. There are several schemes for estimating the difficulty of reading selections (Dale & Chall F14, Flesch F15), and it has generally been assumed that these schemes are equally valid for determining the difficulty of listening selections. Different schemes often produce different estimates of difficulty, and no study has been found in which different schemes have been compared with respect to their ability to select the kind of material that will be most affected by time compression. The evidence currently available comes from studies that cannot safely be compared because they have made use of different listening selections, subject populations, and have explored different ranges of the word rate variable.

Nelson [B297] and Harwood [B211] found the comprehension of a listening selection rated difficult by the Flesch Formula to be more adversely affected by increasing the word rate, within the range from 125 to 225 w. p. m. , than a listening selection rated relatively less difficult by the same formula. Enç & Stolurow (F1) found considerable variability in mean comprehension test scores for ten reading selections presented at a normal word rate and at a slightly accelerated word rate, in spite of the fact that they were rated as equal in difficulty by the Dale-Chall Formula. Using one normal and four accelerated word rates, Foulke et al. (F12) measured the listening comprehension of a scientific selection and a literary selection. In spite of the fact that the two selections were rated as equal in difficulty by the Dale-Chall Formula, comprehension of the scientific selection was generally poorer than comprehension of the literary selection. Although there was a significant interaction between word rate and the nature of the listening selection, it was probably due to the fact that since there was poorer comprehension of the scientific selection than the literary selection at a normal word rate, there was a reduced range within which comprehension scores of the scientific selection could vary.

The estimate of reading difficulty obtained with the Flesch Formula is largely determined by word and sentence length, whereas the estimate obtained with the Dale-Chall Formula depends primarily upon the number of words not found in Dale's lists of words easily understood at various grade levels. In view of these differences, it is not surprising that the formulas often produce different estimates. The finding of a systematic interaction between difficulty and word rate for listening selections rated different in difficulty by a particular formula would provide a kind of rational validity for that formula.

Rodgers (F16) has suggested a procedure for estimating the difficulty of listening selections that takes into account the average idea length, which is found by dividing the number of words in a listening selection by the number of independent clauses in that selection. The effect of increasing word rate upon the comprehension of listening selections at several levels of difficulty, as determined by Rodgers' method, has not yet been explored.

As previously mentioned, it has generally been assumed that reading difficulty and listening difficulty are the same. However, this assumption may not be justified, and the required experimental comparison would appear to be a simple matter.

(4) Reader's Style and Vocal Quality

Oral readers differ considerably with respect to vocal timbre and, of course, there are conspicuous sex differences in vocal pitch. Oral readers also differ with respect to factors such as average word rate, and variation in word rate, pitch, and loudness, that combine to define the personal oral reading style. In a preliminary investigation, Foulke [B118] explored the extent to which these factors interact with word rate in determining listening comprehension. An experiment was performed in which three versions of a listening selection, each read by a different reader (two male and one female), were presented to groups of college students at a normal word rate and a word rate that was accelerated by the sampling method. There were significant differences in comprehension associated with the reader and with the word rate. However, the reader's effect on the comprehension of the listening selection did not depend upon the word rate. The results of this experiment were inconclusive, because of the small number of readers used. There is general agreement among those who have had extensive experience in listening to speech compressed in time by the sampling method that some voices and reading styles withstand the ravages of compression better than others.

Listener Variables Affecting Comprehension

Some listeners show good comprehension of speech presented at a rate of 350 w.p.m. or faster, with little or no prior experience in listening to such speech. Other listeners show poor comprehension of accelerated speech, even after prolonged exposure to such speech (Foulke [B117]). These marked and persistent individual differences are undoubtedly the consequence of the interaction of a host of organismic variables. An effort has been made to clarify the contribution of such variables in determining listening comprehension and accelerated word rates, but it is only a beginning effort and a good deal of research will be required before this class of variables can be taken into account properly.

(1) Sex of the Listener

Comparisons of the comprehension test scores of male and female listeners have revealed no sex related differences in comprehension for word rates varying from 174 to 475 w. p. m. , (Foulke & Sticht [B143], Orr & Friedman F8).

(2) Listener's Age and Educational Experience

In the research relevant to this topic, school children have served as subjects, and their age and amount of education have, of course, varied concomitantly. Therefore, the outcome of such experiments cannot, strictly speaking, be related to either age or amount of education alone. Fergen [B112] and Wood [B449] found a positive relationship between the grade level of school children and the comprehension of accelerated speech. Together, their experiments included grades one, three, four, five, and six. Since the subjects' task was to carry out the instructions communicated by short imperative statements, his measurements probably pertained more to intelligibility than to comprehension.

High school and college students have served as subjects in many experiments in which listening comprehension, as a function of word rate, has been determined. However, due to different experimental materials and conditions, these experiments cannot safely be compared with a view to determining the effects of age and education on the comprehension of accelerated speech. The ability of aged subjects to comprehend accelerated listening selections has not been determined. However, the results obtained by Calearo & Lazzaroni [B48] in testing aged subjects for the intelligibility of short time-compressed sentences, are suggestive. One might reasonably expect a relatively large decline in the ability of aged subjects to comprehend accelerated speech. Of course, such a decline would not be due to age per se, but to the involutional changes in the central nervous system accompanying old age.

(3) Intelligence of the Listener

In the case of children, the evidence presently available is not sufficient to permit a conclusion regarding the effect of intelligence on the comprehension of accelerated speech. Fergen [B112] found no relationship between the IQ's of grade school children and their ability to comprehend accelerated listening selections. However, 230 w. p. m. was the fastest word rate represented in her experiment. Wood [B449] found no relationship between IQ and the ability to follow instructions communicated by short time-compressed imperative statements. However, as previously mentioned, his procedures resemble more closely those used in testing for intelligibility.

A more definite conclusion is possible in the case of adults. Fairbanks et al. [B108,B109], Goldstein [B193], and Nelson [B297] have all found a positive relationship between intelligence and the ability to comprehend accelerated speech. The data of Fairbanks et al. [B108] and of Goldstein [B193] concur in showing a positive relationship between the intelligence of the listener and the magnitude of the decline in listening comprehension as word rate is increased. This relationship is undoubtedly due to the fact that since intelligent subjects earn higher scores on the tests of comprehension of listening selections that have been presented at a normal word rate in order to provide a basis for comparison, the scores they earn on the tests of comprehension of listening selections presented at accelerated word rates have a larger range within which to vary. Those of lower intelligence perform nearer to the chance level with normal rates, and can persist with chance level performance over a wide range of word rates.

(4) Visual Status of the Listener

There are a priori grounds for expecting blind individuals to show better listening comprehension than sighted individuals. In general, blind people depend to a much greater extent than sighted people upon aural communication. Increasingly, blind students, and other blind people who read, do so by listening to recorded books. The practice afforded by such experience might be expected to improve listening ability and this improved ability should be advantageous to listening to accelerated speech as well. Furthermore, whereas accelerated speech may be little more than a curiosity to the average sighted person, it may be perceived by the blind person as a potential solution to the serious reading problem he experiences by virtue of the slow rate at which he reads ordinarily. When such a person serves as a subject in an experiment in which the comprehension of accelerated speech is measured, he might be expected to maintain a more attentive adjustment.

The research related to this question is meager and the results are conflicting. Foulke [B119] offered evidence for superior comprehension by blind subjects of time-compressed listening selections. In a direct comparison, Bellamy [B20] found no difference between blind and sighted subjects with respect to the comprehension of accelerated listening selections. Furthermore, in an experiment performed by Hartlage (F17) blind and sighted subjects did not differ with respect to their comprehension of listening selections presented at a normal word rate.

(5) Reading Rate and Listening Rate

Those perceptual and cognitive factors, whatever they may be, that are responsible for individual differences in reading rate, may also be responsible for individual differences in the ability to comprehend accelerated speech. If this is true, fast readers should be able to comprehend speech at a faster word rate than slow readers. This hypothesis has been tested by Goldstein [B193] and by

Orr, Friedman, and Williams [B315]. In both experiments a significant positive correlation was found between reading rate and the ability to comprehend accelerated speech. In both experiments, it was also found that practice in listening to accelerated speech resulted in an improvement in reading rate. This finding adds further support to the hypothesis that the two performances in question may be mediated, at least in part, by the same underlying factors. Nelson [B297] found no correlation between reading rate and the ability to comprehend accelerated speech. However, his measures of reading rate were taken from college entrance examination data collected some time prior to his study, while Goldstein & Orr et al. obtained their measures of reading rate during their investigations.

Goldstein [B193] and Jester & Travers (F18) compared the comprehension resulting from listening to selections presented at several word rates with the comprehension resulting from reading the same selections, presented at the same word rates. In both cases, comprehension declined as word rate was increased. Listening comprehension was superior to reading comprehension up to approximately 200 w. p. m. Above 200 w. p. m., reading comprehension was superior. Simultaneous reading and listening at 350 w. p. m. resulted in better comprehension than could be demonstrated with either mode of presentation alone. This finding further emphasizes the compatibility of the two processes.

(6) Improving Comprehension of Time-Compressed Speech

In an experiment performed by Fairbanks et al. [B109] a mean comprehension score of 63.8 per cent was obtained by subjects who listened to a selection presented at the uncompressed rate of 141 w. p. m. (Per cent refers to the fraction of items answered correctly on the test of comprehension.) Compressing this selection by 50 per cent to a word rate of 282 w. p. m. resulted in a mean comprehension score of 58 per cent. With two consecutive presentation of the selection at 282 w. p. m., the mean comprehension score was 65.4 per cent. Though the subjects who served in this condition of the experiment did not save any listening time, the two exposures did result in slightly improved comprehension.

In a second study by the same investigators (Fairbanks et al. [B107]), elaborations and commentaries were written for selected facts in a listening selection. The recorded version of this elaborated selection was then compressed by the sampling method enough so that its playback time equalled the playback time of the uncompressed and unelaborated version. The objective was to determine whether or not comprehension could be improved by trading the temporal redundancy in the uncompressed selection for the verbal redundancy in the elaborated selection. The results were positive, showing better comprehension for the compressed selection with verbal redundancy. Analysis of test results indicated decreased comprehension for those portions of the compressed selection that had not been elaborated. The explanation of this finding is probably that subjects associated verbal redundancy with importance and were thus relatively less attentive to the unelaborated material.

Improving the comprehension of time-compressed speech by a training experience of some sort is an obvious possibility, and several investigators have devised and evaluated training experiences. The simplest and least sophisticated training experience that has been evaluated is near exposure. Voor & Miller [B428] exposed subjects to five brief listening selections presented at a rate of 380 w. p. m. The total listening time was 17. 5 minutes. A multiple choice test of comprehension followed each selection. Comprehension increased as a function of exposure up to seven minutes, and remained constant thereafter. These results probably reflect a simple adjustment to the initially unfamiliar task of listening to accelerated speech. Foulke [B119] gave blind school children, with considerable experience in reading by listening, over 25 hours of exposure to speech at a rate of 350 w. p. m. Subjects were tested for listening comprehension at 350 w. p. m. , before and after training, with equivalent forms of the STEP Listening Test. The distribution of pre-training and post-training STEP Test scores were not significantly different.

Simple exposure may have failed as a training experience because listeners were not attending to the training material. Therefore, in a second condition of the same experiment, a comparable group of subjects received the same treatment with the one difference that the listening material used for training was interrupted frequently and subjects were questioned about material just heard. It was hoped that the demand made upon subjects by this procedure would promote a more attentive attitude. Again, the distributions of pre-training and post-training STEP Listening Test scores were not significantly different.

A further modification of the training experience was represented in the two remaining conditions of the experiment. In these conditions, training material was presented initially at a normal word rate. As training progressed, the word rate was gradually increased until, near the end of the training period, material was presented without interruption. In the other condition, training material was interrupted for questioning. The results were the same. In neither case were there differences between pre-training and the post-training STEP Listening Test scores that could be attributed to the training experience.

In an experiment reported by Orr, Friedman & Williams [B315] sighted subjects, with presumably less practice in reading by listening than Foulke's blind subjects, were given a training experience that consisted of exposure to listening material presented initially at 325 w. p. m. , and increased in steps of 25 w. p. m. over a period of several weeks to a final word rate of 475 w. p. m. These subjects were then tested for listening comprehension at 475 w. p. m. and a comparison of their post-training test scores with equivalent pre-training test scores revealed an improvement in comprehension of 29. 3 per cent. Since the subjects in this experiment had probably not had extensive practice in reading by listening, and since there was no control group in which subjects received practice in listening to speech presented at a normal rate, these results cannot be attributed unequivocally to practice in listening to accelerated speech. The improvement that was found may simply have been a consequence of practice in listening.

Friedman, Orr, Freedle & Norris (F9), compared the comprehension test scores of subjects given 35 hours of mass practice in listening to accelerated speech with comprehension test scores of subjects given 12 to 14 hours of distributed practice in listening to accelerated speech. They concluded that the comprehension demonstrated by the distributed practice group was as good or better than the comprehension demonstrated by the massed practice group.

It is clear from the research just reviewed that an adequate training experience for improving the comprehension of accelerated speech has yet to be found. It may safely be concluded that simple exposure, at least in the amount so far tested, is not adequate. Exposure to speech, the word rate of which is slowly increased, may have some benefit, but the evidence so far available will not support a definite conclusion in this regard. Further research is clearly indicated and it will be necessary, among other things, to determine the way in which the amount of prior experience in reading by listening interacts with the kind of training experience provided.

A TWO-PROCESS HYPOTHESIS REGARDING COMPREHENSION OF TIME-COMPRESSED SPEECH

By now, enough research has been accomplished to permit a fairly accurate description of the relationship between word rate and comprehension over a fairly wide range of values for the word rate variable. The relationship that emerges is not a linear one and its explanation is, therefore, apt to be somewhat involved. There are two general classes of results which, when taken together, suggest that the relationship between word rate and comprehension is structured by more than one underlying process. First, there are those studies in which comprehension has been measured at various word rates. Although no single study has included an adequate range of values for the word rate variable, when these studies are considered collectively, the relationship that emerges is one in which comprehension declines at a slow rate as word rate is increased until a word rate of appeoximately 275 w. p. m. is reached, and at a much faster rate thereafter (see Stimulus Variables, p. 489). Then, there are the experiments in which word intelligibility has been determined at several compressions (Characteristics of the Signal, p. 486). When the results of these studies are compared with the results of studies in which comprehension has been measured at several word rates, there is a strong suggestion that comprehension declines more rapidly than intelligibility as the amount of compression is increased. This suggestion has been confirmed by an experiment (Foulke & Sticht [B143]) in which both intelligibility and comprehension were determined at several compressions. As the amount of compression was increased, both intelligibility and comprehension decreased, but intelligibility was always superior to comprehension and was affected much less than comprehension by increasing the amount of compression.

The fact that increasing the amount of compression has a different effect upon comprehension than upon intelligibility suggests that decreased intelligibility is not, in itself, an adequate explanation of the loss in comprehension. One might expect decreased intelligibility to interfere with comprehension to some extent, but the cues that become available to a listener when he hears a succession of meaningful words with high sequential dependency as is the case when comprehension is measured, should at least partially compensate for this interference. In any case, if intelligibility were the only factor, comprehension would not decline at a different rate than intelligibility. The change in the rate at which comprehension declines beyond 275 w. p. m. may mean that when a certain critical word rate is reached, an additional factor begins to determine the loss in comprehension. The perception of speech entails the registration, encoding and storage of speech information, and these operations require time. When the word rate is too high, words cannot be processed as fast as they are received with the result that some of the words and their associated meanings are lost. To put it another way, when channel capacity is exceeded, some of the input cannot be recovered at the output (Miller F19 [&B173]).

Some neurological support for this view is provided by the findings of clinical audiology, reviewed earlier (see Intelligibility and Anatomical Damage, p. 489). When hearing losses are due to peripheral conductive disorders, the curve describing the relationship between amount of compression and the intensity required for 50 per cent intelligibility is elevated, but not changed in shape. On the other hand, when hearing losses are due to central disorders, such as temporal lobe tumors or lesions, or the more diffuse involutional changes that accompany presbycusis, the threshold curve just mentioned is not only elevated, but its shape is substantially altered. In some cases, when compression is moderately high, there is no intensity that will produce 50 per cent intelligibility. It may be that these central disorders have the effect of increasing the time required to process incoming speech elements so that the channel is overloaded at a lower word rate.

The explanation just presented is, of course, quite tentative. A good deal of research regarding sentence, word and syllabic rate will be required in order to provide a substantial basis for the hypothesis. A step in the right direction was made by Diehl et al. [B84] who measured the comprehension of selections, the word rates of which had been varied by varying the time between words. However, since the words they used had not been compressed in time, the maximum word rate that could be achieved by reducing the time between words was still relatively slow. Individual words would have to be subjected to moderately high compression before the method of

varying word rate by manipulating the intervals between words could
be used to produce the word rates that would be required to test the
hypothesis under consideration.   This research has not yet been performed.

Notes

1.   M. E. Enç and L. M. Stolurow.   "A Comparison of the
Effects of Two Recording Speeds on Learning and Retention. "   The
New Outlook for the Blind 54:39-48, 1960.

2.   Emerson Foulke, C. H. Amster, C. Y. Nolan, and R.
H. Bixler.   "The Comprehension of Rapid Speech by the Blind. "
Exceptional Children 29:134-41, 1962.

3.   W. Johnson, F. Darley and D. C. Spriesterbach.   Diagnostic Methods in Speech Pathology.   New York: Harper, 1963.

4.   Ralph G. Nichols and L. A. Stevens.   Are You Listening?   New York: McGraw Hill, 1957.

5.   Library of Congress.   Report on Compressed Speech Activities at the Division for the Blind.   Washington, D. C. :   The Library, 1966.

6.   (Unpublished research.)

7.   R. S. Woodworth and H. Schlosberg.   Experimental Psychology.   New York: Holt, 1954.

8.   David B. Orr and Herbert L. Friedman.   "Research on
Speeded Speech as an Educational Medium. "   Progress Report Grant
Number 7-48-7670-203, Office of Education.   Washington, D. C. :
U. S. Department HEW, 1964.

9.   Herbert L. Friedman, David B. Orr, O. R. Freedle,
and Cynthia M. Norris.   "Further Research on Speeded Speech as
an Educational Medium. "   Progress Report Number 2.   Grant Number 7-48-7670-267, Office of Education.   Washington, D. C. :   Department of HEW, 1966.

10.   Robinson, J. A.   "Category Clustering in Free Recall. "
J. Psychology 62:279-85, 1966.   Category Clustering: a "plan" for
Category Retrieval in Free Recall.   Technical Report No. 1 for
AF-AFOSR-1008-66.   Louisville, Ky. :   University of Louisville,
1966.   Scanning and Clustering: An Exploratory Investigation of Retrieval Strategies in Free Recall.   Technical Report Number Two
for AF-AFOSR-1008-66.   Louisville, Ky. :   University of Louisville,
1966.

11.   H. L. Cramer.   Intelligibility of Compressed Speech as
a Function of Degree and Direction of Delay in Presentation From
One Ear to the Other.   Paper presented to the Annual Meeting of the
American Psychological Association, 1965.

12.   Emerson Foulke.   A Comparison of Two Methods of
Compressing Speech.   Symposium paper presented at the Southeastern
Psychological Association, 1962.

13.   In press.

14.   Dale, Edgar and J. S. Chall.   "A Formula for Predicting Readability. "   Educational Research Bulletin 27:11-20+, 1948.

15.   Rudolph Flesch.   "A New Readability Yardstick. "   J.
Applied Psychology 32:221-23, 1948.

16. J. R. Rodgers. "A Formula for Predicting the Comprehension Level of Material to be Presented Orally." J. Educational Research 56:218-20, 1962.

17. L. Hartlage. "Differences in Listening Comprehension Between Blind and Sighted Subjects." International J. of Education for the Blind 13:1-6, 1963.

18. Robert Jester and R. M. Travers. Comprehension as a Function of Rate and Modality of Presentation. Paper presented to the Annual Meeting of the American Psychological Association, 1965.

19. George A. Miller. "What is Information Measurement?" American Psychologist 8:3-11, 1953.

SUMMARY OF RESEARCH ON TIME-COMPRESSED SPEECH

Sam Duker

This summary has as its scope the research performed on the subject of rate-altered speech which is commonly, if inaccurately, referred to as time-compressed speech. The change on the rate of speech may be either to increase or decrease the amount of time necessary to use in transmitting a particular message. In the first case we refer to the process as expansion.

There are, of course, a number of ways in which expansion and compression of a message can be accomplished. Among them are: 1. Change in the rate of speaking. This procedure has the obvious disadvantage that the range of human voice production is not very great. Besides any person attempting to speak very rapidly becomes less and less intelligible to the listener as he speeds up his speech. The use of this procedure was studied by Goldstein [B193] and Goodman-Malamuth [B194], among others.

2. Rapid playback. This is the procedure whereby a recorded message is played back at a rate differing from that at which it was recorded. It is common knowledge that fast playback, because of the frequency shift involved, turns into an unintelligible "Donald Duck" effect. This procedure has been studied by Tiffany [B422], Fletcher [B114], and Resta [B353], among others.

3. Simplification of the text. Shorter words, a simpler vocabulary, and an easier grammatical structure are among the factors that might be used. Similar procedures have been studied by Reid [B346] and others. 4. Abstract or précis writing. This method of reducing a message to its essentials has been reported on by Wason [B434].

5. Mechanical means. This method was pioneered through the work of Garvey [B167, B168] and Fairbanks [B105]. Both of these

research workers had studied the prior work of Miller & Licklider [B283]. There it had been established that a large portion of a message could be deleted without affecting intelligibility if the interruptions were made at frequent intervals, were random, and of very short duration. From this Garvey and Fairbanks, at about the same time, independently came to the conclusion that time could be saved by using such an interrupted message if the uninterrupted portions were abutted. Such an abuttment was performed by both these individuals by manual means. This was such a demanding and time-consuming task as to be impractical. Subsequently the invention by Fairbanks [B105] of a mechanical device that would perform the task made speech-compression a feasible task.

Since that invention a number of devices have been invented and developed. Foulke ["Compressors--Actual and Imminent," CR-CR Newsletter 6(5):1-4, 1972] has recently given a list of these devices which reads as follows:

COMPRESSORS--ACTUAL AND IMMINENT

For many years, the commercial availability of speech compressors was limited. Around 1960, the Kay Electric Company offered the Vari-Vox, a compressor based upon the Fairbanks principle, but its performance was unsatisfactory, and the few that were sold were collecting dust on laboratory shelves. Starting in the early sixties, the Gotham Audio Corporation in New York began to import the Tempo-Regulator, and later its successor, the Information Rate Changer. These machines also employed the Fairbanks principle; that is, a rotating cylinder which carried four playback heads was used to obtain samples of speech from a recorded tape. The Information Rate Changer was available in this country until 1970.

In 1969, Discerned Sound introduced the Whirling Dervish. This is a compressor of the Fairbanks type that uses a rotating cylinder with four playback heads to obtain samples from a continuous tape loop upon which the signal to be compressed or expanded is temporarily stored. In the past few years, there has been an increasing interest in the development of new speech compressors, particularly electronic speech compressors, and many of these developmental efforts are now coming to fruition. From correspondence and from direct conversations, I gather that there is considerable confusion regarding the speech compressors that are currently available or in advanced stages of development. The information to follow is presented in the hope that it will alleviate this confusion somewhat. The first four paragraphs present information about speech compressors that are commercially available now. The remaining paragraphs present information about speech compressors which exist as successful prototypes, but which have not yet been brought into production for commercial distribution. The list may not be complete, but it includes all of the speech compressors known to the Center for Rate Controlled Recordings.

The Whirling Dervish, manufactured by Discerned Sound, 4459 Kraft Avenue, North Hollywood, California 91602, is an electromechanical compressor of the Fairbanks type. It is available as a separate unit, or as a component in a system which also includes a Teac tape recorder that has been modified to provide continuously variable tape speed. The control of this recorder has been integrated with the control of the compressor, and it is used to play the tape that is to be compressed. At present, the selling price of the Whirling Dervish alone is $3000 and the selling price of the system including the Whirling Dervish and the tape recorder is $3595. A more detailed description of this compressor is presented in the volume 2, number 10, and the volume 5, number 4 issues of the CRCR Newsletter. Now under development at Discerned Sound is a compressor of the same general type as the Whirling Dervish. It will be less flexible than the Whirling Dervish but it will sell at a significantly lower price. Discerned Sound expects to report its availability and price before long.

The VOCOM I is manufactured by PKM, 1976 Ryan Avenue West, St. Paul, Minnesota 55113. This compressor obtains the samples that are represented in the compressed reproduction by starting and stopping a tape as the signal is being recorded on it. The decisions to stop the tape are based upon information obtained from the signal that is being copied. In one mode of operation, compression is achieved by stopping the tape recorder during the unfilled intervals that are distributed throughout fluent speech production. To obtain additional compression, the copying tape recorder may be set to sample vowel sounds by stopping and starting repeatedly while they are occurring. The compressed signal is recorded on a cassette, and the cassette transport is an integral part of the equipment. The VOCOM I accomplishes speech expansion by lengthening the unfilled intervals in fluent speech production. The selling price of the VOCOM I is $995. An article giving a more detailed description of the VOCOM I will appear in the next issue of the newsletter.

Varispeech-I is an electronic speech compressor developed by Professor Francis Lee, a member of the faculty of the Department of Electrical Engineering at M.I.T., and manufactured by Lexicon, Inc., 60 Turner Street, Waltham, Massachusetts 02154. This compressor includes a cassette transport on which the signal to be compressed is reproduced, and a small, special-purpose computer which obtains from the input signal the samples that are reproduced consecutively in the compressed output. The device is also capable of speech expansion. The selling price of the Varispeech-I compressor is $1500. A more detailed description of the Varispeech-I appeared in volume 6, number 4 of the newsletter.

The Cambridge Research and Development Group, 21 Bridge Square, Westport, Connecticut 06880, has announced the suc-

cess of their effort to incorporate the functions required for
the electronic compression of speech in two integrated circuit
chips.   These chips are small enough to be included in even
the smallest cassette recorders.   Cambridge estimates that
volume production of this pair of chips should bring their costs
down to approximately $10 and that inclusion of the chips in a
cassette recorder might raise its cost by as little as $40.
Cambridge Research and Development Group is not a manufacturing concern, but it is currently engaged in the negotiation
of agreements with manufacturers of tape recorders who will
be licensed to incorporate the Cambridge circuitry in the equipment they manufacture.   One licensing agreement has already
been announced.   Crown International, 1718 West Mishawaka
Road, Elkhart, Indiana 46514 is now accepting orders for a
discrete component version of the Cambridge compressor that
will be built into their Crown 800 tape recorder, a professional recorder of the type used in the broadcast industry.   The
Cambridge compressor was described earlier in the volume 6,
number 2 issue of CRCR Newsletter.

The speech compressor under development at Compressed
Time, Inc., 261 West 11th Street, New York, New York 10014,
is an electromechanical compressor of the Fairbanks type.
The prototype I observed incorporates a cassette transport,
modified for continuously variable speed, on which the signal
to be compressed is reproduced.   The samples of the input
signal that appear in the compressed reproduction are obtained
by a sampling wheel with four playback heads, from a storage
loop on which the input signal is temporarily recorded.   Like
other compressors of this type, the one being developed by
Compressed Time, Inc. is also capable of speech expansion.
This compressor is not yet in production, but its developers
are negotiating with manufacturers at present.   Their objective
is a compressor that is cheaper, smaller, and easier to operate than other compressors of the electromechanical type.

The AmBiChron, developed by Mr. Richard Koch, 67 Smith
Street, Lynbrook, New York 11563, is a prototype electronic
compressor.   It is in essence, a special-purpose computer that
obtains from the input signal the samples which are reproduced
consecutively in the compressed output.   It is also capable of
speech expansion.   In its present form, it does not incorporate
a tape transport for playing the tape to be compressed.   However, if a tape recorder with an AC motor is used for this
purpose, this motor may be operated from a variable frequency
power supply in the compressor, and the necessary adjustment
in tape speed is then accomplished with the same control knob
that is used to adjust the electronic circuitry for a desired
compression.   The AmBiChron is not commercially available
as yet, but Mr. Koch is now looking for a manufacturer.   The
volume 5, number 11 issue of the CRCR Newsletter contains a
more detailed description of the AmBiChron.

6. Use of the computer. Because deletions can be made on other than a random basis, there are great advantages to be found in the use of the computer to perform the tasks performed by the mechanical devices just described. The use of the computer for this purpose has been described by Scott [B382], Qureshi [B338], Suen [B415], and Seo [B384].

History and Previous Reviews

The reported research on time-compressed speech is found in both academic theses and in post-doctoral research. The latter type of report originates principally from a few centers where speech compressors have been available. Doctoral and master's theses have been written in a wide variety of universities and colleges throughout the United States.

The principal centers for post-doctoral research are: 1. The Center for Rate Controlled Recordings of the Perceptual Alternatives Laboratory at the University of Louisville. This Center is headed by Dr. Emerson Foulke who is one of the most prolific disseminators of information about time-compressed speech. Under his auspices two conferences on the subject have been held in Louisville [B137, B138] and the CRCR Newsletter [B70] has been issued monthly since 1967. A variety of types of speech compressors is available in the Center.

2. The American Institutes for Research at Silver Spring, Maryland has been an extraordinarily productive center for investigation and dissemination of information concerning time-compressed speech. The work there was begun under the leadership of David B. Orr and continued by Herbert L. Friedman. A summary of some of the research carried on here has been excerpted in Chapter Two of this Part of the Anthology [B153].

3. Other centers are located at a number of universities including: University of Illinois, Syracuse University, University of Utah, and M. I. T. Reviews of research of varying degrees of excellence are found as introductory material in the numerous doctoral dissertations written about a variety of phases of time-compressed speech. The most complete review of research to date is that by Foulke & Sticht [B146], excerpts from which have been included in this chapter.

Evaluation

It is of prime importance to draw a sharp distinction between intelligibility studies and those concerned with comprehension as these are two distinctly separate concepts. Kenneth A. Harwood's explanation of the difference in the significance of these two terms is an excellent one ["A Concept of Listenability," Western Speech 14(2):10-12, 1950; reprinted in Listening: Readings (ed. Sam Duker), Metuchen, N. J. : Scarecrow, 1966; p. 21-24].

No single test or set of tests have been generally accepted as measures of either intelligibility or of comprehension of time-compressed speech. This is illustrative of the unfortunate state of affairs that also exists in the reported research in other areas. I refer to the lack of coordination between studies. Because of this, many studies dealing with the same problem are not comparable because of the use of uncomparable subjects, material, and evaluation. The result is an unnecessary duplication of effort that often fails to produce any contribution to the body of verified findings concerning various aspects of time-compressed speech.

Variables in Research Studies

Fundamentally, there are three variables that can be studied in research work on compressed speech: variables in the material that is compressed; variables in the process of compression; and variables in the listeners to compressed speech.

Variables in material compressed. George [B173] and Reid [B346] have investigated the effect on comprehension of the difficulty of the textual material used in the research study. Meyerson [B277], Goldhaber [B184], and Opubar [B304] have investigated the effect of compressing material spoken in languages other than English. The effect of noise on the intelligibility of time-compressed materials has been studied by a number of researchers. The recent work by Opubar [B304] and Schwimmer [B379] is typical.

Extensive study has taken place concerning the importance of pauses in compressed material. Among investigators of this issue have been Aaronson [B32], Agnello [B5], Diehl et al. [B83], Goldman-Eisler [B189], Miron & Brown [B288], and Overmann [B316]. It is not possible to make any short statement that will adequately summarize the research in this important area. It can, however, be stated with certainty that the message redundancy which makes comprehension of time-compressed speech possible is, at least to a considerable extent, related to the proportion of pause time in the text of the material that is time-compressed.

Many studies have been concerned with the semantic, syntactic, and grammatical content of the material that is compressed. Typical of these are studies by Miron & Brown [B288], Robins [B356], and Lieberman [B258], respectively. Attention has been given by a considerable number of investigators to the effect of simultaneous presentation of visual material as augmentation to the compressed material. Here one finds a variety of reported findings some of which are somewhat contradictory. Among these studies are those by Foulke [B117], Jester [B235], and Woodcock [B450].

The effect of redundancy in the material compressed has been studied among others by Fairbanks [B108], Fant [B110], and Foulke

[B117]. The voice quality of the person who recorded the message
which was then compressed has been studied by Foulke [B117] and
Zemlin [B455] among others. Findings indicate that the sex of the
speaker may be a significant factor. The purpose of the message
as a factor in comprehension has been studied by Wheeless [B442]
and Mack [B272].

Variables in the process of compression. A number of reports have been made concerning the effect of slow playback: Bennett [B23], Fletcher [B114], Tiffany [B422], and Zemlin [B455]; and
of fast playback by Ball [B13], Bellefleur [B21], Foulke [B117], and
Resta [B353]. The various systems of compression have been reviewed by Stevens [B402]. The effect on intelligibility or comprehension of various types of compression has been studied by Chang
[B54], Chapman [B55], Fairbanks [B100], Fant [B110], Foulke [B117],
and Gould [B199] as well as by many others.

Effect on the message of compression by computer has been
studied by Chapman [B55], Foulke [B117], Ingham [B231], Reddy
[B344], and Scott [B382], among others. Dichotic listening has been
investigated by Day [B76], Emmerich [B95], Foulke [B117], Gerber
[B174], Huggins [B227], Jones [B240], and Scott [B382].

Variables in the listeners. Jester [B235] has reported on the
effect of individual differences among listeners to compressed speech.
Specific differences have also been investigated: for instance, sex
by Goldhaber [B186] and McCracken [B270]; intelligence by De Hoop
[B77], Foulke [B117], Gordon [B195], Lovitt [B263], Parker [B319],
Spicker [B393], Sticht [B407], and Woodcock [B450]; emotional stability by Staffen [B399] and McDonald [B271]; age by Foulke [B117]
and Luterman [B266]; reaction time by Lysaght [B267]; and academic
achievement by Goldhaber [B185] and Langford [B249]

The effect of practice on comprehension has been studied in
depth by Friedman [B153]. Additional reports on this aspect of comprehension of compressed speech may be found in Grumpelt [B201],
Klineman [B242], Krall [B247], Orr [B313], Rawls [B343], Robinson
[B358], and Woodcock [B450]. The effect of chunking on listening to
compressed speech has been discussed by Friedman [B153] and Miller [B281]. Rate preferences of listeners to compressed speech are
reported on in studies by Cain and Lass [B47], Foulke [B117], Lovitt
[B263], and Nelson [B296].

Needed Research

A number of areas exist for both new and further research.
The most striking need is for a searching analysis of the factors involved in listening to compressed speech.   There is a plethora of
research on the effects of practice on efficiency of listening to compressed speech but there is no research, that I am aware of, that
is concerned with the teaching of the art of listening to compressed
speech. Such teaching will only be possible after the factors that

are involved are isolated.   An article by Friedman [B154] is a step
in the right direction but has not been followed up to any degree of
the thoroughness that will be required.

The excerpts in Part II of this Anthology will, it is hoped,
present the reader with many ideas for filling gaps in present verified knowledge about the subject of compressed speech.

REVIEW OF THE LITERATURE ON INTELLIGIBILITY
OF SIMULTANEOUS TIME AND FREQUENCY DISTORTION

John T. Tschantz

The testing of speech discrimination is the major interest of
the present review; literature reported on here will be limited to
those articles dealing with time and/or frequency distortion, and
their subsequent findings.

No study of the past experimentation dealing with time and
frequency distortion would be complete without including the early
work of Fletcher [B114] at the Bell Telephone Laboratories.   Fletcher's work with the transmission of speech led him to the discovery
that when a phonograph record was speeded up, or slowed down,
the frequency formants of the recorded speech would retain their
original octave intervals.   The frequencies, in the case of an increase in speed, would be multiplied in direct relation to the increase in speed.   If the record was slowed down, the frequency formants would subsequently be reduced.   In other words if the speed
of the record was doubled, the frequencies formants would be doubled and 300 c. p. s. would become 600 c. p. s.   If the speed was reduced by one-half, the frequency formants were also reduced by
one-half and 300 c. p. s. would become 150 c. p. s.   He found this
shift to be true of all frequency formants of the speech signal, including the harmonics.

Fletcher next recorded articulation lists which he played
through a telephone circuit at various speeds.   By varying the speed
he found that intelligibility was affected as the speed was increased
or decreased from normal.   From the results obtained he was able
to construct a graph which depicted the various speeds of rotation,
and different discrimination scores obtained as the speed was moved
away from normal.   Figure 1 shows that the 50 per cent discrimination score was reached at approximately .65 and 1.6 times the original speed at 1.0.

It is interesting to note that Fletcher found discrimination
was affected to a greater degree at less deviation from normal speed
when the speed and hence the frequency formants were decreased,
and that the discrimination was affected to a much lesser degree as

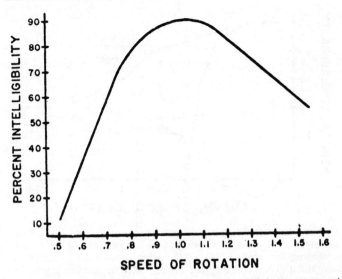

Figure 1. The effect upon articulation of multiplying component frequencies by a common factor (after Fletcher, 1929, p. 293).

the speed and frequency formants were multiplied.

Since Fletcher, little was done to investigate time and frequency distortion and its effect on discrimination until Garvey [B170] developed an experiment called "Speeded Speech." In order to produce his accelerated speech, Garvey cut out portions of previously taped speech, and then spliced the remaining sections together thus producing a new tape. Eleven tapes were constructed in this manner with an acceleration range from 1.5 to 4.0 times the original speed. The speech material used on the tapes were spondaic words which had been recorded at twice the standard rate of speed. The resultant long lengths of tape allowed for the edited intervals. The techniques used were described as follows:

> The position of the words on the tape was determined by slowly passing the tape over the magnetic playback head of the recorder. The beginning and ending of each word could be determined auditorily and then marked on tape. Once the position of the words had been determined, the sections to be removed were marked on the tape and later cut out. The ends of the segments remaining to form a new abbreviated speech pattern were then spliced together. An acceleration of twice the original speed could be accomplished by removing one centimeter, leaving the second, removing the third, leaving in the fourth, and so on throughout the speech record [B170].

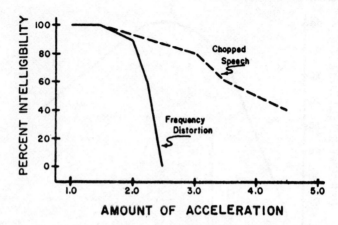

Figure 2. The relationship between intelligibility and the amount of acceleration. The dotted curve represents results obtained without accompanying frequency shift. The solid curve represents the results obtained from accelerating speech with an accompanying frequency shift (after Garvey, 1953, p. 104).

As can be seen in Figure 2 the discrimination results obtained on normal listeners using the cut or accelerated speech were quite different from those found by Fletcher's experiments which included not only a time change, but also a frequency distortion. Garvey in an effort to include frequency distortion in his experiment, accelerated the tape and rerecorded it at 7.5 i.p.s. Five speeds from 1.5 to 2.5 times normal were recorded in this manner with appropriate spacing between words. Garvey then presented 11 conditions of varying degrees of speeded speech, where frequency was held constant, to groups of six subjects each. The other five conditions were frequency distortion conditions where time and frequency varied reciprocally. As can also be seen in Figure 2, frequency distortion more closely approximated Fletcher's results.

The results of Garvey's experiment showed that frequency distortion coupled with time distortion had a much greater effect on discrimination ability than had time distortion by itself. While Garvey's interest was primarily directed to the amount and kind of distortion that could be introduced before intelligibility was grossly affected, it can be inferred from his results that frequency formants have a greater effect on intelligibility. Garvey explained that the large amount of distortion possible was related to the presence of an "excess" of auditory cues in the normal speech pattern.

Calearo [B48] designed a study to investigate the relationship between speed of delivery and intensity in speech discrimination under both normal and pathological conditions. His main interest was to determine the effect of speeded speech on patients with presbycusis, and with lesions of the temporal lobe. The material and technique of the experiment included the use of sentences recorded at three different rates of speech. The first one was recorded at a rate of 140 words per minute (in Italian), which was considered a normal speaking rate. The other two lists of sentences were recorded at rates of 250 and 350 w. p. m. The recordings were made in three different ways: (1) by using a speaker having exceptional possibilities of accelerating his speaking voice; (2) by transferring the primitive recording on a magnetic tape which could be rotated at different speeds; and (3) by employing a special apparatus which allows a direct acceleration of the message without any alteration of frequency [B48]. He does not explain the apparatus used nor how the acceleration was achieved without a subsequent frequency shift.

In tests of normals it was found that a threshold shift of 5 to 10 db from normal values accompanied an acceleration of speech to 250 words per minute, and a shift of 10 to 15 db accompanied an increase to 350 w. p. m. The resulting articulation curves for the three different rates of speed were found to be almost parallel. It was felt that the slight increase in volume neutralized any impairment of discrimination that might have resulted from the increase in speed. He presented the materials at the same three rates to patients with presbycusis, and to patients with temporal lobe tumors. A comparison of the resultant articulation curves for the three groups of subjects, and each of the three speech conditions, shows near normal discrimination ability for all three groups at the 140 word-per-minute presentation. At the 250 w. p. m. presentation the group of subjects with temporal lobe tumors began to have difficulty with discrimination, while the group with presbycusis encountered only slight difficulty. At the 350 w. p. m. presentation the group with presbycusis was able to get only about 50 per cent of the message, while the group with temporal lobe tumors was able to get only a few of the words. Calearo attributed the increased difficulty of the last two groups in understanding speech at high syllabic rates to: "a delay at the levels of the various synapses of the auditory pathways and of the cortex."

Fairbanks [B107], using a device which allowed him to hold frequency constant while he compressed the duration or time of a speech signal, found that subjects were able to discriminate speech without difficulty even though the duration of the signal was greatly reduced. An investigation by Kurtzrock [B248] also indicated that intelligibility was not as greatly affected by an acceleration of time as it was by a multiplication of frequency.

J. D. Harris ["The Importance of Hearing at 3000 cps for Understanding Speeded Speech," Laryngoscope 70:131-41, 1960] in a study designed to investigate the importance of hearing at 3000 c. p. s. devised a discrimination test using a time distortion in the form of speeded speech. He was cognizant of the fact that normal speech contains a great amount of redundancy which affords the mildly hearing handicapped person enough clues in an ideal hearing situation to hear fairly well. However, he points out these same people describe a great deal of difficulty in other than ideal situations.   He was particularly interested in the necessity of good high frequency hearing.

Using Fletcher's sentence lists as a reference, which were devised to test communications equipment, Harris developed 100 sentences of 5 to 15 words each.   Each sentence was accompanied by four words from which a multiple-choice response could be selected. The rules for construction of the sentences and response words were:

> a.   Three key word-ideas per sentence.
> b.   Of the four responses offered on the answer sheet, only one could conceivably be correct if the whole sentence was understood.
> c.   If any one of the key words was missed, at least one and usually two or three of the three other responses would offer a reasonable answer [see note above].

The sentences were then recorded by a speaker with a general American dialect, who habitually spoke rather fast, but clearly. Many recordings of the sentences were made, which were then carefully analyzed on a sound level recorder.   The words per minute were computed which resulted in the selection of six tapes representing a distribution of speeds of 345, 330, 324, 316, 300, and 280 words per minute.   However, it was found that good test-retest reliability was present between two halves of each tape so they were split into Forms 1 and 2 of 50 sentences each.

The subjects for the test were 25 young male adults with normal hearing, and 47 adults with varying degrees of high frequency loss.   Normative data were established on the 25 young adults.   The first group studied were subjects who had only a minor loss at 3000 c. p. s.   It was found that this group had a drop in discrimination of as much as 30 per cent as the sentences were given at progressively faster speeds.   The second group studied were subjects who had normal hearing acuity through 1000 c. p. s. , but with a 20 db or more loss at 2000 c. p. s.   This group dropped from near normal discrimination ability to discrimination scores ranging from 70 to 35 per cent.   While Harris did not feel that frequency distortion per se was responsible for discrimination loss, he did feel that sentence intelligibility was frequency-dependent upon the 3000 c. p. s. range.   He felt that the study did show the special importance of the higher frequencies when speed stress was put upon the speech signal.

Bellefleur [B21] completed the first actual study involving time and frequency distortion on pathological ears.   Although he felt that time was also a distortion factor in his study, it did not appear to significantly influence the end result since previous studies had ruled out time per se as a contributor when it was coupled with frequency distortion.   The purpose of his investigation was to determine how shifts in the formant frequencies of speech affected different hearing handicapped groups.

Fifty-four subjects were used in the experiment. Thirty of the subjects were children, 15 audiometrically normal, and 15 with varying degrees of sensorineural hearing loss present from birth. The remaining 24 subjects were adults. These were divided into groups of six by pathology: six normal, six otosclerotic, six with Ménière's disease, and six with acoustic trauma. The various groups were chosen because it was felt that they were most representative of the various types of clinical audiometric findings. The equipment used in the experiment consisted of a speech amplifier and a record player so designed that the speed of rotation of the turntable was continuously adjustable from 10 to 84 r.p.m. A tone of 1000 c.p.s. on the record could thus be shifted downward to 300 c.p.s. or upward to 2300 c.p.s. A graph was constructed so that any setting along this continuum could be converted to frequency based on the standard 1000 c.p.s. which was recorded at 33 1/3 r.p.m.

Phonograph discs containing the CID research sentence lists and spondaic words were used for testing material. The sentences were used to establish the points where intelligibility would be tested by the spondaic word lists. Three points were determined in the study. The first was described as the most natural setting (MNS). The subject was allowed to control the speed of the record containing the sentences. When he had established the point where he felt that the sentences were the most intelligible, he was given a discrimination test using the spondaic word lists. Next the subject determined the point, either at an increased or decreased speed, where he could just recognize a word or two of the sentences. Once this point had been determined on the frequency scale, the subject was given a spondaic list at the setting to assess intelligibility. Discrimination measurements were taken above and below the setting until it was possible to ascertain the 50 per cent intelligibility point both at the increased frequency and the decreased frequency. Figure 3 shows a graphic display of the results obtained. An examination of the graph shows that all groups set the MNS higher than the 1000 c.p.s. standard. This is interesting when it is noted that particularly the hard-of-hearing children and the adults with acoustic trauma have the most nearly normal hearing in the lower frequencies, and might therefore be oriented to judging "most natural sounding" at a frequency lower than the 1000 c.p.s. standard. The results also indicated that the sensorineural groups had a more restricted range between their high-point 50 per cent score and their low-point 50 per cent score than did the normals and the conductive hearing loss groups.

It is also interesting to note that the 50 per cent low scores for the group of adult acoustic traumas aligned themselves with the normal and conductive groups, suggesting that the 50 per cent low speed is more closely related to speech discrimination than the 50 per cent high speed. Correlations of aspects of the audiometric tests and the 50 per cent high score showed little correlation except

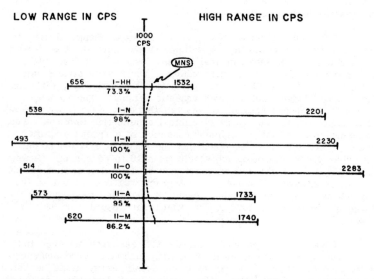

Figure 3. Graphic representation of the MNS, 50 per cent high and
50 per cent low scores. Speech discrimination scores are given for
purposes of comparison (after Bellefleur, 1964, p. 68).

at 4000 c. p. s. The author ends the article stating that "the study
has shown that time-frequency distortion may have implications for
new diagnostic and therapeutic techniques. "

It was with this in mind that Hill [B218] undertook a study of
speech discrimination difficulties in elderly individuals. He hypothesized that elderly individuals, especially those with presbycusis,
might be able to understand speech better if it was manipulated in
such a manner as to shift its component frequencies downward, and
increase the duration of each speech unit. He felt that in so doing,
this might closely approximate the speech conditions that would be
compatible with the general audiometric configuration associated with
presbycusis. He also hypothesized that the upward shift of the component frequencies in addition to the shorter duration of the speech
signal, would have a more limited range for the presbycusi subjects
than would be found for the normal hearing subjects.

The method of Hill's experiment was based on Fletcher's previously described work, in which he found that a decrease or increase in the speed of the rotations of a phonograph record, would
subsequently divide or multiply the frequency components of a speech
signal, and at the same time decrease or increase the duration of
the speech signal. Three sets of subjects were used in this experiment. The first group consisted of young adults (Y) with unimpaired
hearing, and the second, of older adults (O) with hearing normal for
their age. The main criteria for the determination of the group was

fairly normal pure tone thresholds and a discrimination score by PB-50 lists of not less than 84 per cent. The third group were subjects with presbycusis (P) that exhibited a mild but typical high frequency loss and a discrimination score, as determined by the PB-50 lists, of not more than 78 per cent. Each group contained 30 subjects. Four experimental questions were posed:

1. When the subjects are free to manipulate the time and frequency characteristics of speech, and when the experimental task is to select speech which sounds most normal, do elderly subjects with presbycusis choose a time and frequency relationship which is different from the relationships selected by young adult subjects and elderly subjects who do not have significant hearing involvement?

2. When the subjects are free to manipulate the time and frequency characteristics of speech, and when the experimental task is to lower the frequency components of speech and extend the duration of each component to the point where speech is no longer intelligible, do presbycusic subjects exhibit greater tolerance for the distortion than young or elderly adults with no significant hearing involvement?

3. When the subjects are free to manipulate the time and frequency characteristics of speech, and when the experimental task is to shift the frequency components of speech upward and shorten the duration of each component to the point where speech is no longer intelligible, do presbycusic subjects exhibit less tolerance for the distortion than young or elderly adults with no significant hearing involvement?

4. Is the characterizing difference in discrimination ability between presbycusic subjects and young adult subjects or elderly subjects with no significant hearing involvement reflected in a constant difference of similar magnitude when the intelligibility for speech is tested under a variety of time and frequency relationships [B218].

The equipment used in this experiment consisted of a commercial speech audiometer with a standard high quality turntable. In order to vary and control the speed over a wide range, an external method of driving the turntable was devised. When the turntable control knob was in the neutral position, the turntable could rotate freely; then a flat, continuous belt was adjusted around the turntable and the pulley of an externally mounted motor. The motor was operated through a variable output rectifier. This arrangement made it possible to vary the turntable speed from approximately one revolution per minute to more than 100. The subject could then make the various required adjustments of speed by controlling the calibrated variable output rectifier.

Two sets of testing material were used in the experiment.

Both had been put on commercial recording discs using a male speaker with good diction.   The first set of material was the CID research lists of sentences called "Everyday Speech. "   While listening to this list the subject was asked to find the point where speech sounded most normal by controlling the variable output rectifier. He then was asked to increase the speed until he could only understand about half of the words in the sentences.   He was next asked to decrease the speed until he could understand approximately half of the words in the sentences.   The subject was then given a list of ten spondaic words at each of the previously determined speed settings.   He was also given two spondaic word lists at points between the lowest setting and the most normal setting, and between the highest setting and the most normal setting.   These points represented the one-third and the two-thirds distance points in the interim for each range below and above the most normal setting.   Seven discrimination scores were obtained from this procedure.   The results of the experiment are presented in Figure 4.

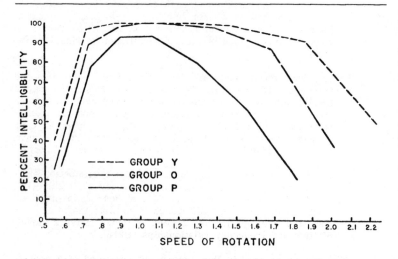

Figure 4.   Graph showing speed of rotation and percentage of spondaic words intelligible at the subject selected settings LRI, MNS, and HRI and at the derived intermediate settings (after Hill, 1964, p. 59).

It was found that as distortion increased in either direction from normal, intelligibility decreased sooner and more rapidly for the older normals than for the young adults, and earlier and more rapidly for the persons with presbycusis than for the older normals. Using the Mann-Whitney U procedure, it was also found that there was a relationship between the high setting and discrimination for the adults with presbycusis and the normal adults, but not for the younger subjects with normal hearing.   No direct relationship occurred between the lowest setting and discrimination for any of the age groups. Hill felt that the experimental evidence indicated that time and frequency distorted speech may lend itself to further investigations of its ability to more correctly determine functional discrimination ability.

In summary, since the object of the present study was to determine the value of time and frequency distorted speech as a clinical tool, it was decided to use time and frequency division and multiplication points based on Hill's study. The points chosen were those that seemed to represent the most significant separation of the three groups he studied. It was decided that three points would be tested. The first point selected to be tested was undistorted speech recorded at 33 1/3 r.p.m. The second point to be tested was the decelerated point which demonstrated the most significant separation of discrimination scores between the three groups, but which was still within a testable range. An examination of Hill's Figure 4 indicated this point to be at a speed of rotation of .7 or 700 c.p.s. The third point to be selected was the accelerated point that also showed the greatest separation of the three groups tested, but which was still within a testable range of discrimination ability. This point was found on Figure 4 to be a speed of rotation of 1.7 or 1700 c.p.s.

Spondaic words are not usually used for discrimination testing, but previous experimenters have used them in this manner, especially in studies where distortions of time were examined. Hirsh described them as being highly intelligible under a variety of conditions, including frequency distortion (filtering), and noise. Garvey utilized spondaic words in his speeded speech experiments. As mentioned earlier, Bellefleur also used these words for discrimination determination in his study in which there was a distortion of both time and frequency. He had previously determined in a pilot study that they were suitable for use in studies of distortion. Hill also used spondaic words for discrimination testing where the speech signal was distorted both by time and frequency, and found them totally suitable for this type of experiment.

The previously reported studies indicate that a determination of discrimination ability can be obtained by the use of spondaic words when they are distorted both in time and frequency. It has been shown particularly by Hill, that they differentiate between persons with normal hearing and those with presbycusis.

Chapter 2

BEGINNINGS OF ORGANIZED RESEARCH ACTIVITIES

In this chapter we examine two items. The first furnishes a rationale for future research and the second summarizes intensive work at the American Institutes for Research over the span of several years.

One of the reasons for accepting the idea that aural reception of speech could be comprehended if ways could be found to change the speech rate upwards without adverse frequency shifting rests on the generally accepted fact that much "mind-wandering" takes place in the ordinary listening process. That thought processes of this kind do not necessarily adversely affect comprehension is easily verified in one's everyday experience. Obviously, however, the listening process becomes more fruitful when the additional thinking time which is available to the listener is concentrated on the listening task by anticipating and by evaluating what is being said.

Dr. David B. Orr, one of the pioneers in the development of research on time-compressed speech wrote a short note on his hypothesis that the speed of the thought processes in so far as they relate to incoming information may be directly related to reading and listening rates that have been acquired by an individual. This note constitutes the first item in this chapter. It is short but the ideas expressed can be profitably mulled over at length as they are of particular significance not only to those concerned with time-compressed speech but also to all those concerned with the more effective teaching of the skills of both reading and listening.

The remainder of this chapter is an excerpt from a lengthy report by Dr. Herbert L. Friedman on the research activities concerning time-compressed speech carried on over a three-year period at the American Institutes for Research at Silver Spring, Maryland. The work there was originally under the direction of Dr. David B. Orr, the author of the note which constitutes the first item in this chapter. After his departure from AIR, Dr. Friedman, who had been associated in this work with Dr. Orr, carried on this research in expanded directions. The research summarized here is concerned primarily with the effect of practice and of various other procedures in improving comprehension of time-compressed speech at increasingly rapid rates. The work was carried out with care and exactitude so that the careful reading of this report will be both profitable and informative.

NOTE ON THOUGHT RATE AS A FUNCTION
OF READING AND LISTENING RATES

David B. Orr

R. G. Nichols ["Ten Components of Effective Listening," Education 75:292-302, 1955] has proposed that connected thought proceeds at speeds on the order of 400 words per minute. If such a rate does indeed prevail, one may ask why. Two possibilities exist: that thought rate for an individual is a sort of psycho-physiological constant for that individual; or that thought rate is a result of potential rate interacting with a number of experiential factors.

What factors might tend to influence thought rate and perhaps limit it? The first is rate of auditory input. The child is early exposed to connected discourse via the auditory channel but almost never at a rate higher than normal speaking rates (100 to 150 w.p.m.). In addition, most modern reading instruction methods fail to build closely on the rather well-developed audio-vergal facility of the young child. The logical consequence of these factors is the conditioning of a rather slow thought rate as a result of comparatively slow input rates (and also unnecessary difficulty in learning to read). In truth, learning to read is often rather difficult, and the average child is around the sixth-grade level before reading becomes his preferred mode of informational input [S. E. Taylor. Listening. Washington, D.C.: National Educ. Assoc., 1964].

Even those children who make the transition to reading rather easily face a limitation. Reading rate (in the sense of every word as opposed to skimming) is also limited physiologically by the number of fixations that can be made per second by the eyes. One authority has estimated that 700 w.p.m. is about maximum for "every word" reading, and haphazard development of eye span and saccadic movements usually leads to lower rates. It is unlikely that very many children have occasion to process information more rapidly than required by their normal reading speeds, and thus a conditioned thought rate at about the normal reading rate is probable.

Exploratory research by the author and his colleagues in the comprehension of highly speeded (but pitch-normal) connected discourse is of interest. For example, auditory comprehension began to fall off rapidly as auditory rate exceeded normal reading rate. Further, however, the use of very rapid auditory material as a pacing procedure while reading resulted in significant increases in reading speed, without loss of comprehension. These tentative findings, when confirmed by current work, may support the notion that the rate of processing of connected discourse is normally habituated, but is trainable.

REPORT ON A FIVE-PART RESEARCH STUDY

Herbert L. Friedman

I. CONCENTRATED PRACTICE STUDY

This report describes the first experiment in a series conducted from March 1965 through February 1967. This research is an outgrowth of the experimentation conducted under grant number OE-7-48-7670-203 (3/63 - 1/65). In earlier research by the investigators, college freshmen and sophomores were exposed to 10 to 15 hours of practice listening material from 325 to 475 w. p. m. Subjects were tested on historical passages and a standard reading test, before and after experimentation, and periodically during practice. The results of this research suggested the following:

1. Zero to three hours of exposure to rapid speech led to comprehension at 325 w. p. m. (or approximately double normal speed) which was between 80 and 100 per cent of comprehension at normal speed.
2. Ten to 15 hours of exposure to rapid speech (325 to 475 w. p. m.) led to a significant improvement on a repeated passage at 475 w. p. m. presented before and after the experiment as compared to that of a control group which received similar tests but did not receive practice.
3. Practice periods which were uninterrupted for about one hour proved more efficacious as training than practice listening which was punctuated with three-minute rest periods every 10 minutes.

The current experiment essentially replicated the first experiment with the alteration of one major independent variable. The practice material, instead of being presented at successively higher speeds (325 to 475 w. p. m.) was presented at the beginning, and throughout the experiment, at 425 w. p. m. This has been described as "high-speed" vs. "graduated" practice listening. The before and after, and periodic benchmark test passages, were presented at the same speeds, as in the first two experiments.

Experimental Design

Eighteen male college freshmen and sophomores were paid $1.50 per hour plus bonuses to participate. Initial measures were taken of reading ability employing alternate forms of the Nelson-Denny Reading Test, of listening ability at normal recording speed (175 w. p. m.), and at very high speed (475 w. p. m.). Subjects also filled out a biographical questionnaire, and were given a pure-tone audiometric test to eliminate subjects with gross hearing defects.

The novel Cheaper by the Dozen was presented in three ses-

sions during the first week's practice at 425 w. p. m.   At the end of
the week a benchmark test passage was given at 325 w. p. m.   The
second, third, and fourth week's procedure was similar in that a
new novel was presented at 425 w. p. m. each week, followed by a
benchmark test passage at the end of each week at successive speeds
of 325, 375, 375, and 425 w. p. m.   At the end of four weeks, the
original high speed passage was again presented at 475 w. p. m. , and
the alternate form of the Nelson-Denny Reading Test was administered to mark change in reading performance.   A new test passage
was presented at normal speed (175) and comprehension measured.
In addition to the above tests, quizzes were given during the fourth
week of training on the listening material.   At the end a comprehensive debriefing questionnaire was administered to examine the subjective responses of the listeners.

Results

The main results of this experiment confirm that of previous
experiments in that performance at 325 w. p. m. at the end of a
week's practice was not significantly different from that at normal
speed.   (All scores were corrected for chance.)   The mean score
at 325 w. p. m. was 108. 5 per cent of the mean score at 175 w. p. m.
The percentage of normal speed score was obtained individually
based on his own normal speed score; these percentages were then
averaged for all subjects.   (Table 1 shows the mean scores for the
high-speed group as well as those for the groups of Spring 1964.)
The other major hypothesis that performance on a repeated passage
at 475 w. p. m. at the end of the experiment would be significantly
better than that before training was also confirmed at the . 01 level.
Table 2 shows various mean comparisons for the high speed group.
The increase in mean score between the pre- and post-administration of the passage at 475 w. p. m. was also significantly greater
than that of the control group run in the spring of 1964 (at the . 05
level of probability based on a Dunnett test).   Performance at 425
w. p. m. at the end of the experiment was approximately 71 per cent
of normal speed performance as compared with 50 per cent for the
original control group.   This difference is significant at the . 05
level.   The major hypothesis that performance on speeded speech
with training can be improved with practice has been reaffirmed.

With regard to whether or not speeded speech practice at one
high speed (425 w. p. m.) throughout the experiment, is more or less
efficacious than presentation at graduated speeds (from 325 to 475
w. p. m.) under the same conditions of uninterrupted practice sessions, subjects in the high speed practice experiment rose from a
mean score on the pre-experimental presentation at 475 w. p. m. ,
which was 25. 7 per cent of normal speed comprehension to a mean
score on the post-experimental presentation, which was 51 per cent
of normal speed.   This may be compared with the graduated practice group of Spring 1964 whose comparable mean performances were
28. 1 and 60. 2 per cent respectively.   Although the mean improvement for the latter group was somewhat higher, the difference is not

Table 1. MEAN SCORES AND MEAN SCORES AS PERCENTAGES OF NORMAL (175 WPM) SPEED SCORES (All Scores Corrected for Chance).

Test Speed (wpm)	Experimental Groups		Control Group
	High-Speed/ Spring 1965/(N=18) Mean (Mean % of Normal[a])	Graduated/ Spring 1964/(N=16) Mean (Mean % of Normal[a])	Spring 1964/(N=16) Mean (Mean % of Normal[a])
175[b]	13. 8(100. 0)	15. 7(100. 0)	17. 4(100. 0)
475(1st)[b]	3. 5 (25. 7)	4. 2 (28. 1)	6. 2 (36. 2)
325	13. 2(108. 5)	14. 1 (87. 0)	13. 9 (83. 5)
375(1st)	11. 4 (83. 7)	13. 6 (88. 0)	12. 9 (73. 7)
375(2nd)	11. 6 (84. 9)	13. 6 (88. 3)	13. 1 (75. 0)
425	8. 6 (70. 6)	12. 2 (79. 4)	8. 6 (50. 0)
475(2nd)	6. 8 (51. 0)	8. 8 (60. 2)	6. 8 (39. 6)

[a] This column represents the mean of individual comparisons of 325 w. p. m. with normal speed performance. [b]Prior to training (all other scores after training).

Table 2. SIGNIFICANCE OF DIFFERENCES BETWEEN MEANS ON LISTENING COMPREHENSION TESTS PRESENTED IN TABLE 1.

Comparison Between Tests (wpm)	Experimental Groups		Control Group	Significance of Differences	
	High Speed/ Spring 1965	(Graduated/ Spring 1964)	Spring 1964	High Speed vs. Graduated	(High Speed vs. Control)
175-325	-. 57	(-1. 7)	-3. 5[d]	N. S.	(N. S.)
175-375(1st)	-2. 38[a]	(-2. 1[a])	-4. 4[d]	--	(--)
175-375(2nd)	-2. 14[a]	(-2. 0[a])	-4. 4[d]	--	(--)
175-425	-5. 14[c]	(-3. 5[c])	-8. 8[d]	N. S.	(<. 05[a])
475(1st)-475(2nd)	+3. 28[d]	(+4. 6[d])	+0. 6	N. S.	(<. 05[a])

[a] <. 05 one-tailed.   [b] <. 05 two-tailed.   [c] <. 01 one-tailed.   [d] <. 01 two-tailed.

---

significant. The decrement in performance from the initial normal speed comprehension measure (at 175 w. p. m.) to the final benchmark test at 425 w. p. m. was greater for the high-speed practice group than for the graduated practice group. The latter did 79. 4 per cent as well as normal at 425 w. p. m. , while the former did only 70. 6 per cent as well. The difference was not significant. Both groups were significantly better at 425 w. p. m. than the control group.

The high-speed group achieved 108 per cent of normal score at 325 w. p. m. (at the end of the first week's practice), while the graduated group reached 87. 0 per cent. The control group reached a level of 83. 5 per cent. Performance at 175 w. p. m. at the end of

Table 3. MEAN SCORES AND STANDARD DEVIATIONS OF HIGH SPEED EXPERIMENTALS.

Nelson-Denny Score	First Administration Mean	(S. D.)	Second Administration Mean	(S. D.)	Significance of Mean Differences 1st vs. 2nd Admin.
Vocabulary	52.05	(17.84)	54.67	(17.63)	.05[a]
Comprehension	49.44	(11.06)	50.79	(11.81)	N.S.
Total Score	101.56	(27.12)	105.48	(27.99)	.05[a]
Reading Rate	312.23	(144.65)	369.11	(134.49)	.05[a]
Last Item Attempted Vocabulary	71.41	(16.13)	78.41	(12.54)	--
Last Item Attempted Comprehension	29.88	(4.25)	33.41	(3.34)	--

[a] one-tailed.

the experiment was not significantly different from initial 175 w. p. m. mean score for any group, suggesting that the procedures had not improved normal speed comprehension. The overall listening test results suggest that while the concentrated practice group performance was significantly better after training than the control group, they do not quite reach the performance of the graduated practice group, although tests of statistical significance do not support the reliability of such a conclusion.

Reading Results

High-speed subjects were also given alternate forms of the Nelson-Denny Reading Test before and after speeded speech practice. There has been some evidence in the past to suggest that reading skills might benefit from such practice. An examination of pre- versus post-administration mean scores on the (see Table 3) four measures of the test shows that reading rate rose from a mean of 312 to 369 w. p. m., statistically significant at the .025 level, one-tailed: vocabulary rose from a mean of approximately 52 to a 55 mean score (significant at the .05 level, one-tail) and comprehension rose from a mean score of 49.5 to 51, an insignificant difference. (The total mean score which is comprised of vocabulary plus comprehension scores rose from 101.56 to 105.48, a significant difference.) Experimental subjects in the graduated experiment had also shown a significant rise on all the Nelson-Denny measures. However, the control subjects also improved their performance on both reading rate and vocabulary significantly. Improvement in vocabulary score is probably closely associated with a higher reading rate, since it is unlikely that the size of the subject's vocabulary appreciably increased during the short time of the experiment. The comprehension test is constructed such that a faster reading speed does not necessarily mean that more questions will be attempted since it may simply take the subject farther into a passage without enabling him

Table 4

MEAN CHANGE IN SCORE REPORTING FOR SUBJECTS
REPEATING AND NOT REPEATING PASSAGES BY SPEEDS

Speeds Compared (w. p. m.)	Non-Repeats (N)	Repeats (N)	Time Elapsed (wks.)
175-325	-2.10 (12)	+2.50 (6)	1
175-375(1st)	-3.99 (12)	+0.84 (6)	2
175-375(2nd)	-3.85 (12)	+1.30 (6)	3
475(1st)-475(2nd)	---	+3.28 (18)	4

Table 5

SELECTED INTERCORRELATIONS
OF READING AND LISTENING PREFORMANCE
FOR HIGH SPEED PRACTICE SUBJECTS (N=18[a])

w. p. m.	175	325	425	475(1st)	475(2nd)	Total	Nelson-Denny Pre-Training Reading Rate
175	--	.27	.38	.24	.34	.30	-.05
325		--	.40	.55	.76	.58	.40
375(1st)							
375(2nd)			.42				
425			--	.19	.31	.30	.36
475(1st)				--	.55	.51	.49
475(2nd)					--	.20	.21
Total Score (N-D)						--	.52
Reading Rate							--
Xe	13.8	13.2	8.6	3.5	6.8	101.6	312.2
Se	4.24	4.76	2.98	2.71	3.65	26.10	144.65

[a] In the intercorrelations between the speeded passages and the Nelson-Denny total, and reading rate, N=17. One subject was disqualified because he had taken the N-D recently.

to reach the questions.

Comparison of the concentrated practice subjects with both the experimental and controls of the graduated practice study failed to reveal any significant difference in the improvement shown on reading rate and vocabulary. The majority of subjects tested in all experiments has shown an improvement in reading rate; however, because this also applied to the control group, we are not justified in saying that the improvement was attributable to speeded speech practice.

Repetition

During each of the first three weeks of the experiment one-third of the subjects (a different third each time) repeated the passage heard at 175 w. p. m. prior to practice. A comparison of subjects repeating with those not repeating shows a higher mean score for the "repeats." (See Table 4.)

Intercorrelations

Intercorrelations were computed between selected listening and reading speed scores (see Table 5). The intercorrelations between normal speed performance and the higher speed listening scores are lower than were those for the graduated practice group. There is a highly positive (+.76) correlation between final 475 and 325, suggesting that a predictor may exist at the 325 w. p. m. level. That is, performance at the early stages appears to be related to higher speed performance. Intercorrelations between listening and reading scores are generally positive, but slightly lower than for the graduated practice groups.

Summary of Results, Part I

Improvement in listening with practice at high speed was again demonstrated; subjects showed significant improvement on a repeated passage at 475 w. p. m. at the end of the experiment, and a significantly smaller decrement on a new passage at 425 w. p. m. at the end of the experiment, than did control subjects on either measure; while improvement in reading rate, vocabulary, and total score was found, results were not significantly different from those of the control group; a comparison of high speed concentrated practice with practice at gradually increasing speed did not show a significant difference, although mean performance with graduated practice seemed to be better.

II. IMMERSION, CRITERION, AND RETENTION STUDIES

Attempts to study rapid speech have invariably reported severe attenuation of comprehensibility with increased rates of presentation. Until recently such studies have used speeded-up tapes or records to increase speech rate and the resulting frequency shift has produced speech of higher and higher pitch. Many investigators concluded that loss of comprehension was as much due to frequency shift as to the acceleration of speech itself. One investigator, Garvey, reasoned that since Miller and Licklider had demonstrated that good intelligibility remained even after considerable loss of the stimulus word, it would be possible to physically cut out small segments of the speech record and play the remainder, thus compressing the total speech time, but leaving the original frequencies unaltered. Using discrete, spondaic words, Garvey found it possible to compress speech up to 2.5 times without losing more than 20 per cent intelligibility.   However, Garvey's compression technique was far too cumbersome to be applied on any large scale.   Subsequently, Fairbanks and his colleagues developed an electronic device for doing essentially what Garvey did by hand, with similarly encouraging results. More recently, Bixler, Foulke, et al. , began investigations of speech compression as an approach to teaching the blind, again demonstrating the feasibility of the technique.

During the past three years under the sponsorship of the U.S. Office of Education, the authors have conducted investigations at the American Institutes for Research inquiring into the ability of college students to understand tape-recorded material at speeds greater than normal.   This research has been made feasible by the use of a device somewhat similar to that developed by Fairbanks, which electronically removes small segments of the tape recorded speech sounds and abuts the remainder of the speech record.   Since the process removes only segments shorter than the shortest speech sounds, the result is relatively distortion-free; in addition pitch and intonation patterns remain normal.   The research reported in the present progress report covers three types of experiments conducted since the last report: The Immersion Study in which subjects listened to many hours of high speed listening for a week; The Criterion Study in which moderately high speed practice was presented until the subjects reached a pre-set criterion; and the Retention Studies in which an attempt was made to determine how well the skill, and the content of material was retained over a period of time.

-- The Immersion Study

It was the purpose of this experiment to determine the effects of listening practice when that practice was given intensively; approximately 8 to 10 hours a day for five consecutive days.   In previous experiments practice had been spread over four weeks.   In this experiment subjects put in a 12-hour day (9:00 a.m. to 9:00 p.m.) including breaks for meals and rest, and were given practice only at 425 w.p.m.   The question was whether concentrated practice in a few days could achieve results similar to or better than those provided by spaced practice.   The rationale for the experiment was two-fold.   In the first place if it should become feasible to apply time-compressed speech as a general educational technique, it might be necessary to have naive students spend time practicing the comprehension of time-compressed speech as a precursor to their regular studies.   It would be desirable to have such a training course occupy a minimum number of days at the beginning of the term. Secondly, the experience of the armed services in recent years in teaching a second language has shown a fair amount of success for intensive or immersion exposure.

Procedures

The immersion study subjects consisted of seven freshmen and sophomore college students. English was their native language and none had a marked regional accent. The average letter grade for the students in their last semester in college was a C+. Two of the subjects had had some training in rapid reading but the course had not been completed. None of the subjects had had any training in listening. The subjects were screened for normal hearing. In the first session a brief talk explaining that the purpose of this study was to provide intensive exposure to speeded speech, and to measure listening performance with periodic benchmark tests was given. A biographical data sheet which called for basic information about their backgrounds was filled out. The Nelson-Denny Reading Test which measures reading comprehension, rate, and vocabulary was then administered. This was followed by the presentation of an historical passage at normal recording speed (175 w. p. m.). A multiple choice test on the information in the passage was given. A similar passage and test was presented at 475 w. p. m. as an initial measure of high-speed performance. Subjects were then asked to return for five consecutive weekdays, beginning on a Monday, from 9:00 a. m. to 9:00 p. m.

During the next week, 12 novels were played at 425 w. p. m. for the subjects. Each day listening material was presented for approximately 48 minutes without interruption. At the end of that time a brief written quiz, including both short answer and essay types of questions, was administered during a 10-minute period. This was followed by a five-minute rest period, after which the cycle was repeated. Subjects were given time for lunch and dinner. During the latter part of each of the five days of exposure, a new benchmark passage and test, similar to the pre-experimental material, was administered. Each test was presented at 425 w. p. m. Near the end of the fifth day, the initial high-speed benchmark passage was presented again at 475 w. p. m. An alternate form of the Nelson-Denny Reading Test was presented as a post-experimental measure of change. Subjects were given an extensive debriefing questionnaire to complete calling for subjective comments on the procedures, materials, and potential usefulness of compressed speech in the educational setting. Upon the completion of the experiment, each subject was paid $100 plus a bonus.

Results and Discussion

Results of the benchmark tests in terms of number of questions correct, based on 25-item tests, corrected for chance, are shown in Table 6. Also shown is percentage of normal speed performance, calculated separately for each individual based on his own performance at normal (175 w. p. m.) speed. It may be noted that there is a progression of means from 40. 4 per cent on Day 1 to 70. 0 per cent on Day 5, which is reasonably steady with the exception of a dropback on Day 2. In addition to this improvement, mean

Table 6

BENCHMARK TEST SCORES CORRECTED FOR CHANCE AND PERCENTAGES OF NORMAL SPEED SCORES

| Subject | | Normal | 475(1st) | 425 WPM | | | | | 475(2nd) |
				Day 1	Day 2	Day 3	Day 4	Day 5	
A		16.25	0.00	6.50	2.75	7.50	8.75	9.37	9.37
	%	100.0	0.0	40.0	16.9	46.2	53.8	57.7	57.7
B		14.00	5.21	9.50	9.75	8.75	7.50	9.58	12.29
	%	100.0	37.2	67.9	69.6	62.5	53.6	68.4	87.8
C		25.00	8.33	15.00	8.75	16.25	10.00	17.70	11.45
	%	100.0	33.3	60.0	35.0	65.0	40.0	70.8	45.8
D		22.50	8.95	16.25	11.50	14.00	13.75	16.09	15.62
	%	100.0	39.8	72.2	51.1	62.2	61.1	71.3	69.4
E		19.25	1.46	0.75	3.75	6.75	14.00	9.58	6.66
	%	100.0	7.6	3.9	19.5	35.1	70.7	49.8	34.6
F		14.25	0.00	1.25	6.50	1.25	3.75	11.45	4.16
	%	100.0	0.0	8.8	45.6	8.8	26.3	80.4	29.2
G		10.00	2.08	3.00	0.50	4.00	6.50	9.16	3.96
	%	100.0	20.8	30.0	5.0	40.0	65.0	91.6	39.6
Mean		17.32	3.72	7.46	6.21	8.36	9.18	11.84	9.07
	%	100.0	19.8	40.4	34.7	45.7	53.2	70.0	52.0

performance on the repeated high speed passage (475 w. p. m.) also improved from 19. 8 to 52. 0 per cent, which is significant at the . 01 level. The progression of means is shown in Figure 1.

With the exception of the 475 w. p. m. passage and test, the figures shown in Table 6 and Figure 1 are based upon different tests and test passages are thus independent estimates of performance. Passages were taken from the same book of early English history, however, and tests were constructed to be equivalent according to item statistics derived from the same population of students. As an illustration of the extent to which variables such as material and subject variability and type of test can affect the results, however, one may consider the results for the short answer tests and essay tests on the practice materials. These were not

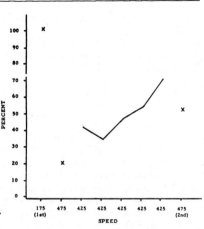

Figure 1.   Mean per cent of normal performance over five days (N= 7).

intended to do more than motivate the subjects to listen to the practice materials, and it was not possible to standardize these measures. The results on these tests showed no discernible trends and great subject variability. The lack of correlation between short answer and essay results (R= O) indicated further that such measures are not dependable.

The results of the present experiment again confirm previous findings that comprehension of time-compressed speech can be improved by simple practice routines to relatively high levels at speeds of about 2. 5 times normal. By the end of a week, all subjects had reached the 50 per cent comprehension mark, although several started from as low at 5 to 10 per cent on the first day. The effects of the training on other variables such as reading test scores and standard listening test scores, while in the right direction, were not great, however.

Another question of interest is the effectiveness of the method here employed to achieve approximately 70 per cent comprehension at 425 w. p. m. During their five days of intensive exposure, these subjects spent approximately 35 hours listening to compressed speech. How does this compare with previous findings? These results can be compared with those of the three previous groups of similar composition, all of which received about 12 to 14 hours of practice distributed at about 1-2 hours, 2-3 days per week, over about 4-5 weeks:

(1) Graduated practice from 325-475 w. p. m.
(2) Graduated practice from 325-425 w. p. m. (with periodic breaks)
(3) High speed practice (425 w. p. m. only)

The mean result for group (1) above was 79 per cent of normal at 425 w. p. m.; for group (2) 80 per cent at 425 w. p. m.; and for group (3) 71 per cent at 425 w. p. m. Thus, the investment of 12 to 14 hours of spaced practice produced results as good or better as the investment of almost three times as much practice in the present "immersion" study. A similar conclusion was reached after looking at the mean improvements from pre- to post-experimental scores on the repeated high speed (475 w. p. m.) passage.

Summary of Immersion Study

The primary findings of this study were two-fold. First, the findings of previous work were confirmed: that time-compressed speech is comprehensible, and the comprehension of time-compressed speech is trainable by means of simple practice. And second, while immersion in concentrated practice is effective in improving comprehension at high rates of speed, it is not an efficient method of practice as compared to less concentrated types of practice. The findings reinforce the conclusion that time-compressed speech offers substantial possibilities as an educational technique. Comparatively high levels of comprehension are possible after limited amounts of training at substantially increased rates of speed. Rather high levels of comprehension at 2.5 times normal speed can be obtained in a period as short as one working week by means of concentrated practice. Thus, the findings confirm the feasibility of a concentrated training course in compressed speech as a prelude to the regular school term, if the use of highly compressed speech should become an educational practice.

-- The Criterion Study (Part 1)

The aim was to determine the amount of practice necessary to reach the criterion of 90 per cent of normal speed comprehension at the 375 w. p. m. level. Previously significant improvement in performance had occurred at 425 and 475 w. p. m., but the mean scores were below 90 per cent. The aim of this study was to achieve 90 per cent comprehension at a moderately high speed, and if successful to go on to still higher speeds. The method of measuring comprehension used has been rather cumbersome, requiring the use of entire passages and the construction of equivalent tests. Therefore, it was planned to examine an intelligibility measure (accurate reporting of the last word heard at certain intervals) as a possible correlate of comprehension.

Procedures

The subjects used were 10 male University of Maryland freshman and sophomores. Subjects were paid $1. 50 per hour. In addition, six bonuses were awarded on the basis of performance on the first administration of the listening tests. Three novels previously recorded by the American Printing House for the Blind in their Talking Book series were selected and compressed to the required speeds as practice material. Quizzes on the information contained in the novels were used. They were comprised of multiple choice and essay questions, but were not standardized.

The texts of the novels were used as follows: each novel was marked at certain intervals at the ends of paragraphs. The tape was stopped at those intervals and the subjects were requested to write down the last word heard. They were asked to guess if uncertain. The ends of paragraphs were chosen to minimize disruption to the subjects and to maximize intelligibility scores since the high degree of contextual restraint could be expected to reduce the number of alternative responses from which the subjects might choose. The intervals were irregular to lessen the predictability of their occurrence. Seven benchmark passages with five-option multiple choice tests were used. Multiple choice tests previously constructed and standardized on a similar population were employed as the chief measures of listening comprehension. One passage was presented at normal recording speed (175 w. p. m.), the remaining seven at 375 w. p. m.

Other materials consisted of pre-numbered pages on which the subjects were to record the "last-word heard" responses--there were always more numbers than responses called for to prevent subjects from knowing when that type of testing was completed. The Nelson-Denny Reading Test containing measures of reading rate, vocabulary, and comprehension was used in a balanced way as a pre- and post-experimental measure. Most of the multiple choice tests contained 25 questions; two contained 30 questions. Scores on those two tests were prorated to give a proportional score for a 25-item test. All test scores were corrected for chance. Each subject's score on the first benchmark passage and test (given at 175 w. p. m.) was taken as the baseline for his comprehension at normal speed. Each subject's subsequent scores were then expressed as a percentage of his score at 175 words per minute. Last words were scored correct or incorrect; hyphenated words were counted right if the last word was right. If the word had the wrong ending, it was counted wrong; if wrongly spelled, even homonyms, it was counted right.

Experimental sessions lasted about three hours. Subjects never listened for more than one hour to any material without being given a ten-minute break. All practice material (novels) was interrupted periodically for recording of "last words" and listening quizzes. Five benchmark passages were presented at 375 w. p. m. after 2, 7, 9. 5, and 16 hours of listening practice. Following the

Table 7

HIGHEST PER CENT NORMAL COMPREHENSION
ATTAINED BY SUBJECT
AND NUMBER OF HOURS PRACTICE TO ACHIEVE IT (375 WPM)

Sub- ject	Normal Speed (175 wpm) Score	Mean Percent Normal 1st Adm.	Mean Percent Normal 2nd Adm.	1st Adm. Highest Per- cent of Normal	Hours to High- est Per- cent
A	12.5	67.4	116.2	104.00**	16.0
B	17.5	46.7	73.0	85.71*	7.0
C	17.5	53.7	98.3	100.00	9.5
D	17.5	66.3	85.8	100.00	16.0
E	13.8	50.6	68.6	83.27*	2.0
F	13.8	58.8	121.9	90.91	16.0
G	17.5	73.1	102.5	95.71	16.0
H	13.8	77.7	112.9	116.36	7.0
I	16.2	61.8	106.4	73.85*	9.5
J	15.0	68.2	94.6	91.67	7.0
MEAN	15.5	62.4	98.0		10.6

* Below criterion.   ** This is the only subject who reached criterion on more than one occasion.   His per cent normal comprehension
was 94.00 after 15 hours of practice.

Table 8

MEAN PER CENT NORMAL COMPREHENSION
BY HOURS OF PRACTICE LISTENING,
FIRST AND SECOND ADMINISTRATIONS, 375 WPM (N=10)

| | Approximate Hours of Practice Novels and Passages | | | | | | |
	2	7	9.5	13	15	16	Mean
Mean %, 1st Adm.	58.8	77.2	58.3	48.7	54.5	77.2	62.4
s.d.	9.8	16.4	27.1	16.6	22.2	20.5	9.5
Mean %, 2nd Adm.	86.5	94.5	102.2	95.6	97.8*	--**	98.0
s.d.	24.4	27.0	25.8	32.0	18.4	--**	16.9

Note: The 2nd administrations came after about 20-25 minutes additional practice.   * No interpolated practice between 1st and 2nd administrations.   ** C-8 was not re-administered because it was to be
used again in a later stage of experimentation.

Table 9

PER CENT LAST WORDS CORRECT BY TEST AND SUBJECT

| Subject | Passage and Test* | | | | | Mean |
	C-3	C-4	C-5	C-6	C-7	
A	89	53	70	86	86	75. 2
B	79	73	75	72	93	78. 4
C	95	73	65	89	79	80. 2
D	89	80	90	78	93	86. 0
E	84	80	85	83	93	85. 0
F	100	80	90	94	93	91. 4
G	79	87	90	94	86	87. 2
H	89	80	100	94	93	91. 2
I	95	73	85	94	93	88. 0
J	95	87	90	94	93	91. 8
No. of trials (Base of %)	19	15	20	19	14	
Mean %	89. 4	76. 6	84. 0	87. 0	90. 2	85. 4

* In chronological order.

administration of each passage and test, 20 to 25 minutes of additional practice material was presented, after which the passage and test were administered a second time, with periodic interruptions during administration for measurement of "last word" intelligibility. An additional passage and test were presented with no interruptions as the final performance measure.

Results

Table 7 shows the normal speed scores corrected for chance for each subject and the mean percentage of these scores attained by the subjects on both first and second administrations separately. It also shows the highest percentage of normal attained by each subject on the first administration and the number of practice hours at 375 w. p. m. taken to reach that level. Table 8 shows the mean per cent normal comprehension over all subjects, by number of hours of practice for first and second administrations of the test passages. Unlike previous experiments, there appeared to be no progressive improvement in these means with practice. Table 9 shows the per cent correct for last words on the test passages. No evidence of progression is apparent, although the generally high level of intelligibility is evident.

Although seven subjects attained criterion in this experiment, it is unlikely that these subjects attained a highly stable degree of comprehension of speeded discourse at 375 words per minute. Six

subjects attained their highest comprehension within the first three
sessions but did not maintain this level.

-- The Criterion Study (Part 2)

      Six subjects who had reached the criterion were asked to par-
ticipate in a second criterion study in which the rate of speeded discourse was 425 words per minute. One could not return, leaving
five. A control group was formed from those subjects from prior
experiments who had met the criterion at 375 w. p. m. Their scores
on a standardized test at 425 w. p. m., after a given number of
hours practice of novel listening, could be compared with the results
of the present experiment in terms of scores on the same standardized test in order to discover if the method of training by similar
materials and testing on those materials was superior to the method
of training by listening to novels.

Procedures

      The experiment was conducted in four three-hour group ses-
sions spread over eight days. Ten practice passages and practice
tests, taken from a variety of library and journalistic materials
were used. The Nelson-Denny Reading Test was not given. The experimental schedule was somewhat more involved than that for Part
1, and is given below:

      Day 1: Subjects' maximum oral reading rates were tested.
Subjects listened to four short passages, of about 10 minutes' duration each. After each passage, multiple choice questions about the
passage were given. Each passage and test were repeated twice in
succession. During the repetition of each passage about 10 interruptions occurred during which subjects were asked to record the last
word they had heard.
      Day 2: Subjects listened to four short unstandardized pas-
sages; the method was the same as on Day 1. Between the second
and third passages, subjects listened to a continuation of Run Silent,
Run Deep at 425 words per minute, for about 20 minutes. It was
thought that maximum oral reading rate might be correlated with
ability to comprehend rapid speech. Therefore the subjects were
given a passage to read out loud. They were asked to read the passage as rapidly as possible. The time from beginning to end of the
passage was recorded for each subject.
      Day 3: Subjects listened to two short passages, in the same
manner as on Days 1 and 2. They then listened to the test passage
for this experiment, taking a standardized multiple choice test. The
passage was repeated with interruptions for recording of the last
word heard. The test was repeated. After all testing for the day
had been completed, subjects listened to the final portions of Run
Silent, Run Deep, at 425 w. p. m.
      Day 4: A passage was repeated for the third time, reading
questions first. A second passage was repeated for the second time.
Subjects were asked to make any comments they wanted to, in writing.

Table 10

PER CENT OF NORMAL SPEED COMPREHENSION SCORES
BY SUBJECT AND AMOUNT OF PRACTICE AT 425 WPM,
CRITERION STUDY, PART 2

Subject****	*Mean, 1st Adm. 9 Practice Pass.	*Mean, 2nd Adm. 9 Practice Pass.	**Test Pass. C-2	Test Pass. C-2 (repeat)	***Test Pass. C-8
D	50. 8 (66. 3)	77. 3 (85. 8)	29. 8 (100. 0)	90. 5	107. 1
F	54. 0 (58. 8)	105. 0 (121. 9)	77. 2 (90. 9)	153. 0	94. 6
G	70. 1 (73. 1)	104. 9 (102. 5)	59. 5 (95. 7)	125. 0	85. 7
H	78. 4 (77. 7)	110. 8 (112. 9)	65. 2 (90. 9)	115. 1	125. 4
J	62. 2 (68. 2)	99. 7 (94. 6)	73. 6 (45. 0)	127. 8	125. 0
Mean	63. 1 (68. 8)	99. 5 (103. 5)	61. 1 (84. 5)	122. 3	107. 6
Average Cumulative Average amount of practice (hrs), Part 2	. 97	1. 1	2. 2	2. 3	3. 0

* Criterion Study, Part 1 mean scores (375 w. p. m.) are given in (Table 7) for comparison.   ** For comparison the last test passage score in Part 1 (375 w. p. m.) is given in (Table 7).   *** This passage was a repeat of the last passage given in Part 1 at 375 w. p. m. **** Refers to Part 1 Identification Code.

Results and Discussion

Table 10 shows the results of Part 2 of the Criterion Study. It is evident that the subjects did slightly less well on the average than they did in Part 1, for both first and second administrations of the practice passages. Of course the Part 2 scores represent tests at 425 w. p. m., while the Part 1 scores were taken at 375 w. p. m. Thus the additional practice was not sufficient to offset the increase in rate. The comparatively large difference between mean per cent of normal for a new test passage in Part 2 as compared to the last test passage in Part 1 for these subjects suggests more than simply a loss attributable to the increase in speed. Possibly there was a diminution in motivation during the Part 2 experimentation, which could have been getting somewhat boring. The efficacy of repetition continued to be clearly evident, as it was in Part 1.

When the performance of the Part 2 group is compared to the ad hoc group of subjects from previous experimental groups who had reached 90 per cent at 375 w. p. m. at some time, we find that the Part 2 group mean on a new passage at 425 w. p. m. was 61.1 per cent, versus 82.8 per cent for the comparison group. This difference cannot be attributed to differences in amount of practice as the Part 2 group had a slightly greater number of total hours of practice. This finding is certainly not stable because of its ad hoc nature, but does not provide any support for the hypothesis that practice on materials similar to the test materials was superior to practice on the novels.

A number of rank order correlations were computed to tentatively examine the relationships in the data. Few consistent relationships were observed. For the Part 1 group, a correlation of .50 was obtained between mean last words on the first administration of practice passages and comprehension score on the first administration of a new test passage. Although this is a relatively stable estimate, when the last words score was correlated with comprehension score on the same passage, the correlations ranged from .72 to -.51 over five passages. It can only be concluded that the last words score is no substitute for comprehension scores. Part 2 results bore out this conclusion. One interesting result of the last words data however was the finding that some subjects did comparatively well on the listening comprehension score for a test passage, but relatively poorly on last words. This indicates that comprehension is not unduly dependent upon the intelligibility of specific words.

The comparatively disappointing results of the Criterion Study may be due to one or more of several factors. First the interruptions associated with determining last words may have been disruptive. Secondly, the repetition of material may have proved boring to the subjects. Third, it was subsequently discovered that the subjects had set up a "bonus pool" amongst themselves to distribute the bonuses. This raises some questions as to the legitimacy of the results. In any case however, the Criterion Study must be taken as tentative and on the order of a pilot study. It did serve the useful function of permitting the try out of a number of new techniques and procedures.

Summary of Criterion Study

1.   Seven of ten subjects reached 90 per cent of normal speed score at least once on a listening test presented at 375 w. p. m. after up to 16 hours of listening practice at 375 w. p. m. Subjects could not be considered to have reached the criterion consistently, however, as little evidence of progressive improvement with practice was found.

2.   There was no clear correlation between the intelligibility measure and comprehension scores, correlations vascillating from positive to negative.

3. The second presentation of a passage almost always resulted in a much higher score. This effect cannot be attributed simply to repeated questions.

4. Subjects generally did not achieve criterion at 425 w. p. m. within the limits of the three or so hours of additional practice material employed.

5. There was no evidence to suggest that practice on materials similar to test passages was superior to practice on novels.

6. A hint of relationship between oral reading rate and listening comprehension at 425 w. p. m. was found.

In addition to the questions of how well it can be understood, and to what degree it is trainable, a major question in using compressed speech as an educational technique is to what extent the skill of listening to compressed speech is retained, and to what extent material learned via compressed speech presentation is retained. The three experiments described below provide some information regarding these questions.

-- Retention Study No. 1

In November of 1964, eleven of the original (Spring 1964) 16 experimentals, and 13 of the original 16 control subjects (from the graduated practice experiments) returned for a single session. The purpose was to measure both degree of retention of content of material heard at a variety of high speeds the previous spring and to measure the degree to which the skill of comprehending high speed speech was retained. For the measurement of content retention, the tests which had originally been administered after presentation of passages C1 to C5 at speeds ranging from 175 to 475 w. p. m., were readministered without any passage presentation. For the measurement of skill retention a new equivalent passage and test were presented at 425 w. p. m.

A comparison of experimental and control mean scores over the five tests (C1-C5) which were administered without presentation of the passages, showed no difference between the groups. The respective mean scores of the experimentals and controls were 6.9 and 8.0 over all passages and were not significantly different. Since the original presentation of the passages occurred under varying conditions of speed and amounts of practice, the percentage of loss cannot be adequately determined. However, the lack of difference at this point suggests that experimentals retained their content as well as controls did. Performance on the new passage was compared with performance on a similar passage presented at the same speed (425 w. p. m.) at the end of training in the spring session. Mean performance for the returning experimental subjects declined from 11.7 in the spring to 9.1 in the autumn (based on 25-item tests, and corrected for chance). Control subjects showed a decline from 8.5 in the spring to 7.5 in the autumn. While the decline for both groups was statistically significant at the 5 per cent level (one-tailed), these losses of 22 per cent and 12 per cent respectively are not statistically different and may be considered modest over an interval of about four months.

Although the experimentals still performed better (9.1 vs. 7.5), they were no longer statistically different from the controls. Even so, it should be noted that there was some indication that the control group was a superior listening group to begin with. (The respective original scores at normal speed for experimental and control groups were: 16.0 and 17.6; at 475 w. p. m. they were 4.2 and 6.5.) There was therefore, a tentative suggestion that even six months after training some training effects may have remained with the experimental subjects. An examination of correlation between initial performance at normal speed with current 425 w. p. m. performance showed about the same correlation for experimentals (.56) as for controls (.39). As the former is significant, while the latter is not, some effect of the practice on the interaction with normal listening is indicated. A comparison of correlations between performance at high speed (425 w. p. m.) immediately after training (spring) and current 425 w. p. m. performance showed a striking difference between experimentals and controls (.73 vs. .17). This significant difference further suggests some residual effect of the practice listening received by the experimentals.

-- Retention Study No. 2

During the Spring of 1965, it became necessary to standardize some additional benchmark tests and passages. Therefore a group of college freshmen and sophomores comparable to those students used as subjects was assembled and given another testing. Passages were administered at 175 w. p. m., each followed by its test. Another passage C-2 was administered at 425 w. p. m. Students were urged to do their best, were paid $7, and a $15 bonus for the best overall score was offered. One month later the group was reassembled and the tests for C-3, C-6, C-7, C-8 and C-2 were readministered without exposure to the passages. Following these a new passage and test was administered at 425 w. p. m. and another new passage and test was administered at 325 w. p. m. Again the students were paid for their time and a bonus was awarded.

The results are summarized in Table 11. It may be seen that on the average about 60 per cent of the content of the four passages presented at 175 w. p. m. was retained over the period of one month. This finding compares favorably with the retentions of similar materials which have been read. The loss in retention of 90 per cent between first and second administrations of the 425 w. p. m. passage is certainly not discouraging evidence of retention of high speed presentations. The level of initial performance at this speed (remembering that these students had had no prior exposure to speeded material) was about 43 per cent of normal speed comprehension, which is just about typical for naive subjects at 425 w. p. m. This percentage jumped to 66 per cent on the re-test however, since com-

Table 11

MEAN SCORES CORRECTED FOR CHANCE AND PRORATED
TO A BASE OF 25 ITEMS FOR RETENTION STUDY NO. 2 (N= 35)

Passage & Speed	1st Session Mean	2nd Session Mean	Percent Loss
C-3 (175)	13.9	9.2*	34
C-6 (175)	16.3	9.7*	40
C-7 (175)	9.5	4.7*	51
C-8 (175)	12.6	7.9*	37
C-2 (425)	5.7	5.2*	9
C-4 (425)		2.4	
C-5 (325)		3.0	

* Retests

paratively greater loss occurred for the normal speed than for the
speeded material. Although the scores were corrected for chance,
it is likely that some of this stability at high speed was a function
of prior knowledge and chance. In any case, however, the retention
of content certainly appears to be no worse for speeded material
than for normal speed material.

The new passage administered at the second session was intended to provide a comparison between the scores for the group on
their first exposure to a speeded passage and their scores on a comparable new passage one month later. Thus, if they had acquired
any skill in the first exposure, the second would measure the retention of that skill. It was recognized that this test was not a strong
one since the amount of skill which could be expected to result from
a single exposure would necessarily be small. However, the comparison was made. Table 11 shows that the group score was significantly lower at the time of second testing at speed 425. This
lower score can also be attributed to the fact that while the experiment was in progress, frequent interruptions occurred due to factors
beyond the control of the experimenter. Similarly the group mean
score for skill at listening to 325 w. p. m. without prior experience
with this particular speed was extremely low. In fact, the mean
score at 325 was lower than the mean score the group obtained upon
first listening to 425 w. p. m. It therefore seems likely that the
tests measuring this group's retention of skill in listening to speeded
speech cannot be said to allow us to interpret in any meaningful way
the retention of this skill. In summary, this experiment provided
tentative evidence that listening retention over a month compares favorably with reading retention; and that retention of speeded presentations appears to be at least as good as for non-speeded presentations.

A further examination of the question of retention was obtained by recalling the Spring 1965 experimental group which had
practiced comprehension of speeded speech on the order of 12 hours,
all at one high speed (425 w. p. m.). It could be called a group of
practiced listeners. The group was recalled one month after the
conclusion of their experimentation and the procedure of Retention
Study No. 2 repeated. Tests on passages which had been originally
heard at some combination of 175, 325 and 375 w. p. m. were readministered without the passages. The same was done for tests on
passages which were originally heard at 425, 475, and 175 w. p. m.
Finally passages were administered at 425 and 325.

Table 12 shows the results of this testing. Again, content
retention of both normal, and particularly speeded passages was high
over this one month period. For highly speeded passages (425 and
475) retention was 116 and 98 per cent, respectively, of first session

---

Table 12

MEAN SCORES CORRECTED FOR CHANCE AND PRORATED
TO A BASE OF 25 ITEMS FOR RETENTION STUDY NO. 3 (N=16)

Passage & Speed	Experimental Sessions Means	Recall Session Means	Percent Loss
C-1 (175)*	9. 8	8. 3	15
C-4 (175)*	11. 2	7. 5	33
C-5 (175)*	9. 1	5. 9	35
C-2 (425)	7. 0	8. 1	-16 (gain)
C-3 (475)	5. 6	5. 5	2
C-6 (175)	12. 9	8. 2	36
C-7 (425)		6. 0	
C-8 (325)		11. 8	

* A mixture of speeds (175, 325, and 375 w. p. m.) occurred on the
1st administration.

---

scores. For passages presented at normal, or for some mixture of
normal and speeds up to 375 w. p. m., retention averaged about 70
per cent of first session scores. A comparison of the mean score
on the new passage at 425 w. p. m. at the second session with the
mean score on a different 425 w. p. m. passage at the end of the experimental sessions one month earlier shows a loss of only 14 per
cent. However, the obtained mean score on this skill retention test
(6. 0) was not significantly different from that obtained by the Retention Study No. 2 group on its first exposure to compressed speech
at 425 w. p. m. (5. 7). This latter score was 43 per cent of normal

speed scores for the Retention Study No. 2 group, while a comparison of the present retention group's mean score at the recall session to their original normal speed scores of the previous month (i.e., to a normal speed naive base) also showed 43 per cent. Thus, there is little evidence available in this study for retention of acquired skill in listening to compressed speech.

Further, comparison of the recall session mean score at 325 w.p.m. (11.8), with the mean score of a composite of several passages at 325 (13.2) on the experimental sessions a month earlier, showed a loss of about 11 per cent over the period of the month. This comparison shows only a slightly better score one month after the experiment than would be expected from a naive group at this speed. Again, little evidence of skill retention is apparent.

III. LISTENING AID STUDIES

Research has indicated the great potential use of connected discourse which is presented faster than, but which is just as intelligible as, normal speech. Concurrently, interest in compressed speech has been growing at an accelerating rate. Within the past year, the technique has received considerable publicity at professional meetings, in the press, and on television. This growing interest has taken two major directions: the application of compressed speech in situations demanding a high output of information in restricted time; and the examination of basic problems in listening research, for which this technique provides a unique means of varying the temporal aspect of speech while holding other variables essentially constant.

-- The Listening Aid Study (A)

In previous experiments performance has been examined under conditions which provided the listener minimal preparation for the content of the material; training was centered exclusively on exposure to appropriately speeded material. In the experiment reported here, preparation for the content of the material was employed in conjunction with practice in speed listening. In this experiment two means of preparing the subjects for the material to be presented were studied. A written summary of the material to be heard was presented to one group, while a list of key words in the passage was presented to another group. The control group received no listening aids prior to exposure. The major hypothesis was that relative to the performance of a control group which did not receive them, these listening aids would improve performance during training and that this improvement would generalize to performance on a new passage presented without any listening aids at the end of the experiment.

In listening to compressed speech several factors play roles. The primary factor is the rate at which input is made to the listener.

We have explored the range of speeds from 325 to 475 w. p. m. , or, approximately two to three times the speed of the original recording. While practice has been found to improve performance, the higher the speed (in this range) the poorer comprehension is likely to be. Because there is less time to process the input, it is to the listener's advantage to recognize, as quickly as possible, words and phrases in the presentation.   It is known that the fewer alternative stimuli which <u>may</u> be presented, the quicker will recognition response be.   It was hypothesized that preparing the subject for material which may be presented will reduce the number of alternatives, thereby providing a listening advantage to the subject.   It was proposed, therefore, to prepare the subject in two different ways by providing a summary of the content of the forthcoming passage without emphasizing the particular language in which it was expressed, and by preparing the subjects for unfamiliar (high information carrying) words to be heard.   The performance of these two groups of subjects, at moderately high speed (375 w. p. m.), was compared with that of a control group with no preparation.

Procedures

        The listening aid study employed 22 male college students as subjects.   The subjects estimated that they could assimilate approximately 62 per cent of their college course work without recourse to reading about the material.   Seventy-seven per cent stated that they would prefer more time devoted to lecture and less to reading in their course work, while the remainder held the opposite opinion. Listening materials consisted of two kinds: eight historical passages of about 3500 words each, taken from a single college level textbook on English history.   They were recorded on magnetic tape and compressed to a speed of approximately 375 w. p. m.   For each of the passages, a five-option multiple choice test of 25 to 30 items was developed and standardized on a similar student population.   In addition, a précis (about 170 words long) of the passage content, and a list of the key words in the passage (a mean of 128 words per passage) were also produced.   The second type of material was used for listening practice and consisted of a single novel recorded on magnetic tape and compressed to a speed of 375 w. p. m.   In addition to the above materials, a biographical data sheet and a debriefing questionnaire were also used.   At the end of the experiment, a battery of psychological tests was administered, and a measure of simple reaction time taken.

        The basic design called for an initial measure of performance at normal recording speed (175 w. p. m.) for purposes of establishing a base line and for dividing the 24 subjects into three matched groups. On the basis of initial normal speed comprehension scores, the 24 students were divided into three groups with equivalent mean scores. These groups were designated the Précis Group, the Key Word Group, and the Control Group.

        The experiment was run in seven days (exclusive of the week-

end). Each session lasted approximately one and one-half hours.
The first session was devoted to the initial measurements. Each of
the next five sessions followed the pattern described below. Approximately 50 minutes of Run Silent, Run Deep was presented at 375
w. p. m. , followed by a 10-minute break. After the break the Précis
Group subjects were each given a typewritten summary (about 170
words in length) of the passages to follow. The Key Word Group
subjects were each given a list of about 130 words consisting mostly
of proper nouns and unusual words to be found in the forthcoming
test passage. The remaining (Control Group) subjects were instructed to sit quietly and were given no listening aid. Subjects in the
first two groups were allowed to scrutinize the listening aids for
two and one-half minutes, after which the listening aid was removed
and the test passage presentation begun. At the conclusion of the
passage all subjects were given a multiple choice comprehension test
based on information in the passage.

On the seventh day of testing, all subjects again listened to
approximately 50 minutes of Run Silent, Run Deep at 375 w. p. m.
and were then given a 10-minute break. A passage and test was
then presented to all subjects; however, in this case, no one received any listening aid. After this test, each of the three groups
was divided into two subgroups matched for current proficiency with
compressed speech. The matching was done by combining the scores
for the previous two sessions' testing as the best indicators of their
abilities to date. One-half of each of the three groups was then
given a précis while the other half was given nothing. The comprehension test based on the passage was then given, but no passage
was presented. The purpose of this measure was to examine to
what extent information in the précis might have contributed to performance on the tests.

Results

Table 13 shows the group means and the order of presentation
of the passages. Percentages were compiled by using each subject's
normal speed score as his own base. Performance on the base line
passage presented at 175 w. p. m. was similar to that of subjects in
previous experiments. The mean score for the 22 subjects who completed the experiment was 14. 3 based on a 25-item test, corrected
for guessing, as compared with overall mean score of 15. 1 for 102
previously tested subjects.

The difference in means between the three groups on the five
days during which listening aids were presented were small, and not
statistically significant, according to a two-factor analysis of variance; this was contrary to the predictions made. Table 14 presents
the summary analysis of variance. On the seventh day of the experiment, the test passage was administered at the same point in the
session except that none of the subjects received any listening aid.
Again, no significant difference among the group means obtained. Although the final test (at 375 w. p. m.) scores were lower than the ini-

Table 13

MEAN LISTENING TEST SCORES[a] AND MEAN PERCENTAGES OF
NORMAL SPEED SCORES BY GROUP AND RATE OF PRESENTA-
TION IN ORDER OF PRESENTATION

Subject Group[b]	175 C-1	Word Rate per Minute and "C" Passage Designation						No Passage[d]	
		375 C-7	375 C-8	375 C-6	375 C-3	375 C-2	375 C-4[c]	C-5[e]	C-5[f]
P	14.1	7.6	12.2	12.0	10.2	12.4	11.8	4.8	6.2
%	100.0	55.6	93.6	90.4	72.9	90.2	91.6	39.0	39.2
KW	14.4	8.2	10.2	10.3	9.2	11.5	13.2	8.0	3.0
%	100.0	57.1	80.7	82.4	62.6	83.1	97.5	55.6	22.2
C	14.3	8.2	10.6	11.4	11.6	14.0	12.9	5.6	7.0
%	100.0	60.9	82.8	87.6	81.3	108.4	88.6	50.0	27.7
AS	14.3	8.6	11.0	11.2	10.3	12.6	12.7	6.2	5.3
%	100.0	57.7	85.4	86.6	71.8	93.4	92.8	48.0	28.8

[a] Scores were prorated to a base of 25 items and corrected for
guessing.   [b] P= Précis (N=7); KW= Keyword (N=8); C= Control (N=7);
AS= All Subjects (N=22).   [c] This passage and test was administered
to all subjects without any listening aids.   [d] Approximately one-half
of each group is represented in each column.   [e] All subjects in this
column received a précis prior to the test.   [f] No subjects in this
column received any listening aids prior to this test.

Table 14

SUMMARY OF ANALYSIS OF VARIANCE:
GROUPS x FIVE TESTS DURING LISTENING PRACTICE

Source of Variation	df	Mean Square	F
Between Subjects	21		
Groups	2	1.47	
Within	19	28.91	
Within Subjects	88		
Tests	4	61.71	6.46**
Groups x Tests	8	4.43	
Tests x Within Subjects	76	9.55	

** $p < .01$

tial test scores at normal speed, the difference did not reach significance at the .05 level.

The final test of the experiment, also administered on the seventh day, consisted of the presentation of a précis to one-half of the subjects in each group, with no listening aid supplied to the remaining half. This procedure was designed to see if the précis provided a significant impact on the number of questions answerable without recourse to the passage. Therefore, no passage was presented. The mean score on this test for the combined one-half of the subjects who received the précis was 6.2, while that for the other half was 5.3, a non-significant difference. This finding suggests that the information provided in the précis was non-specific enough that it did not bias the score obtained by the Précis Group by providing them answers to the questions independent of listening to the passage.

In examining the significant improvement of the subjects with practice, the scores may be looked at in relation to the normal speed listening scores. There was a strong tendency to show improvement with successive sessions. The mean percentage of normal speed performance from the second through the sixth day were

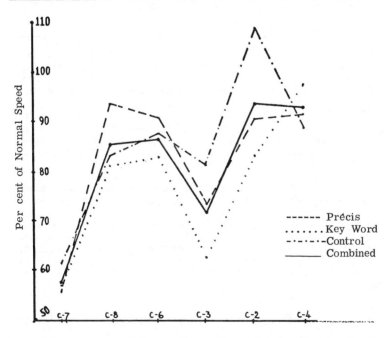

Figure 2. Mean percentages of normal speed comprehension for five passages with listening aids and one without.

Table 15

COMPARISON OF COMPREHENSION RESULTS AT 375 WPM
AS A FUNCTION OF PRACTICE FOR SEVEN GROUPS OF SUBJECTS

| Group | Mean Scores | | | Hours Listening Practice Prior to 375 wpm test | |
	175 wpm (Normal)	375 wpm	% Normal	Novels	Passages
Control (N=11)	17.4	12.7	71.7	0.00	0.50
Graduated Practice (N=10)	15.7	13.2	83.6	9.00	0.50
Interrupted Practice (N=11 Males)	14.1	9.4	71.0	9.00	0.50
Interrupted Practice (N=15 Females)	13.9	10.1	75.1	9.00	0.50
High Speed Practice (N=12)	13.8	9.9	76.0	9.00	0.50
Criterion Study (N=10)	15.5	11.9	77.2	15.25	0.75
Present Study (N=22)	14.3	12.7	92.8	5.00	0.75

as follows: 57.7, 85.4, 86.6, 71.8, and 93.4.   Performance on the
final passage at 375 w.p.m. administered on the seventh day was
92.8 per cent of normal speed score.   Figure 2 shows these data.
These results compare favorably with any achieved in previous experimentation at that speed.   Table 15 shows the percentages of normal speed score achieved by previous subjects on the last new passage administered at 375 w.p.m.   Preformance of the subjects in
the present experiment ranged from 9 to 22 per cent better than that
of previous groups at this speed.   This was achieved with less listening practice than any previous experimental group.

The current experiment combined certain features of previous
experiments which may have led to this advantage: sessions were
approximately one and one-half hours in length; they were held daily,
the proportion of time devoted to listening to test material as opposed to practice material was greater than for previous experimental groups; and the duration of constant listening was approximately
50 minutes without interruption.   The material was all presented at
one speed (375 w.p.m.), intermediate between normal (175) and high
speed (475).

Comprehension of Compressed Speech as a Function of Other Skills

From time to time questions have arisen as to the characteristics of students who do well in compressed speech studies.   While

the present experiment was not specifically designed to answer this question, it was decided to collect data which may be relevant in this respect.

Correlation data are shown in Table 16. At the final stage there were only three significant correlations with listening score: vocabulary, literature information, and English expression. Thus after practice, success in comprehending rapid speech appears to be clearly associated only with a language ability factor, thereby suggesting that, when the task of listening is difficult, but the listener is skilled, general language abilities are the most crucial.

Debriefing Questionnaire. At the end of the experiment proper, the subjects were given a form to complete which called for their evaluation of the experiment and their roles in it. All subjects responded yes to the questions concerning whether or not their abilities to comprehend speeded speech had improved during the experiment and whether or not practice had helped them. The Précis Group for the most part felt that the summary presented just before each passage helped them listen to the passage by giving them some idea of what to look for. The Key Word Group, on the other hand, had a somewhat negative attitude toward their listening aid. It was generally felt that the key word list encouraged a tendency to listen for specific words at the expense of overall meaning. There was some feeling, however, that the key words provided clues in answering the questions. The Control Group was asked what techniques of their own they had devised, if any, to improve their abilities to comprehend compressed speech. Five subjects mentioned that they tried to concentrate and comprehend the subject as a whole rather than to dwell on specific items. The prevalent initial reaction to compressed speech was discomfort at the speed. However, as in previous experiments, a favorable impression soon developed, together with the feeling that the speed was comfortable or would be by the end of the experiment.

Summary and Discussion

The examination of the relationship of listening performance to other aptitude and informational scores suggested that good listeners tend to be generally able and well informed, but that at higher speeds general language ability is increasingly important. The evidence also suggested a tentative hypothesis that good performance at higher speed is associated with listening for meaning rather than concentration on specific words and details.

In general the results reconfirmed previous experimental findings that good comprehension is possible at high speeds and that very modest amounts of practice are efficacious in improving comprehension of compressed speech. The failure of the listening aids to improve performance may possibly be attributable to their focusing attention on aspects of the passage which were irrelevant with respect to the test questions. In addition, they may have functioned to focus

Table 16

CORRELATIONS AND SUMMARY DATA FOR PROJECT TALENT TESTS
VERSUS SELECTED LISTENING COMPREHENSION SCORES (N= 22)

Test	Normal 175	Passage and Word Rate		$\overline{X}$	s
		First 375	Last 375		
Information Tests					
Vocabulary	.37	.29	.63	18.7	1.24
Literature	.49	.44	.47	19.2	1.74
Mucis	.30	.32	.01	9.2	2.36
Social Studies	.50	.71	.36	20.4	3.28
Mathematics	.32	.21	.17	19.5	3.42
Physical Science	.20	.27	-.08	14.7	3.32
Biol. Science	.50	.60	.13	7.9	1.67
Scientific Att.	.20	.04	.04	8.5	1.44
Aero. & Space	.54	.14	-.12	8.6	1.69
Elec. & Elec.	.56	.28	.08	14.9	3.62
Mechanics	.24	.01	.07	15.7	2.35
Farm & Ranch	.20	.06	.19	8.9	1.32
Home Economics	.11	.21	.30	10.3	3.46
Sports	-.17	-.13	.00	11.1	2.19
Total Score	.34	.44	.25	199.3	20.86
Aptitude Tests					
Arith. Comput.	.42	.12	.26	43.5	11.06
Mem. Words	.00	-.28	.16	15.0	6.22
Mem. Sentences	.07	-.43	.25	10.3	2.11
Math. I	.21	.15	.04	14.0	2.04
English Usage	.13	.02	.20	19.4	1.86
English Expression	.10	.04	.44	10.6	1.07
Abstract Reason.	.37	.12	.00	11.3	1.88
Mech. Reason.	.08	-.07	.15	16.6	2.78
Disguised Words	.03	.31	.02	22.1	5.66
Vision 3-D	-.04	.09	.20	10.7	3.66
Word Function	.49	-.04	.21	16.5	4.24
Reaction Time	-.18	.09	-.06	.185	.036

P05: r = .42

attention more on detail than understanding. The present experiment added further weight to the conclusion that practice sessions should be frequent (daily) and of substantial duration (about one hour) without interruption.

The overall results of the studies conducted to date have been highly encouraging with regard to the potential educational value of compressed speech. It is hoped that this research will spur efforts toward a greater understanding of the complexities not only of compressed speech listening, but of the listening process in general.

IV. LISTENING AID STUDY (B)

The research reported here covers a wide gamut of topics; the use of a précis as a listening aid to comprehension of compressed speech, the use of pure tone as an aid in signifying important parts of a passage, the efficacy of compressed speech to be paced by the listener, the ability of trained subjects to retain the listening skill they have acquired after a three week lapse, and the potentialities of compressed speech as a review technique for naive and for trained listeners.

Two of the major findings of previous research were reaffirmed: exposure to compressed speech will improve comprehension of new compressed material, and in general subjects find material presented at more than double normal recorded speed an acceptable way to listen. The listening aids employed in the study in this report were no more helpful than those used in an earlier study. While all groups of subjects improved over time, there was no difference between groups without aids, and those with, in terms of overall comprehension. An examination of self-pacing behavior showed no difference from performance under externally-paced conditions, both with regard to the chosen rate of presentation and ability to comprehend the material. However, this was a new technique for the listeners and it is felt that the more extensive use of this technique in an experiment might provide richer results. The experiments reported here on the feasibility of using compressed speech as a review technique show that both for naive and trained listeners reading for the same amount of time provided superior results. However, the gap between reading and listening groups was greater for the untrained than for the trained listeners.

V. OVERVIEW OF COMPRESSED SPEECH RESEARCH, 1963-1967

The studies in this report describe the preparation of listening and test materials in geology at the college level, and the examination of listening performance with this material, with previously prepared psychological material, and with performance on historical materials previously used in this research. With the exception of an unexplained setback on the final geology test, performance relative to normal speed in listening to compressed materials in psychology and geology is not worse than in history over a similar training period of approximately ten hours spread over a week.   Retention of listening skill, which was tested for these subject matters confirms earlier findings under diverse conditions which suggest that the listening skill usually built up during experimental exposure, is not retained if no intervening training is given.

Under two grants of the new Educational Media branch of the U.S. Office of Education, research has been conducted at the American Institutes for Research since 1963 in which a large number of variables have been examined in compressed speech listening.   At the risk of being redundant, we feel that a brief recapitulation of that research may serve a useful purpose here.

The overall purpose of this research has been to determine the feasibility of using the fairly new technique of speech compression to present lecture and textbook materials to college students. The complexity of speech, not to mention the educational situation itself, present a formidable array of known and unknown variables from which a researcher must select those he feels can be most profitably examined.   Taking as guidelines the availability of technical and educational resources, the limitations of time and money, and the issues we felt were most germane to the problem at hand, we examined the following major questions.   They have loosely been placed in three categories: stimulus, situational, and listener variables.   The superscript numbers refer to Table 17, in which are listed the individual experiments and the reports in which they are described.

Stimulus Variables

Amount, duration, rate, content and continuity of exposure to practice and test listening materials have been examined.   We have found that approximately 10 hours of exposure, of which two-thirds is of lighter material (novels) spread over a period of approximately one week is sufficient to achieve normal comprehension at approximately double speed for most students.[12,13*]   Ten to 15 hours of exposure is sufficient to achieve approximately 80 per cent normal comprehension at two and one-half normal speed (425 w.p.m.).[4] Listening to the practice materials for approximately an hour without interruption presents no difficulty.[12,13,19]   Thirty-five hours of exposure in a week's time offers no advantage in training, and some disadvantages.[7]   Rest period of three minutes after each 10 minutes of exposure is no better and possibly detrimental to the achievement of good comprehension than an uninterrupted flow.[5]   The use of incremental increase in rate over this period from about one and one-third faster than normal to two and one-half is not any better or worse than presenting all material at two and one-half normal from

---

* Refers to entries in Table 17.

Table 17

MAJOR EXPERIMENTS CONDUCTED AT THE AMERICAN INSTITUTES FOR RESEARCH SINCE 1963 IN FACTORS ASSOCIATED WITH THE USE OF SPEEDED SPEECH AS AN EDUCATIONAL MEDIUM

Title of Experiment	AIR Project Designation	Report	Date of Report
1. Exploratory Study	D-50	Progress Report #II	December 1963
2. Paced Reading Study	D-50	Project Report	June 1964
3. Standardization of History Test Materials	D-50	Project Report	June 1964
4. Graduated Practice	D-50	Project Report	June 1964
5. Male vs. Female Interrupted Practice	D-50	Project Report	February 1965
6. Concentrated (high-speed) Practice	E-50	Progress Report #1	July 1965*
7. Immersion Study	E-50	Progress Report #2	January 1966*
8. Criterion Studies 1 & 2	E-50	Progress Report #2	January 1966*
9. Retention Study I	E-50	Progress Report #2	January 1966*
10. Retention Study II	E-50	Progress Report #2	January 1966*
11. Retention Study III	E-50	Progress Report #2	January 1966*
12. Listening Aid Study I	E-50	Progress Report #3	July 1966*
13. Listening Aid Study II	E-50	Progress Report #4	February 1967*
14. Self-Pacing Study	E-50	Progress Report #4	February 1967*
15. Standardization of Psychology Test Materials	E-50	Progress Report #4	February 1967*
16. Use of Compressed Speech as a Review Technique	E-50	Progress Report #4	February 1967*
17. Listening Aid Study II Extension	E-50	Progress Report #4	February 1967*
18. Standardization of Geology Test Materials	E-50	Final Report	September 1967*
19. Materials Comparison Experiments	E-50	Final Report	September 1967*
20. Materials Comparison Follow-Up Studies	E-50	Final Report	September 1967*

* all these reports have been excerpted and are included in this article.

the beginning. [4,6] As noted earlier in this report, we have established most of these findings by using novels as practice listening
material[7] and historical passages as test materials. [3] We have now
examined psychological[15] and geological[16] materials as well, and
while we have much less data in these areas, our results suggest
that both of these disciplines may be amenable to compressed presentation. [19]

Situational Variables

        Under this broad heading we have included the use of listen-
ing aids before and during material presentation, self-determination
of rate, the measurement of retention, and the use of compressed
speech as a method of review. We have found that neither the use
of carefully prepared written summaries of material to be heard[12,13]
scrutinizing a list of key words to appear in the passage[12] nor the
presentation of a short time during the passage to highlight significant portions[13] have altered performance relative to control groups
without any of those listening aids, when speech is presented at better than double speed. (In each of these experiments, however, we
have reconfirmed the basic finding that virtually normal listening
performance at those speeds can be achieved.) In several experiments under a variety of different conditions we have measured both
retention of listening skill and retention of material originally heard
at compressed speeds. In most cases we have found the skill to
disappear rapidly[10,11,12] although we have not tested the possibility
that retaining may be effected more easily. Retention of content,
however, is at least as good as normal speed content. In the single
study in which subjects manipulated the rate of presentation themselves we found no differences in either the rate selected or the listening scores. [14] We feel, however, that self-pacing deserves examination in conditions of greater exposure and an opportunity to become comfortable with the technique. We have found in the past that
repetition of passages, not surprisingly, leads to improvement in
comprehension. [6,8] The likelihood of using compressed speech to
review material already familiar is a logical step from this. The
pilot study performed as an adjunct to another study did not confirm
this;[16] but there again we feel that further experimentation focusing
on this problem is in order.

Listener Variables

        Increasingly as the research progressed and the ability of
groups of college students to learn to comprehend compressed speech
in a relatively short time was confirmed and reconfirmed, we began
to turn our attention to individual differences. We found no difference between male and female students in this respect. [5] We have
found intercorrelations between listening and reading scores generally
positive. [5,6] There is no overwhelming evidence, however, that normal speed listening scores correlate significantly with high speed listening scores. We have found a suggestion that while general lan-

guage handling abilities correlate positively with compressed speech listening performance, skill at giving attention to detail in language does not. [12] We have never found a significant group mean improvement in either normal speed listening or reading skills relative to control groups at the conclusion of compressed speech experimental exposure. We have found significant reading improvement in several experimental and control groups, [4, 5, 6] but it should be borne in mind that the control groups also had some regular exposures to the test materials in compressed form.

Throughout our research we have presented debriefing questionnaires at the end of each major experiment designed to get subjective reactions from our students. The vast majority of students have responded positively to the question of whether they would like to see compressed speech used in some form in their college curricula. Nearly all subjects also expressed the belief that practice listening skill improved their comprehension of compressed material. Overall we have experienced both a willingness to participate in our experiments, and a degree of enthusiasm for the potential use of compressed speech in education which has been most encouraging.

Chapter 3

PAUSE TIME AS RELATED TO INTELLIGIBILITY
AND COMPREHENSION

The four items excerpted in this chapter are concerned with an extremely important phase of time-compressed speech--pause time. In order to accept the possibility of either intelligibility or comprehension of time-compressed material it is necessary first to accept the presence of redundancy in the original message. If we had a message that is not redundant in any respect, then obviously every last bit of it is essential to understanding and any process of interruption or deletion would destroy this understanding.

It is very natural that early thinkers about this problem such as, for example, Diehl, White, and Burk [B83], thought that pause time might very well be the source of a large proportion of redundancy. Hence, it was reasoned, the message might well be speeded up by reducing the time given to pauses. Since the Diehl study used manual methods and did not attain a significant change in rate, no answer containing the truth of this theory was obtained in that study. Subsequently, however, much investigation on the significance of pause time has taken place. Of these the four passages excerpted in this chapter are believed to be representative.

The first item in this chapter was written by Professor Murray Miron of Syracuse University and Professor Eric W. Brown of New York University. Dr. Miron was co-author with Grant Fairbanks and Newman Guttman of three articles excerpted in Part I of this Anthology. He was also the editor and compiler of Experimental Phonetics [B100] which is a collection of papers written by Grant Fairbanks on a variety of phases of speech. The present paper is not easy reading but careful study reveals a thoughtful, carefully performed experiment which is reported in sufficient detail to render a lucid explanation of the role of pause time in creating the syntactic structure of an aural passage.

The second item of this chapter is taken from a doctoral dissertation written by Professor Joseph G. Agnello now on the staff at the University of Buffalo. It is a lucid review of research that has been done on pause time in speech. To the novice this is an excellent introduction and to the sophisticate it should serve as a more than ordinarily useful review. Professor Frieda Goldman-Eisler of London, England is without question the outstanding student of pauses and their significance. She has written extensively on this subject. The third passage in this chapter is an excellent example of her research. The last passage in this chapter is again from Professor

Agnello's dissertation. In this passage he describes the procedure used in his research and lists his hypotheses as well as his results. Particularly useful to most readers is his definition of a number of the terms used in the study of pauses.

DURATIONAL VARIABLES IN SPEECH COMPREHENSION

Murray S. Miron, Eric W. Brown

In the past several years there has been comparatively little work on pause time as a variable in the decoding of speech. Maclay and Osgood [B274] investigated the role of filled and unfilled pauses in spontaneous speech relative to a grammatical and uncertainty analysis; D. S. Boomer ["Hesitation and Grammatical Encoding," Language & Speech 8:148-58, 1965] attempted to refute the transitional probability theory of hesitation phenomena; and Martin and Strange found that perceived pause was displaced to constituent boundaries. However, with the exception of the important and extensive work of Goldman-Eisler [B191], this area of psycholinguistic research seems to have been dominated by the analysis-by-synthesis view, that most of the prosodic features of speech can be regularly predicted by the phonological rules of English from the abstract surface-structure ordering of formatives, N. Chomsky and M. Halle [The Sound Pattern of English, New York: Harper, 1968]. Yet even if this theoretical framework is formally correct as a model of competence, the problem remains as to what cues exist in the speech stream that will guide the listener to the correct deep structure interpretation, hence to a surface structure, phonetic rendering, and a perceptual match and acceptance. It increasingly appears that prosodic features may have a large role in guiding the listener's actual performance, and unfortunately most of the work thus far on pause has concentrated on the planning or hesitation phenomenon in spontaneous speech as an indicator of encoding complexity.

Taken as whole the literature indicates that pause time in the decoding task may serve one of three purposes: (a) it may function as an important indicator of structural complexity--that is, it may literally demarcate computable segments for short term memory (STM); (b) it may provide necessary processing time at the completion of linguistic segments in STM; (c) it may reflect some psychological necessity in the listening habits of subjects and thus function as a redundant aspect of the speech stream. The following analysis was undertaken to explicate and empirically evaluate these three hypotheses in terms of the prediction of pause time in an oral decoding task.

This study specifically investigated the predictability of pause time in a 1537-word spoken message. The so-called "Meteorology Message" has received extensive analysis in the past 15 years, Fair-

banks, Guttman, and Miron [B107-09]; Miron and Brown [B288]. In
this instance a professionally read rendition paced at 164 w. p. m.
was analyzed from three points of view: (a) an immediate constituent (IC), or surface structure, syntactic analysis, R. S. Wells ["Immediate Constituents," Language 23:81-117, 1947] or C. F. Hockett
["Two Models of Grammatical Description," Word 10:210-31, 1954];
(b) a stochastic or information analysis of all lexical items in context; and (c) a deep structure analogue or clause analysis.   An oscillographic recording of the entire message was performed, and text
(i. e. , all sequential lexical items) then appended so that all pauses
could be related to morphemic analysis.

Method

        In a previous series of experiments [B288], stimulus and psy-
chological measures of a battery of 36 rate-manipulated versions of
the message indicated that optimization of the efficiency of aural coding could be accomplished by the simultaneous application of a combination of natural and artificial distortions of the durational characteristics of speech.   Peak efficiency of listening was successfully
pushed to 400 w. p. m. primarily by means of a selective reduction
of speech pause time.   Regression estimates predicting the influence
of pause time, total duration, and talker rate upon judgments of
speech rate and comprehension were calculated, and a number of implications for listening strategies and speech apperception were drawn.
One of the several recorded versions of the message performed for
these earlier studies provided the criterion variable data for the
present experiment.

        Stochastic Measures.   While a more general "uncertainty"
analysis has been applied to the study of hesitation phenomena by a
number of researchers, e. g. , Maclay and Osgood [B274], and Goldman-Eisler [B191], only Tannenbaum [P. Tannenbaum, F. Williams,
C. Hillier, "Word Predictability in the Environment at Hesitations,"
J. of Verbal Learn. & Verbal Behav. 4:134-40, 1965] has used the
information statistic to demonstrate, in that instance, that words
subsequent to hesitations tend to be less predictable than words uttered in fluent context.   In the present experiment, under the hypothesis that knowledge of lexical transitional probabilities within
grammatical constituents might be an important factor in speech perception, an information measure was computed for each of the 1537
words of running text.   For this purpose, an every fifth word deletion scheme was used with five overlapping versions, so that each
word was sampled in a four-word bilateral context.   The resultant
data provide a linear assessment of the information in the message
both within and between sentences.   Ten subjects were asked to fill
in every blank with a single word, and were encouraged to guess
freely when uncertain.   No time limit was set, but it was suggested
that most students would finish in 45 minutes or less.   In all but
several isolated instances, subjects completed the test forms in 50
minutes.

The distribution of the ten subject responses corresponding to each of the 1537 lexical items was summarized and described by several statistical measures. The non-relativized information statistic (H measure) (H = - $\sum_{i=1}$ p$_i$log$_2$p$_i$) earlier used by Miron and Brown [B288] was computed, as well as two relativizing versions of this basic measure. The information statistic relativized with respect to total word tokens (HREL) statistic took as its constant divisor log$_2$10, corresponding to the assumption that were H maximum, all ten responses would be different words or types. This measure simply scales H from 0 to 1 and provides the reader with a better intuitive grasp of the range of the statistic. The information statistic relativized with respect to total word tokens (HTREL) divided the H statistic by the figure log$_2$T, or the log of the number of different types of responses elicited by a particular deletion point. Under this model HTREL equates H for differing numbers of types of response found for a particular item deletion. Hence, to maximize H an equi-probable distribution of word types (I) is assumed, thus removing that variance due to types from the uncertainty measure.

IC Analysis. An "immediate constituent analysis" was performed on each of the 84 sentences in the message. This form of grammatical analysis is well-documented in the linguistics literature, and is customarily associated with the Rulon Wells' [see note, p. 556] formulation of the method. IC analysis involves the successive grouping of words into higher-order constituents, leading to a resultant penultimate set of two or more major constituents for the sentence. These levels of grouping always seek a binary structure or pattern where feasible that may be represented in a tree diagram or equivalent bracketed form. The basic method for determining constituents in the sentence is that of comparing samples, substitutability, or isolating that IC with the greatest freedom of occurrence.

A measure of structural complexity derived from the IC analysis provided a significant variation on the depth hypothesis scoring. Chomsky and Miller [see note, p. 555] suggested that the node-to-terminal-node ratio in the P-marker or tree diagram of the terminal string (sentence) ought to reflect "the amount of computation per input symbol that must be performed by the listener." As later developed by Ruder and Jensen [B365] this method of scoring an IC tree diagram involves determining the lowest node that dominates two adjacent words of interest, and counting the total number of nodes contained in this branch; this figure is then divided by the number of terminal nodes (words) in this branch. The resultant Structural Complexity Index (SCI) has the range 1.0< SCI <2.0, representing low and high syntactic complexity, and generally reflecting a decrease in the amount of branching per non-terminal node as SCI values increase.

Deep Structure Analogue. Bever's hypothesis [T. Bever, J. R. Lakner, W. Stoltz, "Transitional Probability Is Not a General Mechanism for the Segmentation of Speech," J. of Exper. Psychol. 79:387-94, 1969] that "the basic unit of immediate speech processing is any sequence which corresponds to a 'sentence' (single expansion

of 'S') at the level of underlying structure," has a rather firm theoretical base in Chomsky's grammatical theory. Transformational-
generative grammar requires a "deep" or underlying logical form
for sentences. Much of the recent work in psycholinguistics has
been devoted to the establishment of a psychological reality for these
underlying forms, and the development of the necessary performance
algorithms that will recover these deep structures from linguistic input.

     The extrapolation of this hypothesis and method to a general
body of linguistic data had not, however, been attempted, prior to
the present experiment. As previously noted, there has always been
grammatical segmentation of sentences according to clause analysis,
both within and out of present syntactic theory. Clause breaks
would naturally enough correspond to underlying sentence breaks.
However, in the present analysis, a number of other deep structure
analogue (DSA) breaks were noted. Using N. Chomsky's [Aspects of
the Theory of Syntax, Cambridge, Mass.: M.I.T. Press, 1965] illustrative fragment of the deep structure as a guide, additional DSA
breaks were recorded in noun and adjective strings with a depth of
two or more. Chomsky distinguishes sentence adverbials of time
and place as forming "pre-Sentence" units which modify the complete
Verb Phrase or perhaps even the entire underlying "sentence" as a
whole. However, for the DSA analysis of the message in this experiment, a conservative approach was adopted, and these preceding
adverbial phrases were counted as part of each underlying sentence
structure as a whole, since the break between these phrases and the
remainder of the underlying sentence did not separate corresponding
deep structure strings.

     In sum, this experiment sought to determine if pause time in
an oral reading performance could be predicted from the study and
measurement of stochastic and syntactic representations of the message read. As a predictive model it sought to maximize that proportion of the variance of the pause measurements accounted for by
the specification of certain predictor variables. For this purpose a
multiple regression (Mult R) analysis was pursued with each of the
independent variables as predictors of both the occasion and duration
of pause expressed in the form of a linear equation best fitting the
data by the least squares criterion. In short, the research model
adopted in this study asked to what extent pause time in an oral
reading performance was predictable from a set of logically motivated
measures derived from differing models of sentential organization.

Results and Discussion

     Prediction of Specific Pause Loci. A stepped Mult R was
performed with untransformed pause time as the criterion variable.
All seven independent variables were entered into the routine as predictors, and the resultant series of Beta weights for the linear equations along with the appropriately stepped Mult R's are displayed in
Table 1. The rightmost column of this matrix displays the variance

Table 1

MULTIPLE REGRESSION PREDICTION OF PAUSE TIME FROM SEVEN INDEPENDENT VARIABLES

	PAUSE	IC	DSA	SCI	HTREL	H	HREL	T	FINAL BETAS	%V
				Predictor Intercorrelations						
PAUSE	.636	.74	.69	.37	.05	.12	.12	.11		
IC		.743	.70	.68	.01	.12	.12	.11	.66	49
DSA		.74	.782	.41	.04	.15	.16	.15	.31	21
SCI		.50	.34	.797	.02	.10	.10	.10	-.20	-7
HTREL		.66	.32	-.20	.797	.20	.20	.19	.03	0
H		.66	.32	-.20	.03	.797	1.0	.98	.81	10
HREL		.66	.31	-.20	.03	.01	.797	.98	-.80	-10
T		.66	.32	-.20	.03	.81	-.79	.798	.01	0

(Left margin vertical label: BETA WEIGHTS)

NOTE: Variable identifications are as follows: IC=immediate constituent, DSA=deep structural analog, SCI=structural complexity index, HTREL=information statistic relativized with respect to total word types, H=non-relativized information statistic, HREL=information statistic relativized with respect to total word tokens, T=word types.

contribution and the penultimate column the Beta weight for each of
the predictor variables in the final derived equation at Step 7. Successive variables were chosen on the basis of the magnitude of residual variance accounted for by the variable.   The standardized
Beta weight form of the equation is:

$$\text{Pause } (Z) = .66(Z_{IC}) + .31(Z_{DSA}) + .20(Z_{SCI}) + .03(Z_{HTREL})$$
$$+ .81(Z_H) + -.80(Z_{HREL}) + .01(Z_T)$$

the regression coefficient form of the equation is:

$$\text{Pause(m. sec.)} = 54.74(IC) + 179.56(DSA) + -239.46(SCI) +$$
$$32.15(HTREL) + 165.92(H) + -553.15(HREL) + 1.11(T) + 93.82.$$

It will be noted from the successive Mult R predictions as they appear along the diagonal of the matrix that very little increase in
predictive variance results from computation beyond Step 3, when
lexical measures are introduced.   The Mult R at Step 4 was .797
accounting for 64 per cent of the total variance of Pause.   Under the
analysis of variance model the F ratio test of significance for regression ranged from $F = 1888.53$ $(1,1535)$ for Step 1 to $F = 382.50$
$(7,1529)$ at Step 7.

As can be seen by inspection of the regression table, the
first variable entered into the equation, IC, accounted for more than
55 per cent of the total variance in pause time.   It is rather remarkable that this simplest of syntactic measures--often dismissed
by contemporary linguistic theoreticians as not capturing the more
important relations of syntax--should so positively predict the occasion and duration of pause.   The second variable entered, DSA,
brought the R^2 figure to 61 per cent, indicating again that there is
some difference between the predictive variance of the surface structure and deep structure syntactic models.   The third variable entered
into the equation was SCI, which accounted for only a 2 per cent increase in total predictive variance to 63 per cent, indicating that
there was very little linear predictive variance remaining in SCI
which was not accounted for by either IC or DSA.   This is quite reasonable when we consider that IC and DSA are probably the most direct analogues to the two respective syntactic models and ought therefore together to account for most of the syntactic variance.   Finally,
entering the fourth predictive variable, HTREL, increased the predictable pause variance by only 1 per cent--to 64 per cent.   This
variable which had a very low correlation in the original unpartialled
matrix $(r=.05)$ adds the only variance from the lexical measures that
is not accounted for by the syntactic variables.   The other lexical
variables did not appreciably raise the predictive variance figure and
therefore contributed little if any enhancement in the prediction of
specific pause loci not accounted for under the syntactic model.

The Venn Diagram of Figure 1 makes explicit the overlapping
variance among the predictor and criterion variables.   Pause, IC,
DSA, and SCI are all in the same plane, while the lexical variables
form a third dimension of the display.   The negative variance of
SCI as entered in the Mult R determination indicates that SCI acts

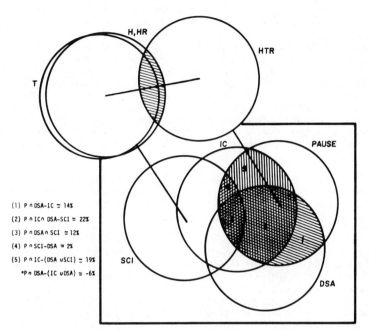

(1) P ∩ DSA-IC ≃ 14%
(2) P ∩ IC∩ DSA-SCI ≃ 22%
(3) P ∩ DSA∩ SCI ≃ 12%
(4) P ∩ SCI-DSA ≃ 2%
(5) P ∩ IC-(DSA ∪SCI) ≃ 19%
*P ∩ DSA-(IC ∪DSA) ≃ -6%

Figure 1.   Criterion and predictor intersections.

as a suppression variable in the prediction of Pause.   Although it
does have some small positive correlation with Pause, its principal
effect in the Mult R determination is to suppress that variance in
IC and, to a lesser extent, the variance in DSA that is not shared
with Pause.   In other words there is some variance in IC which is
uncorrelated, or possibly even negatively correlated with Pause--
variance which is suppressed by entering SCI into the linear equation.   This fact can be seen by inspecting the Beta weight increase
for IC in the multiple determination at the step in which SCI is entered into the equation (see Table 1).   The Beta weight for IC increases from .50 to .66 with the entrance of the negative weight for
SCI, while DSA drops from .34 to .32.   That variance shared by
SCI and Pause is a proper subset of the variance shared by IC,
DSA, and Pause.   Furthermore, that variance shared by SCI and
Pause is more specifically subsumed in the variance shared by IC
and Pause.   Both IC and DSA are substantial predictors of Pause,
and although they share a considerable proportion of variance (as
would be expected from their theoretical assumptions), nonetheless
each variable makes an additional unique contribution, preserving the
grammatical distinction between observed and deep structure.   IC,
however, has the predictive advantage in that a proportion of its
negative co-variation with Pause is suppressed by the SCI measure
of surface structure.

Implications. The present study has demonstrated that up to 65 per cent of the pause time variance in an extended oral reading performance can be predicted from syntactic analyses of the message. It has also been shown that on the average pause events precede lexical items of greater uncertainty than is found with non-pause events. The syntactic predictions of both occurrence and duration of pause are consistent with the widely held hypothesis that fluent oral readers tend to pause at grammatical junctures. However, this is the first study to attempt a large-scale analysis resulting in a predictive equation for pause time. It is also the first study to systematically explore the durational hypothesis--that degree of syntactic complexity has direct behavioral manifestations in performance.

When the results of this last experiment are combined with those of the earlier experiments of our research program a theoretically coherent picture of the role of pause and durational patterns in aural processing begins to emerge.

Beginning with those alterations under the control of the talker, we observe from Figure 2 that as the talker increases his speech rate (from rear to front face of the rate surface of the plot), he affects that increase through a power reduction of the ratio of pause to phonation time. Each of the three faces of this plot represents slices through the continuous rate changes under the control of the talker; rate in words per minute plotted along the ordinates and pause-to-phonation time ratios along the abscissas. The talker rates represent from back to front, respectively, (1) the slowest paced rate the talker could sustain with instruction for communicative effect, (2) the talker's normal and preferred rate, and (3) the fastest sustained rate of which the talker was capable. Horizontal slices through the surface represent experimental distortions of the total duration of the message produced by periodic (and hence random) deletions of the speech signal to produce overall duration reductions of 0, 30, 50, and 70 per cent of the talker resultant durations. Vertical slices of the surface represent selective deletions of the total pause time of 0, 50, and 100 per cent. Thus, for example, the lower, left-most point of the center face represents the obtained rate and pause-to-phonation values for the 0 per cent pause compression (P_c), 0 per cent random deletion (R_cP, and normal talker rate treatment combinations. That is to say, rate increases are normally accomplished through a greater reduction in pause time relative to the reductions in phonation time. Under the self instruction, however, for communicative speech, the talker does not push this process beyond a pause-to-phonation ratio of approximately .3. Our research, however, has shown that an artificial decrease in total duration and a selective decrease in pause time do not linearly degrade comprehension of the resultant speech signal. We first note that proportionate linear reductions in total speech duration, with resultant rates as depicted in the left-most functions in each of the talker rate faces of Figure 2, produce the expected ogival decrease in overall comprehension. This non-linear decrease in comprehension as a function of proportionate reduction in total

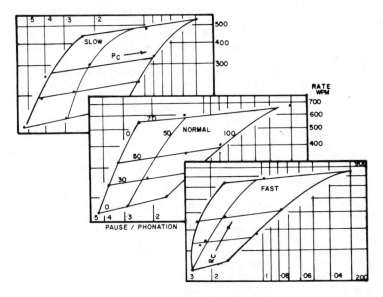

Figure 2.   The rate surface.

duration parallels the classic detection model quite faithfully. What
significantly differs in these experiments is the distinctively different effects of decreases in total duration affected through the proportionate reduction of pause time alone.   We have observed two
salient effects as a consequence of such reduction.   First, the perceived reduction in duration on the part of the listener is not, as it
is in the case for simultaneous reduction in both pause and phonation times, under the control of the measured duration.   Second, the
effect of such selective pause reduction upon comprehension is also
not under the control of measured duration.   When we affect an artificial increase in measured speech rate through the selective reduction of pause duration without changing the total phonation time
originally employed by the talker through the range of his naturally
controlled rate changes, we observe essentially non-significant effects upon the listener either in terms of his judgments of perceived
rate or in terms of his global comprehension of the speech intent.
The generality of these findings is not restricted when we control by
covariance adjustment for such subject competence factors as reading speed, reading comprehension, or vocabulary level, Miron and
Brown [B288].   Thus although the measured rate changes which we
are capable of producing through this means of durational distortion
of normal speech are quite large and although elsewhere we observe
a lawfully predictable relationship between perceived rate and comprehension as a function of measured rate changes, the effects of
pause distortion remain anomolous.

The foregoing detailed account of this last of our experiments makes it clear, however, that the explanation of this anomaly is straightforward. The perception of pause time is predominately under the control of the syntactic structure of the speech material. When the talker and the listener share a common linguistic base, the perception of speech as encoded by the talker is determined by the syntactic expectations of the decoder. The encoder reading meaningful material supplies a decoded "reading" of that material which renders his own perceptions of the syntactic organization of the material. He intentionalizes this reading, in part, through the proportionate distribution of pause intervals between syntactically coherent phrase units. If the listener, for his part, is to share in the intentions of the talker, he must with reasonable fidelity himself recreate those intentions. And it is these decoder generated intentions shared by both the talker and the listener that control speech perception. Our research suggests that there is broad elasticity in the successful matching of such intentions. In the absence of most of the physically realized cues of "reading" intentions, the listener is capable of rendering a correct account of the distorted stimulus. In fact, within rather broad limits his perceptions lead him to believe that the stimulus was undistorted. The limits of this elasticity are apparently dictated by the nature of the distortion. When the speech signal is degraded by an overall reduction in both pause and phonation time beyond approximately 50 per cent of its original duration, fidelity in the match between the encoder's and decoder's separately generated expectations falls precipitously. But when the durational distortion is accomplished through reduction in the physical markers of syntactic organization which preserves the proportionate distribution of the encoders intentions, the process of understanding those intentions suffers little or no disturbance.

When one examines the nature of the predictors which account for this distribution of pause time in normal speech, further light is thrown upon the boundary conditions of the elasticity of the talker-listener contract. Our lexical measures failed to account for much of the intentions of our talker. Beyond predicting sentence word initial choices on the basis of sentence juncture pause time, the perceived lexical uncertainty of choice measure was not very useful. The two most overwhelming determinants of the pause intentions of the talker were those indices which were designed to capture the surface and deep-lying organizations of the syntactic intentions. And although we find, quite reasonably enough, that there is normally a considerable amount of shared co-variance between these two determinants, each nonetheless contributes independent control over the pause time of the talker. This division between shared and independent covariation with pause distribution suggests a compellingly provocative hypothesis as to the roles of these determinants. Simply stated our data suggest the possibility that the marking of surface units of speech must in some manner be realized in any intentional reading if listener decoding of those intentions is to be accurate. If all such marking is removed, the listener would be expected to be able to supply only the major deep structural organizations of the speech material and a series of equally possible putative

Figure 3. Global comprehension as a function of time equated and time dependent rate determination. Message comprehension is plotted as a function of log rate in wpm such that total comprehension is made relative to the maximum efficiency or effectiveness of the message. Effectiveness of comprehension is defined as the raw comprehension of the message chance corrected. Efficiency of comprehension expresses this effectiveness relative to the message display time. Thus while effectiveness varies with message time, efficiency equates message durations at different rates in a measure of comprehension per unit of time. The shoulder of the effectiveness function preceeding the sharp degradation of comprehension is estimated to be at the point corresponding to a 50 per cent reduction of total message duration or a rate of about 320 wpm. For theoretical reasons, this point is assumed to correspond to the crossing point of the two functions. Efficiency rises linearly to a peak of about 400 wpm and subsequently parallels the effectiveness function at an upward displacement of rate which represents the efficiency savings of the undegraded comprehension.

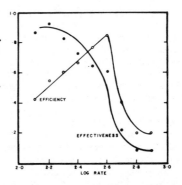

---

derivations leading to divergent surface structures. Without physical cues in the speech stream which would render one of these readings as being more accurate than another, the listener concludes that since all are possible no interpretation is possible. In the normal case the physical markings of the syntactic basis and its singular derivation are supportive of one another, especially in those instances where the otherwise unmarked surface structure could ambiguously imply differing base P markers. Thus, as depicted in Figure 3, normal comprehension of the talker's syntactic intentions can be stretched despite the reduction in total listening item beyond that which would ordinarily have degraded comprehension. These surface markings of putative underlying structures are normally highly redundant. Our experiments have begun to trace the nature and extent of that redundancy with respect to the durational characteristics of aural coding. Further refinement of the role of surface markings as an heuristic to deep structure recovery could be achieved by manipulation of the normal durational patterns of speech which would produce either ambiguous or misleading interpretations of the talker's intentions. And indeed, such experimentation is planned as would employ insertions and expansions of pause time at loci which are predicted from the structural models to be critical for deep structure recovery.

But for the first time, the experiments of this research program supplied a detailed molecular analysis of an extended stream

of an intentional communication. We have completed analyses of the
phonation, pause, lexical, surface and deep structural attributes of
this communication and have manipulated its durational character
through the limits of the range of distortions which could accrue to
such manipulation. We have charted the effects of each of these
attributes across a wide range of subject perceptions and characteristics with regard to rate determinations and global comprehension.
We see this work as supporting and extending the recent experimental attacks on language processing which have been motivated by the
generative school. And beyond its theoretical implications for a
psycholinguistic account of the operations which map meaningful intentions into speech, the research has immediate, practical ramifica-
tions which we should underscore. The oral/aural mode of language processing is almost as little understood as it is important in
everyday communication. Our meager attempts to better understand
that process have not unintentionally produced a set of techniques
which can be utilized to make such coding more efficient. And if
we must conclude that there is more yet to be done, that is a statement of the importance of what we seek and the humble recognition
of its complexity.

REVIEW OF THE LITERATURE ON STUDIES OF PAUSES

Joseph G. Agnello

        Studies that treat pauses fall into five categories: those that
(1) involve instrumental techniques in measuring pauses; (2) express
temporal data; (3) examine the variability of speech rate; (4) relate
certain types of pauses to psychological processes; and (5) relate
pauses to certain lingual characteristics.

(1) Instrumental techniques

        There are numerous ways of measuring pauses: having an
observer simply activate a timer during the elapsed time of a pause,
using photographic tracings taken from an oscilloscope or other materials such as pen-writing devices, galvanometer readings, or
spectrographic analyses. These methods are subjective and are dependent on the individual who makes the measurement. The latter
methods of obtaining the durations of pauses are expensive in terms
of time, especially if long continuous samples of speech are to be
analyzed. The following studies relate to systems designed to detect pauses automatically.

        The Purdue Speech Sound Timer [H. J. Tyler, G. L. Drae-
gert, T. D. Hanley, M. D. Steer, "Purdue Sound Timer," Tech.
Report #Spec Der Cen 104-2-7 (April 1948), Office of Naval Research Contract (this reference not verified. --Ed.)] is a unit that

responds to a voice-operated relay that starts and stops a timer
which measures the time spent in phonation and non-phonation. It
measures phonated time in units of .01 second and can be calibrated
to include some of the voiceless consonants within the measures
called phonation, for example voicing implies vibrating vocal folds
(pitch) whereas phonation is due in part to an "... active muscular
process of closing the glottis and a passive process of opening the
glottis under the influence of air pressure. More specifically,
phonation (plus resonance) provides an acoustic phenomenon called
voice" [L. S. Judson, A. T. Weaver, Voice Science, New York:
Appleton, 1965]. M. Verzeano and J. E. Fenesginer ["An Automatic Analyzer for the Study of Speech in Interaction and in Free Association," Science 110:45-46, July 1949] described an electronic
timer similar to the Purdue timer. This apparatus was designed
to measure the number of units of speech and the total time in
speech during an interview situation. The total time in silence is
obtained by subtracting the total time in speech from the total duration of an interview. A minimum pause was arbitrarily defined as
a silence of .5 second which in turn was used to define a speech
unit.

An apparatus developed by Starkweather [B400], the Speech
Rate Meter, produces a cumulative graphic record of "pulses" in
speech. This apparatus provided a measure of the rate of talking
by the detection of speech "pulses" which were believed to be sylla-
ble-like points of stress within words. The speech "pulses" were
converted into a series of rectangular waves that operated a graphic
plotter displaying the number of speech "pulses" as a function of
time. Hargreaves and Starkweather reported a system called the
Duration Tabulator used for analysis of temporal data. The Duration Tabulator was designed to detect and classify the durations of
pauses of a series on mechanical counters. This method allows for
a quick frequency distribution of pauses. The system included an
automatic triggering circuit activated by a voice signal and a circuit
that discriminated durations of pauses into class intervals. These
authors followed Verzeano and Fenesinger in defining the minimum
pause as .5 second. This duration was established on the basis that
the majority of pauses in conversational speech exceed .5 second.

E. D. Chapple ["Personality Differences As Described by In-
varient Properties of Individuals in Interaction," Proceed. of Natl.
Acad. Sci. 26:10-16, 1940] reported an Interaction Chronograph that
identifies pauses with conversational speech. When pauses were
measured within standardized materials, stable differences were
found to exist among the readings of different subjects. The Sylrater was developed by Irwin and Becklund [B232] and is similar to
Starkweather's Speech Rate Meter. The Sylrater indicated the average, as well as the maximum, repetitive rate in the saying of syllables as in the determination of diadochokinetic rate and in tapping
movements. The essential difference between the Sylrater and the
Speech Rate Meter is that the output of the Sylrater must be monitored by an operator. The Speech Rate Meter can handle similar
types of speech utterances automatically, and, with an operator

pressing a key to identify speakers, it can measure the interaction pauses in conversational speech. I. Goldiamond ["Blocked Speech Communication and Delayed Feedback in Experimental Analysis," Contract No. AF 19(604)-6127 (Feb. 1960), Operational Applications Laboratory, Bedford, Mass.: Air Force Cambridge Research Center, Reports 1 & 2 issued Sept. 1960 (this reference not verified. -- Ed.)] reported a unit that could respond to and automatically classify the pauses in speech into categories. That is, it could classify the durations of pauses into class-intervals. The apparatus could detect silences as short as 50 milliseconds.

Summary. Several similar instruments have been developed for the measurement of pauses. They differ principally in the read-out devices. Although the specific circuitries were not discussed here, they are similar in that they generally function on the principle of a flip-flop circuit. Such circuits, though reliable, are limited in the minimum time to which they can react. The rate of response is limited by the system of measurement and by the rate of occurrence of the events to be measured. This limitation of the minimum duration of a pulse is controlled by the capacitor reaction time incorporated in flip-flop circuits. The rate of response is always limited by the mechanical properties of the read-out devices.

(2) Temporal data on pauses

The following studies on pauses and speech units emphasize mean values. Studies that consider the pause also consider the "non-pause," namely, speech unit. M. Verzeano ["Time Patterns of Speech in Normal Subjects," J. of Speech & Hear. Disord. 15: 197-201, 1950] reported the distribution of speech units, for example, units set off by pauses of at least .5 second. The frequency distribution of the speech units from eight speakers (four- to eight-minute samples), speaking freely about their past, was fitted to a Poisson distribution. The mean speech unit was 2.3 seconds. Verzeano ["Time Patterns of Speech in Normal Subjects, II." J. of Speech & Hear. Disord. 16:346-50, 1951] questioned this minimum pause of .5 second for the definition of a unit of speech. A unit of speech was thus redefined as it was produced by the subject regardless of what the absolute pauses between it might be. This definition is similar to that used in this study. Verzeano reported that the speech units became shorter as the minimum pause defining them was reduced. As the minimum pause defining a speech unit goes beyond .7 second, the departure from a Poisson distribution is greater. Hargreaves [B208] also treated the duration of a speech unit. He described the distribution as similar to an exponential decay process. The distributions of the speech unit durations were reported from a variety of speech samples. He postulated that a simple exponential model provided a workable approximation to these distributions. A more exact model was outlined which accounted for the fact that extremely short speech units lasting only a fraction of a second are less likely to occur than longer units. Also, there tended to be small shifts in expected speech unit durations within a particular speech sample.

      F. Goldman-Eisler ["Continuity of Speech Utterances; Its De-
terminants and Its Significance," Language & Speech 4:220-31, 1961]
reported the frequency of pauses and the duration of words uttered
within phrases (speech sequences) without break. She analyzed
speech produced in a variety of situations and upon a variety of
topics. The differences between speakers with regard to the duration of pauses as well as differences due to the speech situations
were highly significant. The minimum pause was considered to be
250 msec. Allowance was made for "intra-phrase pauses" as long
as 250 msec. which occurred much more frequently than "inter-
phrase" (longer) pauses. In reporting the frequency distribution of
pauses, it was noted that the "inter-phrase" pauses are monotonical-
ly related to the number of words within the phrase. Goldman-
Eisler [B189] also studied the distributions of pauses among different speakers, situations, status or economic level of the speaker,
descriptive or nondescriptive, and speaking during psychological interviews. She concluded that both the duration of pauses and their
frequency of occurrence were useful measures in differentiating the
effect involved in the production of speech.

      The following three studies relate pauses to speech merit.
G. E. Lynch ["A Phonophotographic Study of Trained and Untrained
Voices Reading Factual and Dramatic Material," Archives of Speech
1:9-25, 1934] treated the average duration of pauses between phrases
among trained speakers. Her study indicated that, in each type of
material read, trained readers utilized longer pauses than untrained
readers. E. Murray and J. Tiffin ["An Analysis of Some Basic Aspects of Effective Speech," Archives of Speech 1:61-83, 1934] found
similar results to those reported by Lynch. Their results showed
that a factor which distinguishes between "poor" and "good" speakers was the mean average deviation in "phonation time." "Phonation
time" was not defined and might be similar to a speech unit.
"Good" voices showed more variation in phonation time than "poor"
voices. The mean deviation of pauses and unvoiced intervals also
differentiated "good" and "poor" voices. "Good" voices had longer
pauses. M. Cowan ["Pitch and Intensity Characteristics of Stage
Speech," Archives of Speech Suppl.: 1-91, Dec. 1936] obtained distributions of pauses of the speech of trained actors. The majority
(87 per cent) of their pauses fell within the range of .4 to 1.5 seconds with the modal value being .5 second.

      A. L. F. Snell [Pause: A Study of Its Nature and Its Rhythmi-
cal Function in Verse, Especially Blank Verse, Ph.D., Ann Arbor:
Univ. Mich. Press, 1918] used a kymograph to study pauses in
blank verse. This kymograph was later modified and used in the
Hollister study previously discussed. Her conclusions, expressed
also by some of the previously mentioned researchers, are of interest. For example, she concluded that pauses mark off groups of
words bound together in meaning and that pauses follow certain
grammatical structures. The number of intra-phrase pauses (internal pauses within sentences) is one-third greater than inter-phrase

Table 1

A SUMMARY OF STUDIES REPORTING DURATIONS OF PAUSES AND SPEECH UNITS
(All data reported in hundredths of a second)

Investigator	Measuring Instrument	Minimum Pause	Mean Pause	Mean Speech Unit	Type of Material	Type of Speaker
Verzeano (1950)	Electronic detector	.50	--	2.30	Spontaneous	Normal
Verzeano (1951)	Electronic detector	.10	--	.67	Spontaneous	Normal
		.20	--	1.15		
		.30	--	1.47		
		.40	--	1.79		
		.50	--	2.08		
		.60	--	2.50		
		.70	--	3.11		
		.80	--	3.52		
Hargreaves (1960)	Electronic detector	.05	--	1.50a		--
Goldman-Eisler (1958)	Pen recorder	.25	.75-5.0	--	Spontaneous	Undergraduates (England)
		.25	.40	--	Reading	
Lynch (1934)	Photographic	--	.50		Reading	Undergraduates
Cowan (1936)	Phonophenel-ograph	.05a	.50a	1.50a	Memorized	Trained actors
Murray, Tiffin	Phonophenel-ograph	Reported deviations			Reading	Undergraduates
Snell (1918)	Kymograph	.27	1.45	1.90	Reading	Undergraduates
Cowan (1948)b	Phonophenel-graph	.05a	.50a	--	Reading	Undergraduates

a Estimated by the writer from graphical data.   b Not reviewed here.

pauses (end pauses). The average length of all pauses is .45 second. Pauses ranged from .27 to .65 second. A fall in pitch generally occurs before a pause. The average length of a "speech
unit" is 6.3 syllables, with an average duration of 1.9 seconds, with
a range from .42 to 5.3 seconds.

Summary. The studies reported were quite inconsistent in
regard to what constitutes a pause. Also, mean pause values are
somewhat different. Table 1 is presented to show the contrasts between the mean duration of pauses and speech units from various
studies reviewed.

(3) Studies of speech rate

A speaker typically varies his rate of talking in one or more
ways: he alters the duration of pauses between phrases; he inter-
jects pauses at unusual locations; he increases his breath intake and
speaks on longer periods between breaths, and he may prolong or
shorten vowels. It is difficult to discuss pauses without considering
speech rate. Various units of measure have been used to express
rate of talking: syllables per second, words per second, phonemes
per second, bits per second, lengths of utterances between pauses,
and ratios--namely, phonation/non-phonation.

Brigance [B38] found that the average speaking rate of prize
winners in collegiate oratory contests was between 115 and 135
words per minute, with a range of 83 to 150 words per minute.
He further reported that, when reading, a speaker's normal conversation rate is increased by one-third. Cotton [B66] found it convenient to indicate pauses as a part of the duration of an adjoining
syllable; he plotted syllabic rate on a graph in words per minute.
Thus he postulated that a pause is a part of the preceding syllable;
syllabic rate was the duration of the syllable plus the duration of
the preceding pause; the average speech rate, with the omission of
pause time, is 191 words per minute, and 300 syllables per minute
is equivalent to 191 words per minute. Goldman-Eisler [B192] took
the same position. She defined the rate of articulation as it applies
to absolute rate of speech, for example, rate based on the time of
vocal speech utterance exclusive of pauses. Rate variations were
studied in relation to changes in topic and in the "amount of spontaneity of speech." Articulatory rate was stated as being a "personality constant" of "remarkable" invariance which also reflects the
degree of spontaneity in the production of speech. Variation as a
function of topic was shown to have no effect on articulatory rate.

Goldman-Eisler ["On the Variability of the Speed of Talking
and on Its Relation to the Length of Utterances in Conversations,"
Brit. J. of Psychol. 45:94-107, 1954] further examined the relationships between pause and speech rate, pause and absolute articulatory
rate, and pause and overall rate of speech. Overall rate, namely,
rate of articulation excluding pauses, had an influence on the overall
rate in some speakers. Her primary questions (that implied a posi-

tive relationship between the length of pauses and speech rate) were substantiated on certain speakers, but speakers as a group did not support the question.

Fónagy and Magdics found similar results as those of Goldman-Eisler. The relationship between the length of phrases [phrase, defined: "The unity of the phrase is underlined by the rising pitch in the stressed syllable and the falling intonation of the rest of the phrase. The phrase cannot be interrupted by any pause. If the speaker breaks off a sentence at an unusual place, within a section that would naturally be regarded as a phrase unit, we consider the section as two units. "] and the speed of utterance was studied. Their data were expressed through the mathematical model of an exponential function. That is, as the number of sounds increased per phrase, the mean duration per sound decreased exponentially. Essentially, fast talkers made up their time with long phrases by shortening the time of "speech units. "

Diehl, White, and Burk [B83] examined the relationship of rate of speech and listening comprehension. Rate was uniquely controlled by altering the pause time. This was accomplished by splicing at known pause locations on the tape and inserting longer or shorter pauses at these locations. Altering the pause times did not affect comprehension. Fairbanks and Kodman [B104] found speech rate could be increased or decreased by using an automatic time-frequency compression-expansion device [B105]. Monosyllables were compressed to 75 per cent of their original duration with little loss in intelligibility. In a series of studies, Fairbanks, Guttman, and Miron [B107-109] reported that compressing connected speech from a rate of 141 words per minute to 282 words per minute resulted in very little loss in comprehension. Compression that increased the rate to 350 words per minute resulted in 50 per cent loss in comprehension. The writer, in some extensive pilot studies, found that the ratio of pause time to speech unit time (orally read materials) was .60.

Summary. The studies reviewed noted the variation of speech rate between speakers and also variation with each separate speaker. The studies have not clearly specified the source of variation. One can seldom consider the expression of the unit and/or units of rate without due consideration to pauses. The studies have considered the possibilities of including or excluding pauses in the expression of rate. With the exception of Goldman-Eisler, none of the studies attempted to define a pause. A minimal duration of a pause should be considered if pauses are to be excluded from the expressions of rate.

DETERMINANTS OF THE RATE OF SPEED
OUTPUT AND THEIR MUTUAL RELATIONS

Frieda Goldman-Eisler

The nature of speech production is such that only rarely is
a continuous flow of verbal output achieved. In most cases speech
utterances are series of verbal productions of different lengths which
are broken up into discrete elements by halts and pauses of varying
duration. It is to be expected that these breaks in the flow of
speech determine to some extent the speech rate in any utterance,
if by speech rate we mean the rate at which a certain number of
syllables is produced per unit of time. (In this investigation speech
rate will be the number of syllables per second.) Speech rate calculated in this way was shown to possess a high degree of consistency for individuals, and sensitivity under the impact of changing
conditions [F. Goldman-Eisler, "On the Variability of the Speed of
Talking and on Its Relation to the Length of Utterances in Conversations," Brit. J. of Psychol. 45:94-107, 1954]. As it seemed obvious that the fluctuations in the rate of speech output must, at least
partly, be a function of the duration and of the frequency of the
breaks in the stream of speech, a study of this aspect of speech
output was undertaken. The questions were: (a) To what extent
does the amount of pausing in the flow of speech determine speech
rate and its fluctuations? (b) What is the determining influence of
the absolute speed of talking, i. e. the speed of actual articulation
upon the overall rate of speech, or total speech rate? (c) What
are the internal relations of total or overall speech rate, articulation rate, and the length of halts and pauses in speech?

Experiment

In order to answer these questions, information about the following quantities was required: (a) The number of syllables in each
utterance = Ns (utterances are periods of speech lasting from a preceding question or utterance of an interviewer to the next, which is
usually occasioned by the subject having come to a natural stop or
pause). (b) The total duration of each utterance (in seconds) = t.
(c) The duration of halts and pauses occurring during each utterance = tp. (d) The duration of periods of pure speech = ts.

From these quantities the following measures could be derived: Ns/t = total or overall Speech Rate (SR). Ns/ts = articulation rate (AR), or absolute speech rate. tp/t x 100 = percentage
time, or proportional length of pauses (PP). These quantities were
obtained from eight interviews which were recorded on a speech recorder. Apart from the microphone which fed the tape recorder, a
throat microphone was fixed round the subject's neck to feed the
speech movements into the same polygraph. Thus a record of electrical voice tracings was obtained. Another pen recorded seconds
and half-minutes. A signal between each thirty seconds was fed into

the tape recorder which coincided with the half-minute pen-mark.

The speech recordings were transcribed, the subjects' utterances timed, and the syllables in each utterance counted. In addition, the duration of pauses and halts within each utterance, which appeared on the voice-tracing line, were summed and subtracted from the total duration of the utterance to obtain the duration of the actual speech, and thus the absolute speech rate, or articulation rate. In Figure 1 the kind of record underlying the investigation is illustrated. Interviews were recorded from eight subjects; five of

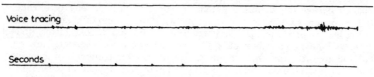

Figure 1. Example of voice tracing used in experiment.

these were patients of the Maudsley Hospital, and three were members of the staff. The interviews lasted from 30 minutes to an hour, and contained between 11 and 54 utterances (Table 1).

Table 1

MEANS (M), STANDARD DEVIATIONS (SD), AND VARIATION COEFFICIENTS (SD/M x 100) OR V OF SPEECH RATES (SR), PERCENTAGE TIME OF PAUSES (PP), AND ARTICULATION RATES (AR), FOR UTTERANCES FROM INTERVIEWS WITH EIGHT SUBJECTS.

	SR			PP			AR			Number of utterances
	M	SD	V	M	SD	V	M	SD	V	
S. I.	4.3	0.78	18.1	4.4	4.01	91.1	4.5	0.75	16.6	26
Co.	3.9	0.53	13.6	19.3	10.4	53.8	4.9	1.12	22.8	53
He.	3.7	0.44	11.8	27.9	18.2	65.2	5.0	1.03	20.6	11
S. II.	3.3	1.09	35.8	29.8	9.7	32.5	4.7	0.54	11.5	15
Jo.	3.3	0.93	28.2	34.3	12.5	36.4	5.0	0.69	13.3	29
Mu.	2.8	0.78	27.8	43.6	12.9	29.6	5.2	1.06	20.4	54
Pea.	2.7	0.45	16.6	53.2	15.0	28.2	5.9	1.48	25.1	46
B. I.	2.3	0.81	35.2	47.6	14.3	30.0	4.4	0.60	13.7	33

Standard Deviations (SD) and Coefficients of Variations (V) of Means for eight subjects

	SR		PP		AR	
	SD	V	SD	V	SD	V
	0.71	21.5%	14.92	45.9%	0.45	9.1%

Results

Table 1 lists the mean and standard deviations of each subject's speech rates (SR), relative duration of pauses (PP), and articulation rates (AR). From these average values it may be seen that there is a close inverse relation between the proportional duration of halts and pauses (PP) in speech utterances and the total speech rate (SR). In other words, the longer and more frequent the pauses, the slower is the total rate of speech production. The rank correlation was -0.940. The absolute speech rate plays no significant part in the rate at which speech is produced over a period of time (rank coeff. $r_{SR/AR}$ = -0.173). This is in harmony with the result of an investigation by R. Henze ["Experimentelle Unterschungen zur Phonomenologie der Sprachgeschwindigkeit," Zeitsch. für Experim. & Angewandt Psychol. 2:214-43, 1953], who found that the total time of utterances correlated with the time taken up by pauses was 0.730, while its correlation with the absolute speaking time was 0.207 (insignificant).

This seems not surprising if we compare the variability of the absolute speech rate with that of the pauses. As these two series of measurements are in two different units with greatly differing means, the variation coefficient (SD/M x 100) was used to compare their relative dispersions. The variation of the mean percentage times of pauses (PP) and the mean articulation rates (AR) in the group of eight subjects can be expressed by the variation coefficients 45.9 per cent (M = 32.5, SD = 14.92) for PP, and 9.1 per cent (M = 4.95, SD = 0.45) for AR. The variation coefficient for the total speech rate (SR) was 21.5 per cent (M = 3.3, SD = 0.71).

The articulation rate proved of remarkable invariance, not only when the means for the eight subjects were compared but also within any one of these subjects. As the column of variation coefficients shows, the variability of absolute speech rates from utterance to utterance in any one subject as expressed by this index ranged from 11.5 to 25.1 per cent, with a mean variation coefficient for all subjects of 18.0 per cent, while that of the halts and pauses ranged between 28.2 and 91.1 per cent, with a mean coefficient of variation of 45.9 per cent. The difference in the degree of variability between the speed of articulation (or absolute speech rate) and the relative duration of breaks in the utterances (PP) is highly significant (t = 3.85, P = beyond 0.01). The variability of the total speech rate for the different individuals was thus shown to be a function of the high degree of variability in the durations of halts and pauses in the speech performances to which these individuals were inclined.

A STUDY OF INTRA- AND INTER-PHRASAL PAUSES
AND THEIR RELATIONSHIP TO THE RATE OF SPEECH

Joseph G. Agnello

         The primary scope of this study was to relate pauses to (1)
the rate of speech, (2) the rhythm of speech, (3) utterances loaded
with particular consonantal sounds, as classified according to the
"manner of production," and (4) to determine the minimal duration
of a pause as the word is used to denote a noticeable stoppage of
speech.   Defining a minimal pause appears simple but becomes difficult since silence is viewed as relative.   The auditory threshold
is involved--it is vital in determining what constitutes silence--as
well as the temporal threshold.   Since speech units occur in rapid
sequence and in noise--some vocal and some not--the listener's
threshold for time, as well as for pressure, related to the definition of a pause.

         A distinction is made between the temporal threshold of si-
lence in speech and a noticeable stoppage of speech (pause).   A listener obviously can detect short interruptions not generally associated with noticeable stoppages associated with pauses.   The experimenter has been able to train himself to attend to extremely
short interruptions.   Kinesthesis, the perception of movement and
position, involves the senses.   In an attempt to define an observed
pause the sense of "hearing" silence and then reacting with a hand
movement is of import to this study.   The sense of hearing cannot
be discussed apart from stimuli.   Morse Code operators are capable of distinguishing the extremely rapid dot-dash pulses of a tone.
R. D. Hollister [Relation Between Hand and Voice Impulse Movements, Ph. D. , Ann Arbor: Univ. Mich. Press, 1935] determined
whether subjects could simultaneously coordinate hand impulses with
voice impulses.   In general, the hit of the hand comes at the point
of a syllabic unit, for example, where the combined energies of
breath pressure, vocalization, and articulation reach their moment
of climax.   The average variation between the synchronized hit of
the hand and the beginning of the mouth tone is plus or minus . 02
second.   G. Von Bekesy [Experiments in Hearing, New York: Mc-
Graw-Hill, 1960] interprets the periodicity of acoustic stimuli after
the concept of conscious present introduced by L. W. Stern ["Psy-
chische Prasenzzeit," Zeitsch. für Psychol. 13:325-49].   Von
Bekesy stated:

                  The sudden presentation of a weak continuous tone makes
                  this readily observable.   The constant character of the
                  amplitude comes to consciousness only periodically.   The
                  period of time during which consciousness lapses can be
                  reduced with practice, so that what is observed approaches
                  more closely to the physical reality.   If the duration of
                  the audible decline exceeds 0. 8 sec. the process of decline
                  can no longer be perceived as a whole, as it is split up
                  into parts by the momentary lapses of consciousness....

The fact that unitary perception applies only to phenomena
lasting no more than 0. 8 sec. is clearly apparent subjectively, and it is well known to psychologists.   Stern referred to this period of time as the conscious period.
The general significance of this period of time is apparent
in the structure of speech, for the number of syllables
that enter into the formation of words is such as mainly
to require the conscious present for their enunciation.
Only then is the word apprehended as a whole.   It is apparent that words of more than four syllables are comparatively rare.   In normal speech a syllable takes about
0. 21 sec. , so that in this way we obtain the value of the
conscious present as 0. 84 sec.

The temporal threshold for the discrimination of pauses has
been set arbitrarily by some researchers.   The writer, in a pilot
study, estimated a minimal duration of a pause to lie between 150
and 200 milliseconds.   Boomer and Dittman [B32] tested three durations of pauses, 100 msec. , 200 msec. , and 300 msec. , and concluded through the method of paired comparison that the minimal
duration was about 200 msec.   F. Goldman-Eisler ["On the Variability of the Speed of Talking and on Its Relation to the Length of
Utterances in Conversations," Brit. J. of Psychol. 2:214-43, 1953]
estimated a minimal pause at 200 msec. and M. Verzeano ["Time
Patterns of Speech in Normal Subjects, II. " J. of Speech & Hear.
Disord. 15:197-201, 1950] at 500 msec.   W. Jassem [From Proceedings of 4th International Congress of Phonetic Sciences (ed. A.
Sovijarni & P. Aalto) Netherlands: Moulton, 1960] as a result of
spectrographic analysis, stated: "... besides longer stretches of
zero energy (corresponding to pauses) there also are gaps of limited duration rarely exceeding 150 msec. "

Definition of Terms

In this study a PAUSE was any response made by an instrument that was sensitive to a reduction of energy in the amount of
30 db from a level of 45 db re 1 volt input, provided the condition
held for at least 5 msec.

A PHRASE was an utterance spoken on one continuous breath.
A phrase was seldom interrupted by a noticeable pause and was generally bounded by noticeable pauses.

An INTER-PHRASE PAUSE was a stoppage of speech bounded
by two phrases and generally exceeded 150 msec.   An inter-phrase
pause always occurred between two words or two phrases, never
within a word.

An INTRA-PHRASE PAUSE was the short intermittent gap occurring within a phrase which in turn contained no noticeable pause
or inter-phrase pauses.

A SPEECH UNIT was a segment of an utterance bounded by
pauses.   The term TALKSPURT is of common usage in communication research and is analogous to speech unit.

An UTTERANCE was any meaningful segment of speech; it

might correspond to a public discourse, a sentence, a phrase, or to any orally read materials.

RHYTHM was an alteration of the articulators, pauses, stress-unstressed, and rate, as a cyclical alternation of strong and weak elements in the flow of sound and silence in speech.

PHONETICALLY STRUCTURED PHRASES were selected stimuli of six to seven words in length, each containing more than a normal number of a particular consonant.

CONSONANTAL CLASSIFICATIONS consisted of four major divisions of consonants, as classified according to the nature of the sound, namely plosive, fricative, nasal, glide.

A SYLLABLE was defined through the tabulations of two observers who had phonetic training and felt confident in their sense of recognizing a syllable.

RATE OF SPEECH was determined by a panel of listeners who scaled utterances for rate on equal-appearing intervals.

Hypotheses of the Study

Testing of the following main hypotheses was of primary interest:

1. The minimal duration of a pause does not exceed 150 msec.
2. There is no difference between the mean durations of pauses from four orally read passages (three of poetry and one of prose) that were previously determined to be differentiated in rhythm.
3. There is no difference between the mean durations of pauses among sentences that were individually loaded with one or another of four types of consonants: plosive, fricative, nasal, and glide.
4. There is no difference in the mean durations of pauses among materials that have been found to differ in the speed of utterance.
5. The number of syllables incorporated within a speech unit was significantly different between plosive, fricative, nasal, and glide-type speech.
6. The number of syllables incorporated within a speech unit was significantly related to speech rate.

Summary of Results

The main conclusions are summarized as follows:

1. A minimal pause was estimated to be 190 msec.
2. The durations of pauses, exceeding 5 msec., did not distinguish spoken materials equated in rhythm.
3. The durations of intra-phrase pauses failed to distinguish spoken materials among phonetic classifications of plosive, fricative, nasal, and glide-type phrases.

4. The durations of intra-phrase pauses failed to distinghish between voiced and voiceless consonants.
5. Trained judges could scale reliably the rate of utterances from short phrases on six equal-appearing intervals.
6. Speakers, as a group, consistently spoke some phrases at similar rates.
7. The durations of intra-phrase pauses related significantly to utterances scaled on six equal-appearing intervals.
8. The durations of inter-phrase pauses did not relate significantly to rate of speech.